S0-AAG-396

Microsoft®

Microsoft® Systems Management Server 2003 Administrator's Companion

Steven D. Kaczmarek

PUBLISHED BY
Microsoft Press
A Division of Microsoft Corporation
One Microsoft Way
Redmond, Washington 98052-6399

Copyright © 2004 by Steven D. Kaczmarek

All rights reserved. No part of the contents of this book may be reproduced or transmitted in any form or by any means without the written permission of the publisher.

Library of Congress Cataloging-in-Publication Data
Kaczmarek, Steve.
    Microsoft Systems Management Server 2003 Administrator's Companion / Steven D. Kaczmarek.
        p. cm.
    Includes index.
    ISBN 0-7356-1888-7
    1. Computer networks--Management.   2. Microsoft Systems management server.   I. Title.

    TK5105.5.K3323   2003
    005.7'1-dc22   2003059352

Printed and bound in the United States of America.

4 5 6 7 8 9   QWT   8 7 6

Distributed in Canada by H.B. Fenn and Company Ltd.

A CIP catalogue record for this book is available from the British Library.

Microsoft Press books are available through booksellers and distributors worldwide. For further information about international editions, contact your local Microsoft Corporation office or contact Microsoft Press International directly at fax (425) 936-7329. Visit our Web site at www.microsoft.com/mspress. Send comments to *mspinput@microsoft.com*.

Active Directory, BackOffice, Microsoft, Microsoft Press, MS-DOS, SQL Server, Visual Basic, Windows, Windows NT, and Windows Server are either registered trademarks or trademarks of Microsoft Corporation in the United States and/or other countries. Other product and company names mentioned herein may be the trademarks of their respective owners.

The example companies, organizations, products, domain names, e-mail addresses, logos, people, places, and events depicted herein are fictitious. No association with any real company, organization, product, domain name, e-mail address, logo, person, place, or event is intended or should be inferred.

This book expresses the author's views and opinions. The information contained in this book is provided without any express, statutory, or implied warranties. Neither the authors, Microsoft Corporation, nor its resellers or distributors will be held liable for any damages caused or alleged to be caused either directly or indirectly by this book.

Microsoft Learning   **nSight, Inc.**
Acquisitions Editor: Martin DelRe   **Project Manager:** Susan H. McClung
Project Editor: Valerie Woolley   **Technical Editor:** Bob Hogan
                                                Copy Editor: Joe Gustaitis
                                                Indexer: Rebecca Plunkett

Body Part No. X10-08390

I would like to dedicate this book to my parents, who proudly tell anyone who will listen that there is an author in the family. I am especially grateful to my partner, William, for his support and encouragement, and to Scruffy, our cairn terrier, who kept me from working too many continuous hours at my many computers by subtly reminding me of the importance of the occasional walk.

Contents at a Glance

Table of Contents

Part II

Resource Discovery, Client Installation, and Remote Control

Part IV
Site Database Maintenance, Recovery, and Upgrade

Part V
Appendixes

Acknowledgments

Having authored and participated in the publication of several books in recent years, I can assert with conviction that the process takes the commitment of many people. This book was certainly no exception.

My sincere thanks to the editorial team at Microsoft Press. Their dedication and hard work were outstanding in every respect. The editorial review process can be frustrating, but they made it comfortable for me and I greatly appreciate their efforts, their comments, and their patience. In particular, thanks to Jeff Koch and later Martin DelRe for accepting and shepherding my book proposal and to Valerie Woolley, Bob Hogan, Joe Gustaitis, and all the others, the excellent editorial team who made sure I dotted the i's and crossed the t's.

Thanks also to John Howie, for his contributions to the chapters about software updates and the patch management process in SMS 2003. I appreciate the time and effort he committed in assisting me with this material in a very short time frame. I would also like to express my gratitude to all my training and consulting colleagues. It is through the healthy and often spirited exchange of information in a variety of forums—along with my own training and consulting experiences—that I have developed a deeper appreciation for this product and gained greater insight into its strengths and foibles. In this vein, a special thank you to the contributors of the SMS MCT forum as well as MYITForum.com for your generous commitment to keeping the SMS community informed about SMS.

Last, but by no means least, many thanks to my colleagues on the SMS 2003 documentation team at Microsoft Corporation. As many of you know, I joined this team in March 2003 and became the project leader for all SMS 2003 documentation. This is a terrific group of talented individuals who are passionate about SMS and dedicated to producing the highest quality documentation for you, their customers. By sharing their expertise with me, as well as proofreading several of the more tricky chapters for me (on their own time, of course), I am certain that this book will complement and enhance the rich set of documentation already published about SMS 2003 by Microsoft. So thanks Terri, Susie, Anat, Cathy, Stacey, Bill, Carol, Liz, Scott, Suzanne, and Kim—and Kristina (especially for hiring me in the first place)!

Introduction

Microsoft has traditionally geared its development of Microsoft BackOffice applications toward providing network administrators with tools that can facilitate the functionality and management of their Microsoft Windows networks. For example, applications such as Microsoft Exchange 2003 and Microsoft SQL Server 2000 provide exceptional mail and database support through centralized management. Microsoft Systems Management Server (SMS) 2003 is just such a product. In this new release you have a superior product that provides centralized management and support for your install base of computers. Those of you who have grown up with SMS will be particularly impressed with the improvements made in this version that enhance the functionality and scalability within large enterprise networks of its predecessor, SMS 2.0.

This book is designed to provide you with both a learning and practical guide to the administrative tasks you'll be performing with SMS 2003. You'll find "Real World" examples that illustrate how to apply a concept in a realistic scenario, "Tips," "Cautions," and resource suggestions for obtaining more information about a topic. Where appropriate, as SMS 2003 performs a specific function or process, the process flow and its components are outlined, monitoring techniques are suggested, and troubleshooting considerations are highlighted. Many chapters include a "Checkpoints" section, in which potential problem areas are reviewed and new troubleshooting tips are presented.

Part I: Installation, Planning, and Management

Part I introduces the reader to SMS 2003, outlining its features and functionality and comparing and contrasting it to the previous version, SMS 2.0. This part also covers a wide range of topics specific to the installation and planning of an SMS site. Chapter 1, "Overview," presents an overview of SMS 2003. Chapter 2, "Primary Site Installation," provides a detailed discussion of the installation process for an SMS primary site, including preinstallation requirements as well as postinstallation system modifications. You'll also learn how to navigate administrative functions using the SMS Administrator console, which uses the Microsoft Management Console (MMC) format. In Chapter 3, "Configuring Site Server Properties and Site Systems," you'll learn how to define and configure the SMS site and site systems. Chapter 4, "Multiple-Site Structures," suggests planning considerations for a multiple-site structure, including developing parent-child relationships among primary sites, creating secondary sites, and establishing SMS 2003 communication mechanisms between sites. Chapter 5, "Analysis and Troubleshooting Tools," and Chapter 6, "System Performance and Network Analysis," introduce the reader to the various tools available in SMS 2003 that enable the administrator to monitor activity in the SMS site, track the flow of information, and analyze network and server performance. These tools will be examined in more detail in subsequent chapters.

Part II: Resource Discovery, Client Installation, and Remote Control

Part II discusses three main areas of client system support through SMS 2003: resource discovery, client installation, and remote control. Chapter 7, "Resource Discovery," and Chapter 8, "Client Installation Methods," describe the discovery and assignment process for SMS client systems. Before a client can be installed as an SMS client, it must be discovered and assigned to an SMS 2003 site. The three client setup methods are described, along with their process flow. SMS 2003 supports software inventory and hardware inventory, and the collection process for the various SMS client types is defined for both hardware and software inventory in Chapter 9, "Inventory Collection." In Chapter 10, "Remote Control of Client Systems," you'll learn how to monitor and troubleshoot a client system remotely through the SMS Administrator Console.

Part III: Software and Package Management

Part III discusses what is probably an SMS administrator's primary reason for purchasing SMS 2003—the distribution of software and other packages to client systems through the network with little or no user intervention and the management of that software once it's installed. This part is divided into four areas of concern. Chapter 11, "Collections," explains the concept of a collection in SMS 2003 and describes how collections are created and maintained. Chapter 12, "Package Distribution and Management," describes the package distribution process, including creating packages and programs, identifying package recipients through collections, and executing package commands at the client system. Chapter 13, "Patch Management," discusses the newest feature of SMS 2003—software update management. This feature provides you with a mechanism to automatically roll out patches and other software updates to your SMS clients through SMS. Chapter 14, "Microsoft Systems Management

Server Installer," illustrates the use of SMS Installer to script an installation process and make it potentially invisible to the user. Chapter 15, "Software Metering," discusses a feature introduced in SMS 2.0 and completely rewritten for SMS 2003: software metering. This feature enables you to monitor and report on software usage on client systems.

Part IV: Site Database Maintenance, Recovery, and Upgrade

Part IV covers a wide variety of topics related to the SMS 2003 database. Because the database itself must be maintained on a server running SQL Server 7.0 or 2000, this part approaches database management from two perspectives: management and reporting from within the SMS 2003 Administrator console and maintenance and events related directly to SQL Server. In Chapter 16, "Queries and Reports," you'll learn how to query for and report on information kept in the database from within the SMS Administrator Console. In Chapter 17, "Security," we'll look at securing access through Windows and through custom consoles, and in Chapter 18, "Disaster Recovery," we'll examine disaster recovery techniques. Chapter 19, "Maintaining the Database Through Microsoft SQL Server," covers SQL Server topics, including event triggers, SQL Server resources and components used by SMS 2003, maintenance and optimization techniques, and SQL Server backup and restore methods. These chapters aren't intended to be a primer for SQL Server; instead, they're designed to provide the SMS administrator with a basic understanding of SQL Server–related maintenance tasks. Chapter 20, "Migration Issues," identifies planning considerations, discusses postmigration issues, and describes client handling and upgrading as well as supporting mixed SMS environments.

Appendixes

This book contains two appendixes:

- **Appendix A: Backup Control File** Contains the text for the backup control file used by the SMS Site Backup service when performing a site server backup scheduled through the SMS Administrator Console, as discussed in Chapter 18.

- **Appendix B: Recommended Web Sites** Lists some of the Internet sites that the author considers particularly useful for gathering additional information about or obtaining support for SMS 2003, Windows 2000 and Windows Server 2003, and SQL Server.

About the CD-ROM

This book includes a 120-day evaluation edition of SMS 2003 that you can use to explore features and management methods discussed in the text. The SMS 2003 evaluation edition is unsupported by both Microsoft and Microsoft Press and should not be used on a primary work computer. In addition, this CD does not include the documentation guides cited in this book. For online support information related to the full version of SMS 2003 (much of which will also apply to the evaluation edition), or to download any of the support guides, you can connect to *http://www.microsoft.com/smserver*.

System Requirements

It's recommended that you read the release notes included on the evaluation edition CD for the most current information regarding system requirements, installation instructions, and operating instructions.

System Requirements for the Evaluation Edition CD

Component	Requirement
Processor	550 MHz or faster processor (Intel Pentium/Celeron family or compatible processor recommended).
Operating system	Windows Server 2003 Standard Edition. Windows Server 2003 Enterprise Edition. Windows Server 2003 Datacenter Edition. Windows 2000 Server with Service Pack 2 (SP2) or later. Windows 2000 Advanced Server with Service Pack 2 (SP2) or later. Windows 2000 Datacenter Server with Service Pack 2 (SP2) or later.
Memory	256 MB of RAM; 4 GB of RAM maximum
Hard disk space	2 GB of available hard disk space.
Drive	CD-ROM or DVD-ROM drive.
Cards	Network interface card.
Adapters	Windows 2000–compatible video graphics adapter.
Database	SQL Server 7.0 with SP3 or later, or SQL Server 2000 with SP3a or later.
Software	Internet Information Services (IIS) must be installed as part of the Windows Server installation for certain SMS site system roles. For specific details, see the "Getting Started" chapter in the *Microsoft Systems Management Server 2003 Concepts, Planning, and Deployment Guide*, included on the SMS CD and available from the SMS Web site (*http://www.microsoft.com/smserver*) and through Microsoft TechNet.

System Requirements for the Evaluation Edition CD

Component	Requirement
Peripheral devices	Keyboard and mouse or compatible pointing device or hardware that supports console redirection.
Additional Requirements	Management points require Windows 2000 Server SP3 or later. It's recommended that all server computers with SMS site server roles have only NTFS partitions. SMS 2003 has been extensively tested with the supported operating system versions listed above. Although SMS 2003 is supported on all of the platforms listed, it's strongly recommended that you upgrade to the latest operating system service pack at the earliest opportunity in order to benefit from the latest security fixes. If an issue is reported to Microsoft that is exhibited only on an earlier operating system revision and the root cause of the issue is determined to be an operating system component, the recommended solution might be to upgrade to a more recent operating system service pack.

Technical Support

As a member of the SMS product team, I encourage you to send your comments, expectations, and wishes about the software to smswish@microsoft.com. The product team monitors this e-mail alias, although it's not intended as a means of engaging in a problem-solving or troubleshooting conversation. That's what Microsoft's Premier Support Services is for. In addition, I would appreciate receiving your comments about the SMS 2003 core documentation—those documents I've been referencing throughout this book, including the SMS 2003 online Help. I, and the documentation team I represent, want to know how you use the documentation, whether it's useful in its present form, and what we can do to make your experience with the documentation better. We have many good ideas of our own for improving the documentation usage experience for you, but once again, your input as a customer is the most valuable. You can send comments about the SMS 2003 core documentation to smsdocs@microsoft.com or to me directly at stevenka@microsoft.com.

Every effort has been made to ensure the accuracy of this book. Microsoft Press provides corrections for books through the World Wide Web at

http://www.microsoft.com/mspress/support.

To query the Help and Support Knowledge Base about a question or issue that you may have, go to

http://support.microsoft.com/default.aspx?pr=kbhowto.

If you have any comments, questions, or ideas regarding this book, please send them to Microsoft Press using either of the following methods:

E-Mail:

msinput@microsoft.com

Postal Mail:

Microsoft Press

Attn: *Microsoft Systems Management Server 2003 Administrator's Companion* Editor

One Microsoft Way, Redmond, WA 98052-6399

Please note that product support isn't offered through the preceding addresses. For support information, visit Microsoft's Web site at *http://support.microsoft.com.*

Part I
Installation, Planning, and Management

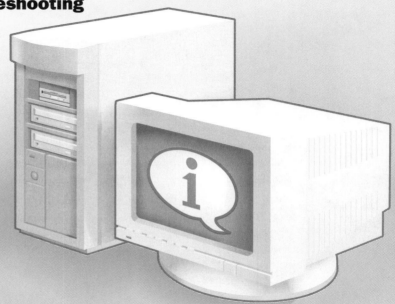

Chapter 1
Overview

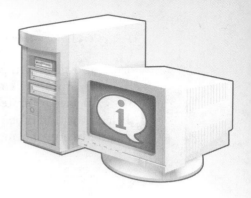

Welcome to the newly engineered version of Microsoft Systems Management Server (SMS) 2003. This book gives you the insight and tools necessary to successfully administer SMS 2003. We'll explore the fundamental components and features of SMS, such as package distribution, hardware and software inventory, remote diagnostics and software metering, as well as new features such as management points, reporting points, and server locator points, enhanced console functionality, and—finally—*real* support for Advanced Clients. We'll discuss the installation procedures for site systems and clients, as well as examine the implementation of an SMS site hierarchy. We'll also look at relevant SMS 2.0 migration and update readiness issues, as well as disaster recovery and database maintenance recommendations.

SMS has gone through many generations and enhancements since its initial 1.0 release. Noting the shortcomings of the SMS 1.x family—unabashedly reported to Microsoft by all of you SMS administrators—Microsoft released SMS 2.0. This was a complete renovation of the product that addressed many of the issues that SMS administrators raised. That version dropped some functionality (most notably the clunky Program Group Control), enhanced existing functionality (package distribution, inventory, and remote control), and added functionality (logon points, client access points, distribution points, and software metering).

Through the application of five service packs, these components of SMS 2.0 were further enhanced and various "undocumented user features" were addressed and resolved. SMS 2.0 finally became compatible with Microsoft Windows 2000–based networks, although it was never fully integrated with Windows 2000 Active Directory directory service. SMS 2003 represents the next generation of this product and reconfirms Microsoft's commitment to addressing your client management needs.

To those of you who purchased the previous edition of this book, *Microsoft Systems Management Server 2.0 Administrator's Companion,* let me assure you that this book isn't a repetition of the previous edition. I have rethought the order and flow of the original book and have made adjustments—many suggested by my alert readers. Also, Microsoft has "touched" every component in SMS 2.0 as it generated SMS 2003, so there is new material throughout. Nevertheless, there will be new SMS administrators among you, so we begin in this chapter by introducing SMS 2003 and describing what SMS 2003 is all about.

What Is Systems Management Server 2003?

The computing industry has undergone many changes since the days of UNIVAC mainframes. In the early 1980s the desktop computer as a viable business tool was relatively new. In fact, typical corporate discussions at the time centered around issues such as whether to purchase a desktop computer with a 10 MB disk drive at an additional cost of $1,700 because "users will just never need that much space."

Since that time, the desktop computer as a productivity tool has become a necessity in most organizations as well as in schools and at home. The need to provide processing power at the user's fingertips is a foregone conclusion. As a result, desktop computing has grown into a major industry and, consequently, a potentially huge administration headache. Desktop computer users can be territorial about their systems and the applications used. It's not unheard of to have an IS group that supports a user running three different word-processing programs in several versions because that user is unwilling to risk converting the documents to a single word-processing version. On the other end of the spectrum, more businesses are taking advantage of tools like SMS, Windows Installer Service, and Active Directory Group Policies to provide their users with a standard desktop that can not only be centrally maintained but also can't be modified at all by the user. Both of these scenarios exemplify the fact that supporting multiple desktop computers installed with a variety of program applications can be a challenge for even the best-equipped and best-funded IS support groups.

In addition to application support, IS groups often provide hardware support for their organization's users. This too can be a daunting prospect when the install base of computers is in the thousands or tens of thousands, deployed within different departmental, geographic, or international locations. It's not always practical—or even possible—to physically access every computer in an organization.

Many IS managers have acknowledged the need to provide standards for desktop computing and have begun to look for and to implement some kind of centralized desktop management system. IS support groups need to be able to respond actively and proactively to implement and update software on client systems and to respond to their users' requests for assistance as quickly, effectively, and consistently as possible. IS support groups should be able to perform as much user desktop management as possible while sitting at their own desktop computers. The key to effective remote desktop management is to provide a reliable set of remote management tools that enable an IS support group to be as effective as if they had actually laid hands on the user's desktop.

Microsoft has long recognized this need and has responded by providing tools to assist IS groups in centralizing desktop management. These tools include the use of Active Directory Group Policies to provide standard desktop environment settings and registry values. Microsoft Operations Manager (MOM) 2000 offers a server-based means of monitoring server performance remotely and responding to selected events appropriately—for example, restarting a service remotely if that service stops unexpectedly. Microsoft Application Center 2000 is designed to support the development and implementation of Web-based applications by using a cluster of servers that can serve the same elements of those applications (Web pages, COM+ components) to appropriate clients in the network. Windows Management Instrumentation (WMI) services provide a robust schema for managing desktop configurations from a central location.

SMS 2003 is a powerful management product that offers a newly enriched set of desktop management features, with the capability of leveraging Active Directory. SMS 2003, together with the other client management solutions that Microsoft offers, provides IS managers with perhaps their most effective set of centralized management tools to date. With SMS 2003, you'll be able to remotely diagnose and troubleshoot desktop systems, install applications, and manage software.

With these general specifications in mind, let's take a closer look at the various features that SMS 2003 offers.

Features and Functions

SMS 2003 offers remote desktop administration in six primary areas:

- **Inventory and resource management**   The ability to gather and maintain a workstation's hardware and software configuration in a central database that's easily accessible and interpreted.

- **Diagnosis and troubleshooting**   The tools to effectively analyze hardware and software concerns on remote workstations.

- **Package distribution** The ability to install applications and updates and execute programs remotely on a user's workstation.

- **Application management** The ability to track and restrict software usage on users' workstations, as well as to detect and monitor unregistered or unsupported applications.

- **Security** With Standard Security, the reliance on internal and optional user accounts to run services, connect between systems, and perform client-based functions as happened with SMS 2.0; with Advanced Security, the ability to leverage the local system account and computer accounts and to perform the same functions.

- **Reports** The ability to create and manage meaningful reports directly through the SMS Administrator Console through two new components: the Report Viewer and dashboards.

We'll explore these SMS features more closely throughout this book. First, let's look at the various SMS components; we'll refer to these components as we look at features.

Components and Definitions

The term *process* refers to a program that performs a specific SMS task. The term *component* refers to a computer running SMS software, in particular, server computers. In this section we'll review some basic SMS 2003 component and process definitions. If these descriptions seem brief, don't despair! Each is discussed in detail later in this book.

SMS Client

An *SMS client* is any computer that SMS 2003 will manage. An SMS client can be a user's desktop or portable computer, workstation, or a network server, including an SMS site server or site system. SMS clients fall into two categories: Legacy and Advanced. The distinctions between these two client types will be discussed in greater detail later in this book. For now, let's define Legacy Clients as those that SMS 2003 will manage in the traditional manner, using client access points (CAPs), distribution points, and internal user accounts to perform various client functions, and so on. Legacy Clients are most often stationary desktop systems. Legacy Clients also communicate with Server Locator Points and Reporting Points.

By contrast, SMS 2003 manages Advanced Clients by leveraging Active Directory. Advanced Clients communicate with the site through Management Points, Server Locator Points, Reporting Points, and Active Directory.

Advanced Clients are most often portable computers, but they can also be stationary desktop computers. Table 1-1 represents the operating system platforms supported by SMS 2003 for Legacy and Advanced Clients.

Table 1-1. Supported client operating system platforms

Legacy Client	Advanced Client
Windows 98	n/a
Windows NT 4.0 Workstation or Server SP6a or later	n/a
Windows NT Terminal Server SP6a	n/a
Windows 2000 Professional	Windows 2000 Professional
Windows 2000 Server, Advanced Server, Datacenter Server	Windows 2000 Server, Advanced Server, Datacenter Server
Windows XP Professional	Windows XP Professional
Windows Server 2003, Standard, Enterprise, Datacenter, and Web Editions	Windows Server 2003, Standard, Enterprise, Datacenter, and Web Editions

Note SMS 2003 doesn't support any Windows family operating system not specifically listed in Table 1-1, including Windows Millennium Edition (Windows Me) and Windows XP Home Edition, nor does it support any version of Macintosh, Novell NetWare, or Microsoft Small Business Server. In addition, SMS 2003 doesn't support Alpha-based computer systems, IP version 4 or earlier, or the Netscape Browser for Web-based reporting.

SMS Site

An *SMS site* defines the computers, users, groups, and other resources that SMS will manage so that the SMS site can remotely control a client, advertise a package, view all IP devices, inventory system resources, track software usage, and report on this data. SMS 2003 sites are defined either by Active Directory sites or IP subnet address, or both. This means that you have a lot of flexibility as far as defining which resources you wish to manage and allows SMS 2003 to scale more efficiently to your enterprise network. An SMS site consists of an SMS site server, SMS site systems, and SMS clients and resources.

SMS Site Server

The *SMS site server* is the Windows server on which SMS 2003 has been installed and that manages the SMS site and all its component attributes and services. The SMS site server is the primary point of access between you and the SMS database. It must be a Windows server (SP2 or later) or a Windows Server 2003 server that's a member of either a Windows NT 4.0 domain or an existing Windows 2000 or higher Active Directory domain. If the SMS site server will be a primary site, it will need access to a SQL server running Microsoft SQL Server 7.0 with SQL Service Pack 3 or later (required to support a primary site server in standard security mode) or SQL Server 2000 with SQL Service Pack 3 or later (required to support a site server in advanced security mode). You can install an SMS site server on either a domain controller or a member server, but not on a stand-alone server.

Note Servers running Windows Server 2003 don't support Microsoft SQL Server 7.0.

Included with SMS 2003 is the Deployment Readiness Wizard. This tool is designed to be run on servers in an SMS 2.0 site server prior to upgrading to SMS 2003 to identify potential incompatibilities, such as unsupported operating systems. The results are stored in Extensible Markup Language (XML) format and so can be viewed using a Web browser. Specific installation requirements for site servers are discussed in Chapter 2, "Primary Site Installation."

SMS Site System

An *SMS site system* is a Windows 2000 server (SP2 or later) or Windows Server 2003 server that performs one or more SMS roles for an SMS site. These SMS roles include CAPs, distribution points, management points, server locator points, and reporting points. The CAP and distribution point roles are installed on an SMS site server by default. (Chapter 3, "Configuring Site Server Properties and Site Systems," covers all these roles in detail, as well as discusses additional server requirements necessary to support some new features of SMS 2003.) You can then identify additional SMS site systems within the SMS site and assign various SMS roles or combinations of roles.

Note SMS 2003 no longer supports the logon point role or software metering server roles, as these components of SMS no longer exist. The software metering function has been reengineered as a configurable client agent that you can install on your SMS clients.

An *SMS client access point (CAP)* is an SMS site system and functions as the exchange point between SMS Legacy Clients and the SMS site server. You install components of SMS Legacy Clients from a CAP. Inventory, status, and discovery information is collected on the Legacy Client and forwarded to a CAP. The Legacy Client obtains advertisement information and other instructions from the CAP. When a Legacy Client receives an advertisement for a program, it will also include a list of distribution points at which that client can find the package files.

An *SMS distribution point* is an SMS site system that stores the package files, programs, and scripts necessary for a package to execute successfully at an SMS client computer. By default, SMS places these files on the drive with the most free space and shares them using a hidden share. A new feature of distribution points is the ability to enable Background Intelligent Transfer Service (BITS). Advanced Clients use BITS to control the download of package files from a distribution point, using idle bandwidth. If the download is interrupted for any reason, BITS keeps track of where the download stopped and restarts it at the next opportunity, beginning with the file that was interrupted. For example, if a user connects a portable computer for a short time while in the office and then disconnects and leaves the office while a package download was initiated, that download is interrupted. The next time the user connects the portable computer, the download will continue, beginning with the file that was interrupted.

An *SMS management point* is an SMS site system used by Advanced Clients to communicate with their assigned SMS site. It provides the same kinds of functionality as a CAP does for a Legacy Client. A management point is only supported in an SMS primary site because it requires access to the SMS site database. However, a proxy management point can be deployed in a secondary site when roaming boundaries are enabled to support Advanced Clients that roam to that site. The concept of roaming and roaming boundaries will be explored in more detail in Chapter 2.

An *SMS server locator point* is an SMS site system that's used primarily in client installation. It provides site assignment information to clients and locates a CAP for Legacy Clients, or a management point for Advanced Clients, and directs the client there to complete installation. The server locator point requires that Microsoft Internet Information Server (IIS) be installed. This site system replaces the SMS 2.0 system role of logon point and so eliminates most of the network traffic and server performance issues that affected domain controllers.

An *SMS reporting point* is an SMS site system that hosts the Report Viewer component for Web-based reporting functionality. As it communicates with the local site database, it can only be implemented on primary sites. Like the server locator point, a reporting point requires installation of IIS. Specific implementation requirements for this and all site system roles are discussed in Chapter 3.

SMS Administrator Console

An SMS administrator is the individual trusted with the implementation, maintenance, and support of an SMS site or specific objects in the SMS database. An *SMS Administrator Console*, as shown in Figure 1-1, is the primary tool that an SMS administrator uses to maintain an SMS site.

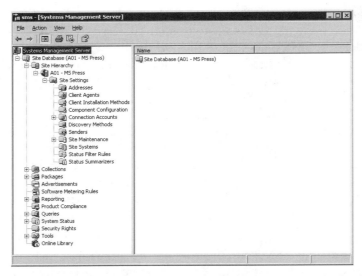

Figure 1-1. *A representative SMS Administrator Console displaying the different top-level objects that the SMS administrator can manage.*

The SMS Administrator Console can be installed on the following platforms:

- Windows 2000 Professional, SP2 or later
- Windows 2000 Server, SP2 or later
- Windows 2000 Advanced Server, SP2 or later
- Windows 2000 Datacenter Server, SP2 or later
- Windows XP Professional
- Windows Server 2003, Standard Edition
- Windows Server 2003, Enterprise Edition
- Windows Server 2003, Datacenter Edition

The SMS Administrator Console is actually Microsoft Management Console 2.0 (MMC) with the SMS Administrator snap-in added. The 12 top-level SMS objects in the SMS site database that can be administered are described in Table 1-2; each top-level object contains additional objects. Since the SMS Administrator Console is an MMC, you can create a custom console that includes it and additional snap-ins from third-party SMS developers such as Altiris, the Microsoft SQL Enterprise Manager snap-in, or Windows 2000 or Server 2003 management tools. Also, all the functionality of an MMC is available to you, including creating taskpads, exporting lists to a file, and printing standard lists in the details view pane of the console. Specific details concerning the use and navigation of the SMS Administrator Console are discussed in Chapter 2 and Chapter 6, "System Performance and Network Analysis."

Table 1-2.   Top-level SMS objects

Object	Description
Site Hierarchy	Display the site hierarchy and contain site properties and component configurations, such as client agents, installation methods, discovery methods, site systems, status filters, and summarizers.
Collections	Create, delete, view, and modify predefined or SMS administrator–defined groupings of SMS resources, as well as view resource information, create advertisements, and initiate remote tools functions. Collections can consist of any SMS-discovered resources.
Packages	Display package and program settings. A *package* is a set of files, programs, or commands that you want executed on an SMS client. Package programs are advertised to collections. Package files are stored in distribution points.
Advertisements	The means by which you let an SMS client know that a package is available for it. An advertisement can be offered not only to SMS client computers, but also to any users or user groups that SMS has discovered. Advertisements are maintained on CAPs.
Product Compliance	Determine the compliance level of Microsoft applications installed and inventoried on SMS clients.
Software Metering Rules	Monitor the usage of programs on SMS clients.
Reporting	Create, modify, and run reports and dashboards.
Queries	Provide a means of displaying database information based on a set of predefined criteria. Several queries are defined by default, and the SMS administrator can also create new queries.
System Status	SMS equivalent to the Windows Event Viewer. Virtually every SMS service or process generates a robust set of status messages that outline the progress of that service or process. The information provided by the System Status object is the best place for an SMS administrator to begin troubleshooting.
Security Rights	Provide the capability to define and refine the level of access that users have when working with SMS objects. This gives you the ability to delegate specific tasks to specific groups of users.
Tools	Run the SMS Service Manager, for monitoring component and service status, stopping and starting SMS services and threads, and logging component and service activity.
Online Library	View and search comprehensive documentation provided for SMS 2003, including Release Notes, Concepts, Planning and Deployment Guide, and Administrator Help, as well as access online documentation and order printed versions of online documentation.

SMS Site Hierarchy

An *SMS site hierarchy* resembles an organizational flowchart and exists whenever two or more SMS sites have been defined in a parent-child relationship. SMS site hierarchies provide a means of extending and scaling SMS support across a wide variety of organizational structures.

Parent and child sites are defined by their relationship within an SMS site hierarchy. A *parent site* is any site with at least one child site defined, and it has the ability to administer any child site below it in the SMS site hierarchy. A *child site* is any SMS site that has a parent defined. Child sites send discovery, inventory, and status information up to the parent site. Any SMS primary or secondary site can also be a child site. An SMS primary site can have a child site reporting to it, but an SMS secondary site can't.

An *SMS primary site* is an SMS site that has access to a SQL Server database. An SMS primary site can be directly administered through the SMS Administrator Console as well as by any SMS site above it in the SMS site hierarchy. An SMS primary site can also administer any child site below it in the site hierarchy. SMS primary sites can be children of other primary sites. They can also have child sites of their own. Only SMS primary sites can support site systems assigned the management point, server locator point, and reporting point roles.

An *SMS secondary site* is an SMS site that doesn't have access to a SQL Server database. An SMS secondary site is always a child of a primary site and is administered solely through its parent or through another primary site above it in the SMS site hierarchy. A secondary site can't have child sites of its own nor can it support site systems assigned the management point, server locator point, and reporting point roles, although it can be assigned a proxy management point.

An *SMS central site* is an SMS primary site that resides at the top of the SMS site hierarchy. Inventory data, status messages, site control data, and discovery data roll from child to parent and are collected ultimately at the central site's SMS database. An SMS central site can administer any site below it in the SMS site hierarchy.

Figure 1-2 illustrates a simple SMS hierarchical model showing both primary and secondary sites as child sites of a central site. An SMS site system's roles don't all have to be enabled on the site server. Rather, these roles can be enabled on other servers in the domain.

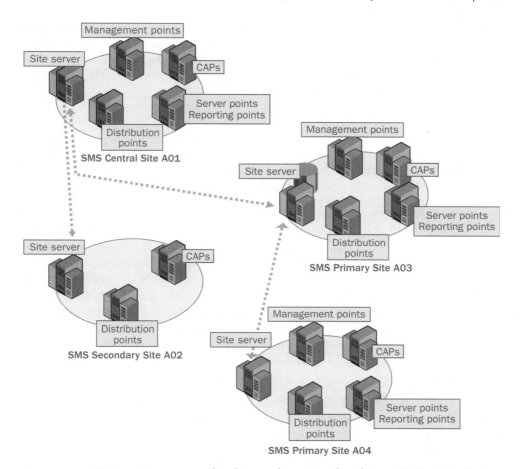

Figure 1-2. *Various site system roles that can be assigned within an SMS site and a representative SMS site hierarchy.*

That's it for general terminology. All these components and terms will be explored in more detail later in this book.

Inventory and Resource Management

SMS 2003 can collect and display resources deployed within your network. These resources include, of course, the workstations and servers that have been installed. You have the ability to discover and view your Windows domain users and groups, as well as any IP-addressable component connected to your LAN or WAN. SMS 2003 offers several configurable discovery methods. SMS 2003 also provides three kinds of Active Directory discovery: Active Directory System Discovery, Active Directory User Discovery, and Active Directory System

Group Discovery. Although not all discovered resources might be manageable, the administrator can display and view some basic properties. For example, a computer's discovery data includes its IP address, network card address (the MAC address), its computer name, and the domain of which it's a member. The process of discovering resources will be discussed at length in Chapter 7, "Resource Discovery."

Note The process of discovering a resource such as a computer doesn't automatically mean that SMS is installed on that computer. Nor does it mean that inventory is collected. Rather, it means that the "fact" of the resource being there is recorded along with some basic properties of that resource.

In addition to discovery data, SMS 2003 can collect hardware and software data from an SMS 2003 client. Two of the five client agents that can be installed on an SMS client computer are the Hardware Inventory Client Agent and the Software Inventory Client Agent. The SMS administrator enables and configures both and then installs them on an SMS client. Collected inventory is stored, viewed, and maintained in the SMS site database. This database is created and maintained on a SQL Server. The SMS Administrator Console acts as a front end to this database and provides the SMS administrator with the tools to manage that data. For example, you view an SMS client's inventory through the SMS Administrator Console by selecting that client in an appropriate collection and executing a tool called the Resource Explorer.

When troubleshooting needs to be performed, it's not always possible, or even appropriate, that users have full knowledge of their hardware or software configuration. Having an SMS client's inventory readily available and up-to-date, however, provides an administrator with the computer configuration data needed to assist a user with a problem.

The Hardware Inventory Client Agent executes according to an administrator-defined frequency and collects system configuration such as hard disk space, processor type, RAM size, CD type, monitor type, and so on. In addition, you can configure the Hardware Inventory Agent to collect more granular information from SMS clients using a template file called SMS_DEF.MOF, such as the installation date of the system's BIOS, asset and serial number information, program group names, and printers installed. It does so by using the WMI service. WMI is Microsoft's implementation of Web-Based Enterprise Management (WBEM). (You'll learn more about these services in the section entitled "Understanding WBEM and WMI" later in this chapter.) Briefly, WMI allows for more detailed system configuration data to be reported and stored on the workstation for use by management applications such as SMS. Once the Hardware Inventory Client Agent on a 32-bit client has collected the full inventory, only changes to the inventory on the client will be reported in subsequent inventories. The hardware inventory process and configuration are discussed thoroughly in Chapter 9, "Inventory Collection."

The Software Inventory Client Agent also executes according to an administrator-defined interval and essentially audits the SMS client for applications installed on its local hard disks. The SMS administrator can configure the Software Inventory Client Agent to audit other file types and report on specific files, as well as to collect copies of specific files. As with the Hardware Inventory Client Agent, the first time the Software Inventory Client Agent runs, a complete software audit or file collection takes place and the full inventory is gathered and reported. At each successive inventory interval, only changes to the audited files will be reported. The software inventory collection and configuration process is discussed more completely in Chapter 9.

Diagnosis and Troubleshooting

Provided with SMS 2003 are several tools that can help the SMS administrator diagnose problems in the SMS site, problems with communications within and among sites, and problems with SMS client computers—and troubleshoot those problems with little direct physical intervention.

Network Monitor

Network Monitor provides the means to track, capture, and analyze network traffic that occurs between individual client computers or within the network itself. This version has been enhanced both in functionality and security. For example, a set of functions called experts has been included to assist you in tracking down and parsing events such as top users, protocol distribution, and so on. Network Monitor is discussed in detail in Chapter 6.

Network Trace

Network Trace offers a snapshot flowchart of the SMS site system structure that maps the communication path of each site system, checks for communication status between site systems, and displays the status of SMS components running on each site system. Think of Network Trace as a miniature SNMP manager. See Chapter 6 for more information about working with Network Trace.

System Monitor

When SMS has been installed on a site server, it also adds several new objects that contain counters to the Windows 2000 and Server 2003 Performance Monitor utility. These objects are listed here:

- SMS Discovery Data Manager
- SMS Executive Thread States
- SMS In-Memory Queues
- SMS Inventory Data Loader
- SMS Software Inventory Processor
- SMS Software Metering Processor
- SMS Standard Sender
- SMS Status Messages

These objects and their corresponding counters, along with the traditional Windows 2000 and Server 2003 objects and counters (Processor, Process, Memory, Logical Disk, Physical Disk, and so on) can assist the SMS administrator in performance testing site systems and determining optimization alternatives. See Chapter 6 for more information about working with Performance Monitor.

Remote Tools

Remote Tools has been perhaps the most appreciated feature of any SMS version. This utility enables the SMS administrator to gain keyboard and mouse control of an SMS client from the administrator's workstation. Through a video transfer screen, the administrator can "see" the user's desktop and diagnose and troubleshoot problems without having physical access to the remote client. The administrator can also "talk" to the user through a remote chat screen, execute programs on the remote client, transfer files to and from the remote client, and restart the remote client. As with the Hardware Inventory Client Agent and Software Inventory Client Agent, the amount of remote access that can be initiated is configured by the SMS administrator and rendered on the client by a Remote Tools Client Agent.

Remote Tools also includes remote diagnostic utilities specific to Windows NT 4.0 and later computers and other Windows operating systems that provide real-time access to system attributes such as interrupt usage, memory usage, services running, and device settings. You can also configure Remote Tools to manage the remote connection features of Windows XP Professional. This feature is discussed more thoroughly in Chapter 10, "Remote Control of Client Systems."

SMS Trace

SMS Trace allows the SMS administrator to view one or more SMS log files in real time in order to follow, diagnose, and troubleshoot service activity. You can use this tool to search for text strings and to highlight found values. See Chapter 5, "Analysis and Troubleshooting Tools," for more information about SMS Trace. This tool, along with several others, is available for download from the Microsoft SMS 2003 Web site *http://www.microsoft.com/smserver*.

All SMS services and processes create and update a wide variety of log files and generate detailed event status messages. These files and messages provide the SMS administrator with an extensive source of diagnostic data that's critical to the successful maintenance of the SMS site and also provide an ideal means to learn about the inner workings of SMS. Server-based log files aren't enabled by default to conserve server resources, but the SMS administrator can enable and configure them. Client-based log files are enabled by default and can be disabled through the client registry. You can view log files with any text editor.

Package Distribution

One important way of reducing the total cost of owning and maintaining client computers is to minimize the amount of time an administrator needs to physically spend at a computer. When part of the administrator's job involves installing and upgrading software at a computer, the amount of time spent at each computer can be significant. We've already looked at some of the remote tools available to reduce the time spent at a user's computer. Another way to reduce this time is to acquire the ability to remotely install, maintain, and upgrade software. SMS 2003 enables you to do just that. Through its package distribution feature, you can run programs on client computers to install and upgrade software, update files, execute tasks such as disk optimization routines, and modify configuration settings such as registry entries or INI files.

The SMS administrator defines a package's properties, including the location of source files; sending priority; where the package should be stored and shared on the distribution point; and version and language values. The SMS administrator identifies which distribution points should receive the package and also creates one or more programs for the package that define how the package should be executed at a client computer. For example, a software application installation might have several types of installations that can be run, such as Typical, Custom, and Laptop. Each of these installations would represent a program that the SMS administrator would create for the package. The same package definition could then be used to install the application in different ways on different clients.

Clients are made aware of the existence of an application through advertisements. The SMS administrator creates an *advertisement*, and it identifies both the program that should be executed by the target resources and the SMS collection that defines the target resources. Programs can be advertised only to collections, and a valid collection can consist of SMS clients and Windows 2000 or Server 2003 users and groups or Active Directory discovered resources. The advantage of this arrangement is that when a new computer, user, or user group is added to a collection, it will automatically receive any advertisements for that collection. Packages and advertisements are discussed in detail in Chapter 12, "Package Distribution and Management."

Application Management

SMS 2003 offers several tools for managing applications installed on SMS clients. In SMS 2.0, Microsoft introduced the software metering server component. The software metering server provided two main functions: application usage tracking and application licensing. When an application was executed at the client, a client agent reported that fact to the software metering server, which was, in turn, passed to the SMS site server and stored in its own SQL database. The data could then be summarized and displayed for the SMS administrator through the SMS Administrator Console. The SMS administrator could also register an application. The SMS administrator could then set restrictions on it or enforce tracking of licenses.

This function was never fully integrated into the SMS site server "suite" of components. Note, for example, the use of a separate SQL database for storing usage and license information rather than incorporating that information into the main SMS database. The interaction between the client and a software metering server, as well as between the site server and its software metering servers, could generate a fair amount of network traffic. For example, licenses would be propagated and periodically balanced among existing software metering servers in the site, and the software metering client agent would need to contact a software metering server whenever a registered application was executed on the client. When I taught the Microsoft Certified classes for SMS 2.0, I would frequently refer to the software metering component as a glob of Silly Putty stuck onto the otherwise smooth globe of SMS.

In SMS 2003, the software metering component has been redeveloped and is now fully integrated with the rest of SMS. It uses WMI to monitor running applications. You can now create software metering rules that are downloaded to specified clients. You can configure a software metering rule to monitor all or specific applications that are executed on an SMS client, detect and report on unregistered or unsupported applications, and collect application usage information. The software metering data that's collected is now stored in the SMS site database, and you can generate more useful reports regarding the usage of applications on SMS clients. You can use software usage data to determine:

- How many copies of a program have been deployed in your organization
- How many licenses you need to purchase to remain compliant
- How many users actually use the program
- What times of day the program is most frequently used

Software metering will be explored in detail in Chapter 15, "Software Metering."

An additional application management tool, Product Compliance, is installed with SMS. The product compliance database allows you to import or configure your own product information for applications running within your organization and use it to identify those clients that are running noncompliant applications.

This process actually involves several SMS components. You can use the Software Inventory Client Agent to collect a list of programs installed on each client. This list is compared to the product compliance database using SMS queries. Once you have identified programs that are unsupported or nonstandard, you can use software metering rules to restrict the execution and use of those programs. If you identify programs that need to be upgraded, you can use the package distribution process to send and apply the appropriate upgrades.

Understanding Windows Management Instrumentation

Windows Management Instrumentation (WMI) is Microsoft's implementation of Web-Based Enterprise Management (WBEM), an industry initiative adopted by the Distributed Management Task Force (DMTF) to implement a common interface between management applications, such as SMS, and management entities, such as SMS objects. SMS objects include discovery data, client computers, packages, advertisements, sites, and site control information. This common interface is called the Common Information Model (CIM) repository. It defines a standard schema for storing and exposing object data. Providers are components that collect object information from managed objects and store them in the CIM repository. A management application can then obtain that information from the CIM repository and make it available for view and analysis.

This interface feature is similar to installing a Windows device driver such as a printer driver. The print device manufacturer provides a printer driver that's compatible with Windows. All Windows applications use this same printer driver to generate print jobs on the print device. Using a similar premise, with WMI installed, any management application program can collect and set configuration details for a wide variety of hardware types, operating system components, and application systems because it uses providers to work with those systems. Providers can be written to store and expose data in the CIM repository, and management applications (written with Microsoft Visual Basic, SQL Server, Java, Open Database Connectivity (ODBC), Active Directory Service Interface (ADSI), and so on) can be created to obtain that data from the CIM repository.

To illustrate, a hardware provider on the SMS client stores SMS object information such as hardware inventory in the CIM repository. SMS agents such as the Hardware Inventory Client Agent extract that data from the CIM repository and report it to the SMS database. The SMS Provider, which can be installed on the SMS site server or the SQL Server, accesses the SMS database to provide the data to the SMS Administrator Console. Figure 1-3 demonstrates this relationship.

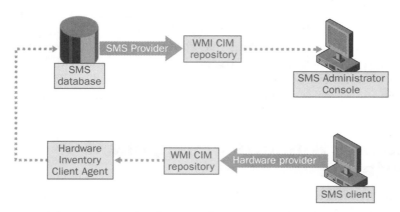

Figure 1-3. *Relationship between the SMS Provider, the WMI, and the SMS database.*

The SMS site database objects, views, and tables aren't directly accessible or modifiable except through the WMI layer. SMS provides an open architecture, however, that makes it possible to create tools other than the SMS Administrator Console that can access and manipulate the SMS database objects. In essence, you could use any WMI-compliant and ODBC-compliant application to access these objects. So you could view the data with a Web browser using ActiveX controls or Java, through applications written using C++, Visual Basic, or the Component Object Model (COM).

WMI is installed with Windows 2000, Windows XP, and the Windows Server 2003 family operating systems. It's also installed on all Windows 98 and

Windows NT 4.0 clients when the SMS client is installed. The registry is modified to reflect the WMI component installation, and the Windows Management Instrumentation service is installed and started. Of course, it's already available on Windows 2000 and later clients. If WMI has already been installed on the desktop, SMS requires that it be WMI version 1.50.1085 or later.

What's Changed Since System Management Server 2.0?

SMS 2003 differs from SMS 2.0 in several key areas. SMS 2003 is capable of leveraging your existing Active Directory structure. This means that you can model your SMS structure and manage your SMS resources without having to create and maintain a separate hierarchical structure. In addition, using the functionality of Active Directory and the new Advanced Client allows for exceptional manageability of so-called mobile client computers, most notably portable computers.

Security Modes

This difference is manifested in two installation modes now available for SMS 2003: standard security and advanced security. If you choose to implement standard security, for example, because your network still consists of some Windows NT 4.0 servers or hasn't been upgraded to Active Directory native mode, or because you are upgrading an existing SMS 2.0 site, the installation will effectively result in an SMS site that functions not much differently from the way SMS 2.0 sites did. For example, SMS 2003 will still create a slew of internal accounts and use them to manage connections between clients and servers and the functioning of SMS services and components.

However, if you choose to implement advanced security, for example, because your network is a fully implemented native mode Active Directory network, or because all your SMS component servers are running Windows 2000 or later and are registered in Active Directory, you'll be able to take advantage of the features of SMS 2003 designed to use Active Directory functionality. You can enable one or more of the three new Active Directory discovery methods mentioned earlier in this chapter and assign and use the new management point site system role that's used to manage Advanced Clients. Important for resource management, advanced security relies on the use of local system context to run services and components and computer accounts rather than user accounts to manage communication between servers.

SMS Component Changes

As you read earlier in this chapter, several additions and enhancements have been made to existing SMS components. The most notable of these include the ability to base SMS site boundaries on your Active Directory sites as well as IP addresses, the ability to use the enhanced features of the MMC, the full integration and reconfiguration of software metering, the extended functionality of package distribution to support Advanced Clients, and the ability to audit inventoried software based on specific file names and wildcards.

Here are some of the notable enhancements made to the package distribution process:

- SMS 2003 can use BITS to make more efficient use of network bandwidth and to transfer files from BITS-enabled distribution points and any management point.

- You can restart a package download if it's interrupted at the point it left off by beginning with the last file being downloaded if BITS has been started. BITS is set to manual by default.

- Only delta updates to packages between sites need to be sent rather than resending the entire package.

- Clients can receive packages from any distribution point rather than just from distribution points in their assigned sites.

- SMS 2003 packages can be created from Windows Installer packages and existing SMS 2.0 packages can be converted to Windows Installer compatible packages.

- Packages are now published to Add Or Remove Programs in Control Panel.

Backup and Recovery

SMS 2.0 included a fully automated backup routine for primary site servers that you could schedule through the SMS Administrator Console. This backup process captured the SMS database and related databases; SMS-specific registry keys and related registry keys, such as SQL keys; the entire SMS installation directory structure; and the site control file. In other words, it backed up every possible bit of information related to the site in case it might be needed for recovery. In addition, Microsoft provided an interactive online Recovery Expert that would essentially "ask" you a series of questions regarding the site and what you need to recover and then generate a comprehensive checklist of steps the administrator should take to recover the site.

SMS 2003 builds on these recovery features in the following ways:

- You can now automate the backup of secondary sites.

- The backup process now backs up only what's necessary to restore the site in an effort to reduce the backup time and storage space required.

- The SMS Recovery Expert is now available on the SMS CD and can be executed from the SMS setup menu.

- The often reported, but heretofore unavailable, SMS Site Repair Wizard is now integrated into the SMS site server installation and can be executed from the SMS startup menu. The SMS Site Repair Wizard allows you to automate many of the tasks outlined in the SMS Recovery Expert checklist, and it's integrated into the SMS Recovery Expert as well.

- You can use these tools as effectively for your SMS 2.0 sites as well.

Unsupported Features

Of course, when Microsoft "giveth" functionality, it sometimes must also "taketh" away. In order to keep the program size and processing requirements of SMS 2003 to reasonable levels, as well as to address changing operating system and support trends—both as stated within Microsoft and as noted within the networking market—some features of SMS 2.0 are indeed no longer supported under SMS 2003. Table 1-3 lists these unsupported features.

Table 1-3.   SMS 2.0 features no longer supported

Feature	Heads Up!
Any Windows operating system client running Windows 95 or earlier, Windows Millennium Edition (Windows Me) or MS DOS.	If you have any of these legacy systems around, you'll need to upgrade them or retain one or more SMS 2.0 sites in your SMS hierarchy to manage them. Of course, if you still have some of these systems around, you have other issues to deal with....
Novell NetWare Client and Server support	Be sure to remove any SMS 2.0 site systems roles assigned to NetWare servers before you upgrade. If you don't, you'll face the prospect of having to manually remove SMS components from those servers. Unless uninstalled before upgrading from SMS 2.0, these clients will become orphaned and will deinstall in 60 days as part of the regular client maintenance cycle.
IPX site boundaries	Any clients that use IPX to define their site boundaries (usually NetWare or Alpha clients) will become orphaned and eventually uninstalled as part of the client's regular maintenance cycle.

Table 1-3. SMS 2.0 features no longer supported

Feature	Heads Up!
Alpha-based system support	Like NetWare clients, Alpha-based clients will become orphaned after upgrading to SMS 2003.
Crystal Reports	Microsoft has replaced this old warhorse with a new reporting solution. No, your old reports will not be portable.
Logon Discovery, logon installation, and logon points	The concept of discovering and installing SMS clients through the use of an SMS logon script is now passé (although clients can be discovered when users log on when using CAP-based or manual installation). If you don't disable the Windows NT Logon Discovery and Installation methods so that SMS can remove those components from domain controllers, the domain controllers will, in effect, become "orphaned," and you'll need to manually remove those components.
Software Metering Servers	Although software metering hasn't been completely removed, it has been significantly reworked, as indicated earlier in this chapter, and the Software Metering site system role is no longer supported. As with logon points, you should remove the Software Metering role from all assigned servers before upgrading to SMS 2003.

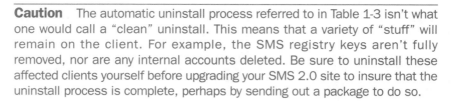

Caution   The automatic uninstall process referred to in Table 1-3 isn't what one would call a "clean" uninstall. This means that a variety of "stuff" will remain on the client. For example, the SMS registry keys aren't fully removed, nor are any internal accounts deleted. Be sure to uninstall these affected clients yourself before upgrading your SMS 2.0 site to insure that the uninstall process is complete, perhaps by sending out a package to do so.

Client Changes

On the client side, aside from streamlining the way client agents run, the most notable change is the added support for portable computers and any other computer that changes location frequently in your network called Advanced Client. Advanced Client support will be discussed in detail in Chapter 13, "Patch Management." In brief, Advanced Clients use Server Locator Points to receive component updates and advertisements. Because SMS 2003 leverages Active Directory, these clients don't need to be connected to their "home" subnet to be managed. For example, they can receive packages from any available distribution point. In addition, any Windows 2000 or later computer can take advantage of Advanced Client functionality—not just portable computers. This gives the SMS administrator significantly greater control over the management of SMS clients than in the past.

Summary

As you can see, SMS 2003 represents yet another significant advance from previous versions of SMS. It has a robust feature set, increased functionality, improved client support, and extensive status messaging and troubleshooting tools. It can take advantage of Active Directory, and it provides reliable support for Advanced Clients such as portable computers. We've reviewed most of the enhancements and new features that an SMS 2.0 administrator will encounter when implementing and managing an SMS 2003 environment. We'll explore all of these more extensively as we progress through this book.

Chapter 2
Primary Site Installation

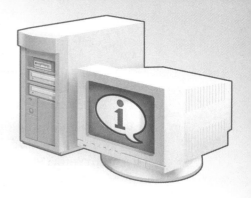

This chapter focuses on the process of installing a Microsoft Systems Management Server (SMS) 2003 primary site server. Although SMS is relatively easy to install, its implementation is far from trivial—as you'll see in the course of reading this book. Because creating an SMS site requires a great deal of thought, we begin this chapter with a discussion of planning considerations. Planning includes identifying such issues as your current network and domain structures, your Active Directory directory service structure, which SMS features you plan to install, what kinds of computers and operating systems your client base consists of, and personnel and training concerns. Next, we'll review preinstallation considerations, including hardware and software requirements and Microsoft SQL Server setup issues. We'll then look at the installation process itself, examining both express and custom setups. We'll also discuss the steps involved in removing SMS from the server if necessary. Then we review changes that take place after installation, such as what SMS services were added, what registry changes were made, and what service accounts or other Active Directory objects were created. We'll also take our first look at the SMS 2003 directory structure. Last, you'll learn how to navigate the SMS Administrator Console.

> **Note** Installation of secondary sites and the implementation of site hierarchies are discussed in Chapter 4, "Multiple-Site Structures," and migration from SMS 2.0 sites to SMS 2003 is detailed in Chapter 20, "Migration Issues."

Planning Considerations

Perhaps the most commonly heard complaint at training sessions for new users of any version of SMS is, "I installed SMS out of the box and I can't get it to work." Unlike Microsoft Word or Microsoft Excel, products that you can install and start to work with almost immediately, SMS 2003 is a more complex product consisting of a rich set of services and components. As we've seen, it contains many features and functions and requires more than just a casual walk-through. Indeed, the importance of determining where and how you'll deploy SMS 2003 can't be stressed enough. In short—planning, planning, planning!

To illustrate this point, the *Microsoft Systems Management Server 2003 Concepts, Planning, and Installation Guide*, one of the Online Library documents included with SMS 2003, has no less than seven excellent chapters (Chapters 7-13) that thoroughly outline a deployment and implementation planning strategy before even discussing the rather straightforward installation steps. Chapter 1 of the *Microsoft Systems Management Server 2003 Operations Guide*, available as a downloadable file from the SMS documentation Web site, as an orderable book, and through Microsoft TechNet, provides a step-by-step set of procedures for deploying an SMS site based on a set of common deployment scenarios. The information contained in these documents is quite detailed, so there's really no need for us to "recreate the wheel" in that respect. I strongly encourage you to read those chapters—perhaps two or three times—for the details of SMS planning and site designing. Here, however, we'll highlight those key essentials that you should take into consideration in any deployment strategy. Let's take a look at each of these key elements and ponder some of the questions that can help us develop a strong implementation and deployment strategy.

Network Infrastructure

The first, and probably the most important, material you'll need is information about your network's infrastructure (boundaries, hierarchy, and connectivity). You should have concise answers to each of the following questions:

- How is your network structured?

  Is it one large LAN, or is it segmented by routers and remote links into a WAN? This information will influence your placement of SMS sites and site systems.

- What network protocols are you employing?

  SMS 2003 requires the use of IP.

- Into how many subnets is your network divided?

  Can you identify departments, regions, or other organizational divisions by their subnet? SMS 2003 assigns clients based on IP address or Active Directory site boundaries, or both.

- How reliable is your network infrastructure?

  SMS 2003 will take advantage of well-maintained and optimized networks but will exploit poorly maintained networks. For example, if you're using 100 Mbps switches but have installed 10 Mbps network cards in your computers, your throughput will be only 10 Mbps. If you've installed 100 Mbps network cards, your throughput will be 100 Mbps. As another example, if your network is poorly routed, data collected from clients may take longer than expected to propagate from the client to the SMS site database.

- What Microsoft Windows NT/2000 domain model is in use in your organization?

  Although not strictly speaking a network infrastructure issue, the Windows NT/2000 domain model is generally influenced by the network topology. The Windows NT/2000 domain model in use might influence your design of an SMS site hierarchy. If your Windows NT/2000 domain structure is no longer efficient or appropriate for your organization's needs, now would be a good time to reconsider and restructure your Windows NT, Windows 2000, and Windows Server 2003 domains.

- Are you using Active Directory?

  SMS 2003 can leverage the use of Active Directory objects such as registered servers and computers and user and group accounts for discovery purposes.

- Do you use Active Directory sites?

  If so, how many sites do you have and would, or should, your planned SMS site hierarchy mirror your Active Directory sites?

Once you have a clear understanding of your network infrastructure, you'll be better equipped to design an SMS site structure that takes advantage of the strengths of your network infrastructure while avoiding its weaknesses. In addition, you'll be better able to discern whether you'll need to make any changes to that infrastructure.

Organizational Structure

Just as important as having an intimate understanding of your network infrastructure is to fully comprehend your organizational structure. Areas of discussion would include the geographical, physical, and hierarchical or reporting structures of the organization, the current or proposed server and client environments (or both), and matters of security. You should have ready answers for these related questions:

- What are the potential geographical implications for your proposed SMS site(s)?

Are there any language or international operating system version concerns that you should address?

- Where are your offices and potential SMS sites physically located?

  How do these sites communicate through the network (really part of the network infrastructure, but valid to restate here)?

- What's the company's departmental or hierarchical layout?

  What kind of management structure is in place? What kind of departmental communication and reporting takes place and is required? What does your IT organization look like? Who in IT is responsible for what areas of the network infrastructure, servers, clients, Internet access, and backup/recovery?

- How poorly or well does the organization structure fit your Active Directory domain and organizational unit (OU) structure?

- What long term plans for your organization might impact the current structure (mergers, acquisitions, sales)?

- What political implications need to be considered?

Needless to say, the answers to these questions will have a significant impact on your design strategy, especially the last item. In addition, as with your network infrastructure, you'll be better able to identify those areas that you should perhaps address prior to your implementation of any SMS site.

Server Environment

You'll need to know what kind of server environment you currently have and whether it can support your SMS site. Among the questions to be asked are:

- How many servers do you have and where are they located within the organization?

  Do you plan to manage any of these servers through SMS?

- Who is responsible for managing these servers and what's their level of responsibility?

  Will these managers assume any of the responsibilities inherent in managing SMS servers?

- What are the hardware and operating system levels of these servers— that is, memory, disk space, CPU speed, operating system version, and service pack level?

Are any upgrades required? Even though SMS 2003 supports a Windows NT domain structure, it can be installed only on servers running Windows 2000 with Service Pack 2 (or later) or Windows Server 2003.

- What roles and functions have been assigned to these servers—that is, DHCP, DNS, IIS, WINS, Terminal Services, clustering? Which are domain controllers?

- How are these servers currently being utilized, and what's their projected change in resource allocation over the next three to five years?

  Tools such as System Monitor can be valuable in ascertaining resource utilization.

- If you plan to manage mobile (for example, laptop) clients by utilizing SMS 2003's advanced security, does your network run in Active Directory native mode? If not, can it do so?

Understanding and documenting this data about your servers gives you valuable assistance in determining placement of your SMS servers and whether you can use existing hardware or need to invest in upgrades or new equipment.

Client Environment

As important as your server configuration is the client environment that you'll be supporting. You should be able to have answers to this list of questions:

- How many clients do you have and where are they located within your organization? How many of these do you plan to manage through SMS?

- Who is responsible for managing these clients now and what's their level of responsibility? Will these managers assume any of the responsibilities inherent in managing SMS clients?

- What are the operating system and service pack levels of these clients—that is, do they fall within the levels supported by SMS? What are the main applications installed? Should you consider any proprietary applications?

- How many of your clients are considered "mobile," that is, using laptop computers? How do your mobile clients connect to the network?

In Chapter 1, "Overview," we briefly discussed the fact that SMS 2003 provides support for a wide range of clients, including mobile clients, but within a smaller range of operating systems than with SMS 2.0. The answers to these questions help to identify which clients can and can't be managed by SMS 2003, where you might need to perform upgrades, and potentially where you might need to maintain a down-level SMS 2.0 site for legacy clients.

Security

Securing your SMS site is explored in detail in Chapter 17, "SMS Security." Nevertheless, you should ask some security-related questions during your planning and documentation phase. These questions include:

- What security policies are currently in place that might affect the deployment of SMS sites, servers, and clients? What kinds of security groups have been created?

- Who has administrative access, and to what degree have administration-related activities been delegated?

- What group policies and client lockdown levels are in force for users and computers?

The extent to which users have or don't have control over their desktops will have a significant impact on many areas of SMS—most importantly, installation of the client and deployment of packages, as we'll see later in this book. Also, you might need to address the delegation of administrative tasks to determine whether and how to best address the delegation of SMS-related administrative activities.

Systems Management Server 2003 Functionality

As part of your planning process, you should consider SMS 2003 functionality—which is to say, you must determine what SMS 2003 features and functions you intend to implement, and where. Some of the questions to be considered include:

- Do you need to track hardware or software configurations or collect files from your clients? Which clients would be affected?

- Do you need to deliver and install software packages on your clients or automatically initiate client-based programs or routines? Which clients would be affected?

- Do you need to remotely troubleshoot your clients by taking control of their desktops, viewing system information, transferring files, running programs, or restarting the client? Which clients would be affected?

- Do you need to track the use of installed applications on your clients and monitor and disallow use of unsupported programs? Which clients would be affected?

- Do you need or want to manage site boundaries, target collections, and manage mobile clients through the functionality of Active Directory?

- Do you have a need to produce and publish reports based on inventory and other client properties that can be viewed using a Web browser?

Your answers to these questions will certainly drive your decisions as far as the number of SMS sites to implement, the number and type of site systems to deploy in each site, and the site's ultimate hierarchical structure.

Putting It Together

At this point we can begin to tie some of these planning considerations together. An organization with more diverse requirements might require more SMS 2003 sites to be installed. For example, client options such as Remote Tools are site-wide options. In general, you can't deploy Remote Tools for only some clients in a site; instead, you must deploy Remote Tools for *all* clients in a site. This is where a good understanding of your network infrastructure will be beneficial. It might be possible to use your network's subnets or Active Directory sites to your advantage. In the Remote Tools scenario, if the clients that require Remote Tools support can be segmented to their own subnet or Active Directory site, you can install a separate SMS 2003 site to provide Remote Tools support.

As another example, suppose the finance department requires that its employees maintain and deploy their own packages within their department. Their packages are specific to their environment and their users. You could manage all the packages from a central site, but doing so would mean that the finance-specific packages might also need to move through a wider network path than is necessary. If the finance department is defined by its own subnet or Active Directory site, you can give it its own SMS 2003 site. Employees can then deploy their packages only within their own subnet and not affect the rest of the network. Remember that creating multiple sites like this isn't always desirable, or even practical. These examples simply demonstrate the need for a clear understanding of your organizational structure and all its implications.

As a third example, consider how well-connected your network servers are. Suppose that a significant number of users move from subnet to subnet and still need access to packages and client component updates. Suppose, too, that some of those subnets are connected to the network through slow or unreliable connections. In this scenario you need to think carefully about the placement of

SMS component servers such as client access points (CAPs), management points, and distribution points. Indeed, you might well decide that a better solution is to implement SMS sites in those poorly connected locations so that you have more control over how network bandwidth is utilized across those network connections.

The Hardware Inventory Agent collects hardware inventory on the SMS client, with changes copied to a CAP or management point. The CAP or management point, in turn, sends the changes on to the site server. The site server updates the SMS database with the change information. The amount of data that's generated, and the corresponding network bandwidth that will be used, will be determined by the number of clients involved and how frequently inventory information is collected. Bandwidth considerations will generally be less of a concern within a LAN than across a wide area link. In other words, it will be more efficient and perhaps less disruptive to the network to collect this inventory if the client, CAP, site server, and database are all located in the same LAN.

Now suppose that your company needs to send packages from a central location to various geographic regions around the world. Package files are copied to distribution points within the SMS site. These files include source files, programs, and installation scripts and can represent a fairly large amount of data. Microsoft Office XP, for example, could require more than 300 MB of storage space. This data must be moved across the network to the distribution points and generally moves in an uncompressed state. You could certainly plan for one large SMS 2003 site, with distribution points in each geographic region. Your packages will then need to be copied to these distribution points across WAN links and will have to contend with any other WAN traffic that might be occurring. Alternatively, you could plan for an SMS site in each geographic region. Each SMS site can have one or more local distribution points. Package files are compressed before they're sent from one site to another. Also, you can adjust how much bandwidth is actually used when communicating from one site to another. This arrangement should significantly improve WAN performance related to package distribution. As you can surmise, a thorough understanding and documentation of your network infrastructure, number and location of your servers and clients, and the structure and location of your Active Directory sites will be extremely valuable in evaluating design decisions.

Personnel, Training, and Testing

As you develop your deployment strategy, keep in mind who needs to use SMS 2003. You can easily delegate the features and functions of SMS 2003 to various users. Help desk personnel, for example, can be given access to Remote Tools but not to any other features. An SMS administrator in the finance department might be given the ability to create packages and advertisements and to deploy them only to finance department users. This distribution of tasks is an essential part of determining where and how to implement SMS 2003 and to establish the appropriate levels of training and security required. Security options are explored in Chapter 17.

Another aspect of personnel considerations might be staffing issues. In a small site, one person might be responsible for most or all SMS-related support issues, including not only things like package distribution and remote control, but also site design, database maintenance, network analysis and troubleshooting, status message analysis, SQL administration, package scripting, and general troubleshooting. But in a medium-sized SMS site structure—let's say three SMS sites with perhaps a thousand clients—one person will be hard-pressed to adequately maintain all aspects of the SMS sites. In fact, each site should have at least one SMS administrator assigned. In an ideal setting, SMS 2003 will be provided with a support team among whose members tasks will be divided throughout the SMS site structure. Remember that SMS 2003 is designed to be a network management tool. This product is not trivial to set up or to maintain. Treat it with the same consideration that you give your Windows domain support and your network infrastructure support. It truly requires no less.

Let's also not forget the need to properly staff the implementation process. The planning and design stage of your implementation is the ideal time to involve some, if not all, of the interested and affected parties in the deployment process, not only to receive their input, but also to facilitate a higher comfort level with the product and the way it works *before* it goes live. This leads us into a nice segue and a topic that's near and dear to this author's heart—training.

Along with appropriate staffing comes appropriate training. Even if management and budget constraints don't welcome the possibility, SMS 2003 is definitely not the kind of product that you can install out of the box and begin using immediately. (You'll hopefully come to this conclusion yourself by the end of this book.) And although you could teach yourself how to use SMS 2003, the most effective learning environment will be one that's structured and controlled and one in which you can freely destroy SMS if you like!

Several Microsoft-certified training centers offer courses in SMS 2003. Other training centers offer their own versions of SMS 2003 training. You should seriously consider some kind of formal training for yourself and your staff before rolling out SMS 2003. This training might include administrative tasks for those users involved in the day-to-day operations of SMS 2003, such as using Remote Tools or creating advertising packages. For those staffers involved in the background support of SMS 2003, training should include a thorough review of SMS services and processes, security, site system roles, network traffic considerations, and performance issues. Guides such as this book will serve to supplement and reinforce that training.

> **Tip** From time to time, Microsoft publishes online webcasts that you can view live or later at your leisure (if network administrators can ever find leisure time!). These can be informative and serve as a source of "continuing" education. Watch for webcast notices on the Microsoft SMS Web site: *http://www.microsoft.com/smserver*.

Seriously consider setting up a lab environment in which you can simulate your network environment, experiment with different site and site system configurations, perform stress testing on site systems and network load—without worrying about damaging SMS. Such an undertaking isn't always possible, of course, but think of how much time, energy, and expense you might save by testing your SMS strategy in a lab rather than in live production. And after your SMS sites have been implemented, you can continue to use your lab to test the viability of package scripts, to stage new clients, and to test troubleshooting and recovery strategies. This strategy will have a positive impact on productivity while reducing the potential for problems in the production environment. All in all, this will be money well spent with a quantifiable return on your investment!

Preinstallation Requirements

In this section we'll explore the specific hardware and software requirements for SMS 2003 sites and site systems, beginning with SQL Server because it's an integral part of SMS and the SQL Server database serves as the repository for most of the data that SMS collects. To that effect, we'll explore database size and security considerations as well as SQL Server optimization considerations. We'll also explore the hardware and software requirements of the Windows server that will become your SMS site server.

SQL Server Requirements

SMS 2003 requires the existence of a SQL Server 7.0 with Service Pack 3 or later applied or SQL Server 2000 with Service Pack 3a or later applied. As with SMS 2.0, if SQL Server is installed on the same computer as the SMS site server, SMS can create the database for you. If SQL Server is installed on a separate computer, you must create the database before you install SMS 2003 and be sure that the SQL Server settings are appropriate for SMS.

If you install SMS 2003 on the same computer as SQL Server, SMS 2003 will not only create the database for you, but it will also tune SQL Server for use with SMS 2003. This does not, of course, relieve you of all responsibility for maintaining SQL Server or the SMS database, but it does ease some of the setup concerns regarding SQL Server, which is especially helpful if you have little experience with SQL Server.

Note During the setup process for SMS 2.0, if SQL was not already installed on the proposed site server, the SMS 2.0 installation process prompted you for the SQL Server source files and installed a dedicated SQL Server database for itself on that same server. The SMS 2003 installation process doesn't do this. It's recommended that you install SQL Server before running the SMS 2003 setup.

More Info Although a working knowledge of SQL Server isn't required to install and work with SMS 2003, in the long run you'll need a good working knowledge of at least SQL Server administration tasks. SMS 2003 is not itself a database server; rather, it acts as a front end to the SMS site database maintained in SQL Server. Therefore, you'll need to initiate many database maintenance tasks through the SMS Administrator Console or through SQL Server. Consider taking a class in SQL Server administration, such as Microsoft-certified course 2072, "Administering a Microsoft SQL Server 2000 Database," or 2071, "Querying Microsoft SQL Server 2000 with Transact-SQL." Microsoft Press offers several books about SQL Server. One that I especially recommend is *Microsoft SQL Server 2000 Performance Tuning Technical Reference* (Microsoft Press, 2001). Many of the performance tuning methods and formulas presented in that book are directly applicable when planning for capacity and hardware requirements for SMS component servers.

There are two main issues to consider for the SQL Server installation.

1. Should the installation of SQL Server be dedicated to the SMS site database and not shared with other SQL databases?

2. Should you install SQL Server on the same computer as the site server or should you install it on a separate server?

Microsoft recommends that you have a dedicated installation of SQL Server just for SMS 2003. This is because of the significant increase in information SMS 2003 now stores in the database, the over 200 SQL transactions and triggers related to SMS 2003 processes and services, the 40-50 connection accounts required just for the site server, the resource requirements of SQL Server itself, and the fact that SMS 2003 uses Windows Management Instrumentation (WMI) to provide access to the database for the SMS Administrator Console. However, there's nothing inherent in the way the SMS site database is maintained that precludes your sharing an instance of SQL Server with other SQL databases or, for that matter, with other SMS site databases. You'll need an adequate hardware configuration for that server to handle the load appropriately.

Similarly, Microsoft recommends installing SQL Server on the same computer as the site server. Doing so provides more efficient access to the database for the site server and significantly reduces network traffic involved with SMS-SQL transactions. However, this arrangement will also require an increased investment in hardware on the proposed site server computer to accommodate the resource requirements for both SMS 2003 and SQL Server. This cost will be felt in three areas:

- **Processing memory (RAM)** SMS 2003 requires a minimum of 256 MB of RAM. SQL Server requires a minimum of 64 MB of RAM and is driven largely by the size of the database(s) it will maintain. So the total RAM requirement will be significant. On the other hand, RAM is relatively inexpensive.

- **Disk storage and I/O** SMS 2003 requires a minimum of 2 GB of disk storage. SQL Server can require up to 270 MB, depending on the type of installation, and this doesn't take into account the amount of storage required for the database itself. SMS 2003 has an automatic minimum of 50 MB for the database and 20 MB for the transaction log. Most SMS 2003 and SQL processes are disk intensive, so the faster the disk access, the better the performance gained. Unlike RAM, disk upgrades can be costly. For example, hardware-based redundant array of independent disks (RAID) systems offering disk mirroring (RAID 1) or disk striping with parity (RAID 5), or both, provide excellent I/O performance as well as fault tolerance in the event of a disk failure. However, such a system can be expensive.

- **Processor** The type of processor used will obviously affect the performance of the site server. SMS 2003 requires a minimum 550 MHz processor-Intel/Celeron family or compatible, while SQL Server requires a minimum 166 MHz processor. Two or more processors installed in your server would be preferable for optimum performance, as Windows 2000 and Windows Server 2003 will certainly take advantage of their presence. Again, multiple-processor systems can be expensive.

Ultimately you'll need to balance resource requirements, network traffic concerns, and overall performance considerations when deciding whether to use a single computer for both SQL Server and SMS 2003 or separate computers.

Sizing the Database

SMS 2003 requires a minimum practical database size of 50 MB and a transaction log of 20 MB. I say practical, because this is the published minimum to support a small (100-1000, perhaps) client install base. However, you can successfully install SMS 2003 with smaller database sizes, especially for demo or testing purposes. Microsoft recommends anticipating around 220 KB per client for the database. The transaction log should be at least 20 percent of the database size. Additional factors in determining the amount of database space required include the amount of hardware and software inventory collected; the number of packages, programs, and advertisements that will be deployed; the size and number of collections; the type and number of discovered resources; and the number of queries and status messages to be maintained.

The *Systems Management Server 2003 Concepts, Planning, and Deployment Guide* offers the following formula for determining database size:

50 MB + (x × 220 KB) (where x is the number of clients in the site)

This formula is based on a weekly hardware and software inventory schedule, default aging interval (90 days) of discovery and inventory out of the database, and 20 status messages reported by each client each week. If we apply this formula to a single site with 1000 clients, we get:

*50 MB + (1000 * 220 KB) = 270 MB*

Keep in mind that the actual database size will be affected by changes you make in the default settings for hardware and software inventory, aging, and the actual number of status messages generated. Sizing the database is not an exact science, and it will require that you monitor database usage periodically.

As if this weren't enough to consider, don't forget your site hierarchy. If you have identified child sites, these sites will report their inventory, discovery records, status messages, and site configuration to their parent site. You must allow space for this additional information in the parent site's SMS database. Needless to say, the greatest cause for concern regarding database space will be at the central site, as it will collect and maintain database information for every site below it in the site hierarchy.

Database Security

You'll need to create an account that SMS will use to generate, access, and maintain its database. This is known to SMS as the SQL Server Account. However, if you haven't created a specific account and you installed SMS with standard security, SMS will use the SMS Service Account. If you haven't created a specific account and you installed SMS with advanced security, SMS will use the SMS site server's local system account.

Two basic types of security are available for the SQL Server database: SQL Server and Windows and Windows Only authentication. SQL Server and Windows authentication uses SQL Server-specific accounts that are maintained within SQL Server. The SQL Server account must be specified when making the connection to SQL Server. SQL Server and Windows authentication is present for backward compatibility and for Windows 95 and Windows 98 clients. In this scenario the default SQL login ID is "sa," which stands for system administrator and, by default, has no password assigned. Windows Only authentication indicates that the database may be accessed by using a Windows account. Windows Only authentication is always available. SQL Server and Windows authentication can be enabled and disabled.

If you use SQL Server and Windows authentication, you can create a Windows account that SMS will use to create and access the database in SQL Server and then map that account to the sa account using the SQL Security Manager by making the account a member of the administrators group on the server running SQL, or you can let SMS use the existing SMS Service account if SMS was installed with standard security or the local system account if SMS was installed with advanced security. By default, all members of the Administrators group in the server running SQL are mapped to the sa account. If the server running SQL is a member of the same domain as the SMS site server, SMS can use the SMS Service account to access the database, as this account becomes a member of the Domain Admins global group, which is, by default, a member of the local Administrators group on every member server in the domain. If the server running SQL isn't a member of the same domain, you can either establish a trust relationship between the domain in which the server running SQL resides and the domain in which the SMS site server resides and add the Domain Admins group from the SMS domain to the Administrators local group on the server running SQL, or you can explicitly create a duplicate account (and password) in the SQL Server domain so that Windows pass-through authentication can allow access to the server running SQL and thus the database, though the latter is not recommended as a best practice.

Tuning SQL Server

As stated earlier, if you let SMS install SQL Server for you, or if SQL Server is already installed on the intended SMS site server, SMS will set SQL Server parameters to their optimum settings for you. If you install and configure SQL Server yourself, you should pay attention to some specific SQL Server configuration parameters and set them appropriately before installing SMS 2003. Now if you installed SQL Server without changing any of its defaults, SQL Server will be able to automatically and dynamically modify and allocate the required parameters. However, if you choose to maintain and monitor some or all of the

SQL Server settings yourself, Table 2-1 lists those parameters that are specific to SMS and provides guidelines as to how they should be set.

Table 2-1. **SQL Server configuration parameters**

Parameter	Guidelines
User Connections	SMS 2003 requires a minimum of 40 user connections for the site server and two connections for each SMS Administrator console you plan to install. It also requires five additional user connections for each instance of the SMS Administrator Console, if more than five consoles will be running concurrently on your site. You can set SMS 2003 to calculate this number and configure it automatically during setup. Each installation of SMS 2003 requires 20 user connections. By default, SQL Server will dynamically allocate the appropriate number of connections.
Open Objects	Open Objects indicates the number of tables, views, stored procedures, and the like that can be open at a time. If you exceed the number of open objects specified, SQL must close some objects before it can open others, resulting in a performance hit. By default, SQL Server will dynamically allocate this value. However, if you need to manually manage this value, for large SMS sites, this number should be 5000 or more. Use SQL Server Performance Monitor counters to track the number of open objects in use to determine the optimum number for the SMS site.
Memory	Memory indicates the amount of RAM that should be used for database caching and management. SMS automatically allocates 16 MB of RAM for SQL Server use. SQL Server allocates memory dynamically in 8 KB units. You can define a range for SQL Server to use.
Locks	Locks prevent users from accessing and updating the same data at the same time. Because of the volume of information contained in the database, Microsoft recommends setting this value from 5000 to 10,000 depending on the size of the database and the number of SMS Administrator Consoles. By default, SQL Server will dynamically allocate the appropriate number of locks.
Tempdb Size	The temporary database and log are used to manage queries and sorts. By default, the tempdb database and log information are maintained in the same SQL device. For best performance, each should be kept in this default location. Set the tempdb database size to at least 20 percent of the SMS database size. Set the tempdb log size to at least 20 percent of the tempdb database size. SQL Server, as you have by now surmised, sizes the tempdb database dynamically by default.

Although system clock synchronization isn't a function of SQL Server per se, it's nevertheless important that you synchronize the system clocks between the server running SQL and the SMS site server if they're on separate computers. When an SMS service or process schedules a task, it will use the system clock of the server running SQL to trigger the task.

Real World   Synchronizing Time

Conventional and unconventional wisdom alike suggest that you identify a time server for your SMS site that synchronizes the system clocks not only between the server running SQL and the SMS site server, but also among all SMS site systems and SMS clients. This should be an essential part of your deployment strategy for SMS 2003. SMS services use the system clock of the server running SQL when scheduling tasks. However, SMS clients and site systems will look to their own system clocks when determining when scheduled tasks should run. Scheduling tasks is perhaps most critical with SMS clients.

When you advertise a program to a collection of SMS clients, you can assign a schedule for that program to run, or you can make the program mandatory to run at an assigned time. The SMS client agent (Advertised Programs Client Agent) that checks for available advertisements will determine whether the program is scheduled to run at an assigned or a mandatory time. However, the agent will determine this schedule based on the SMS client's system clock. If the system clock on the client isn't correct for some reason, the program might not run at the expected time, and might never run.

Here's an example. Suppose you have a user who obtains trial software that's time-stamped to run for a specific trial period—say 120 days. The user decides that she likes the product, but she doesn't want to actually buy it. To keep using the software beyond the proscribed time period, the easy thing to do is to set the system clock back—perhaps a couple of months, perhaps a year. Not touching on the legal or ethical issues involved here, this tampering can wreak havoc on your advertised programs. As you can see, something scheduled to run today might in fact never run on this user's SMS clients. Presumably, if your clients are Windows NT 4.0 or higher, the user will not have the security rights to change the time on her system clock. Nevertheless, in many organizations users are routinely given administrative rights on their own desktops and so would be able to configure their clock settings.

The steps involved in creating devices, databases, security accounts, and so on are outlined in Chapter 19, "Maintaining the Database Through Microsoft SQL Server."

Caution   A final thought about SQL preparations: be sure the SQL services have been set to autostart after installing SQL Server manually. If you don't, you could be in for a big surprise after you install SMS 2003 and then restart the server.

Site Server Requirements

SMS 2003 site servers have specific hardware and software requirements. Some of these include disk space, memory, processor, and operating system. We'll outline these requirements, as well as explore other platform considerations, such as Windows Terminal Server and Cluster Server support, in this section.

Hardware Requirements

SMS 2003 has the following hardware and platform requirements:

- Be sure that your computer hardware is included on the Windows 2000 or Windows Server 2003 Hardware Compatibility List (HCL). It's sometimes possible to install Windows on computers whose hardware components might not be on the HCL. However, when you install a Microsoft BackOffice product onto such a server, you might experience anomalous activity—like the "blue screen of death." It's not worth the gamble.

- The server platform must be X86-based. Alpha systems are no longer supported.

- SMS 2003 requires a minimum processor type of Pentium 550 MHz. The more powerful (and plentiful) the processor(s), the better performance you'll see. Dual-processor systems are strongly recommended.

- SMS 2003 requires a minimum of 256 MB of RAM. Of this, 16 MB is automatically allocated to SQL Server. SMS 2003 running on a 64 MB server is not a pretty sight. As RAM is a relatively inexpensive upgrade, you should install at least 256 MB, testing performance under various load conditions and then upgrading RAM as necessary.

- SMS 2003 must be installed on a Windows 2000 or Windows Server 2003 file system (NTFS) partition. SMS 2003 uses NTFS permissions to secure access to SMS directories and shares. An SMS 2003 site server or site system may be a member server in a Windows NT 4.0 domain, Windows 2000, or Windows Server 2003 domain, or it may be a Windows 2000 or Windows Server 2003 domain controller.

- SMS 2003 requires that a minimum of 2 GB of hard disk space be available on an NTFS partition. Keep in mind that the actual amount of disk space required ultimately depends on such factors as the system roles the site server will employ, the number of clients and resources that will be managed, and the number of packages, programs, and advertisements that will be generated. For example, 2 GB of free space might be sufficient if the site server functions as a server locator point and a CAP in a medium-sized stand-alone site. However, if the site server will also function as a management point, reporting point, and distribution point in a large enterprise environment, you'll almost certainly require additional disk space for storing the package files.

Note A medium-sized stand-alone site refers to a site with a few thousand clients that's collecting hardware and software inventory, status messages, and discovery data based on the SMS 2003 default settings. The assumption is that the site averages two to three packages a week of about 20 to 30 MB in size and two to three advertisements a week. These examples should be taken as soft guidelines only. As always, you must test your SMS 2003 configuration within the unique requirements of your own organization and modify it to provide you with satisfactory performance parameters.

- Microsoft also recommends a higher video resolution than you might have on most Windows servers. SMS 2003 will function just fine with a standard VGA resolution monitor. However, if you plan to use the SMS Administrator Console on the site server itself for regular site tasks, consider setting video resolution to at least 256 colors, 800-by-600 pixels.

- Microsoft also always mentions the following two devices in its requirements list, although it's hard to imagine purchasing a server nowadays without them: a mouse and a CD-ROM drive. (Performing SMS 2003 tasks using only keyboard shortcuts is possible but would be ill-advised.)

Software Requirements

In addition to the hardware requirements we outlined previously, you need to consider the following software requirements before beginning the SMS 2003 installation process:

- The SMS 2003 Site Server must be installed on a Windows 2000 Server, Advanced Server, or Datacenter Server with Service Pack 2 or later installed, or Windows Server 2003 (Standard, Enterprise, or Datacenter Editions).

- IIS is required for server locator points, management points, and reporting points. It's also required for distribution points that have Background Intelligent Transfer Service (BITS) enabled.

- Management points require Windows 2000 Service Pack 3 or later. Also, you must enable BITS (the Windows component) on your management points if you intend to use BITS-enabled distribution points.

- All SMS Standard Clients must have Microsoft Internet Explorer 5.0 or later installed.

- SMS 2003, as we've seen, requires SQL Server 7.0 Service Pack 3 or later applied, or SQL Server 2000 Service Pack 3a or later. You can install either as part of the SMS 2003 setup routine. See the section "SQL Server Requirements" earlier in this chapter for a discussion of the merits of having SMS 2003 perform the SQL Server installation for you.

Windows Cluster Service Considerations

SMS 2003 doesn't directly support Windows Cluster Service. If you must run SMS 2003 on clustered servers, be sure to take the following precautions:

- Do not install the site server or any site systems on the shared drive of any cluster with the exception of distribution points.

- Install the site server or any site systems on only one node of a cluster. If one node of a cluster is a site system, the other node must be an SMS client.

- Note that cluster fail-over isn't supported at all except for distribution points.

More Info For more information about how SMS 2003 interacts with Windows 2000 Server Clustering, read the technical paper "Microsoft Windows 2000 Server Clustering Interoperability with SMS" available from the Microsoft SMS Web site (*http://www.microsoft.com/smserver*).

Installing a Primary Site Server

Now that you have created a viable deployment strategy for your SMS 2003 site, decided how to install and configure your SQL Server, and confirmed the hardware and software requirements necessary for a successful installation of SMS 2003, it's time to begin the installation process itself. This section will concentrate on the installation of an SMS 2003 primary site server. Installing secondary site servers and other site system roles will be discussed in Chapter 3, "Configuring Site Server Properties and Site Systems," and Chapter 4.

Installation Options

You can install your SMS 2003 site server using a variety of techniques and options. You may install directly from the CD, or you can first copy the source files from CD to the local hard disk of the proposed site server or a network drive. If you choose to copy the source files to a drive location, be sure to copy the entire SMS 2003 CD, as the installation process might require files located in support folders. You can also run a scripted automated setup. Figure 2-1 shows the autorun screen that appears when you insert the SMS 2003 CD. Notice that besides starting the setup wizard, you can also run the integrated Recovery Expert as well as view documentation included as part of the Online Library.

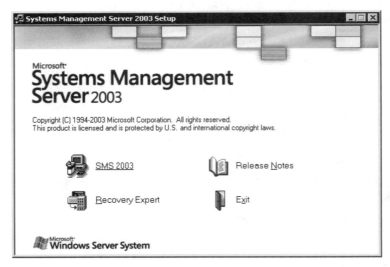

Figure 2-1. *The setup screen that appears when you first insert the SMS 2003 CD.*

Once you have located the source files, you can run the installation interactively through the Systems Management Server Setup Wizard by inserting the SMS 2003 CD and choosing SMS 2003 from the autorun menu shown in Figure 2-1, or, if you prefer to run Setup.exe from the \SMSSetup\Bin\I386 folder or choose to run an unattended setup, you can also initiate the installation from a Windows command prompt. The command-line syntax is shown here:

SETUP [/?] [/SCRIPT scriptname] [/UPGRADE] [/NODISKCHECK] [/NOACCTCHECK]

The command-line method provides five switch options to initiate the setup process under different circumstances, as outlined in Table 2-2. If you execute the SMS 2003 Setup.exe from the command line, you'll still launch the Systems Management Server Setup Wizard, which presents you with a series of nice, "user-friendly" installation pages that guide you every step of the way.

Table 2-2. Command-line switch options

Switch	Description
/?	Displays a pop-up dialog box listing that describes each switch along with the command-line syntax.
/SCRIPT scriptname	Allows you to specify a path and script file, which provides the different pieces of information required during setup for unattended installation.
/UPGRADE	Allows to you specify an unattended upgrade from an earlier version of SMS.

Table 2-2.   Command-line switch options

Switch	Description
/NODISKCHECK	Allows you to perform the installation without having SMS 2003 check for available disk space first. Assumes that you have already confirmed that you have the required amount of disk space available.
/NOACCTCHECK	Allows you to perform the installation without having SMS 2003 check the specified service account for the appropriate level of permission and rights. Assumes that you have already created the account and have given it the appropriate administrative permissions and the Log On As A Service user right.

Unattended Installation

If you choose to run an unattended installation, you'll need to run setup from the command line using the /SCRIPT option, which references an information file called an SMS initialization file. This is actually just a standard .INF file, similar to those you might have worked with before when running unattended installations of other products.

The SMS initialization file consists of three sections: [Identification], [Options], and [SQLConfigOptions]. For those of you who have installed previous versions of SMS, these sections should sound familiar, as each refers to a different set of setup information you normally provide when manually running setup. Those of you who haven't installed SMS before will notice the link as you continue through this chapter. Chapter 15 of the *SMS 2003 Concepts, Planning, and Installation Guide* describes how to construct this information file in some detail. Here are just some of the data that you can specify in each section.

In the [Identification] section, you can identify what kind of installation you want to perform—primary site, secondary site, or SMS Administrators console.

In the [Options] section, you can identify setup options specific to primary and secondary site installations. For example, for a primary site installation, you can define product registration and organization information, which additional SMS components to install— Remote Tools, Package Automation Scripts—the security mode you wish to use, standard or advanced—service account name, domain, and password, the site code, site domain, and site name, and the folder location where the SMS server files will be installed. For a secondary site installation, you can define the default connection address that the parent site should use for the secondary site, the connection account name and password to be used by the sender at this site, and the parent site code.

In the [SQLConfigOptions] section, you can identify setup options related to SQL information that setup needs to complete successfully. This information includes the SMS database name, number of simultaneous SQL connections your SMS site database requires, and the type of security or authentication mode to use.

Here is an example of an SMS initialization file for a primary site:

```
[Identification]
Action=InstallPrimarySite

[Options]
FullName=Steven Kaczmarek
OrgName=Enact Solutions Corp
ProductID=123-4567890
SiteCode=S00
SiteName=ENACT Primary Site
SiteDomain=ENACTCorp
SecurityMode=Standard
ServiceAccount=smsservice
ServiceAccountDomain=ENACTCorp
ServiceAccountPassword=Scruffy&4315Glem
NumOfClients=100
OptionalUnits=Remote Control
OptionalUnits=Scripts
SMSInstallDir=F:\SMS
InstallSQLServer=0
NumberOfAdminUI=5
SDKServer=ENACT1

[SQLConfigOptions]
SQLServerName=ENACT1
SQLServerVersion=2000
UseSQLIntegratedSecurity=1
CreateSQLDevice=1
DatabaseName=SMS_S00
DatabaseDevice=SMSdata_S00
LogDevice=SMSlog_S00
SQLDevicePath=F:\MSSQL\SMSDATA
NumberOfSqlConnections=75
AutoConfigSqlConnections=1
```

Express vs. Custom Setup

When you begin the setup process on a server, you'll be presented with two installation options: Express Setup and Custom Setup. Express Setup installs most SMS 2003 components and features, enables all discovery methods except Network Discovery, enables all client agents except Software Inventory and

Software Metering, and creates all applicable service accounts depending on the security mode you choose. Custom Setup lets you choose which components and features to install. Custom Setup doesn't automatically enable any discovery methods (except Heartbeat Discovery) or client agents.

Table 2-3 describes which SMS components are available with each setup option. Table 2-4 outlines the default values that are set during an express installation versus a custom installation. These features, discovery methods, installation methods, and client agents have additional options that you can configure; these elements are discussed in their respective chapters later in this book.

Table 2-3. SMS 2003 setup option defaults

Option	Express Install—Primary Site	Custom Install—Primary Site	Secondary Site Installation
SMS site server	Installed	Installed	Installed
SMS Administrator Console	Installed	Installed	Available
Remote Tools	Installed	Optional	Optional
Package automation scripts	Installed	Optional	Not Available

Table 2-4. SMS 2003 components installed during setup

Feature	Express Install	Default Value	Custom Install
Discovery Methods			
Windows Networking User Discovery	Enabled	Once a day at midnight	Disabled
Windows Networking User Group Discovery	Enabled	Once a day at midnight	Disabled
Heartbeat Discovery	Enabled	Once a week for Custom Setup; once a day for Express Setup	Enabled
Network Discovery	Disabled	No default; configured by administrator	Disabled
Active Directory System Discovery	Enabled if Advanced Security mode is selected	Once a day at midnight	Disabled
Active Directory System Group Discovery	Enabled if Advanced Security mode is selected	Once a day at midnight	Disabled
Active Directory User Discovery	Enabled if Advanced Security mode is selected	Once a day at midnight	Disabled
Installation Methods			
Client Push Installation	Enabled	N/A	Disabled

Table 2-4. SMS 2003 components installed during setup

Feature	Express Install	Default Value	Custom Install
Client Agents			
Advertised Programs Client Agent	Enabled	Polls every 60 minutes for advertised programs; scheduled programs have 5-minute countdown; user can make changes to settings	Disabled
Hardware Inventory Client Agent	Enabled	Once a day	Disabled
Software Inventory Client Agent	Disabled	N/A	Disabled
Remote Tools Client Agent	Enabled	All remote options enabled; user permission required; user notified; user can make changes to settings	Disabled
Software Metering Client Agent	Disabled	N/A	Disabled

Express Setup is a fast and easy way to install SMS 2003 and is recommended for evaluation installations or test environments. Express Setup requires that SQL Server 7.0 Service Pack 3 or later or SQL Server 2000 Service Pack 3a or later be already installed on the same server. It then creates and configures SQL Server database files for SMS, sets the SQL Server parameters (as discussed in the section "SQL Server Requirements" earlier in this chapter), and creates all applicable service accounts. When installation is complete, the site server will assume the site system roles of CAP and distribution point.

The Custom Setup option installs SMS 2003 with the basic site server and SMS Administrator Console installed. All other SMS 2003 features and components are options that you can select as desired. You can always leave an option cleared and install it at a later time. If the option is selected, it will be installed, but not enabled, by default. Once an option is installed, however, you can't uninstall it without removing and reinstalling SMS 2003. The site server will assume the site system roles of CAP and distribution point.

Custom Setup doesn't require that SQL Server 7.0 or SQL Server 2000 be installed on the same server (if SQL Server isn't already available). However, if

SQL Server has been installed on the same server, Custom Setup creates and configures SQL Server database files for SMS, sets the SQL Server parameters, and creates all applicable service accounts.

Running Setup

To install a primary site server, follow these steps:

1. Insert the SMS 2003 CD and choose SMS 2003 from the autorun menu (shown in Figure 2-1), or in Windows Explorer navigate to the SMS 2003 source files and execute Autorun.exe to display the autorun menu or execute Setup.exe from a command prompt.

2. The Welcome page appears, as shown in Figure 2-2.

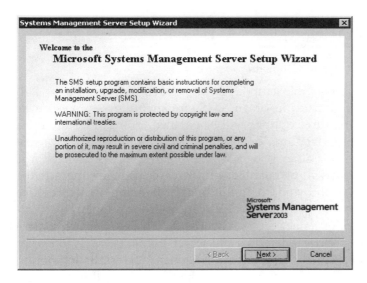

Figure 2-2. *The Setup Wizard Welcome page.*

3. Click Next to display the System Configuration page, as shown in Figure 2-3. At this time, Setup checks to see whether you have any earlier versions of SMS installed or if the server is already functioning as an SMS site system.

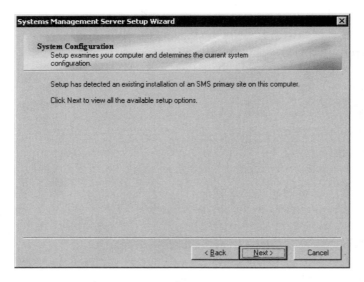

Figure 2-3. *The System Configuration page.*

4. Click Next to display the Setup Options page, as shown in Figure 2-4. If no current installation of an SMS site server or site system is detected, the first three options will be enabled. You can install a primary site, a secondary site, or just the SMS Administrator Console and related tools. If an existing SMS 2003 site server is detected, the last three options will be enabled. In this case, you can upgrade the existing installation by adding additional SMS components, remove SMS 2003, or modify or reset the installation—for example, by changing service account names and passwords or rebuilding a site control file. If the Setup Wizard detects a site server installation for an earlier version of SMS, only the Upgrade An Existing SMS Installation option will be enabled. For this example, select Install An SMS Primary Site.

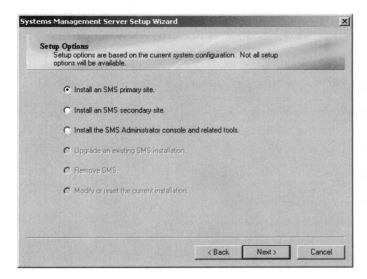

Figure 2-4. *The Setup Options page.*

Note If the Setup Wizard detects an existing installation of an SMS site system such as a CAP or a server locator point, you will not be able to continue the installation until you remove that site system from the SMS site it is a member of.

5. Click Next to display the Installation Options page, as shown in Figure 2-5. Choose Express Setup or Custom Setup.

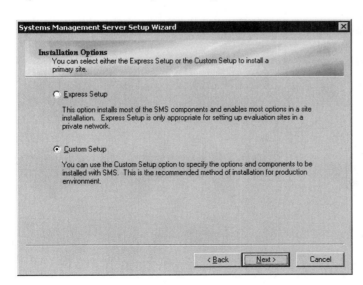

Figure 2-5. *The Installation Options page.*

6. Click Next to display the License Agreement page, as shown in Figure 2-6. Read this agreement carefully and signify your acceptance by selecting I Agree.

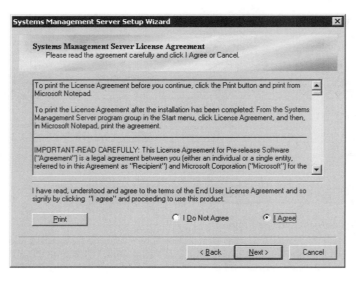

Figure 2-6. *The License Agreement page.*

7. Click Next to display the Product Registration page, as shown in Figure 2-7, and enter the Name, Organization Name, and the CD Key located on the back of your SMS 2003 CD case.

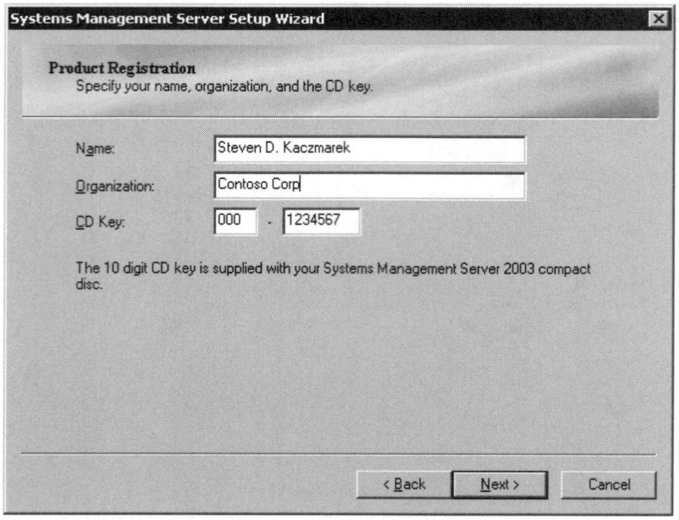

Figure 2-7. *The Product Registration page.*

8. Click Next to display the SMS Site Information page, as shown in Figure 2-8, which asks you to supply the three-character site code you want to assign to this site, a descriptive site name, and the Windows domain in which you're installing the site.

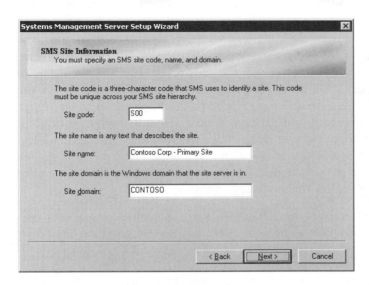

Figure 2-8. *The SMS Site Information page.*

The site code is limited to three characters and must be unique across your SMS hierarchy. The site name is descriptive, limited to 50 characters (including spaces) and should reflect the site's location or function, such as *Contoso Corp Central Site* or *Finance Primary Site*. It's usually a good idea to specify whether the site is central, primary, or secondary. Once this information is entered, it sticks.

Caution Do not use the same site code name for more than one site in your enterprise. If you're sharing or replicating WINS between two Active Directory forests and you use the same site code in your production SMS site as the site code of a pilot SMS site in a different forest, the WINS registrations for the sites might overwrite each other. This can cause the Advanced Client to use the wrong WINS database and therefore the wrong management point, causing the Advanced Client policy to be reset in the wrong SMS site. The Advanced Client is no longer a member of the pilot site and can't participate in the pilot project.

Caution If you need to change the site code, site name, or domain name later, you'll need to remove this installation of SMS and reinstall it.

9. Click Next to display the SMS Active Directory Schema page, as shown in Figure 2-9. Here you have the option to extend the Active Directory schema to support the use of automatic site assignment or roaming boundaries for advanced security. As the page implies, the account that you're performing the installation under must be a member of the Schema Admins group for your forest. In addition, if you're installing SMS 2003 on a domain controller, you'll need to use the Windows 2000 Active Directory Schema administration MMC snap-in to allow schema modifications to take place through that domain controller. If you have met these requirements, select the Extend The Active Directory Schema checkbox and then click next. If you're unable to update the schema, you can update it after installation. In this case, don't select this option; just click Next.

Tip You can extend the Active Directory Schema later by running the Extadsch.exe command line tool from the SMS\bin\i386 folder on the site server after you have met the requirements specified in step 9.

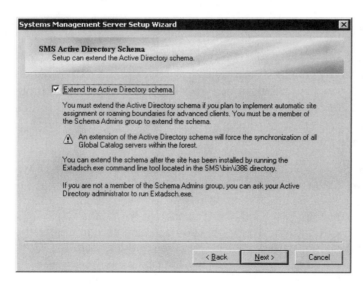

Figure 2-9. *The SMS Active Directory Schema page.*

10. On the SMS Security Information page, shown in Figure 2-10, select the security mode that you plan to implement. If you choose Advanced, go on to step 11; advanced security mode doesn't require

that a service account be created. If you choose Standard, enter the name of the account you'd like SMS to create, for example, SMSService. SMS will automatically assign it the appropriate group memberships and user rights. If you have already created this account using Active Directory Users And Computers, specify it here. Be sure you have already assigned the account the appropriate group memberships in the SMS site domain (Domain Admins, Domain Users, Administrators) and have given the account the Log On As A Service user right using the local group policy editor. Enter and confirm a password (preferably something other than *password*).

Tip   Always enter account information in SMS using the format *domain/account*.

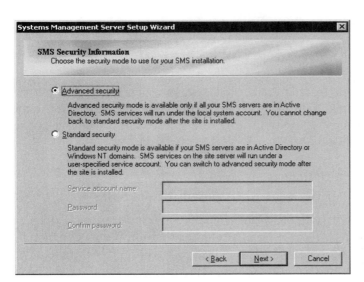

Figure 2-10.   *The SMS Security Information page.*

Note   The SMS service account must be a member of the local Administrators group on the site server, the Domain Admins group, and be given the Log On As A Service User Right.

11. Click Next to display the SMS Primary Site Client Load page, as shown in Figure 2-11. Enter the number of SMS clients that this site will manage, as you determined in your deployment strategy. The number that you enter here ultimately affects the size of the SQL database that SMS will create or that you have created ahead of time. An incorrect database device or file size will cause the installation to fail.

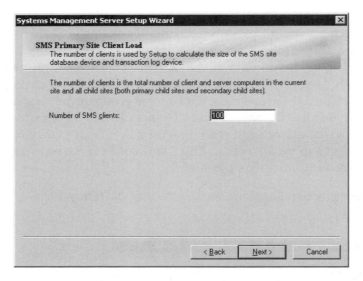

Figure 2-11. *The SMS Primary Site Client Load page.*

At this point, the installation process will vary depending on whether you chose Express Setup or Custom Setup in step 5 above. Let's continue first with the Express installation options and then look at the Custom installation options.

Express Installation Options

Follow these steps to perform an express installation of SMS:

1. Click Next to display the Concurrent SMS Administrator Consoles page, as shown in Figure 2-12, and enter the number of concurrent SMS Administrator Consoles you expect to be running in the site. SQL Server will allocate five user connections for each instance of the SMS Administrator Console in addition to the 50 required by the SMS site server and its components.

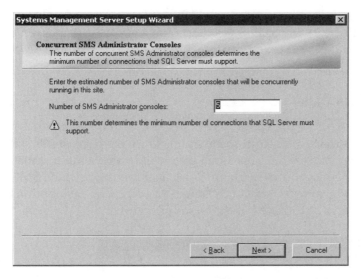

Figure 2-12. *The Concurrent SMS Administrator Consoles page.*

2. Click Next to display the Completing The Systems Management
   Server Setup Wizard page, as shown in Figure 2-13. Confirm your settings, and then click Finish. You can click the Back button from this
   and any previous pages to go back and modify your entries—and even
   to switch from Express to Custom installation. You can also double-
   click any entry in the text box on this page.

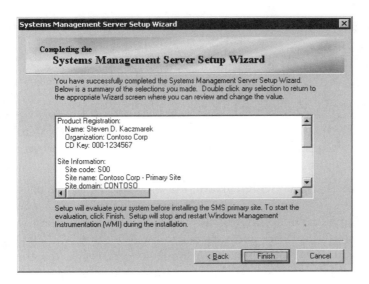

Figure 2-13. *The Completing The Systems Management Server Setup
Wizard page.*

3. If you chose Standard Security in step 10, the Setup Wizard will ask whether it is to create the SMS Service Account for you, if you haven't already created it. Choose Yes. Setup will then proceed with the SMS installation.

Custom Installation Options

Follow these steps to perform a custom installation of SMS:

1. If you're performing a Custom installation, the next page you'll see after the SMS Primary Site Client Load page will be the Setup Installation Options page, as shown in Figure 2-14. You can select which SMS components you want to install at this time. As you check each option, a brief description is displayed in the Description box.

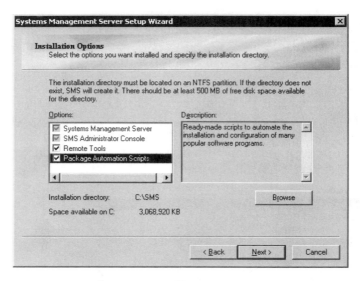

Figure 2-14. *The Setup Installation Options page.*

The Setup Wizard will automatically select the NTFS partition with the most free disk space as the installation directory. Click the Browse button to select a different location.

2. Click Next. The SQL Server Information For SMS Site Database page is displayed, as shown in Figure 2-15. This page requires that you identify the name of the computer running SQL Server, the version (7.0 or 2000) that's installed, and whether to use Windows Authentication to access the SMS site database. You may choose either Yes, the default, or No. Make your selections as appropriate on this page and click Next. Depending on your selections, one or more of the following steps will follow.

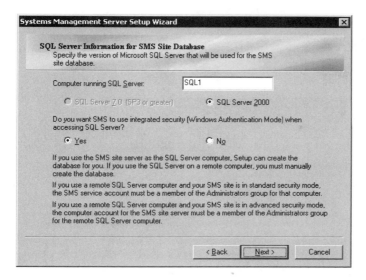

Figure 2-15. *The SQL Server Information For SMS Site Database page.*

3. If you chose No for the Windows Authentication option, you need to specify the SQL Server Login ID or accept the default sa account and supply the password for SMS to use. In this case the SQL Server Account for SMS Site Database page is displayed, as shown in Figure 2-16. Supply the appropriate information and then click Next.

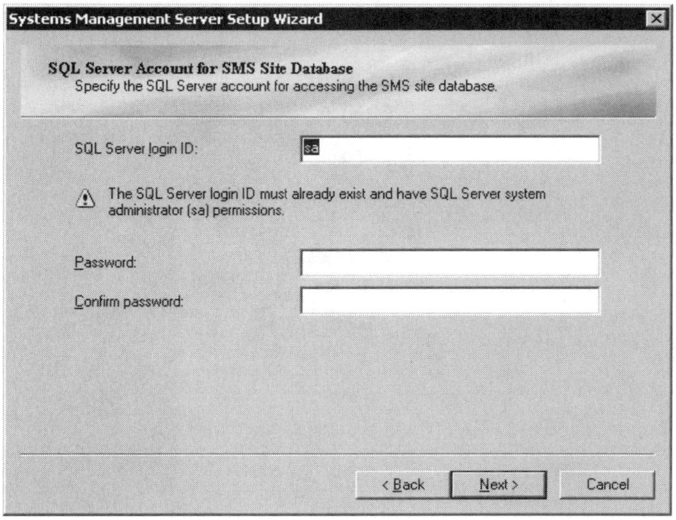

Figure 2-16. *The SQL Server Account For SMS Site Database page.*

4. If you choose to create the SMS site database, select Yes in the Creation of SMS Site Database page, as shown in Figure 2-17. Enter the name you'd like to use for the SMS site database or accept the defaults and then click Next.

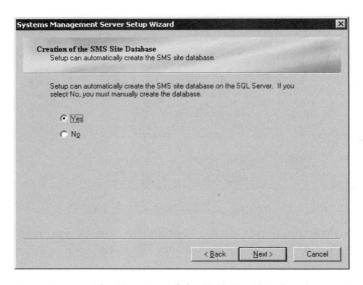

Figure 2-17. *The Creation of the SMS Site Database page.*

5. The SMS Site Database Name page is displayed, as shown in Figure 2-18. Enter the name you'd like to use for the SMS site database and then click Next.

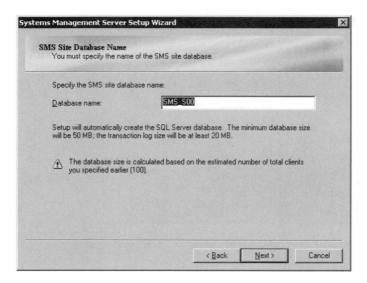

Figure 2-18. *The SMS Site Database Name page.*

6. Clicking Yes in step 4 triggers the display of the SQL Server Directory Path For SMS Site Database page, as shown in Figure 2-19. Enter the location and path to the directory in which you intend to store the database. Again, the Setup Wizard defaults to the partition with the most free disk space.

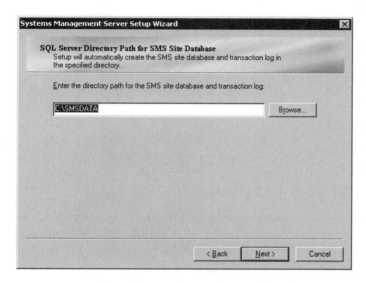

Figure 2-19.   *The SQL Server Directory Path For SMS Site Database page.*

7. Click Next to display the Concurrent SMS Administrator Consoles page, as shown in Figure 2-20, and enter the number of concurrent SMS Administrator Consoles you expect to be running in the site. SMS will add five user connections for each instance of the SMS Administrator Console to its default of 50 when configuring this parameter in SQL Server. If you leave the check box selected that allows the Setup Wizard to automatically configure SQL Server for the correct number of user connections, SMS will dynamically fill in the correct number in the Minimum Number Of SQL Server Connections text box. If you clear the check box, be sure to enter an appropriate number of user connections or your site server might not be able to access the SMS database.

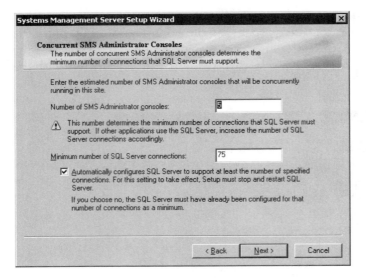

Figure 2-20. *The Concurrent SMS Administrator Consoles page.*

8. If the SMS site database has been installed on a different server, clicking Next will take you to the SMS Provider Information page, as shown in Figure 2-21. If the SMS site database is installed on the same computer, go on to step 9.

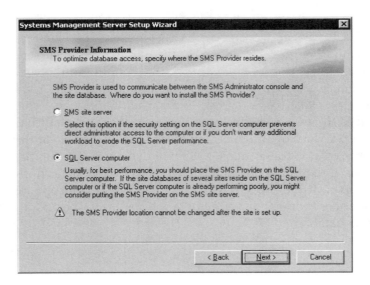

Figure 2-21. *The SMS Provider Information page.*

Recall from Chapter 1 that the SMS Provider effects access to the SMS database through the WMI Common Information Model (CIM) repository for the SMS Administrator Console. In this page, you specify whether to install the SMS Provider on the site server or the server running SQL. In general, optimum performance access is achieved when the SMS Provider is installed on the server running SQL. However, if doing so would result in poorer performance, if the server running SQL is home to other SMS site databases, or if security on the server running SQL prevents the administrator from directly accessing that computer, you should place the SMS Provider on the site server.

9. Click Next to display the Completing The Systems Management Server Setup Wizard page, as shown in Figure 2-13, and confirm your choices. You can click the Back button in any of these pages or double-click any entry in the list box to return to a previous page and modify your entries. Click Finish to complete the installation.

Note   If you chose standard security mode during setup, the Setup Wizard will ask whether it is to create the SMS Service Account for you, if you haven't already created it. Choose Yes. Setup will then proceed with the SMS installation.

If you have followed these steps closely, you have now successfully installed an SMS 2003 primary site server! If you performed a custom installation, you made choices as to which SMS components you wanted to install. The next section discusses what to do when you need to add components to your site server.

Planning Scenario—Installing Service Packs and Feature Packs

As we all know, products such as SMS will continue to mature. As the product becomes more widely used in different networking environments, unusual or anomalous activity, affectionately referred to by many of us as "undocumented user features," will be discovered and addressed. Short-term fixes for problems of this nature usually come in the form of patches. Longer term fixes, including product enhancements, usually take the form of a service pack. Additional functionality to existing product versions is generally added through feature packs.

Microsoft released four service packs for SMS 2.0 by the time SMS 2003 entered its beta testing period and a fifth before the release of SMS 2003. Besides consolidating hotfixes and other patches, each successive service pack also enhanced the product. Service Pack 2, for example, provided compatibility with Windows 2000 servers; Service Pack 3 enhanced Remote Tools support for Windows 2000 clients. My experience with these service packs has been that Microsoft's SMS development team rigorously tested the service pack before releasing it and that in the vast majority of SMS sites the application of the service packs has been smooth.

There will always be problem scenarios in some sites simply because it's impossible to test any software upgrade for every possible permutation of a product's installation and use. However, because SMS has a relatively narrow focus, its service packs tend to be less prone to such scenarios.

Nevertheless, before applying any service pack to SMS 2003—or any other product for that matter—the wise administrator will first perform a complete backup of the site. SMS 2003 provides an automated backup process that's explored in Chapter 18, "Disaster Recovery." Your backup should certainly include the SMS site database, any related registry keys, and the SMS system directory structure.

A terrific source for monitoring successes and failures that your peers might have encountered with service packs, feature packs, and patches is the Web site *http://www.myitforum.com*. Run by Rod Trent and monitored by Altiris and Microsoft, this is a great place to go for support for SMS and other Microsoft management products and to interact with your fellow SMS administrators.

After obtaining the service pack, feature pack, or patch source files in whatever media provided by Microsoft—generally through purchase of an upgrade CD, through download, or by virtue of a service agreement between your company and Microsoft—you can launch the upgrade process by running setup. This is similar to starting the installation procedure described earlier in this chapter. For example, when you reach the Setup Options page, as shown previously in Figure 2-4, when executing a service pack installation, the Upgrade An Existing SMS Installation option that's dimmed for a site server installation is now enabled.

After the upgrade has finished, although it's not always necessary, it's suggested that you restart the system to ensure that all upgrades are properly applied and that all services and processes start successfully. Then check your configuration to be sure that everything looks like it should. If you encounter any problems or issues with the installation, you can always roll back to the previous installation using your backup.

Modifying the Installation

When you first install SMS 2003, you should select only those components or features that you know you'll be using right way. For example, you might decide to install the Remote Tools but not the Package Automation Scripts. Later, your needs or your organization's needs might change, and you might find that you need to add a component.

Adding a component that has not yet been installed to your site installation is a relatively easy process. You simply rerun setup from the source file CD or folder and select that product from the Installation Options page. However, once a component has been installed, it can't be easily removed. For example, if you chose to install Remote Tools during the initial installation of your site and then later decided that you really don't want that component any longer, you can't just rerun setup and clear that option. To remove an option, you must uninstall the SMS site, and then reinstall it *without* selecting that option during installation.

To modify your installation, follow these steps:

1. Either insert the SMS 2003 CD or run Setup.exe from the SMS-Setup\Bin\I386 source file directory. The SMS Setup Wizard Welcome page is displayed as it was during the actual installation. Click Next.

2. Because the Setup Wizard detects that you have already installed an SMS 2003 site server on this computer, it displays that information in the System Configuration page, as shown in Figure 2-22.

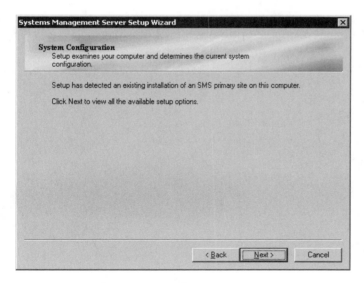

Figure 2-22. *The System Configuration page.*

3. Click Next to display the Setup Options page, as shown in Figure 2-23, and choose Modify Or Reset The Current Installation.

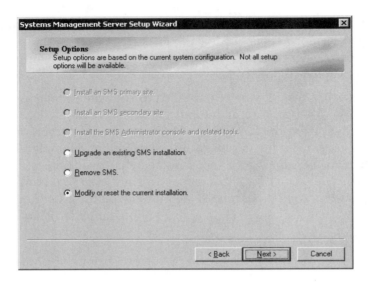

Figure 2-23. *The Setup Options page.*

4. Click Next to display the Installation Options page, as shown in Figure 2-24, and select the additional SMS 2003 components or features you want to install. Note that you can't actually remove an option once it has been installed without removing SMS 2003 and reinstalling it. The instructions here merely remind you that you can both select and clear *available* options while on this page.

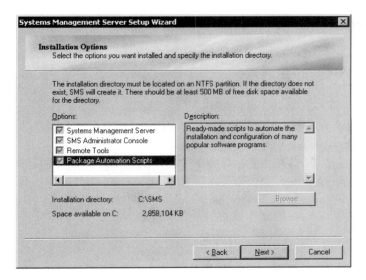

Figure 2-24. *The Setup Installation Options page.*

5. Click Next to display the SMS Security Information page, as shown in Figure 2-25, where you can identify to SMS any changes you have made to the SMS Service account name or password if you installed using standard security, or switch to advanced security at this time if you desire.

Caution Recall that the SMS Service account's information was originally provided by you. A site reset merely informs SMS of any changes you might have made to the SMS service account. It doesn't make the changes in Windows for you. If you need to modify the SMS service account name or password, you must do so using Active Directory Users And Computers prior to running setup.

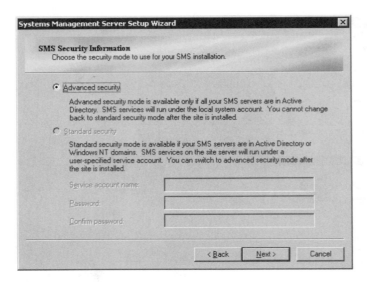

Figure 2-25. *The SMS Security Information page.*

6. Click Next to display the Database Modification page, as shown in Figure 2-26. Make any SMS database modifications here. For example, if you moved the database to a different server running SQL, enter that server's name in the SQL Server Name text box.

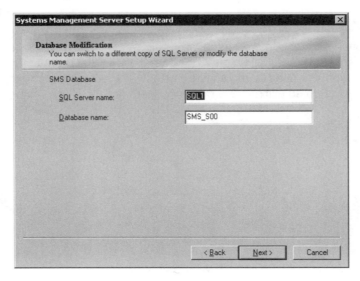

Figure 2-26. *The Database Modification page.*

7. Click Next to display the Authentication Mode For SMS Site Database page, as shown in Figure 2-27. This page gives you the opportunity to switch between Windows Authentication (recommended) and SQL Server Authentication for accessing the SMS database. As with other database changes, this page assumes that you have already made the appropriate security and account changes in SQL Server.

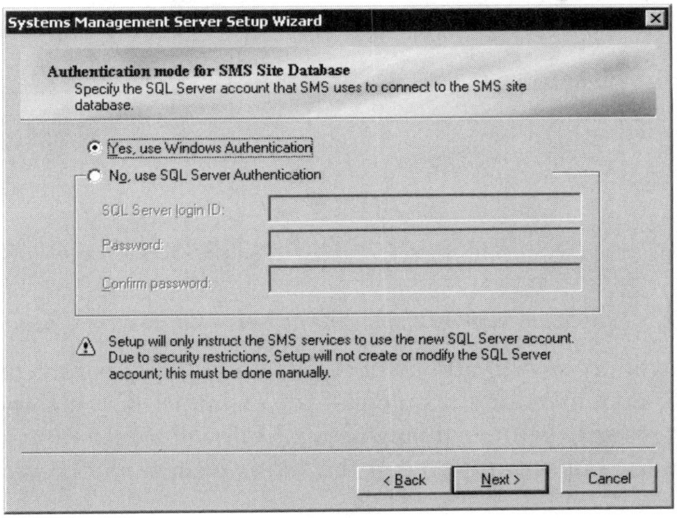

Figure 2-27. *The Authentication Mode For SMS Site Database page.*

8. Click Next to display the Completing The Systems Management Server Setup Wizard page, as shown in Figure 2-28. Remember that you can click the Back button from any of these wizard pages to return to a previous page and modify your entries. Confirm your choices and then click Finish.

Figure 2-28. *The Completing Systems Management Server Setup Wizard page.*

The Setup Wizard will proceed to add components and modify parameters as you specified. If it encounters any problems—for example, if you forgot to modify SQL Server security before running Setup, SMS will display a warning message giving you the opportunity to exit the Setup Wizard and correct the problem.

Server Modifications After Installation

The SMS 2003 Setup program makes several modifications to your server upon completion. Unlike SMS 2.0, the SMS client software isn't automatically installed on the SMS site server. However, you can choose to install the client software later.

Additional modifications are made in the following areas:

- Program group
- Services
- Directory
- Shared folders
- Windows Registry

In this section we'll look at each of these areas of modification in detail.

Program Group

After the primary site server installation is complete, the Setup Wizard adds the Systems Management Server program group to the Start menu. Table 2-5 describes the program group shortcuts that are created during installation.

Table 2-5.   Systems Management Server program group shortcuts

Shortcut	Description
SMS Administrator Console	Launches the SMS Administrator Console, which is used to access and administer the SMS database and its site components.
SMS Courier Sender	Launches the SMS Courier Sender Manager, which creates and receives parcels from packages using the Courier Sender. The Courier Sender can be used to send packages between sites that have slow or unreliable network links, although it isn't meant to be used exclusively in place of other network connections.
SMS Setup	Launches the SMS 2003 Setup Wizard, through which you can modify and reset site settings, such as the service account name and password, and remove SMS.
SMS Online Library	Launches the new SMS Online Library utility, from which you can view and read the Release Notes; the Concepts, Planning, and Installation Guide; the Operations Guide; the Troubleshooting Guide; and the Administrator Help. It also contains information about ordering related books, implementing accessibility for people with disabilities, and links for additional Internet-based resources.
SMS Site Repair Wizard	Starts the new Site Repair Wizard, which helps you recover settings and data that might have been lost since the last site backup. Chapter 18 discusses how to recover a site in detail.

> **Tip**   After you install your SMS 2003 primary site server, be sure to scan and possibly print out the Installation and Operation Release Notes. Not only is it a terrific cure for insomnia, but it's also an invaluable source of additional information about, and corrections to, the existing documentation. This book incorporates the most significant entries from the Release Notes.

Services

During the SMS installation, SMS services, or processes, are installed and enabled. By default, the SMS Setup program will load and start three services on a primary site server—SMS Executive, SMS Site Component Manager, and SMS SQL Monitor—and load, but not start, SMS Site Backup. If you're running SMS in advanced security mode and enable the management point, reporting point, and server locator point roles, these two additional services will be loaded and started: SMS Management Point and SMS Reporting Point.

The SMS Executive is the primary SMS service—sort of like the CIO for the SMS site. It accesses and updates the database, and it manages up to 43 different process threads depending on the components installed. These process threads are listed here:

- Client Configuration Manager
- Client Install Data Manager
- Collection Evaluator
- Courier Sender Confirmation
- Despooler
- Discovery Agents
  - Active Directory System Discovery
  - Active Directory System Group Discovery
  - Active Directory User Discovery
  - Network Discovery
  - Windows Server Discovery
  - Windows User Discovery
  - Windows User Group Discovery
- Discovery Data Manager
- Distribution Manager
- Hierarchy Manager
- Inbox Manager
- Inbox Manager Assistant
- Inventory Data Loader
- Inventory Processor
- Installation Managers
  - Client Push Installation
- Management Point Control Manager
- Management Point File Dispatch Manager
- Offer Manager
- Policy Provider
- Replication Manager

- Scheduler
- Senders
  - Asynchronous RAS Sender
  - Courier Sender
  - ISDN RAS Sender
  - SNA RAS Sender
  - LAN Sender
  - X25 RAS Sender
- Site Control Manager
- Status Summarizers
  - Component Status Summarizer
  - Offer Status Summarizer
  - Site System Status Summarizer
- Software Inventory Processor
- Software Metering Processor
- Status Manager

You'll learn about the significance of each of these process threads as we encounter them in future chapters.

SMS 2003 Site Configuration

The Site Component Manager carries out most site configuration requests posted in the database and written to the site's Site Control file. These requests would include adding a site server address, enabling a client agent, or adding a site system.

The SMS SQL Monitor acts as a wake-up service for the SMS Executive and its process threads. Based on SQL event triggers and stored procedures, the SMS SQL Monitor writes a wake-up file to the inbox of the SMS process that needs to carry out a specific task. As a result, you should think of SMS 2003 as being event-driven rather than cycle-driven. Think of each of the SMS components and services involved in carrying out a task on the site server as a domino. As each domino falls, it hits another domino, causing it to fall and hit another, and so on until all dominos have fallen. Similarly, as each component executes, it will write a wake-up file to an inbox or otherwise trigger the next component to execute until the task has been completed.

> So when you click OK in a properties dialog box, although the change you "requested" isn't immediate, in most cases you won't be waiting around for hours for the task to be completed.

SMS Directory Structure and Shares

When you run the SMS Setup program, it creates the registry, shares, and services needed to make configuration changes. Among the items created are two SMS directories: \SMS and \CAP_*sitecode*. The \SMS directory is the main SMS installation directory. It is created on the NTFS drive with the most free disk space and contains all the site component files, inboxes, system files, data files, and so forth needed to maintain and service the SMS site. It's shared as SMS_*sitecode*, where *sitecode* represents the three-character site code you assigned to the site.

> **Note** You can prevent SMS from installing files on a specific drive by creating an empty file called No_SMS_on_drive.sms, and placing this file in the root folder of any drive that you want to prevent SMS from installing files on. SMS does not install files in a drive that contains a file of this name.

The \CAP_*sitecode* directory is created on every site system configured as a CAP. The site server becomes a CAP by default. This directory contains all the client component configuration files, advertisements, site assignment lists, component inboxes for client data, and any other instruction files the Standard Client might require. It's shared as CAP_*sitecode*.

The \SMS_CCM directory is created on every site system configured as a management point. Like the CAP, this directory contains all the client component configuration files, advertisements, site assignment lists, component inboxes for client data, and any other instruction files the Advanced Client might require.

The Inetpub\wwwroot\SMSComponent and Inetpub\wwwroot\SMSReporting_*sitecode* folders are created on every site system configured as a reporting point. Reporting points are used to provide access to SMS web reports.

The Setup program also shares the \SMS\Inboxes\Despoolr.box\Receive directory as SMS_SITE. SMS site servers use this share to connect to another site and copy package information and other data to that site. Suffice it to say that the setup program creates no superfluous directories. Every SMS component and thread has its directory or directories, and every directory has its component or thread.

Windows Registry

The setup program creates and configures four main areas of the Windows server registry—specifically in the HKEY_LOCAL_MACHINE hive. Setup adds the Network Access Layer (NAL) and SMS keys to HKEY_LOCAL_MACHINE\ Software\Microsoft in the registry. The NAL key contains information relating to logical disk and network providers used by SMS, connection account information, and CAP lists. The SMS key contains all the site configuration and control information, including components installed, site parameters, SQL information, and so on. Setup will also add the appropriate service-related keys to HKEY_LOCAL_MACHINE\System\CurrentControlSet\Services. In addition, a number of Windows Management providers are installed and the WBEM registry key is updated appropriately.

As always, it's possible, and sometimes necessary, for you, the SMS administrator, to modify SMS site and component settings through the Windows Registry Editor. As always, please use due caution when making changes. Before browsing the registry to look up current settings or to determine whether a change should or could be made, it would be wise to set the Registry Editor to read-only mode. This precaution will prevent you from accidentally modifying an existing entry, adding an incorrect entry, or deleting a significant entry from the registry—the results of which could range from minor annoyance to critical disaster. This is not a lesson you want to learn the hard way.

Removing a Primary Site

At some point you might need to remove an SMS 2003 site server for one reason or another. Perhaps you're moving your site server to another computer, or perhaps you need to remove a component. The removal process consists of three main parts: removing the site server client software, removing the SMS site server components, and cleaning up the server. This last task generally consists of removing any leftover SMS accounts, folders and files, and registry keys.

Caution This section merely outlines the steps necessary to uninstall a primary site. It doesn't address the implications of doing so if the site currently has clients reporting to it or if it's part of an existing site hierarchy. Refer to Chapter 4 for a more thorough discussion of these implications in different scenarios.

Removing the SMS Site Server Client Software

When SMS 2003 installs your SMS site server, it doesn't automatically install the SMS client software on it. However, if you chose to install the SMS client components on the SMS site server yourself, then the first step in uninstalling your primary site is to remove the client piece. You may have installed either the Advanced Client or the Standard Client software on your site server. The steps to remove each client are different. Let's start with the Standard Client. To remove the Standard Client software from the site server, follow these steps:

1. Start the Windows Registry Editor (Regedt32.exe or Regedit.exe).

   Caution Modifying the Windows registry without due caution is like signing your server's death warrant. Be careful!

2. Find and highlight the following key: HKEY_LOCAL_MACHINE\ Software\Microsoft\SMS\Client\Configuration\Client Properties.

3. Choose Edit from the Registry Editor menu, and then choose Add Value to open the Add Value dialog box. Enter SMS Client Deinstall as the Value Name, select REG_SZ as the Data Type, and click OK to open the String Editor dialog box.

4. In the String Editor dialog box, enter *True* and then click OK.

5. Close the Windows Registry Editor.

6. Start the Services console from the Administrative Tools program group and find and highlight the SMS Client Service entry.

7. Right-click SMS Client Service and choose Restart. Restarting the SMS client service causes it to reread the registry and find the deinstall value you entered. This initiates the deinstall process. Once the service starts, close the Services console.

Only a user with administrative credentials on the computer can remove the Advanced Client software. Remove the Advanced Client software by using the Ccmclean.exe tool. This tool is available for download on the Microsoft Web site at *http://www.microsoft.com/smserver/downloads*.

If you monitor processes through Windows Task Manager, you'll notice that the deinstall process has begun. This might take several minutes to complete—when the SMS client service (Standard Client) or the SMS Agent Host service (Advanced Client) is no longer running, the deinstall process will be complete. You can see whether this service has completed deinstallation by checking the Control Panel for the absence of the Systems Management icon or checking the

Task Manager for the absence of the process file Clisvcl.exe (Standard Client) or Ccmexec.exe (Advanced Client). You can then proceed to clean up any residual client files as outlined in Chapter 8, "Client Installation Methods."

You can actually use these same processes to remove the SMS client software from any Windows computer. Once the client components have been removed from the site server, you can proceed to the next task at hand—removing the site server components.

Removing the Primary Site Software

To remove a primary site, follow these steps:

1. Initiate SMS 2003's uninstall process by executing SMS 2003 Setup.exe from the SMS 2003 CD or by running the SMS Setup from the Systems Management Server program group on the site server.

2. From the Setup Options page, shown in Figure 2-29, select Remove SMS.

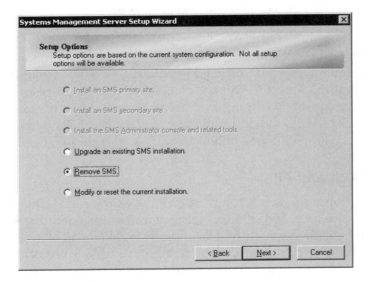

Figure 2-29.   *The SMS Setup Options page.*

3. Click Next to display the SMS Database Deinstallation Options page, as shown in Figure 2-30. Here you're given the opportunity to delete the SMS database as part of the removal process. Clear the check box if your intent is to reinstall the site server and point it to the existing database.

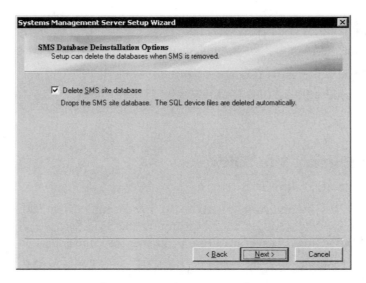

Figure 2-30. *The SMS Database Deinstallation Options page.*

4. Click Next and then click Finish to complete the removal process.

The SMS 2003 removal process will uninstall SMS services and components, remove the SMS Administrator Console, and remove the Systems Management Server program group. However, it will not completely remove all vestiges of SMS 2003 from your server. You'll need to attend to three areas of cleanup: removing folders and files, removing Windows registry keys, and removing SMS accounts and groups. We'll look at how to perform this cleanup next.

Removing Folders and Files

Use Windows Explorer to search for the drive on which SMS 2003 was installed. If you still see the SMS folder, delete it and all its subdirectories. Remember that any non-SMS files or folders in the SMS folder will be removed also. To avoid the removal of non-SMS data, be sure that SMS is installed in a folder that doesn't hold any other data, preferably off the root directory. You might also find the following folders on this drive: CAP_*sitecode*, if the site server was assigned the CAP site system role, and one or more SMSPkgx$ directories (*x* represents the drive letter) if the site system was assigned the distribution point site system role. All SMS-related folders should have been removed when you ran the Remove SMS option in Setup. Nevertheless, be sure to confirm that they're gone.

You can choose to install SMS client software on the site server. The Standard Client component files are stored in a subfolder named MS created in the operating system folder, %Systemroot%\MS. The Advanced Client component files are generally stored in a subfolder named CCM created in the System32 subfolder in the operating system folder, %Systemroot%\System32\CCM. However, if the site server is also the management point, the CCM folder might be created in the same folder as the management point files. The client removal process should have already cleaned out these subfolders, but it's good practice to check for their existence and remove them if necessary.

Under %Systemdrive%\System32, delete all SMSSetup.* files, smsmsgs, and smsexec_PROCHIST.DAT. In %Systemroot%, delete SMSCFG.ini (only present if SMS 2003 client components are not installed on the computer).

Under C:\Documents and Settings, delete all profiles with an SMS prefix. Also, remove the SMSPKG folder on the SMS installation drive if one exists. After these folders and files have been deleted, you must then turn your attention to the registry. SMS does add several entries to the registry. However, the uninstall process doesn't completely remove them. The next section discusses how to clean up the registry.

Removing SMS Windows Registry Keys

Using the Windows Registry Editor (with all due caution, of course), find the HKEY_LOCAL_MACHINE\Software\Microsoft key. Within this key, remove the NAL and SMS subkeys if they exist. Then find the HKEY_LOCAL_ MACHINE\System\CurrentControlSet\Services key and be sure to delete any service keys beginning with *SMS*, if any exist.

Now that we have cleaned up the leftover folders, files, and registry keys, we have one final task left to perform. SMS uses many accounts and groups to perform different tasks. We have so far talked about only the SMS Service account. Others are described throughout this book, especially in Chapter 17. You should remove these accounts and groups to complete the cleanup process.

Removing SMS Accounts and Groups

Through the Local Users And Groups node in the Computer Management console on Windows 2000 or Server 2003 member servers or through the Active Directory Users And Computers MMC on domain controllers, find and remove any user or group accounts that begin with *SMS*. The number of accounts and groups will vary, depending on how you configured your primary site. If you created any additional accounts of your own for use with SMS, be sure to delete those as well.

After you perform these cleanup steps successfully, your server should be free of any leftover SMS folders, files, registry keys, and accounts. Be sure to review the entire process before you remove your site servers and perhaps create a checklist for yourself of the tasks involved. Always pay particular attention when editing or deleting any registry key to avoid errors.

Navigating the SMS Administrator Console

The SMS 2003 Administrator Console is actually a snap-in to the Microsoft Management Console (MMC). As you're probably aware, MMC is a productivity utility that enables you to customize management tools for your environment. The idea is to have all your management tools accessible through a single interface or to display only those tools that apply to a specific user or group of users. So you can add in the snap-ins you need or display only the functionality of the snap-in you require. SMS 2003 third-party utilities will largely be available as snap-ins to the SMS Administrator Console.

Note   If you're using different versions of SMS in the same hierarchy, it's recommended that you use the SMS 2003 Administrator Console to maintain both SMS 2003 and SMS 2.0 sites. The SMS 2.0 Administrator Console can't view SMS 2003 sites. The SMS 2003 Administrator Console checks the SMS version to determine which features and properties should be displayed for each site.

The SMS Administrator Console, like any MMC, can be run in author mode. To run the SMS Administrator Console in author mode, open a command prompt, switch to the \SMS\Bin\I386\ folder, and execute the command: *sms.msc /a*. Author mode lets you customize the look of the console. For example, SQL Server 2000 also uses the MMC to run the SQL Server 2000 Enterprise Manager. To simplify your administrative tasks, you might decide to add the SQL Server 2000 Enterprise Manager to the SMS Administrator MMC. Alternately, you might prefer to create taskpads in a custom MMC for specific SMS administration functions that you plan to delegate to a specific group of users—for example, the Helpdesk group initiating a Remote Tools session for the clients they support. We'll spend more time on the subject of customizing and securing the SMS Administrator Console in Chapter 17. The purpose of this section is to familiarize you with the SMS Administrator Console and how to navigate it.

The SMS Administrator Console is installed to run with author mode turned off by default. You launch it from the Systems Management Server program group or by choosing Start, Run, and then entering d:\SMS\bin\i386\sms.msc, where d represents the drive on which SMS was installed.

As shown in Figure 2-31, the SMS Administrator Console looks much like a Windows Explorer window. Objects that the SMS administrator can access and manage are displayed in the left pane, which is also called the console tree. As you select each object in the left pane, the contents of that object are displayed in the right pane, also called the details pane. These contents generally consist of additional objects that can be accessed and maintained.

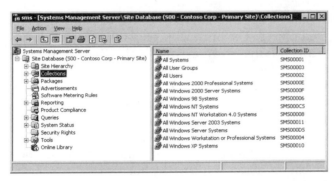

Figure 2-31. *The default SMS Administrator Console, displaying all top-level objects that the SMS administrator can access.*

Notice that highlighting the Collections object in the left pane displays the 12 default collections that SMS 2003 created during setup in the right pane. Refer back to Table 1-2 for descriptions of each top-level object.

You navigate through the objects as you would navigate through a Windows Explorer pane—the same shortcuts apply. For example, click a plus sign or a minus sign to expand or collapse an object or a folder. Double-click the object or folder name to expand or collapse it. Press the Tab key to move between panes or to move from entry to entry in a dialog box.

The SMS Administrator Console has two key menu options: Action and View. Highlighting an object and choosing the Action menu will display the Action menu options for that object. These options might include opening the item (same as double-clicking it), refreshing the object (updating its contents or properties), deleting the object, or performing some additional task, such as displaying messages or launching a tool. Most objects have Properties windows in which you can view and change an object's attributes. Right-clicking an object also displays the object's Action menu.

The View menu lets you customize how the console appears. For example, you can show or hide the description bar, status bar, or console tree, and you can decide which toolbars to display, including menus or toolbars from other snap-ins.

In addition to the two menus, the SMS Administrator Console provides nine toolbar buttons, shown in Figure 2-31. The blue left and right arrows are jump buttons that switch you backward and forward through the last console tree selections you made. The yellow folder with the up arrow lets you navigate up one object or folder level from where your cursor is currently placed. The list with an left arrow next to it toggles the console tree (left pane) on and off for easier reading of the details pane. The hand holding a piece of paper displays the properties of a highlighted object. The print icon prints the current details pane. The white paper with revolving green arrows is the Refresh button. Because the SMS Administrator Console isn't dynamically updated, remember to refresh your screen to view new and updated data. You can also refresh any object by highlighting it and pressing F5 on the keyboard or by right-clicking the object and then choosing Refresh. The Export List button (list with the right arrow) allows for exporting of the selected objects details pane list. Of course, there's also the Help button—the one with the yellow question mark. This button invokes SMS help for whichever object you have highlighted.

This seems like an ideal opportunity to put in a plug for SMS 2003's help engine. Compared to other help products you might have used (even from Microsoft), this one is really quite good. Combined with the Online Library (and, of course, this book), you'll have the resources you need to answer the majority of your questions about SMS. Get yourself the Software Development Kit (SDK) through the Microsoft Developer Network (MSDN) program and you'll be on your way to becoming an SMS guru. For more information on the MSDN program, please check the following Web site: *http://msdn.microsoft.com*.

That's all there is to it. Navigating the SMS Administrator Console is actually quite easy once you get used to it. The hardest part might be finding out where to look for various SMS component settings, especially if you're new to SMS. Give yourself a little extra time to become comfortable with the new MMC and be sure to check out how to customize and secure your console in Chapter 17.

Summary

This chapter explored the ins and outs of the installation process for an SMS primary site server. We expressed the seriousness of the planning process and identified key questions to be asked that can help develop your implementation strategy not only in the area of domain and network considerations but also in hardware and software requirements, server and client considerations, personnel and training requirements, and testing. We have thoroughly examined the installation process itself, highlighting changes made to the server through services loaded; files, folders, and shares created; and registry keys added. We've even identified how to remove SMS from the server if the need arises.

Chapter 3 focuses on the different functional roles that the site server and other identified site systems can assume. We'll define these roles and examine how to assign them to servers within our growing SMS site. Then in Chapter 4 we'll look at how to link your SMS sites together to create a management hierarchy.

Chapter 3
Configuring Site Server Properties and Site Systems

Now that you have successfully installed your Microsoft Systems Management Server (SMS) primary site server, the next step in your deployment strategy is to begin configuring your site. This configuration might consist of two parts. Certainly, you'll need to configure the single SMS site. This means identifying which components should be enabled, what the SMS site boundaries should be, and what additional servers should be enabled as component or site systems for the site. You might also need to establish an SMS site hierarchy for your organization. This means, among other things, identifying parent-child relationships, establishing a reporting and administration path, configuring communication mechanisms, and identifying primary and secondary sites.

This chapter concentrates on the first part of the configuration process—that is, configuring the single SMS site, including setting site boundaries, monitoring status and flow, and identifying site systems. In Chapter 4, "Multiple-Site Structures," you'll learn how to implement a site hierarchy.

Defining and Configuring the SMS Site

The first step in configuring your new SMS 2003 site is to identify which clients should become members of the site. SMS 2003 determines which clients should be assigned to the site according to the site boundaries you configure. You can assign SMS clients to only one site. SMS 2003 site boundaries are defined by either IP subnet or Active Directory site. A subnet is a segment of a network whose members share the same network address and is distinguished from other subnets by a subnet number and subnet mask. An Active Directory directory service site defines a physical relationship among domain controllers based on their IP subnets and represents a unit of optimum network performance for Active Directory replication and authentication.

More Info For a more thorough examination of the purpose and configuration of Active Directory sites, please attend Microsoft Certified Course 2154, *Implementing and Administering Microsoft Windows 2000 Directory Services* or read *The Microsoft Windows 2000 Server Administrator's Companion* (Microsoft Press, 2000). Also see Chapter 8, "Designing Your SMS Sites and Hierarchy," in the *Microsoft Systems Management Server 2003 Concepts, Planning, and Deployment Guide* part of the SMS 2003 documentation set, as well as the online help included with SMS 2003.

Don't confuse site assignment with the discovery process. SMS uses any of several configurable discovery processes to "look for" and record an instance of a resource. A resource might be a client computer. However, it might also be a user; a global group; an Active Directory user, group or system; or an IP-addressable device such as a switch or a network printer. Discovering a resource doesn't make it an SMS client. A client computer can't become an SMS client until it has been assigned to an SMS site based on the IP subnet or the Active Directory site with which it's associated. Once it has been assigned, it can then be installed with the SMS client software. To sum up, the SMS site server can discover clients as a site resource, but does not necessarily have to install them immediately. Likewise, it can install them as SMS clients without discovering them first. But in all cases, a client must be assigned to an SMS site before it can be installed. The discovery process is explored in detail in Chapter 7, "Resource Discovery."

Site systems, on the other hand, do not need to be located within the boundaries of the site with which they're associated—unless, of course, they will also become clients of that site. In some cases, site system roles can be shared across sites, or SMS clients can reference site systems that are members of another SMS site in the site hierarchy.

You can configure two kinds of boundaries: site boundaries and roaming boundaries. The main difference between the two has to do with the kind of SMS client support that will be provided. Recall from Chapter 1, "Overview," that SMS 2003 supports two kinds of clients: Legacy Client and Advanced Client. Legacy Clients are SMS 2.0-type clients and may include Microsoft Windows NT 4.0 SP6 and Windows 98 Second Edition computers. Advanced Clients are Windows 2000 and higher computers that participate fully in Active Directory. Site boundaries are used to assign Legacy Clients to the site based on their IP subnet or Active Directory site association. Using Active Directory sites to define site assignment provides you with the easiest way to assign new clients that join the network regardless of their IP address.

Note The Advanced Client software is actually installed on a potential SMS client using SMS package distribution, Client Push Installation, or by manually installing the client.

For example, if you use only IP subnets, every time a new client or set of clients joins the network, in addition to associating them with an appropriate Active Directory site, you must ensure that the IP subnets of those clients is represented in the site boundary for the appropriate site. However, if you've defined the site boundary based on Active Directory sites, you need only associate the new clients with the appropriate Active Directory site. The SMS site will already "know" that the SMS client should be assigned to it.

Roaming boundaries are used to support Advanced Clients that can—and do—move from site to site and might not have access to a distribution point in the site to which they're assigned. Advanced Clients use roaming boundaries to locate distribution points in other sites in the SMS hierarchy that can provide them with distributed programs. Like site boundaries, roaming boundaries can be defined by IP subnet, Active Directory sites, or both. However, because Advanced Clients can access the network by a variety of connection methods, such as a RAS server or a VPN, you can also use IP address ranges to define a roaming boundary.

When you configure the site boundaries for a site, all the client agent settings that you define will be applied to all the assigned clients when the SMS software is installed. In other words, agent and component settings are site-wide settings and apply equally to all members of the site. If different sets of clients require different client components, you might need to create a separate site for those clients. For example, if 100 out of 1000 clients require Software Metering to be enabled, and the remaining clients do not, you need to segment these clients into their own subnet, create an SMS site for that subnet, assign those 100 clients to that site, and enable Software Metering for that site. There are ways to get around this limitation, of course, both supported and unsupported. Nevertheless, your goal as an administrator should not be how to "get around" a product's boundaries. This is one of the reasons a well-conceived deployment strategy will be extremely valuable to you as you construct your SMS site hierarchy.

Real World   Site Boundaries and Subnet Masks

When you use IP subnets to determine site assignment, SMS 2003 checks the client's discovery record to see whether the client's IP address falls within the IP boundaries set by the SMS administrator. It does so by checking the client's subnet mask. (The subnet mask determines the subnet address for that segment of the network.) Checking the client's subnet mask is significant because most companies don't use a subnet mask of 255.255.0.0 or something similar to define their network segments. In fact, they likely will use a mask such as 255.255.248.0 to segment the network into different subnets for organizational reasons, network routing considerations, security, localization of resources, and so on.

Using a subnet mask such as 255.255.0.0 makes it easy for us to identify the subnet address. With this particular mask, every number in the third and fourth octets will constitute a host device address. Every number in the first and second octets will constitute a different IP subnet address. For example, consider these two IP addresses: 172.16.20.50 and 172.16.10.50. Using subnet mask 255.255.0.0, it's easy to see that they're both in the same subnet. If you set the SMS site boundary to 172.16.0.0, you'll be sure to discover and assign both clients.

Now take the same two IP addresses, but use subnet mask 255.255.248.0 instead. This subnet mask places each client address into a different subnet. If your site boundary is 172.16.8.0, it will discover and assign clients whose IP addresses fall within the range 172.16.8.1 through 172.16.15.254. Thus the client with address 172.16.10.50 would be assigned and the client with address 172.16.20.50 would not. To include the latter client, you would need to add its subnet address—172.16.16.0—to the site boundaries.

You might need to refresh your IP addressing skills to fully appreciate the significance of subnet masking and SMS 2003. But rest assured, the subnet mask does make a difference.

Now consider using Active Directory sites as your SMS site boundary. Without going into a lengthy discussion about Active Directory sites, suffice it to say that they also depend in part on subnet objects. These subnet objects consist of both subnet addresses and masks. This makes it easier to associate computer objects with a particular Active Directory site and so makes it easier for the SMS administrator to assign those clients to an SMS site.

Configuring Site Properties

In SMS 2003 you can configure other site properties besides site boundaries, including site accounts and security. In this section you'll learn how to configure all these properties.

To display the site properties for an SMS site, follow these steps:

1. Open the SMS Administrator Console.

2. Under the Systems Management Server group, expand the Site Database node, and then expand the Site Hierarchy node to display the site object (in the form, *sitecode—sitename*).

3. Right-click the site object and choose Properties from the context menu. Or, highlight the site object, and from the Action menu choose Properties to display the Site Properties dialog box for the site, as shown in Figure 3-1. Let's start with the General tab.

Figure 3-1.   *The General tab of the Site Properties dialog box.*

The General Tab

The General tab displays some descriptive information about your site server. For example, in Figure 3-1 we can see that the site server is a primary site. We can identify its version and build numbers, the server name, the SMS installation directory, and the current security mode. We can also see whether this site participates in a site hierarchy as a child site to another site. Since in Figure 3-1 the Parent Site label is set to "None," we can conclude that this site is either a stand-alone site, since it has no parent site, or that it might be the central or topmost site in an SMS site hierarchy. You use the Set Parent Site button to identify the parent site that this site should communicate with in an SMS site hierarchy. We'll talk about creating parent-child relationships in Chapter 4.

Descriptive comments always add value to objects in SMS 2003, as they help provide additional information that might otherwise not be available. In this case we can use the Comment text box to indicate the name of the company (Contoso Corporation), its site hierarchy role (Primary Site), and its location (Corporate Headquarters—USA).

If you installed your site using standard security mode, you can switch to advanced security mode by clicking the Set Security button. When you do, the Set Security Mode dialog box shown in Figure 3-2 is displayed. Note the requirements for switching to advanced security as outlined in this dialog box.

Be sure that these requirements are set before you change security modes. Note too that this is a one-time option. Once you change to advanced security mode you cannot change back to standard security. The Set Security button becomes disabled (as displayed in Figure 3-1).

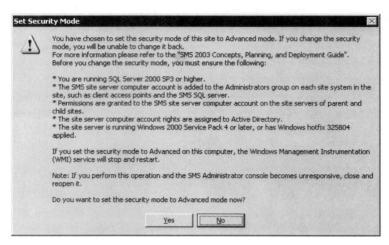

Figure 3-2. *The Set Security Mode dialog box.*

The Site Boundaries Tab

To configure the site boundaries, complete the following steps:

1. Click the Site Boundaries tab in the Site Properties dialog box, as shown in Figure 3-3. The IP subnet of the segment in which the site server was installed will be displayed by default.

Figure 3-3. *The Site Boundaries tab of the Site Properties dialog box.*

2. To add a new IP subnet or Active Directory site, click the yellow star button on the right to open the New Site Boundary dialog box, as

shown in Figure 3-4. Select a Boundary type from the drop-down list and enter either the subnet ID or the Active Directory Site name (shown in Figure 3-4) as appropriate. Then click OK.

Figure 3-4.   *The New Site Boundary dialog box.*

3. The new boundary will be displayed in the Site Boundaries list in the Site Boundaries tab. Click OK or Apply to save your changes.

The Accounts Tab

SMS 2003 in standard security mode makes use of several accounts to access other sites, install clients, install packages, access the database, generate reports, and so on. The Accounts tab, shown in Figure 3-5, provides the SMS administrator with the means of modifying two accounts specific to the site itself: the SMS Service account and the SQL Server account.

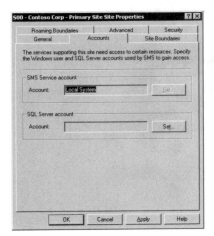

Figure 3-5.   *The Accounts tab in the Site Properties dialog box.*

SMS Service Account   SMS creates the SMS Service account during setup, and it's the primary service account for the SMS site. It provides the site server with access to most SMS services running on the site server as well as on other site systems, including the SMS Executive, SMS Site Component Manager, and the SMS SQL Monitor services.

If you chose to install SMS in standard security mode, SMS can create the account for you, and it calls it SMSService by default, as described in Chapter 2, "Primary Site Installation." This account is made a member of the local Administrators group on the site server and the domain's Domain Users global group, and it's granted the Log On As A Service and Act As Part Of The Operating System user rights for the site server as well.

However, if your site is running in advanced security mode, the SMS site server uses the Local System account to provide access to the same SMS services rather than create a separate SMSService account.

If you're running in standard security mode and need to modify the SMS Service account name or password that you or SMS created, follow these steps:

1. Create the new account or modify the existing account using Active Directory Users And Computers. Be sure that any new account is a member of the local Administrators group on the site server and the domain's Domain Users global group. Also be sure that you have given the account the Logon As A Service and Act As Part Of The Operating System user rights on the site server.

2. In the Site Properties' Accounts tab, click the Set button in the SMS Service Account frame to display the Windows User Account dialog box, as shown in Figure 3-6.

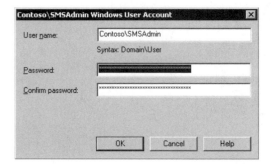

Figure 3-6. *The Windows User Account dialog box.*

3. Enter the new account name in the form *domainname\username*, and then enter and confirm a password. Click OK to save your changes and then click OK again to close the Site Properties dialog box.

Alternatively, you can let SMS create the new account for you or specify the new account for SMS to use by running the SMS Setup program in the Systems Management Server program group. To do so, follow these steps:

1. From the Systems Management Server program group, on the Start menu, choose SMS Setup.

2. From the Setup Wizard Welcome page, click Next twice to get to the Setup Options page. Select the Modify Or Reset The Current Installation option, as shown in Figure 3-7.

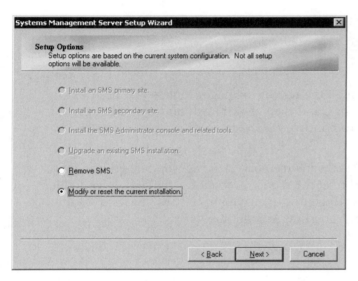

Figure 3-7.   *The Setup Options page of the Setup Wizard.*

3. Click Next to display the SMS Security Information page, as shown in Figure 3-8. Enter the new account and password that you have created and want SMS to now use or that you want SMS to create for you.

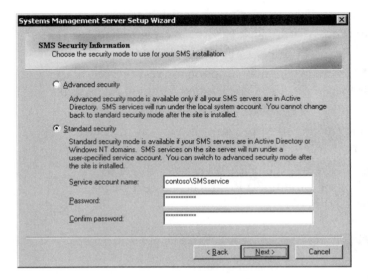

Figure 3-8. *The SMS Security Information page of the Setup Wizard.*

4. Click Next to pass through the rest of the pages (unless you need to make other modifications), and then click Finish on the final page. SMS will prompt you to confirm the creation of the new account. Click Yes.

SMS will create the account, make it a member of the appropriate groups, grant it the appropriate rights, and reset the service account for the site server and its services. The new account will then be displayed in the SMS Service Account field when you open the Site Properties' Account tab.

Caution Microsoft recommends using Site Reset to notify the site server of any changes to either the SMS Service account or the SQL Server account rather than making the changes through the Accounts tab Set buttons. See Chapter 17, "Security," for more information about using Site Reset and its implications for your site, and for more information about the SMS Service account and other SMS accounts.

Tip   If you're using advanced security, SMS will use the Local Security account as its service account. However, if you must run SMS in standard security, be sure to exercise appropriate security with the SMS Service account. It does, after all, have administrative access across the domain as well as in the SMS site. Use an identifiable name as well as a complex password, preferably using some combination of alphanumeric and special characters (for example, gle43kaz$) In addition, consider making the SMS Service account a direct member of the local Administrators group on each site system (client access point, server locator point, and so on). By doing this, you can remove the account from the Domain Admins global group for the domain so that this account won't affect the security of other systems in the domain.

When SMS attempts to access a site system in another Windows domain, SMS uses the SMS Service account you specified to complete its tasks. If your site server and site systems are in separate Windows domains, particularly in a mixed mode Windows environment (supporting both Windows NT 4 and Windows 2000 servers and domains), the SMS Service account you specify must have access to the other Windows domains. This access can be accomplished by using Windows trust relationships or pass-through authentication.

If the Windows domain that contains the site system trusts the site server Windows domain, you can use the same SMS Service account you (or SMS) created in the site server Windows domain to access the site system. All the rules apply, of course. Be sure that the SMS Service account from the trusted domain is a member of the trusted domain's Domain Admins global group, or make it an explicit member of the local Administrators groups on the site system in the trusting domain and grant it the appropriate user rights.

Note   Recall that all Active Directory domains in the same forest automatically maintain two-way transitive trusts.

If no trust relationship exists between the two Windows domains, you must duplicate the SMS Service account in the site system's Windows domain, giving it the appropriate group access and user rights. Duplicating the account means creating an account with the same name and password so that SMS can use pass-through authentication to access the site system.

Running SMS in advanced security presupposes that all your SMS servers have been upgraded to Windows 2000 or higher and participate in a native mode Active Directory forest structure. In this case, SMS will use the directory to locate and connect to site systems in different domains.

SQL Server Account The SMS 2003 site server uses the SQL Server account to gain access to the SMS database and this account is created during setup. The SQL Server account varies depending on the type of SQL Server security implemented during the setup. If SQL Server is using SQL Server authentication, you could specify the default sa account or another SQL login ID that you create and configure. If SQL Server is using Windows authentication, SMS will use whatever account the SMS administrator logs on with to access the database.

Note If SMS 2003 is installed using the Express Setup, SMS uses the SQL sa login ID as the SQL Server account by default.

There should be little need to modify this account. However, if you must change the account that SMS uses, you should follow the same basic steps and cautions as you would for changing the SMS Service account above. After you've created or modified the account, you can inform SMS to use it by following these steps:

1. In the Accounts tab, click the Set button in the SQL Server Account frame to display the SQL Server Account dialog box, which resembles the one shown in Figure 3-6.

2. Enter the new SQL account user name, and then enter and confirm a password. Click OK to save your changes and then click OK again to close the Site Properties dialog box.

Alternately, run a Site Reset from SMS Setup and provide the updated SQL Account information when prompted.

More Info If your working knowledge of creating the SQL Server account falls short, you might want to attend a training class on SQL Server, as mentioned in Chapter 2.

The Roaming Boundaries Tab

The Roaming Boundaries tab, shown in Figure 3-9, allows you to configure boundaries for roaming Advanced Clients that will allow those clients to access the site's distribution points. Use the action buttons to add a new roaming boundary, view and edit the properties of a selected roaming boundary, or to delete a roaming boundary.

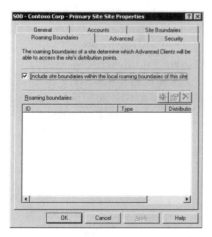

Figure 3-9.   *The Roaming Boundaries tab in the Site Properties dialog box.*

To add a new roaming boundary, follow these steps:

1. In the Roaming Boundaries tab, click the yellow star button to display the New Roaming Boundary dialog box.

2. Select the boundary type you wish to add from the Boundary Type drop-down list: IP Subnet, Active Directory Site, and IP Address Range.

3. Enter the appropriate information for the boundary type you selected. Figure 3-10 shows the entries for an IP address range.

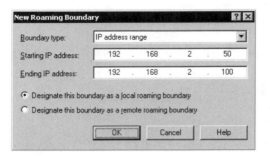

Figure 3-10.   *The New Roaming Boundary dialog box displaying an IP address range.*

4. The Designate This Boundary As A Local Roaming Boundary and Designate This Boundary As A Remote Roaming Boundary options let you specify whether the roaming Advanced Client should treat this site's distribution as local or remote. If the local option is selected, the

distribution points will be designated as local, and the Advanced Clients will use the When A Distribution Point Is Available Locally setting you choose in the Advanced Client tab of the Advertisement Properties shown in Figure 3-11 when it receives an advertisement. If this local option is not is not selected, the Advanced Client will use the When No Distribution Point Is Available Locally setting you choose in the Advanced Client tab of the Advertisement Properties. This option can be useful when the roaming boundaries you specify represent slow or unstable links to the network.

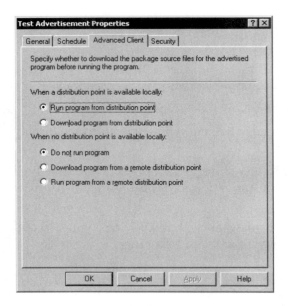

Figure 3-11.   *The Advertisement Properties dialog box showing the Advanced Client tab options.*

5. Click OK to save your changes.

The Advanced Tab

The Advanced tab, shown in Figure 3-12, allows you to specify two options for dealing with child sites. By default, all new SMS 2003 sites use private/public key pairs to sign data that's sent between sites. The option Publish Identity Data To Active Directory, enabled by default, ensures that this SMS data is published in the Active Directory. Using private/public key pairs helps to ensure that potentially harmful data is rejected when sent between sites within your SMS hierarchy. However, this data signing is not enabled for SMS 2.0 sites that haven't been upgraded to SP 5 or higher. If you haven't disabled signed communications between SMS 2003 sites, select the option Do Not Accept Unsigned Data From Sites Running SMS 2.0 SP 4 And Earlier to ensure that those sites don't send unencrypted data to their parent sites. If you need to maintain down-level SMS 2.0 sites within your site hierarchy, and you want those sites to continue to report data, such as inventory, discovery information, and status messages, to your SMS 2003 site, you'll need to disable signing of data between that site and its SMS 2003 parent; in this case, disable the previous option.

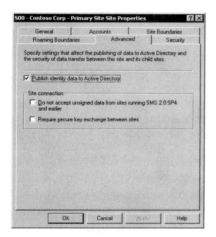

Figure 3-12.   *The Advanced tab of the Site Properties dialog box.*

Select the option Require Secure Key Exchange Between Sites to ensure that communication is allowed only when keys can be securely exchanged between sites. If you wish to enable data to be sent without this data signing process, leave this option cleared. Chapter 4 discusses the encryption of site-to-site data communications in more detail.

The Security Tab

The Security tab, shown in Figure 3-13, displays the current security rights for the Site Properties object. Every object in the SMS database has both class and instance security that can be applied. Applying security to SMS objects is similar to creating an access control list (ACL) for Windows files, folders, or shares. To set object class security rights, click the yellow star button in the Class Security Rights frame to display the Object Class Security Right Properties dialog box. You can specify permissions such as Administer, Create, or Delete by selecting the boxes in the Permissions list. To set object instance security rights, click the yellow star button in the Instance Security Rights frame and follow the same procedure for setting the class security rights.

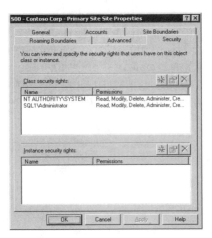

Figure 3-13. *The Security tab of the Site Properties dialog box, showing the two default accounts granted permissions to manage the Site Properties class of object.*

Class vs. Instance Security Rights

Class security rights indicate the access granted to all objects of this type. In the example displayed in Figure 3-13, the class security rights apply not only to this specific site, but also to any other site that might enter into a parent-child relationship with this site.

Instance security rights indicate the access granted to that specific instance of the object. In this example, the instance security rights would apply only to this particular site (S00—Contoso Corp).

As another example, consider the Collections object. The class security rights indicate which users and groups have been granted specific permissions for working with *all* collections. Each individual collection, however, has an instance security right that identifies which users or groups have been granted specific permissions to that *one* collection.

By default, the administrative-level account that was used to perform the SMS site server installation as well as the local system account (NT Authority\System) are granted full class security rights for all SMS objects in the database. The list of permissions that are granted, or that can be granted, varies from object to object. Full permissions to the Site Properties class include Administer, Create, Delegate, Delete, Manage SQL Commands, Manage Status Filters, Meter, Modify, and Read. Full permissions to the Collections class include Administer, Advertise, Create, Delegate, Delete, Delete Resource, Modify, Modify Resource, Read, Read Resource, Use Remote Tools, and View Collected Files.

So, permissions granted to a user for a class of object will apply to all objects of that class. Permissions granted to a user for a specific object in a class will apply to that object alone. If a user is a member of two or more groups, each with different permissions, permissions are cumulative for the user—that is, the least restrictive of the permissions will apply. For example, if the user is a member of a group called FINHELP that has the read permission assigned to it and a member of a group called FINMGRS that has full permissions assigned to it, the user's permissions are full permissions. The least restrictive permission prevails. However, permissions at the instance level of an object will override the class permissions granted. For example, suppose you want a specific help desk group named FINHELP to be able to initiate RemoteTools sessions with only the clients in the Finance collection. You would grant FINHELP no permission to the Collection class, but full permission to the Finance collection. This would not only restrict members of FINHELP to only the Finance collection, but also their SMS Administrator Consoles would display only the Finance collection. As you can see, class and instance security give the SMS administrator far more control over securing objects in the SMS database than in earlier versions of SMS. Chapter 17 explores class and instance security and other security options in more detail.

Site Settings

Typically, you'll think of SMS site settings and component attributes such as client agent settings, site addresses, site systems and their roles, and so on, as properties of the site, and rightly so since these settings are indeed specific to each site. However, as you've seen, these other settings aren't part of the Site Properties dialog box for an SMS 2003 site. The SMS 2003 Site Properties dialog box might better be thought of as relating to the site object properties than to settings and attributes of components within that site.

To access the component settings, expand the Site object in the console tree and then expand the Site Settings object. Under the Site Settings object, you'll find SMS 2003 component settings, as we discussed above. Each of these site settings will be discussed in detail in later chapters. Remember that these site settings are integral and unique to each specific SMS site and can rightly be termed properties of the site.

The Site Configuration Process Flow

Different SMS 2003 services and processes carry out different tasks depending on the site property or site setting you enable or configure. However, there is still one basic process flow that takes place when any site setting changes. The change is requested by you and posted to the SMS database, the change is carried out by the appropriate SMS site server component processes, and the database is updated with the change. Let's explore this process more closely.

Site settings are stored in the site control file. This file is named Sitectrl.ct0 and is maintained in the SMS\Inboxes\Sitectrl.box directory on the site server. This file is a text file that you can view using any text editor. The beginning of a representative site control file is displayed in Figure 3-14. The file is quite complete and detailed. It's the single most significant file for the site, apart from the database itself, because it contains every site setting parameter.

Figure 3-14. *An example of some of the site properties contained in the site control file, showing the site code and site name (S00 and Contoso Corp), the site server platform (X86), the installation directory (V:\SMS), and the site server name and domain (SQL1 and Contoso).*

The site control file can be modified either through a change initiated by the SMS administrator or through a change initiated by an SMS component. Figure 3-15 outlines the process flow for initiating and carrying out a change to the site control file. The SMS SQL Monitor service and the Hierarchy Manager and Site Control Manager threads are the three SMS 2003 components responsible for maintaining and updating the site control file.

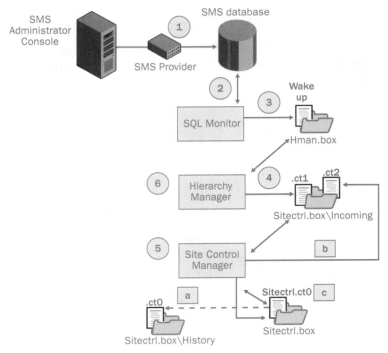

Figure 3-15.   *The process flow for carrying out changes to the site control file in an SMS site.*

This process is broken down into the following steps:

1. When the SMS administrator makes a change to a site setting through the SMS Administrator Console, the SMS Provider directs that request to the SMS database through Windows Management Instrumentation (WMI). It matches the change against the current database settings, called the site control image, and then creates a delta site control image that contains the changes to be made.

2. A SQL stored procedure (one of over 200) is triggered, which wakes up the SMS SQL Monitor Service.

3. The SMS SQL Monitor, in turn, writes a wake-up file to Hierarchy Manager's inbox, SMS\Inboxes\Hman.box. This filename is in the form *sitecode*.ssu or *sitecode*.scu, where *sitecode* is the three-character code you assigned to the site during setup.

4. The Hierarchy Manager component on the site server monitors Hman.box for any new files. When the wake-up file is written to that folder, the Hierarchy Manager thread accesses the database and looks for any proposed changes to the site settings. If a delta image exists in

the database, Hierarchy Manager creates a delta site control file with the extension .CT1 and writes this file to Site Control Manager's inbox, SMS\Inboxes\Sitectrl.box\Incoming.

5. The Site Control Manager component on the site server monitors Sitectrl.box\Incoming for any new files. When the .CT1 file is written, the Site Control Manager thread wakes up, reads the .CT1 file, and performs three actions:

   - It copies the current Sitectrl.ct0 file to the SMS\Sitectrl.box\History folder. SMS retains the last 100 site control files. As you'll discover, these files can multiply quickly.

   - It merges the changes into the current site control file and creates a .CT2 file in Hierarchy Manager's inbox, SMS\Inboxes\Hman.box.

   - It creates a new Sitectrl.ct0 file in the SMS\Sitectrl.box directory.

6. Hierarchy Manager wakes up when the .CT2 file is written to its inbox and updates the SMS database with the new site control data.

Note   Hierarchy Manager and Site Control Manager wake up whenever a file is written to their respective inboxes on the site server. However, they also have wake-up cycles. Hierarchy Manager will wake up every 60 minutes by default, and Site Control Manager will wake up once a day at midnight by default to generate a heartbeat site control file for Hierarchy Manager.

Site Control Filenames

As you monitor the Hierarchy Manager and Site Control Manager inboxes, you'll see the .CT1 and .CT2 files created. You'll also notice the rather strange filenames that are assigned to these files. When the files are created, they're assigned randomly generated filenames. This is done both to ensure uniqueness and to provide security. By scanning the status messages that are generated, or the log files, for Hierarchy Manager and Site Control Manager, you'll be able to follow the creation of these files as they move from inbox to inbox.

The history copy of the site control file that Site Control Manager writes to the SMS\Inboxes\Sitectrl.box\History folder, however, has a definite naming convention. Here each site control history file is named *.ct0, where * represents the site control file serial number in hexadecimal format. Thus, site control file 9 would be saved with the filename 00000009.ct0, and site control file 10 would be saved with the filename 0000000A.ct0.

The site control file's serial number is simply its sequential order in relation to other site control files. The site control file created during setup is serial number 0. The next one representing a change in site settings would be serial number 1, and so on. The serial number is recorded in the sixth line of the site control file, which can be read using any text editor.

This is not the whole story, of course. When you initiate a change, you might be asking SMS to enable a component, schedule a task, or initiate discovery or installation. Other SMS components also monitor the Sitectrl.ct0 file for changes, or the SQL Monitor Service might write a wake-up file directly to the appropriate component's inbox. When Site Control Manager generates the new site control file or SQL Monitor writes a wake-up file to an inbox, these other components wake up, read the file(s) for changes that pertain to that component, and then carry out the change. These same components might themselves create .CT1 files to update the site control file with changes that have been carried out.

As you can see, the Site Control Manager process is very much event driven, meaning that services and threads wake up when a change is detected rather than waiting a predetermined period of time before waking up and checking for any activity that needs to take place. This process was introduced with SMS 2.0 and further enhances the performance of SMS 2003, as many of these processes have been streamlined.

More Info   Throughout this book, we'll explore process flows relating to specific processes such as package distribution and client installation. We'll look at the highlights of these process flows—those elements that most facilitate troubleshooting. However, many of these process flows are far more complex. For a thorough treatment of various SMS process flows, refer to the *Microsoft Systems Management Server 2003 Troubleshooting Guide*, available through the SMS Web site (*www.microsoft.com/smserver*) and through Microsoft TechNet.

Monitoring Status and Flow

SMS 2003 offers an excellent set of tools for monitoring the status and flow of the Site Control Manager process: site status messages and site component log files. Together, these tools provide you the means not only to effectively troubleshoot an SMS process but also to learn the process and become familiar with the way SMS components interact with, and react to, one another.

Status Messages

Each of the SMS components responsible for carrying out the Site Control Manager process generates a set of status messages specific to this process. To view these status messages, expand the System Status object in the SMS Administrator Console, expand Site Status, and then expand your site. Click Component Status to view a list of status messages for all the components, as shown in Figure 3-16. You'll find entries for Hierarchy Manager and Site Control Manager listed here.

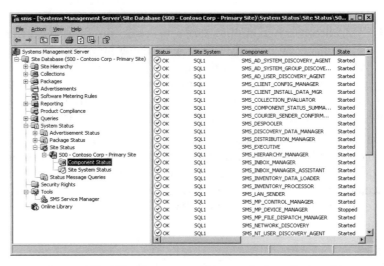

Figure 3-16. *The Site Component Status window, listing the general status level for all the SMS components.*

To view all the detailed status messages generated for a component, right-click the component, choose Show Messages from the context menu, and then choose All. SMS will display the rich set of detailed messages that that component has generated during a predefined period—by default, since midnight that day. Figures 3-17 and 3-18 show the messages generated by Hierarchy Manager and Site Control Manager, with the content of one message displayed. You can view message content by double-clicking the message or by positioning your cursor on the description area of each message to open a pop-up window. Viewing and configuring status messages are discussed in detail in Chapter 5, "Analysis and Troubleshooting Tools."

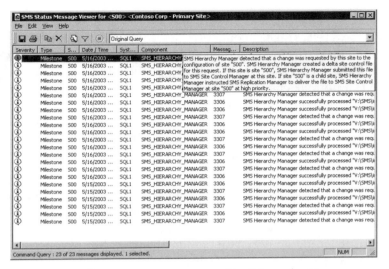

Figure 3-17. *Status messages generated by Hierarchy Manager.*

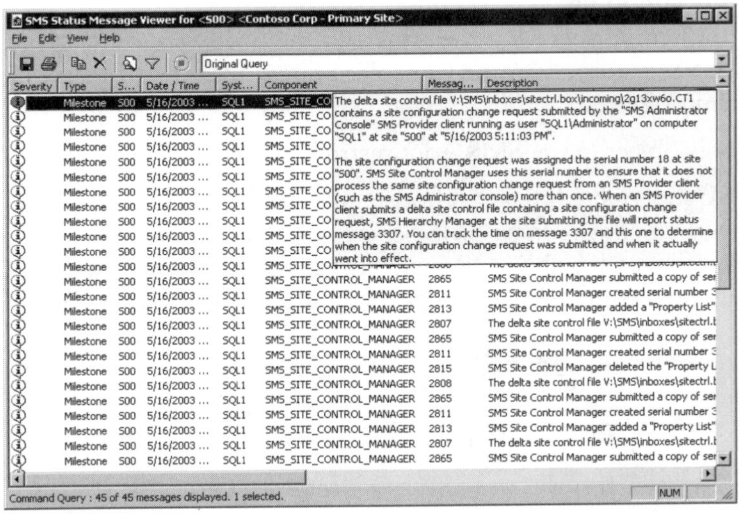

Figure 3-18. *Status messages generated by Site Control Manager.*

Log Files

In addition to status messages, you can configure each component to create and maintain log files. Unlike status messages, which are generated automatically and enabled by default, log files aren't automatically enabled for the site server in SMS 2003. This is a notable change from earlier versions of SMS. Logging component activity does require an additional expense of resources on the site server. Depending on the SMS 2003 features you installed and the components you have enabled and configured, SMS could generate 30 or more log files—more than twice as many as were generated in SMS 1.2.

Needless to say, it's not always practical, or even necessary, to enable logging for every SMS component. Logging is intended primarily as a troubleshooting tool. However, you would do well to practice using logging in a test environment to learn how the SMS components interact with one another. Logging is certainly not the most exciting activity you could engage in, but nevertheless this exercise will be enlightening from an SMS perspective.

Enabling SMS 2003 Log Files

You enable SMS 2003 component log files through the SMS Service Manager tool launched in the SMS Administrator Console. Follow these steps to enable SMS 2003 component log files:

1. Expand the Tools object in the SMS Administrator Console.

2. Right-click SMS Service Manager, choose All Tasks from the context menu, and then choose Start SMS Service Manager, as shown in Figure 3-19. SMS launches the SMS Service Manager console. Notice that it makes its own connection to the SMS database.

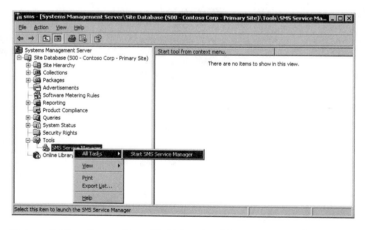

Figure 3-19. *Launching SMS Service Manager console.*

3. Expand the site node and highlight Components, as shown in Figure 3-20.

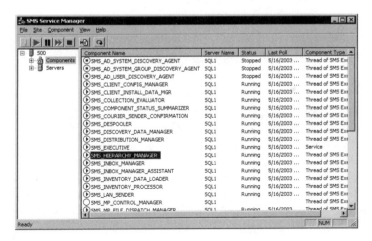

Figure 3-20.   *The SMS Service Manager console.*

4. Right-click the component for which you want to enable logging—for example, SMS_Hierarchy_Manager—and then choose Logging from the context menu to display the SMS Component Logging Control dialog box, as shown in Figure 3-21.

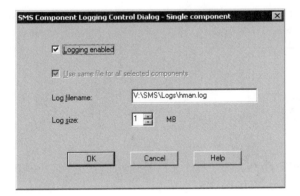

Figure 3-21.   *The SMS Component Logging Control dialog box for single components.*

5. Select the Logging Enabled check box. Note the location and name of the log file that will be created. Modify this entry only if you need to. Note also the default log size of 1 MB. This setting ensures that the log doesn't compromise disk storage space. Again, you can modify this entry (in MB) if you need to.

6. Click OK and then close the SMS Service Manager console.

Enabling Logging for Multiple Components

Obviously, there's much more to SMS Service Manager, which we'll look at more closely in Chapter 5. However, one feature that's definitely applicable here is the ability to enable logging for multiple SMS components at one time.

You can enable logging for multiple components at one time by holding down the Ctrl key and clicking the components you want to log, just like selecting multiple files in Windows Explorer. You can enable logging for all components by clicking the Component menu in the SMS Service Manager console and then choosing Select All or by right-clicking a component and choosing Select All from the context menu. With all the components selected, you can either right-click any one of them and choose Logging from the context menu or click the Component menu once again, choose Logging, and then enable logging as described earlier.

When you enable logging for multiple SMS components in this way, the option Use Same File For All Selected Components will be selectable in the SMS Component Logging Control dialog box, as shown in Figure 3-22.

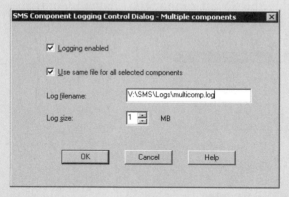

Figure 3-22. *The SMS Component Logging Control dialog box for multiple components.*

Selecting this option will cause the components that you selected to write their logging data to a single file. With more than two or three components, this log file can become confusing and somewhat unwieldy. Nevertheless, for something like the site configuration change process, in which two SMS threads are involved, this file can provide a single source of tracking information.

Log files are text files that are written, by default, to the SMS\Logs folder. You can save these files anywhere you want when you enable logging, but unless you have disk resource concerns, why make changes? You can view log files using any text editor or using the SMS Trace utility. SMS Trace is included as one of several tools for download from the SMS Web site (*http://www.microsoft.com/ smserver*). The advantage of using SMS Trace is that it displays one or more log files in real time—that is, while they're being updated. A text editor will display the file only as it appears up to that point in time. For details on how to use SMS Trace effectively, refer to Chapter 5.

Defining and Configuring Site Systems

New site systems for the SMS site are defined as site settings for the site. As such, you could consider these site systems to be properties of the site as well. In this section we'll review the site systems that you can define and examine how each becomes a site system for your SMS site. The various site roles that you can assign to an SMS 2003 site system are listed here:

- SMS Site Server
- SMS SQL Server
- SMS Client Access Point (CAP)
- SMS Component
- SMS Distribution Point
- SMS Management Point
- SMS Reporting Point
- SMS Server Locator Point

Each of these roles is supported to a greater or lesser extent depending on the operating system platform the site system is using. Chapter 2 described the server requirements for the SMS Site Server and SMS SQL Server in detail. Like the SMS Site Server, you can assign the site system roles to any server running Windows 2000 Server or the Windows Server 2003 family of servers. Table 3-1 outlines additional requirements for specific site system roles.

Table 3-1. Additional requirements for site system roles

Site System Role	Requirement
Distribution Point	If you intend to use the Background Intelligent Transfer Service (BITS) for Advanced Clients, both the site server and the distribution point must have Internet Information Services (IIS) installed and enabled.
Management Point	If you intend to use a server as a management point, you must install and enable IIS on that server.
Reporting Point	If you intend to use a server as a reporting point, you must install and enable IIS. Any server or client that will use the Report Viewer component must have Internet Explorer 5.01 with Service Pack 2 or later installed, as well as Office Web Components to use graphs in the reports.
Server Locator Point	If you intend to use a server as a server locator point, you must install and enable IIS.

We've already looked closely at installing and configuring the site server and the site database server (the SQL Server). Let's now focus on the other site system roles. The SMS administrator generally assigns site system roles. The SMS administrator can assign all the site system roles mentioned so far to any server that meets the requirements already outlined.

However, some site system roles are assigned automatically when another component is enabled. When you first install the site server, it's automatically assigned as a CAP and distribution point. When a sender is installed on a server, or when the CAP role is assigned to a site system, that site system is automatically assigned the role of component server. A component server is generally defined as any site system running the SMS Executive service, although we typically refer to a server acting as an alternate sender for facilitating site-to-site communication within a hierarchy as a component server. Chapter 4 will talk more about senders.

In either case, you must be sure that the proposed site system meets the requirements outlined in Table 3-1. In addition, check for space and partition requirements as outlined in the relevant sections later in this chapter for each site system role. For example, CAPs require an NTFS partition because of security that SMS 2003 applies to the directories it creates on those site systems. Clients must be able to access site systems such as CAPs, distribution points, and management points in order to access advertisements and client component files and configuration updates, to write discovery and inventory data, and to read and execute package scripts. In large part, SMS 2003 assigns the appropriate level of permissions, but this doesn't totally absolve you from checking and testing permissions and access.

Site System Connection Accounts

If you administered SMS 2.0 sites in the past, you're already well acquainted with the great number of accounts that SMS 2.0 created and supported. In contrast, the number of accounts required and used by SMS 2003 depends on whether you're running in standard security mode or advanced security mode. The number, type, and purpose of SMS 2003 accounts related to standard and advanced security are discussed in detail in Chapter 17. However, since we're talking about site systems here, it's appropriate to speak about the accounts used by SMS 2003 to facilitate communications between the site server and its site systems. Consequently, we'll now have a brief discussion about SMS 2003 accounts as they relate to site systems.

No matter which security mode you're using, SMS 2003 uses some account type to facilitate communications between the site server and its site systems. Site servers need to connect to site systems to transfer information such as advertised programs, package information, client component option updates, and so on. Site systems, on the other hand, need to connect to site servers to transfer information that they've collected, such as client inventory data and discovery information. These connection accounts fall into three categories: common accounts, advanced security accounts, and standard security accounts.

Common Accounts

SMS 2003 creates and uses some common accounts regardless of the security mode in which it's running. Whether you can use these accounts effectively depends on whether your servers are running Active Directory or not, whether any SMS servers are running Windows NT 4 or not, and whether you're running advanced security or not. Chapter 17 provides a complete list and description of all the accounts used by SMS.

There are three security groups that facilitate communications between the SMS site server and a site system. They are as follows:

- **Site System to Site Server Connection** This group gives site systems the ability to connect to the site server to read and write resources such as advertised programs and inventory. Its members are preferably the site system computer accounts, although they can be Site Server Connection accounts that you create and manage.

- **SMS Server Connection** In sites running standard security, this account gives CAPs access to the SMS site server. This account is preferably the computer account of the SMS site server, but it can also be the SMS Service account.

- **Site System Connection** The SMS site server uses this account to connect to its site systems. This account is preferably the computer account of the SMS site system, but it can also be a specific account created and managed by the SMS administrator.

Advanced Security

As we've mentioned several times already, one great advantage of using advanced security is that you don't need to rely on anything other than Active Directory computer accounts when communicating between servers. In fact, as we stated earlier, the preferred membership of the SMS Site System To Site Server Connection group account is the computer accounts of the site systems. By making these computer accounts members of this group, site systems will automatically have the appropriate level of access to the appropriate shares and folders on the site server. You don't need to worry about creating separate connection accounts, making sure that they have the correct level of security and access, and so on.

Standard Security

When you're using standard security mode, especially when in a mixed mode Active Directory, accounts are created and maintained largely as they were in SMS 2.0. When you identify and assign site system roles, the site server automatically creates a SMS Server Connection Account called SMSServer_*sitecode*. Site systems such as CAPs use this account to connect to the site server and transfer data such as inventory and discovery data. SMS creates and maintains this account on its own so you should not modify it in any way.

When you installed SMS 2003 on the site server, the Setup program created the SMS Service account. Among other tasks, the site server uses this account to connect to site systems to transfer data. You can, however, create additional accounts, called SMS Site System Connection Accounts, depending on your site's security requirements. You do so through Active Directory Users And Computers. The account must be a member of the site system's local Administrators group and must be granted the Log On As A Service user right. It should also have the Password Never Expires option selected since service accounts can't change their own passwords. You can also use the site server's computer account to accomplish this communication by making it a member of the local Administrator's group on the site systems. This is a more secure method than using the SMS Service account.

When a site server needs to connect to a site system, SMS will attempt a connection first through any existing service connection. It then tries the Site System Connection Account if one exists. If the attempt fails, SMS tries the SMS Service account.

After you have created the connection account in Windows, you need to identify the account to the SMS site server using the following steps:

1. In the SMS Administrator Console, navigate to the Site Settings folder, and expand it.

2. Expand the Connection Accounts object, highlight and right-click the Site System object, as shown in Figure 3-23, and choose New\Windows User Account from the context menu. This option will be dimmed if SMS 2003 is running in advanced security mode.

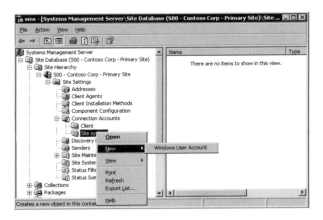

Figure 3-23.   *The SMS Administrator Console, showing the Site System object selected and the available connection account type.*

3. In the Connection Account Properties window, click the Set button to display the Windows User Account dialog box. Enter the account name in the dialog box *Domainname\Username* and enter and confirm a password, as shown in Figure 3-24. Click OK.

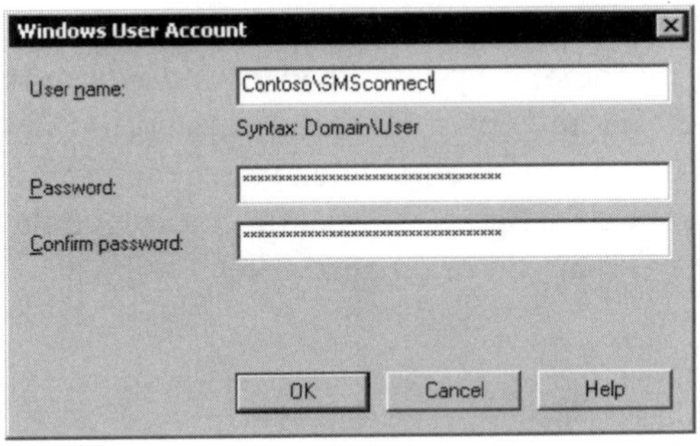

Figure 3-24.   *The Windows User Account dialog box.*

4. Click OK again to close the Connection Account Properties window.

Assigning Site System Roles

Now that you have identified the servers that will become site servers and created any necessary connection accounts, you must tell SMS that the server should be considered a site system. To do so, follow these steps:

1. In the SMS Administrator Console, navigate to the Site Settings folder and expand it.

2. Select the Site Systems folder. Initially, the only entry you'll see is the site server itself.

3. Add a new site system by right-clicking the Site Systems folder and choosing New from the context menu to display the two site system options list available, as shown in Figure 3-25.

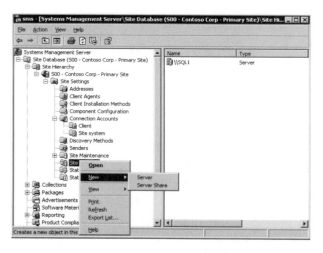

Figure 3-25.   *The Site System context menu options.*

4. Choose either Server or Server Share.

   - Choosing Server will display the Site System Properties dialog box shown in Figure 3-26. Click Set and enter the name of the Windows server that you want to make a site system. Then select the tab for the site system role you want to assign to the server and make the appropriate option choices. When you're finished, click OK.

Figure 3-26. *The Site System Properties dialog box for a server.*

- Choosing Server Share will display a slightly different Site System Properties window, as shown in Figure 3-27. Click Set and enter the name of the server and share (which you have already created) that you want to define as the site system. Select the tab for the site system role you want to assign to the server and make the appropriate option choices. Notice that only the CAP and distribution point roles can be assigned to a share. When you're finished, click OK.

Figure 3-27. *The Site System Properties dialog box for a server share.*

Planning It's not necessary that you assign a site system role immediately. You might choose to wait until you have completed your assessment as to the best number and placement of site system servers. This is particularly useful when you're planning a phased rollout of your site.

The main difference between the Server and Server Share options is that by creating a share on a server first and defining that share as the site system, you can direct where SMS will create and write the support files for the CAP and distribution point roles. However, if you use Server Share, SMS will not create a discovery record for that site system.

Tip If you need a discovery record for the site system created as a Server Share, perhaps because you want to use the Network Trace utility to monitor its health, create the site system as both a Server Share and Server. Simply assign the desired roles to the Server Share site system entry; don't assign any site system roles to the Server site system entry.

5. Click OK to close the Site System Properties window and save your new site system.

In the next few sections we'll explore each site system role and the options that are available to you when you assign that role to a server.

Client Access Points

The CAP is an SMS site system that functions as the main exchange point between SMS Legacy Clients and the SMS site server. If you're using Advanced Clients only in your SMS site, you don't need to configure any additional CAPs. Components of SMS Legacy Clients such as the Remote Tools and Hardware Inventory agents are installed from a CAP. Inventory, status, and discovery information that's collected on a client is written to a CAP. Advertisement information and other client instructions are obtained from the CAP. When a client receives an advertisement for a program, it also includes a list of distribution points at which the client can find the package files.

When the site server is installed, it becomes a CAP by default. Typically, however, you'll want to assign other site systems the CAP role and remove this role from the site server to reduce its resource requirements and improve its performance as well as load balancing the CAP function within your site network. CAPs are installed through the SMS Administrator Console as a site system setting. To assign the CAP role, follow these steps:

1. In the SMS Administrator Console, navigate to the Site Settings folder and expand it.

2. Highlight the Site Systems folder to display the list of site systems you have defined.

3. Right-click the site system you want to assign as a CAP, and choose Properties from the context menu to display the Site Systems Properties window, as shown in Figure 3-28.

Figure 3-28.   *The General tab of the Site System Properties dialog box.*

4. Select the Client Access Point tab, as shown in Figure 3-29. Select the Use This Site System As A Client Access Point check box, and then click OK.

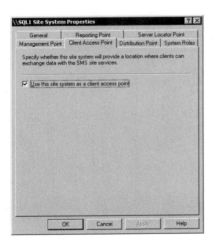

Figure 3-29.   *The Client Access Point tab of the Site System Properties dialog box.*

5. Click OK again to save this setting and begin the Site Control Manager process that will set up the new CAP.

If you want to remove the CAP role from the site server, right-click the site server and just follow the same procedures that you used to assign a CAP role to the site system; however, you should clear the Use This Site System As A Client Access Point check box when you're in the Client Access tab.

When you enable a new CAP, you have identified a change to the site control information for the site. A new site control file will be created according to the process described in the section entitled "The Site Configuration Process Flow" earlier in this chapter. Recall that during that process, after the new site control file is generated, other components wake up and read the file to determine whether they need to perform any tasks. One of these components is Site Component Manager.

In this scenario, Site Component Manager wakes up and installs the SMS Executive service and the Inbox Manager Assistant thread on the new CAP if it's a Windows server. The SMS Executive runs the Inbox Manager Assistant, which is used to copy inventory files, discovery records, and so on from the CAP to the site server. In addition, the Inbox Manager thread on the site server wakes up and creates the directory structure and share needed on the CAP for the Windows, as shown in Figure 3-30. The directory name and share is CAP_*sitecode*. This directory includes all the inboxes needed for client agents to write information generated on the client to the CAP and to write instructions that the client needs from the site server to the CAP. As you can see, the folder names in the CAP directory structure are fairly descriptive of the data that's written.

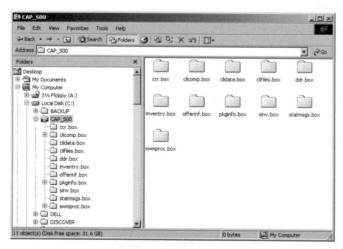

Figure 3-30. *The CAP directory structure, which contains the inboxes needed to write data from both the client and the site server.*

Inbox Manager and Inbox Manager Assistant

Those of you who come from an SMS 2.0 or earlier environment might recognize the functions of Inbox Manager and Inbox Manager Assistant. For SMS 2003, both Inbox Manager and Inbox Manager Assistant are responsible for writing information from the site server to the CAP (Inbox Manager) and from the CAP to the site server (Inbox Manager Assistant), maintaining the integrity of the data and ensuring that it's written to the appropriate inbox on the appropriate server.

Inbox Manager copies client component and configuration information, the site assignment list, advertisements, package instructions, and the SMS_def.mof file (hardware inventory definition) to the CAP. It wakes up when the site control file changes and when any inbox is written to or modified, and it reports status messages and logs activity in the Inboxmgr.log file if logging was enabled for this thread.

Inbox Manager Assistant copies client data records from the client inboxes on the CAP (Ccr.box, Ddr.box, Inventry.box, Sinv.box, and Statmsgs.box) to their counterpart inboxes on the site server. It wakes up when an inbox on the CAP has been written to or modified, reports its status messages, and logs activity to the Inboxast.log file on the CAP if logging was enabled for this thread.

For example, the client uses Ddr.box, Inventry.box, and Sinv.box to write discovery data records, hardware inventory files, and software inventory data. The site server uses Clicomp.box, Offerinf.box, and Pkginfo.box to write client configuration parameters, instruction and offer files for advertisements and packages, and package contents and location information.

The amount of time that the CAP installation takes will, of course, depend on your network's performance level and on whether the installation will need to take place across a WAN connection. As with all site systems, Microsoft strongly suggests that CAPs be located on a LAN or be accessible through a fast and reliable remote connection.

The actual number of CAPs that you create will depend on several factors. Certainly the most significant factor will be the number of Legacy Clients that the site manages and their location within your network. Recall that CAPs provide the main point of contact between the SMS Legacy Client and the SMS site. The CAP provides client component configuration, advertisement, and package information to the Legacy Client, and it records and relays inventory, discovery, and status information from the client. The more Legacy Clients managed, the greater the resource requirement on the CAP. From another perspective, the larger the number of packages and advertisements the site generates, the greater the resource requirement will be at the CAP. In other words, there is no cookie-cutter approach in determining the optimum number of CAPs that should be created. You need to monitor resource usage on the CAP itself (using the Windows Performance console's System Monitor utility, for example), monitor the network traffic that's generated (using the SMS Network Monitor, for example), and consider the needs of the site and your organization.

Distribution Points

The distribution point is an SMS site system that stores the package files, programs, and scripts necessary for a package to execute successfully at an SMS client computer. When the site server is installed, it becomes a distribution point by default. As with CAPs, however, you'll want to assign other site systems as distribution points and remove this role from the site server to reduce its resource requirements and improve its performance as well as to load balance the potentially significant network traffic generated by clients downloading package source files.

BITS-Enabled Distribution Points

Advanced Clients, also known as roaming clients, can take advantage of a new feature called Background Intelligent Transfer Service (BITS). BITS is a service that can be enabled on distribution points that serve Advanced Clients. It's used to help control the amount of bandwidth used by an Advanced Client during download, as well as to insure that the Advanced Client doesn't necessarily have to wait a lengthy period for a package while, say, being connected to the network through a slow or unreliable connection. BITS provides a checkpoint restart of a package. If the download of package files is interrupted—the connection is lost accidentally or because the user needs to disconnect—the download can continue at the point it was interrupted once a new connection is established rather than starting over from the beginning.

 Caution The checkpoint restart will restart the download with the last file that was being accessed at the time the connection was lost. If this was the 10th file out of 20, the download will restart with the 10th file when the connection is reestablished. However, if your package consists of a single executable file such as an .EXE or .MSI file, the download will restart at the beginning, since that was the file that was interrupted.

The Advanced Client remains assigned to its original site. However, when the Advanced Client needs to retrieve an advertised package, it can download or run the package from a local distribution point, rather than from its assigned site. Remember this when you choose remote servers to be distribution points.

To protect your Advanced Clients from excessive bandwidth consumption, enable BITS on your distribution points that serve Advanced Clients. This provides an efficient file transfer mechanism through client-sensitive bandwidth throttling. It also provides checkpoint restart download of packages, which allows files to be transferred to the client in a throttled manner.

Protected Distribution Points

The protected distribution point is designed to protect network links to distribution points from unwanted traffic. The SMS administrator specifies which roaming boundaries or site boundaries Advanced Clients must be in to use the protected distribution point. Any clients outside those boundaries are unable to download or run packages from that distribution point.

To restrict access to a distribution point that's across a slow or unreliable network link, plan to enable it as a protected distribution point. This is beneficial at remote locations, where a small number of SMS clients and a distribution point are connected to the primary site by a WAN. For example, consider configuring a protected distribution point on secondary site servers that are connected to their parent primary site by a WAN link.

Distribution points are installed through the SMS Administrator Console as a site system setting.

To assign the distribution point role, follow these steps:

1. In the SMS Administrator Console, navigate to the Site Settings folder and expand it.

2. Highlight the Site Systems folder to display a list of the site systems you have defined.

3. Right-click the site system you want to assign as a distribution point and then choose Properties from the context menu to display the Site Systems Properties dialog box.

4. Select the Distribution Point tab, shown in Figure 3-31. Select the Use This Site System As A Distribution Point check box. If you want to enable BITS, select the Enable Background Intelligent Transfer Service (BITS) check box as well. Then click OK.

Figure 3-31. *The Distribution Point tab of the Site Systems Properties dialog box.*

5. Click OK again to save this setting and begin the site configuration change process that will set up the new distribution point.

If you want to remove the distribution point role from the site server or disable BITS, right-click the site server and just follow the same procedures as you did to assign a distribution point role to the site system; however, you should clear the Use This System As A Distribution Point or the Enable Background Intelligent Transfer Service (BITS) check boxes (or both) when you're in the Distribution Point tab.

When you enable the new distribution point, you have identified a change to the site control information for the site. A new site control file will be created according to the process described in the section entitled "The Site Configuration Process Flow" earlier in this chapter. However, no SMS components are installed on the distribution point.

The distribution point is not written to until a package is actually distributed. At that time, the Distribution Manager thread on the site server checks the distribution point for the partition with the most free space. On that partition, it creates a shared folder named SMSPkgx$, where *x* is the drive letter of the partition. The share is a hidden share—a change from earlier versions of SMS. Then the Distribution Manager component on the site server copies the package and program files to a subfolder beneath SMSPkgx$. If in the course of copying packages to the distribution point, you begin to run low on disk space, the

Distribution Manager will find the next partition with the most free space and create another shared SMSPkgx$ folder there. We'll encounter the Distribution Manager again in Chapter 12, "Package Distribution and Management."

> **Tip** If you want or need to specify where the package files will be copied on the distribution point, create the SMSPkgx$ folder and share yourself. Be sure to give your users at least Read access to the folder and give the SMS Service account Full Control access. Alternately, you can create your own share structure using your own naming conventions on each distribution point (the same structure on each distribution point). Then when you create your package you can reference the appropriate share that you want the package files distributed to.

You can also use the Distribution Point tab in the Site Properties window to create what are known as *distribution point groups*. Basically, distribution point groups let you group your distribution points into more manageable units. Packages can then be targeted to a distribution point group rather than to individual distribution points.

To create a distribution point group, follow these steps:

1. In the SMS Administrator Console, navigate to the Site Settings folder and expand it.

2. Highlight the Site Systems folder to display a list of the site systems you have defined.

3. Right-click any site system you have assigned as a distribution point and choose Properties from the context menu to display the Site Systems Properties dialog box.

4. Select the Distribution Point tab, shown in Figure 3-31.

5. In the Group Membership frame, click the yellow star button on the right to display the Distribution Point Group Properties dialog box, as shown in Figure 3-32.

6. Enter the name of the distribution point group you want to create. If you want the site system you selected to be included in the group you're creating, select the Include This Site System In This Distribution Point Group check box. Then click OK.

7. Click OK again to save this setting and begin the site configuration change process that will set up the new distribution point group.

Figure 3-32. *The Distribution Point Group Properties dialog box.*

Now when you create a new distribution point or display the properties of an existing distribution point site server, any distribution point groups you created will be displayed in the Group Membership list in the Distribution tab of the Site Systems Properties dialog box, as shown in Figure 3-33, and you'll have the opportunity to include the distribution point in one or more of the distribution point groups.

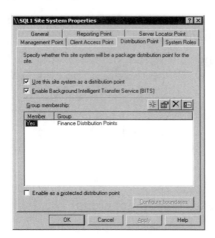

Figure 3-33. *The Group Membership list in the Distribution Point tab.*

Unlike CAPs, distribution points can be shared among SMS 2003 sites. This sharing enables you to leverage equipment and place distribution points closer to the users and clients that will need to access them. The most significant resource consideration for a distribution point is disk space. Since you're copying source files and scripts for package installation there, you'll need enough disk space to accommodate all the packages. The next most significant resource consideration will be network access and traffic. You can use Network Monitor to track and gauge this factor. This tool can also help you determine when an additional distribution point might be necessary. The amount of network traffic that's generated will depend on the size of your packages, the number of clients accessing the DP to execute a program, and whether you scheduled the package to run at an assigned time.

Management Points

Similar to the relationship between a CAP and a Legacy Client, the management point is an SMS site system that functions as the main exchange point between SMS Advanced Clients and the SMS site server. Components of SMS advanced clients such as the Remote Tools and Hardware Inventory Agent are installed from a management point. Inventory, status, and discovery information that's collected on an advanced client is written to a management point. Advertisement information and other client instructions are obtained from the management point. When a client receives an advertisement for a program, it will also include a list of distribution points at which the client can find the package files.

Unlike a CAP, when the site server is installed, it doesn't become a management point by default. This is a role that you'll assign to other site systems. Several factors might influence the placement and number of management points that you decide to implement. Generally, you choose one server to be the default management point for that site, and that management point will support all your Advanced Clients. However, you might choose to have additional management points for network load balancing or backup purposes—in case the default server is down or unavailable, especially if you have large numbers of Advanced Clients that need to be supported.

When you configure the management point role, you'll notice reference to a SQL database. Again, since typically you'll have one management point implemented, it will use the data in the SMS site database. However, if you do need to implement additional management points, you might choose to off-load some of the SQL Server resource requirements for the management point from the SMS site database to a replicated copy of the site database, perhaps installed on the management point itself.

Management points are installed through the SMS Administrator Console as a site system setting. To assign the management point role, follow these steps:

1. In the SMS Administrator Console, navigate to the Site Settings folder and expand it.

2. Highlight the Site Systems folder to display the list of site systems you have defined.

3. Right-click the site system you want to assign as a management point and then choose Properties from the context menu to display the Site Systems Properties dialog box.

4. Select the Management Point tab, as shown in Figure 3-34. Select the Use This Site System As A Management Point check box.

Figure 3-34. *The Management Point tab of the Site System Properties window.*

5. From the Database drop-down list, select the Use The Site Database option if the management point should access the SMS site database for reading and writing client data. Select the Use A Different Database option and supply the requested information if the management point should access a database other than the SMS site database—for example, if the server is to be an management point for a secondary site that doesn't have its own site database or if you have replicated the SMS site database to another SQL server for load balancing or failover.

6. Click OK, then, if prompted, click Yes, to save these settings and begin the Site Control Manager process that will set up the new management point.

If you want to remove the management point role from the site server, right-click the site server and just follow the same procedures as you did to assign an management point role to the site system; however, you should clear the Use This Site System As A Management Point check box when you're in the Management Point tab.

As with other site systems, when you enable a new management point, you have identified a change to the site control information for the site. A new site control file will be created according to the process described in the section entitled "The Site Configuration Process Flow" earlier in this chapter. Recall that during that process, after the new site control file is generated, other components wake up and read the file to determine whether they need to perform any tasks. As with other site systems, Site Component Manager is responsible for the setup of a management point.

The SMS Agent Host (Ccmexec.exe) is loaded and started and is used to provide change and configuration management services. Two directories are created on the new management point. The folder %Systemroot%\System32\CCM is created and is the location for the agent support files. This folder acts as the "clearinghouse" for data provided to the client and received from the client.

Management Point Component Configuration

In addition to assigning the management point role to a site system, you also have the option of configuring the default settings for the management point role function. You can do this through the Management Point Component configuration properties by completing the following steps:

1. In the SMS Administrator Console, navigate to the Site Settings folder and expand it.

2. Highlight the Component Configuration folder to display the list of SMS components that you can configure.

3. Right-click the entry Management Point and choose Properties from the context menu to display the Management Point Properties dialog box, as shown in Figure 3-35. If there is to be no default management point, select the option None. If you want to name a default management point for the site, select the option Management Point and select the name of the site system that will function as the default management point. If you'd like the management point to be a Network Load Balancing (NLB) virtual cluster rather than a physical server, select the option Network Load Balancing Cluster Virtual Server and enter the cluster server's virtual IP address.

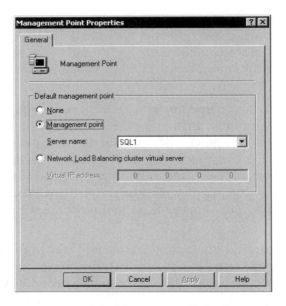

Figure 3-35. *The Management Point Properties dialog box.*

4. Click OK to save these settings.

The site control information will then be updated to reflect your component configuration choices.

Proxy Management Points

Advanced Clients located at a secondary site and reporting to a management point at a parent primary site across a WAN link might have an effect on the available bandwidth of the WAN link between the secondary site and its parent primary site. Significant network traffic can be produced when client status and hardware or software inventory data is sent to the parent primary site. Because an Advanced Client can be assigned only to a primary site, network traffic generated by Advanced Client policy requests also reduces the available bandwidth between the two sites.

Installing a proxy management point at the secondary site can significantly reduce the effect on available network bandwidth created by Advanced Clients located within that site's roaming boundaries or site boundaries. Advanced Clients send inventory data, software metering data, and status data to the proxy management. The proxy management point uses the site's sender functionality to transfer the data to the parent primary site. By using the sender's bandwidth control functionality, you can specify when the data is sent to the primary. The proxy management point also caches some Advanced Client policy information.

Advanced Clients obtain this Advanced Client policy information from the proxy management point, rather than from the management point at the primary site.

Component Server

Any site system that runs the SMS Executive is considered a component server. As we've seen, the CAP is also considered a component server for this reason. The other type of component server that you might define in your site would support the site server by running senders. *Senders* are communication routines used by one site server to contact another site server in a site hierarchy to transfer information. For example, a child site will send inventory data, discovery data, status messages, and site control information to its parent through a sender. A parent site will send package information, advertisements, collections, and configuration data to its child sites through a sender.

When a sender is installed on another Windows server, the SMS Executive and all required support files for that sender are copied to the server and the server becomes a component server—a site system for that SMS site. The best example of using a component server effectively in a production environment is when a Remote Access Service (RAS) server connection is required or is available as an alternative connection mechanism between two sites. It would probably not be practical or advisable to install the SMS site server on the RAS server. The combined resource requirement would no doubt result in reduced performance. So with RAS on one server and SMS on another, you could install the RAS server with an SMS RAS sender, making it a component server for the SMS site. Outside of this scenario, the network traffic that might be generated between the site server and the component server (depending on the size and number of packages, advertisements, and so on) might counterbalance any benefit derived from having the additional sender capability. We'll discuss senders more closely in Chapter 4.

Reporting Points

A reporting point is a site server that stores the report files used for the Web-based reporting feature in SMS 2003. Since a reporting point can communicate only with the local site database, this role can be used only within primary sites. In a large site hierarchy, you might consider placing reporting points at each site in hierarchy for access by specific users within those sites, or higher up in the hierarchy so that information about several sites can be reported on.

Reporting points are installed through the SMS Administrator Console as a site system setting. To assign the reporting point role, follow these steps:

1. In the SMS Administrator Console, navigate to the Site Settings folder and expand it.

2. Highlight the Site Systems folder to display the list of site systems you have defined.

3. Right-click the site system you want to assign as a reporting point and then choose Properties from the context menu to display the Site Systems Properties dialog box.

4. Select the Reporting Point tab, as shown in Figure 3-36. Select the Use This Site System As A Reporting Point check box. The Report Folder text box displays the name of the folder created on this site system where the report information will be stored. Recall that IIS must be installed and enabled on the site system to support the reporting point role. SMS creates the folder under \Inetpub\wwwroot beneath the site server root. The name of the folder is also used as the name of the virtual directory, as displayed in IIS. The URL text box displays the Uniform Resource Locator (URL) used to access reports as determined by the Report Folder name.

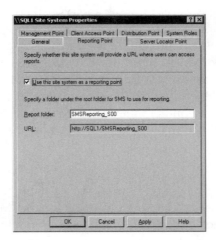

Figure 3-36. *The Reporting Point tab of the Site System Properties dialog box.*

5. Click OK to save these settings and begin the Site Control Manager process that will set up the new Reporting Point.

If you want to remove the reporting point role from the site server, right-click the site server and just follow the same procedures as you did to assign the reporting point role to the site system; however, you should clear the Use This Site System As A Reporting Point check box when you're in the Reporting Point tab.

As with other site systems, when you enable a new reporting point, you have identified a change to the site control information for the site. A new site control file will be created according to the process described in the section entitled "The Site Configuration Process Flow" earlier in this chapter. Recall that during that process, after the new site control file is generated, other components wake up and read the file to determine whether they need to perform any tasks. As with other site systems, Site Component Manager is responsible for the setup of a reporting point. The SMS Reporting Point Service is loaded and started, and the Report Folder is created under the IIS folder structure.

Server Locator Points

A server locator point is used to implement a client installation point for Legacy or Advanced Clients when using a logon script to initiate client installation or to provide autoassignment of Advanced Clients to a site when the Active Directory schema has not yet been extended. Like the reporting point, a server locator point communicates directly with the local site database and is in contact only with the sites beneath it in the SMS site hierarchy. Consequently, this role can't be assigned to site systems in a secondary site. Server locator points support the client installation process by locating a CAP or management point for the client to connect to to receive component installation files.

Typically, you install the server locator point at the central site. If the server locator point creates too much load at the central SMS site database, you have the option to use a replicated SQL Server database for that site. If there are excessive client requests, causing excessive traffic on a single server locator point, you can set up multiple server locator points at the central site, but this is not generally recommended.

Server locator points are installed through the SMS Administrator Console as a site system setting. To assign the server locator point role, follow these steps:

1. In the SMS Administrator Console, navigate to the Site Settings folder and expand it.

2. Highlight the Site Systems folder to display the list of site systems you have defined.

3. Right-click the site system you want to assign as a server locator point and then choose Properties from the context menu to display the Site Systems Properties dialog box.

4. Select the Server Locator Point tab, as shown in Figure 3-37. Select the Use This Site System As A Server Locator Point check box.

Figure 3-37. *The Server Locator Point tab of the Site System Properties dialog box.*

5. From the Database drop-down list, select the Use The Site Database option if the server locator point should access the SMS site database for reading and writing client data. Select the Use A Different Database option and supply the requested information if the server locator point should access a database other than the SMS site database—for example, if you have replicated the SMS site database to another SQL server for load balancing or failover.

6. Click OK to save these settings and begin the Site Control Manager process that will set up the new server locator point.

If you want to remove the server locator point role from the site server, right-click the site server and just follow the same procedures as you did to assign a server locator point role to the site system; however, you should clear the Use This Site System As A Server Locator Point check box when you're in the Server Locator Point tab.

As with other site systems, when you enable a new server locator point, you have identified a change to the site control information for the site. A new site control file will be created according to the process described in the section entitled "The Site Configuration Process Flow" earlier in this chapter. Recall that during that process, after the new site control file is generated, other components wake up and read the file to determine whether they need to perform any tasks. As with other site systems, Site Component Manager is responsible for the setup of a server locator point. The SMS Server Locator Point service is loaded and started, and a SMS_SLP support virtual directory is created under the IIS default Web site structure. This virtual directory points to \Sms\Bin\i386\ SMS_SLP.

Checkpoints

If you've been reading carefully, you'll have encountered several notes and cautions describing situations that, if not considered, can result in strange and unusual things happening in your site. These administrative lapses might be called "gotchas" because of the sneaky way they have of jumping up to get you. Let's recap the most significant gotchas here.

Planning and Identifying Site Systems

First and foremost, be sure that your deployment strategy has identified which servers will serve as site systems, how many servers you might need, and which roles they will play. Your answers will depend on the size of your site; the number of clients, packages, advertisements, and so on involved; and the current state of your network and network traffic. The soundest approach is to test, track, and analyze. Use the tools available to learn how your site server and site systems will perform under different conditions.

The Performance console's System Monitor utility is an ideal Windows tool to assist you with this analysis on Windows servers. Use Network Monitor to track and analyze traffic generated between the site server and its site systems. Identify, wherever possible, those times when site traffic might take advantage of lighter traffic loads. As we delve more deeply into SMS processes, such as inventory collection and package distribution, you'll learn how to identify and analyze network traffic.

Disk Space

The amount of disk space required for each type of site system varies. Be sure that the site systems you have in mind have adequate disk space to carry out their function and store their data. CAPs and management points, for example, need space to store inventory data, discovery data, and status messages from clients, as well as package information, advertisements, site lists, and client configuration files. Of course, the number of clients you're managing and the number of packages and advertisements that you generate will affect the disk space requirements, but this quantity can—with some effort and resource analysis—be determined.

Distribution points require as much disk space as each package you store. Again, with some calculation effort and planning, you can determine this number. The space required by a reporting point will depend on the number of reports that you have configured and the location of the reporting point within the hierarchy. Server locator points probably require the least amount of additional space since their primary function is to direct a client to an appropriate CAP or management point.

Connection Accounts

Connection accounts were discussed in detail in the section entitled "Site System Connection Accounts" earlier in this chapter. For SMS site servers running in standard security mode, additional connection accounts beyond the default account that SMS creates or the SMS service account aren't really required unless you have specific security issues to address on specific site systems. Site systems running in advanced security mode make use of computer accounts rather than user accounts, as well as the new SMS_SiteSystemToSiteServerConnection group account to which the computer accounts of site systems should be added.

Summary

In this chapter we explored how to configure site server properties such as the site boundaries, roaming boundaries, and site accounts. We explored the site configuration process flow and identified three main SMS components involved in most site property changes—SMS Hierarchy Manager, SMS Site Component Manager, and SMS Site Control Manager.

We also discussed how to identify and configure site systems for our SMS site. The site server could, of course, be assigned all site system roles, and in many environments this might be appropriate. However, other concerns might lead us to assign one or more site system roles to other servers in our site. These concerns, as we have seen, include performance limitations of the site server, the number and location of our clients and users, network infrastructure, and network traffic patterns. Now that we understand how to manage systems within our site, we can explore the process of joining different SMS sites into an enterprise-wide site hierarchy—the topic of Chapter 4.

Chapter 4
Multiple-Site Structures

For most large organizations, maintaining a single Microsoft SMS site to manage all network resources won't be practical. In an organization whose network infrastructure consists of subnets that communicate through WAN connections, routers and so on, implementing multiple SMS sites might well prove to be the stronger strategy.

With that in mind, in this chapter we'll examine the strategies and processes involved in designing and implementing a site hierarchy for your organization. We'll explore the concepts of parent-child relationships and creating secondary sites, and we'll look at methods of communicating between sites. We'll also examine the factors that will affect your site structure strategy, such as network performance, domain model, number and location of clients, and the client components you wish to install. Let's begin with the basic building block of the SMS site structure—the parent-child relationship.

Defining Parent-Child Relationships

Parent and child sites are defined by their relationship within an SMS site hierarchy. We've already explained the related terms and concepts in Chapter 1, "Overview." Let's review them first and then explore them in more detail. A *parent site* is any site with at least one child site defined; the parent site has the ability to administer any child sites below it in the SMS hierarchy. A *child site* is any SMS site that has a parent defined.

An SMS *primary site* has three main distinguishing characteristics:

- A primary site is an SMS site that has access to a Microsoft SQL Server database.

- A primary site can be administered through the SMS Administrator Console as well as by any SMS primary sites above it in the site hierarchy. A primary site can also administer any child sites below it in the site hierarchy.

- A primary site can be a child of other primary sites, and it can have child sites of its own.

The requirement that a primary site has access to a SQL Server database might translate into an additional investment in hardware and software for each SMS site, site server, or both. On the other hand, because a primary site can be both a parent and a child site, it's relatively easy to restructure your site hierarchy if all your sites are primary sites, as we'll see in the section "Implementing a Parent-Child Relationship Between Primary Sites" later in this chapter.

An SMS *secondary site* is also distinguished by three main characteristics:

- A secondary site doesn't have access to a SQL Server database.

- A secondary site is always a child of a primary site and is administered solely through its parent or through another primary site above it in the SMS site hierarchy.

- A secondary site can't have child sites of its own.

Because a secondary site doesn't require access to a SQL Server database, it might not command the same investment in hardware and software as a primary site. However, a secondary site can be administered only through its parent site or through another primary site above it in the site hierarchy. If an SMS administrator on the same local subnet as the secondary site wants to administer the site, that SMS administrator will first need to connect to the site database for the secondary site's parent site. If the SQL database for the parent site is accessed across a WAN link, response might be slow or inefficient. On the other hand, if no local SMS administrator is available, a remote SMS administrator can rather easily manage the secondary site in the same manner.

Caution To switch primary and secondary site roles, you must first uninstall and then reinstall SMS.

A *central site* is an SMS primary site that resides at the top of the SMS hierarchy. Database information rolls from child to parent and is collected ultimately at the central site's SMS database. A central site can administer any site below it in the SMS hierarchy and can send information down to its child sites.

Figure 4-1 shows a typical SMS site hierarchy model. In this site hierarchy, site A01 is the central site. All information rolls up to this site. Sites A02, A03, and A04 are primary sites, as they have access to a SQL database for SMS. Site A05 is a child site to site A03; it's also a secondary site, as it doesn't have access to a SQL database for SMS.

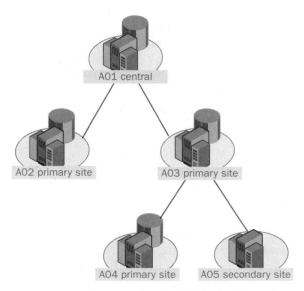

Figure 4-1.   *An example of an SMS site hierarchy.*

Child sites send inventory data, discovery data, site control data, and status messages to their immediate parent sites. A child site never sends information directly to its "grandparent" site. Parent sites, in turn, send information about collections, package definitions, advertisements, and site control files to their child sites. Although child sites send data only to their immediate parent, a parent site can send information to any child below it in the SMS site hierarchy, provided it has an address for that site. Addresses are discussed later in this chapter.

Because child sites send inventory data to their parent sites, database storage space becomes a greater concern at the parent sites at each successive layer up in the hierarchy. In the hierarchy shown in Figure 4-1, site A04 reports its inventory data to site A03. Site A03's database needs to be large enough to accommodate its own information plus the information coming from site A04. Similarly, site A03 reports its inventory data to site A01. Since site A01 is also the central site, it receives information from all sites below it in the hierarchy. Site A01's database therefore needs to be large enough to accommodate its own information plus that of all sites below it in the hierarchy.

Tip   Try to keep your site hierarchy as flat as possible. A flatter hierarchy will require information to flow through fewer layers (sites) before reaching the central site. Child site information will be reported to the central site more quickly and efficiently. In addition, the simpler the hierarchy, the less concern you'll have about database space requirements at parent sites at each level of the hierarchy.

Installing a Secondary Site

In Chapter 2, "Primary Site Installation," you learned how to install an SMS 2003 primary site. In this section we'll explore the process of installing an SMS 2003 secondary site. Recall that a secondary site can be a child only of a specific primary site, and it is managed primarily through that primary site or through any site above it in the site hierarchy. Because of this, it's most appropriate to think of the SMS 2003 secondary site as being a property of a primary site.

You can initiate an SMS 2003 secondary site installation through the SMS Administrator console. However, you can also install it directly from the SMS 2003 CD. The setup program gives you the option of installing a secondary site. You might choose this option if you need to install the secondary site but don't yet have a WAN connection available to the primary site, or if the existing WAN connection is "network traffic challenged" and you want to avoid the additional traffic involved in performing the installation from the primary site server. Also, when installing a secondary site from CD, you'll be able to choose which SMS components you want to install on the secondary site server much like the custom installation we reviewed in Chapter 2. When you install the secondary site from the parent site, all SMS components are installed on the secondary site server.

Installing the Secondary Site from Its Parent Primary Site

Follow these steps to install an SMS 2003 secondary site server from a primary site:

1. In the SMS Administrator Console, navigate to the site entry folder (this should fall directly below the Site Hierarchy folder), right-click it, choose New from the context menu, and then choose Secondary Site. The Welcome To The Create Secondary Site Wizard page appears, as shown in Figure 4-2.

Figure 4-2.   *The Welcome To The Create Secondary Site Wizard page.*

2. Click Next to display the Site Identity page, as shown in Figure 4-3. Enter a three-character site code, a descriptive name for the site, and optionally a descriptive comment.

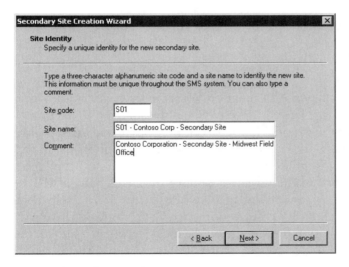

Figure 4-3.   *The Site Identity page.*

3. Click Next to display the Site Server page, as shown in Figure 4-4. Enter the name of the domain in which the secondary site server is located, the site server name, the processor platform (Intel X86 and compatible is your only choice here), and the NTFS installation directory (be sure that you reference an NTFS directory).

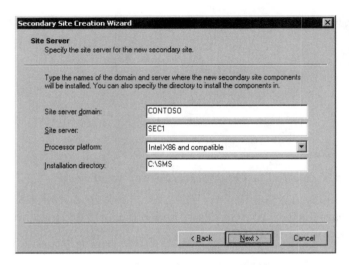

Figure 4-4. *The Site Server page.*

Note   Be sure to enter the server name correctly. The Secondary Site installation process doesn't verify that the server actually exists.

4. Click Next to display the Installation Source Files page, as shown in Figure 4-5. This page lets you specify where the source files for installing the secondary site reside. If you select the Copy Installation Source Files Over the Network From The Parent Site Server option, Setup will obtain the installation files from the primary site server and copy them across the network to the target secondary site. This option will, of course, generate a fair amount of network traffic. If you select the Install The Source Files From A Compact Disc... option, Setup will look for the installation files on the on the local (secondary site) server. This option assumes, of course, that you have inserted the SMS CD into the CD drive on the target secondary site server, have copied the SMS source files to a local drive on the target server, or mapped a drive to a shared folder that contains the SMS source files.

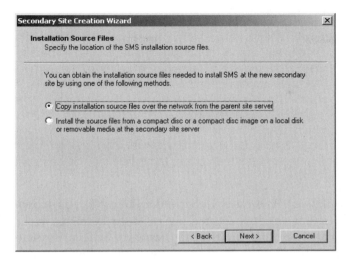

Figure 4-5. *The Installation Source Files page.*

5. Click Next to display the SMS Security Information page, as shown in Figure 4-6. If you intend the site to run in standard mode security, select that option and enter the name of the SMS Service account (which you have already created) that the secondary site server will use and confirm the password. If you intend the site to run in advanced security mode, select that option. Then click Next.

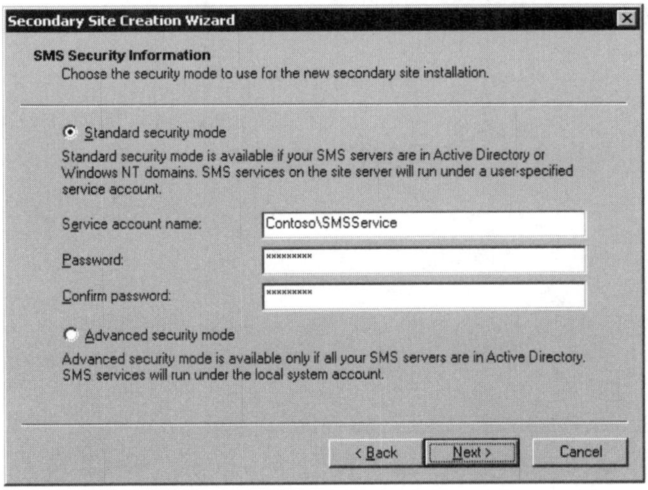

Figure 4-6. *The SMS Security Information page.*

Caution The SMS Service account you specify during the installation of the SMS 2003 secondary site must already have been created for the target server, as we discussed in Chapter 3, "Configuring Site Server Properties and Site Systems." Be sure to make the account a member of the Domain Admins global group in the secondary site's Microsoft Windows domain, if not in the same domain. Also be sure that the account is a member of the local Administrators group on the secondary site server itself—either explicitly or by virtue of its being a member of the Domain Admins global group—and that it has the Log On As A Service user right on the secondary site server. If any of these prerequisites is missing, the installation process will fail—miserably!

6. Click Next to display the Addresses To Secondary Site page, as shown in Figure 4-7. If you have already created one or more addresses to the target secondary site—for example, using the Standard Sender (through LAN or WAN connections) or the Asynchronous RAS Sender (through dial-up)—these will be listed in the Addresses To list. If you haven't already created an address to the secondary site or if you want to create a new address, select the Yes Create A New Address option and go on to step 7. Otherwise, select the No Proceed With Site Creation option to use the existing address and proceed to step 9. If there is no existing address to select, you must create a new address.

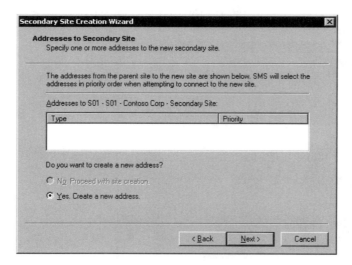

Figure 4-7. *The Addresses To Secondary Site page.*

7. If you chose Yes in the preceding step, clicking Next takes you to the New Address To Secondary Site page, as shown in Figure 4-8. Here

you must select a sender address type, confirm the secondary site server name, and, if you're installing the site to run in standard security mode, identify the name of the account on the secondary site server that you want the primary site to use when connecting to the secondary site. This account will generally be the SMS Service account, but it can be any account that has at least Change access to the SMS_Site share. Once again, this account must have been created before you begin the secondary site installation. If you're installing the site to run in advanced security mode, the account referenced will be the Local System account as shown in Figure 4-8 and you won't be able to reference any other account.

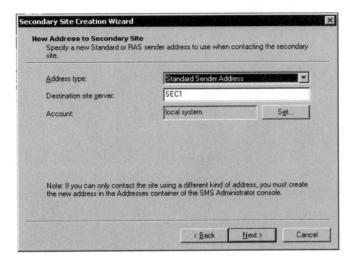

Figure 4-8.   *The New Address To Secondary Site page.*

Note   When you create an address using Setup, you'll have only the options Standard Sender Address and Asynchronous RAS Sender Address in the Address Type drop-down list. If you choose to use a RAS sender, the RAS service must be installed on the server you'll use for the secondary site server or on another server accessible to the proposed secondary site server. If you need any other sender type, you must create the address through the SMS Administrator Console before beginning the secondary site installation process.

8. Click Next to display the New Address To Parent Site page, as shown in Figure 4-9. Specify a sender address type, confirm the primary site server name, and, if you're installing the site to run in standard security mode, identify the name of the account on the primary site server

that you want the secondary site to use when connecting to the primary site. This account will generally be the SMS Service account, but it can be any account that has at least Change access to the SMS_Site share on the primary site server. Once again, this account must have been created before you begin the secondary site installation. If you're installing the site to run in advanced security mode, the account referenced will be the Local System account as shown in Figure 4-9 and you won't be able to reference any other account.

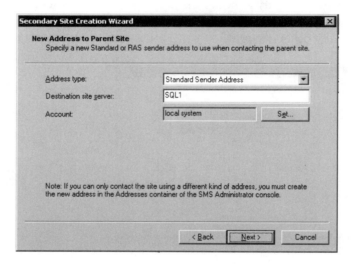

Figure 4-9. *The New Address To Parent Site page.*

9. Click Next to display the Completing The Create Secondary Site Wizard page. Review your selections in the New Secondary Site Characteristics section, and then click Finish to begin the installation process. You can also click Back to return to previous pages to make changes.

Installing the Secondary Site Locally from the SMS CD

Follow these steps to install an SMS 2003 secondary site server from the SMS CD:

1. Begin Setup from the SMS CD. You'll see the Systems Management Server Setup Wizard's Welcome page, as you did when you were installing the primary site.

2. Click Next until the Setup Options page is displayed, as shown in Figure 4-10. Select the Install An SMS Secondary Site option.

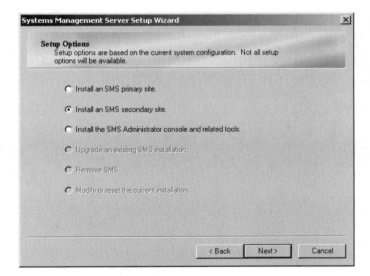

Figure 4-10.   *The Setup Options page.*

3. Click Next to display the Systems Management Server License Agreement page, as shown in Figure 4-11. Read the agreement carefully and select the option I Agree.

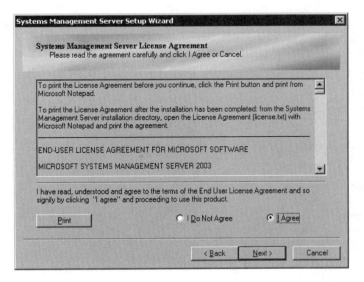

Figure 4-11.   *The Systems Management Server License Agreement page.*

4. Click Next to display the Product Registration page, as shown in Figure 4-12, and enter the name, organization, and CD Key information.

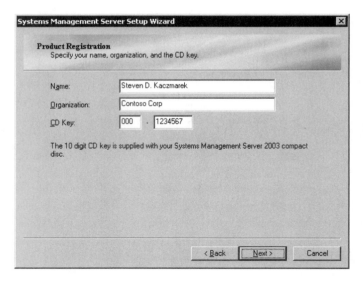

Figure 4-12. *The Product Registration page.*

5. Click Next to display the SMS Site Information page, as shown in Figure 4-13. Enter the three-character site code you'll assign to the secondary site server, a unique descriptive name for the site, and the name of the Windows domain in which the secondary site server is located.

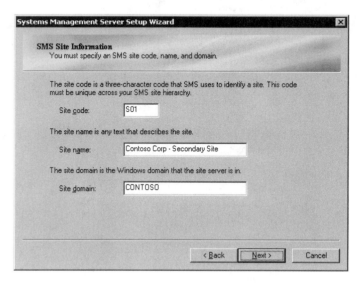

Figure 4-13. *The SMS Site Information page.*

6. Click Next to display the SMS Security Information page, as shown in Figure 4-14. If you intend the site to run in standard security mode, select that option, enter the name of the SMS Service account that the secondary site server will use, and confirm the password. If you intend the site to run in advanced security mode, select that option.

![Systems Management Server Setup Wizard dialog box showing the SMS Security Information page with options for Advanced security and Standard security]

Systems Management Server Setup Wizard

SMS Security Information
Choose the security mode to use for your SMS installation.

⊙ Advanced security

Advanced security mode is available only if all your SMS servers are in Active Directory. SMS services will run under the local system account. You cannot change back to standard security mode after the site is installed.

○ Standard security

Standard security mode is available if your SMS servers are in Active Directory or Windows NT domains. SMS services on the site server will run under a user-specified service account. You can switch to advanced security mode after the site is installed.

Service account name:

Password:

Confirm password:

< Back   Next >   Cancel

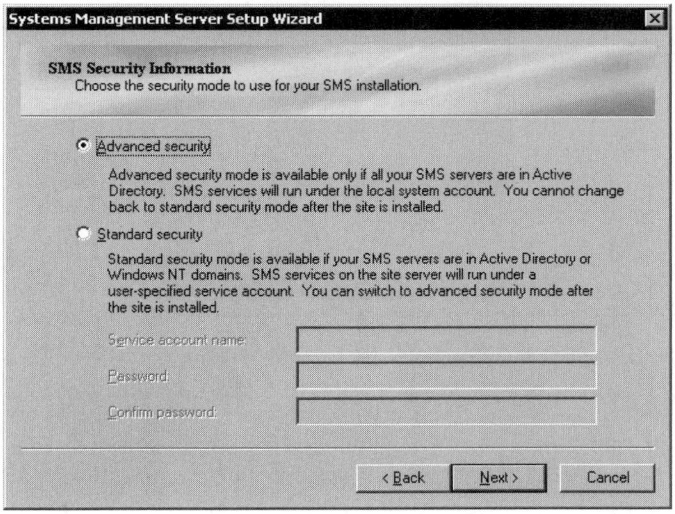

Figure 4-14.   *The SMS Security Information page.*

Note   You can't install a secondary site in advanced security mode if the parent site is running standard security.

Note   When you install a secondary site from its parent site as discussed in the previous section, the SMS Service account you specify must already have been created for the target server. However, when installing the site from the CD, as we are here, it isn't necessary to have created the account ahead of time. If the account hasn't yet been created, the setup program can do that for you just as it does during the installation of a primary site (as described in Chapter 2).

7. Click Next to display the Installation Options page, as shown in Figure 4-15. Select the SMS 2003 options that you want to enable on the secondary site server. You can also change the directory in which the components are installed on your site server.

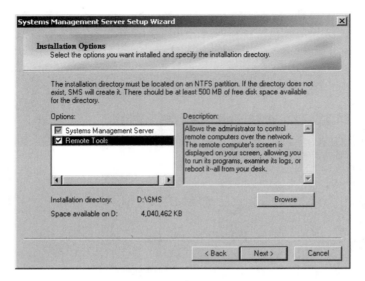

Figure 4-15. *The Installation Options page.*

Note When installing SMS from the CD, you can select which SMS options you want to install, much like a custom installation for a primary site server. Notice, however, that only those options that don't require access to an SMS site database or that are applicable to the SMS Administrator Console are listed as valid options.

8. Click Next to display the Parent Site Information/Identification page, as shown in Figure 4-16. Enter the site code and server name of the parent primary site and select the network connection type that the secondary site will use to connect to that parent site. Your connection choices include Local Area Network, the default, Asynchronous RAS link, ISDN RAS link, X.25 RAS link, and SNA Over RAS link. If your primary and secondary sites are in the same Active Directory forest, be sure that the This Computer And The Parent Site Server Are In The Same Active Directory Forest option is enabled. If your primary and secondary sites are not in the same forest, clear this option. See Chapter 8, "Designing Your SMS Sites and Hierarchy," in the *Microsoft Systems Management Server 2003 Concepts, Planning, and Deployment Guide* (on the SMS 2003 CD) for more information about parent and child sites that exist in different forests.

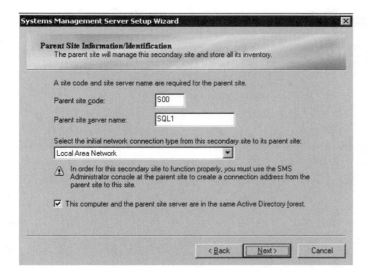

Figure 4-16.   *The Parent Site Information/Identification page.*

Caution   You'll still need to create a valid address at the primary site server that identifies connection parameters that allow the primary site to connect back to the secondary site server. The steps for creating an address will be discussed in the section entitled "Creating an Address" later in this chapter.

9. If you selected Standard Security in step 6, the Connection Account Information page will be displayed when you click Next, as shown in Figure 4-17. If you selected advanced security in step 6, the site won't require any additional connection accounts and you can go on to step 10.

   On the Connection Account Information page, you must enter the name and password of the account that the secondary site server will use to connect to the parent site. This account will generally be the SMS Service account, but it can be any account that has at least Change access to the SMS_Site share on the primary site server.

   If you're running advanced security, the computer account of the parent site must be a local administrator on the secondary site server, and the computer account of the secondary site server must be a local administrator of the parent site. For more information about how to set up computer accounts, see Chapter 16, "Queries and Reports."

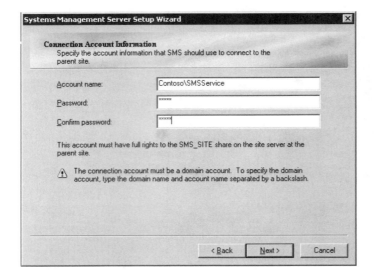

Figure 4-17. *The Connection Account Information page.*

10. Click Next to display the Completing The Systems Management Server Setup Wizard page, review your selections, and then click Finish to begin the installation process. Again, you can click the Back button from this page or any previous page to go back and modify your entries. As with the primary site installation, if the service account hasn't been created ahead of time, Setup can create an account for you. Setup will display a dialog box prompting you to do so; choose Yes.

Note When you apply a service pack to your SMS sites, secondary sites aren't automatically upgraded when the parent site is upgraded. To upgrade your secondary site server, first upgrade its parent primary site. When you right-click the secondary site object in the SMS Administrator Console for the primary site, you'll have an option to upgrade the site. When you select this option, an upgrade wizard will walk you through the upgrade process.

The Secondary Site Installation Process Flow

The process of installing a secondary site from the SMS CD is relatively straightforward. Setup simply creates the subdirectory structure, loads services and components as necessary, and connects to the parent site to complete the parent-child relationship. This process is similar to the primary site server installation. However, installing a secondary site from a primary site server involves SMS primary site server components, network traffic, and installation routines installed and run on the secondary site server. This section provides a basic overview of that process.

When you initiate the installation of a secondary site through the SMS Administrator Console, you are in effect changing the primary site's properties, and the site configuration process flow described in Chapter 3 is started. Hierarchy Manager queries the sites table and site control file in the SMS site database. From this information, it determines that a secondary site installation process needs to be initiated and generates a request to do so in the Scheduler's inbox (SMS\Inboxes\Schedule.box). The Scheduler, in turn, creates the package and instruction files that support the installation and that need to be sent to the secondary site server and creates a send request file for the sender that will connect to the secondary site server. The sender will be the same connection mechanism you chose when you initiated the setup process.

The sender connects to and copies the package and instruction files to the secondary site server and loads a bootstrap service that creates the SMS folder structure, starts the setup process, and loads and starts the SMS Site Component Manager. Site Component Manager completes the installation and configuration of SMS components, loads and starts the SMS Executive service, and generates a new site control file. Finally, the connection back to the parent site is configured, and the SMS Replication Manager sends the new secondary server site control information back to the parent site through the Scheduler and sender at the secondary site.

You can follow the flow of this process by monitoring the status messages and log files (if enabled) on the primary site server for Hierarchy Manager, Site Control Manager, Discovery Data Manager, the Scheduler, and the appropriate sender, such as the SMS Standard Sender.

Differences Between Primary and Secondary Sites

The SMS 2003 secondary site server is installed much like the SMS 2003 primary site server. Setup builds the SMS and CAP_*sitecode* directory structures (where sitecode represents the three-character site code of the secondary site), including the component support files and inboxes, and installs the secondary site server as an SMS client. Setup installs the secondary site as a site system with the client access point (CAP) and distribution point roles by default and doesn't enable any discovery or installation methods or client agents until the SMS administrator does so through the SMS Administrator Console. The SMS Executive, SMS Site Component Manager, and SMS Site Backup components are loaded, the SMS Executive and SMS Site Component Manager are started, and the SMS, Network Access Layer (NAL), and SMS service keys are added to the Windows server registry. The same shares are created on the secondary site server as on the primary site server.

However, the secondary site server is fully administered through a parent site, as shown in Figure 4-18. Thus, no Systems Management Server program group is created, and no SMS Administrator Console is installed by default. The SMS SQL Monitor service isn't installed, nor are any references to SQL Server or SQL Server triggers placed in the Windows server registry. Also missing from the SMS directory structure are folders or files, or both, that reference SMS components and options that aren't applicable to the secondary site, such as the product compliance database.

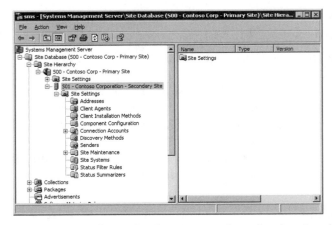

Figure 4-18. *The SMS Administrator Console, showing the secondary site.*

Because the secondary site is administered through its parent site, site property changes will take place across the network, generating some network traffic. This network traffic generally includes writing the change to the site control file on the secondary site server or writing a file to a component inbox on the secondary site server. The secondary site server will experience performance similar to the primary site server, and you should plan your hardware investment for a secondary site server in much the same way as you would for a primary site server. Since you don't have the added overhead of SQL Server database access, the resource requirements for the secondary site server won't be as high as for a primary site server. Nevertheless, you'll sell yourself, your organization, and the secondary site short if you don't include the same planning and testing strategies when implementing the secondary site as you do when implementing a primary site.

When viewing the site properties of the secondary site through the parent site's SMS Administrator Console, you'll notice that any site tasks related to the presence of a database will be missing. For example, let's consider the folder Site Settings\Site Maintenance. For a primary site, you can schedule SQL commands and enable and configure a variety of database tasks, such as backing up the database and setting aging intervals for discovery data and inventory records. For a secondary site, you can schedule only a site backup.

Additionally, the only other site system role supported by a secondary site besides the default CAP and distribution point roles is management point (in this scenario, called a proxy management point). As you can see in Figure 4-19, if you assign this role, you must specify whether to use the parent site's database or some database on another server.

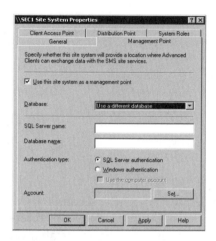

Figure 4-19.   *The Site Systems Properties dialog box for the management point role for a management point site system in a secondary site.*

Uninstalling a Secondary Site

Although there might be several reasons for wanting to remove a secondary site, one main consideration must be kept in mind—the relationship between the secondary site and its parent. Since the secondary site can't exist without a parent site, it's more closely related to its parent than two primary sites would be in a parent-child relationship. For example, if you want to move the secondary site from one parent to another, you must completely uninstall the secondary site first and then reinstall it for the new parent.

The process for uninstalling a secondary site is similar to that for uninstalling a primary site, as described in Chapter 2. You can initiate an uninstall by running setup from the SMS 2003 source CD, navigating to the Setup Options page, and selecting Remove SMS. You can also initiate the uninstall process through the SMS Administrator Console. Start the SMS Administrator Console for the parent site of the secondary site that you want to remove. Right-click the secondary site entry in the console and select Delete from the action menu. This starts the

Delete Secondary Site Wizard. When you click Next, the setup process displays the Choose Whether To Delete Or Deinstall page, as shown in Figure 4-20.

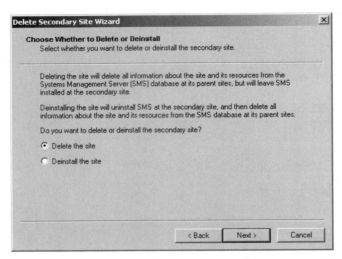

Figure 4-20.   *The Choose Whether To Delete Or Deinstall page.*

With SMS 2003, you have the option to completely remove the secondary site installation (the Deinstall option on this page) or to simply remove all references to the secondary site from its parent while leaving the server installation intact (the Delete option). You would use the Delete option if, for example, the secondary site server is no longer functioning or no longer exists. In that case the Deinstall option wouldn't work because the secondary site server wouldn't be able to respond to commands to uninstall. Only error messages would be generated at the parent, and the deinstall would fail from the parent's point of view. However, the Delete option bypasses the uninstall portion of the process and simply removes the reference of the secondary site from the parent site. Of course, you might still need to do some cleanup on the secondary site server.

When the removal process is complete and you refresh the parent site console, the secondary site entry will no longer be present. You can then proceed to perform your server cleanup tasks as described for cleaning up an uninstalled primary site in Chapter 2.

Implementing a Parent-Child Relationship Between Primary Sites

When you install an SMS 2003 secondary site, it becomes a child of the primary site it's installed from, and, voila, you have a parent-child relationship. As we discussed, however, primary sites can also enter into parent-child relationships. Two main requirements must be met to successfully implement a parent-child relationship between two primary sites: each site must have an address to the other site, and the child must identify its parent.

Creating an Address

An address in SMS 2003 is yet another site setting—that is, a property of the site. A site server needs to know which other site servers it needs to communicate with—for sending package information, inventory data, status messages, and site control information—and how to establish that communication.

Both the parent and the child need an address to each other. The child sends inventory data, status messages, discovery data, and site control information to its immediate parent. The parent site sends package, collection, advertisement, and site control information to its child. A parent site can also send this information to any other site below it in the hierarchy. It does so by routing the information through its child sites or by configuring an address directly to the other site.

This flow of information is illustrated in Figure 4-21. Sites A04 and A05 will report data directly to their parent, site A03. Site A03 will, in turn, report its data (which includes the data from sites A04 and A05) directly to its parent, central site A01, as will site A02. Sites A04 and A05 need an address to site A03, and sites A02 and A03 need an address to site A01. Similarly, site A01 needs an address to sites A02 and A03, and site A03 needs an address to sites A04 and A05. Site A01 can administer any site below it in the hierarchy. It can send package and advertisement information to sites A04 and A05 by routing that information through site A03, for which it has an address. However, if the SMS administrator configures an address in site A01 for site A04, site A01 could send information directly to site A04.

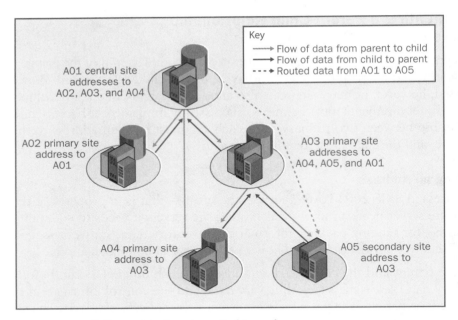

Figure 4-21. *Information flow in a site hierarchy.*

An SMS 2003 site delivers information to another site by connecting to that site using a communication mechanism called a *sender*. The five available senders are Standard Sender (regular LAN/WAN connection), Asynchronous RAS Sender, ISDN RAS Sender, X.25 RAS Sender, and SNA RAS Sender. These senders, along with a sixth sender named Courier Sender, will be discussed in detail in the section entitled "Communicating Through Senders" later in this chapter.

These senders connect to a default share point on the target site named SMS_Site. This shared folder references the SMS\Inboxes\Despoolr.box\Receive directory and is created automatically during the installation of a primary or secondary site server. If you're running your sites in standard security mode, the SMS administrator must identify a connection account that has at least Change access to this share. That could, of course, be the SMS Service account, but it doesn't have to be. Using this account to access the target site server share, the sender copies the data in question to the target site, keeping track of its progress. When it has finished, the sender disconnects from the target site. If you're running your sites using advanced security mode, SMS will use the Local System account and computer accounts to connect to this share.

Tip Since the SMS Service account is a domain administrator as well, it's not the most secure account to use. The more secure approach in standard security mode would be to create a new account (just a regular user), password protect it, and give it Change access to the SMS_Site share.

Creating an Address to Another Site

To create an address to another site, follow these steps:

1. In the SMS Administrator Console, navigate to the Site Settings folder and expand it.

2. Right-click the Addresses folder and choose New from the context menu. A list of sender address types is displayed, as shown in Figure 4-22.

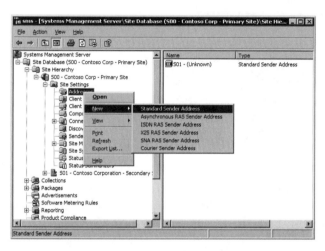

Figure 4-22.   *Displaying a list of sender address types.*

3. Choose the sender address type you need, to display its Properties dialog box. Fill in the General tab in the appropriate Properties dialog box as follows:

   - In the Standard Sender Address Properties dialog box, shown in Figure 4-23, select the site from the Destination Site Code drop-down list for the target site. In the Destination Access frame, enter the name of the destination site's site server name. Click the Set button to specify the name and password of the account on the target site that has at least Change permission for the SMS_Site share on the target site.

Figure 4-23.   *The Standard Sender Address Properties dialog box.*

- In the Asynchronous RAS Sender Address Properties dialog box, shown in Figure 4-24, select the site from the Destination Site Code drop-down list for the target site. In the RAS Access frame, enter the RAS phone book entry that references dial-up information for accessing the target site. Click the Set button to specify the dial-up access account and phone number to be used when dialing in to the target site. In the Destination Access frame, enter the name of the target site's site server name and the domain of which it is a member. Click the Set button to specify the name and password of the account on the target site that has at least Change permission for the SMS_Site share on the target site. If you're running in advanced security mode, this account will be displayed as Local System and you won't be able to change it.

Figure 4-24.   *The Asynchronous RAS Sender Address Properties dialog box.*

- In the ISDN RAS Sender Address Properties dialog box, shown in Figure 4-25, select the site from the Destination Site Code drop-down list for the target site. In the RAS Access frame, enter the RAS phone book entry that references dial-up information for accessing the target site. Click Set to specify the dial-up access account and phone number to be used when dialing in to the target site. In the Destination Access frame, enter the name of the target site's site server and the domain of which it is a member. Click Set to specify the name and password of the account on the target site that has at least Change permission for the SMS_Site share on the target site. If you're running in advanced security mode, this account will be displayed as Local System and you won't be able to change it.

Figure 4-25.   *The ISDN RAS Sender Address Properties dialog box.*

- In the X.25 RAS Sender Address Properties dialog box, shown in Figure 4-26, select the site from the Destination Site Code drop-down list for the target site. In the RAS Access frame, enter the RAS phone book entry that references dial-up information for accessing the target site. Click the Set button to specify the dial-up access account and phone number to be used when dialing in to the target site. In the Destination Access frame, enter the name of the target site's site server and the domain of which it is a member. Click Set to specify the name and password of the account on the target site that has at least Change permission for the SMS_Site share on the target site. If you're running in advanced security mode, this account will be displayed as Local System and you won't be able to change it.

Figure 4-26.   *The X.25 RAS Sender Address Properties dialog box.*

- In the SNA RAS Sender Address Properties dialog box, shown in Figure 4-27, select the site from the Destination Site Code drop-down list for the target site. In the RAS Access frame, enter the RAS phone book entry that references dial-up information for accessing the target site. Click the Set button to specify the dial-up access account and phone number to be used when dialing in to the target site. In the Destination Access frame, enter the name of the target site's site server and the domain of which it is a member. Click the Set button to specify the name and password of the account on the target site that has at least Change permission for the SMS_Site share on the target site. If you're running in advanced security mode, this account will be displayed as Local System and you won't be able to change it.

- For details on how to create a Courier Sender address, please refer to the section entitled "Courier Sender" later in this chapter.

Figure 4-27. *The SNA RAS Sender Address Properties dialog box.*

4. Select the Schedule tab, as shown in Figure 4-28. As you can see, by default the sender is available for all priority send requests at all times. Select the time period you want to modify by highlighting it using the mouse. In the Availability list, select the appropriate option: Open For All Priorities, Allow Medium And High Priority, Allow High Priority Only, Closed. The priority of a send request such as a package is set when the package is created. Choose Closed for periods when you don't want the sender to send anything, such as during regular backup times. If there are multiple addresses to a target site, SMS will automatically choose the next sender in order of priority (based on the Relative Address Priority setting in the General tab) if the current sender is unavailable for some reason. Select the Unavailable To Substitute For Inoperative Addresses check box to prevent this sender from being used as an alternative sender (used when a higher priority sender is in use or unavailable.)

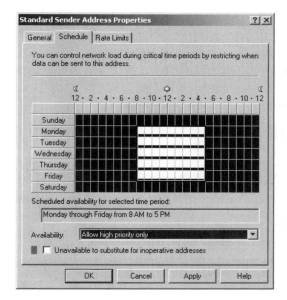

Figure 4-28.   *The Schedule tab of the Standard Sender Address Properties dialog box.*

5. Select the Rate Limits tab, as shown in Figure 4-29. Notice that by default SMS can use as much bandwidth as it wants when transferring data to the target site. Select the Limited To Specified Maximum Transfer Rates By Hour option and highlight the period of time you want to modify using the mouse. In the Rate Limit For Selected Time Period frame, select a preferred bandwidth percentage from the drop-down list.

6. Click OK to create the address.

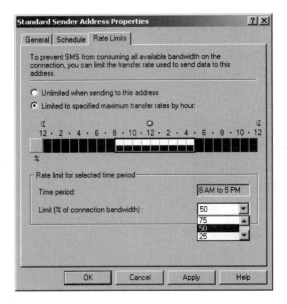

Figure 4-29. *The Rate Limits tab.*

If multiple addresses exist for a target site, the order of priority in which SMS will use them to connect to the target site is the order in which the addresses were created. This is known as the *relative address priority*—that is, the priority of one address relative to another. You can change the relative priority of an address by right-clicking one of the addresses in the address pane of the SMS Administrator Console and choosing either Increment Priority or Decrement Priority from the context menu. If you have only one address listed, the priority options will be dimmed.

Multiple addresses to the same target site provide SMS with alternative ways of connecting to a site and transferring data if one sender is busy or unavailable. This flexibility can improve performance in the sending process, but with one caveat. You can install only one sender of each type on the same site server. For example, you can't install two Standard Senders on the same site server, but you can install the Standard Sender once on as many component site systems as you want.

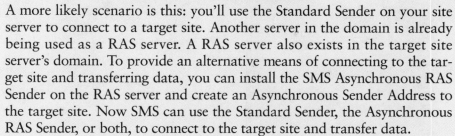

Real World   Alternate Senders to a Target Site

A more likely scenario is this: you'll use the Standard Sender on your site server to connect to a target site. Another server in the domain is already being used as a RAS server. A RAS server also exists in the target site server's domain. To provide an alternative means of connecting to the target site and transferring data, you can install the SMS Asynchronous RAS Sender on the RAS server and create an Asynchronous Sender Address to the target site. Now SMS can use the Standard Sender, the Asynchronous RAS Sender, or both, to connect to the target site and transfer data.

You'll want to closely monitor the traffic generated between the site server and the RAS server—which, in this case, is functioning as a component server for the SMS site. Assuming that both servers are on the same subnet, the traffic shouldn't be significant. Nevertheless, you don't want to find yourself in a situation where the benefit you gain in improved sending performance to the target site is negated by excess traffic or degraded network performance between the site server and the RAS server.

Identifying the Parent Site

Before you identify a site's parent, you must have created an address to that parent site. The child site will use that address to connect to the parent and transfer its site control information—including the fact that the parent now has a new child site. You can then set the parent site by following these steps:

1. In the SMS Administrator Console, navigate to the site entry and choose Properties from the context menu.

2. The Site Properties dialog box appears, as shown in Figure 4-30. In the General tab, click the Set Parent Site button.

Figure 4-30. *The General tab of the Site Properties dialog box.*

3. In the Set Parent Site dialog box, shown in Figure 4-31, select the Report To Parent Site option, enter the three-character site code of the parent site, and click OK to return to the Site Properties dialog box.

Figure 4-31. *The Set Parent Site dialog box.*

4. Click OK again to set the parent site, which starts the site configuration change process.

The site configuration change process includes not only updating the child site with the new parent site information but also sending data to the parent site and updating the parent site's database and site control information. This process shouldn't take more than a few minutes, but factors such as the resource capabilities of both the child and parent sites, available bandwidth, and other database activity will affect the length of time it takes for the parent-child relationship to be established and "recognized" by both parent and child. When you first create the address entry for the parent or the child, the site entry should include the site code and should indicate that the site name is unknown. After the relationship has been established and site control data has been transferred, this information will be updated to reflect the actual site name of the addressed site.

You can follow the flow of the site configuration change process and the transfer of information that takes place by monitoring the status messages that the SMS components record at each point in the process. For a detailed explanation on how to view status messages, please refer back to the section entitled "Status Messages" in Chapter 3. Table 4-1 lists the SMS components and the status messages that relate to this process.

Table 4-1.   Status messages generated during the establishment of a parent-child relationship

SMS Component	Status Message Codes	Description
Discovery Data Manager	2603, 2607	Transferring discovery data to the parent site
	2611, 2634	Updating child discovery data (at the parent site)
Inventory Data Loader	2708, 2709, 2711, 2713	Transferring inventory data to the parent site
Replication Manager	4000	Creating jobs to send data to parent site
Hierarchy Manager	3306, 3307	Processing site control files (at the parent site)

You can also monitor the log files associated with the appropriate SMS components for information regarding the flow of this process if you have enabled logging for those components. These log files can be found in the directory SMS\Logs and include Hman.log (Hierarchy Manager), Sched.log (Scheduler), Sender.log (Sender), DDM.log (Discovery Data Manager), or Replmgr.log (Replication Manager), depending on which components you have enabled logging for.

These log files are text-based and can be viewed using any text editor such as Notepad. You can also view them using a utility you can download from the SMS Web site (*http://www.microsoft.com/smserver*) called SMS Trace. Refer to Chapter 5, "Analysis and Troubleshooting Tools," for details on how to use SMS Trace.

Developing Site Hierarchies

In Chapter 2 you learned about the importance of developing a viable deployment strategy for SMS 2003. A significant part of that design process should include determining the kind of site hierarchy—if any—that you need to implement for your organization. An SMS site hierarchy exists whenever two or more SMS sites have been defined in a parent-child relationship; its structure resembles an organizational flowchart. Site hierarchies provide a means of extending and scaling SMS support across a wide variety of organizational structures. Figure 4-32 shows what our completed SMS hierarchy looks like when viewed through the SMS Administrator Console from the central site server. As you can see, the central site has the ability to view and manage any site below it in the hierarchy.

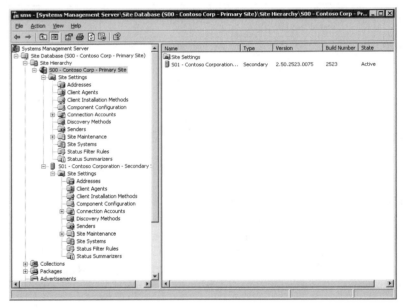

Figure 4-32. *SMS hierarchy viewed through the SMS Administrator Console.*

SMS sites, as we have seen, are identified by the site boundaries that you assign. Clients are assigned to an SMS site based on either IP subnet or Active Directory directory service site boundaries. As such, a multinational organization with locations in different countries could be managed by one large SMS site or by individual SMS sites in each location connected to a central site. Figure 4-33 illustrates an example hierarchy. Contoso, Ltd. has a corporate office in Chicago and regional offices in New York, London, and Tokyo. Each office has its own IP subnet. The single SMS site, located in Chicago, could manage all Contoso locations because it includes all the IP subnets in its site subnet boundaries.

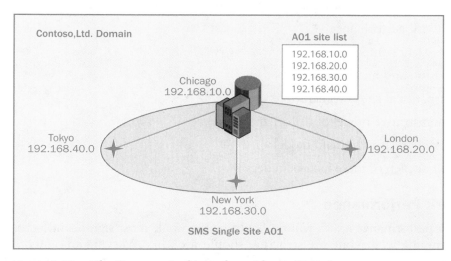

Figure 4-33.   *The Contoso site hierarchy, with one SMS site.*

In contrast, Figure 4-34 shows the same organization, but this time with individual SMS sites in each region, each reporting back to a central site located at Contoso headquarters in Chicago.

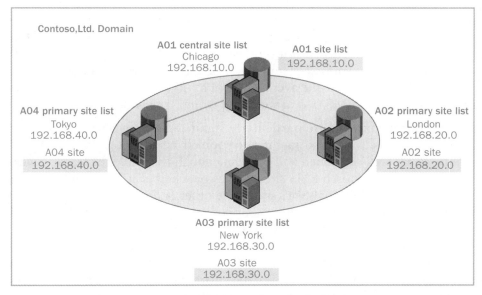

Figure 4-34.   *The Contoso site hierarchy, with multiple SMS sites.*

Many factors and circumstances can affect your site structure strategy. Each must be considered carefully before implementing the hierarchy. These factors are likely to include, but are certainly not limited to, the following:

- Network performance
- SMS client components
- Location and number of clients
- International site considerations
- Administrative model of the organization
- Active Directory domain model

Let's look at each of these factors in detail.

Network Performance

Network performance issues will no doubt be the single most significant factor in determining what your site structure should look like. Varying amounts of network traffic are generated among SMS site servers, SMS site systems, and SMS clients. Site servers communicate package, advertisement, and site configuration data to their site systems. The amount of traffic that's generated depends on the nature of the data being sent. For example, a site that distributes three packages a day with an average size of 50 MB to 10 distribution points is generating 500 MB of network traffic three times a day. This traffic could be significant on an already crowded network infrastructure. Or suppose that hardware inventory files representing only changes that have occurred are collected from a group of 32-bit SMS clients. If inventory is collected once a week from 5000 clients, the amount of traffic generated is probably not going to be significant. Even at 100 KB per client—the average size of a full default inventory file—this traffic would total 500 MB once a week and would largely be randomized.

Network traffic concerns are particularly significant when SMS traffic must cross WAN connections. You might ask yourself whether the existing WAN connections are well connected and efficient enough to handle the traffic generated between the proposed SMS site systems or whether it would make more sense to create an additional SMS site at the other end of a WAN connection. Let's return to our Contoso example. Suppose that you need to send a 50 MB package from the site server in Chicago to 10 distribution points in New York, as illustrated in Figure 4-35. This transaction will generate about 500 MB of package distribution traffic across the WAN connection between Chicago and New York because SMS must deliver the entire package to each distribution point individually within the same site—and generally uncompressed.

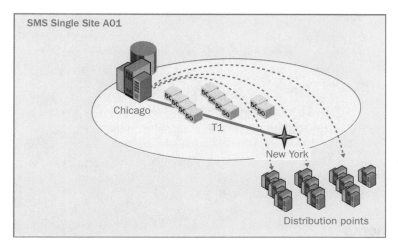

Figure 4-35.   *A package distributed from a site server to multiple distribution points.*

On the other hand, SMS sends packages from one site to distribution points in another site by sending the package to the target site once and letting the target site distribute the package to its local distribution points. Furthermore, it generally sends the package to the target site in a compressed format. As illustrated in Figure 4-36, the amount of WAN traffic generated for the same package scenario is considerably less—only about 25 MB as opposed to around 500 MB. Your site deployment strategy should already have assessed and predicted how you'll use SMS and the amount of data that you'll be generating within the site. Armed with this information, consider its effect on the current network traffic patterns and volumes, especially across WAN links, when deciding whether to implement one large SMS site or several SMS sites participating in a site hierarchy.

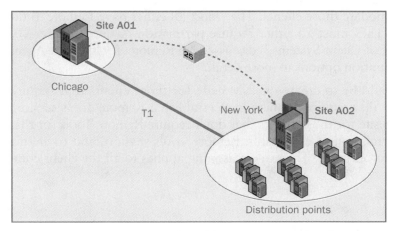

Figure 4-36.   *A package distributed from one site to distribution points in another site.*

More Info The scenarios suggested here aren't exhaustive. SMS 2003 introduces new server roles and additional server properties, such as proxy management points and protected distribution points, both of which affect network traffic and server performance in their own ways. For a more detailed discussion of factors that can affect network traffic and server performance, see Chapter 9, "Capacity Planning for SMS Component Servers," in the *Microsoft Systems Management Server 2003 Concepts, Planning, and Installation Guide* available from the SMS 2003 Online Library, and on the product CD.

Tip Microsoft recommends implementing a single SMS site across WAN links only if the WAN links are fast and reliable and can handle network traffic within acceptable thresholds (as identified by you, of course).

Client Components

Client component settings within a given SMS 2003 site apply to all the clients assigned to that site—they are sitewide settings. As such, there are no means of installing certain components on one set of clients and other components on another set. For that matter, there are no means of enabling one set of attributes for a component for some clients and a different set of attributes for the same component for other clients.

The most frequent example of this situation concerns the Remote Tools component. If Remote Tools is enabled as a client agent for the SMS site, all SMS clients will be enabled with Remote Tools. If the Do Not Ask For Permission configuration option is disabled for the Remote Tools Client Agent, permission will be required on all clients before a Remote Tools session can be established. In other words, if your site has 1000 clients and 100 don't require Remote Tools, or if 100 don't require permission to establish a Remote Tools session, you can't accommodate those clients. They must all either have Remote Tools installed or not. They must all either require permission or not. Chapter 10, "Remote Control of Client Systems," discusses the Remote Tools Client Agent and all its configuration options in more detail.

One solution would be to create one SMS site for those clients that require Remote Tools (or that require permission to establish a Remote Tools session) and another SMS site for those clients that don't require Remote Tools (or that don't require permission to establish a Remote Tools session) and to enable Remote Tools appropriately. The same reasoning applies to all the client component options.

Real World   Enabling Client Features as Sitewide Settings

At first glance, it might seem that enabling client features as sitewide settings isn't that big a concern. Consider this case, however: suppose you choose to enable Remote Tools for your SMS site and require that permission at the client be granted before a Remote Tools session can be established. Of course, all clients will be enabled with the Remote Tools Client Agent and all will be required to grant permission before the Remote Tools session can be established. So far, so good.

You also have a need, however, to establish Remote Tools sessions with your Windows servers, which are also clients in your SMS site. As SMS clients, they too will have been installed with Remote Tools and will require that permission be granted before a Remote Tools session can be established. The latter setting will cause problems at the servers because typically no user is logged on at a Windows server to grant the permission request.

One solution, of course, would be to create a separate SMS site to manage the Windows servers. This would involve being able to identify the servers on a subnet or subnets separate from those that the other SMS clients are segmented on. This segregation might also involve a separate investment in hardware and software to install the SMS site server for that site, which might not be practical. Another solution would be to *not* require permissions at any of the clients in your site—which could raise other security or privacy concerns—or to forgo the use of Remote Tools for your servers altogether.

A third solution might be to require permission but also allow the user to change Remote Tools options at the client. This would let you as the administrator turn off the permission requirement at each Windows server. Unfortunately, this solution also lets users modify Remote Tools attributes without regulation, which could pose other Remote Tools problems on a client-by-client basis. In either case, the agent settings would be reset to their sitewide settings at the client's next update cycle (see Chapter 8, "Client Installation Methods," for more information).

Fortunately, Microsoft provides a tool that allows you to modify Remote Agent settings at specific clients so that they are different from the sitewide settings. This tool will be discussed in Chapter 10.

Location and Number of Clients

Another factor that might affect the structure of your SMS site hierarchy is the number and location of SMS clients and resources. Each SMS site can potentially handle 10,000 or more clients. But if you think this gives you license to create one large site and be done with it, go back and read the section entitled "Network Performance" earlier in this chapter.

The true number of clients that any one SMS site server can manage will be dictated more realistically by the server hardware—how powerful it is—as well as by the number of SMS features and options you have decided to enable on that server. The minimum hardware requirements for an SMS site server are a 550 MHz Pentium processor, 256 MB of RAM, and a recommended 2 GB of disk space. Let's say that you have two site servers with this configuration. Suppose you install and enable Remote Tools on one server and install all options and enable all client components on the other. The resource requirements for the latter site server will obviously surpass those of the former server. It follows logically, then, that the second site server could manage fewer SMS clients than the first site server (perhaps 10 as opposed to 20—which also gives you some idea of how minimal the minimum hardware requirements are).

Location of clients can also be a factor, as it was with network performance. Your site server can easily manage 10,000 SMS clients or more. However, their location in the network might suggest the creation of multiple SMS sites depending on the SMS features you're implementing, the amount of network traffic generated, the efficiency of your WAN link, and the number of clients that need to be managed. For example, suppose you have three regional locations. If these are relatively small offices—say, 10 to 20 clients—with a modest WAN link between them and the corporate SMS site server, you might create a single SMS site, perhaps placing a distribution point and a CAP in each local subnet. On the other hand, if these regional locations had 100 or more clients, you might begin to weigh the possibility of creating separate SMS sites in each location and linking them together into a site hierarchy—depending, of course, on what features (such as package distribution) you have enabled, the size of packages, the frequency of advertisements, and so on.

International Site Considerations

Just as Windows supports a wide variety of language versions in its operating system, so too does SMS 2003 support a wide variety of language versions for both the site server and SMS clients. SMS 2003 site servers support the following languages:

- Chinese (simplified and traditional)
- English

- French
- German
- Japanese

Each of these site server languages supports clients in its language, as well as English-language clients, with the exception of French, which doesn't support English-language clients. Note also that English is the default language for the server-side user interfaces for Chinese and Korean site servers, but you can choose to display the local language characters. The client-side user interfaces have been localized to the local language.

In addition to English, SMS 2003 clients are available in 21 additional language versions:

- Chinese (simplified and traditional)
- Czech
- Danish
- Dutch
- Finnish
- French
- German
- Greek
- Hungarian
- Italian
- Japanese
- Korean
- Norwegian
- Polish
- Portuguese-Brazilian
- Portuguese-Portugal
- Russian
- Spanish
- Swedish
- Turkish

For the most part, you can create a site hierarchy with any combination of language versions. Keep in mind, however, that some data that's recorded in one language version will be transferred between sites in that language version. For example, site code, collection, package, and advertisement names and Management Information Files (MIFs) will always be transferred in the language version in which they were created. This untranslated information can cause a problem if the parent and child site servers are using different language code pages. If they're using the same code pages, data will be passed on and displayed correctly. If not, the names might appear corrupted.

Default collection names are defined at each site; however, in a parent-child relationship, the default collection names from the parent site overwrite those of the child sites. Again, if both sites are using the same code page to view the default collection names, the names will appear correctly. If the child site is using a different code page, the default collection names might be corrupted.

If the site servers are using different code pages, you do have a couple of options. You could use all ASCII characters or a combination of ASCII and the language characters either in the Name or Comment field of collections, advertisements, packages, and programs properties to provide easier identification. You could also use a separate Windows computer running the SMS Administrator Console with the appropriate code page enabled. Also, be aware that extended and double-byte character names aren't supported in domain and site server names. When your sites represent a mix of languages, use ASCII characters when naming domains and site servers.

More Info The *SMS 2003 Online Library*, which includes the *Microsoft Systems Management Server 2003 Release Notes*, discusses language considerations; consult these references for more specific information. If language versions are a concern within your organization, you should also periodically review the Microsoft Knowledge Base articles published for SMS 2003 for references to specific issues you might be encountering (See *http://support.microsoft.com* and *http://www.microsoft.com/smserver* for more information.)

Planning If you have installed an International Client Pack (ICP) for your SMS 2003 site and are planning to upgrade to an SMS service pack, be sure to upgrade your ICP with the service pack version as well. If you don't, the ICP files will be overwritten and only English language clients will be supported. Also, in order to correctly process and display characters in the appropriate language in the SMS Administrator Console on a Windows 2000 or higher computer, the Locale Regional Options setting on that computer, located on the Control Panel, must be set to match the language of the data you want to view or input.

Administrative Model

The structure of your organization's Information Services (IS) support (as well as company policies) will no doubt influence your SMS site structure. Whether or not a proposed SMS site has a designated SMS administrator locally might determine, for example, whether you install a primary or a secondary site at that location. The size and location of the administrative staff might also determine the number of child sites in the hierarchy, as well as its depth.

This is a good opportunity to make a recommendation regarding SMS administrative staff. The reality of many corporate environments is that a small number of persons manage large numbers of computers and networks and typically fulfill many roles: database administrator, network administrator, mail server administrator, and so on. The role of the SMS administrator is just as significant and time-consuming. As you've already seen, implementing SMS 2003 is far from trivial. A successful installation requires a significant amount of planning and testing.

The ongoing management of SMS clients and resources, troubleshooting, and maintenance are no more trivial. Therefore, you could recommend that many SMS tasks be delegated to other support personnel. For example, help desk staff might be given the ability to initiate Remote Tools sessions to facilitate their task of troubleshooting client problems. Resource administrators in specific departments might be given the ability to create and distribute packages to users and clients within their departments. Nevertheless, these are administrative tasks, and they make up only a small percentage of the overall management of an SMS site or an SMS site hierarchy.

Active Directory Domain Model

Certainly the Active Directory site structure that you're using within your organization will have a significant impact on the look of your SMS hierarchical structure since you can use Active Directory site names to define SMS site boundaries. Similarly, the domain model that supports your organization will also influence your SMS 2003 hierarchical structure. You might, from an administrative point of view, decide to simply let your SMS structure reflect your Active Directory site structure or domain model. If your organization spent a great deal of thought and planning when implementing its Active Directory site structure and domain model, and it's well organized and optimized, then following that model for your SMS site hierarchy will make the most sense. However, if your current Active Directory site structure and domain model is less than optimal, you might want to consider cleaning it up before you implement your SMS site hierarchy or choose not to base your SMS hierarchy or your site boundaries on your Active Directory structures.

If you're implementing SMS in a multiple-domain environment, especially in a mixed mode environment (Active Directory and Windows NT domains), and you're running SMS in standard security mode, remember that SMS will still require the use of the SMS Service account and several internal accounts to connect between sites and site systems within a site. When multiple domains are involved, and you wish to reference in one domain an SMS account such as the SMS Service account from another domain, you'll need to understand how trust relationships have been implemented between those domains (especially where Windows NT domains are involved) or create duplicate accounts that Windows can use through pass-through authentication, or both. Refer to your Windows documentation for more detail on the authentication process and how it can affect your SMS sites. Also, refer to Chapter 8 of the *Microsoft Systems Management Server 2003 Concepts, Planning, and Installation Guide* included with the SMS Online Library for a more detailed discussion of domain-specific issues.

Communicating Through Senders

As we've seen, SMS uses a sender to connect to another site and transfer information to that site. A sender is a highly reliable and fault-tolerant communication mechanism that transfers data in 256 KB blocks, making it more efficient than dragging and dropping or using an XCOPY command. Senders can communicate using the standard LAN/WAN connection that exists between two sites, or they can use one of four RAS Sender types: Asynchronous RAS Sender, ISDN RAS Sender, X.25 RAS Sender, and SNA RAS Sender. There is also a Courier Sender type, which enables you to create and send package information to another SMS site if you have a slow or unreliable (therefore not well-connected) link between a site and its parent. However, one of the other sender types must still be installed and available for regular intersite communication.

Sender Process Flow

Three main SMS components are involved in sending data from one site to another: Replication Manager, Scheduler, and a sender. With the exception of the Courier Sender, the sender component wakes up when it receives a send request file in its outbox. The process begins earlier than that, however, as illustrated in Figure 4-37. When a request to send data is made, an SMS component will create a replication file and place the file in Replication Manager's inbox.

When the parent-child relationship is established, for example, the Inventory Data Loader places an .MIF file in Replication Manager's inbox (SMS\Inboxes\Replmgr.box\Outbound) so that it can send the child site's inventory data to the parent site. As another example, when a package is identified for distribution to another site, Distribution Manager places a replication object file (.RPL or .RPT) in Replication Manager's inbox.

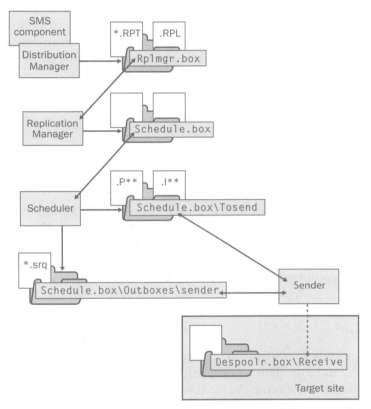

Figure 4-37. *The sender process flow, showing the flow of information among SMS components.*

Replication Manager will in turn bundle the data if necessary and then create information files for the Scheduler. The Scheduler creates packages, the instructions needed for sending the data in question, and a send request file (.SRQ) for the sender. The package and instruction files are placed in the SMS\Inboxes\Schedule.box\Tosend directory. The send request file is an instruction file for the sender that contains information such as the priority of the request, the site code and preferred address of the target site, a job identifier, the location of the sender's outbox, the location and names of the package and instruction files, action codes, and routing information if a direct address to the target site doesn't exist. This file is written to the preferred sender's outbox (SMS\Inboxes\Schedule.box\Outboxes\sender, where sender is the sender type, such as LAN, RASAsynch, RASISDN, and so on).

When this file is written, the sender wakes up and reads the send request file. It also checks to see whether the address properties have placed any restrictions on when requests of this priority can be sent and whether any bandwidth limits have been set. The sender then changes the extension of the send request file to .SRS and writes status information to the file, including when the sending process started, when it ended, and how much data has been transferred at any point in time.

Note The Total Bytes To Send and Bytes Left To Send values in the send request file serve an important fault-tolerance role. If the sending process is interrupted for any reason—for example, if a send request of higher priority is created—the sender knows how to pick up where it left off.

The sender connects to the target site's SMS_Site share—the SMS\Inboxes\ Despoolr.box\Receive directory—where the Despooler component will complete the processing of information at the target site. If the sender comes across an error while transferring the data, it will write an error status to the .SRS file. When the data has been completely transferred, the send request file is updated to Completed status and is then deleted.

Defining a Sender

When the SMS site server is first installed, Setup creates the Standard Sender and Courier Sender by default. The SMS administrator can then choose to install additional senders as necessary. As mentioned, only one sender of each type can be installed on the same server. However, you can install the same sender type on multiple servers. These servers will become SMS component servers when you install a sender on them.

There is nothing special involved in adding a Standard Sender on an SMS component server. The only requirement is that you have an existing LAN or WAN connection between the Standard Sender component server and the target site server. Then, of course, you must configure an additional address to the target site using the new Standard Sender.

The other four sender types are RAS senders: Asynchronous RAS Sender, ISDN RAS Sender, X.25 RAS Sender, and SNA RAS Sender. Enabling the use of one or more of these sender types assumes that you have already established a RAS server at each site installed with the appropriate hardware and software support—that is, a modem, ISDN, X.25, or SNA connection. It's not necessary, or even desirable, that the site server itself be installed as a RAS server; it's only necessary that the site server for each site have access and connectivity to a RAS server (appropriately configured) on their local networks.

Senders on Other Servers

When you install an SMS sender on another server, such as the Asynchronous RAS Sender on a RAS server, that server becomes an SMS component server. The SMS Executive, support files, and directories for the sender are all installed on that server. Since the sender doesn't reside on the site server, it won't wake up when a send request file is created. Instead, the sender wakes up on a 5-minute polling cycle.

This polling cycle will require some additional resources on the sender's server. Also, network traffic will be generated between the site server and the sender server to transfer send request, package, and instruction data. The ultimate effect on the network's and sender server's performance will depend on the amount of usage the sender will experience and, of course, the current usage of the server itself. Alternative senders do provide a means for the Scheduler to improve sending performance from one site to another. The SMS administrator will need to determine the significance of any trade-off between having an alternative sending mechanism and the network and server performance hits that might occur.

The immediate benefit that your SMS site will have when you install additional senders on other servers is that the site will then have one or more alternative ways to send data to a target site—assuming that you created addresses to those sites referencing each available sender. Data can be sent using an alternative sender when the primary sender is unavailable. Data can also be sent concurrently to the same site or to different sites using all available senders. Again, the trade-off will be in the area of network traffic and network performance. As always, be sure to monitor network usage to be sure that you're gaining the most out of your senders' configuration.

You add new senders to the site through the SMS Administrator Console as a site setting. To establish a new sender, follow these steps:

1. In the SMS Administrator Console, navigate to the Site Settings folder and highlight the Senders object. One sender will be displayed—the Standard Sender installed by default. (Please note that the Courier Sender isn't displayed. Although the Courier Sender is installed by default, it can't be modified. For details, refer to the section entitled "Courier Sender" later in this chapter.)

2. Right-click the Senders object and choose New from the context menu to display the five sender type options, as shown in Figure 4-38. Select the type of sender you want to establish.

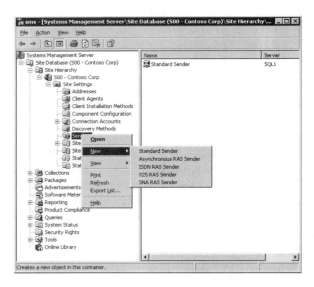

Figure 4-38.   *The list of sender type options.*

Note   Because all the sender types will display a similar series of Property dialog boxes, we'll show only the pages for the Asynchronous RAS Sender here.

3. Right-click a sender in the details pane and select Properties from the context menu. In the General tab of the Sender Properties dialog box, shown in Figure 4-39, enter the name of the server on which you want to create the sender—in this case, the name of the RAS server.

Figure 4-39.   *The General tab of the Sender Properties dialog box.*

4. Select the Advanced tab, as shown in Figure 4-40, and enter values for the Maximum Concurrent Sendings and Retry Settings options.

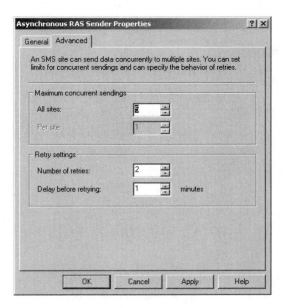

Figure 4-40.   *The Advanced tab of the Sender Properties dialog box.*

Maximum Concurrent Sendings represents the number of concurrent transmissions that can be made to all sites through this sender or to any single site (Per Site). The Per Site setting is set to 1 and disabled for RAS senders by default. The Retry Settings options consist of the number of retries to attempt if a connection fails and the number of minutes to wait between retries (Delay Before Retrying). Your choices for these options depend primarily on the kind of network connection you have between the sites. For example, if you have a well-connected network connection and the amount of bandwidth used is low, you might increase the Maximum Concurrent Sendings value and decrease the Retry Settings options.

5. Click OK to begin the site configuration process.

Establishing a new sender initiates the same site configuration change process we've seen in earlier examples. Part of this process includes creating an outbox for the sender in the SMS\Inboxes\Schedule.box\Outboxes directory. If the sender is being installed on another server, the process will include installing the SMS Executive on the sender server (making it a component server), installing the sender support files and the sender's support directory, and then updating the site server's site control file appropriately. Status messages for the new sender will include a notice of successful installation, as shown in Figure 4-41. Of course, you can also follow the process by checking status messages and logs for Hierarchy Manager, Site Control Manager, and Site Component Manager.

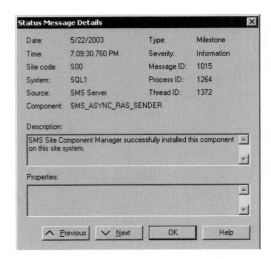

Figure 4-41. *Status message indicating that the RAS Sender has been successfully installed on the component server.*

Courier Sender

As mentioned, the Courier Sender enables you to create and send package information to another SMS site through non-network channels, such as regular postal service or a package delivery service if you have a slow or unreliable link between a site and its parent. It can also be used to send packages that are so large that an existing address might not provide adequate performance levels. It's not, however, meant to be used as a consistent alternative to existing network communication mechanisms, nor can it be used to transmit data packages generated internally by SMS.

As with other senders, to use the Courier Sender as an alternative means of sending packages, you must create an address to the target site using the Courier Sender as the sender type, as shown in Figure 4-42. We have discussed how to create an address to the target site using other sender types in the section entitled "Creating an Address to Another Site" earlier in this chapter. Similarly, in the SMS Administrator Console, navigate to the Site Settings folder and expand it. Right-click the Addresses object and choose New and then Courier Sender Address from the context menu, which will bring you to the Properties dialog box shown in Figure 4-42.

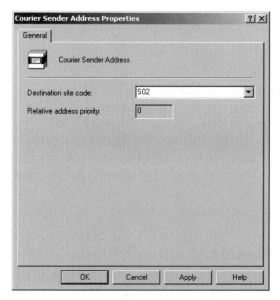

Figure 4-42.   *The General tab of the Courier Sender Address Properties dialog box.*

When you create the package, you can also identify the Courier Sender as the preferred sender type for that package, as shown in Figure 4-43. (For details on creating packages, please refer to Chapter 12, "Package Distribution and Management.")

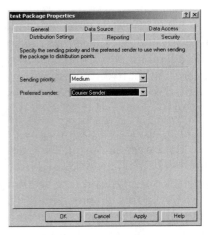

Figure 4-43. *The Distribution Settings tab of the Package Properties dialog box.*

You'll also need to identify the target site as a distribution point for the package. Please refer back to Chapter 3 for details.

> **Tip** If you have more than one address to a target site and you want to send a package using the Courier Sender, choose Courier Sender as the preferred sender type when you create the package.

When you use the Courier Sender as the sending mechanism to transfer a package, the package files are compressed into a single package (.PCK) and placed in the SMS\Smspkg directory. A send request file is also created and placed in the Courier Sender's outbox. Because no automatic connection needs to be made to the target site, you must next launch Courier Sender Manager from the Systems Management Server program group. To create outgoing parcels, follow these steps:

1. In Courier Sender Manager, choose Create Outgoing Parcel from the File menu.

2. Select your package from the list and click Next.

3. In the Parcel Properties section, enter the name of the package, a tracking name, the method you're using to send the parcel (for example, UPS or Federal Express), and a descriptive comment. Click Next.

4. Enter the path where you want to save the parcel. The default is SMS\Inboxes\Coursend.box\Out. Click Next.

5. Click Finish to create the parcel (.PCL) file.

You can now copy this parcel to some other medium, such as CD-ROM, and then send it on using some non-network method, such as the U.S. Postal Service. The SMS administrator at the target site will in turn copy this parcel to a directory on the target site server. (The default used by Courier Sender Manager is SMS\Inboxes\Coursend.box\In.) The SMS administrator will then launch Courier Sender Manager on the target site server, essentially reversing the sending process by following these steps:

1. In Courier Sender Manager, choose Receive Incoming Parcel from the File menu to display the Courier Sender Wizard's Receive An Incoming Parcel page.

2. Click Browse, select the package from the list, and click Open.

3. Click Next and then Finish to complete the package receiving process.

Courier Sender Manager will process this parcel as though a package had been sent using one of the other senders. If necessary, a SMSPkg$x$\$ directory will be created (where x stands for the drive letter) and the package files will be uncompressed and copied to a subfolder below the directory. When the process has been completed, you can check the parcel's status by choosing Parcel Status from the Courier Sender Manager's File menu at the sending site. Since the nature of Courier Sender is that the package is being sent by some non-network method, parcel status is also updated by a non-network method—that is, you need to manually update the status.

When you first create the parcel, the parcel status will be displayed as "created." After you send the parcel to the target site, you can change the status to either "sent" or "confirmed." After you change the status to "sent," your only other option can be "confirmed," which you might select, for example, when the administrator from the target site notifies you that the parcel was received and processed.

Change the status of a parcel by following these steps:

1. In the Courier Sender Manager, right-click the parcel whose status you want to change and select Properties from the Action menu.

2. In the Parcel Properties dialog box, click Change Status.

3. In the Change Status dialog box, select the option that reflects the parcel's new status.

Note   For more information about using and troubleshooting the courier sender process, see the online help available when you launch the Courier Sender Manager.

Summary

In this chapter you've explored how to implement multiple site structures. Various factors influencing your choice of site hierarchy have been introduced and discussed. We've also examined the concept of parent-child relationships in SMS 2003, and you've learned how to establish that relationship through addresses and senders. You've also learned how to install a secondary site and the site configuration process involved. Last, we looked at defining and implementing SMS senders and traced the sending process. Chapter 5 and Chapter 6 will introduce several diagnostic tools that will become invaluable to you as you maintain and troubleshoot your site.

Chapter 5
Analysis and Troubleshooting Tools

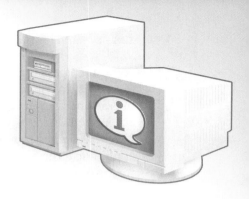

In the preceding chapters we've viewed log files and status messages as a way of interpreting and troubleshooting process flows and component activity in your Microsoft Systems Management Server (SMS) 2003 site. In this chapter we'll spend a little more time exploring the uses of these tools, and we'll look at some additional tools that will help you maintain your site. In particular, you'll learn how to view status messages, use status summarizers, filter status messages, report status to other SMS components, and use queries to customize the status messages displayed. You'll also learn how to use SMS Service Manager to start, stop, and monitor the status of the components as well as to enable logging and how to use the SMS Trace utility to view log files.

Working with Status Messages

Virtually every SMS 2003 component and service generates status messages as it goes about its business. These messages aren't the sometimes vague or unhelpful variety you might have come to dread in the Windows Event Viewer. On the contrary, SMS 2003 status messages are rich with details. In the event of error messages, the details often offer potential reasons for the error and suggest possible remedies.

Status messages represent the flow of process activity for each site system and client. They're automatically consolidated and filtered for display using status summarizers and status filters (discussed in detail in the sections entitled "Understanding Status Summarizers" and "Filtering Status Messages" later in this chapter). As you'll see throughout this book, these status messages will provide your first, and often best, insight into how a process or task works and what to do in the case of a problem.

There are three levels of severity for status messages in SMS 2003: informational, warning, and error. *Informational messages* are just that—informational. They simply record the fact of an event occurring, such as a service or component starting, the successful completion of a task, and so on. *Warning messages* are of concern, but they aren't necessarily fatal to the site server's operation. They generally indicate potential problems, such as low disk space, a component that failed or that is retrying a task, or a file that was corrupted. *Error messages* are usually of great concern, as they indicate problems that could harm the SMS site. These require the attention of the SMS administrator for resolution. Error messages include authentication problems, the complete failure of a service or component to complete a task, database access problems, and so on.

Every status message that's generated will fall into one of three message type categories: milestone, detail, and audit. *Milestone message types* usually relate to the start or completion of a task. For example, a successful completion would generate a milestone informational message, whereas an unsuccessful task would generate a milestone warning or error message. *Detail message types* generally refer to the steps in a process and make sense only in the context of the status message process flow. Again, these might be informational, warning, or error messages, depending on the severity of the process steps being reported. *Audit message types* refer to objects being added, deleted, or modified in some way, usually by the SMS administrator—for example, assigning a site system role or modifying a collection membership.

Tip Status messages sometimes stand alone and can be readily interpreted from the detail message. In many cases, however, a status message will make sense only in the context of a process flow. It's always a good idea, therefore, to look not only for a specific message reference, but also at the status messages preceding and following the reference to gain further insight into the specific message. Throughout this book, when we explore process flows, you should review the status messages for *all* the SMS components and services involved in that process flow to develop a well-rounded understanding of the process.

You can view status messages through the System Status node in the SMS Administrator Console, as shown in Figure 5-1. From this node, you can view the advertisement status, the package status, and the component and site system status for the SMS site, and you can execute status message queries. We'll discuss status messages for advertisements and packages as we get to those topics in Chapter 12, "Package Distribution and Management."

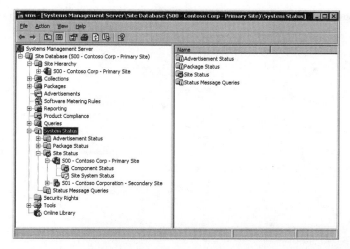

Figure 5-1. *The expanded System Status node in the SMS Administrator Console.*

Viewing Site Status Messages

Site status messages fall into two categories: component status and site system status. If all is well with your site, you should see a green check mark (an OK indicator) in front of each node, as you do for the Site System Status node in Figure 5-1. If any problems have been detected, this check mark might change to an x in a red circle (an Error indicator), as you see for the Site Status node in Figure 5-1, based on the thresholds you set. (For a detailed discussion of thresholds, see the section entitled "Status Message Thresholds" later in this chapter). The icons for OK, Warning, or Error will help you to determine which components need attention.

You will always begin troubleshooting by viewing the summary information. First select Component Status in the SMS Administrator Console to display a list of all SMS components and services and a summary of their current status, as shown in Figure 5-2. In the Component Status window, you can see at a glance the component status; the site system on which the component is running; the component name; its current state; the number of error, warning, and informational messages that have been generated; how the component wakes up (type); when a scheduled component next runs; the last time the component woke up; and the last time a message was written. In this case, we can see that while most components are running properly, the component—SMS_Site_Component_Manager—has been elevated to Critical status.

The Show/Hide Console Tree icon

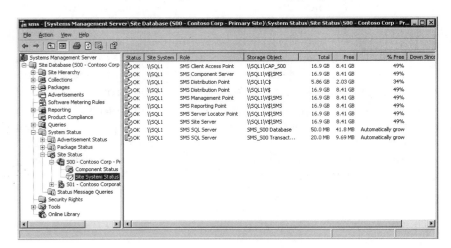

Figure 5-2. *The Component Status window in the SMS Administrator Console.*

Tip Click the Show/Hide Console Tree icon (fifth from the right on the toolbar at the top of the SMS Administrator Console) to hide the console tree so that you can more easily view the Component Status window.

Click the Site System Status node to display a list of all the site systems identified for the site and their summary status by site system role, as shown in Figure 5-3. In the Site System Status window, you can view the site system status, the site system name, the role that has been assigned to the site, the location of the storage object (partition and folder or database), total and free storage space, free space represented as a percentage of the total, and whether the system has been down. In this case, all site systems are running properly.

Figure 5-3. *The Site System Status window.*

The detailed information behind each summary entry in the Component Status window pertains specifically to that component. However, the detailed messages behind each summary entry in the Site System Status window reference messages from any number of SMS components and services that are running on, or affect, that particular site system.

We examined how to view status messages in Chapter 3, "Configuring Site Server Properties and Site Systems"; let's review here. To view the detailed messages for a specific component in the Component Status window, for example, for the SMS_Site_Component_Manager component in Figure 5-2 that indicates a critical status, follow these steps:

1. Right-click the component's summary entry and choose Show Messages from the context menu to display a list of message types, as shown in Figure 5-4.

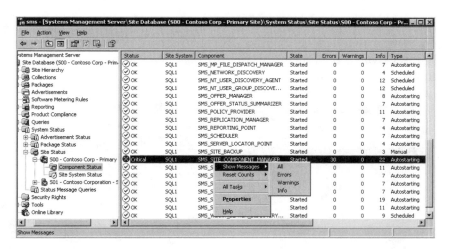

Figure 5-4.   *Displaying a list of message type options.*

2. The All option displays all messages collected for this entry, Errors displays only error messages, Warnings displays only warning messages, and Info displays only info messages. For this example, choose Info. The Status Message Viewer appears, as shown in Figure 5-5.

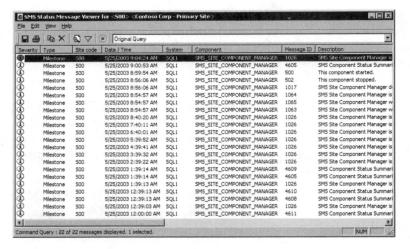

Figure 5-5. *The Status Message Viewer.*

3. To view a detailed description of the message, position the mouse pointer over the Description field to display a pop-up window, as shown in Figure 5-6.

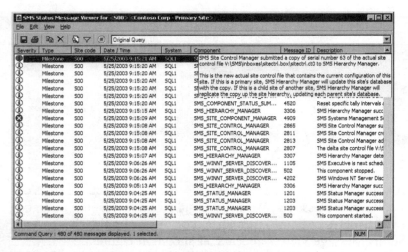

Figure 5-6. *A pop-up window containing a detailed description of a status message.*

Alternatively, you can double-click the message to display the Status Message Details dialog box, as shown in Figure 5-7. This dialog box provides you with more specific details about the message. It also provides buttons to enable you to view the previous and the following messages. For this example, click OK to close the dialog box.

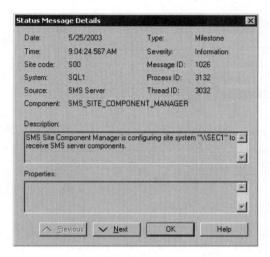

Figure 5-7.   *The Status Message Details dialog box.*

4. Close the Status Message Viewer when you've finished reviewing the message details.

To view the detailed messages for a site system in the Site System Status window, follow these steps:

1. Right-click a site system's summary entry and choose Show Messages from the context menu to display a list of message types.

2. Choose All to display all messages collected for this entry, choose Errors to display only error messages, choose Warnings to display only warning messages, or choose Info to display only informational messages.

3. After you choose an option, the Set Viewing Period dialog box is displayed, as shown in Figure 5-8. Select the Specify Date And Time option to display only messages generated after the date and time you enter. Select the Select Date And Time option to display messages generated within a more generic time period from 1 hour ago to 1 year ago.

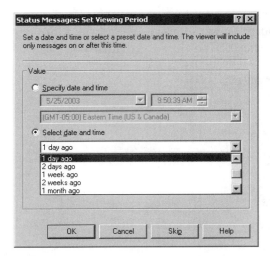

Figure 5-8. *The Set Viewing Period dialog box.*

4. Click OK to display the Status Message Viewer, as shown in Figure 5-9. You can also click Skip if you prefer not to limit the scope of the messages displayed.

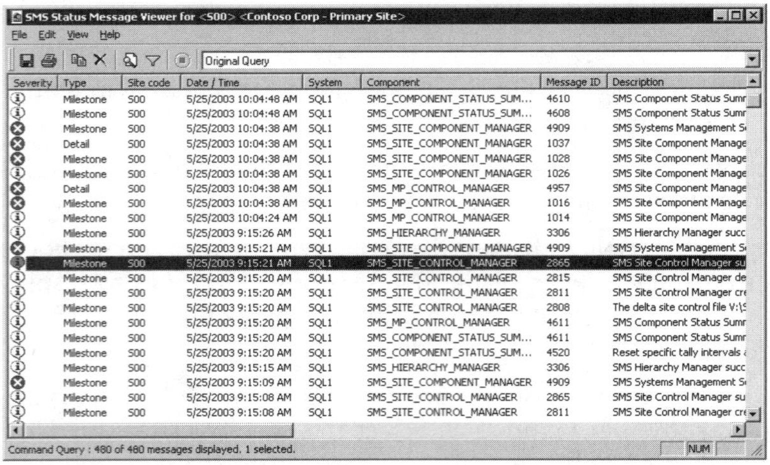

Figure 5-9. *The Status Message Viewer for a site system status window summary entry.*

5. View the detailed description for each message either by positioning your mouse pointer on the message's Description field to display a pop-up window or by double-clicking the message to display the Status Message Details dialog box.

6. Close the Status Message Viewer when you've finished reviewing the message details.

In this section we've discussed how to view status messages in the Status Message Viewer. We'll continue to explore how to utilize this viewer in the next section.

Setting Status Message Viewer Options

When SMS components or services generate status messages, they're written to the site database. The Status Message Viewer uses the SMS Provider to query the database for the detailed messages when you use the technique described in the preceding section.

As shown in Figure 5-9, the Status Message Viewer for the site system status displays all the SMS components that are running on that site system or that affect it in any way. These messages are the same as those displayed for each component in the Component Status window. For example, the highlighted SMS_Site_Control_Manager message in Figure 5-9 is the same as the message highlighted in Figure 5-6.

Regardless of whether you're viewing component status or site system status, the Status Message Viewer always displays the following information:

- **Severity**   Specifies whether the message category is info, warning, or error

- **Type**   Specifies whether the message type is milestone, detail, or audit

- **Site Code**   Specifies the three-character site code of the site for which the message was generated

- **Date / Time**   Specifies the time and date stamp indicating when the message was generated

- **System**   Specifies the server name of the site system for which the message was generated

- **Component**   Specifies the name of the SMS component or service that generated the message

- **Message ID**   Specifies the numeric code related to the task performed by the SMS component or service that generated the message

- **Description**   Provides a detailed description of the message

The Status Message Viewer provides many features that can facilitate your analysis of messages. Let's begin with some of the GUI features. You can change the sort order of each column simply by clicking the column header. Each column has three sort options: click once to sort from lowest to highest, click again to sort from highest to lowest, and click once again to return to the default column order. You can, of course, resize the columns by clicking the border between each column heading and dragging to make the column wider or narrower. You can also move the columns to customize the display simply by dragging and dropping a column header to a new position.

By right-clicking any message entry to display its context menu, you can copy it, delete it, or display its Status Message Details window. You can also set a filter for the Status Message Viewer or refresh all the messages from this menu. You can select multiple messages for copying, deleting, and printing by using the Windows Explorer Ctrl-click method.

The Status Message Viewer also provides a variety of options and features that are enabled through the menus on its menu bar. Because most of these settings are self-evident, we'll look here only at those that are unique or of particular interest to the SMS administrator—in particular, the options in the Status Viewer Options dialog box and the Filter Status Messages window.

The Status Viewer Options Dialog Box

Let's start by discussing the Status Viewer Options dialog box. Begin by displaying the Status Message Viewer for a component or site system. Choose Options from the View menu to display the Status Viewer Options dialog box shown in Figure 5-10. The General tab is shown by default.

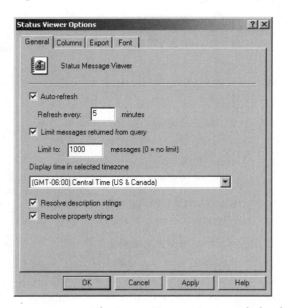

Figure 5-10. *The Status Viewer Options dialog box.*

The General Tab

The Status Message Viewer doesn't refresh the interface with new messages by default unless you tell it to—for example, by pressing F5. The General tab lets you enable auto-refresh and specify a refresh interval. However, having the viewer automatically refresh itself will incur additional resource cost, so you shouldn't select this option unless you intend to leave the viewer open for a long time—perhaps to follow the flow of a task or the generation of messages. You can also limit the number of messages that are collected and displayed.

> **Caution**   The Status Message Viewer might not display data correctly when you execute it on the SMS Administrator Console running on Microsoft Windows XP Professional with no service pack applied and when your SMS site database or SMS Provider is on a server running Windows Server 2003. To ensure that the Status Message Viewer executes correctly, be sure to update the Windows XP Professional computer running the SMS Administrator Console with Service Pack 1 or higher.

The Status Message Viewer displays messages stamped with the local time and date. The General tab lets you specify different time zones if you want to see when a message was generated on a site or site system in a different geographic location.

Most status messages are generated based on generic text strings in which variables have been inserted to customize the detail to a specific component, time, and so on. For example, message ID 4611 for the SMS Component Status Summarizer contains the text:

```
SMS Component Status Summarizer reset the status of component %1, running on
computer %2, to OK.
```

This message always reads the same, except that the percent values are replaced with a specific SMS component value and server value. Displayed in the Status Message Viewer for SMS Site Component Manager on site server SQL1, this message would read:

```
SMS Component Status Summarizer reset the status of component "SMS Site
Component Manager", running on computer "SQL1", to OK.
```

If you clear the Resolve Description Strings and Resolve Property Strings check boxes in the General tab, the status messages would resolve more quickly but would leave empty quotation marks in the variable positions, rendering the messages not especially helpful to the SMS administrator.

The Columns Tab

The Columns tab of the Status Viewer Options dialog box, shown in Figure 5-11, enables you to customize the information displayed in the Status Message Viewer by adding columns to view thread and process IDs or by removing columns that might not be of interest.

Figure 5-11. *The Columns tab of the Status Viewer Options dialog box.*

The Export Tab

By default, status messages are deleted after seven days, but you can adjust this setting to suit your needs. Because some components can generate a multitude of messages, you might decide to delete messages more frequently to better manage database space. If you need to save or copy status messages to file for future reference and analysis or to print them out, the Export tab of the Status View Options dialog box, shown in Figure 5-12, provides options for doing so.

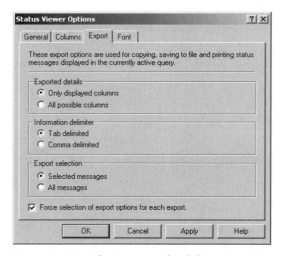

Figure 5-12. *The Export tab of the Status Viewer Options dialog box.*

The Exported Details frame lets you specify whether to include all possible data about a status message or only the data associated with the displayed columns. Under Information Delimiter, you can identify whether columns should be exported as tab delimited or comma delimited. This option is helpful if you expect to import this data into some other reporting or analysis tool such as Microsoft Excel or Microsoft Access. The Export Selection frame lets you specify whether to export only messages that you've selected in the viewer or all messages. By default, every time you choose to copy, print, or save a message, this Export tab is displayed, allowing you to modify the options before continuing. If you want the same options to apply to every copy, print, or save operation, clear the Force Selection Of Export Options For Each Export check box.

The Font Tab

The Font tab, shown in Figure 5-13, enables you to set the typeface, style, and size of the font that will be used to display messages in the Status Message Viewer. Be careful to choose something readable. A decorative font might look pretty at first, but if you'll be scrutinizing messages for long periods of time, a poorly chosen font can give you a headache.

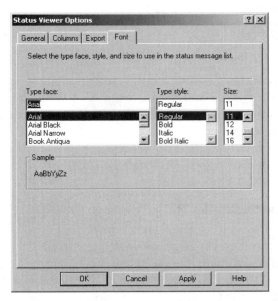

Figure 5-13. *The Font tab of the Status Viewer Options dialog box.*

Filter Options

Another neat feature of the Status Message Viewer is the set of filter options, which let you customize which messages are displayed in the Status Message Viewer. If you've used the filter options in the Windows Event Viewer, these filter options will be familiar. To set the filter options, choose Filter from the View menu to display the Filter Status Messages dialog box, as shown in Figure 5-14, or click the Filter icon from the tool bar (the one that looks like a funnel).

Figure 5-14. *The Filter Status Messages dialog box.*

You can filter messages based on any status message detail. Figure 5-14 shows a filter that displays error messages of any type (milestone, detail, and audit) for site S00 and generated by the component SMS Site Backup on site system SQL1. Click the Advanced button to display the Advanced Filter Options dialog box, where you can also specify filtering based on Process ID and Thread ID, message properties, and a range of time.

Real World   **Using Queries to Customize the Status Message Viewer**

The status messages that are displayed for a particular component, site system, package, advertisement, and so on are built based on an SMS query for that status message object. By default, the reference "Original Query" is listed in the drop-down list on the Status Message Viewer toolbar, as you see in Figure 5-9. To view the Original Query's criteria, choose Query Information from the View menu to display the Query Information dialog box, as shown in Figure 5-15.

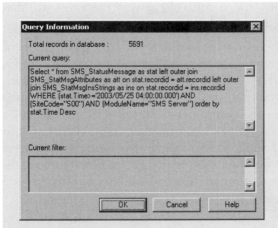

Figure 5-15.   *The Query Information dialog box.*

The Original Query usually shows all messages for a specific component on a specific site system. However, many predefined queries are available that you can run against any status message object; we'll look at some of these predefined queries later in this section. You can display and compile the status messages based on a query by selecting the query you want from the drop-down list of queries on the Status Message Viewer toolbar. For example, Site Component Manager status messages might include messages generated on several site systems in your site as well as on child sites. Perhaps you need to see only the status messages for your site or for a specific site system. Status message queries are available, from the drop-down query list, for both of these situations: All Status Messages From A Specific Component At A Specific Site and All Status Messages From A Specific Component On A Specific System. To resolve these queries, from the drop-down query list, select one of these queries to display its corresponding query resolving window, specify the prompted values, and then click OK to execute the query. The Status Message Viewer screen is refreshed accordingly.

Understanding Status Summarizers

You can configure status messages in a variety of ways. For the most part, the default configuration of the status message system will serve the average site quite well and generate a sufficient number of messages to facilitate reporting and troubleshooting. However, you might need to modify or enhance the reporting of status messages. One way to control the way messages are displayed in the SMS Administrator Console is by using status summarizers.

Status summarizers provide a mechanism to consolidate the copious amounts of data generated by status messages into a succinct view of the status of a component, a server, a package, or an advertisement. In the Component Status window (shown in Figure 5-2), for example, you're presented with a single entry for each component that indicates the component's status (OK, Warning, or Error), its state (Started or Stopped), and the number of error, warning, and info messages that have been generated. Remember that behind each of these entry summaries can be a host of detailed messages. Let's explore some techniques for modifying how the status summarizers consolidate and display the data you see in the SMS Administrator Console.

Display Interval

The status messages that are displayed are filtered first by a display interval. By default, only status messages generated since midnight are displayed. This limitation doesn't mean that all previous status messages have been deleted. On the contrary, all status messages are written to the SMS database by default (You'll learn more about the status message reporting process in the section entitled "Status Message Process Flow" later in this chapter). The display interval merely facilitates your view of recent messages. You can modify the display interval for status summaries displayed in the Component Status node and the Advertisement Status node. Since summaries displayed in the Site System Status node and the Package Status node are based solely on state, you can't modify the display interval for these status messages.

To modify the display interval, right-click the Component Status node or the Advertisement Status node and choose Display Interval from the context menu to display a list of interval options, as shown in Figure 5-16.

Select the interval option that best suits your viewing needs. Be aware that choosing an interval such as Since Site Installation is likely to net you a significant number of messages to scroll through when you choose Show All Messages from the context menu.

Strictly speaking, the display interval is not so much an attribute of the status summarizer mechanism as it's a way to facilitate your view of the status messages kept in the database. You can also view package status based on display interval; we'll discuss package and advertisement status in detail in Chapter 12.

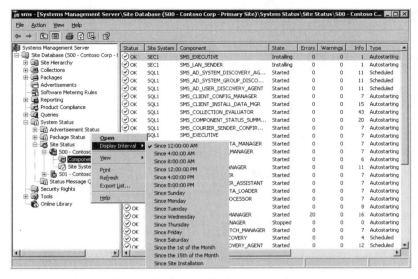

Figure 5-16.   *Displaying the list of display interval options.*

Status Message Thresholds

A *status message threshold* is a limit that defines when the status summary for a component or site system should indicate OK, Warning, or Critical status. This threshold is set by determining the number of actual OK, Warning, and Critical messages that have been generated for each component or site system. When a predetermined number of messages has been collected, the status changes from OK to Warning or from Warning to Critical.

For example, consider the Status Threshold Properties dialog box shown in Figure 5-17, which you can get to by right-clicking a status summary entry in the Component Status window and choosing Properties. The Status Message Threshold settings indicate that if one error type status message is generated for SMS Site Component Manager, the status summarizer will change the component's status from OK to Warning. If five error type status messages are generated, the component's status will change from Warning to Critical. Similarly, if 2000 informational type status messages are generated for SMS Site Component Manager, the status summarizer will change the status of SMS Site Component Manager from OK to Warning, and if 5000 informational type status messages are generated, the status will change from Warning to Critical.

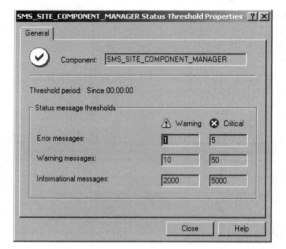

Figure 5-17. *The Status Threshold Properties dialog box, showing the default number of status message thresholds.*

Status thresholds for site system status are calculated similarly, but are based on available free space in the SMS site system and the site and software metering databases. Figure 5-18 shows the Free Space Thresholds Properties dialog box, which you can access by right-clicking any status summary entry in the Site System Status window and choosing Properties. Notice that the free space thresholds for all site systems generate a warning status message if free space falls below 20 MB (20,480 KB) and a critical status message if free space falls below 10 MB (10,240 KB).

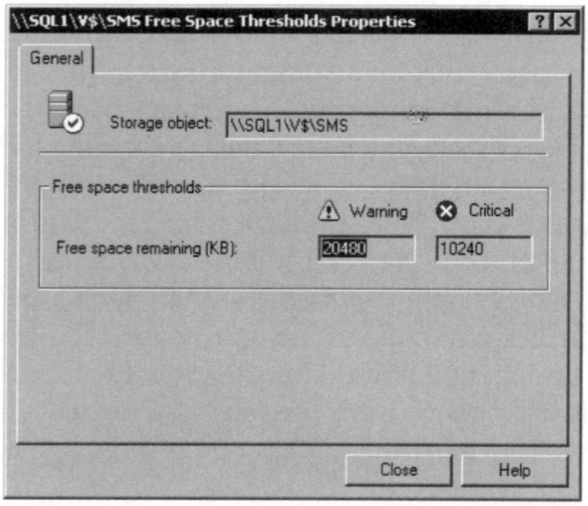

Figure 5-18. *The Free Space Thresholds Properties dialog box for the Site System Status.*

Other thresholds are specific to the databases based on a percentage of the database size. You'll learn how to modify these values or add new threshold values in the next section.

Configuring Status Summarizers

You can configure three status summarizer components: Component Status Summarizer, Site System Status Summarizer, and Advertisement Status Summarizer. To access these status summarizers, in the SMS Administrator Console expand the site's Site Settings node and then expand the Status Summarizers node. We'll look at the specific property settings for each of these status summarizers in the following sections.

Component Status Summarizer

To configure the Component Status Summarizer, follow these steps:

1. Right-click Component Status Summarizer in the Status Summarizers node and choose Properties from the context menu to display the Component Status Summarizer Properties dialog box, shown in Figure 5-19.

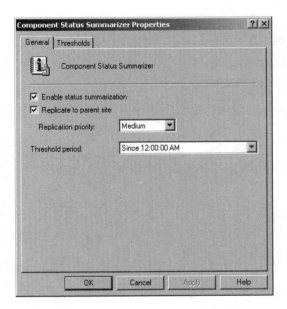

Figure 5-19. *The General tab of the Component Status Summarizer Properties dialog box.*

Notice that the Enable Status Summarization and Replicate To Parent Site options are selected by default. If you want to disable component status summarization, clear the option Enable Status Summarization. If you do so, however, the status message system won't be of much help to you as you'll no longer be tracking the activity of SMS components.

If you don't want to send status information to administrators in a parent site, clear the option Replicate To Parent Site. You might choose to do so if all site troubleshooting occurs at your site or if your parent site administrators don't want to receive status information from your site, or both. If you're replicating status messages to a parent site, you can set the replication priority for those messages. The default, as you see in Figure 5-19, is Medium. You might choose Low as a replication priority if you've set address options limiting the priority of intersite communications (refer to Chapter 4, "Multiple-Site Structures," for more information) and you want to control when status messages are sent to the parent. This dialog box also gives you another place to modify the display interval, here called the threshold period.

2. Select the Thresholds tab to configure summary thresholds for each component, as shown in Figure 5-20.

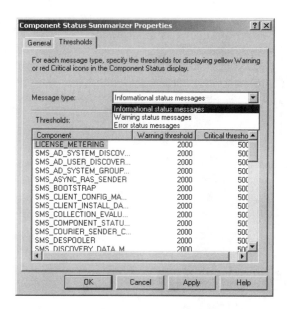

Figure 5-20. *The Thresholds tab of the Component Status Summarizer Properties dialog box.*

3. Select the Message Type you want to set the threshold for—Informational, Warning, or Error—from the drop-down list and then double-click the component whose thresholds you want to change to display the Status Threshold Properties dialog box.

The default status message thresholds differ for each message type. Figure 5-21 shows the default settings for informational status messages for the SMS Hierarchy Manager.

Figure 5-21. *The default status message thresholds for informational status messages.*

Note   By default, the thresholds are the same for all components.

Figure 5-22 shows the default settings for warning status messages.

Figure 5-22. *The default status message thresholds for warning status messages.*

Figure 5-23 shows the default settings for error status messages.

Figure 5-23. *The default status message thresholds for error status messages.*

4. Specify the number of warning and error messages that need to be generated (the threshold) before the Component Status Summarizer changes the summary status from OK to Warning or to Critical.

5. Choose OK to close the Status Threshold Properties dialog box and then choose OK in the Component Status Summarizer Properties dialog box to save your modifications.

Site System Status Summarizer

To configure the Site System Status Summarizer, follow these steps:

1. Right-click Site System Status Summarizer in the Status Summarizers node and choose Properties from context menu to display the Site System Status Summarizer Properties dialog box, as shown in Figure 5-24.

    Notice that the Enable Status Summarization and Replicate To Parent Site options are selected by default. If you want to disable site system status summarization, clear the option Enable Status Summarization. If you do so, however, the status message system won't be of much help to you as far as tracking site system thresholds. However, you'll still be collecting component status. You might decide that tracking component status is enough, and because, let's say, you have resource concerns on the site server, you might choose to turn off site system status summarization to conserve on resource usage.

If you don't want to send status information to administrators in a parent site, clear the option Replicate to Parent Site. You might choose to do so if all site troubleshooting occurs at your site or your parent site administrators don't want to receive status information from your site, or both. If you're replicating status messages to a parent site, you can set the replication priority for those messages. The default, as you see in Figure 5-24, is Medium. You might choose Low as a replication priority if you've set address options limiting the priority of intersite communications (refer to Chapter 4 for more information) and you want to control when status messages are sent to the parent.

Figure 5-24.   *The General tab of the Site System Status Summarizer Properties dialog box.*

Click the Schedule button to display the Schedule dialog box, where you can specify a schedule for when and how often site system status summarization takes place.

2. Select the Thresholds tab to configure space thresholds for each database and for each site system, as shown in Figure 5-25.

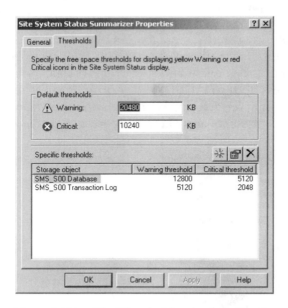

Figure 5-25. *The Thresholds tab of the Site System Status Summarizer Properties dialog box.*

SMS has already set general default values for site systems. You can modify these settings by entering new values in the Warning or Critical text boxes. SMS has also defined specific threshold values for the SMS database. If you need to change these values, double-click the entry to display the Free Space Threshold Properties dialog box, where you can specify the values you prefer. Then click OK to close the dialog box.

3. To add a specific site server to monitor its status, click the New button (the yellow star) in the Specific Thresholds frame to display the Free Space Threshold Properties dialog box, as shown in Figure 5-26.

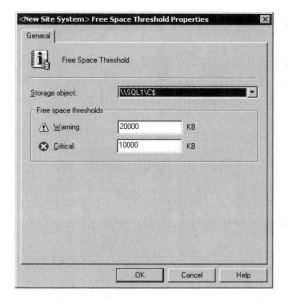

Figure 5-26. *The Free Space Threshold Properties dialog box.*

Select the site system to monitor from the Storage Object drop-down list, enter the desired free space thresholds to monitor for in the Warning and Critical text boxes, and then click OK.

4. Click OK again to save your changes.

Advertisement Status Summarizer

To configure the Advertisement Status Summarizer, follow these steps:

1. Right-click Advertisement Status Summarizer in the Status Summarizers node and choose Properties from the context menu to display the Advertisement Status Summarizer Properties dialog box, shown in Figure 5-27.

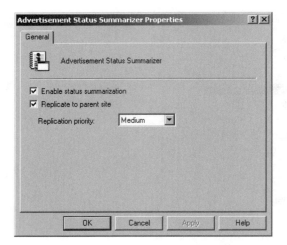

Figure 5-27. *The General tab of the Advertisement Status Summarizer Properties dialog box.*

Notice that the Enable Status Summarization and Replicate To Parent Site options are selected by default. If you want to disable site advertisement status summarization, clear the option Enable Status Summarization. If you do so, the status message system will no longer track advertisement status. If you manage a lot of packages at this site, disabling this option will effectively rob you of the ability to follow the progress of a package advertisement to a target collection.

As with Component and Site System status, if you don't want to send status information about advertisements to administrators in a parent site, clear the option Replicate To Parent Site. You might choose to do so if all package maintenance occurs at your site or your parent site administrators don't want to receive information about advertisements from your site, or both. If you're replicating status messages to a parent site, you can set the replication priority for those messages. The default, as you see in Figure 5-27, is Medium. You might choose Low as a replication priority if you've set address options limiting the priority of intersite communications (refer to Chapter 4 for more information) and you want to control when status messages are sent to the parent.

2. Choose OK to save your modifications.

Status summarizers help us to define how component, system, and advertisement status is displayed to the SMS administrator based on their message type—OK, Warning, and Critical. The next section shows us how to further refine which status messages are captured and displayed in the Status Message Viewer.

Filtering Status Messages

SMS components and site systems generate a constant stream of status messages. Most of these messages will prove to be extremely helpful in resolving issues or troubleshooting problems you might be having with your SMS site. Some messages, however, might simply be flooding the Status Message Viewer with interesting but not particularly useful information, or too much information, or not the kind of information you're looking for.

There are several ways to filter status messages and display just the status information of interest. We looked at one technique in the section entitled "Setting Status Message Viewer Options" earlier in this chapter. You can also accomplish status filtering in a more global fashion by modifying the status reporting properties or by defining status filter rules.

Configuring Status Reporting Properties

To configure the status reporting component properties, in the SMS Administrator Console, expand the Site Settings node and then select the Component Configuration node. Right-click Status Reporting and choose Properties from the context menu to display the Status Reporting Properties dialog box, as shown in Figure 5-28.

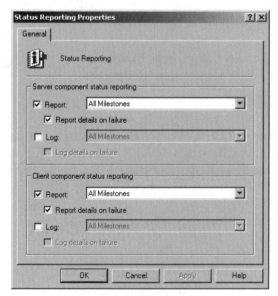

Figure 5-28.   *The Status Reporting Properties dialog box.*

By default, reporting is enabled for both the site server and the client components for the following types of messages:

- All milestones

- All milestones and all details

- Error and warning milestones

- Error milestones

By selecting the appropriate message types from the drop-down lists, you can control how much data is reported. For example, to only show milestone messages that are errors or warnings, select the Error And Warning Milestones option from the drop-down list in the Server Component Status Reporting frame of the dialog box.

Caution The default settings for message reporting are considered appropriate for most SMS sites. Enabling too many messages or filtering out too much information can make the status message system less effective as a problem-solving tool.

The Report Details On Failure option is also selected by default. This powerful feature ensures that when a failure occurs or an error is reported, the affected component reports details as to the nature of the failure as well as possible causes and remedies. You will probably not want to disable this feature—unless, of course, you can troubleshoot without knowing the details of a problem.

You can also enable logging for the same message types to the Windows Event Log and include failure details in the log by selecting those options.

Status Filter Rules

The second way to globally affect how status messages are reported is by using status filter rules. SMS creates 15 status filter rules of its own to control how status messages are reported and viewed, as shown in Figure 5-29. In the SMS Administrator Console, expand the Site Settings node, then select the Status Filter Rules node to display these status filter rules. These default filter rules are used to control how many, and which, status messages are reported and displayed in the Status Message Viewer.

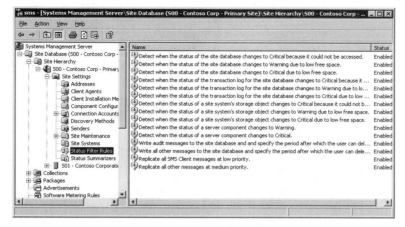

Figure 5-29. *The SMS default status filter rules.*

When an SMS component generates a status message, the SMS Status Manager tests the message against these status filter rules to determine how that message should be handled. The SMS Status Manager then performs one or more of the following actions.

- Writes the message to the SMS database
- Writes the message to the Windows Event Log
- Replicates the message to the parent site
- Sends the message to a status summarizer
- Executes a program

Most of the default status filter rules generate a system message that's displayed on the site server using a NET SEND command. You should not modify any of these default status filter rules. Each has been created for a reason, and they're all significantly useful. But you might find that you want to create additional filter rules. You can customize status filter rules to discard certain types of messages that you don't want or don't need to see, to replicate certain types of messages to a parent site at a higher priority than others or not replicate certain messages at all, and to execute a program based on a message type.

Begin by deciding just what messages you need to see and what messages you don't need to see. For example, if your site participates in a parent-child relationship but is fully administered within the site—that is, no administration occurs at the parent site—it might be unnecessary to replicate any status messages to the parent site. Eliminating this replication would certainly decrease the amount of network traffic generated between the parent site and your site.

Caution Do not modify existing status filters or define any new filter rules until you're fully comfortable with and knowledgeable about the status message system. If you make a change without knowing its full effect, you could render the status message system useless to you as a troubleshooting tool.

Follow these steps to create a new status filter rule:

1. In the SMS Administrator Console, expand the Site Settings node.

2. Right-click Status Filter Rules, choose New from the context menu, and then choose Status Filter Rule to display the Status Filter Rule Properties dialog box, as shown in Figure 5-30.

Figure 5-30. *The General tab of the Status Filter Rule Properties dialog box.*

3. In the General tab, enter a descriptive name for your filter.

Tip The status filter name should adequately explain the function and purpose of the status filter rule you're creating. Use the default filter names as a guideline for creating your own.

You can narrow your filter criteria further by selecting any combination of options available in the General tab. These options are described below in Table 5-1.

4. Select the Actions tab, as shown in Figure 5-31, and specify what Status Manager should do when the message criteria defined in the General tab are met.

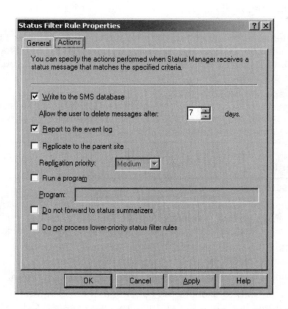

Figure 5-31.   *The Actions tab of the Status Filter Rule Properties dialog box.*

In this example, Status Manager has been instructed to write the message to the SMS database as well as to the Windows Event Log. By default, the message will also be forwarded to the appropriate status summarizer to be included in the Status Message Viewer. Other actions available to you are described below in Table 5-2.

5. Choose OK to save the new filter rule.

Table 5-1.   Status filter rule options

Filter Option	Description
Source	The source of the status message: SMS Server, SMS Client, or SMS Provider
Site Code	The site code corresponding to the source of the status message
System	The name of the SMS client or server that generates the status message
Component	The name of the SMS component that generates the status message
Message Type	The status message type: Milestone, Detail, or Audit
Message Severity	The message severity: Informational, Warning, or Error

Table 5-1.   Status filter rule options

Filter Option	Description
Message ID	The specific status message ID you're reporting on—for example, an ID of 500 generally relates to a component starting up
Property	The name of a specific property, such as Advertisement ID, Collection ID, Package ID, Policy Assignment ID, or Policy ID, that might be present in some status messages you want to report on
Property Value	A specific property attribute for the property name you specified, such as Advertisement ID, Collection ID, Package ID, Policy Assignment ID, or Policy ID, that might be present in some status messages you want to report on

Table 5-2.   Status filter action options

Action Option	Description
Write To The SMS Database	Includes the status message as a record in the SMS database. By default, messages are kept in the database for seven days and then deleted, unless this value is modified.
Report To The Event Log	Writes the status message to the Windows Event Viewer application log.
Replicate To The Parent Site	Sends a copy of the status message to the site's parent.
Run A Program	Directs SMS to execute the command entered in the Program text box when the status message is generated.
Do Not Forward To Status Summarizers	Prevents the status message from being handled by any status summarizer. This means that it might not be included in determining warning or error thresholds in the status viewer.
Do Not Process Lower-Priority Status Filter Rules	Effectively ends any further processing of this status message. This means that it won't be evaluated by any additional filter rules.

The new status filter rule will be added at the end of the list of existing rules. However, the actual order in which the rules are listed is determined by their relative priority. Status messages will be passed through all the filters if you don't select the Do Not Process Lower-Priority Status Filter Rules check box for a filter in the Actions tab. If you do select this option for a filter, the message won't pass through any filters below this one in the filter list. You can change the order of filter processing by right-clicking a filter, choosing All Tasks from the context menu, and then choosing Increment Priority to move the filter up in the list or Decrement Priority to move the filter down in the list.

Tip   The Run A Program option in the Actions tab can be a useful alert tool if you're using a Windows-compatible paging application or some other notification tool that can be executed through a command line. For example, you can enter the command-line sequence for executing a page to notify you when a specific status message is generated.

Real World   **Using Status Filter Rules**

Chapter 14 of the *Microsoft Systems Management Server 2003 Operations Guide*, available from the Microsoft SMS Web site (*http://www.microsoft.com/smserver*), contains several useful example filter rules in the section titled "Sample Status Filter Rules." The filter rule on how to discard status messages from a component that's flooding the system is particularly useful. After you've become comfortable with the status message system and the way in which the various SMS components work and interact, you might want to filter out simple informational messages, such as messages generated when a component starts or wakes up. Follow the steps outlined earlier to define this simple filter. In the General tab, specify a name in the form "Discard message *xyz* from component *abc* on server *123*." Fill in the System, Component, and Message ID fields, as shown in Figure 5-32. For this example, we're excluding startup messages for Site Control Manager that are generated on the system SQL1.

Figure 5-32.   *Defining a sample status filter rule.*

In the Actions tab, select the Do Not Forward To Status Summarizers check box. This setting ensures that the message is disregarded and that it won't be displayed in the Status Message Viewer. Depending on where this new rule sits in relation to the other rules, you might also want to select the Do Not Process Lower-Priority Status Filter Rules check box to prevent any subsequent filters from picking this message up and possibly writing it to the database or displaying it in the Status Message Viewer.

Working with Status Message Queries

You already know how to effectively use the Status Message Viewer to customize status messages and troubleshoot components and site systems. The Status Message Viewer displays messages on a per-component or per-system basis. Sometimes, however, you might need to see all messages of a specific type generated across all the site systems or from several components.

The SMS development team, being one step ahead of the rest of us in this thinking, created status message queries as a means of accomplishing just that. In fact, there are currently 70 existing default queries that might well satisfy most of your message viewing needs. These queries are listed in the Status Message Queries window, shown in Figure 5-33. In the SMS Administrator Console, navigate to the System Status node and expand it, then select he Status Message Queries node to display this window. For example, the query highlighted in Figure 5-33 will generate a list of all SMS clients on which the Hardware Inventory Agent reported some problem when trying to generate the Management Information Format (MIF) file needed to report the client's hardware information to the site database. Running a query of this type is certainly easier than scanning for the error status message for every client reporting messages to the Component Status Summarizer.

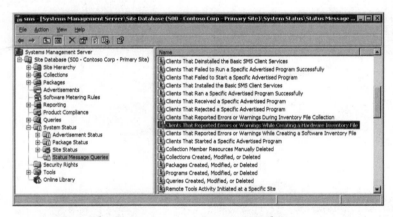

Figure 5-33. *The Status Message Queries window.*

Most of these default queries are prompted—meaning that you must provide information such as a site code, the server name, and so on. To execute a status message query, right-click the query in the Status Message Queries window and choose Show Messages from the context window. Any values that need to be resolved are listed, and you must enter the information or values requested.

You can also create your own status message queries. To do so, follow these steps:

1. Right-click Status Message Queries, choose New from the context menu, and choose Status Message Query to display the Status Message Query Properties dialog box, as shown in Figure 5-34.

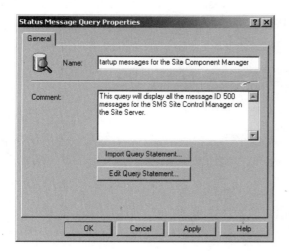

Figure 5-34.   *The Status Message Query Properties dialog box.*

2. Enter a descriptive name for your query and a comment that further explains the query's purpose.

3. Click the Import Query Statement button to display the Browse Query dialog box that lists all the available status message queries, as shown in Figure 5-35. Select the query you would like to import into your new query and click OK.

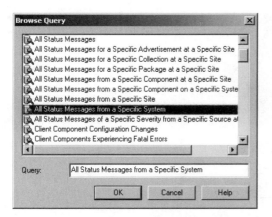

Figure 5-35.   *The Browse Query dialog box.*

4. Click the Edit Query Statement button to display the Query Statement Properties dialog box. In this dialog box, you can modify the properties of the query you imported in step 3. If you did not import an existing query, then here you can create your own new query.

By default, a status message query displays only status messages in its results list; thus all the options in the General tab are unavailable, as shown in Figure 5-36.

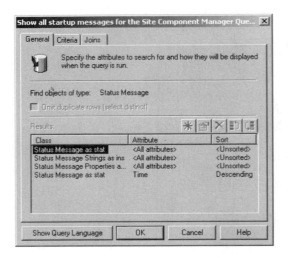

Figure 5-36. *The General Tab of the Query Statement Properties dialog box.*

5. Select the Criteria tab to create or modify the query statement. Any existing query statements are displayed in the Criteria list, as seen in Figure 5-37.

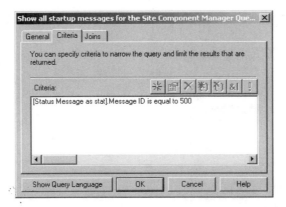

Figure 5-37. *The Criteria tab of the Query Statement Properties dialog box.*

6. Click the New button (yellow star) to add a new criteria statement or highlight an existing criteria statement and click the Edit button (hand holding paper) to display the Criterion Properties dialog box, as shown in Figure 5-38.

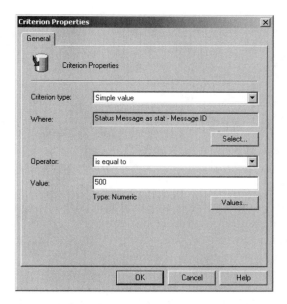

Figure 5-38.   *The Criterion Properties dialog box.*

7. Select the criterion type (in most cases, this will be Simple Value) from the drop-down list and specify the attribute class and the attribute by clicking the Select button to display the Select Attribute dialog box shown in Figure 5-39. The attributes describe an SMS object type and are grouped into one or more attribute classes. In this example the attribute class Status Message consists of attributes that include component, machine name, severity, and site code, any of which can be used to qualify the results of the query. Select an appropriate Attribute Class and Attribute and then click OK to go back to the Criterion Properties dialog box. Next, specify an operator by choosing one from the drop-down list. Click the Values button to display all the values related to the attribute you selected that have been recorded in the SMS database. Then Click OK.

Figure 5-39. *The Select Attributes dialog box.*

8. To add criteria to your query, repeat steps 6 and 7 for each additional criteria statement. When you've finished, click OK twice to save your query.

The new status message query is now available in the Status Message Queries window. Figure 5-40 shows the results of running our sample query by right-clicking the sample query and choosing Show Messages from the context menu. Notice that the result of the query is to display the message "This Component Started" for every component on the site server.

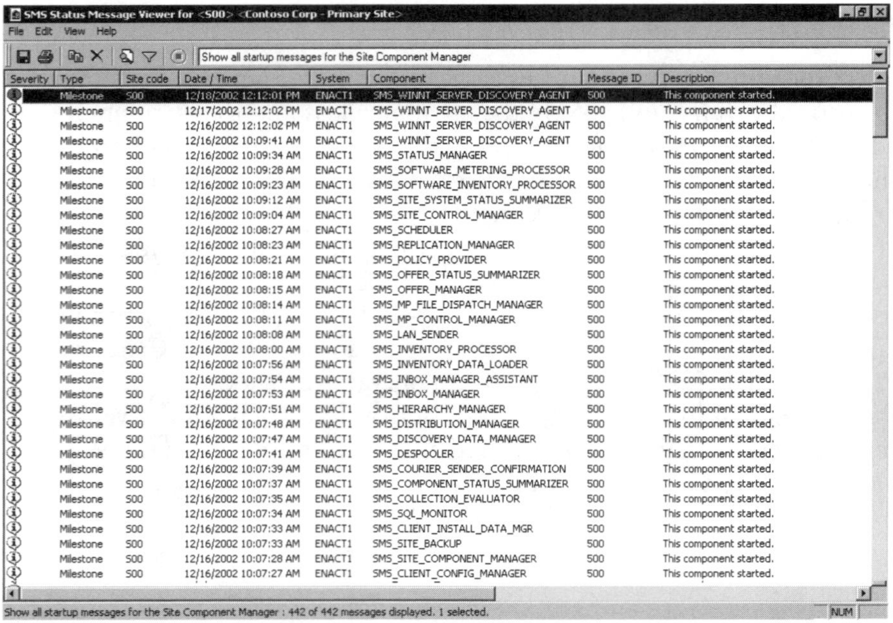

Figure 5-40. *The results of running a sample status message query.*

Status Message Process Flow

Now that we've examined the different tools for handling status messages, let's look at the status message process flow. Nearly every SMS 2003 service and component generates status messages. Not only does the site server itself generate messages, as one would expect, but the components and services running on site systems (management points, client access points, and so on) and agents running on SMS clients also generate status messages. The status message system in SMS 2003 has the capacity to generate a multitude of messages; however, as we've seen, status summarizers and filters keep these messages to a manageable level by default. Nevertheless, status message reporting can add to your existing network traffic bandwidth issues.

Reporting Status on Site Servers and Site Systems

Status messages generated on the site server are processed within the site server itself and then updated to the SMS database. If the SMS database resides on the same server, no additional network traffic is generated. However, status messages that SMS services and components generate on site systems are copied to the site server so that they can be updated to the SMS database. Figure 5-41 depicts the process flow for status messages generated on the site server and site systems.

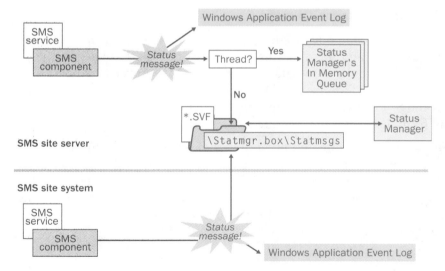

Figure 5-41. *Status message process flow for status messages generated on the site server and site systems.*

As we've mentioned in the section entitled "Configuring Status Reporting Properties" earlier in this chapter, several options are available to the SMS administrator when configuring status message reporting. Remember that one option enables the SMS administrator to specify whether to convert the status message to a Windows event. When an SMS service or thread generates a status message, that service or thread checks its properties to see whether this option has been set. If it has, the status message is first converted to a Windows event and written to the Windows Application Event Log. If no other reporting options have been configured, the process stops here. If other reporting options have been configured, the status message must be handed off to the Status Manager component on the site server. If the server on which the status message was generated is the site server, the status message is placed either in Status Manager's In Memory Queue if a thread component generated the message or in Status Manager's inbox (SMS\Inboxes\Statmgr.box\Statmsgs) as an .SVF file if a service component generated the message.

If the server on which the status message was generated is a site system, the status message is copied to Status Manager's inbox on the site server. If for some reason the component is unable to copy the status message to the site server, it stores the status message(s) in the %Systemroot%\System32\Smsmsgs subdirectory on the site system and retries until it can successfully copy the status message to the Status Manager's inbox on the site server.

Reporting Status from Clients

As we've seen, SMS components and agents residing on SMS clients also generate status messages, and these messages too must be reported back to the site server for updating to the SMS database. Figure 5-42 illustrates the flow of status messages from the SMS Legacy Client to the site server. Status messages generated on the SMS Advanced Client are propagated to the site's management point and from there moved to the site server.

Status information is collected not only from SMS client components and agents, but also as the result of application installations in the form of status MIF files. For example, both the package program created through the SMS Administrator Console and the packages compiled through the SMS Installer have the ability to generate status MIF files upon the execution of the program or package.

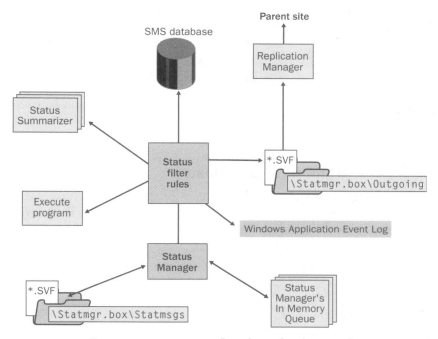

Figure 5-42. *Status message process flow from the client to the site server.*

When a status message is generated on the SMS client by an SMS client component, its properties are checked by that component to determine whether the message needs to be converted to a Windows event. If so, and if the SMS client is also a Windows NT client or higher, the status message is written to the Windows Application Event Log. Next, the status message and status MIF files are written to an .SVF file and stored in the %Systemroot% or in the Temp or TMP directory. The client component then initiates a request for the Copy Queue component on the client to move the .SVF file to the Status Manager's inbox on the client access point (CAP) (CAP_*sitecode*\Statmsgs.box). Copy Queue is an SMS client component that writes data to CAPs and management points reliably. When Copy Queue has trouble writing its error messages to the CAP, it will write to the CPQMgr32.log file in the %Systemroot%\MS\SMS\Logs file on the client in question. After the file is written to the management point or the CAP, the Inbox Manager Assistant thread wakes up and moves the .SVF file to Status Manager's inbox on the site server.

Tip Each client component generates a log file in the %System-root%\MS\SMS\Logs directory on the client computer by default. Check these log files to determine whether the .SVF file was created during trouble-shooting of status message generation. In addition, in the log file of the component that should have generated the status message, look for a line that begins with "STATMSG" on or around the time that the status message should have been generated. If it doesn't exist, or if the next line begins with the text "CserverStatusReporter," the component might have had trouble generating and reporting the status message.

Reporting Status to the SMS Database

Once the status message is written to its in-memory queue or to its inbox, Status Manager wakes up and reads the status message or .SVF file. It evaluates the message against the status filter rules established by SMS during setup or modified by the SMS administrator. As we've discussed, a status message can be handled in one of five ways, as shown in Figure 5-43.

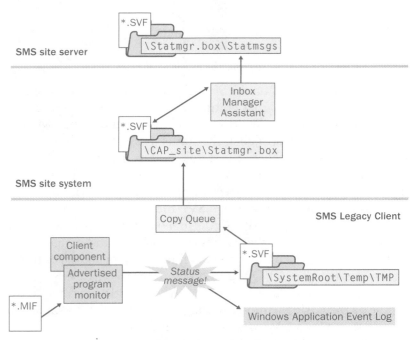

Figure 5-43. *Using status filter rules to handle the disposition of a status message.*

The status message could be written to the SMS database or discarded. If the Status Manager has not already done so, the status message could be converted to a Windows event and written to the Windows event log. The status message could be handed to a status summarizer to be condensed for viewing through the SMS Administrator Console. If a parent site exists, the message could be sent to the parent site for inclusion in its SMS database or viewing through its SMS Administrator Console. The SMS administrator could also configure a program to be executed upon receipt of a status message. This program might be a system pop-up notification on the SMS administrator's desktop, the execution of a batch file, or a notification using paging software.

As you can see, the status messaging system in SMS 2003 is quite robust and is capable of inundating you with information about your site server, site systems, and clients. Fortunately, you can control which status messages are reported and how these messages are handled, and you can tailor their generation to fit your specific reporting needs.

Using SMS Service Manager

Status messages will be, and should be, your first stop when you're trying to understand an SMS process or to troubleshoot a problem on your site. However, in addition to status messages, you can also study the log files that each component can generate. Log files provide an even greater level of detail in describing how an SMS component is functioning, especially in relation to other components.

Remember from Chapter 3 that log files aren't enabled in SMS 2003 by default in order to conserve server resources. After all, there are over 40 different SMS components and services that can generate log files. In addition, each log file can hold up to 1 MB of data before archiving that data to an archive log. Altogether, if all component logs and archive logs were full, the server would require over 80 MB worth of storage space just for these files.

On the other hand, log files are enabled on SMS clients by default because the number of client components is considerably less and so that the SMS administrator doesn't have to visit a client to enable logging. Also, each log file defaults to 256 KB in size. We also explored using SMS Service Manager to enable SMS 2003 log files through the SMS Administrator Console in Chapter 3.

SMS Service Manager is also used to monitor the status of components. Unlike the Status Message Viewer, SMS Service Manager provides an at-a-glance view of SMS components and services running on the site server and on each site system. As shown in Figure 5-44, you can see the status of each component represented both as an icon preceding each entry and in the Status field, the server the component is running on, the last time the component was polled, and the component type. The icon preceding each entry appears only after you query each component for its current status by right-clicking it and choosing Query from the context menu. Using the same technique, you can also stop, pause, and resume component activity.

Tip If you want to stop all the SMS Executive threads, stop the SMS_SITE_COMPONENT_MANAGER first and then stop SMS_EXECUTIVE using SMS Service Manager, because the Site Component Manager might attempt to restart the SMS Executive if it's stopped. The Windows Services administrative tool also enables you to stop these services; however, using SMS Service Manager is the preferred method.

Tip Just because an SMS component is listed as stopped doesn't necessarily mean that there's a problem with the service. Some services, like SMS_NETWORK_DISCOVERY, highlighted in Figure 5-44, run on a predetermined or administrator-defined schedule. It's important to familiarize yourself with viewing status messages and log files so that you can determine whether a component problem exists.

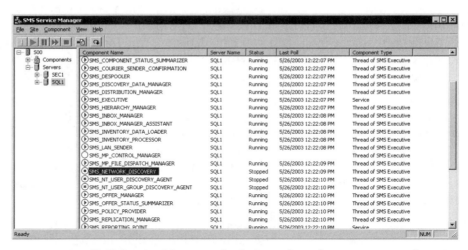

Figure 5-44. *SMS Service Manager, displaying a list of components and services running on the site server.*

Using SMS Trace

As discussed in Chapter 3, log files are simply text files that can be read using any text editor. However, trying to scroll through several long log file entries using Notepad can become tedious, if not frustrating. Fortunately, there is a utility named SMS Trace that provides a nicer interface for viewing log files. Each log entry is easy to read, ordered, and time-stamped. In addition, the view is dynamically updated as components modify the log file. You can even view multiple log files at one time—a great way to learn how various components interact with one another.

Obtaining SMS Trace

SMS Trace is one of several tools that Microsoft has made available to help you manage your SMS site. This set of tools is called the SMS 2003 Toolkit 1, and you can obtain it through the SMS Web site (*http://www.microsoft.com/ smserver*). You can download these tools as a bundle to your site server or desktop and extract them by running the self-extracting executable and following the instructions given.

After you install SMS Trace, you might want to place a shortcut to it on the desktop of your site server or your SMS Administrator console computer. If you've used the version of SMS Trace that came with SMS 2.0, you'll notice a couple of welcome enhancements with this updated version. For example, all error and warning entries are now highlighted in the SMS Trace viewer to make it easier for you to find. To use SMS Trace to view log files, follow these steps:

1. Start SMS Trace using either of the methods described above. The SMS Trace window appears, as shown in Figure 5-45.

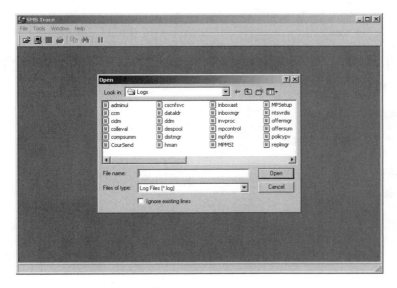

Figure 5-45. *The SMS Trace window.*

2. Choose Open from the File menu or click the File Open icon on the toolbar to display the Open dialog box. SMS Trace automatically defaults to the SMS\Logs directory.

3. Select the log file you want to open and click Open or double-click the filename. The contents of the log file are displayed in the SMS Trace window, as shown in Figure 5-46.

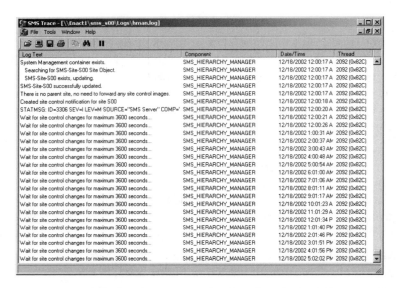

Figure 5-46. *The log file contents displayed in the SMS Trace window.*

Notice how nicely this utility displays the contents of the log file. Each entry is easy to read, ordered, and time-stamped. In addition, the view is dynamically updated as the component modifies the log file. Compare this window to the same log file opened in Notepad, as shown in Figure 5-47.

Figure 5-47. *The log file contents displayed using Notepad.*

The SMS Trace interface offers several nice features. You can, of course, print the log file and modify how much data appears on the screen. SMS Trace also lets you search for text, highlight text, and filter what's displayed on screen.

Searching for Text

If you're looking for a particular text string—perhaps a filename or an extension or a package or advertisement ID—you can ask SMS Trace to find the log entry that contains that text string. To do so, follow these steps:

1. Start SMS Trace and open the log file you want to search. Highlight the first log entry.

2. Choose Find from the Tools menu to display the Find dialog box, as shown in Figure 5-48.

Figure 5-48.   *The Find dialog box.*

3. Enter the text string you want to search for. This can be a partial string. To make this a case-sensitive search, select the Case Sensitive check box.

4. Click Next. The entry that contains the text string you entered will be highlighted in the log file if it exists.

5. To view the next entry with this text string, choose Find from the Tools menu, and then click Find Next in the Find dialog box. To view the previous entry, choose Up as the Direction and then click Find Next in the Find dialog box.

Highlighting Text

Perhaps, as you open multiple log files, you would like to highlight any entry that references a particular text string. For example, when a site setting is modified, Hierarchy Manager and Site Control Manager both create and reference files back and forth. While monitoring the flow of this interaction, you might choose to highlight the lines that reference specific files or file extensions to better view how the two components work with each other and hand files back and forth. To use SMS Trace to specify text that should be highlighted as it occurs in the log file, follow these steps:

1. Start SMS Trace.

2. Choose Highlight from the Tools menu to display the Highlight dialog box, as shown in Figure 5-49.

Figure 5-49.   *The Highlight dialog box.*

3. Enter the text string you want SMS Trace to look for. This can be a partial string. To make this a case-sensitive search, check the Case Sensitive check box.

4. Click OK.

5. Open the desired log file or files. As the log files are opened, any entry that contains the referenced string will be highlighted with a box surrounding the entry.

Filtering the SMS Trace View

Log files can get filled up quickly and contain hundreds of entries. Perhaps you're interested only in certain types of entries—for example, status message entries or entries that contain a reference to a particular package ID. SMS Trace provides a filter tool that can facilitate your view of these kinds of entries. To filter the SMS Trace view, follow these steps:

1. Start SMS Trace and open the log file or files you want to filter.

2. Choose Filter from the View menu to display the Filter dialog box, as shown in Figure 5-50.

3. Notice that you can filter what you see in the log window based on Entry Text, Component, Thread, and Time values. For each filter that you want to apply, select an appropriate operator and then enter the value you're filtering on. For example, in Figure 5-50 we're looking only for lines in the log file in which the entry text contains the string value "S0000001". Make your selections and click OK. SMS Trace will refresh the screen and show only the entries you filtered for.

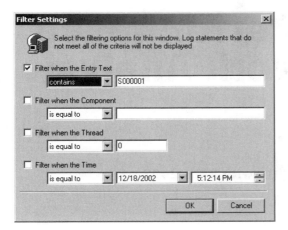

Figure 5-50.   *The Filter dialog box.*

Note   Once you have filtered a log in this manner, you can't turn off the filter without first closing the log file. After you close the log file, you can go back into the Filter Settings dialog box and change your filter options or clear them to turn them all off.

Summary

In this chapter you've learned about two of the most useful troubleshooting and learning tools you will have at your disposal through SMS: status messages and log files. Although status messages will provide you with most of the information you will need to successfully monitor and troubleshoot SMS component activity, the log files, when enabled, will give you that extra level of granularity that can so often provide the elusive bit of data needed to pull all the pieces of a puzzle together.

In Chapter 6, "System Performance and Network Analysis," we'll continue our exploration of troubleshooting and analysis tools as we discuss System Monitor, Network Trace, and Network Monitor.

Chapter 6
System Performance and Network Analysis

In the last chapter we began a discussion about monitoring and troubleshooting SMS using status messages and log files. In this chapter we'll round out that discussion by looking at some additional tools that can be used to assist SMS administrators as they monitor the performance of their systems and networks. We'll start by briefly reviewing the Windows System Monitor snap-in in the Performance console and defining the SMS performance objects that are added during SMS setup. We'll explore how to use Network Trace to determine the status of our site systems. Finally, we'll review how to use the Network Monitor utility to monitor network performance.

Using System Monitor with SMS 2003

In my experience, the Windows System Monitor tends to be an underappreciated utility. This is generally because administrators really haven't taken the time to learn how to use it effectively. With a product such as Microsoft SMS 2003, which requires a significant amount of resources to function efficiently, the System Monitor can be one of the most effective tools at your disposal to identify server resource usage and load. I'd like to approach this discussion, therefore, with two objectives. The first thing I want to do is reintroduce you to the System Monitor tool and ensure that you understand how to navigate it. My second objective is to identify some System Monitor objects and counters that can be of specific use when monitoring resource usage and load on your site systems.

Using System Monitor

Perhaps one of the more important tasks involved in troubleshooting problems on your server, whether it's any Microsoft Windows server or an SMS Site System, is to spot potential problem sources and develop and analyze trends before the problems materialize. Two basic steps are involved in achieving this kind of analysis—baseline creation and real-time tracking. Always create a baseline chart or log of so-called "normal" activity on your server. In our case, this should include the objects and counters specific to SMS 2003 server activity. When you're analyzing performance, you can create real-time charts using the same objects and counters as you used for your baseline chart and then compare it to the baseline to determine how server performance has been affected.

Here are some basic suggestions on how to create and use System Monitor charts. As I refer to a System Monitor object and one of its counters, I will use the following syntax: Object:Counter. For example, the *Processor* object has several counters that you can chart, one of which is the *% Processor Time*. I would refer to this object and counter set as *Processor:% Processor Time*.

Over 20 different System Monitor objects come with Windows by default. These facilitate the monitoring of basic system resources such as memory, processor, disk, and network. In fact, these are the four areas that you'll want to monitor on any given Windows server, especially your SMS servers. In addition to these, other objects with their corresponding counters are added when other applications are installed—for example, SMS 2003 or Microsoft SQL Server 2000. These represent additional items to monitor that can give you more information about what might be causing a specific resource situation.

Tip Monitoring objects alone with no other object data against which to reference is an exercise in futility for the administrator because you can't obtain any useful or specific information. For example, if the *Processor: % Processor Time* value is consistently higher than 80 percent, you might conclude that the processor might be overutilized. However, you have no information as to what might be overutilizing the processor. Add the *Process: % Processor Time* object for suspected processes, and you now have connected data upon which to begin your analysis.

Baselines are also important in determining when a given system is being "resource-challenged." It should seem obvious, but bears repeating, that unless you know what "normal" resource utilization is like on any given system, you can't begin to analyze problems or bottlenecks, develop trends, or implement load balancing across systems. Let's begin our review by creating a chart.

Creating a System Monitor Chart

To create a system monitor chart, complete the following steps:

1. Start the Performance console from the Administrative Tools group and then select the System Monitor node.

2. Click the Add button (the "plus" sign) from the chart window tool bar to display the Add Counters dialog box shown in Figure 6-1.

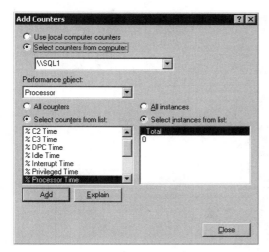

Figure 6-1. *Add Counters dialog box.*

3. Confirm the system you're monitoring in the Select Counters From Computer drop-down list box or choose Use Local Computer Counters if you're monitoring the local computer.

> **Tip**   Since running the System Monitor on a Windows server requires additional resources in and of itself, it's recommended that you remotely monitor your systems from your workstation rather than at the actual system in question.

4. Select the Object, Counter, and an appropriate Instance if necessary, and then click Add. If you're unsure of a counter's purpose or function, select it and click Explain to display a brief description at the bottom of the dialog box.

5. Repeat step 4 for each object:counter combination you wish to track. Then click Close.

6. Specify the desired color, scale, width, and style for your chart lines by selecting an object:counter in the legend at the bottom of the graph, right-clicking it and selecting Properties to display the System Monitor Properties dialog box, as shown in Figure 6-2.

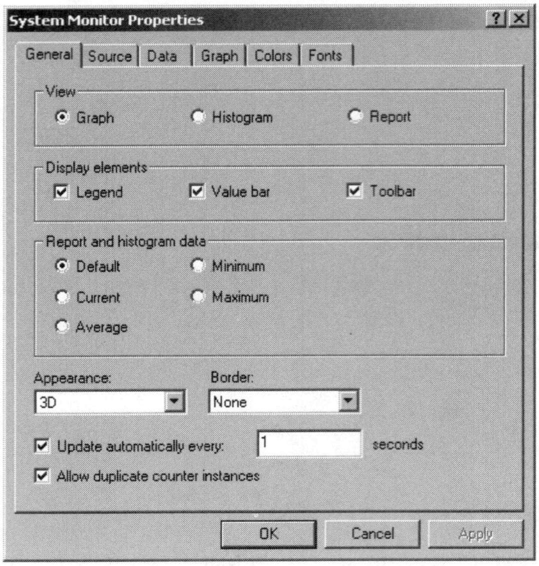

Figure 6-2. *System Monitor Properties dialog box.*

Figure 6-3 shows a representative chart. Three objects are being monitored—*Processor: % Processor Time, Process: % Processor Time* for the SMS Executive instance (smsexec), and *Memory: Pages/sec*. After I created the chart, I switched back to my SMS Administrator Console and updated the Collection memberships. You can see on the chart at what point I did so by the peaks recorded for each object.

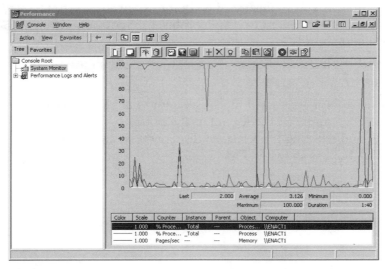

Figure 6-3. *A simple chart that monitors three object:counter values.*

Tip As more objects are monitored in a chart, the busier the chart becomes. You can facilitate the reading of chart lines by turning on a highlight feature. With the chart open, press Ctrl+H. Now when you select a line on the chart, it will display with a heavy white highlight making it easier to read. Press Ctrl+H again to turn off the highlight feature.

SMS 2003 performance, like most Windows systems, tends to revolve around a specific set of system resources that you can monitor and analyze with the help of System Monitor. These resources include processor usage, disk I/O, physical memory, and network. Table 6-1 outlines the more useful objects and counters to use when tracking and analyzing SMS Site System server performance using System Monitor.

Table 6-1. System Monitor objects

Object:Counter	Description	Instance	Threshold Suggestions
Memory:Committed Bytes	This represents the amount of virtual memory that has been committed for use for paging RAM.	N/A	This value should be less than the amount of physical RAM. The higher the value, the more likely that the system is experiencing a high level of paging and thrashing.
Memory:Page Reads/ sec	This represents the frequency that data had to be read from the page file back into RAM to resolve page faults.	N/A	A value less than 5 generally represents acceptable performance. Values over 5 might indicate a need for more RAM.
Network Interface: Packets Received/ second	This represents the total number of network packets received on this network interface.	Each network card	This value should remain relatively consistent and reflect average network traffic being generated. Prolonged increases in this number might indicate that a process or server on the network segment is generating additional traffic and using potentially more bandwidth.
Network Interface: Bytes Received/ second	This represents the number of bytes received per second on this network interface.	Each network card	This value should remain relatively consistent and reflect average network traffic being generated. Prolonged increases in this value may indicate that a process or server on the network segment is generating additional traffic and using potentially more bandwidth.

Table 6-1. System Monitor objects

Object:Counter	Description	Instance	Threshold Suggestions
Physical Disk:% Disk Time	This represents the amount of time the disk is engaged in servicing read/write requests.	Each physical disk	Levels less than or equal to 80 percent generally represent acceptable system performance.
Physical Disk:Current Disk Queue Length	This represents the number of read/ write requests currently waiting to be processed on the physical disk.	Each physical disk	Subtract from this value the number of spindles on the disks. For example, a RAID device would have two or more spindles. The resulting value should be less than 2.
Process:% Processor Time	This represents the percentage of time spent by the processor(s) executing threads for the process selected.	_Total, or for each process currently running.	Use with Processor:% Processor Time to determine which SMS process in particular is utilizing processor time, and to what extent.
Processor:% Processor Time	This represents the percentage of time spent by the processor or processors executing nonidle threads.	_Total, or each installed processor	Levels less than or equal to 80 percent generally represent acceptable system performance.
SQL Server:Cache Manager:Cache Hit Ratio	This represents how often SQL Server requests could be resolved from the SQL Server cache rather than having to query the database directly.	N/A	This value should be high— 98 percent or greater, which indicates efficient and responsive processing of SQL queries.
System:Processor Queue Length	This represents the number of threads waiting to be processed.	N/A	There should generally be no more than two requests waiting to be processed. Use this object while also monitoring the *SMS Executive Thread States*.
Thread:Context Switches/sec	This represents the number of context switched between threads, such as one thread requesting information from another or yielding to a higher priority thread.	_Total/_Total	The lower the value, the better.

These and other System Monitor objects and counters are meant to be used together to determine overall system performance as well as to track down problem processes and potential resource bottlenecks.

As I've said earlier, you can't perform effective problem or trend analysis of a system if you don't have statistics relating to so-called "normal" performance of that system. To get this data, you should create and save chart information during periods of "normal" and peak performance. This gives you the baseline data you need to begin with. You can create these baselines by saving them as System Monitor logs.

Creating a System Monitor Log

To create a System Monitor log, complete the following steps:

1. Start the Performance console from the Administrative Tools group.

2. Expand Performance Logs And Alerts in the console tree and select Counter Logs.

3. Right-click Counter Logs and choose New Log Settings to display the New Log Settings dialog box shown in Figure 6-4.

Figure 6-4. *The New Log Settings Dialog box.*

4. Enter a name for your log file and then click OK to display the log Properties dialog box shown in Figure 6-5.

5. Use the Add button to add objects and counters to the log just as you did in the section entitled "Creating a System Monitor Chart" earlier in this chapter.

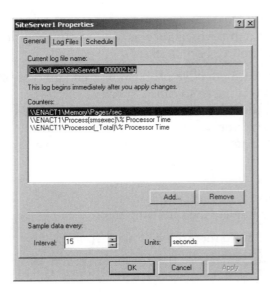

Figure 6-5. *The log Properties dialog box for the SiteServer1 log.*

6. In the Log Files tab shown in Figure 6-6, select a location to store the log file, a file name, file type, and size limit.

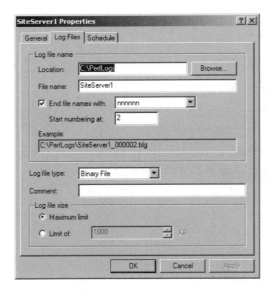

Figure 6-6. *The Log Files tab settings.*

7. Use the settings in the Schedule tab, shown in Figure 6-7, to determine when System Monitor should begin to write information to the log, when it should stop, and whether another log file or command option should run.

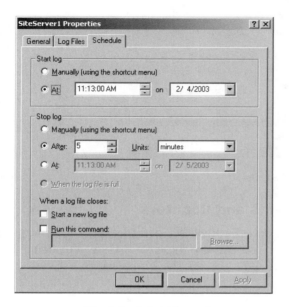

Figure 6-7. *The Schedule Tab settings.*

8. Click OK to schedule the log.

Viewing a Log File

After the log has run, you can view the associated data in the performance window by selecting System Monitor in the console tree and clicking the View Log File Data button (the disk drive icon). Navigate to the location of the log file you created, select it, and choose Open to display the collected data in a static chart, as shown in Figure 6-8.

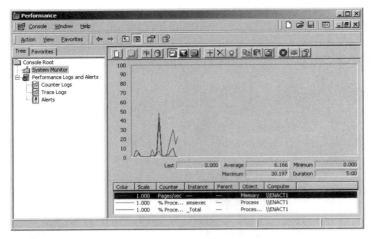

Figure 6-8. *Static chart from a log file.*

SMS 2003 Specific Objects and Counters

When SMS 2003 is installed, Setup adds a set of SMS-specific objects and counters to the System Monitor. You can use these to assess performance levels of your SMS site system. Table 6-2 outlines these objects and some of their more useful counters for you.

Table 6-2. SMS-specific System Monitor counters

Object	Counter	Description
SMS Discovery Data Manager	Total DDRs Processed	The total number of Discovery Data Records (DDRs) processed by the Discovery Data Manager during the current session. This number should generally be high.
SMS Executive Thread States	Running Thread Count	When using the _Total instance, this indicates the total number of SMS threads currently running. By scrolling through the instances, you can assess thread count on a thread-by-thread basis. You can also monitor sleeping threads—blocked by *Yield*()—and yielding threads—ready to run but not allowed due to a need to limit running threads.
SMS In-Memory Queues	Total Objects Dequeued	This represents the total number of objects added to the queue by a specific component since the component last started. You can monitor numbers for each component by selecting it in the instance list.
SMS Inventory Data Loader	Total MIFs Processed	This represents the total number of inventory records processed by the Inventory Data Loader during the current session. You can also monitor the number of Management Information Format (MIF) files processed per minute and the number of bad MIF files processed.

Table 6-2.   SMS-specific System Monitor counters

Object	Counter	Description
SMS Software Inventory Processor	Total SINVs Processed	This represents the total number of software inventory records processed by the Software Inventory Processor during the current session. You can also monitor the number of software inventory records processed per minute and the number of bad records processed.
SMS Standard Sender	Sending Thread Count	This represents the number of threads currently sending to a destination. You can monitor the total number or monitor on a site-by-site basis by selecting the appropriate instance.
	Average Bytes/sec	This represents the average throughput of the sender. This number, generally, should be high. You can also monitor total bytes attempted, failed, and sent to establish baselines for the sender.
SMS Status Messages	Processed/sec	This represents the number of status messages that the Status Message Manager has processed per second. Depending on the instance selected, you can monitor the total number of status messages processed or break it down between those processed from the In Memory Queue and from the Status Manager's Inbox.

Some of these objects are informational, providing additional data for you to help you understand how a component is working. They can all by and large assist you in establishing how resources are being utilized on your SMS servers. Remember, the idea here is to use these SMS specific objects and counters along with the traditional objects and counters used to monitor processor, memory, disk, and network performance to establish a baseline of normal activity on your SMS servers and then use that baseline to help you determine when performance is outside the norm and when it becomes unacceptable.

> **Note**   Disk performance object counters are *not* enabled by default on Windows systems. This is to reduce the number of resources monitored and the overhead needed to monitor them. If you create a chart using disk objects such as Logical Disk and Physical Disk, no data will be created until you enable disk counters. To do this, enter the following command at a Windows command prompt: *diskperf -y*. You'll need to restart the system in question before the disk counters are enabled. Enter *diskperf -n* to disable the disk counters when you're finished, again remembering to restart your system for the change to take effect.

More Info System Monitor contains additional features and options. For a more complete discussion of System Monitor, refer to the online Help files included with Windows. Also, see Chapter 9, "Capacity Planning for SMS," in the *Microsoft Systems Management Server 2003 Concepts, Planning, and Installation Guide* included as part of the SMS 2003 documentation, for a complete list of SMS objects and counters and for a thorough discussion of performance-related issues to consider when planning your SMS site.

Network Trace

Some of you might work with an SNMP management application. These types of applications are used to map out and monitor IP-addressable hardware devices such as routers, switches, and printers. Often they can provide you with a graphical map of what your network infrastructure looks like.

The Network Trace utility is similar in that it can help you map out and monitor your SMS site system structure—kind of like "SNMP-lite." This utility provides the following:

- A graphical map of the relationship between the SMS Site Server and its site systems, including subnets

- A graphical view of the assigned role of each site system

- A polling mechanism to check the running status of SMS components on each site system

- A polling mechanism to check the connectivity between site systems

You can access this utility through the SMS Administrator Console by navigating to the Site Systems folder under Site Settings and right-clicking any site system. Choose All Tasks and then Start Network Trace. A site map similar to that shown in Figure 6-9 is generated.

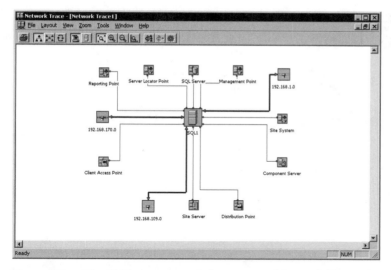

Figure 6-9. *The SMS site system infrastructure Network Trace view.*

In this particular mapping, there is only one site system, called SQL1. We can see that it is has been assigned the site system roles of site server, client access point, distribution point, management point, reporting point, and server locator point. It's also the server running SQL and is part of the subnet 192.168.1.0.

The Network Trace interface is fairly easy to navigate. You can, of course, print the map, which is actually quite convenient, especially for documentation purposes. You can switch between Trace view and Site view. Trace view is the default view, as displayed in Figure 6-9. Site view reconfigures the map to show all the elements of the site. You can also zoom in and out to view the map more easily or with more detail.

The monitoring aspect of this utility comes on the Tools menu. There are two connectivity check options: Ping All Servers And Routers and Ping Selected Servers And Routers. Either option generates a network connectivity check to determine whether the site systems can be accessed across the network. The result is a green check mark on top of each site system that was successfully accessed, as shown in Figure 6-10, and a red X on top of those that couldn't be accessed.

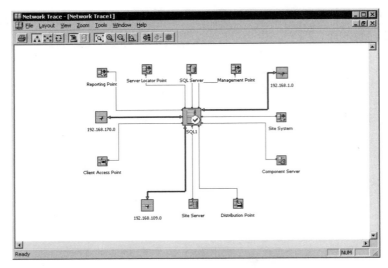

Figure 6-10. *The Trace View displaying site systems successfully accessed across the network.*

There is also a component check option. By clicking a given site system in the Network Trace map window and then selecting Tools, Poll Components of Selected Server(s), a Component Poller window similar to that shown in Figure 6-11 is displayed. In this window you can click a specific component or several components and then click Poll Selected to check the running status of particular SMS components on that particular site system, or you can check the running status of all components by clicking Poll All. Figure 6-11 shows the result of clicking Poll All. The status of each component is listed along with the last time it was polled, the name of the site system, and whether the component is a service or a thread.

In this example you can see that there are two components SMS_NETWORK_ DISCOVERY and SMS_SITE_BACKUP—that indicate a status of "Stopped." This doesn't necessarily indicate a problem with the component. In this case these components run at predetermined schedules and at the time of the poll were simply not scheduled to run. As you might be discerning at this point, a component's status as displayed here might or might not be indicative of a problem with the component. To get to that next level of information, the savvy SMS administrator would check the status messages for those components and perhaps the log files to determine whether a problem exists.

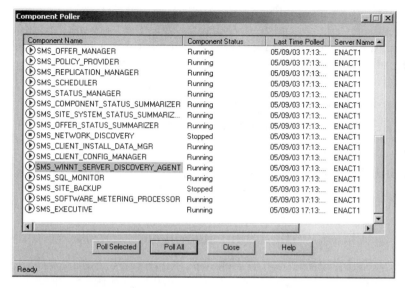

Figure 6-11.   *Network Trace Component Poller dialog box.*

But then, the purpose of this utility is to convey a high-level view of the status and mapping of an SMS site and its site systems. It's one more tool—a neat one, at that—available for SMS administrators as they balance day-to-day administration with the wider issues of site structure, connectivity, and interaction.

Network Monitor

The Microsoft Network Monitor utility version 2.1 that comes with SMS 2003 is yet another tool for the SMS administrator that provides a mechanism for analyzing and monitoring network traffic among computers in your network. It's similar in function to other more expensive hardware-based tools currently available in the market. It's used to identify heavily used subnets, routers, and WAN connections, recognize bottlenecks and potential bottlenecks, and develop trends to optimize the network infrastructure and placement of computers and servers, and, in our particular case, SMS site systems.

Network Monitor, by default, captures network traffic that passes through the NIC on the computer running Network Monitor. This means that, by default, Network Monitor captures only network traffic that's generated on the same network segment as the computer running Network Monitor. If you want to monitor traffic on a different network segment, you can do so by using Network

Monitor to capture traffic passing through the NIC of a remote computer on that other network segment. The remote computer must have the Network Monitor driver installed on it. You can install the Network Monitor driver like any other network protocol through the properties dialog box of the local Network Connections Control Panel program on that computer.

Network Monitor 2.1 provides the following functions:

- Capture, filter, and display network frames
- Edit and forward frames
- Monitor traffic for remote computers
- Determine which users and protocols used the most bandwidth
- Determine location of routers
- Resolve device names to Media Access Control (MAC) addresses

This version of Network Monitor also includes "*experts*." These aren't little network gurus that come popping out of the box. They are post-capture analysis tools that can facilitate the administrator's understanding of the data collected. Table 6-3 describes these experts and what they're designed to accomplish.

Table 6-3. Network Monitor experts

Expert	Description
Average Server Response Time	Identifies the average time each server in the capture took to respond to requests and the number of clients interacting with each during the capture
Property Distribution	Calculates protocol statistics for a specified protocol and property
Protocol Coalesce Tool	Combines all the frames of a single transaction that might have been fragmented into a single frame and creates a new capture file using this information
Protocol Distribution	Calculates which protocols generated the most traffic during the capture session
TCP Retransmit	Identifies which Transmission Control Protocol (TCP) frames were transmitted more than once during the capture, indicating congestion or connectivity issues
Top Users	Identifies the senders and recipients of frames that generated the most traffic during the capture session

Using Network Monitor

In order to run Network Monitor 2.1, you and your computer must meet the following requirements:

- The computer is running Windows 2000 Server or later.

- You must have local Administrator privileges on the computer running Network Monitor 2.1 or local Administrator privileges on any remote computer that will be monitored using the Network Monitor Driver, or both.

- The computer has a NIC that supports promiscuous mode (p-mode). This allows the NIC to receive any and all frames that pass through it on that network segment.

- You have already installed Network Monitor 2.1 (run setup from the Netmon\i386 folder on the SMS 2003 CD).

Given that these requirements are met, you can begin using Network Monitor. This tool has its own online help, which can assist you with the more detailed uses of the product and which I highly recommend you use for future reference. However, in this chapter I want to visit some of the more common uses and features. Let's review some fundamentals for using Network Monitor.

Capturing Data

The most fundamental purpose for Network Monitor is to capture network traffic for analysis and troubleshooting.

To capture network traffic using Microsoft Network Monitor, complete the following steps:

1. Start Network Monitor from the Microsoft Network Monitor program group.

2. The Network Monitor capture window is displayed as shown in Figure 6-12.

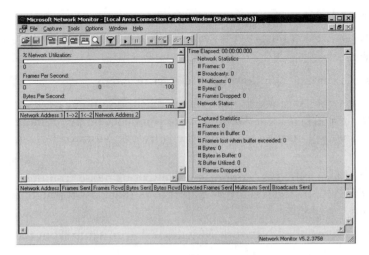

Figure 6-12. *The Network Monitor capture window.*

3. Choose Start from the Capture menu. The captured frames will be evident in each section of the Network Monitor capture window.

4. When you have captured enough data, choose Stop from the Capture menu to end the capture session. You can then view statistics or save the captured data as a file for viewing individual frames later.

   Alternatively, choose Stop and View from the Capture menu to end the capture session and immediately view individual frames that were captured.

Without any further filtering, all frames generated on the network and received by the monitored computer will be captured and potentially saved and displayed. This can add up quickly, as any network administrator can attest. The capture file's default size is 1 MB. As the file reaches capacity, it drops the oldest data and adds the newest. You can use filters to manage the amount of data that's collected in the capture file, and you can change the capture file's default size.

Frequently, you might be interested in the traffic generated between two specific computers—for example, between the Site Server and the server running SQL that's hosting the SMS database, or between the Site Server and its site systems, or between an SMS client and a client access point (CAP). You can easily accomplish this by adding a filter before initiating a capture session. Filters can be based on protocol(s) used, specific frame property, such as Service Advertising Protocol (SAP) or Etype, or by the originating or destination address. You can also filter based on network segment if you're capturing remotely.

To establish a capture filter, complete the following steps:

1. Start the Network Monitor.

2. Select Filter from the Capture menu to display the Capture Filter dialog box, as shown in Figure 6-13.

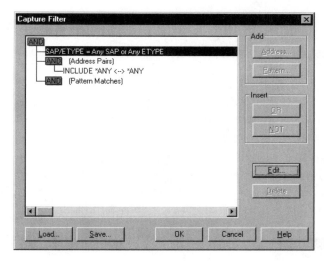

Figure 6-13. *Capture Filter dialog box.*

3. Select the property you wish to filter against.

   If you choose SAP/ETYPE, you can then click Edit to specify the protocols that will be captured during the capture session, as shown in Figure 6-14. By default, all protocols are enabled.

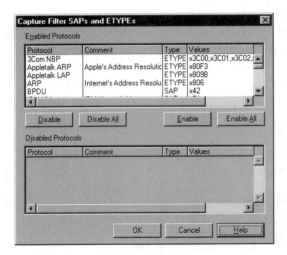

Figure 6-14. *Capture Filter SAPs And ETYPES dialog box.*

If you choose Include under Address Pairs, you can click Edit or Address to modify the computers monitored from the default of ANY to a specific set of addresses.

If you choose Pattern Matches, you can click Pattern to specify that only frames that contain a particular pattern of ASCII or hexadecimal data be captured. The pattern can start at the beginning of the frame or at a specified offset. The Pattern Match dialog box is shown in Figure 6-15.

Figure 6-15. *Pattern Match dialog box.*

4. Choose OK. Then start your capture session. Only frames that meet your criteria will be collected during the capture session.

Establishing Capture Triggers

You can also configure Network Monitor to perform an action when the capture file fills to a certain level or when a particular pattern match is detected. The trigger can sound an audible signal, stop capturing data at that point, or execute a command line program or batch file.

To establish a capture trigger, follow these steps:

1. Start Network Monitor.

2. Select Trigger from the Capture menu to display the Capture Trigger dialog box, as shown in Figure 6-16. By default, no triggers are enabled.

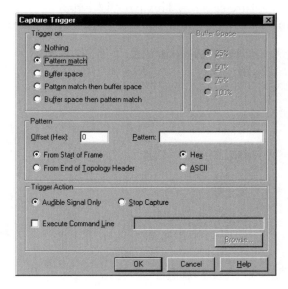

Figure 6-16.   *Capture Trigger dialog box.*

3. Select the type of trigger that you want to enable. Buffer Space refers to the filled size of the capture file and Pattern Match refers to those frames that contain a particular pattern of ASCII or hexadecimal data to be captured. The pattern can start at the beginning of the frame or at a specified offset.

   If you choose a buffer trigger, select the desired percent of buffer space.

   If you choose a pattern match trigger, enter the hexadecimal or ASCII text pattern that you need to match and an offset value, if necessary.

4. Select a Trigger Action. These are fairly self-explanatory. One example of a command line action might be a net send command to the SMS Administrator noting that a capture trigger event occurred, that is, net send SMSAdmin1 Capture Trigger Event Occurred.

5. Choose OK.

Viewing Captured Data

When you stop a capture session, you can view capture statistics in the Capture Window, an example of which is displayed in Figure 6-17. This window is divided into four sections sometimes called "panes." The top left pane, referred to as the Graph pane, represents five different graphic charts of the frames generated and received during the capture session. This pane is dynamic and only active during the capture session itself. The data monitored is self-explanatory.

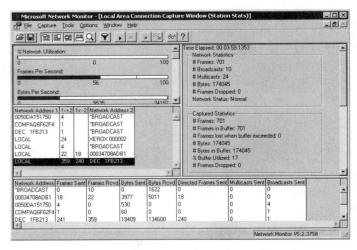

Figure 6-17. *Network Monitor Capture window, showing results of capturing data.*

The middle left pane, called the Session Statistics pane, displays a summary of the frames sent and received between this computer and any other specified computers. In the example in Figure 6-17, 18 frames were sent from a computer with MAC address 00034708ADB1 to the LOCAL server and 22 frames were sent form the LOCAL server to the other computer.

The bottom pane, called the Station Statistics pane, displays more detailed frame information on a computer-by-computer basis, such as frames sent and received, bytes sent and received, directed frames, broadcast frames, and multicast frames.

Finally, the right pane, referred to as the Total Statistics pane, displays summary information about the capture session as a whole. These are divided into network statistics, captured frames statistics, per second statistics, network card statistics, and network card error statistics (frames dropped, CRC errors).

You might have noticed from Figure 6-17 that Network Monitor identifies source and target computers largely by their MAC address. This is the network card address, of course. You can make this screen, as well as the frames view, friendlier to read by helping Network Monitor to resolve the MAC address to a NetBIOS name. You can accomplish this by completing the following steps:

1. Choose Addresses from the Capture menu.

2. In the Address Database dialog box, as shown in Figure 6-18, click Add to display the Address Information dialog box, as shown in Figure 6-19.

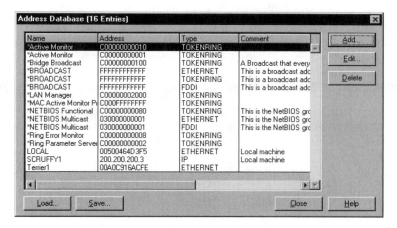

Figure 6-18.   *Address Database dialog box.*

Figure 6-19.   *Address Information dialog box.*

3. Enter the NetBIOS name, or whatever friendly name you would like, in the Name text box. Enter the MAC address in the Address text box, and select a network type from the Type drop-down list if necessary.

4. Click OK.

5. You can then close the Address Database screen to use the name values for this session or save them to facilitate viewing of future captures.

However, although this statistical information can certainly help identify the amount of traffic generated, there are still the frames themselves to view. By viewing the frames that were captured, you can understand the type of traffic that was generated and which frames are associated with certain kinds of activity on various servers. For example, when did the CAP forward discovery data to the Site Server, and how much traffic was generated as a result?

You can view frames by opening a saved capture file or by choosing Stop and View when ending a capture session. Figure 6-20 shows a sample capture file of individual frames. In this view you can see the frames generated and received between the two servers Scruffy1 (the LOCAL server) and Terrier1.

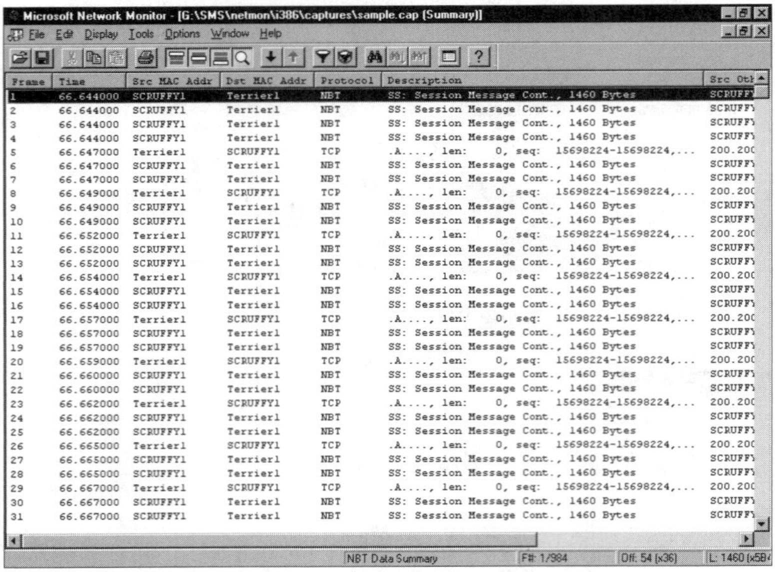

Figure 6-20. *A sample capture file showing individual frames.*

This screen begins with a frame number, a time offset, the source and destination MAC addresses (which could be resolved to names as they are here), the protocol type of the frame, a brief description of the frame, and the MAC address resolved to a NetBIOS name or IP address.

Each frame is "viewable" in that if you double-click a frame, you can view the frame's contents. Figure 6-21 shows one individual frame's contents. At the top is the Summary pane, a tiled view of the capture file where we started.

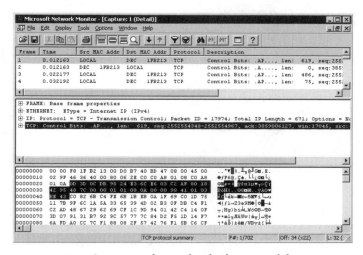

Figure 6-21. *Contents of an individual captured frame.*

The middle pane is the Detail pane, showing us an expandable view of the contents of the frame, including its size, Ethernet information such as MAC address, IP information, such as IP address, and SMB information, such as the frame offset and flags if the frame is part of a fragmented group of frames, and the frame data. The bottom pane is the Hexadecimal pane, displaying the frame contents both in hex and in text where possible.

Using Network Monitor Experts

The Network Monitor Experts included with Network Monitor 2.1 are post-capture analysis tools designed to help facilitate the understanding of the data collected. The experts were outlined previously in Table 6-3.

You can enable the experts by following these steps:

1. Open a capture file.

2. Select Experts from the Tools menu. The Network Monitor Experts dialog box is displayed, as shown in Figure 6-22.

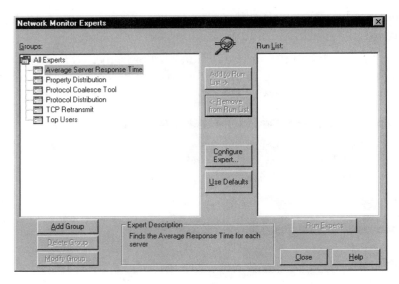

Figure 6-22. *Network Monitor Experts dialog box.*

3. Click the expert you would like to enable, such as Average Server Response Time, and choose Configure Expert, as shown in Figure 6-23. In this case you can add or delete Transmission Control Protocol/Internet Protocol (TCP/IP) port numbers and IPX socket numbers. Other experts will offer other configuration choices.

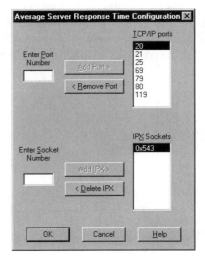

Figure 6-23. *Configure Expert dialog box.*

4. Click Add To Run List.

5. When you're ready to run the expert, choose Run Experts.

6. When the expert has completed processing, an event screen is displayed similar to Figure 6-24 showing the information you requested. In this example all experts were selected to run. You can access the result of each by selecting its respective tab in the viewer.

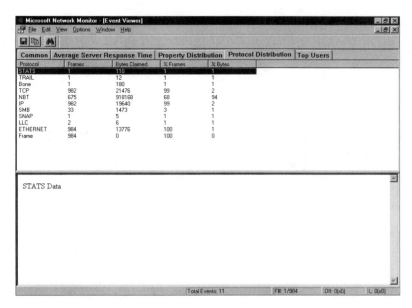

Figure 6-24.   *Expert results screen.*

Summary

With the completion of this chapter and the previous chapter, you should have a full set of tools to help you understand, monitor, analyze, and troubleshoot your SMS site and site systems. This particular chapter reintroduced you to System Monitor as a server optimization tool and Network Monitor as its network counterpart, as well as the Network Trace tool.

The next four chapters will concentrate on the discovery of resources in your SMS site and—at last!—the installation of clients, inventory collection, and remote control services.

Part II
Resource Discovery, Client Installation, and Remote Control

Chapter 7
Resource Discovery

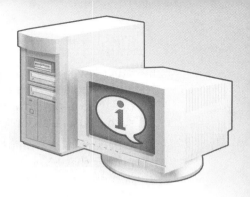

Now that our SMS site has been implemented and our monitoring, analysis, and troubleshooting tools are ready and at our disposal, it's time to begin adding resources and clients to our site. After all, we can't use any of the neat features we've been talking about—package delivery, remote control, software metering—unless we identify and install valid Microsoft Systems Management Server (SMS) 2003 clients. In Part II we'll focus on discovery methods and client installation and look at two specific client management options—inventory collection and remote control.

The installation process, as we'll see in Chapter 8, "Client Installation Methods," consists of discovering a client, assigning it to an SMS site, and then installing SMS client components on that computer. In this chapter we'll look specifically at the resource discovery methods and process and Discovery Data Manager.

Overview

When we talk about the SMS 2003 database, we're generally referring to the population of client computers in our environment that we want to manage. These clients are probably the most significant resources that we deal with in our SMS sites on a day-to-day basis. In fact, with SMS 1.2 and earlier, you really couldn't do anything at all unless the client computer was not only "discovered" and installed, but also inventoried into the SMS database.

With SMS 2003, our computer clients are still our most significant resource. However, the processes of discovering, installing, and inventorying these clients are now separate and distinct functions. For example, it's no longer necessary to complete an inventory of a client before an SMS administrator can initiate a Remote Tools session with that client or advertise a program to it. Indeed, a client computer can be discovered without ever being installed.

In addition to discovering client computers, we can also discover other resources and add them to the SMS database. These other resources include user accounts and global groups from a Windows domain account database, other site systems, routers, hubs, switches, network printers, and any other IP-addressable devices on the network. They could include mainframe computers or UNIX workstations. SMS 2003 can also discover Active Directory objects such as users, groups, and computers.

Of course, we won't be able to send a package of TrueType fonts to a network printer that SMS discovers—not yet, anyway. But we can know that the printer is there and make it part of the database of information about our network. More significantly, unlike in earlier versions of SMS, we now have the ability to advertise programs not only to clients, but also to users and groups. As an SMS administrator, having access to those two new resources might become as important to you as your SMS client computers.

When an SMS discovery method discovers a resource, a record is created for it and included in the SMS database. This record is called a discovery data record (DDR), and the DDR file generated by the discovery method has a .DDR extension. The information that is "discovered" varies depending on the resource, but it might include such data as the NetBIOS name of a computer, IP address and IP subnet of a computer or device, user name, SMS GUID, operating system, MAC address, Windows account domain, and so on.

The seven methods that can be used to discover resources are

- Windows User Account Discovery
- Windows User Group Discovery
- Network Discovery
- Heartbeat Discovery
- Active Directory System Discovery
- Active Directory User Discovery
- Active Directory System Group Discovery

These discovery methods are configurable by the SMS administrator. SMS also creates DDRs for site server and site system computers when you assign a site system role to that computer, as well as when inventory is collected from an SMS client. This method of discovery is automatic and not configurable.

Note In SMS 2.0, when a site server or site system was automatically discovered, the SMS client software was also automatically installed on that computer. SMS 2003 no longer automatically installs SMS client software on a site server or site system unless you've also enabled the Client Push Installation method described in Chapter 8.

When a DDR is created, SMS assigns that resource a GUID to distinguish it from other resources in the database. Depending on the discovery method chosen, discovery records are periodically regenerated to keep the discovery data up-to-date in the database and to verify that the resource is still a valid resource within the site.

Recall that when you install SMS using the Custom Setup option, none of the discovery methods is enabled except for Heartbeat Discovery, which is set to run on a client once a week, and the automatic site system and inventory discovery mentioned earlier. Therefore, the SMS administrator must determine which methods to use and how to configure them. When SMS is installed using the Express Setup option, however, all discovery methods are enabled by default except for Network Discovery.

> **Tip**   Table 2-4 in Chapter 2, "Primary Site Installation," lists the SMS 2003 features and components that are installed or enabled during Express and Custom setup and their main default values.

Resource Discovery Methods

In this section we'll examine the individual discovery methods. You'll learn how to configure each discovery method if applicable, the mechanics involved in carrying out the discovery process, the network traffic generated, and the elements you might need to troubleshoot when you work with each discovery method.

> **More Info**   For a detailed discussion of planning issues to consider when choosing a discovery method, see Chapter 10 in the *Microsoft Systems Management Server 2003 Concepts, Planning, and Installation Guide* included on the SMS CD, and available from the SMS Web site (*http://www.microsoft.com/smserver*) and through Microsoft TechNet.

Windows User Account and User Group Discovery

The Windows User Account Discovery and Windows User Group Discovery methods are designed to discover domain user accounts and domain global group accounts and to add them as resources to the SMS database. When you enable either of these discovery methods, you can specify which Windows domains to poll for user and group account information. A corresponding DDR is generated for each user and group account discovered. By default, these resources will be added to the All Users and All User Groups collections, which you can view through the SMS Administrator Console.

The primary purpose in enabling either of these discovery methods is to provide the SMS administrator with an alternative target for advertising programs through SMS. Although we haven't discussed package distribution in great length yet, we have talked briefly about the advertisement process. (Chapter 12, "Package Distribution and Management," covers the details of package distribution.) As noted in Chapter 1, "Overview," in SMS 2003 a package reaches a target destination by advertising a program associated with that package. This program might be a Typical installation of Microsoft Office, for example, or a Custom installation of Microsoft Project. Programs are always advertised to collections. If you want a specific group of SMS clients to receive a particular program, you must create a collection that contains those clients and then advertise the program to that collection.

Real World **Packages for Discovered Users or User Groups**

The beauty of SMS 2003 in the context of package distribution is that you can also advertise programs to collections that contain discovered users or user groups from a Windows domain or from Active Directory directory service. This gives the SMS administrator an alternative target for certain packages. For example, suppose you have a budget spreadsheet that must be distributed and available to all finance department users, regardless of which computer they're logged into. If you've discovered those users through SMS or discovered a Windows global group named Finance that contains these users, you can create an SMS collection with those users or that group as its members. You can then create a package that contains the spreadsheet and advertise it to your user or group collection. Whenever a member of that collection checks for advertisements on whatever SMS client the member happens to log in on, that spreadsheet will be made available. Furthermore, if the collection gains any new members, those users (or group members) will automatically receive all advertisements targeted to that collection.

Enabling Windows User Account and User Group Discovery

To enable the Windows User Account Discovery and Windows User Group Discovery methods, follow these steps:

1. In the SMS Administrator Console, navigate to the site's Site Settings folder, expand it, and then select the Discovery Methods folder.

2. Right-click Windows User Account Discovery or Windows User Group Discovery, as appropriate. The two procedures are essentially the same, so in this example we'll select Windows User Account Discovery.

Choose Properties from the context menu to display the Windows User Account Discovery Properties dialog box shown in Figure 7-1.

Figure 7-1. *The Windows User Account Discovery Properties dialog box.*

3. In the General tab, select the Enable Windows User Account Discovery check box (or Enable Windows User Group Discovery, if you're enabling the other discovery method).

4. Click the New button (the yellow star) in the Properties dialog box to add a Windows domain to the list for the discovery agent to poll. The New Domain dialog box appears, as shown in Figure 7-2.

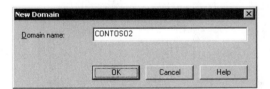

Figure 7-2. *The New Domain dialog box.*

Enter the name of the Windows domain for which you want to discover user accounts and then click OK.

5. Select the Polling Schedule tab, shown in Figure 7-3. Notice that you can choose to have SMS run the discovery method as soon as possible by selecting the option Run Discovery As Soon As Possible or set a specific time for discovery to run.

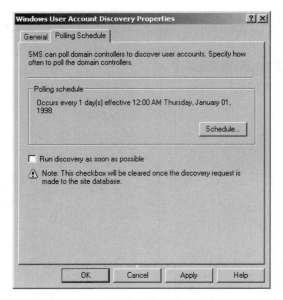

Figure 7-3.   *The Polling Schedule tab.*

6. To set a specific time for discovery to run, click the Schedule button to display the Schedule dialog box shown in Figure 7-4.

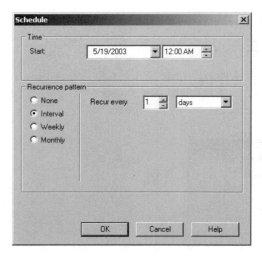

Figure 7-4.   *The Schedule dialog box.*

7. Define the frequency with which the User Account Discovery Agent or User Group Discovery Agent should poll the specified domains for user accounts, and then click OK.

8. Click OK to begin the discovery process.

Windows User Account and User Group Discovery Process

The discovery process for these two methods is fairly straightforward as SMS processes go. When you enable either method, the corresponding discovery agent on the site server makes a secure connection to the Primary Domain Controller (PDC) emulator of the Windows 2000 or higher domain you specified and according to the schedule you specified when you enabled the discovery method.

The discovery agent enumerates the user accounts or global groups in the Windows domains and generates a DDR for each one it discovers. These DDRs are written directly to Discovery Data Manager's inbox on the site server (SMS\Inboxes\Ddm.box). Discovery Data Manager in turn updates the SMS database with the new discovery information. User accounts are automatically added as discovered resources to the All Users collection, viewable through the SMS Administrator Console, and user group resources are automatically added to the All User Groups collection. To view this discovery data, right-click the user resource under All Users in the SMS Administrator Console and then choose Properties from the context menu. A sample user resource discovery record is shown in Figure 7-5.

Figure 7-5.   *A sample user resource discovery record Properties dialog box.*

In terms of network traffic, each user and group that is enumerated generates, on average, 2 KB of traffic. If your Windows account database contains, say, 10,000 users and 100 groups, you'll experience around 22 MB of network traffic to generate the corresponding DDRs. The frequency at which this traffic is generated, of course, depends on the polling schedule you've defined. Remember, too, that for this discovery method, SMS will poll the domain controller that has been assigned the PDC emulator role. That computer might or might not be on the same network subnet as the SMS site server, and you should account for the additional cross-subnet traffic that will be generated. If your Windows account databases are relatively stable and rarely change, you don't have to poll frequently, and network traffic relating to user or user group discovery will be largely a one-time experience. On the other hand, if your Windows account database is volatile, you might need to enumerate users and groups more frequently, and, of course, you'll generate a corresponding amount of network traffic.

Each agent generates status messages when it starts, stops, and generates DDRs. You can view these status messages through the SMS Administrator Console. Look for message IDs in the 410x range for SMS_NT_USER_GROUP_DISCOVERY_AGENT and message IDs in the 430x range for SMS_NT_USER_DISCOVERY_AGENT. The sample status message window shown in Figure 7-6 tells us that in this case 24 Windows user accounts were enumerated and discovered from the Windows domain. These agents also write detailed processing information to their respective log files (Ntusrdis.log and Ntug_dis.log) if you've enabled logging through the SMS Service Manager tool in the SMS Administrator Console.

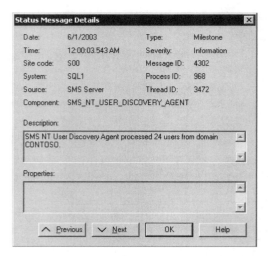

Figure 7-6. *A sample status message window and the Status Message Details dialog box.*

Checkpoints

The main problems you might encounter with these discovery methods have to do with access. The SMS Service account or the site server's computer account must have Administrator rights on the PDC emulator that it's polling for resources. If this condition isn't met, user and group discovery will fail. Other possible problems, of course, are that the discovery agent hasn't been enabled or that the scheduled polling time hasn't yet been encountered.

Network Discovery

The Network Discovery method is designed to provide the SMS administrator with the means of discovering any network resources that are IP addressable, which means that you can discover not only computers, but also printers, routers, bridges, and so on. The discovery that takes place using this method can be far-reaching. You can discover these resources on the local subnet in which the site server resides, or you can discover resources throughout your enterprise network using DHCP, SNMP, and other mechanisms. Resources discovered using this method are automatically added to the All Systems collection, which is viewable through the SMS Administrator Console.

Network Discovery includes the following information as part of the discovery record:

- SMS GUID
- NetBIOS Name
- IP Addresses
- IP Subnets
- IPX Addresses
- IPX Network Numbers
- Last Logon User Domain
- Last Logon User Name
- MAC Addresses
- Name
- Resource Domain
- User Domain
- Operating System Name and Version
- Resource ID
- SMS Assigned Sites
- SNMP Community Name
- System Roles

This discovery method can be useful in a variety of contexts. It can be used, for example, to find computers that could become SMS clients. When a computer is discovered, its IP address and subnet mask are included in the discovery record. This information can help you identify where your potential SMS clients are located and how they are distributed among the subnets, enabling you to formulate a more specific plan for locating and implementing your SMS sites, site servers, and site systems.

You can also use this information to plan the best client installation method for implementing SMS 2003 on those computers. For example, if you plan to use the Client Push Installation method, described in Chapter 8, you need to have first discovered the clients. You can use Network Discovery to create the DDRs for clients that will be installed using the Client Push Installation method.

Network Discovery can make your Network Trace map more meaningful. As we saw in Chapter 6, "System Performance and Network Analysis," the Network Trace utility provides a graphical mapping of your SMS site structure showing the routes between site systems and site servers. This mapping can include any routers, switches, and the like that the route between systems encounters.

If you don't enable Network Discovery to discover these links between systems, they will be represented in the Network Trace window as "clouds." The Network Trace map is built based on the DDRs that have been generated for site systems and devices on the network. Again, since Network Trace provides a means of testing connectivity, you can identify problem links more easily if all possible routes between systems are displayed in the Network Trace window. As you can see, you can gain some unique benefits by enabling the Network Discovery method.

Enabling Network Discovery

Like the other discovery methods, Network Discovery is enabled through the SMS Administrator Console. To enable Network Discovery, follow these steps:

1. Expand the site's Site Settings folder and then select the Discovery Methods folder.

2. Right-click Network Discovery and choose Properties from the context menu to display the Network Discovery Properties dialog box shown in Figure 7-7.

3. In the General tab, select the Enable Network Discovery check box.

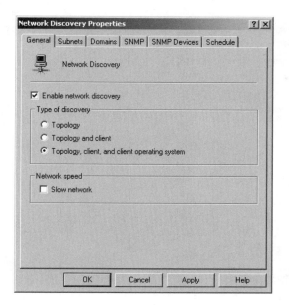

Figure 7-7. *The Network Discovery Properties dialog box.*

4. Specify the type of discovery you want. Selecting the Topology option will cause Network Discovery to discover IP-addressable resources such as subnets and routers using SNMP. (You would also configure options in the Subnets, SNMP, SNMP Devices, and DHCP tabs, as we'll see shortly.) The Topology And Client option additionally discovers computers and resources such as printers and gateways using SNMP, DHCP, and the Windows Browser. Topology, Client, And Client Operating System also picks up the computer's operating system name and version using SNMP, DHCP, Windows Browser, and Windows Networking calls.

Note   The DHCP tab is available only if your site is running in standard security mode.

5. Select the Slow Network check box for networks with speeds less than 64 Kbps. This option will cause Network Discovery to decrease the number of outstanding SNMP sessions it generates by doubling SNMP time-outs.

6. Select the Subnets tab, shown in Figure 7-8. Here you can add, enable, and disable the subnets you want Network Discovery to search. By default, Network Discovery will search the local subnet in which the site server is a member. If you want to ignore that subnet, clear the Search Local Subnets check box.

Figure 7-8. *The Subnets tab.*

Network Discovery displays the subnets it discovered during each previous search. As it discovers the subnets, it marks them with a lock to indicate that they can't be modified or deleted—in fact, subnets discovered by Network Discovery, unlike those you add yourself, can't be modified or deleted once they've been discovered. However, you can enable or disable those subnets that you want Network Discovery to search on subsequent cycles.

7. To add subnets to the list, click the New button to display the New Subnet Assignment dialog box shown in Figure 7-9. Provide the appropriate subnet address and subnet mask and click OK.

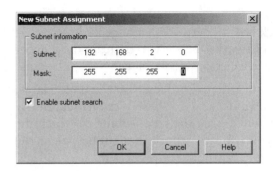

Figure 7-9. *The New Subnet Assignment dialog box.*

8. If you've selected a discovery type other than Topology in the General tab, select the Domains tab, shown in Figure 7-10, and enter the name of the Windows domain that you want to search for resources.

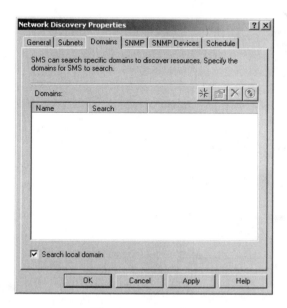

Figure 7-10.   *The Domains tab.*

By default, the local Windows domain to which the site server belongs is searched. If you want to ignore that domain, clear the Search Local Domain check box.

Note   Network Discovery can find any computer that you can find using Network Neighborhood to browse the network. Once it finds a computer, it still must obtain its IP address and will use one of the other methods (DHCP, SNMP, and so on) to do so. Network Discovery will ping each computer to determine whether it's active, find its subnet mask, and generate a DDR for it.

9. To add Windows domains to the list, click the New button to display the Domain Properties dialog box shown in Figure 7-11. Enter the appropriate domain name. The domain must be accessible through the network. By default, the Enable Domain Search check box is selected. This option enables Network Discovery in the domain. Click OK to close the dialog box.

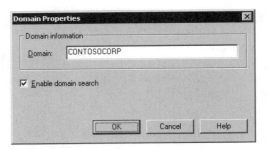

Figure 7-11. *The Domain Properties dialog box.*

10. Select the SNMP tab, shown in Figure 7-12, and specify the SNMP community you want Network Discovery to search.

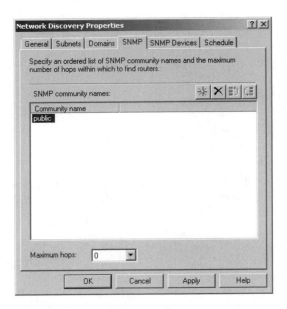

Figure 7-12. *The SNMP tab.*

11. To add SNMP communities, click the New button to display the New SNMP Community Name dialog box shown in Figure 7-13. Enter the appropriate community name and click OK to return to the SNMP tab. If you enter multiple communities, you can specify the order in which you want them searched by using the two Order buttons.

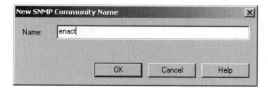

Figure 7-13.   *The New SNMP Community Name dialog box.*

Note   It's not necessary to have the SNMP Service installed on the site server performing Network Discovery. This discovery method uses its own SNMP stack to make requests and discover data.

12. Network Discovery attempts to access the local router to obtain IP addresses and data from the device. If the Maximum Hops value is set to 0, Network Discovery searches only the default gateway. You can set this value as high as 10. Each successive increment extends discovery to another set of routers. For example, setting Maximum Hops to 1 enables Network Discovery to search the default gateway and any routers connected to it.

13. Select the SNMP Devices tab (a companion to the SNMP tab) shown in Figure 7-14.

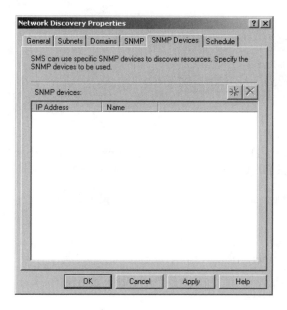

Figure 7-14.   *The SNMP Devices tab.*

In this tab you can identify specific SNMP devices that you want to discover by clicking the New button and supplying the IP address or name of the device. The SNMP devices can include routers, hubs, and token-ring media access units.

14. If your site is running standard security mode, you can select the DHCP tab, shown in Figure 7-15, and identify which Microsoft DHCP servers you want Network Discovery to query for a list of IP addresses leased to computers.

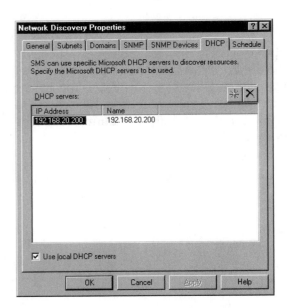

Figure 7-15. *The DHCP tab.*

If the site server is itself a DHCP client, Network Discovery automatically queries the site server's DHCP server. If you want to ignore that DHCP, clear the Use Local DHCP Servers check box.

Note The DHCP tab isn't displayed if you're running advanced security mode.

15. To add Microsoft DHCP servers to the list, click the New button and provide the appropriate subnet address or server name.

16. Select the Schedule tab, shown in Figure 7-16, and identify the frequency at which you want Network Discovery to run.

Figure 7-16.   *The Schedule tab.*

17. To add a new schedule, click New to display the Schedule dialog box, shown in Figure 7-17.

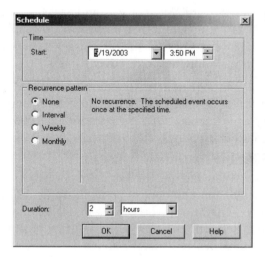

Figure 7-17.   *The Schedule dialog box.*

18. To modify a schedule's properties, click the Properties button (the hand holding a piece of paper) to display the same Schedule dialog box.

In the Schedule dialog box, enter the time you want discovery to begin. You can also specify a recurrence pattern. Selecting None directs Network Discovery to search only one time for resources. You might select this option as a first pass to find all subnets, for example. The other options direct Network Discovery to perform subsequent searches according to your specified schedule. Duration indicates the period of time Network Discovery has to complete its search for resources. On a local subnet, two hours might be sufficient. However, if you're performing a search of an enterprise network across several router hops with several thousand potential resources, you might need to increase this number so that Network Discovery has enough time to complete its search. If Network Discovery runs out of time, it will log a message to that effect and complete DDRs only for the part of the search that was completed.

19. Click OK twice to save your settings and initiate the Network Discovery process.

Network Discovery Process

The discovery process itself is once again fairly straightforward. Depending on the discovery options you enabled, Network Discovery will attempt to search for subnets, routers, computers, and other devices. It needs to retrieve an IP address and subnet mask for each resource in order to generate a DDR for it. Network Discovery uses the information it receives from DHCP servers and SNMP to communicate directly with a device, such as a router, and then uses the router's ipNetToMedia table and Router Interface table to obtain subnet masks. It also uses RIP, SNMP, and OSPF protocol multicast addresses to discover routers.

Network Discovery uses Windows Management Instrumentation (WMI) to store discovered resource information and generates DDRs based on this information. When Network Discovery generates a DDR, it writes the DDR to Discovery Data Manager's inbox (SMS\Inboxes\Ddm.box). Discovery Data Manager in turn adds the record to the SMS database.

Network Discovery is capable of discovering literally thousands of devices on your network, and in doing so, it can generate a fair amount of network traffic. For this reason, your choice of schedule will be significant. If you need to find large numbers of devices, you might opt to schedule Network Discovery to run during quiet periods on the network. And as suggested earlier, you might also need to increase the Duration value (shown in Figure 7-17) to accommodate processing of larger numbers of resources. Like the other discovery methods, Network Discovery generates status messages that you can view through the SMS Administrator Console. Figure 7-18 shows a representative set of messages generated by Network Discovery. Message IDs in the 13xx range relate specifically to the discovery of resources.

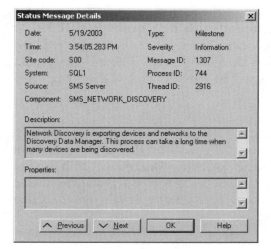

Figure 7-18.   *A sample Status Message Details dialog box.*

Also, if you've enabled logging for Network Discovery, more detailed information will be written to the Netdisc.log file.

Checkpoints

When you're performing a Topology, Client, And Client Operating System search, the operating system on Windows 95, Windows 98, and Windows Millennium Edition (Windows Me) clients will be returned only if file sharing has been enabled on those computers. In addition, the operating system will be returned as Windows 9x until the SMS client software has been installed, with the exception of Windows 95 clients, which aren't supported by SMS 2003.

Verify that you've identified not only the correct subnet address to search, but also the correct subnet mask. Network Discovery is more concerned with the subnet mask when retrieving device IP address information.

The All Systems collection displays discovered system resources. System resources include any IP-addressable device. Network Discovery also discovers logical networks and subnets. To view these resources, you'll need to create a query to display the logical networks and subnets that were discovered. Refer to Chapter 16, "Queries and Reports," for more information about creating queries in SMS 2003.

Heartbeat Discovery

Heartbeat Discovery is designed to keep DDRs up to date. This discovery method is significant because it ensures that resource records won't be accidentally aged out of the SMS database.

Heartbeat Discovery is installed as part of the SMS client installation and is used to keep existing DDRs up-to-date rather than to create new DDRs. By default, Heartbeat Discovery will run once a week but is configurable. However, even if you configure it to run less than once every 25 hours—the default client refresh cycle—the updated DDR will be reported no less than once every 25 hours.

Enabling Heartbeat Discovery

Heartbeat Discovery is enabled by default and generates DDRs from each client every seven days. If you choose to disable Heartbeat Discovery, you'll need to have enabled some other discovery method to keep the DDR information up-to-date. Furthermore, Heartbeat Discovery is active only on computers that have already been installed as SMS clients.

To configure Heartbeat Discovery, follow these steps:

1. In the SMS Administrator Console, expand the site's Site Settings folder and then select the Discovery Methods folder.

2. Right-click Heartbeat Discovery and choose Properties from the context menu to display the Heartbeat Discovery Properties dialog box shown in Figure 7-19.

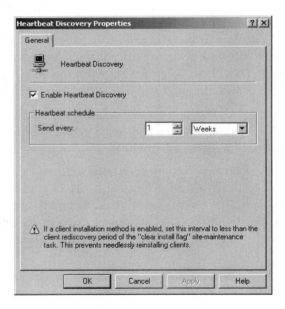

Figure 7-19. *The Heartbeat Discovery Properties dialog box.*

If you want to disable Heartbeat Discovery, clear the Enable Heartbeat Discovery check box.

3. Specify the frequency at which you want Heartbeat Discovery to generate DDRs.

4. Click OK to implement your schedule.

Heartbeat Discovery Process

Heartbeat Discovery runs on installed SMS clients according to the schedule you specified. With this method enabled, Client Component Installation Manager (CCIM) on the client causes the Cliex32.dll to generate a DDR, which is written to the client access point (CAP) by the Copy Queue component (refer to Chapter 8 for details on Copy Queue). The network traffic generated is the size of a normal DDR—that is, about 1 KB per client.

Checkpoints

The only potential problem here is ensuring that Heartbeat Discovery has in fact been enabled and not disabled by accident. Also, be sure that the schedule you create causes the DDRs to be generated frequently enough that the DDR isn't accidentally deleted from the SMS database.

Active Directory Discovery Methods

There are three Active Directory discovery methods: Active Directory User Discovery, Active Directory System Discovery, and Active Directory System Group Discovery. Unlike the Windows User Account and User Group discovery methods, which poll the PDC emulator, each of the Active Directory discovery methods polls the closest Active Directory domain controller.

These methods are configurable by the SMS administrator. The objects returned reflect those objects contained in Active Directory when the discovery method last ran. Therefore, don't consider this method to be dynamic.

Active Directory User Discovery returns the following information about the user account:

- User name
- Unique user name (including domain name)
- Active Directory domain
- Active Directory container name

Active Directory System Discovery returns the following information about the system account:

- Computer name
- Active Directory container name
- IP address
- Assigned Active Directory site

Active Directory System Group Discovery returns the following information about the group account:

- Organizational unit
- Global groups
- Universal groups
- Nested groups
- Nonsecurity groups

Enabling an Active Directory Discovery Method

To enable the Active Directory User Discovery, Active Directory System Discovery, and Active Directory System Group Discovery methods, follow these steps:

1. In the SMS Administrator Console, navigate to the site's Site Settings folder, expand it, and then select the Discovery Methods folder.

2. Right-click the appropriate Active Directory discovery method. The procedures for each method are essentially the same, so in this example we'll select Active Directory User Discovery. Choose Properties from the context menu to display the Active Directory User Discovery Properties dialog box shown in Figure 7-20.

3. In the General tab, select the Enable Active Directory User Discovery check box.

Figure 7-20. *The Active Directory User Discovery Properties dialog box.*

4. Click the New button in the Active Directory Containers frame of the Properties dialog box to specify the location in Active Directory that SMS should search for the container. The Browse For Active Directory dialog box appears, as shown in Figure 7-21. Choose Local Domain, Local Forest, or enter a Custom LDAP Or GC Query in the Domain text box.

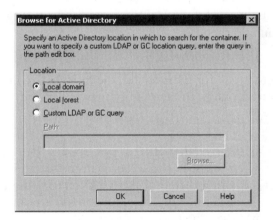

Figure 7-21. *The Browse For Active Directory dialog box.*

5. Select the Polling Schedule tab shown in Figure 7-22. Notice that you can choose to have SMS run the discovery method as soon as possible by checking the option Run Discovery As Soon As Possible or set a specific time for discovery to run.

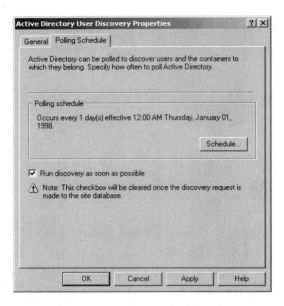

Figure 7-22. *The Polling Schedule tab.*

6. To set a specific time for discovery to run, click the Schedule button to display the Schedule dialog box. Define the frequency with which the discovery method should run and then click OK.

7. Click OK again to begin the discovery process.

Like the other discovery methods that poll for information, the three Active Directory discovery methods can generate a significant amount of network traffic.

Checkpoints

SMS must have at least read access to the containers that you specify when you configure each discovery method when the SMS site server is in the same Active Directory domain. If the site server is in a different Active Directory domain from the domain that you're polling, SMS must be at least a domain user in that domain. Other than that, check that the scheduling options and Active Directory locations are configured correctly.

Discovery Data Manager

The most prominent and common SMS site server component in the discovery process is Discovery Data Manager. Its role is to process DDRs written to its inbox on the site server (SMS\Inboxes\Ddm.box) and to create site assignment rules based on the site boundaries as specified in the site control file. It also forwards the site assignment rules to secondary sites and creates Client Configuration Manager requests for discovered Windows clients if Client Push Installation has been enabled. (*Site assignment rules* are the list of subnets, IP ranges, and Active Directory sites that define the site boundaries to determine whether discovered computers are assigned to SMS sites. See Chapter 8 for details.) Discovery Data Manager will also forward discovery information through Replication Manager to the parent site, if one exists.

Since it's a site server component, Discovery Data Manager generates status messages and writes more detailed information to its log file (SMS\Logs\Ddm.log) if logging has been enabled for this component. Look for status message IDs in the 26*xx* range for specific information related to the processing of DDRs.

Summary

This chapter explored the first step in populating the SMS database and installing SMS clients—discovering resources. We looked at a variety of discovery methods that you can use to carry out the discovery process. In Chapter 8 we'll examine the various client installation methods available to the SMS administrator.

Chapter 8
Client Installation Methods

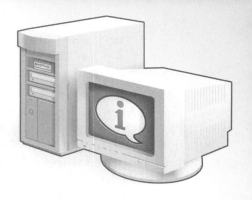

In Chapter 7, "Resource Discovery," you learned how to discover resources and add them to the Microsoft Systems Management Server (SMS) database. To manage a computer resource, however, you must make that computer an SMS client, which means installing SMS client components on that computer. In this chapter we'll focus on the installation process. We'll begin by exploring the concept of site assignment. Then we'll look at the installation methods, and you'll learn how to manage the client configuration and how to remove SMS from the client if necessary.

Site Assignment

Before you can install a computer as an SMS client, you must first assign it to an SMS site. A computer's site assignment is determined by its IP subnet address and mask and the boundaries you set for the SMS site. (Refer to Chapter 3, "Configuring Site Server Properties and Site Systems," for detailed information on subnet addresses and subnet masks.) If the computer is assigned to the site, installation continues. If it isn't, the installation process stops. Site assignment depends on the site boundaries configured for your SMS site. This group of site boundaries is also known as the *site assignment rules*—the list of subnets, roaming boundaries, and Active Directory directory service sites that define the site boundaries of an SMS site. These rules are maintained at the site server level and are written to the client access points (CAPs) for SMS Legacy Clients and to the management points for Advanced Clients.

Site boundaries determine which clients are to be installed as SMS clients to the site. They aren't used to specify which site systems can be assigned site roles in the site. In fact, site systems can be members of other accessible subnets. Unlike SMS 2.0, an SMS 2003 client can't belong to more than one site. You can assign a client to a site manually or let SMS assign the client to a site automatically, but the client can't be made a client of more than one site.

Microsoft recommends that all subnets identified as site boundaries be local to the site and that site boundaries not span WAN connections unless the link is fast and reliable. Network and site server performance could be adversely affected if the WAN connection is already heavily utilized. When you plan Active Directory sites, you usually keep this same recommendation in mind. For that reason, and because SMS supports it, you should consider using the Active Directory sites you already configured as your SMS site boundaries. Another advantage of using an Active Directory site as your SMS site boundary is that as you add subnets to the Active Directory site, those subnets are automatically included as part of the SMS site boundaries.

Setting Site Boundaries

You create the site assignment rules by setting the site boundaries for the site. Site boundaries are a property of the site and are set through the SMS Administrator Console. To set site boundaries based on IP address, follow these steps:

1. In the SMS Administrator Console, navigate to your site entry in the Site Hierarchy node. Right-click the site entry and choose Properties from the context menu to display the Site Properties dialog box.

2. Select the Site Boundaries tab, shown in Figure 8-1.

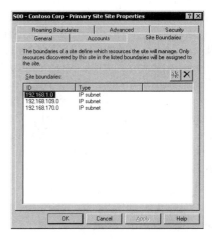

Figure 8-1. *The Site Boundaries tab of the Site Properties dialog box.*

3. To add a subnet to the Site Boundaries list, click the New button (the yellow star) to display the New Site Boundary dialog box, shown in Figure 8-2.

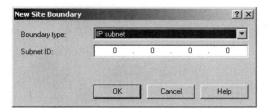

Figure 8-2. *The New Site Boundary dialog box.*

4. Select a boundary type from the drop-down list—either IP Subnet or Active Directory Site.

5. In the Subnet ID text box, enter the IP subnet address or Active Directory site name, and then click OK to close the dialog box.

6. Click OK again to begin the site control process, which will update the site assignment rules.

Advanced Clients use roaming boundaries to access distribution points that are members of this site. You can also specify whether the Advanced Client will treat a distribution point as local or remote. If you treat distribution points as local, the Advanced Client uses the When A Local Distribution Point Is Available setting in the Advanced Client tab of the Advertisement Properties dialog box. If you treat distribution points as remote, the Advanced Client uses the When No Local Distribution Point Is Available setting in the Advanced Client tab of the Advertisement Properties dialog box.

To set the roaming boundaries of the site, follow these steps:

1. In the SMS Administrator Console, navigate to your site entry in the Site Hierarchy node. Right-click the site entry and choose Properties from the context menu to display the Site Properties dialog box.

2. Select the Roaming Boundaries tab, shown in Figure 8-3.

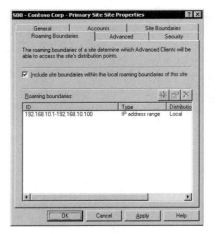

Figure 8-3. *The Roaming Boundaries tab of the Site Properties dialog box.*

3. Select Include Site Boundaries Within The Local Roaming Boundaries Of This Site to make the boundaries you configure part of the local boundaries for the site.

4. To add a new boundary to the Roaming Boundaries list, click New to display the New Roaming Boundary dialog box, shown in Figure 8-4.

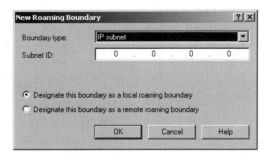

Figure 8-4. *The New Roaming Boundary dialog box.*

5. Select a boundary type from the drop-down list—either IP Subnet, Active Directory Site, or IP Address Range.

6. In the text box below the Boundary Type, enter the IP subnet address, Active Directory site name, or IP address range. Select Designate This Boundary as a Local Roaming Boundary to have Advanced Clients treat this site's distribution points as local. Select Designate This Boundary as a Remote Roaming Boundary to have Advanced Clients treat this site's distribution points as remote. Click OK to close the dialog box.

7. Click OK again to begin the site control process, which will update the site assignment rules.

Installation Methods

Just as several discovery methods are available for adding resources to the SMS database, several client installation methods are available for loading the SMS Legacy and Advanced Client components on computers that have been assigned to the SMS site. There are six client installation methods. You can use three of these methods to install both the Legacy Client and the Advanced Client software on assigned computers. The six methods and the SMS client types that they can be used with are described in Table 8-1.

Table 8-1.   SMS Client installation methods

Installation Method	Used to Install:
Client Push Installation	Both Legacy and Advanced Client
Logon Script Initiated	Both Legacy and Advanced Client
Manual	Both Legacy and Advanced Client
Windows Group Policy	Advanced Client
Software Distribution	Advanced Client
Imaging	Advanced Client

Note   It is strongly recommended that you do not install the Legacy Client on computers running Windows 2000 or later except in cases where you are upgrading an existing SMS 2.0 site to SMS 2003. In this case, the upgrade will install the Legacy Client automatically on such computers. However, this should be considered an interim step. SMS includes a report and query to help you identify those computers that have the Legacy Client installed on Windows 2000 or later computers so that you can target those for upgrade to Advanced Client. Advanced Client is considered a more secure client for those operating system environments.

As we saw in Chapter 7, it isn't necessary for a resource to have been discovered before it can be installed. The installation process will automatically generate a discovery data record (DDR) for the client. The exception to this is Client Push Installation. In order for SMS to push the client software to a computer, that computer must have been discovered first. A DDR must already exist for the computer in the SMS database for that site. In many larger SMS sites, you might choose to discover all your potential SMS clients first so that you can determine which of those can become Legacy or Advanced Clients or to develop a roll-out plan for installing SMS clients.

More Info   For more information about how to plan the installation of clients in your SMS site, see Chapter 10, "Planning Your Deployment and Configuration," in the *Microsoft Systems Management Server 2003 Concepts, Planning, and Deployment Guide* included on the SMS 2003 CD.

All SMS clients receive a core set of components when the SMS client software is installed. Advanced Clients receive all the client agents whether or not the agents have been enabled and configured. Legacy Clients receive only those agents that have been enabled and configured. Although not essential to the successful installation of an SMS client, it would be productive to configure the client agents that you intend to enable prior to installing the client computers. Doing so will ensure that all the agents and their properties will be installed at one time. If you enable a client component later, the client update process will update the client on its next polling cycle—every 25 hours—or when the update is forced on the client.

There are five client agents:

- Advertised Programs Client Agent
- Hardware Inventory Client Agent
- Remote Tools Client Agent
- Software Inventory Client Agent
- Software Metering Client Agent

Tip   Client agents are enabled by default when you install SMS using the Express Setup option. No client agents are enabled if you performed a Custom installation.

The process of enabling and installing each of these agents on your SMS clients will be covered in later chapters.

Client Push Installation

Client Push Installation is designed to push either the Legacy Client or the Advanced Client to newly discovered computer resources. The Client Push Installation method supports computers running Microsoft Windows NT 4.0, Windows 2000, Windows XP Professional, or operating systems in the Windows Server 2003 family. Although this method doesn't automatically install SMS client software on domain controllers and site systems, it can be configured to do so. Also, you can use this method to upgrade SMS clients from the Legacy Client to the Advanced Client, but not from the Advanced Client to the Legacy Client.

This method attempts to connect to the computer using the SMS Service account, if the site is running standard security mode, or a Client Push Installation account that you create. Chapter 16, "Queries and Reports," discusses these accounts in more detail. It's important that these accounts have local administrative privileges on the computers that will become SMS clients.

You can enable Client Push Installation to run automatically until you decide to turn it off, or you can initiate a client push by targeting a specific collection or resource in a collection using the Client Push Installation Wizard. Both methods work essentially the same way regarding the manner in which the client is installed. The latter, however, runs only when the administrator initiates it.

If you're pushing the Advanced Client, SMS uses two primary files: Ccmsetup.exe and Client.msi. Client.msi is a Windows Installer package that contains the Advanced Client software. Ccmsetup.exe is a wrapper for Client.msi and runs as a service. Ccmsetup.exe copies Client.msi to the computer on which you're installing the Advanced Client software.

Configuring Client Push Installation

You configure Client Push Installation through the SMS Administrator Console. Follow these steps to enable Client Push Installation:

1. In the SMS Administrator Console, navigate to the Client Installation Methods node under Site Hierarchy.

2. Right-click Client Push Installation and select Properties from the context menu to display the Client Push Installation Properties dialog box shown in Figure 8-5.

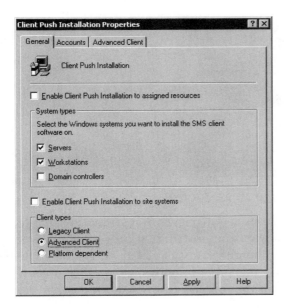

Figure 8-5. *The Client Push Installation Properties dialog box.*

3. In the General tab, select Enable Client Push Installation To Assigned Resources to enable this method to run. Select the system types that SMS should push the client software to. Select Enable Client Push Installation To Site Systems if you want site systems to automatically receive the SMS client software. Finally, select the client type to push. If you choose Platform Dependent, SMS will push the Advanced Client software to the discovered computer if the computer's operating system supports Advanced Client. Otherwise, SMS will push the Legacy Client.

4. In the Accounts tab, shown in Figure 8-6, use the New button to specify one or more accounts for SMS to use when connecting to the computer to install the client software. Note the requirements for Legacy and Advanced Clients outlined in this tab.

Figure 8-6. *The Client Push Installation Properties Accounts tab.*

5. In the Advanced Client tab, shown in Figure 8-7, in the Installation Properties text box enter any custom installation properties that you want SMS to use when installing the Advanced Client. For example, enter *CCMINSTALLDIR=C:\MS\SMS* if you want the Advanced Client support files installed in the folder C:\MS\SMS rather than the default %Windir%\System32\CCM.

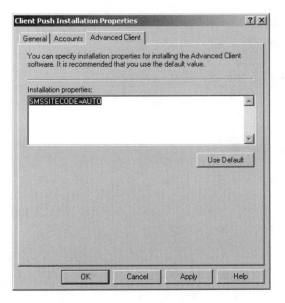

Figure 8-7. *The Client Push Installation Properties Advanced Client tab.*

6. Click Apply and then OK when you're finished.

More Info For detailed information about the various configuration options that are available for installing the Advanced Client, see Chapter 17, "Discovering Resources and Deploying Clients," in the *Microsoft Systems Management Server 2003 Concepts, Planning, and Deployment Guide* included with the SMS CD.

Using the Client Push Installation Wizard

You can push SMS client software to discovered computers using the Client Push Installation Wizard. This method is a variation of the Client Push Installation method and works in much the same way. The main difference is that the Client Push Installation Wizard runs only when the SMS administrator initiates it. By contrast, the Client Push Installation method runs so long as it remains enabled.

You initiate the Client Push Installation Wizard by targeting a collection of computers or a specific computer in a collection. To do that, follow these steps:

1. Navigate to the Collections node in the SMS Administrator Console.

2. Select the collection or computer in a collection that you want to push the client software to. Right-click the selection and choose All Tasks, then Install Client from the context menu to launch the Client Push Installation Wizard shown in Figure 8-8.

Figure 8-8. *The Client Push Installation Wizard.*

3. Click Next to display the Installation Options page shown in Figure 8-9. Select the appropriate client type or choose Collect System Status Without Installing The SMS Client if you want to determine whether the discovered resource already has client software installed.

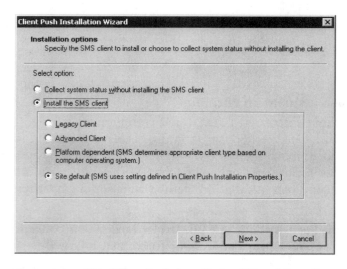

Figure 8-9. *The Client Push Installation Wizard Installation Options page.*

4. Click Next to display the Client Installation Options page shown in Figure 8-10. Here you can choose to install the client software only to assigned clients—the default—or you can include domain controllers as well. If you selected a collection when you launched the wizard, you can also target resources contained in subcollections.

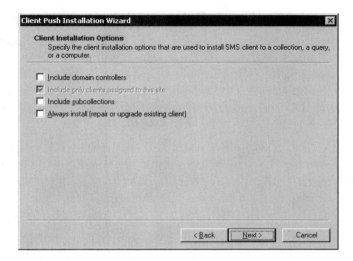

Figure 8-10.   *The Client Push Installation Wizard Client Installation Options page.*

If you are upgrading existing SMS 2.0 clients to the Legacy Client, select the option Always Install (Repair or Upgrade Existing Client). Do not select this option if you are upgrading from the Legacy Client to the Advanced Client.

5. Click Next to display the Completing page, shown in Figure 8-11, and then click Finish to begin the client push process.

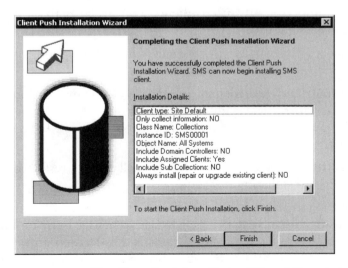

Figure 8-11.   *The Client Push Installation Wizard Completing page.*

Logon Script Initiated Client Installation

This installation method is similar to the Windows NT Logon Installation method you could enable in SMS 2.0, which used the logon point site system installed on a domain controller to initiate client installation. SMS 2003 no longer supports the logon point role. However, SMS 2003 does support installing the Legacy or Advanced Client software using the file Capinst.exe in a logon script as the installation trigger.

Legacy Clients use the CAP site system to install and receive client component updates. Advanced Clients use the management point site system for this function. Logon script-initiated installation uses the server locator point site system to locate either a CAP or management point as appropriate for the client.

Consequently, you need to set up the logon script so that an appropriate server locator point can be found. You can do this either by supplying a specific server locator point as an argument for Capinst.exe or by simply letting Capinst.exe find the first server locator point registered in the Active Directory global catalog. However, if the Active Directory schema hasn't been extended for SMS, Capinst.exe will fail to find a server locator point. For this reason, it's recommended that you always specify a server locator point as part of the Capinst.exe statement in your logon script.

The following steps occur when a user runs the logon script:

1. Capinst.exe finds a server locator point.

2. The server locator point returns a list of the CAPs (for Legacy Clients) or management points (for Advanced Clients) that are available for the site the client is assigned to.

3. Capinst.exe launches Smsman.exe (for Legacy Client installation) or CCMSetup.exe (for Advanced Client installation).

4. If the user has administrative credentials on the client, the installation proceeds. If the user doesn't have administrative credentials on the client, Capinst.exe generates a Client Configuration Request (CCR) that's sent to the site server.

5. If the site server receives a CCR, the client installation is restarted using the Client Push Installation method.

When you configure a logon script, include a call to Capinst.exe along with any command-line options that are necessary. Table 8-2 describes the most common command-line options you're likely to use. Capinst.exe is located on the site server in the SMS\client\i386 folder. If you want to run Capinst.exe from another server—for example, a domain controller—you must copy that file to the appropriate server. However, keep in mind that if Capinst.exe is later updated, you'll need to manually copy the updated file to the appropriate servers yourself. The syntax for Capinst.exe is: Capinst.exe /option. For example, to specify a server locator point, use the syntax: Capinst.exe /SLP=server1.

Table 8-2.   Capinst.exe command-line options

Option	Description
/AdvCli	Installs the Advanced Client software. If the option isn't used or the client computer's operating system doesn't support Advanced Client, the Legacy Client is installed.
/SLP=<*SLP Server Name*>	Specifies the server locator point that should be used.
/AdvCliCmd	Lets you include any installation properties specific to Client.msi that you'd like to pass to Ccmsetup.exe to customize the installation of the Advanced Client. If you don't include any installation properties, Ccmsetup.exe will install the Advanced Client using default settings.
/AutoDetect=<*Executable Name*>	Lets you specify a script or program that should be executed as part of the installation to help determine which type of client software is installed. For example, you might reference a script that looks for a specific hardware property stored in Windows Management Instrumentation (WMI) on the client and then return a value. A value of 1 installs Advanced Client if the client operating system supports Advanced Client or the Legacy Client if the client operating system does not. A value of 0 installs the Legacy Client, and any other value returned installs no client software.
/DC	Installs Advanced Client on a domain controller.

> **More Info**   For more information about these and other logons script options that you can use, see Chapter 17, "Discovering Resources and Deploying Clients," in the *Microsoft Systems Management Server 2003 Concepts, Planning, and Deployment Guide* included with the SMS CD.

Manual Client Installation

The third method of installing SMS client software on a computer is manual client installation. You can install either the Legacy Client or the Advanced Client using this method. The Legacy Client uses Smsman.exe, and the Advanced Client uses Ccmsetup, also called the Advanced Client Installer.

Using Smsman.exe to Install the Legacy Client

Use Smsman.exe to manually install the Legacy Client directly from a CAP through a UNC path. Alternately, you could use a command-line switch to specify the location of a CAP for the client to use. Smsman.exe is located on the site server in the SMS\Client\i386 folder and on the SMS CD in the SMS-Setup\Client\i386 folder.

By default, Smsman.exe launches the Systems Management Installation Wizard, which will provide a series of prompts for you to answer. However, you could also execute Smsman.exe from a command prompt using the options described in Table 8-3.

Table 8-3. Smsman.exe command-line options

Option	Description
/A	Sets the installation location to the path used to launch the Systems Management Installation Wizard.
/D	Generates a discovery record but doesn't install the Legacy Client.
/H or /?	Displays help.
/M	Specifies the path to a specific CAP. Syntax: Smsman.exe /M \\server\ CAP_sitecode.
/Q	Runs installation in silent mode with no windows or messages displayed.
/T	Allows installation to run in a Terminal Services session.
/U	Removes SMS client software.
/F	Forces the client to be assigned to the SMS site of the CAP.

Using Ccmsetup.exe to Install the Advanced Client

Use Ccmsetup.exe to install the Advanced Client manually to a computer. Ccmsetup.exe uses the Client.msi program to install the Advanced Client software. Client.msi is located on the site server in the SMS\Client\i386 folder, on management points in the SMSClient\i386 folder, or on the SMS CD in the SMS-Setup\Client\i386 folder. Ccmsetup.exe copies all the files necessary to complete the installation, including the Client.msi and language-specific files and folders, to the client computer.

Ccmsetup.exe provides several command-line switches that you can use to customize the way it runs. These switches are described in Table 8-4.

Table 8-4. Ccmsetup.exe command-line options

Option	Description
/source	Sets the location for Client.msi and other supporting files. Syntax: Ccmsetup /source:folder
/mp	Specifies a management point as the source file location. Ccmsetup.exe will automatically look in the SMSClient\i386 folder on the server you specify. Syntax: Ccmsetup.exe /mp:server
/useronly	Runs Ccmsetup.exe using the logged-on user's credentials. If the user doesn't have administrative credentials, Ccmsetup.exe will fail.
/service	Runs Ccmsetup.exe in the local system account security context. This option assumes you're using Active Directory and that the client computer account has access to the SMSClient\i386 folder on the management point.

In addition to the Ccmsetup.exe command options described in Table 8-4, you can also customize Client.msi using one or more installation property options. Table 8-5 describes these options. Ccmsetup.exe passes the installation property options to Client.msi. Thus, you append the installation property options to the Ccmsetup.exe command that you create using the options in Table 8-4. For example, if you want to specify a management point source location (/mp from Table 8-4) and specify where the Advanced Client files should be located on the client computer (CCMINSTALLDIR from Table 8-5), the syntax would look like this: Ccmsetup.exe /mp:*server* CCMINSTALLDIR=*folderpath*.

Table 8-5.   Ccmsetup.exe installation property options for Client.msi

Option	Description
CCMINSTALLDIR	Identifies the folder where the Advanced Client files are installed
CCMADMINS	Specifies an account to grant administrative access to
CCMALLOWSILENTREBOOT	Allows the computer to be rebooted even if a user is logged on
CCMDEBUGLOGGING	Enables debug logging
CCMENABLELOGGING	Enables logging for Ccmsetup.exe and stores the log files in the CCM\Logs folder on the client
CCMLOGLEVEL	Specifies the level of logging required from 0, the most verbose, to 3, which only logs errors
CCMLOGMAXHISTORY	Specifies the number of log versions to keep
CCMLOGMAXSIZE	Specifies the maximum log file size
DISABLESITEOPT	Prevents users with administrative credentials from changing the site assignment
DISABLECACHEOPT	Prevents users with administrative credentials from changing the cache settings
SMSCACHEDIR	Specifies the location for downloaded files to be cached on the client
SMSCACHESIZE	Specifies the cache size
SMSCACHEFLAGS	Allows control of cache usage through SMSCACHEFLAG properties
SMSCONFIGSOURCE	Specifies where and in what order Ccmsetup.exe looks for configuration settings
SMSNOWINSLOOKUP	Controls failover from Active Directory to WINS
SMSPREFERREDCLIENT	Sets the preferred client to Advanced Client if the Legacy Client isn't already installed
SMSSITECODE	Specifies the site to assign the client to

More Info   For a detailed discussion of all the options described in Table 8-5, including examples of how to use them, see Chapter 17, "Discovering Resources and Deploying Clients," in the *Microsoft Systems Management Server 2003 Concepts, Planning, and Deployment Guide* included with the SMS CD.

Advanced Client Installation Methods

The next three installation methods apply only to deploying the Advanced Client software components to computers. These three installation methods are

- Windows group policy
- Software distribution
- Computer imaging

In a way, you could think of the first two methods as variations on the manual installation method described earlier because they use the Ccmsetup.exe file and its options to run an installation.

Active Directory Group Policy

Active Directory provides a way to distribute programs to clients through group policy. Similar, in a way, to SMS software distribution, you can publish or assign a program to computers based on their organizational unit location in Active Directory. Although you can't use Ccmsetup.exe in this scenario (unless you include it as part of a custom .MSI file that you create), you can use the Advanced Client installation file Client.msi that Ccmsetup.exe calls. However, this method doesn't offer you the same scope of customization that the other methods already described do. This method would probably be best used for small groups of similar computers that require the default installation of Advanced Client. For more information about using Active Directory group policy to distribute programs, refer to your Windows server documentation.

Software Distribution

To install Advanced Clients through software distribution, use Ccmsetup.exe as the program when you create your software distribution package. Configure the Advanced Client installation using the Client.msi properties and command-line options described earlier.

Alternatively, SMS 2003 includes a package definition file called Smsclint.sms that you can use to create the basic software distribution package based on pre-defined defaults. This file is installed on your SMS site server only if you selected the setup option Package Automation Scripts during SMS setup. It's also available on the SMS 2003 CD. Chapter 12, "Package Distribution and Management," describes how to create software distribution packages from scratch and by using a package definition file.

Computer Imaging

Computer imaging is more commonly known as "cloning" or "ghost imaging." Basically, this process involves setting up a source, or reference, computer with all the applications, settings, registry keys, and so on that are commonly required for computers in an organization. A snapshot, or "image," of this computer configuration is created, which can then be loaded onto other computers. The result is a standard computer configuration across the set of computers that received the image.

Several tools allow you to create a computer image and distribute it to other computers in your organization, including Remote Installation Services (RIS), a feature of Windows 2000 Server and later. You can deploy the Advanced Client by installing it without a site assignment on the reference computer before you create the image using manual installation as described earlier. Then, when you load the image on subsequent computers, they'll have the Advanced Client components already installed. The only additional step you'll need to take is to assign those clients to an appropriate site. As we've seen already, you could use client push, a logon script, or a command-line option to carry out this last task. You could also use the Systems Management icon in Control Panel to assign a site code to the client.

Understanding and Managing the Client Configuration

Now that you've finished installing SMS on your clients, let's explore what happened on the client. Just what have we accomplished here? Actually, all we've done is make the client ready to receive or enable any of the optional client agents that allow you to more fully manage the client. The Legacy Client receives a core set of components when it's installed. Other client agents, such as the Hardware Inventory Client Agent, are installed after you enable them at the site and the client runs its next update cycle. The Advanced Client, however, receives all client components when it's installed. The components are enabled after you enable them at the site, and the Advanced Client runs its next update cycle.

Changes to the Client

So what does happen to the client? The installation process causes several changes to occur on the client, affecting its directory structure and disk space, its services, its registry, and its Control Panel. Let's start by looking at changes to the client's directory structure.

Directory Structure Changes

First and foremost, perhaps, is the creation of an SMS directory structure within the operating system directory. The default operating system directory name tends to vary among the Windows operating systems, so we'll refer to it here as the system directory, or by its system variable name, %Windir%.

The form that the SMS directory structure takes depends on whether you installed the Legacy Client or the Advanced Client. If you installed the Legacy Client software, base and optional client component support files installed on the computer are stored in their respective folders under %Windir%\MS\SMS\Clicomp. Client installation history and its DDR are maintained in the %Windir%\MS\SMS\Core\Data folder. SMS sites that the client has been assigned and installed to are reflected under %Windir%\MS\SMS\Sitefile. Client components and services generate their log information in files written to the %Windir%\MS\SMS\Logs folder. The %Windir%\MS\SMS\IDMifs and NOID-Mifs folders are used for customizing entries to the SMS database.

If you installed the Advanced Client software, base client component support files installed on the computer are stored in their respective folders under %Windir%\System32\CCM\Clicomp. Client installation history and its DDR are maintained in the %Windir%\System32\CCM \Core folder. Client components and services generate their log information in files written to the %Windir%\System32\CCM\Logs folder. Client agent components are stored in their respective folders under %Windir%\System32\CCM. For example, files that support the inventory agents, including the IDMifs and NOIDMifs folders, are stored in %Windir%\System32\CCM\Inventory.

You'll find numerous other folders as well, but these are the most pertinent to our discussion in this book. As you can see, just like the SMS directory structure on the site server or any site system, there are no superfluous directories. Each has a purpose and, in this case, is monitored or used by one or more client components.

Service and Component Changes

As we've seen in our examination of logon discovery and logon client installation processes in Chapter 7 and in this chapter, several .EXE and .DLL files are installed and loaded to aid in the discovery and installation process. These files include Clicore.exe and Clisvc.exe on the Legacy Client and CCMExec.exe on the Advanced Client.

Registry Changes

In addition to the directories created and the services and components installed, the client installation process adds several keys to the client's registry under

HKEY_LOCAL_MACHINE\Software\Microsoft\SMS\Client for both Legacy and Advanced Clients, SMS\Mobile Client for Advanced Clients, and WBEM for Windows 98 and Windows NT 4.0 clients. The installation process also adds the appropriate client service entries under HKEY_LOCAL_MACHINE\System\CurrentControlSet\Services.

The SMS\Client and SMS\Mobile Client keys maintain all client component configuration settings—both configurable and nonconfigurable by you, the administrator. The WBEM key, of course, supports the Windows Management implementation on Windows 98 and Windows NT 4.0 clients. The Services key contains service-specific information, such as startup parameters and service accounts for the SMS Client Service and the Windows Management Service. You can find this information in the appropriate subkeys of the Services key: the Clisvc subkey on Legacy Clients, the CCMExec subkey on Advanced Clients, and the Winmgmt subkey.

Control Panel Changes

Last but by no means least, the client installation process updates the client's Control Panel to include the Systems Management icon, as shown in Figure 8-12. This program is used to install, update, or repair components on the client. The only other programs that can be added to the Control Panel are Remote Tools and Advertised Programs if these optional components have been enabled and installed on the client. Administrators familiar with earlier versions of SMS will notice that the old SMS Client program group is no longer added to the client's Start menu. In fact, in SMS 2.0, user access to, and control of, SMS client components is far more limited than it was in earlier client installations.

Figure 8-12. *The updated Control Panel.*

All these changes combined require about 20-25 MB of disk space on the client computer, depending on the client type you installed and the components you enabled.

Systems Management Icon

You use the Systems Management icon to install, update, and repair SMS components installed on the client. Double-clicking this icon in Control Panel will display the Systems Management Properties dialog box, which differs depending on whether you installed the Legacy Client or the Advanced Client.

Systems Management Icon for Legacy Client

When you run the Systems Management program on the Legacy Client, the dialog box that displays contains three tabs: General, Sites, and Components.

General Tab   The General tab, shown in Figure 8-13, displays a list of the client's system properties. This is a subset of the discovery data reported to the site server and includes the client's IP address and subnet, MAC address, operating system, and domain or workgroup membership—and the SMS GUID assigned to the client. This GUID is a randomly generated, 32-character identifier used internally by SMS to identify the client. Unlike in earlier versions of SMS, the SMS 2003 administrator doesn't need to refer to the client by its GUID at any time. You can use the discovered information to manage and troubleshoot your computer.

Figure 8-13.   *The General tab of the Systems Management Properties dialog box for the Legacy Client.*

The General tab also provides a mobile computing option that you can enable for the Legacy Client if that client will be connecting to the network—and potentially to different SMS sites—from different subnets. Enabling this mode can prevent the client from changing its site assignment if it roams to a different site.

You can enable the traveling mode by selecting the This Computer Connects To The Network From Different Locations check box. If this mode is enabled, the user will be presented with a dialog box when the client connects to a different site and the client update cycle runs or a client installation method is executed. The user can either change site assignment to the new site (become a member of a different SMS site) or keep the existing site assignment. If the user doesn't install to the new site, he or she won't be prompted again for 30 days, even if the client roams to that site again.

Note   On computers running Windows NT or higher, the user must have administrative credentials on the client to enable or disable travel mode.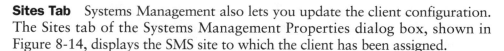

Sites Tab   Systems Management also lets you update the client configuration. The Sites tab of the Systems Management Properties dialog box, shown in Figure 8-14, displays the SMS site to which the client has been assigned.

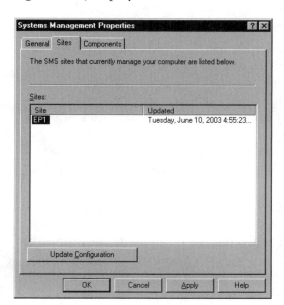

Figure 8-14.   *The Sites tab of the Systems Management Properties dialog box for the Legacy Client.*

Tip   If the client belongs to multiple sites, the Update Configuration button will refresh the client components from all the sites.

The SMS client polls for component updates every 25 hours to see whether there are any new components to install, components to remove, or components whose configurations need to be modified in some way. As you enable and configure components on the site server, you can be assured that the client will be updated on a daily basis. However, if you want or need to update the client immediately, you can force the client to perform an immediate update by clicking the Update Configuration button at the bottom of the Sites tab.

Real World   When Does "Immediate" Mean Immediate?

CCIM32, the SMS client component on Legacy Clients that keeps components up to date, connects to a CAP or management point, checks for any component updates that need to be made on the client, and applies those updates. The amount of time that elapses before the changes are effected at the client depends on the components involved and the number of changes that need to be made. In general, use this rule of thumb for timing: "immediate" in SMS generally means over the next few minutes (or hours). All kidding aside, even if it seems as if nothing is happening on the client, if you monitor client component logs or view the Processes tab in the Windows Task Manager, you'll see that things are indeed happening under the hood.

As an example, let's say that you've changed the inventory frequency at the site server. You then go directly to your client and click Update Configuration. When should you expect to see the changes on the client? In this case, probably not until tomorrow—that's right, sometime within the next 25 hours. Remember, CCIM32 is going to check for updates. You initiated the change at the site server. Even though that change is event driven, we have to wait for several SMS site server components to wake up, process the change, and write it to the CAP or management point before CCIM32 knows about it.

In particular, the regular site update process involving Hierarchy Manager and Site Control Manager (described in detail in Chapter 3) will take place. When the site control file (Sitectrl.ct0) is updated, Client Install Data Manager reads the file, identifies client agent updates, and writes configuration and offer files to the SMS\Inboxes\Clicfg.src folder on the site server. Inbox Manager forwards these files to the CAP_Site\Clicomp.box folder on the CAP. Only after this happens (you can view the date and time stamps on the appropriate files in these directories to confirm) can you update the client configuration through Systems Management on the client computer.

Components Tab   You can repair the configuration through the Components tab of Systems Management. The Components tab, shown in Figure 8-15, displays a list of components that have been installed on the client, their version numbers, and their current status.

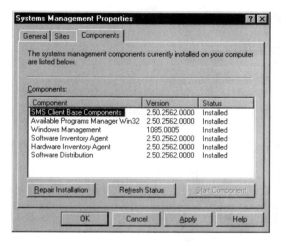

Figure 8-15.   *The Components tab of the Systems Management Properties dialog box for the Legacy Client.*

A basic installation of SMS on the client will result in the following components being installed:

- Available Programs Manager Win32
- SMS Client Base Components
- Windows Management

The Available Programs Manager manages the programs available to run on the client. It isn't the same as the Advertised Programs Client Agent, which is used to run advertised programs. This entry represents the support file SMSapm32.exe that's used to run installation programs for various client components.

As you enable additional client components and they're installed, they'll be displayed in this list as well.

At the bottom of the Components tab are three buttons: Repair Installation, Refresh Status, and Start Component. Clicking Refresh Status will cause the client components to be rechecked and their status updated. Table 8-6 describes the different status indicators you might see.

Table 8-6.   Table 8-6.   Client component status indicators

Status	Description
Installed	The component has been successfully installed on the client.
Install Pending	SMSapm32.exe has initiated the installation process for the component, but it hasn't yet been completed.
Repair Pending	CCIM32 is verifying the component and reinstalling it.
Reboot Required	The component has been repaired, but it won't initialize until a reboot has taken place on the client.
Not Available	The component, although enabled at the site server, isn't compatible with this computer's current configuration. Could also indicate that the client's IP address no longer falls within the site assignment rules for the SMS site and that the client components have been subsequently uninstalled.

If you suspect or determine that you're having a problem with a particular component—for example, if yesterday the component's status was Installed and today it is Not Available—you can select that component and click Repair Installation. This will cause that component's status to change to Repair Pending, while CCIM32 attempts to verify and reinstall that component. This technique is the best way to recover from corrupted component support files. You can either keep clicking Refresh Status until the status changes to Installed or close Systems Management and wait a few minutes for CCIM32 to complete the reinstallation.

Tip   You can observe the CCIM32 and SMSapm32 processes through Windows Task Manager to gauge when the repair starts and finishes.

System Management Program for Advanced Client

When you run the Systems Management program on the Advanced Client, the dialog box displays four tabs: General, Components, Actions, and Advanced.

General Tab   The General tab, shown in Figure 8-16, displays a list of the client's system properties similar to that shown for the Legacy Client. However, because Advanced Clients handle roaming differently from Legacy Clients, there's no travel mode option.

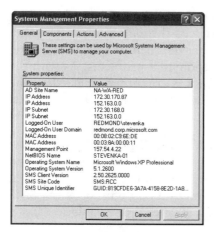

Figure 8-16.   *The General tab of the Systems Management Properties dialog box for the Advanced Client.*

Components Tab   Like the Legacy Client, the Components tab, shown in Figure 8-17, provides a list of the SMS client components available on the client along with each component's current status. Background components such as services are displayed as Installed. Recall that all client agents are installed on the Advanced Client whether or not you've enabled them at the site server. So, as you see in Figure 8-17, the agents display a status of Disabled if you haven't yet configured and enabled the agent for the site or Enabled if the agent has been enabled at the site and the client update cycle has subsequently enabled the agent at the client.

Figure 8-17.   *The Components tab of the Systems Management Properties dialog box for the Advanced Client.*

If you've enabled a client agent and you notice that within 25 hours the client agent status still displays as Disabled when viewed through Systems Management on the client, you should investigate whether the client received its update, whether the client update cycle ran, and other potential problems. As with the Legacy Client, if you suspect that a component is corrupted or needs to be reinstalled, you can select that component in the Components list and then click Repair.

Actions Tab The Actions tab, shown in Figure 8-18, displays a list of procedures that you can run that are related to the various components installed and enabled on the Advanced Client. If, for example, you wanted to get an updated machine policy for this client outside of the interval configured by the SMS administrator, you would select Machine Policy Retrieval & Evaluation Cycle in the Actions list and then click Initiate Action.

Figure 8-18. *The Actions tab of the Systems Management Properties dialog box for the Advanced Client.*

Advanced Tab The Advanced tab, shown in Figure 8-19, allows a user with administrative credentials to change some Advanced Client settings for the client. The SMS Site section of this tab displays the current site that the client is assigned to. You can also click the Discover button to have the client search for the appropriate local site. You could use this option to assign a client that was created from a computer image and wasn't yet assigned to a site or to change the client's site assignment. You can also remove the site assignment for this client by deleting the site code value and leaving it blank, or null. If you do this, however, discovery records, inventory, and status messages aren't generated and advertisements and Advanced Client policies aren't downloaded. The client is therefore considered dormant.

In the Temporary Program Download Folder section you can modify the folder location on the client where advertised programs will be cached when they're downloaded to manage the size of that folder and to delete files from the folder if necessary. The client will automatically delete older files from the folder specified when the disk space limit is reached.

Figure 8-19.   *The Advanced tab of the Systems Management Properties dialog box for the Advanced Client.*

Removing Systems Management Server from the Client

At some point you might need to uninstall SMS from the clients. Removing an individual component is simply a matter of disabling that client agent at the site server. Since client agent settings are sitewide in nature, disabling a client agent at the site server will cause that component to be removed from all Legacy Clients, and disabled at all Advanced Clients, assigned to that SMS site.

Your intention, however, might be to remove SMS entirely from all your SMS clients or from individual SMS clients. Removing the client software varies depending on the client type installed.

Removing the Advanced Client

As we just discussed, if you change the Advanced Client's site assignment to null through the Advanced tab of Systems Management its client components remain installed, but the client becomes dormant. There is no automatic method of removing the Advanced Client software. However, any user with administrative credentials on the client can remove the Advanced Client software manually by using the Ccmclean.exe program. This program is included as part of the SMS 2003 ToolKit and can be downloaded from Microsoft's SMS Web site (*http://www.microsoft.com/smserver/downloads*). It's executed at the client from a command prompt. Once executed, it will initiate an uninstall routine.

Note   Ccmclean.exe is a powerful tool that can also be used to perform other uninstall tasks, such as uninstalling a management point. To ensure that only the client is uninstalled from a management point, use the command line syntax: Ccmclean.exe client.

Removing the Legacy Client

In contrast to the Advanced Client, if the Legacy Client's site assignment changes, say because the client roamed to different site boundaries, that client's site assignment changes and its component configuration is updated according to the new site's settings.

However, if the Legacy Client's IP address or Active Directory site assignment no longer falls within the boundaries of its assigned site and the client is no longer assigned to any site, the client software is automatically removed from the client. So one way to remove SMS from a large number of Legacy Clients at one time is to change the site server's site boundaries so that the clients' subnets or Active Directory site assignments are no longer represented, meaning that the client is no longer assigned to the site. During the client's next maintenance interval, the SMS components will be uninstalled from the Legacy Client. Similarly, if the Legacy Client is unable to contact a CAP in its assigned site for 60 days, the client software is automatically removed.

Note   If you change the site boundaries to effect an uninstall of the Legacy Client, be sure to factor in extra time for those clients that might be turned off or not connected to the site. Also, this method won't work if travel mode has been enabled.

A couple of other techniques are available for uninstalling the Legacy Client software from individual clients. You could run the SMSMan.exe programs as described earlier in this chapter. Uninstall options are available both through the wizard and through the command prompt versions of this program. You can run SMSMan.exe by connecting to the CAP or by navigating to %Systemroot%\MS\SMS\Core\Bin\00000409 folder on the client itself.

Another method of uninstalling SMS from the clients is through a registry modification made on the client, as we saw in Chapter 2, "Primary Site

Installation." To use this method, follow these steps (which may vary depending on the operating system you are using):

1. As an administrator, open the client's registry.

2. In the Registry Editor, navigate to the HKEY_LOCAL_MACHINE\ Software\Microsoft\SMS\Client\Configuration\Client Properties key.

3. Select the Client Properties key, and choose Add Value from the Edit menu to display the Add Value dialog box. In the Value Name text box, enter *SMS Client Deinstall*. Leave the Data Type setting as REG_SZ. Click OK to return to the Registry Editor.

4. In the String Editor dialog box, enter *TRUE* in the String text box and then click OK.

5. Close the Registry Editor to save your changes.

6. Stop and restart the SMS Client Service (Clisvc.exe). The SMS Client Service will read the new registry entry and initiate an uninstall boot-strap process.

Tip   You could also use the 20clicln.bat utility and its support files that are included with the SMS 2.0 Support Tools available from Microsoft's SMS Web site (*http://www.microsoft.com/smserver/downloads*).

Regardless of the method you choose, the uninstall process might take several minutes depending on the number of components installed.

Checkpoints

If you've read this chapter carefully, you've already compiled a list of potential problems regarding client installation. The most obvious sources of error occur in four areas:

- Be sure that an appropriate client installation method or methods has been selected, enabled, and properly configured. It would be a good idea to review all your clients (servers and workstations) to determine whether your selected installation method is appropriate for all your clients. For example, a logon script initiated installation method might not be appropriate for installing the SMS client on Windows servers at which administrators rarely or never log on locally.

- Be sure that the client can actually be assigned to your SMS site by confirming the site boundaries. Remember that SMS uses not only the subnet address and mask of the client but also its Active Directory site assignment to determine a client's site assignment.

- If you're managing Advanced Clients that will roam from site to site and subnet to subnet, be sure to enable and configure appropriate roaming boundaries for the site and the clients.

- Be sure that whatever client installation account you're using—the SMS Service account or your own designated SMS Client Push Installation account—has local administrative rights on the client.

Summary

In this chapter we've thoroughly explored the client installation methods for both the Legacy and the Advanced Client and enabled them and our client installation accounts accordingly. We've examined the installation process and also seen how that process ties in to the discovery and site assignment processes. We've noted the changes that take place on the client after SMS has been installed, including modifications made to the client's registry and the amount of disk space required. We've even seen how to go about removing SMS from the client should the need arise. Now that we've installed our clients, the next step is to enable and configure the client agents that will enable us to more completely manage these clients—agents such as the Remote Tools Client Agent and the Advertised Programs Client Agent. We'll begin with the inventory agents in Chapter 9, "Inventory Collection."

Chapter 9
Inventory Collection

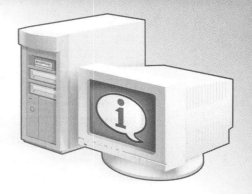

Collection of hardware and software inventory from Microsoft Systems Management Server (SMS) clients is certainly one of the more popular client options that SMS administrators can enable for their SMS sites. Inventory collection offers the obvious advantage of reporting to a central database certain specific pieces of information that can be of interest or use to the SMS administrator. Data such as disk space, memory, processor type, NIC, operating system, IP address, and software installed can be reported to the SMS database. You might then use that information to identify which clients need an upgrade or a patch for a particular piece of software or an upgrade to Microsoft Windows XP, for example, or to identify which clients have the hardware requirements to support a program installation or an upgrade.

In this chapter we'll explore the inventory collection process for hardware and software, including how to enable the hardware inventory and software inventory, how to view inventory, and how to customize the hardware inventory. As in previous chapters, we'll also look at the log files and status messages that are generated throughout the inventory collection process and discuss how to interpret them.

Note Hardware and software inventory provide the same functionality on the Advanced Client and the Legacy Client.

Hardware Inventory

The Hardware Inventory Client Agent (Inventory Agent on the Advanced Client) collects a broad assortment of hardware properties from the client. For the purposes of this discussion, I'll refer to the client agent for both client types as Hardware Inventory Client Agent, and I'll make distinctions between the behaviors of each when necessary.

When we think of hardware inventory, most of us, especially those of us familiar with earlier versions of SMS, think of the basic data: disk information such as space used and space available; memory, video, processor, and operating system data; and MAC, IP, and subnet addresses. To be sure, some of this hardware information sounds a lot like the discovery data stored in the discovery data records (DDRs) we looked at in Chapter 7, "Resource Discovery." However, hardware inventory is *nothing* like discovery data.

In fact, a great deal more hardware information is collected than just these basics. The hardware inventory process is designed to query the Windows Management Instrumentation (WMI) that's part of the SMS client installation to obtain its data. Windows Management itself can expose a vast amount of information about the client, obtaining information from various providers, including the WIN32 subsystem of Windows, the registry, the computer's basic input/output system (BIOS), and so on.

SMS uses an inventory collection file to determine how much information is collected from WMI classes and queries for approximately 1,500 different hardware properties. The inventory collection file is a Managed Object Format (MOF) file and is named SMS_def.mof. The master version of this file is stored on the SMS site server. The amount of data reported about each of the basic hardware components is considerable and can actually be extended further. For example, you could report on program groups created on the client, or network printer connections, or account information such as the user's full name or security ID (SID). This extension is done by modifying the SMS_def.mof file to include additional WMI classes. We'll talk more about this file later in this chapter.

You can also add data to the inventory data normally collected. For example, you could add asset-related information, or contact names, and so on. You accomplish this reporting through the creation of text files known as Management Information Format (MIF) files that you present to SMS as an update to the database record for a specific SMS client.

If information isn't available directly through the Hardware Inventory Client Agent, you can update client records with your own manually generated data—or even create whole new classes of object types, such as "multimedia equipment." Or you can obtain one of several new third-party add-ons to SMS 2003 to obtain data such as OEM-specific DMI-based information. Once hardware inventory has been collected at the client, it's passed on to the client access point (CAP) if the client is a Legacy Client or the management point if the client is an Advanced Client. The CAP or management point, in turn, forwards the hardware inventory to the site server. Hardware inventory is ultimately stored in the SMS site database, so it's important to draw a distinction between primary and secondary site servers. As we saw in Chapter 4, "Multiple-Site Structures," the main difference between a primary and a secondary site server is that a primary site server maintains access to an SQL Server database.

In the case of hardware inventory, this doesn't mean that you can't enable the Hardware Inventory Client Agent on a secondary site server for its clients. In fact, you can, and the agent's configuration settings can even be different from the secondary site's parent site. When hardware inventory is passed to the secondary site server, the secondary site server forwards the information to its parent primary site, where it can be added to the SMS database. The Advanced Client will pass its inventory to the management point of the parent site, unless a proxy management point has been installed at the secondary site.

Enabling Hardware Inventory

Let's begin by getting the Hardware Inventory Client Agent enabled and installed on our SMS clients. Then we'll explore how inventory is actually collected. You can enable the Hardware Inventory Client Agent through the SMS Administrator Console. To do so, follow these steps:

1. Under Site Settings, navigate to the Client Agents folder and expand it.

2. Right-click Hardware Inventory Client Agent and choose Properties from the context menu to display the Hardware Inventory Client Agent Properties dialog box shown in Figure 9-1.

Figure 9-1.   *The Hardware Inventory Client Agent Properties dialog box.*

3. Select the Enable Hardware Inventory On Clients check box.

4. The default inventory collection schedule on the client is once a week. With the Simple Schedule option, you can specify collection to run once every 1 to 23 hours, 1 to 31 days, or 1 to 4 weeks. Or you can select Full Schedule and then click the Schedule button to display the Schedule dialog box, shown in Figure 9-2. Here you can designate a more specific start time and recurrence pattern. When you've finished, click OK.

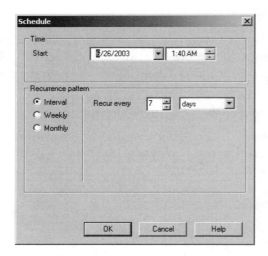

Figure 9-2. *The Schedule dialog box.*

5. You can modify the default value for the Maximum Custom MIF File Size if you anticipate using custom MIFs larger than 250 KB to append data to the inventory data being collected.

6. Use the options in the MIF Collection tab shown in Figure 9-3 to identify whether to collect custom MIF files (IDMIF and NOIDMIF) from the Legacy Client and the Advanced Client.

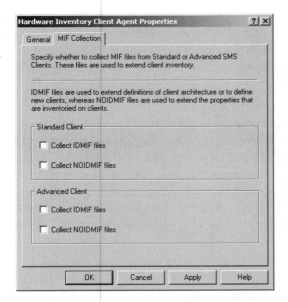

Figure 9-3.   *The Hardware Inventory Client Agent Properties dialog box MIF Collection tab.*

7. Click OK again to begin the site update process.

When you enable the Hardware Inventory Client Agent, you are, of course, making a change to the site properties, and the site's site control file (Site-ctrl.ct0) will be updated as a result (as described in Chapter 3, "Configuring Site Server Properties and Site Systems"). The following three files are written to the SMS\Inboxes\Clicfg.src directory on the site server:

- **Hinv.cfg**   Contains the Hardware Inventory Client Agent configuration settings
- **Hinv.nal**   Contains the CAPs from which the Hardware Inventory Client Agent can be installed
- **Hinv.pkg**   Contains the instructions for installing the Hardware Inventory Client Agent on the client for various platforms

In the same directory, the client offer (.OFR) file for Legacy Clients and the Advanced Client policy is also updated to indicate that the Hardware Inventory Client Agent needs to be installed on all SMS clients for the site. This file is named Cli_*xxx*.ofr, where *xxx* represents the client operating system platform.

The site server uses the client offer file to notify its clients of any client components that need to be installed, updated, or removed. It's created on the site server and copied to each CAP for the site. The Advanced Client policy acts similarly for Advanced Clients and is propagated to the management point.

The next time the SMS client restarts or at the next client update interval—every 25 hours—the client obtains the updated client component information and the agent is installed. In the case of the Advanced Client, the agent was already installed but not enabled when the Advanced Client software was first installed, so it's simply enabled. At this time, the SMS_def.mof file is compiled into the WMI layer on the client, the agent support files are installed, the hardware inventory log files are updated, and the agent is started. Ten minutes after the Hardware Inventory Client Agent is started, the first complete inventory is collected from the client as specified by the SMS_def.mof file through WMI and is then copied to the CAP.

Client Requirements and Inventory Frequency

A complete default inventory will generate a hardware information file about 200 KB in size. A copy is stored on the client as part of the WMI Common Information Model (CIM) repository. The initial inventory is also passed to the CAP and then to the site server. Subsequent inventory files generally report only changes to the hardware inventory, however, so you can expect a corresponding amount of network traffic associated with the installation (one time), with the first complete inventory (one time), and with subsequent delta inventories (according to your schedule). The *delta inventory* is an inventory cycle that creates a delta inventory file containing the information that has changed since the previous inventory.

The schedule you specify should reflect the frequency with which you need to collect or update your clients' inventory record. If your clients have fairly standard hardware installations and don't make, or aren't allowed to make, substantial changes on their own, you could collect inventory less frequently—say, once a week or even once a month.

However, if your client computers are volatile regarding hardware changes, you might need to report changes to the inventory more frequently—perhaps once a day or once every 12 hours. The more frequent the inventory, the more potential network traffic will be generated. The Hardware Inventory Client Agent reports inventory regardless of whether a user is actually logged on to the client. If the client isn't currently connected to the network, the agent will still run and store the collected data on the client until the next time the client can connect.

Tip   The Hardware Inventory Client Agent can be forced to run through Systems Management in the Control Panel. Double-click the Systems Management icon to display the Systems Management Properties dialog box and then select the Components tab. On Legacy Clients, select the Hardware Inventory Agent entry in the Components list and then click the Start Component button. On Advanced Clients, select the Hardware Inventory Cycle in the Actions tab and then click the Initiate Action button.

Caution   Inventory stored in the SMS database is historical in nature, meaning that it's only as accurate as the last time you collected the inventory record. If your clients are volatile, as described earlier, and you rely on the inventory to identify clients' available disk space for installation applications, you might require an inventory schedule that's more frequent.

Hardware Inventory Collection Process Flow

Now let's explore the hardware inventory collection process in more detail. Recall that the Hardware Inventory Client Agent uses WMI to obtain hardware inventory data about various classes of objects designated in the SMS_def.mof file. When the Hardware Inventory Client Agent is scheduled to run, it reads the SMS_def.mof file and queries the CIM Object Manager component of WMI for the object properties it needs to report on. The CIM Object Manager, in turn, retrieves the current information from the appropriate object providers, such as WIN32, and then passes the data to the Hardware Inventory Client Agent.

The first time the Hardware Inventory Client Agent runs—approximately 10 minutes after its installation—a complete inventory is collected and its history is maintained in the CIM repository on each client. Each subsequent inventory generates a delta file only, detailing only those inventory properties that have changed since the last interval.

At this time, the agent looks for any NOIDMIFs that might reside in the %Windir%\MS\SMS\Noidmifs folder on a Legacy Client or the %Windir%\System32\CCM\Inventory\Noidmifs folder on an Advanced Client. Refer to the section entitled "MIF Files" later in this chapter for details about MIF files. If the client deems the MIF file to be valid, it's included as part of the inventory file. If not, a Badmifs subfolder is created under the Noidmifs or Idmifs folder, depending on the MIF type, and the invalid file is moved there.

Note   The Badmifs folder is created only if a bad NOIDMIF or IDMIF is detected. By default, the maximum MIF file size is set to 250 KB, although you can change this value through the Hardware Inventory Client Agent properties described earlier. A NOIDMIF or an IDMIF is considered bad if it exceeds the maximum size or if it can't be parsed successfully because of syntax errors or because, in the case of IDMIFs, it's being used to update the system architecture for an existing client record.

The MIF data is appended to the inventory data already collected and a temporary inventory file is created on the client. The Legacy Client sends the inventory file to the CAP_site\Inventry.box folder on the CAP. The Advanced Client sends the inventory file to the SMS_CCM\Inventory folder on the management point.

Note   Once the inventory file is copied to the CAP or management point, the temporary inventory files are deleted. This process generally happens in a matter of seconds, so you might not see the files unless you're watching closely.

Inbox Manager Assistant running on the CAP, and the SMS Management Point File Dispatch Manager on the management point, in turn moves the file to Inventory Processor's inbox (the SMS\Inboxes\Inventry.box folder) on the site server. If the site server is a primary site server, Inventory Processor adds a binary header to the .NHM file, renames it with the extension .MIF, and moves it to Inventory Data Loader's inbox (the SMS\Inboxes\Dataldr.box folder). Inventory Data Loader then reads the .MIF file, parses the data, and writes it to the SMS database on the server running SQL. If a parent site exists, Inventory Data Loader forwards the .MIF file to Replication Manager, which forwards it to Inventory Data Loader's inbox on the parent site server.

If the site server is a secondary site server, Replication Manager forwards the .MIF file to the parent primary site server's Inventory Data Loader inbox, where it's processed as described earlier.

Hardware Resynchronization

Occasionally, Inventory Data Loader might determine that the inventory data it receives is somehow "bad" or out of sync with the SMS database. In these instances, a resynchronization (resync) will be triggered automatically. *Resync* is a corrective process that can cause the client agent to ignore the history file and collect a complete hardware inventory. Specific events that trigger hardware inventory resync include the following:

- The SMS_def.mof file has changed since the last inventory (Legacy Clients only).

- The inventory delta contains updates for a database record that doesn't exist.
- The inventory delta itself contains bad or corrupted data.
- The client has attached to a new SMS site.
- The client has upgraded from SMS 2.0 to SMS 2003.

Note Resync doesn't change the hardware inventory schedule—the next inventory cycle will start at the scheduled time.

When a resync is triggered for a Legacy Client, Inventory Data Loader creates a .CFG file for the client and writes a resync request to it. This file is maintained in the SMS\Inboxes\Clidata.src folder on the site server. Inbox Manager writes this file to the corresponding folder on the CAP (CAP_Site\Clidata.box). At the next client update cycle or when an update is forced, the .CFG file is read, the client's registry is updated with the resync information (on 32-bit clients), and the SMS Client Service directs the Hardware Inventory Client Agent on the Legacy Client to generate a complete hardware inventory.

When a resync is triggered for an Advanced Client, the Inventory Data Loader purges any NOIDMIF data that was received from the client. The Policy Provider on the site server creates a resync policy and sends it to the management point. At the next policy refresh period on the Advanced Client, the resync request is received, and a full hardware inventory is run.

Status Messages and Log Files for Hardware Inventory

Status messages and log files are generated throughout the inventory installation and collection process. Let's begin with the log files. Unlike log files generated on the site server, client logs are enabled by default and written automatically to the \MS\SMS\Logs folder on each Legacy Client and to the %Windir%\System32\Ccm\Logs folder on each Advanced Client. When monitoring hardware inventory on the Legacy Client, you should view the Ccim32.log file for entries related to the detection of the Hardware Inventory Client Agent offer. For example, the notification that the Hardware Inventory Client Agent needs to be installed is made to the client through the client offer file, as discussed in the section entitled "Enabling Hardware Inventory" earlier in this chapter. Monitor the SMSapm32.log file for entries related to Advertised Programs Monitor scheduling the installation of the Hardware Inventory Client Agent. Inhinv32.log tracks the installation of the agent.

Hinv32.log tracks the generation of inventory files as well as updates to the SMS_def.mof file, as illustrated in Figure 9-4. Notice the start of the inventory cycle as well as the enumeration of object classes.

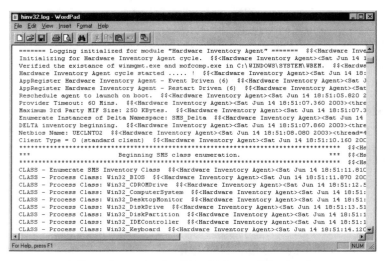

Figure 9-4. *Sample entries for Hinv32.log in Wordpad.*

Cqmgr32.log tracks the copying of inventory and status messages to the CAP, as illustrated in Figure 9-5. Notice when the client connects to the Inventry.box folder on the CAP.

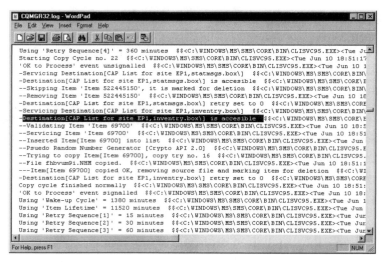

Figure 9-5. *Sample entries for Cqmgr32.log in Wordpad.*

You should also monitor the respective log files for Inventory Processor (Invproc.log), Inventory Data Loader (Dataldr.log), Inbox Manager (Inboxmgr.log), and Inbox Manager Assistant (Inboxast.log) to monitor their part in the inventory collection process.

On the Advanced Client, monitor the Policyagent.log file for updates received by the client, which would include enabling Inventory Agent on the client and configuring hardware inventory collection. Monitor the Inventoryagent.log file, a portion of which is shown in Figure 9-6, for collection of inventory data.

Figure 9-6. *Sample entries for Inventoryagent.log in Notepad.*

You can view status messages regarding inventory activity on a client by running a status message query through the SMS Administrator Console. To do so, follow these steps:

1. Navigate to the System Status folder, expand it, and select the Status Message Queries folder.

2. Right-click the query All Status Messages From A Specific System and choose Show Messages from the context menu to display the All Status Messages From A Specific System properties page, as shown in Figure 9-7.

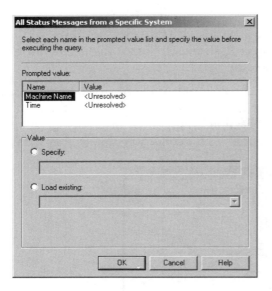

Figure 9-7. *The All Status Messages From A Specific System properties page.*

3. In the Prompted Value list, select Machine Name. Click Specify and enter the name of the client computer you want to report on or select Load Existing to have SMS query the database and compile a list of all client names it has recorded.

Note This process can take a while for large databases.

4. Select Time in the Prompted Value list. The options in the Value frame will change. Either specify a starting date and time from which you want to see status messages or choose Select Date And Time to enter a range of hours (1, 2, 6, or 12 hours ago).

5. Click OK. The SMS Status Message Viewer will display all the status messages recorded for that client during the period specified.

Look for message IDs of 10500, indicating that inventory has been successfully collected; 10505, indicating that the inventory schema (SMS_def.mof) has been updated; and 10204 from Client Component Installation Manager (CCIM), reporting that the Hardware Inventory Client Agent was successfully installed. Note that CCIM made this report an hour later, which is its verification cycle.

For a list of clients that have installed the Hardware Inventory Client Agent, run the status message query Legacy Clients That Installed The Hardware

Inventory Client Agent. To view status messages for clients based on their collection membership, run the status message query All Status Messages For A Specific Collection At A Specific Site. Of course, you could create your own status message query as well. Refer back to Chapter 5, "Analysis and Troubleshooting Tools," for more information on how to create status message queries.

On the site server, monitor the status messages of Inventory Data Loader. Look for messages in the 27*xx* range identifying successful processing of MIFs. Monitor the status messages for Inventory Processor for resynchronization or the processing of .RAW files from 16-bit clients and monitor status messages for Replication Manager for forwarding of MIF files to a parent site.

You can also use the SMS Report Viewer to view status information related to the inventory process. To launch the SMS Report Viewer, follow these steps:

1. Navigate to the Reporting folder in the SMS Administrator console.

2. Right-click the Reporting folder. From the context menu, select All Tasks, then Run, then the name of the reporting point site system (if there's more than one) to display the SMS Report Viewer shown in Figure 9-8.

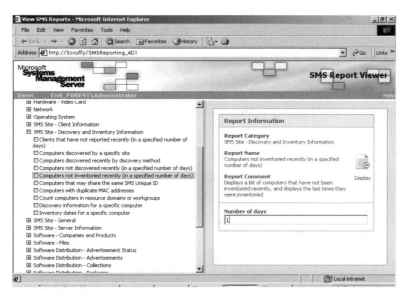

Figure 9-8. *The SMS Report Viewer.*

3. Expand SMS Site-Discovery and Inventory Information and select an appropriate report. In Figure 9-8, I selected Computers Not Inventoried Recently. Enter whatever prompted information is required and then click Display. The results are displayed in a results window, as shown in Figure 9-9.

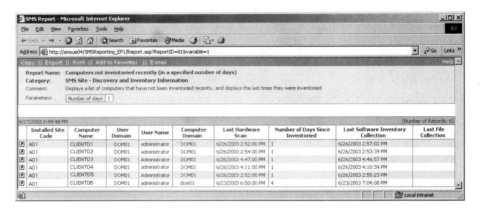

Figure 9-9. *The results window for a report run through the SMS Report Viewer.*

Viewing Hardware Inventory

You view hardware inventory through the SMS Administrator Console. To do that, complete the following steps:

1. Navigate to the Collections folder and expand it.

2. Select the collection that contains the client or clients whose inventory you want to view.

3. Right-click the appropriate client entry in the right pane, choose All Tasks from the context menu, and then choose Start Resource Explorer.

4. In the Resource Explorer window, expand Hardware to view a list of object classes for which properties have been collected, as shown in Figure 9-10. Select each object to view its instances and properties.

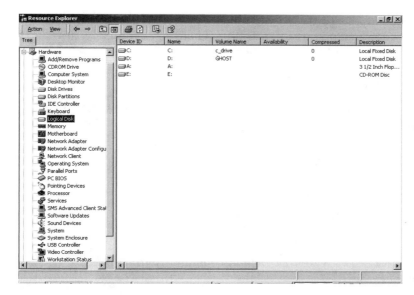

Figure 9-10.   *The Resource Explorer window, with Logical Disk selected.*

The Resource Explorer window lists properties horizontally across the viewing screen, requiring you to scroll across to see all the properties. However, if you right-click an object and choose Properties from the context menu, you can view the same properties listed in a vertical column, as shown in Figure 9-11.

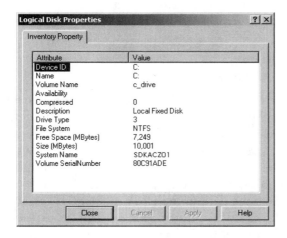

Figure 9-11.   *The Logical Disk Properties dialog box.*

5. Expand Hardware History to view information collected from previous inventories such as Logical Disk History, Memory History, and Operating System History, as shown in Figure 9-12.

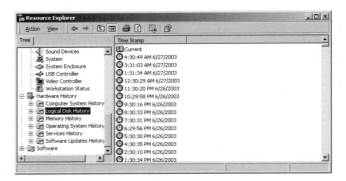

Figure 9-12. *The Resource Explorer window, with Hardware History expanded.*

Tip You could use Hardware History to develop resource usage trends for your clients—for example, to track how much disk storage is utilized over a period of time or whether paging might be excessive due to a lack of RAM.

The entries listed under Hardware in the Resource Explorer window represent the object classes identified through the SMS_def.mof file and any MIF files that were created to be appended to or modify the client's inventory record. As you can see, it's quite a thorough list. You can actually collect more than 10 times the amount of data than you could through the hardware inventory process in earlier versions of SMS.

Customizing Hardware Inventory

There are two ways to customize the inventory that you collect from a client or add to the database as a new class of object: you can modify the default SMS_def.mof file or you can create custom MIF files. Either method requires some planning and testing on the part of you, the SMS administrator. As we've seen, the default SMS_def.mof file collects a large amount of data—around 200 KB per client. Modifying the file could result in larger amounts of data to track, more network traffic when sending the data to the CAPs and site server, and so on. Adding an MIF file can also result in additional inventory data being reported. Also, although the SMS_def.mof exists as a template that can be modified, in general, MIF files must be created.

SMS_def.mof

As mentioned, you can consider the SMS_def.mof file a template that defines for Windows Management on SMS clients which inventory objects, or hardware classes, should be queried and how much data should be collected for each. The master SMS_def.mof file is maintained in the SMS\Inboxes\Clifiles.src\Hinv folder on the site server. This file is copied to the CAP (CAP_Site\Clifiles.box\Hinv) and ultimately to each Legacy Client (%Windir%\MS\SMS\Sitefile*site*\Hinv). For Advanced Clients, the SMS_def.mof file is used to create an inventory rules policy that's propagated to each Advanced Client through the management point.

You can modify the class and property settings contained in the SMS_def.mof file or add new classes and properties by opening the file with any text editor such as Microsoft Notepad. Figure 9-13 shows a portion of an SMS_def.mof file as displayed using Notepad. Each class and property includes a flag named SMS_Report. When this flag is set to True, the property is collected as part of inventory. In Figure 9-13, you can see that the SMS_Report flag for the class SMS_LogicalDisk is set to True and that the values for the properties Availability, Description, DeviceID, DriveType, FileSystem, and FreeSpace will be collected from the client. Figure 9-14 displays a list of the Class Qualifiers and their descriptions as outlined in the SMS_def.mof file.

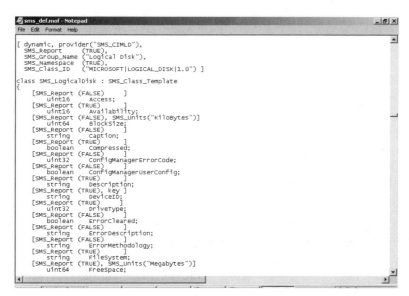

Figure 9-13.   *Sample of SMS_def.mof file displayed using Notepad.*

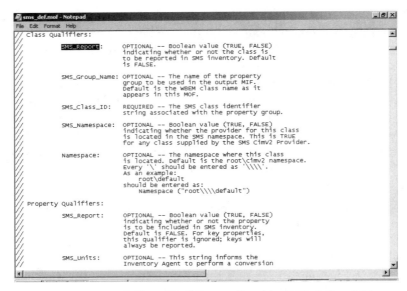

Figure 9-14. *List of Class Qualifiers as listed in SMS_def.mof file.*

If you want to prevent a class or property from collecting inventory data, set the SMS_Report flag to False. If you want to enable a class or property to collect data for inventory, set the flag to True.

More Info A detailed explanation of the use and editing of the SMS_def.mof file is included in Chapter 2 of the *Microsoft Systems Management Server 2003 Operations Guide*, available for viewing and download through Microsoft TechNet, and available as a print book from Microsoft's SMS Web site (*http://www.microsoft.com/smserver*) as well.

MIF Files

Another way to modify the hardware inventory is through the creation of MIF files. MIF files modify the database by creating architectures, object classes, and attributes. Architectures define entire new classes of objects, whereas object classes and attributes are generally added to existing architectures.

You can create two types of MIF files: NOIDMIFs and IDMIFs. NOIDMIFs are used to modify or append object classes and properties to existing client inventory records—hence the term "no id." You're not creating a new architecture; you're simply appending to an existing architecture—namely, System

Resources. You could use a NOIDMIF to add a client system's asset number, information about peripheral devices attached to the computer, or even the department name or code to the existing client record.

IDMIFs, on the other hand, are used to create new architectures of object classes and attributes. For example, suppose you want to report on all the multimedia equipment you have in your organization. Through an IDMIF, you could create a new architecture (say, Multimedia Equipment) with its own object classes—(perhaps *Audio*, *Video*, *CD*, *Tape*, or *PC Conferencing*), each of which would have one or more attributes (*Model*, *Manufacturer*, *Asset number*, *Cost*, and so on). You can also use IDMIFs to update existing architectures—for example, to add stand-alone computers to the database or to associate an architecture with existing computer records for the purpose of creating queries and collections that can be linked to unique properties.

> **More Info**   Although it would be nice to present examples showing how each of these types of MIFs can be used and explain their basic structure, we don't want to reinvent the wheel here with an in-depth explanation of MIF usage and interaction. You can find that level of detail, along with a detailed discussion of MOF files, in the *Microsoft Systems Management Server 2003 Operations Guide*, available as a print book from Microsoft's SMS Web site (*http://www.microsoft.com/smserver*) and also through Microsoft TechNet. Be sure to read Chapter 3, "Advanced Inventory Collection," which discusses customizing hardware inventory, if you want to use MIF and MOF files to their greatest advantage.

The basic structure of IDMIFs and NOIDMIFs is essentially the same. Because they're text files, you can create them using any text editor. Actually, most third-party add-ons for SMS 2003 are capable of generating MIF files that update the database with various kinds of information. SMS Installer can notify the site server about the successful or failed installation of an application through a status MIF file. The MIF file format is an industry standard format. If you've created any kind of scripts or batch files in the past, you'll find it easy to create an MIF file. Let's start with the NOIDMIF.

Creating a NOIDMIF   NOIDMIFs are perhaps the most commonly used MIF file because they add to existing computer records and they're the easiest to create. Figure 9-15 shows a sample of a NOIDMIF designed to add the client computer's department name and department code to its existing hardware record in the SMS database.

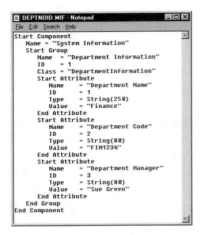

Figure 9-15. *A sample NOIDMIF file.*

NOIDMIFs always begin with Start Component and a general component name. The next step is to create an object class. You do this by adding the Start Group statement, a name describing the group, an ID, and a class. The Name attribute is the string displayed in the Resource Explorer that refers to this class. The ID attribute represents this group in relation to any other group in this MIF. For example, if you add another group, you would give it an ID of 2, and so on—the number is unique. The Class attribute is used by SMS internally for processing the group information.

Next you list each attribute that you're adding for this object. In this case we're adding three attributes: *Department Name*, *Department Code*, and *Department Manager*. Each attribute entry begins with Start Attribute and ends with End Attribute. For each attribute you must provide at a minimum *Name*, *ID*, *Type*, and *Value* settings. These attributes are fairly self-explanatory. *Name* is a descriptive attribute name. *ID* represents the attribute in relation to other attributes. *Type* indicates whether the value is a text string, a number, or a list, and gives the value's length when appropriate. *Value*, of course, is the current value you're assigning to the attribute. You end the MIF file with End Group and End Component statements.

Save the NOIDMIF with a descriptive filename and the .MIF extension. You must place the file in the %Windir% \MS\SMS\Noidmifs folder on each client you want to update. You can do this using SMS 2003's package distribution process, which will be discussed in Chapter 12, "Package Distribution and Management." At the next hardware inventory cycle, the MIF file will be read, evaluated for syntax, and added to the client's inventory file, as described in the section entitled "Hardware Inventory Collection Process Flow" earlier in this chapter, and then updated to the client's SMS database record. You can then view it through Resource Explorer, where it will be listed along with the other classes that were collected.

> **Caution**   Be sure that the MIF file you create using a text editor is saved with the .MIF extension. Text editors such as Notepad append a .TXT extension. It's easy to miss this, and if you do, you'll spend an inordinate amount of time trying to figure out why the MIF file isn't working.

Creating an IDMIF   As mentioned, the basic structure of an IDMIF is similar to that of a NOIDMIF. The main difference comes at the beginning of an IDMIF file, as you can see in the example shown in Figure 9-16.

IDMIFs require that you include the following two statements at the top of the MIF:

- **//Architecture**   Identifies the name of the new architecture (object class) you're creating

- **//UniqueID**   Defines a single unique value that identifies this specific instance of the architecture in the database

Figure 9-16.   *A sample IDMIF file.*

IDMIFs also require that you include a top-level group that has the same name as the architecture and that has at least one attribute defined. Also, if a class has more than one instance within an architecture, you must have defined at least one key attribute to avoid overwriting previous instances with subsequent information. A key value is simply one of the group attributes. As with NOIDMIFs, you must save the file with an .MIF extension. You can place the file in the %Windir%\MS\SMS\Idmifs folder on any SMS client.

Viewing an IDMIF   Unlike NOIDMIFs, which are associated with specific clients, IDMIFs generally add new object classes to the database. Therefore, you can't view this information through Resource Explorer. Instead, you must create a query to extract and view the relevant data from the SMS database. For details on creating queries, refer to Chapter 16, "Queries and Reports."

As mentioned, NOIDMIFs are generally associated with individual client records, and, as such, they must be placed in the %Windir%\MS\SMS\Noidmifs folder on each client. Of course, you can use SMS package distribution to accomplish this. IDMIFs can also be placed in the Idmifs folder on the SMS client. However, since IDMIFs generally aren't associated with any one client, you can place an IDMIF in the Idmifs folder on any SMS client. For that matter, you could also place the IDMIF in the CAP_*Site*\Inventry.box folder on the CAP or in the SMS\Inboxes\Inventry.box folder on the site server. The result will be the same.

Software Inventory

SMS 2003 offers greatly enhanced software inventory capabilities. Like its hardware counterpart, the Software Inventory Client Agent (Inventory Agent on the Advanced Client) runs automatically on the client according to a schedule you create and collects information according to options you select. For the purposes of this discussion, I'll refer to the client agent for both client types as Software Inventory Client Agent, and I'll make distinctions between the behaviors of each when necessary. Unlike the Hardware Inventory Client Agent, the Software Inventory Client Agent scans local drives rather than querying the WMI for its inventory data.

The Software Inventory Client Agent collects application information that includes the following data:

- Filename, version, and size
- Manufacturer name
- Product name, version, and language
- Date and time of file creation (presumably at installation)

The Software Inventory Client Agent can also collect copies of specific files.

As with hardware inventory, once software inventory has been collected at the Legacy Client, it's passed on to the CAP. Inventory collected at the Advanced

Client is, of course, passed on to the management point. The CAP or management point, in turn, forwards the information to the site server. Software inventory is ultimately stored in the SMS database, so it's again important for us to draw a distinction between primary and secondary site servers. Recall that the main difference between a primary and a secondary site server is that a primary site server maintains access to an SQL Server database.

As with hardware inventory, you can enable the Software Inventory Client Agent for the clients on a secondary site. As a matter of fact, the configuration settings for the Software Inventory Client Agent can even be different from the secondary site's parent site. When the CAP passes software inventory to the secondary site server, the secondary site server forwards the information to its parent primary site, where it can be added to the SMS database. The Advanced Client will pass its inventory to the management point of the parent site, unless a proxy management point has been installed at the secondary site.

Enabling Software Inventory

To begin, let's get the Software Inventory Client Agent enabled and installed on our SMS clients. Then we'll explore how inventory is actually collected. To enable the Software Inventory Agent through the SMS Administrator Console, follow these steps:

1. Under Site Settings, navigate to the Client Agents folder and expand it.

2. Right-click Software Inventory Client Agent and choose Properties from the context menu to display the Software Inventory Client Agent Properties dialog box, shown in Figure 9-17.

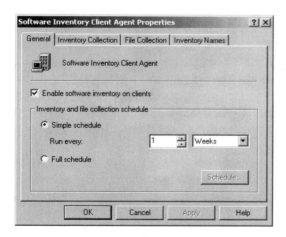

Figure 9-17.   *The Software Inventory Client Agent Properties dialog box.*

3. Select the Enable Software Inventory On Clients check box.

4. Notice that the default inventory collection schedule on the client will be once a week. You can specify from 1 to 23 hours, 1 to 31 days, or 1 to 4 weeks under Simple Schedule. Or you can select Full Schedule and then click the Schedule button to display the Schedule dialog box and designate a more specific start time and recurrence pattern, and then choose OK.

5. Select the Inventory Collection tab, shown in Figure 9-18.

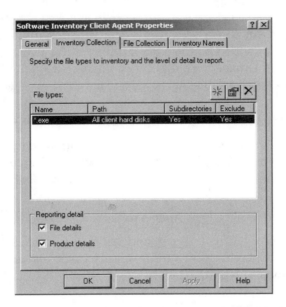

Figure 9-18. *The Software Inventory Client Agent Properties dialog box Inventory Collection tab.*

6. Notice that the default files that the agent will scan for are those with an .EXE extension. You can click the New button (the yellow star) to display the Inventoried File Properties dialog box shown in Figure 9-19. Here you can identify the file or files to inventory using wildcards and specific paths and choose whether to exclude encrypted or compressed files from the inventory scan.

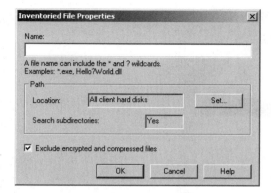

Figure 9-19.   *The Inventoried File Properties dialog box.*

7. On the Inventory Collection tab, check the appropriate options under Reporting Detail. These two options can tailor how data is collected and represented to you:

   - *File Details*—Reports information that the agent can determine for all files that match the criteria, including "unknown" files. Unknown files include those for which the header information contains no product information—for example, some game files. File details include the file name, location, and size.

   - *Product Details*—Reports information that the agent can read from the file header of all files that match the criteria. Product details include company name, product name, version, and language.

   You must enable at least one of the two options to enable SMS to report information on inventoried files. By default, both options are enabled.

8. Select the File Collection tab, shown in Figure 9-20, if you want to also collect a copy of specific files from each client. The Maximum Traffic Per Client value displayed at the bottom of this tab is informational and represents the estimated amount of traffic that the specified files might generate.

Figure 9-20. *The Software Inventory Client Agent Properties dialog box File Collection tab.*

9. To add the name of a specific file, click the New button to display the Collected File Properties dialog box, similar to the Inventoried Files dialog box. Here you can identify the file or files to inventory using wildcards and specific paths and choose whether to exclude encrypted or compressed files from the inventory scan and the maximum file size. Click OK to return to the File Collection tab.

10. Select the Inventory Names tab, shown in Figure 9-21, to standardize the names of the company or product that are displayed when you view software inventory information. Sometimes, as companies update their software applications or create new versions, the developers include variations on the company's or the product's name in the header information included in the program executable. Of course, when you view the software inventory, the products will be sorted and displayed according to each variation of the company or product name. This can make it difficult for you to find all versions of the product.

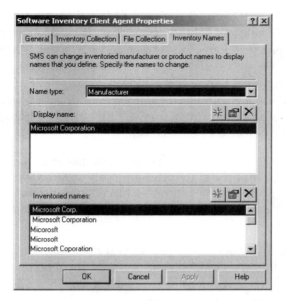

Figure 9-21. *The Software Inventory Client Agent Properties dialog box Inventory Names tab.*

This example lists several variations of the company name for Microsoft—Microsoft Corp., Microsoft Corporation, Microsoft, and so on—that will be displayed as Microsoft Corporation when viewing software inventory information.

11. Select which name type you want to standardize; your choices are Product and Manufacturer. In the Display Name section, click New to display the Display Name Properties dialog box. Enter the name you want to be displayed on the product information screen and then click OK to return to the Inventory Names tab. In the Inventoried Names section, click New to display the Inventoried Name Properties dialog box. Enter the names that have been inventoried by the Software Inventory Client Agent that you want standardized to the display name you entered in the Display Name section and then click OK to return to the Inventory Names tab.

12. Click OK to begin the site update process.

Collected files are stored on the site server in the SMS\Inboxes\Sinv.box\FileCol folder. If the file changes at all on the client, the Software Inventory Client

Agent will collect it again at the next cycle. By default, SMS will retain the last five copies of the file that were collected. Think about that. If you collected 1 MB per file and 5 collected copies per client, for 1000 clients you would require 5 GB of storage space just for your collected files. Not pretty! Obviously, you wouldn't use this as an alternative backup process. However, you can use it to look for files that should not be on a client, like a game executable. The number of such collected files ought to be significantly smaller. All collected files are kept in the database for 90 days before they're aged out.

Note To modify the number of copies of collected files maintained at the site server, you need to modify the following registry entry: HKEY_LOCAL_MACHINE\Software\Microsoft\SMS\Components\ SMS_Software_Inventory_Processor. Look for the value *Maximum Collected Files* and change it as desired.

When you enable the Software Inventory Client Agent, you're making a change to the site properties, and the site's site control file (Sitectrl.ct0) will be updated as a result (as described in Chapter 3). The following three files are written to the SMS\Inboxes\Clicfg.src directory on the site server:

- **Sinv.cfg**   Software Inventory Client Agent configuration settings

- **Sinv.nal**   CAPs from which the agent can be installed

- **Sinv.pkg**   Instructions for installing the agent on the client for various platforms

In the same directory, the client offer file is also updated to indicate that the Software Inventory Client Agent needs to be installed on all SMS clients for the site. The offer file is Cli_*xxx*.ofr, where *xxx* indicates the client operating system platform.

The offer file is copied to the CAP for use by Legacy Clients, and a software inventory rules policy is created and placed on the management point for use by Advanced Clients.

Thirty minutes after the Software Inventory Client Agent is started, the first complete inventory is collected from the client as specified by the inventory and collected files options you specified.

Client Requirements and Inventory Frequency

The client computer will require about 200 KB for the Software Inventory Client Agent support files. The size of the software inventory file that's generated will depend on what you told the agent to scan for, how much data it found, and whether you chose to collect files. Software inventory history is maintained on each client. The initial inventory is also passed to the CAP or management point and then to the site server. Like hardware inventory, subsequent software inventory cycles generally report only changes to the inventory. Therefore, you can expect a corresponding amount of network traffic associated with the installation (one time), with the first complete inventory (one time), and with subsequent delta inventories (according to your schedule).

As with hardware inventory, the schedule you choose should reflect the frequency with which you need to collect or update your clients' inventory record. If your clients have fairly standard software installations and don't make or aren't allowed to make substantial changes on their own, you could collect inventory less frequently—say, once a week or even once a month.

If your client computers keep changing in terms of software installations, updates, and uninstalls, you might need to report changes to the inventory more frequently—perhaps once a day or once every 12 hours. The more frequent the inventory is collected, the more potential network traffic will be generated. Like the Hardware Inventory Client Agent, the Software Inventory Client Agent will continue to run and report inventory regardless of whether a user is actually logged onto the client.

> **Tip**   You can force the Software Inventory Client Agent to run through Systems Management in the Control Panel. Double-click Systems Management to display the Properties dialog box and then select the Components tab. On Legacy Clients, select the Software Inventory Agent entry in the Components list and then click Start Component. On Advanced Clients, select the Software Inventory Cycle in the Actions tab and then click Initiate Action.

Software Inventory Collection Process Flow

The first time inventory collection runs—30 minutes after installation of the Software Inventory Client Agent—a complete software inventory is collected and its history is maintained on the client. Each subsequent inventory generates a delta file containing the details for only those inventory properties that have changed since the last interval. When a complete inventory file has been generated, the agent writes a temporary file with an .SIC (software inventory complete) extension to the %Windir%\MS\SMS\Clicomp\Sinv folder on the client until it's moved to the CAP. For subsequent inventory cycles, this delta file will have an .SID (software inventory delta) extension. On the Advanced Client, the temporary file is written to the %Windir%\System32\Ccm\Inventory\Temp folder until it's moved to the management point.

Note Once the inventory file is moved to the CAP or management point, the temporary files are deleted.

Inbox Manager Assistant running on the CAP, and the SMS Management Point File Dispatch Manager on the management point, in turn moves the file to Software Inventory Processor's inbox (the SMS\Inboxes\Sinv.box folder) on the site server. If the site server is a primary site server, Software Inventory Processor writes the data to the SMS database on the server running SQL. If the file is deemed corrupt, it's written to the SMS\Inboxes\Sinv.box\Badsinv folder. If a parent site exists, or if the site receiving the software inventory is a secondary site, Software Inventory Processor forwards the MIF file to Replication Manager, which forwards the file to the Software Inventory Processor inbox on the parent site server. Collected files are removed from the inventory file and written to the SMS\Inboxes\Sinv.box\FileCol\ID folder. Files collected from SMS clients are stored in a separate ID folder for each client. The ID folder name represents the resource ID assigned to the client when the client was discovered.

Tip You can find each client's resource ID by viewing its discovery data in the Collections folder in the SMS Administrator Console or by creating a query to display the resource IDs for all the clients.

Software Resynchronization

Occasionally, Software Inventory Processor might determine that the inventory data it receives is somehow "bad" or out of sync with the SMS database. In these circumstances, a resync will be triggered automatically. The following events can trigger a software inventory resync:

- The software inventory collection properties have changed since the last inventory (Legacy Clients only).

- The inventory delta contains updates for a database record that doesn't exist.

- The inventory delta itself contains bad or corrupted data.

- The client has attached to a new SMS site.

- The client has upgraded from SMS 2.0 to SMS 2003.

When one of these events triggers a resync, the rest of the process proceeds much like the hardware resynchronization process we discussed earlier. The difference, of course, is that the Software Inventory Processor on the site server creates the resync request.

Status Messages and Log Files for Software Inventory

As we've seen, status messages and log files are generated throughout the inventory installation and collection process. As we did for hardware inventory, let's begin here with the log files. As you know, client logs are enabled by default and are written automatically to the %Windir%\MS\SMS\Logs folder on Legacy Clients and the %Windir%\System32\Ccm\Logs folder on Advanced Clients. As you monitor the installation of the Software Inventory Client Agent on Legacy Clients, look for entries related to the detection of the Software Inventory Client Agent offer in the Ccim32.log file. Monitor the SMSapm32.log file for entries that show when the Advertised Programs Monitor scheduled the installation of the Software Inventory Client Agent on the client. Insinv32.log tracks the agent installation.

To track the generation of software inventory files on Legacy Clients, monitor the Sinv32.log. Cqmgr32.log tracks the copying of inventory and status messages to the CAP. Monitoring the log files for Software Inventory Processor (Sinvproc.log), Inbox Manager (Inboxmgr.log), and Inbox Manager Assistant (Inboxast.log) can help you determine the role of these files in the software inventory collection process.

On the Advanced Client, monitor the Policyagent.log file for updates received by the client, which would include enabling Inventory Agent on the client and configuring hardware inventory collection. Monitor the Inventoryagent.log file, a portion of which was shown previously in Figure 9-6, for collection of inventory data.

As we did for hardware inventory, you can view status messages regarding inventory activity on a client by running a status message query through the SMS Administrator Console using the process we described previously. A message with ID 10600 indicates that inventory has been successfully collected; 10605 indicates that a file has been collected; 10204 from CCIM reports that the Software Inventory Client Agent was successfully installed.

On the site server, monitor the status messages of Software Inventory Processor. Look for messages in the $37xx$ range, which identify successful processing of MIF files. Also monitor status messages for Replication Manager for forwarding of MIF files to a parent site.

As with hardware inventory, you can also use the SMS Report Viewer to view status information related to the inventory process

Viewing Software Inventory

You can view software inventory through the SMS Administrator Console in much the same way as you view hardware inventory. The procedure is described here:

1. Navigate to the Collections folder and expand it.

2. Select the collection that contains the client or clients whose inventory you want to view, right-click the client entry, choose All Tasks from the context menu, and then choose Start Resource Explorer to display the Resource Explorer window, shown in Figure 9-22.

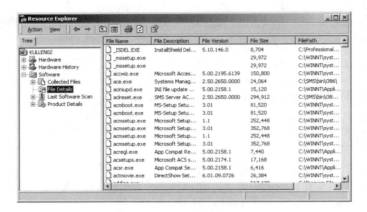

Figure 9-22. *The Resource Explorer window.*

3. Expand Software and select Collected Files to view a list of files collected for the client.

4. Select File Details to see a list of inventoried files and their properties, such as file name, size, and location, as shown in Figure 9-22.

Tip Properties are listed horizontally across the viewing screen, requiring you to scroll across to view all the properties. If you right-click an object and choose Properties from the context menu, you can view the same properties listed vertically in a Properties window.

5. Select Last Software Scan to determine the last time the agent ran.

6. Expand Product Details to view the product data collected by the Software Inventory Client Agent, as shown in Figure 9-23. Expand each entry to see more specific version information. As you select each version, you can view the filename (and other attributes) associated with this product, assuming that you enabled the File Details option for the agent.

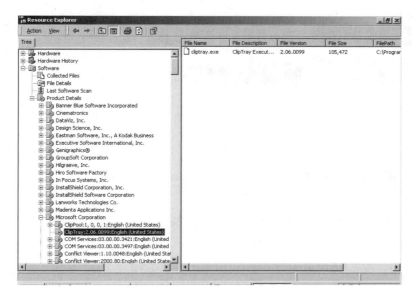

Figure 9-23. *The Resource Explorer window, with Product Details expanded and a product selected.*

Summary

Well, that's it for the inventory collection process. As you can see, SMS 2003 can report on a lot of "stuff"—both hardware-related and software-related. Using the SMS_def.mof file and customized NOIDMIF and IDMIF files, you can append data to the existing client architecture and add new architectures, object classes, and attributes to the database. You can view inventory through Resource Explorer, and you can further refine what you see through the use of queries.

> **More Info**   Because the inventory process is fairly straightforward, this chapter didn't include a "Checkpoints" section. You can easily spot and correct any problems you might encounter by monitoring the log files and status messages. You're more likely to encounter issues as you work with MOF Manager and create custom MIF files, and, in that regard, there are no better resources than the *Microsoft Systems Management Server 2003 Operations Guide* available through the Microsoft SMS Web site (*http://www.microsoft.com/smserver*) and through Microsoft TechNet.

In Chapter 10, "Remote Control of Client Systems," we'll continue our exploration of client management tools as we look at Remote Tools.

Chapter 10
Remote Control of Client Systems

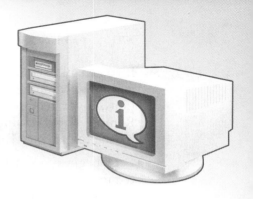

As most of us know from experience, many computer-related problems can be solved only through a hands-on approach. We have to see the error message displayed or re-create the scenario that caused a crash or watch the user perform a task. So it's no surprise that being able to remotely control client systems appeals to the typical administrator. Tools that provide remote access and diagnostic abilities have actually been around for a while. Some are built into the operating system, such as Remote Assistance in Microsoft Windows XP. Some tools are separate applications that provide a broader scope of functionality.

Remote control has long been a key feature of Microsoft Systems Management Server (SMS) and has been enhanced in SMS 2003. With SMS 2003's Remote Tools, the SMS administrator can remotely diagnose a client, start and stop services, view the user's desktop, run programs, transfer files, and specify how much control to allow the user over the session. The user also can be given the ability to determine who can access the client and what remote functions are made available.

In this chapter you'll learn about the remote control tools available with SMS 2003 and how to use them. We'll look at the configuration of remote control for the client, including system requirements, protocol considerations, and configuring the remote options at the client system. Then we'll take a look at the Remote Tools installation process itself and how to monitor status of the remote client and network performance.

Configuring a Client for Remote Control

SMS Remote Tools enables you to deliver help desk support from the SMS administrator's desktop to all supported SMS 2003 clients. As with other SMS components, you begin by configuring the client agent component through the SMS Administrator Console. Keep in mind that, like other client agent settings, the Remote Tools Client Agent settings are configured and effective on a site-wide basis.

If you enable Remote Tools for a site, the Remote Tools Client Agent is enabled and installed on all SMS clients that belong to that SMS site—with no exceptions. If you require users to give permission for an administrator to initiate a Remote Tools session, permission will be required on all SMS clients that belong to that site. This is the nature of all SMS client agents.

Let's begin our discussion of configuration by looking at the client system requirements, including network connection considerations. Then we'll look at the configuration of the Remote Tools Client Agent and the remote options.

Client System Requirements

Clients must meet the following general requirements to use Remote Tools for monitoring and control:

- The client must be installed as an SMS client. This will allow the client to receive and run the Remote Tools Client Agent.

- The Remote Tools Client Agent must be installed and started on the client computer. Each client platform uses different agents, services, or utilities to support remote functions.

- Access to the client must be allowed. The level of remote access to the client must be defined, including who has the ability to initiate a session.

- The SMS Administrator Console computer and the client must use a common protocol, and that protocol is generally TCP/IP; 32-bit Windows clients also allow Windows Sockets over TCP/IP.

 Note SMS can remotely monitor and control clients that are connected to the network locally or through a WAN. SMS can also perform remote functions when an SMS administrator connects to the client's network using RAS through a minimum 28.8-Kbps connection; however, performance degrades significantly for connections lower than 56 Kbps.

If your clients meet these requirements, you can proceed with enabling and configuring the Remote Tools Client Agent, as we'll see in the next section.

Configuring the Remote Tools Client Agent

The Remote Tools Client Agent is the only component that needs to be configured to enable remote control functionality for your site. To verify that you have installed this agent when you installed your site server, check the list of client agents in the Client Agents node under Site Settings in the SMS Administrator Console, as shown in Figure 10-1. If you don't see the Remote Tools Client Agent listed there, rerun the SMS Setup application from the SMS 2003 CD to add the component to your site server. (Refer to Chapter 2, "Primary Site Installation," for more information about the installation process.)

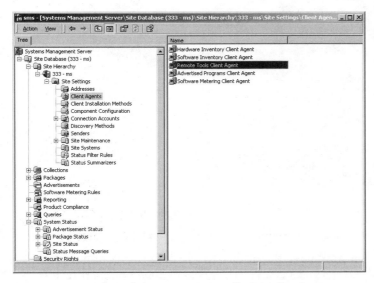

Figure 10-1.   *A list of client agents installed on the site server.*

Note   If you install SMS using the Express Setup option, Remote Tools will be installed and enabled automatically. If you choose the Custom Setup option, you must choose the Remote Tools option; Custom installation doesn't enable Remote Tools by default.

Once the Remote Tools component has been installed, we must specify what remote features we want to enable for the clients in our site and how the Remote Tools sessions should be established. To enable and configure the Remote Tools Client Agent, follow these steps:

1. In the SMS Administrator Console, navigate to the Site Settings folder and expand it, and then select the Client Agents folder to display the list of client agents (shown previously in Figure 10-1).

2. Right-click Remote Tools Client Agent and choose Properties from the context menu to display the Remote Tools Client Agent Properties dialog box, shown in Figure 10-2.

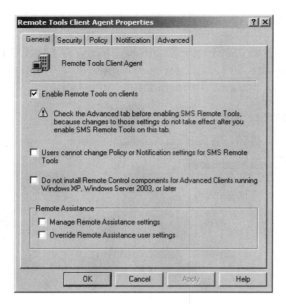

Figure 10-2. *The Remote Tools Client Agent Properties dialog box.*

3. In the General tab, select the Enable Remote Tools On Clients check box.

4. In SMS 2003, you now have the ability to "lock" your configuration of Remote Tools so that users can't arbitrarily change your settings. If you want to enable this feature, select the Users Cannot Change Policy Or Notification Settings For SMS Remote Tools check box.

   If the client computers are running Windows XP or Windows Server 2003 or higher, a remote assistance tool is already included as part of the operating system. SMS 2003 can leverage this built-in tool for its Advanced Clients without installing the SMS Remote Tools component. In fact, it's recommended that you don't install SMS Remote Tools on such clients. Therefore, if you support client computers running Windows XP or Windows Server 2003 or higher, and if it isn't already selected, select the option Do Not Install Remote Control Components For Advanced Clients Running Windows XP, Windows Server 2003, Or Later.

   The last two Remote Assistance options in this tab let you decide whether you want SMS to manage or override, or both, Remote Assistance settings on the client computers. Select these options as appropriate for your environment.

5. Select the Security tab, shown in Figure 10-3. Here you create the Permitted Viewers list. This list defines which users or user groups are allowed to perform remote functions on Windows clients. Before a Remote Tools session can be established on a Windows client, the client agent will evaluate this list to determine whether the administrator initiating the session is a valid member.

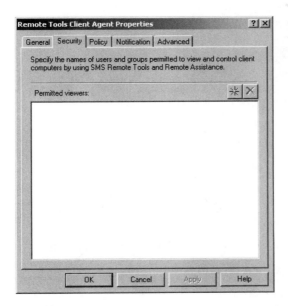

Figure 10-3.   *The Security tab of the Remote Tools Client Agent Properties dialog box.*

6. To add users or user groups to this list, click the New button (the yellow star) to display the New Viewer dialog box and enter the name of the Windows user or security group. Although it's recommended that you manage this list using security groups, you can use user accounts when necessary.

Note   In order to run Remote Tools on a client computer, the SMS administrator must either be a local Administrator on the client computer or appear in the permitted viewers list explicitly or as a member of a group.

7. Select the Policy tab, shown in Figure 10-4. This tab contains settings that define the scope of remote access and the permission level.

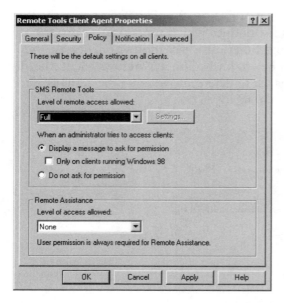

Figure 10-4. *The Remote Tools Client Agent Properties dialog box Policy tab.*

Three levels of access are available:

- *Full*—Allows all remote functions and diagnostics to be run
- *Limited*—Selects individual functions
- *None*—Prohibits remote control

8. If you choose Limited, click the Settings button to display the Default Limited SMS Remote Tools Settings dialog box, shown in Figure 10-5, which contains a list of remote functions to enable or disable.

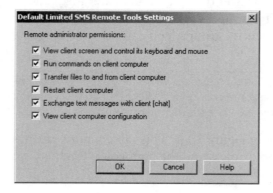

Figure 10-5. *The Default Limited SMS Remote Tools Settings dialog box.*

As you can see, all these options are enabled by default. Each of the options you select here generates a different level of network traffic, and the first option probably generates the most traffic. Click OK to return to the Policy tab.

9. You can indicate whether you want the user to give permission for the Remote Tools session to be initiated. If you select Display A Message To Ask For Permission, the user will have to respond Yes or No in a pop-up message box before the session can begin. This option might be required in organizations that must comply with C2-level security guidelines. Notice that you can restrict this functionality to Windows 98 clients.

10. In the Policy tab, in the Remote Assistance frame, you can choose to allow full control, remote viewing, or no control for client computers that support Remote Assistance.

11. Select the Notification tab, shown in Figure 10-6. In this tab, you specify how the client will be notified that a Remote Tools session has been established.

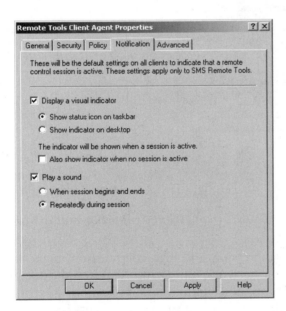

Figure 10-6. *The Remote Tools Client Agent Properties dialog box Notification tab.*

By default, both a visual and an audible indicator will be enabled on the client. The visual indicator can be either a taskbar status icon (the

Show Status Icon On Taskbar option) or a high-security icon (the Show Indicator On Desktop option) that appears in the top-right corner of the user's desktop and can't be hidden. You can optionally have the indicators display when no Remote Tools session is active. Audible indicator choices include playing a sound when the session begins and ends or repeatedly throughout the session (the default).

Note The settings in the Notification tab apply only to SMS Remote Tools and not to Remote Assistance.

---

12. Select the Advanced tab, shown in Figure 10-7. This tab allows you to specify several advanced feature settings that affect the performance of remote functions.

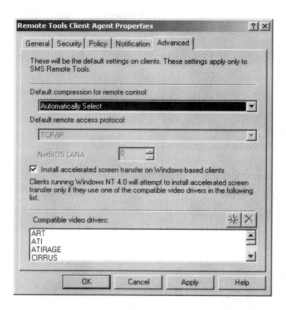

Figure 10-7. *The Remote Tools Client Agent Properties dialog box Advanced tab.*

13. Remote Tools uses low-compression and high-compression methods to control the demands on network bandwidth generated during Remote Tools sessions. Using the Default Compression For Remote Control option, you can select either method for all clients to follow or you can allow SMS to select the optimal compression method on a per-client basis. By default, the agent will negotiate for the most appropriate compression method based on the client's processor speed.

If you select Low (RLE), SMS uses the Run Length Encoding (RLE) compression method. You should typically use this setting for clients running Windows NT 4.0 or Legacy Clients with CPUs that are slower than a 150-MHz Pentium processor. This method works well on slower CPUs because of the lower demand on CPU cycles. It can also help resolve video transfer problems that might arise from hardware incompatibilities on the client.

If you select High (LZ), SMS uses the Lempel-Ziv (LZ) compression method. This is a math-intensive compression algorithm, and therefore it requires more intensive CPU processing. This method of compression should be configured for clients running Windows 2000 or higher. This setting minimizes network utilization; however, it might also impact client performance during the Remote Tools session.

By default, SMS 2003 clients will use TCP/IP; you can't change this value for SMS 2003 sites.

14. For your Windows clients, you can optionally enable the Install Accelerated Screen Transfer On Windows-Based Clients option. If any client computers are running Windows NT, they'll install video acceleration only if they use one of the drivers that appears in the Compatible Video Drivers list, a list of drivers that have been tested by Microsoft and that can run with the screen transfer "wrapper" Idisntkm.dll that SMS installs on the client when this option is enabled. The *wrapper* is a piece of program code that helps to speed up the screen transfer during a Remote Tools session.

Caution   You can add drivers to this list by clicking the New button. However, the screen transfer software works only with the video drivers listed and any other drivers compatible with those listed. If you add a driver to the list, be sure to test and ensure that the Remote Tools session works properly.

15. Click OK to begin the site update process.

As usual, the Remote Tools Client Agent will be installed on SMS Legacy Clients, and enabled on SMS Advanced Clients, during the next update cycle on the client or when the client forces an update through the Systems Management program in the Control Panel. At this point, an SMS administrator will be able to initiate a Remote Tools session according to the options you configured for the agent.

> **Caution** If you make changes to any of the options in the Advanced tab of the Remote Tools Client Agent Properties dialog box after the Remote Control Client Agent has been installed on the clients, the clients won't receive the new settings. In this case you could uninstall the agent by disabling it at the site server, updating the clients, and then reenabling the agent so that the clients can get the new settings.

Remote Tools Client Agent Installation Process Flow

Like the other client agents, Remote Tools is installed but not enabled on Advanced Client computers. When you enable Remote Tools in the SMS Administrator Console, an Advanced Client policy is generated and applied to the client at the client's next policy update interval (once an hour by default). However, the update process is a bit more involved for Legacy Clients.

The Legacy Client executes Remctrl.exe to install the Remote Tools Client Agent and its support files, including Remote Control support (Wuser32.exe), File Transfer Slave Agent (Wslave32.exe), and Remote Chat (Wchat32.exe). All in all, about 1.8 MB of disk space will be required on the client, and a corresponding amount of network traffic will be generated.

On Windows NT 4.0 and Windows 2000 clients, Wuser32 is installed as a service, the appropriate registry keys are created and updated, and the agent is started. Additionally, two other services are loaded to support virtual keyboard and mouse devices—KBStuff.sys and RCHelp.sys. On Windows 98 clients, Wuser32 is installed as a client service, the appropriate registry keys are created and updated, and the agent is started.

The Remote Control application on Legacy Clients contains two programs, Hardware Munger and Security Munger. A *munger* basically reconciles configuration settings relating to network interface cards (NICs) and protocols on the client with settings from multiple sites that the client might belong to. The Hardware Munger runs once at installation or when a Repair Installation procedure is run through the Systems Management program in Control Panel. The Hardware Munger manages all hardware settings for the Legacy Client and implements the sitewide settings that you configured for the Remote Tools Agent. It also determines the compression type and video acceleration for Windows NT 4.0 clients and higher.

The Security Munger runs whenever a change is made to the SMS-related registry keys on the client. It updates the Remote Tools Client Agent settings on the client and determines whether the user attempting a remote session has the appropriate level of permissions—that is, if a local administrator appears in the Permitted Viewers list.

> **Tip** For more information about mungers and other processes related to Remote Tools, refer to Chapter 9 of the *Microsoft Systems Management Server 2003 Operations Guide,* available for viewing and download through Microsoft TechNet, and available as a print book from Microsoft's SMS Web site (*http://www.microsoft.com/smserver*) as well.

Each step in the installation process is recorded on the Legacy Client in the %Windir%\MS\SMS\Clicomp\RemCtrl\Install.log file, and remote control activity is recorded in the %Windir%\MS\SMS\Logs\Remctrl.log, as shown in Figures 10-8 and 10-9. Notice in Figure 10-9 the notation regarding the initialization of the Hardware Munger (Rchwcfg.exe) process. Remote control activity on the Advanced Client is recorded in the %systemroot%\system32\ccm\logs\Remctrl.log file, an example of which is shown in Figure 10-9.

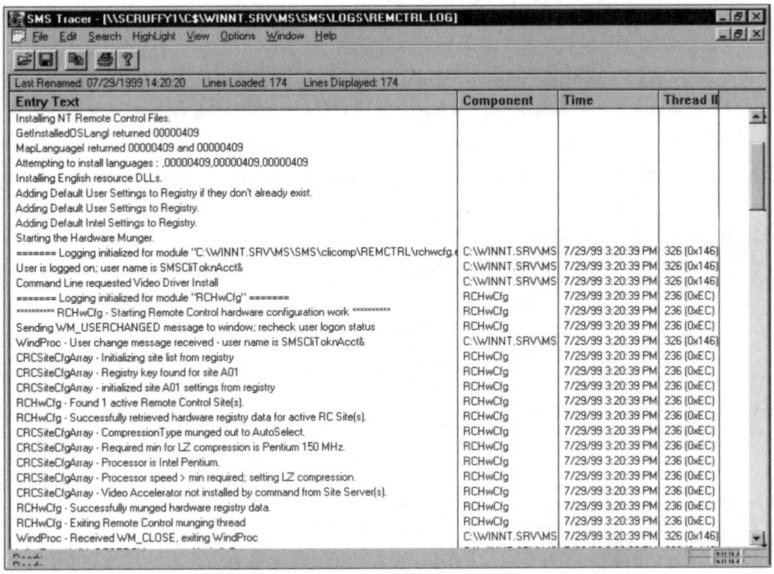

Figure 10-8. *Sample Remctrl.log file.*

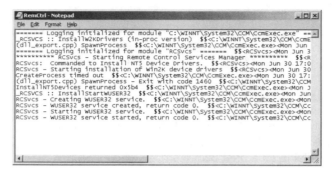

Figure 10-9. *Sample Remctrl.log file from the Advanced Client.*

Setting Remote Options at the Client System

If the SMS administrator doesn't enable the option Clients Cannot Change Policy Or Notification Settings in the General tab of the Remote Tools Client Agent Properties dialog box, the user at the client computer will be able to choose some site settings for the Remote Tools session. For example, the user can specify which remote functions to enable, whether permission for the Remote Tools session must be granted first, and how the Remote Tools session will be announced on the client system. The user can modify the remote control options on the client from the Remote Control program in Control Panel, which is added when the Remote Tools Client Agent is installed, as shown in Figure 10-10. The client's remote control settings will take precedence over the site's default settings. You'll have to determine whether allowing the user such latitude is practical or desirable.

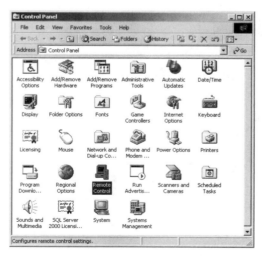

Figure 10-10. *The Remote Control program added to the client's Control Panel.*

To configure the Remote Tools options on a client, follow these steps:

1. From the client's Control Panel, double-click the Remote Control program to display the Remote Control Properties dialog box, shown in Figure 10-11.

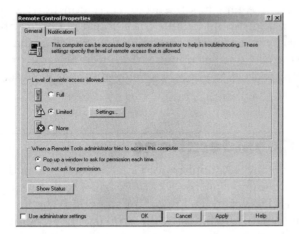

Figure 10-11.   *The Remote Control Properties dialog box.*

The settings in the General and Notification tabs will reflect those configured in the SMS Administrator Console.

2. To make a change, clear the Use Administrator Settings check box at the bottom of either tab and configure the policy and notification settings as described in the previous section.

3. Click the Show Status button in the General tab to display the Remote Control Status dialog box, shown in Figure 10-12, which contains connection information regarding the agent. This information will include the client's IP address and name, the level of compression and acceleration used, and whether a session is currently active. From this screen the user can also click Close Session to terminate the session.

Figure 10-12.   *The Remote Control Status dialog box.*

If the Show Indicator On Desktop visual indicator notification is enabled, users can display the same screen by double-clicking the face of the indicator.

4. Click OK to save your settings.

When the Remote Tools Client Agent has been correctly configured and installed on your SMS clients, you should be able to establish remote control sessions. However, one of the client requirements mentioned earlier was that the client and the SMS Administrator Console computer both use the same protocol. This requirement isn't always as clear-cut as we might think, as we'll see in the next section.

Client Protocol Considerations

When you use Remote Tools, the SMS Administrator Console computer and the client computer must share a common protocol. At first glance, this requirement probably seems obvious. However, it's important to note that when the client agent is installed, it automatically binds to the primary protocol on the client computer, and this is the protocol under which the Remote Tools session will be attempted. SMS 2003 clients listen only for TCP connection attempts. However, NetBIOS and IPX connections are made for backward compatibility with SMS 2.0 clients. The remainder of this discussion is apropos for SMS 2.0 clients.

Suppose that the SMS Administrator Console computer has TCP/IP installed and the SMS 2.0 client computer has NetBEUI and TCP/IP installed, with NetBEUI as the primary protocol. In this case the Remote Tools Client Agent will use NetBEUI as its protocol. When a Remote Tools session is attempted, it won't be established because the SMS Administrator Console computer and the client don't have a common Remote Tools protocol.

Note You can either change the protocol order on the client or reconfigure the settings in the Advanced tab in the Remote Tools Client Agent Properties window to use a different LANA number. The problem, of course, is that these settings are sitewide, and perhaps not all your clients experience the same problem. Changing the LANA number might clear up the issue for some SMS 2.0 clients and introduce it for other clients.

Clients with Multiple Network Interface Cards

A similar issue might arise if your network has clients with more than one NIC installed. By default, the Remote Tools Client Agent binds to the first NIC in the binding order. Changing the NIC to which the client agent binds varies depending on platform.

On Windows clients, using the Registry Editor, locate the key HKEY_LOCAL_MACHINE\Software\SMS\Client\Client Components\Remote Control. Add new string type values to this key named *Subnet* and *SubnetMask*, each containing the appropriate address value for the NIC you want the agent to bind to. This forces the client agent to bind to the NIC specified by the subnet and subnet mask.

Using Remote Tools over RAS Connections

As an SMS administrator, you might need to diagnose a problem or assist a client over a RAS connection. Remote Tools enables you to connect to client computers over such connections. Consider the following requirements when you're using Remote Tools over RAS:

- To use Remote Tools over a RAS connection, the link should be at least 28.8 Kbps. Keep in mind that this is a minimum specification—as with any remote connection, faster is better. Also, remember to disable any wallpaper settings.

- The SMS Administrator Console computer will connect to the RAS server, so you must install and configure the RAS client software on this computer.

- The SMS Administrator Console computer, the RAS server, and the remote client computer must be running the same transport protocol.

- At the site containing the remote client, a RAS server must be located on the same LAN as the remote client computer.

Exploring Remote Tools Functions

The SMS administrator is frequently called on to diagnose problems on client computers. Remote Tools enables you to run diagnostics on Windows 98, Windows NT 4.0, Windows 2000, Windows XP, and Windows Server 2003 clients. You can then use this diagnostic information to help analyze and troubleshoot client hardware and other problems.

Running Diagnostic Tools for Windows Clients

The diagnostic tools for Windows clients are based on the standard System Information utility (WinMsd). This utility provides a static view of the system configuration parameters, services, resources, environment settings, and other system information.

To run the System Information utility, follow these steps:

1. In the SMS Administrator Console, navigate to Collections and select the collection that contains the Windows client for which you want to initiate remote diagnostics.

2. Select the client, right-click it, choose All Tasks from the context menu as shown in Figure 10-13, and then choose Start Windows Diagnostics.

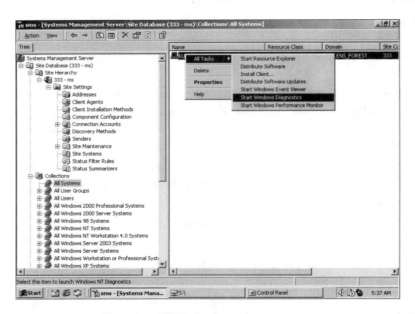

Figure 10-13. *Choosing All Tasks from the context menu to access the Start Windows Diagnostics utility.*

3. The System Information window appears, as shown in Figure 10-14. This is the same System Information window you would see if you were logged on at the client and executed the utility there. You can view information about the hardware connected to the computer and identify device drivers and services that should be started when you

start the computer. For more information about using this utility, see the Windows product documentation.

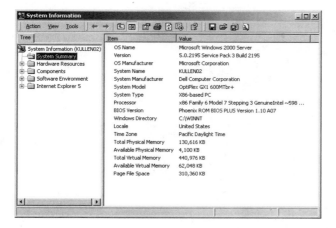

Figure 10-14.   *The System Information window.*

4. Close the window when you've finished.

Note   You can also run the Windows Event Viewer and Performance Monitor utilities remotely for Windows clients by choosing All Tasks from the context menu.

Running Diagnostic Tools for Windows 98 Clients

You run the diagnostic tools for Windows 98 clients from the Remote Tools window. From the toolbar or the Tools menu, you can run diagnostic routines on the client computer to view information about memory allocation, CMOS data, interrupt usage, and so on.

To start a Remote Tools session, follow these steps:

1. In the SMS Administrator Console, navigate to Collections and select the collection that contains the client for which you want to initiate remote tools.

2. Select the client, right-click it, choose All Tasks from the context menu, and then choose Start Remote Tools to display the Remote Tools window, shown in Figure 10-15.

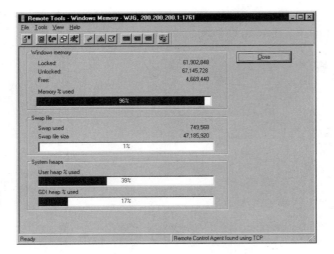

Figure 10-15. *The Remote Tools window, showing the result of running the Windows Memory diagnostic for the client WJG.*

On the toolbar in the Remote Tools window, the diagnostic tools for Windows clients begin with the sixth icon from the left. They are, in order: Windows Memory, Windows Modules, Windows Tasks, CMOS Information, ROM Information, and DOS Memory Map. Table 10-1 lists the diagnostic tools for Windows 98 clients.

Table 10-1.   **Diagnostic tools for Windows 98 clients**

Diagnostic Test	Description
Windows Memory	Displays the allocation of memory on the client, providing information about locked, unlocked, and free memory on the remote client; swap file size; user and Graphical Device Interface (GDI) heap usage; and the largest amount of contiguous memory available on the remote client.
Windows Modules	Displays the drivers and libraries loaded on the client at the time the diagnostic was run and provides information such as the module handle, use count, path to the module, and memory objects reserved by the module.
Windows Tasks	Displays the tasks currently running on the client, providing information such as handle, instance, queue location and size, waiting events, current directory, and command-line options in effect.

Table 10-1.   Diagnostic tools for Windows 98 clients

Diagnostic Test	Description
CMOS Information	Displays the data stored in the client CMOS for only Intel-based AT-class and later chip sets.
ROM Information	Displays the IRQ hooks (if they exist) and ASCII strings for ROM entries on the client.
DOS Memory Map	Displays which programs are loaded into conventional (first 640 KB) and upper memory only.

When you select one of these diagnostic tools, the client will first be asked to allow permission if that option was enabled for the Remote Tools Client Agent, as shown in Figure 10-16. When permission is granted, or if that option wasn't enabled for the agent, the Remote Tools window will display the desired information.

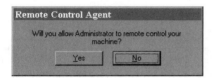

Figure 10-16.   *The Remote Control Agent dialog box.*

Ping Test

Another useful Remote Tools function is the Ping Test utility. You can use this utility to determine whether a client is accessible for a Remote Tools session. The Ping Test icon is the rightmost icon on the Remote Tools window toolbar; you can also run the utility from the Tools menu. Ping Test generates and sends packets to the client, waits for a response, and then sends additional packets over a 4-second period to determine the connection's reliability and speed.

Figure 10-17 shows the results of running a ping test. These results include test statistics and a thermometer that visually represents the effectiveness of the connection—red means poor connectivity, yellow means fair, and green means good. To the right of the thermometer, two level indicators can be seen. The yellow (top) arrow indicates the maximum number of packets per second that the test generated; the green (bottom) arrow indicates the average number.

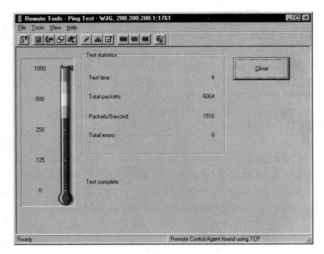

Figure 10-17.   *The results of running a ping test.*

Remote Functions

Five remote functions are available to the SMS administrator. In order of their position on the toolbar and on the Tools menu, they are (from left to right): Remote Control, Remote Reboot, Remote Chat, Remote File Transfer, and Remote Execute. All these functions are initiated from the Remote Tools window, but before we can use any of them, SMS must establish a remote connection with the client. If the client session can't be established, the Remote Tools window will be closed. Remember that the inability to establish a Remote Tools session is typically due to network or client agent configuration problems, as we discussed in the sections "Client System Requirements" and "Client Protocol Considerations" earlier in this chapter. In this section we'll look more closely at each of these functions.

Remote Control

To initiate a Remote Control session through the Remote Tools window, either click the first toolbar icon or choose Remote Control from the Tools menu. The client will first be asked to grant permission for the Remote Control session if that option was enabled for the Remote Tools Client Agent. When permission is granted, or if permission isn't required, the Remote Control window appears on the SMS Administrator Console computer, bordered with a moving yellow and black marquee. Figure 10-18 shows an example of a Remote Control window for a Windows XP client.

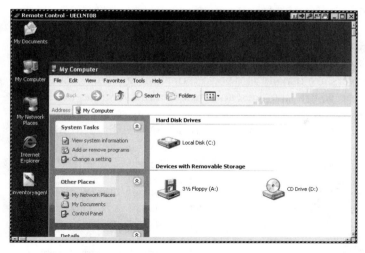

Figure 10-18.   *A Remote Control window for a Windows XP client.*

Here you're viewing the client computer's actual desktop, and you can manipulate that client's mouse and keyboard. Currently, there's no way to lock the keyboard and mouse from user input. If both the administrator and the user are manipulating the keyboard and mouse, some fascinating control wars can result. To avoid this conflict, it's a good idea to present some kind of visual or audible signal to the user, and probably to require user permission as well, to notify the user that you're establishing the Remote Control session. Otherwise, you could end up creating a whole new set of problems on the client.

> **Note**   All mouse and key sequences are passed to the client except Ctrl+Alt+Del, Ctrl+Esc, Alt+Tab, and any hot key sequences you identify.

The Remote Control window might not be large enough to display the entire client desktop. With SMS 2003, however, the window can be maximized. To help facilitate control of the desktop, the Remote Control window includes four toolbar buttons in the top-right corner for Windows 98 clients and five toolbar buttons for Windows NT 4.0 clients and higher.

The first button displays the Start menu on the client. The second button (an arrow) acts like the Alt+Tab combination on the client and toggles between active windows. The third button allows Alt-key combinations to be passed through to the client instead of being run locally. The fourth button (a hand) activates an area box that can be used to navigate in the Remote Control window when maximizing the screen isn't sufficient or practical.

If you established a Remote Control session with a Windows NT 4.0 or higher client, you'll also see a gold key button. Under certain circumstances, it's necessary to log on to these clients as well as lock and unlock the desktop. For example, you might have a Windows Server 2003 server system acting as an application server. Servers are usually in a locked or "unlogged-in" state, making any user intervention to the Remote Tools function unavailable. Locking or unlocking a Windows computer and logging on require a Ctrl+Alt+Del sequence, which we know we can't initiate from the SMS Administrator Console computer. This is what that gold key button is for. When you click the gold key button, you send a Ctrl+Alt+Del sequence to the Windows client.

Caution After the Remote Tools Client Agent has been installed on a Windows NT 4.0 client, it's necessary to restart the Windows NT 4.0 client at least once before all remote functionality, like the gold key button, becomes enabled. This extra step is needed because a new KBStuff.sys driver is written to the registry and it can only be read and enabled by restarting the system. A restart isn't required for Windows 2000 or higher computers.

In addition to the toolbar buttons, configuration options are available through the Remote Control window's control menu, sometimes referred to as the system menu. This menu is displayed when you click the icon on the left in the title bar. The system menu contains the usual Minimize and Maximize options and also provides Configure, Hot Keys, and Help options.

If you choose Configure, the Control Parameters dialog box will appear, as shown in Figure 10-19.

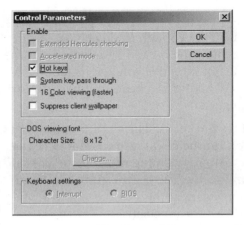

Figure 10-19. *The Control Parameters dialog box.*

From this dialog box, you can set configuration options. These options, which will vary slightly based on your clients, include:

- **Accelerated Mode**   Sends screen refreshes from the client at the fastest speed supported by the network

- **Hot Keys**   Enables hot-key sequences defined under the Hot Keys option to be passed to the client

- **System Key Pass Through**   Disables passing of system key sequences to the client

- **16 Color Viewing (Faster)**   Forces 16-color display resolution on the client to help speed screen transfer

- **Suppress Client Wallpaper**   Disables the client's wallpaper during the Remote Control session—again to help speed screen transfer and minimize network traffic

- **Keyboard Settings**   Switches between BIOS and interrupt methods of sending key sequences to Windows 98 clients and is available for Windows 98 clients only

If you choose Hot Keys from the system menu, the Hot Key Settings dialog box appears, as shown in Figure 10-20. In this dialog box you can define hot key sequences for seven remote control commands, all of which are fairly self-explanatory.

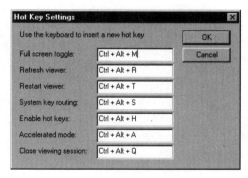

Figure 10-20.   *The Hot Key Settings dialog box.*

To end the Remote Control session, simply close the Remote Control window.

Remote Reboot

You can restart the client computer in a couple of ways. One way is to establish a Remote Control session and then, through the Remote Control window, choose Shutdown from the client's Start menu. The advantage of this method is that you can follow the shutdown process and see any messages that might appear, such as a request to close a file or a message indicating an error shutting down a service.

You can also click the Remote Reboot button or choose the Remote Reboot option from the Tools menu in the Remote Tools window. This method has the same result, but since you don't have a Remote Control window open, you won't see the shutdown process. Indeed, you might not know for sure whether the client actually shut down—it might be waiting for some kind of user input.

Remote Chat

Remote Chat is similar to a chat room on the Internet. It provides an avenue through which the SMS administrator can communicate with the user. It can be used when a voice connection isn't available, for example. When you start a chat session, the user is prompted first for permission, if that option was enabled. Then the SMS administrator and the user are presented with a chat window similar to the one shown in Figure 10-21. The top text box always represents the remote person, and the bottom text box represents the local person. When the session is over, either party can click Exit Chat to terminate the session.

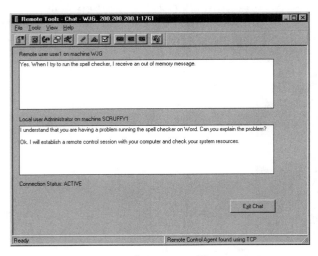

Figure 10-21. *A sample Remote Chat session.*

Remote File Transfer

The Remote File Transfer tool provides a means to initiate file, folder, and tree copies between the SMS Administrator Console computer and the client computer. When the Remote File Transfer feature is started, and after the user has given permission (if necessary), the Remote Tools screen displays a Windows

Explorer–type window, as shown in Figure 10-22. The SMS Administrator Console computer's directories are controlled through the top pane, and the remote client's directories are controlled through the bottom pane. You navigate this window in the same way you would Windows Explorer. You transfer files simply by dragging them from one pane to the other. This tool is especially effective when the client doesn't have file sharing enabled or doesn't have the necessary shares available to create network mappings.

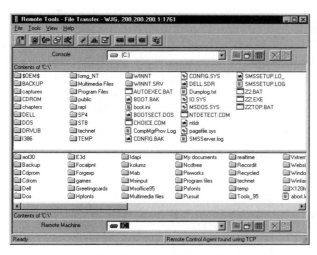

Figure 10-22.   *The Remote File Transfer interface.*

Remote Execute

The Remote Execute tool enables the SMS administrator to run a program on the client, such as a disk defragmentation program or a virus scan—or even a game of solitaire. When the Remote Execute option is selected and user permission is granted, a simple dialog box named Run Program At User's Workstation is displayed. Enter the path and name of the program and click Run to execute that program on the client.

Remote Tools Session Process Flow

Now that we've examined how to configure and run a Remote Tools session on an SMS client, let's take some time to explore the process of initiating a Remote Tools session. An understanding of this process will enable you to analyze problem situations when you're attempting to remotely control a client computer.

When the SMS administrator starts a Remote Tools session, a specific sequence of events occurs. This flow of events will allow the communication between the

SMS Administrator Console computer and the remote client computer. This section will guide you through the steps that take place in the SMS Administrator Console computer and on the primary site server when a Remote Tools session is initiated with a client computer. It will also give you a fair indication of the network traffic that's generated.

As you know, you initiate a Remote Tools session by selecting a client in the Collection folder in the SMS Administrator Console. So really the first step that occurs is that SMS determines whether the SMS administrator has permission to start a Remote Tools session through that collection. This permission is different from the Permitted Viewers list that can be configured as part of the Remote Tools settings; it involves object security set on the collection itself through SMS security. This type of security allows you to create customized SMS Administrator Consoles and delegate specific tasks, such as remote troubleshooting, to specific individuals without having to give them access to everything else. (This aspect of security is discussed in detail in Chapter 17, "Security.")

Now when the SMS administrator begins a Remote Tools session, Remote.exe makes a connection through the SMS Provider to the SMS site database using the resource ID of the client in question. The SMS Provider returns the IP address or, in the case of an SMS 2.0 client, an IP or IPX address, and the NetBIOS name of the client. This information is passed to LDWMNT.dll, which attempts to connect to the client. LDWMNT.dll resolves the NetBIOS name through WINS or DNS, for example, and attempts a connection over each protocol (connection point).

 Note   SMS 2003 now establishes a TCP session with the client by default, instead of the UDP sessions used by earlier versions of SMS. This guaranteed connection ensures that communications exist between the SMS Administrator Console and the client and should result in fewer lost session events.

In the meantime, the client agent is "listening," waiting for a connection attempt. When a connection is attempted using this protocol, the client agent responds, and returns the Permitted Viewers list to Remote.exe. The list is evaluated to determine whether it includes the logged-on SMS administrator. If not, the logged-on SMS administrator is prompted for the name of a valid user. If the administrator is included, the client determines which remote tools are enabled, and Remote.exe displays the Remote Tools window to the SMS administrator with the appropriate tools enabled or disabled.

The SMS administrator initiates a remote tool such as Remote Chat or Remote Control. If user permission is required, the client displays a Remote Control Agent dialog box asking the user for permission.

If user permission is granted, the appropriate tool is launched. If permission is denied, a message box similar to the one shown in Figure 10-23 is displayed on the SMS administrator's desktop.

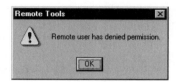

Figure 10-23.   *A message box notifying the SMS administrator that user permission has been denied.*

As you can see, a fair amount of network traffic is involved in establishing the Remote Tools session. In addition, the Remote Tools session itself can generate a rather significant amount of CPU usage on the client. For example, on a computer running Windows with compression set to high and screen acceleration enabled, it's not uncommon to experience a CPU usage increase of between 90 and 100 percent. Setting compression to low can bring that down to the 50 to 65 percent range, but changing the compression setting might also generate additional network bandwidth usage.

Monitoring Status and Flow

As we've seen, when the Remote Tools Client Agent is configured, SMS status messages are generated at the site server by the site update process—Hierarchy Manager, Site Control Manager, and so on. These status messages will help you determine whether the Remote Tools Client Agent is available for installation on the client. Additionally, status messages are generated for each Remote Tools session between a user at an SMS Administrator Console and a client computer. Status messages will provide the necessary information for tracking Remote Tools sessions. Unfortunately, no log files are generated for the Remote Tools session itself.

Monitoring Installation

You can view two log files at the SMS site server to verify that the Remote Tools Client Agent is ready for installation at the client: SMS\Logs\Cidm.log (Client Install Data Manager) and SMS\Logs\Inboxmgr.log (Inbox Manager). You can view these log files using a text editor. Search for entries with the text string "Remctrl," as shown in the sample log in Figure 10-24.

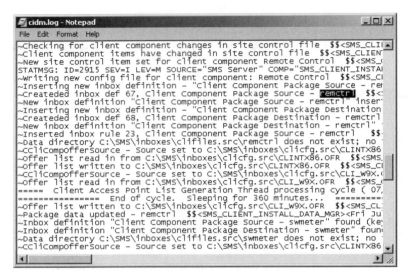

Figure 10-24. *Sample Cidm.log file with the reference to Remote Control selected.*

Log activity is also generated at the client computer when the Remote Tools Client Agent is installed or updated, just as with any other client agent. At the Legacy Client, for example, you can view the %Windir%\MS\Sms\Logs\Ccim32.log. Open this log using any text editor or SMS Trace and search for a wake-up event. In other words, look for specific entries that record when the Remote Control Client Agent was found, when the offer for Remote Control was read, and when the offer was submitted to Advertised Programs Manager for installation (Launch32).

You can also view the Advertised Programs Manager log file for remote control activity. Open %Windir%\MS\Sms\Logs\Smsapm32.log on the Legacy Client and search for the string "remote control." You should see a request to schedule Remote Control, an attempt to execute Remctrl.exe for service context, and the reporting of installation status. On the Advanced Client, view the log files Ccmexe.log and PolicyAgent.log.

As we've seen, you can also open the Remote Control log file, Remctrl.log. You can use this log file to identify the following events that occur during the Remote Tools Client Agent installation:

- Detection of the operating system on an Intel processor

- Installation of appropriate language support for the client's installed languages

- Installation of the discovered platform's remote control files
- Configuration of registry settings, including security and permissions
- Configuration of hardware-specific Remote Tools settings from the registry
- Registration of the agent with the SMS application launcher (Launch32 or Launch16)
- Start-up of the agent

If you come across any problems during the installation of the Remote Tools Client Agent, remember to review this file on the client computer. You can also monitor the Remote Tools session itself, as we'll see in the next section.

Monitoring a Remote Tools Session

When the SMS administrator initiates a Remote Tools session of any kind with the client, the Remote Tools Client Agent will generate status messages. You can, of course, view these messages through the Status Message Viewer. However, although SMS log activity will be generated on the client computer as a result of installing the agent, the act of establishing and terminating a Remote Control session is recorded as part of the Windows Application Event log on Windows clients. Relying on the Status Message Viewer in this case will give you more useful information.

You can view status messages specific to a Remote Tools session by executing one of the following status message queries related to Remote Tools sessions:

- Remote Tools Activity Initiated At A Specific Site
- Remote Tools Activity Initiated By A Specific User
- Remote Tools Activity Initiated From A Specific System
- Remote Tools Activity Targeted At A Specific System

The status messages displayed by these queries are in the range 300*xx* and will provide you with the following details:

- The domain name and user account of the user that's viewing the client
- The machine name of the SMS Administrator Console that's being used
- The machine name of the client computer on which remote functions are being carried out
- The types of functions being performed

Figure 10-25 shows an example of the status messages returned by the status message query Remote Tools Activity Targeted At A Specific System. Notice the entries in the Description column for initiating and ending each type of remote function.

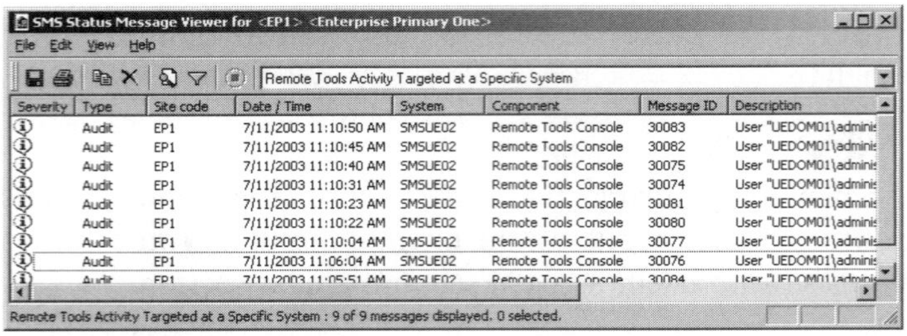

Figure 10-25. *Sample status message query results.*

To view the client log activity generated by a Remote Tools session recorded in the Windows Application Event log, follow these steps:

1. In the SMS Administrator Console, navigate to the Collections folder, expand it, and then select All Windows Workstation Systems or another collection that contains the Windows client.

2. In the Details pane, right-click the client entry and choose All Tasks from the context menu.

3. Choose Start Windows Event Viewer. Navigate the Windows Event Viewer as you normally would.

4. Choose Application from the Log menu to open the Application log as shown in Figure 10-26 and display the details for Event ID 5.

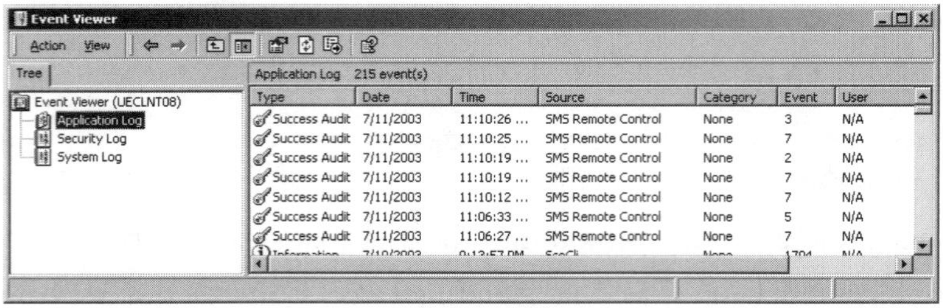

Figure 10-26. *The Event Viewer System log.*

5. The Event Properties dialog box appears, as shown in Figure 10-27. Notice that the text for the event indicates a Remote Control session with the client started by the SMS administrator using Windows security.

Figure 10-27.   *The Event Properties dialog box.*

Table 10-2 shows the Remote Tools session events that can be recorded in the Windows Security log.

Table 10-2.   Windows security events generated by a remote function

Event ID	Remote Function
1	Remote Reboot
2	Remote Chat
3	Remote File Transfer
4	Remote Execute
5	Remote Control Session Start
6	Remote Control Session End
7	Local User Granted Permission For Remote Session
8	Local User Denied Permission For Remote Session

You can also monitor remote session activity by enabling logging of Wuser32.exe. You do this by modifying the registry on the client computer. To enable logging for Wuser32.exe, set the value of LogToFile to 1 in the client's registry under \HKEY_LOCAL_MACHINE\SOFTWARE\Microsoft\SMS \Client\ Client Components\Remote Control. The resulting log file is named Wuser32.log, and it's stored in %Systemroot%\MS\SMS\Logs on Legacy Clients and %Systemroot%\system32\ccm\logs on Advanced Clients.

Remote Assistance and Terminal Services Support

As I mentioned earlier, SMS 2003 supports the Remote Assistance and Terminal Services features available in the applicable Windows operating systems. SMS 2003 leverages these features by integrating them into the SMS Administrator Console. You initiate a remote session using Remote Assistance or Terminal Services essentially the same way you initiate a Remote Tools session. Follow these steps:

1. Navigate to the Collections node in the SMS Administrator Console.

2. Open the collection that contains the SMS client with which you want to initiate a remote session.

3. Right-click the client and select All Tasks from the context menu.

4. Select either Start Remote Assistance or Start Remote Desktop Connection.

The command that you can select from the context menu depends on the combination of operating systems running on the client computer and the computer running the SMS Administrator Console. If the client computer and the computer running the SMS Administrator Console are both running Windows XP Professional or Windows Server 2003, the command Start Remote Assistance appears on the context menu of the client you've selected in the collection.

However, the command Start Remote Desktop Connection will appear if the client computer has Terminal Server client installed and enabled and it and the SMS Administrator Console computer are both running one of these operating systems:

- Windows NT Server 4.0, Terminal Server Edition
- Windows 2000 Server family
- Windows XP Professional
- Windows Server 2003 family

Selecting Start Remote Assistance initiates a remote session using the Remote Assistance feature. Selecting Start Remote Desktop Connection initiates a Terminal Services session.

Checkpoints

If you've been reading carefully and experimenting with Remote Tools as we go along, you should already be aware of the most frequent problem areas. Let's recap the main "gotchas."

Configuring the Client as an SMS Client

Remember that in SMS 2003, unlike earlier versions of SMS, the SMS client isn't required to collect any kind of inventory to the SMS site database. Nevertheless, the client does have to be discovered and installed as an SMS Legacy or Advanced Client.

Using NetBIOS Names for Session Communication

All the remote tasks you can perform have been enhanced or rewritten in SMS 2003. However, one fact remains the same as in earlier versions of SMS: Remote Tools sessions are still NetBIOS-based. This means that SMS will require a NetBIOS name resolution server such as WINS or DNS to successfully initiate the session, particularly for any SMS 2.0 clients that you need to support.

Remote Control Protocol

The SMS Administrator Console computer and the client computer must share a common protocol. If all clients are SMS 2003 clients, all clients will be using TCP/IP. However, down-level clients (SMS 2.0 clients) can still use IPX and Net-BEUI. You must ensure that these down-level clients "listen" for connection attempts using TCP/IP.

Reconfiguring the Client Agent

Normally, if you make a change to any client agent setting, that change is propagated to the client at its next maintenance cycle. This is true for most Remote Tools settings. However, changes to settings made in the Advanced tab in the Remote Tools Client Agent Properties window after the client agent has been installed on the client will propagate only to new clients.

To update existing clients, you need to either uninstall and then reinstall Remote Tools from all the clients, run the Repair Installation procedure through the Systems Management program in Control Panel on each client (called Repair on Advanced Clients), or create an SMS package to force an update of the client agent settings. The SMS package program should contain the command line %Windir%\MS\SMS\Clicomp\Remctrl\Rchwcfg.exe with the command option Install.

Summary

In this chapter we've explored the various Remote Tools as well as the configuration settings for the Remote Tools Client Agent. We've also explored the process for installing and initiating a Remote Tools session with a client, monitoring the session's status, and troubleshooting potential problems. In Part III we'll shift our focus to another set of SMS functions that deal more specifically with program management on client computers.

Part III
Software and Package Management

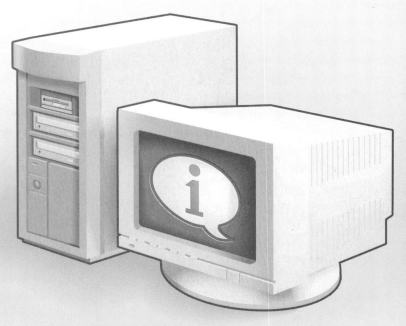

Chapter 11
Collections

In Part III we'll explore application management on Microsoft Systems Management Server (SMS) clients. In particular, we'll look at how to deploy packages to SMS clients and then manage or track their usage. Fundamental to the package distribution process in SMS 2003 is the creation and use of collections. So before we begin our examination of the package distribution process in earnest, we need to turn our attention to collections. In this chapter you'll learn how to define, create, and update collections; how collections are handled in an SMS site hierarchy; and how to troubleshoot potential problems.

Defining Collections

Although our focus here is on the use of collections in the package distribution process, collections have many other uses. Collections are groups of SMS resources and can consist not only of computers, but also of Microsoft Windows users and user groups, as well as any resources discovered through the Network Discovery method or the Active Directory directory service discovery methods, as we discussed in Chapter 7, "Resource Discovery." Package programs can be advertised to collections that consist of users, user groups, or computers. Computer collections, however, are the starting point for performing many client management tasks. For example, you can initiate Remote Tools, view inventory information through Resource Explorer, and view Event Viewer and diagnostic information for each client by selecting the client through a collection.

> **Caution** Collections represent discovered resources. The computer resources that are discovered and displayed in a collection might not actually be installed as SMS clients. If a client hasn't been installed and the appropriate client component hasn't been enabled, you won't be able to initiate a Remote Tools session, collect inventory, and so on, even though the discovery data record (DDR) exists.

We know that if a computer is discovered but not installed as an SMS client, that computer can't be the recipient of an advertisement since the Advertised Programs Client Agent is an SMS client component. On the other hand, a discovered Windows *user* obviously can't be installed as an SMS client, since there's no equivalent user installation method. However, a discovered user can be the recipient of an advertisement when that user is logged on at an SMS client. For example, suppose that a company's auditing department has developed a spreadsheet that its auditors use when auditing other departments. If SMS has discovered the auditors' user accounts, those user accounts can be grouped into a collection called Auditors. The audit spreadsheet can then be advertised to the Auditors collection and would subsequently be available to each auditor at whatever SMS client they log on to, in whatever department they're visiting.

In many ways, collections are similar to Windows global groups. You use Windows groups to organize users into easily managed units. Groups are used to assign access permissions to Windows resources such as printers, folders, files, and shares. When a new user joins a group, that user automatically inherits all the permissions assigned to that group.

The same concept applies to SMS collections. You use collections to organize your SMS discovered resources into manageable units. For example, suppose you've installed 1000 clients as SMS clients. These clients will appear as part of the All Systems collection in the SMS Administrator Console. If each of these clients belongs to a different business unit or department within your organization and you need to send these computers packages based on their affiliation with their business unit or department, you could create a collection for each business unit or department and add each client to the appropriate collection. Your clients are now grouped into manageable units to which you can easily target packages.

Collections can contain subcollections to give the SMS administrator more flexibility (or more headaches, depending on your point of view). Subcollections work in much the same way as nested groups in Windows. Actions performed on a main collection can also be performed on its subcollections. The most common use for subcollections is in connection with advertisements. Package programs are advertised to collections, but you can also configure an advertisement to target a collection's subcollections as well.

Subcollections are not considered to be *members* of the collection that contains them. Think of subcollections more as a convenient way to link different collections so that they can be treated as one unit. Membership rules are unique for each subcollection and don't affect any other collection. We'll look at collection membership in the next section.

Collection Membership

Collection membership rules can be either direct or query-based. *Direct membership* is a manual membership method, meaning that you define which resources are to be members of the collection. You're also responsible for maintaining the collection over time. If, for example, computers are added or removed from the business group or department, you'll need to add or remove those computers from their corresponding collections.

Query-based membership, on the other hand, is more dynamic in nature. You define the rules by which the collection membership is established, and then SMS keeps the collection up-to-date by periodically rerunning the query. For example, suppose your company standard for naming computers is to include a business unit or departmental code—say, all computers in the finance department are named FIN203-PC*x*, where *x* is a value that's incremented each time a new computer name is needed. You could create a collection named Finance whose membership rule is based on a query that searches the database for all computers whose names begin with FIN203. SMS would automatically populate the collections with the appropriate computers. If computers are added or removed from the finance department, the collection would be updated automatically when the collection query was next executed.

As you can see, query-based collections are generally more practical and efficient than those based on direct-membership rules.

> **Real World Automating Collections and Packages**
>
> Let's build on our query-based collection example, in which all computers in the finance department are named FIN203-PCx and a Finance collection has been created whose membership rule is based on a query that searches the database for all computers whose names begin with FIN203. Since package programs are always advertised to collections, all members of the Finance collection would receive any advertisement to that collection. If computers are added or removed from the finance department, the next time the Finance collection is (automatically) updated, this change will be reflected to the collection and any new computers that were added to the collection will receive advertisements made to the collection. Similarly, if a computer has been removed from the Finance collection, that computer will no longer receive any advertisements made to the collection.

This process makes it easier for the SMS administrator to automate some client management tasks, such as applying virus updates. Suppose your advertisement is to copy a new virus update to each client in the finance department once a month. You already have the Finance collection, so all you need to do is create a recurring advertisement (you'll learn how to do this in Chapter 12, "Package Distribution and Management") that copies a new virus update file to the clients on a specified day of each month.

Working together, the advertisement and the collection ensure that all computers in the finance department will receive the virus update file once a month. If new computers are added to the finance department, the next time the collection is automatically updated they will automatically receive the same advertisement for the virus update file that every other member of the Finance collection will receive. Similarly, if a computer is moved to another department, the next time the collection is automatically updated that computer will no longer receive advertisements for the virus update. The only administrative task that you need to worry about is obtaining the virus update file once a month and making it available to the advertised package.

Predefined Collections

As mentioned, collections represent discovered resources that haven't necessarily been installed as SMS clients. For example, Windows users and user groups can be discovered as resources for an SMS site and the discovered users and user groups are automatically made members of the All Users and All User Groups collections—two examples of predefined collections.

Collections are used to group resources into more easily managed units. When you install SMS 2003, 12 default collections are created. These default collections are described in Table 11-1.

Table 11-1.   Default collections created during SMS site server installation

Collection	Description
All Systems	Displays all computers and IP-addressable resources discovered through any discovery method except Windows User Account Discovery and Windows NT User Group Discovery
All User Groups	Displays all Windows users discovered through the Windows User Group Discovery method

Table 11-1.   Default collections created during SMS site server installation

Collection	Description
All Users	Displays all Windows users discovered through the Windows User Account Discovery method
All Windows 2000 Professional Systems	Displays all discovered computers running the Windows 2000 Professional operating system
All Windows 2000 Server Systems	Displays all discovered computers running the Windows 2000 Server family operating system
All Windows 98 Systems	Displays all discovered computers running the Windows 98 operating system
All Windows NT Systems	Displays all discovered server or workstation computers running the Windows NT operating system
All Windows NT Workstation 4.0 Systems	Displays all discovered computers running the Windows NT Workstation 4.0 operating system
All Windows Server 2003 Systems	Displays all discovered computers running th Windows Server 2003 family operating system
All Windows Server Systems	Displays all discovered computer systems running the Windows NT 4.0 Server, Windows 2000 family, and Windows Server 2003 family operating system
All Windows Workstation or Professional Systems	Displays all discovered computers running the Windows NT Workstation 4.0, Windows 2000 Professional, and Windows XP Professional operating system
All Windows XP Systems	Displays all discovered computers running the Windows XP operating system

As you can see, these default collections are designed to group resources by operating system. The collections can be used as targets for receiving advertisements. They're updated once a day by default, but you can change that frequency by clicking the Schedule button in the Membership Rules tab in the collection's Properties window, as we'll see in the section entitled "Creating a Query-Based Collection" later in this chapter. Note that you can manage the default collections only from the central site. You can't modify them from child sites.

Creating Collections

The default collections provide some basic resource groupings, but these won't always be the best way to manage your resources, especially when it comes to advertising package programs to SMS clients. Instead, you can create your own collections, grouping together your resources in as many logical units as makes sense within your SMS site or site hierarchy.

Part of creating a collection involves defining the collection membership using membership rules. Recall that a collection's membership rules can be either direct, a manual method that requires more maintenance, or query-based, which provides greater flexibility and less maintenance. In this section we'll look at how to create collections with both types of membership rules.

Creating a Direct Membership Collection

To create a direct membership collection, follow these steps:

1. Navigate to the Collections folder in the SMS Administrator Console.

2. Right-click the Collections folder, choose New from the context menu, and then choose Collection to display the Collection Properties dialog box shown in Figure 11-1.

Figure 11-1. *The Collection Properties dialog box.*

3. In the General tab, enter a descriptive name for your collection along with a descriptive comment if you like.

4. Select the Membership Rules tab and click the Direct Membership button (the PC with the yellow star) to launch the Create Direct Membership Rule Wizard. Figure 11-2 shows the Create Direct Membership Rule Wizard welcome page.

Figure 11-2. *The Create Direct Membership Rule Wizard welcome page.*

5. Click Next to display the Search For Resources page, shown in Figure 11-3. Select the resource class for the resource you want to add to the collection. In the Resource Class drop-down list, the User Group Resource and User Resource options will let you add members discovered by the Windows User Account Discovery and Windows User Group Discovery methods. The System Resource option relates to discovered computers. For this example, select System Resource.

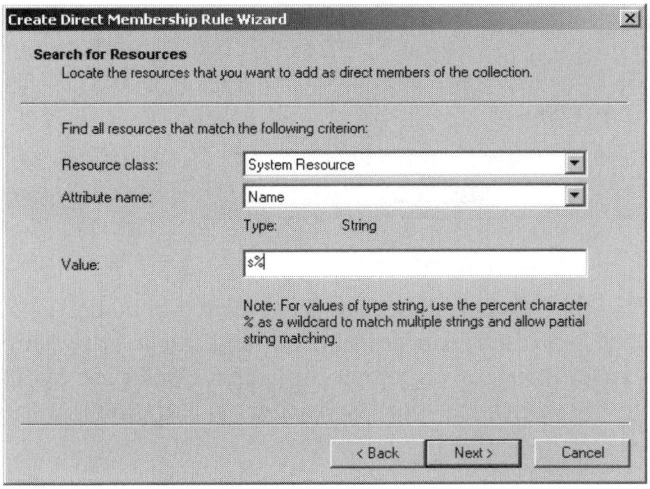

Figure 11-3. *The Search For Resources page.*

6. Select the resource attribute on which you'll base your membership choice. Attributes include resource name, resource ID, IP information, domain information, and so on. The attributes listed reflect the discovery data collected for that class of resource. For this example, specify Name.

7. Enter the appropriate attribute value to look for when selecting members for this group. The % sign is a wildcard character. In this case we're looking for all computers whose name begins with the letter "S."

8. Click Next to display the Collection Limiting page, shown in Figure 11-4. From this page you specify which existing collection to use to look for the resources you identified. You can leave the field blank if you have sufficient permissions to search the entire SMS database. Otherwise, you must enter the name of a collection that you have permissions to view.

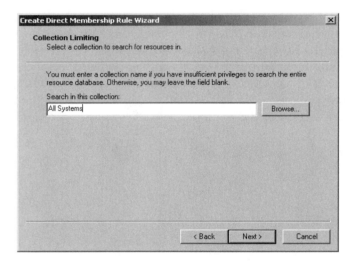

Figure 11-4. *The Collection Limiting page.*

9. Click Next to display the Select Resources page, as shown in Figure 11-5. This page shows a list of the resources that match your membership criteria—in this case, a list of all the computer names that begin with the letter "S." Select the resources you want to include in the collection.

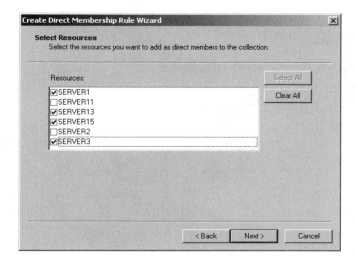

Figure 11-5.   *The Select Resources page.*

10. Click Next to display the Completing The Create Direct Membership Rule Wizard page, shown in Figure 11-6. You can also click the Back button to review or change your settings. Review your choices and then click Finish.

Figure 11-6.   *The Completing The Create Direct Membership Rule Wizard page.*

11. The resources you selected will now appear in the Membership Rules tab of the Collection Properties dialog box, as shown in Figure 11-7.

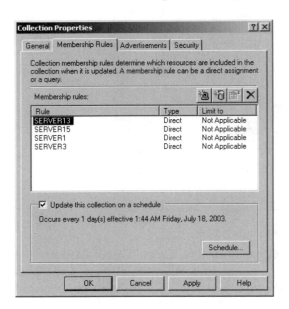

Figure 11-7. *The Membership Rules tab of the Collection Properties dialog box.*

12. In step 8 you specified a collection to use to look for resources you identified. In the Membership Rules tab, the Update This Collection On A Schedule check box indicates the frequency with which Collection Evaluator will browse the collection you specified to see if the resource still exists. If the resource is no longer a member of the specified collection, it will be removed from this new collection. Collection Evaluator is the SMS thread component that performs collection management tasks such as updating or refreshing collection data. By default, the collection will be updated once a day. Click the Schedule button to modify the collections update schedule.

Note   The minimum update interval is every 15 minutes. If you specify an update interval of less than 15 minutes, the collections won't be updated at that interval. In addition, if you change the membership update schedule, the first evaluation will have a delay up to 15 minutes.

13. Click OK to create the collection and add it to the Collections folder.

The Advertisements tab of the Collection Properties dialog box lists all advertisements that have targeted that collection. The Security tab lets you specify who can access this collection—and collections in general—and to what extent they can administer the collections. Security will be discussed in detail in Chapter 17, "Security."

Creating a Query-Based Collection

To create a query-based collection, follow these steps:

1. Navigate to the Collections folder in the SMS Administrator Console.

2. Right-click the Collections folder, choose New from the context menu, and then choose Collection to display the Collection Properties dialog box, shown previously in Figure 11-1.

3. In the General tab, enter a descriptive name for your collection along with a descriptive comment if you like.

4. In the Membership Rules tab, click the Query Rules button (the database with the yellow star) to display the Query Rule Properties dialog box, shown in Figure 11-8.

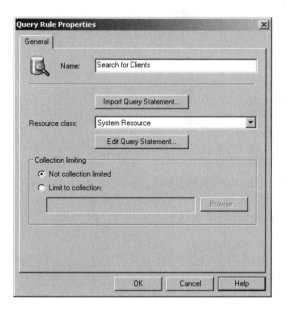

Figure 11-8.   *The Query Rules Properties dialog box.*

5. In the General tab, enter a name for your query, or click Import Query Statement to choose from a list of existing SMS queries.

6. Select the resource class for a set of related objects you want to add to the collection. The Systems Resource option is selected by default. In the Collection Limiting frame, select Limit To Collection if you want to narrow the query to a specific collection's membership. Click Browse to select from a list of existing collections.

7. Click Edit Query Statement to display the Query Statement Properties dialog box, shown in Figure 11-9.

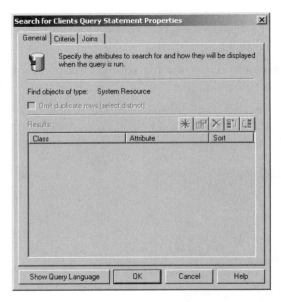

Figure 11-9. *The Query Statement Properties dialog box.*

8. In the General tab, you'll notice that you don't have the ability to create or modify a Query Results list. This is because the query is being used to populate a collection membership instead of displaying resource attributes.

9. Select the Criteria tab, as shown in Figure 11-10, where you can define how to populate the collection.

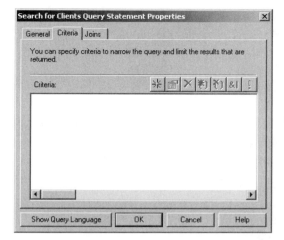

Figure 11-10. *The Query Statement Properties dialog box Criteria tab.*

10. Click the New button (the yellow star) to display the Criterion Properties dialog box, shown in Figure 11-11.

Figure 11-11. *The Criterion Properties dialog box.*

11. Select the criterion type. The available choices are Null Value, Simple Value, Attribute Reference, Subselected Values, and List of Values. (See Chapter 16, "Queries and Reports," for a description of each criterion type.)

12. Click the Select button to define the attribute class and attribute on which you're basing the query.

13. Select an operator and enter a value appropriate to the attribute class and attribute you defined or click Values to make your selection from a list of values recorded in the SMS database. When you've finished, click OK.

Caution String values require an exact value entry. If you wish to use a wildcard character, use the operator Is Like or Is Not Like, and then use the percent sign (%) like you see in Figure 11-11 or one of the other wildcard characters described in Chapter 16.

14. Repeat steps 10 through 13 to add selection criteria.

Note As mentioned, a collection can be mixed—that is, it can contain computers, users, and groups.

15. Click OK to return to the Query Rule Properties dialog box. Click OK again to return to the Collection Properties dialog box.

16. Select the Membership Rules tab, shown in Figure 11-12.

Figure 11-12. *The Collection Properties dialog box Membership Rules tab.*

Select the Update This Collection On A Schedule option to define the frequency at which you want Collection Evaluator to run the query and update the collection. By default, the collection will be updated once every hour.

17. Click OK to create the collection and add it to the Collections folder.

As with direct membership collections, the Advertisements tab of the Collection Properties dialog box lists all advertisements that have targeted that collection. The Security tab lets you specify who can access this collection—and collections in general—and to what extent they can administer the collections. Security will be discussed in detail in Chapter 17.

Creating Subcollections

When a collection has one or more subcollections associated with it, any actions (such as advertisements) performed on the collection can also be performed on the subcollection. However, each subcollection is still its own collection and as such is governed by its own membership rules. Placing them as subcollections within a new collection provides a way to link different collections rather than a method of nesting collections.

Suppose a particular business unit can be further subdivided into smaller units. Management Information Services (MIS), for example, might be divided into various support areas—say, PC Support, Network Support, and Server Support. Let's say that you create a collection for each of these groups—MIS, PC Support, Network Support, and Server Support. The last three collections could become subcollections of the MIS collection. This reclassification enables you to advertise packages to the MIS collection, which includes the members of the three subcollections. If you don't need to hit all the collections, you can opt not to when you create the advertisement. And you still have the ability to advertise to each collection directly.

To link one collection to another, thus creating a subcollection, follow these steps:

1. Navigate to the Collections folder in the SMS Administrator Console and expand it.

2. Right-click the collection that you want to associate with a subcollection, choose New from the Context menu, and then choose Link To Collection to display the Browse Collection dialog box, shown in Figure 11-13.

3. The Browse Collection dialog box contains a list of all the available collections. Select the collection you want to add as a subcollection and then click OK.

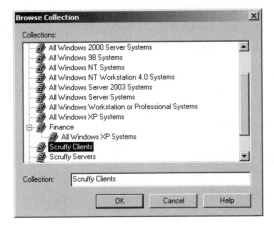

Figure 11-13. *The Browse Collection dialog box.*

You can easily view which collections have subcollections and what those sub-collections are by expanding the collection entries in the SMS Administrator Console, shown in Figure 11-14. In this example, the Scruffy Clients collection has a subcollection named Finance that itself has a subcollection named All Windows XP Systems, which is one of the default collections.

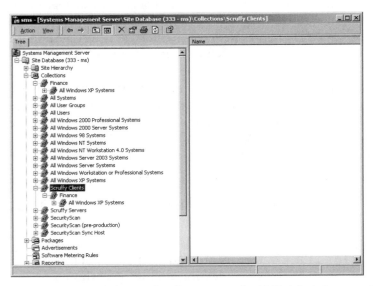

Figure 11-14. *Viewing subcollections in the SMS Administrator Console.*

> **Tip** You can view subcollections of a collection by clicking the plus sign (+) preceding the collection name.

Unlinking Subcollections

If you need to "unlink" a subcollection to reorganize your collection structure, follow these steps:

1. Navigate to the Collections folder, expand it, and select the subcollection you want to delete.

2. Right-click the subcollection and then choose Delete from the context menu to initiate the Delete Collection Wizard, as shown in Figure 11-15.

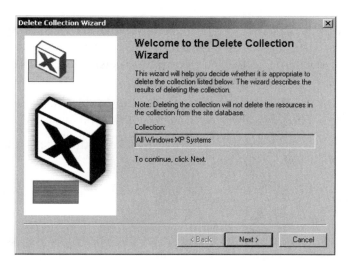

Figure 11-15. *The Delete Collection Wizard Welcome page.*

3. Verify the subcollection name and then click Next to display the Delete Collection Instance page, as shown in Figure 11-16.

Figure 11-16. *The Delete Collection Instance page.*

4. Select Yes to delete this instance of the collection. Note that you'll be deleting only this instance of the collection. You won't delete any other instance of the same collection that appears elsewhere in the Collections folder.

5. Click Next and then click Finish. The Collections folder will be refreshed, and the subcollection will no longer be displayed or linked.

Now that we've created and deleted collections and subcollections, let's take a look at how we can keep them up-to-date through SMS.

Updating Collections

As we've seen, collections that are based on direct-membership rules need to be maintained by the SMS administrator since they're manually created and defined. Collections that are based on queries, however, can be updated automatically based on the schedule that you define. The SMS component responsible for carrying out this updating task is Collection Evaluator.

Collection Evaluator will execute the query and update the collection whenever the scheduled interval occurs or when the SMS administrator forces an update through the SMS Administrator Console. When the SMS administrator forces an update or modifies a collection, creates a new collection, or deletes an existing collection, SQL Monitor notifies Collection Evaluator of the event.

Forcing an Update

Collection Evaluator will execute a collection's query and update the collection membership according to whatever schedule you define. However, sometimes you need or want to update the collection membership outside of that schedule. The SMS administrator can force Collection Evaluator to update all the collections or any individual collection at any point in time.

Updating All Collections

To update all the collections at once, follow these steps:

1. Navigate to the Collections folder in the SMS Administrator Console and expand it.

2. Right-click the Collections folder, choose All Tasks from the context menu, and then choose Update Collection Membership.

3. A message box will appear confirming the update of all collections. Choose OK. This update might take some time to complete depending on the number of collections, network traffic if the SMS database is on another computer, and so on.

4. When the update is complete, all the collections in the SMS Administrator Console will show an hourglass alongside the collection icon in the SMS Administrator Console, as shown in Figure 11-17. These hourglasses indicate that the collection was updated, but that the SMS Administrator Console window needs to be refreshed.

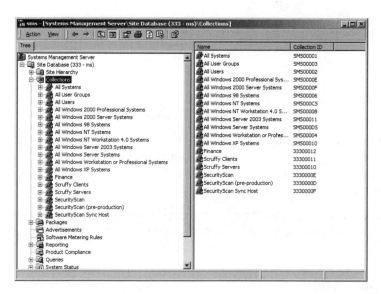

Figure 11-17. *The SMS Administrator Console with updated collections before being refreshed.*

5. To refresh the SMS Administrator Console window, right-click the Collections folder again and choose Refresh from the context menu. The collections will now display their updated memberships.

Updating an Individual Collection

To update an individual collection, follow these steps:

1. Navigate to the Collections folder in the SMS Administrator Console and expand it.

2. Right-click the collection you want to update, choose All Tasks from the context menu, and then choose Update Collection Membership.

3. As shown in Figure 11-18, a message box appears confirming the update of this collection and giving you the option of simultaneously updating the collection's subcollections. If you want the subcollections updated as well, select the Update Subcollection Membership check box. Click OK to begin the update.

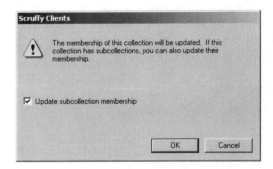

Figure 11-18.   *Message box confirming the collection update.*

4. When the update is complete, the collection in the SMS Administrator Console will show an hourglass icon alongside the collection entry. This indicates that the collection was updated but that you still need to refresh the SMS Administrator Console.

5. To refresh the SMS Administrator Console window, right-click the collection again and choose Refresh from the context menu. The collection will then display its updated membership.

Deleting a Collection

That which the SMS administrator gives, the SMS administrator can take away. This, of course, is true of collections. While you maintain collections, you might need to reorganize your collection structure by creating new collections and deleting existing ones. Deleting a collection can have consequences other than just removing that collection. When you delete a collection, you'll also effect the following events:

- Any advertisements that have targeted only this collection will also be deleted. (If an advertisement is also targeting another collection, it won't be affected.)

- When you create a query, you can limit its scope by associating it with a particular collection. When the collection is deleted, the query's scope is no longer limited.

- Any collections whose membership rules (queries) are limited to the collection that's being deleted will still process the rule but will display no resources.

- Through the object class or instance security (discussed in Chapter 16) you can identify which SMS administrators have the ability to view the membership of each collection. After you remove a collection, the administrators you identified will no longer be able to view that collection's resources if the resources aren't in other collections that the administrators can view.

Note   If the collection you're deleting has a subcollection linked to it, that subcollection is also deleted unless the subcollection itself has its own subcollections. If the latter is true, when you delete the top-level collection, the subcollection isn't deleted and will still exist in the collection tree.

Fortunately, when you delete a collection, the Delete Collection Wizard warns you of these effects and shows you what properties of the collection might be affected.

Note   When you right-click a collection, you see an option called Delete Special. Be careful when using this option. It bypasses the Delete Collection Wizard and simply deletes all the resources from the collection from the SMS database, along with the resources' discovery and inventory information. Consequently you could inadvertently delete resources from the SMS database.

Follow these steps to delete a collection:

1. Navigate to the Collections folder in the SMS Administrator Console and expand it.

2. Right-click the collection you want to delete and choose Delete from the context menu. The Delete Collection Wizard Welcome page is

displayed, as shown previously in Figure 11-15. Verify the name of the collection to be deleted.

3. Click Next to display the Effects Of Deleting This Collection page, shown in Figure 11-19. This page warns you about the effects of deleting a collection and lets you choose whether to display details about the effects.

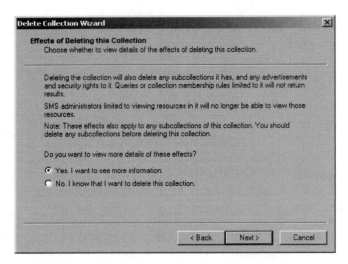

Figure 11-19. *The Effects Of Deleting This Collection page.*

4. Select the Yes option to view individual pages describing what will be affected by the deletion. Select the No option to proceed with the deletion.

If you selected the No option, you'd proceed to step 11, where you would simply delete the collection. For this example, select the Yes option.

5. Click Next to display the Subcollections page, as shown in Figure 11-20. This page displays a list of this collection's subcollections. Note the warning that deleting this collection will also delete the subcollections.

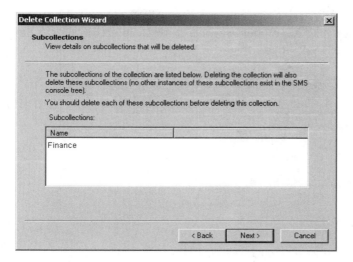

Figure 11-20.   *The Subcollections page.*

6. Click Next to display the Advertisements page, as shown in Figure 11-21, which displays a list of all the advertisements that have targeted this collection. Again, note the warning that deleting this collection could also delete the advertisements (if they're not also targeted to another collection).

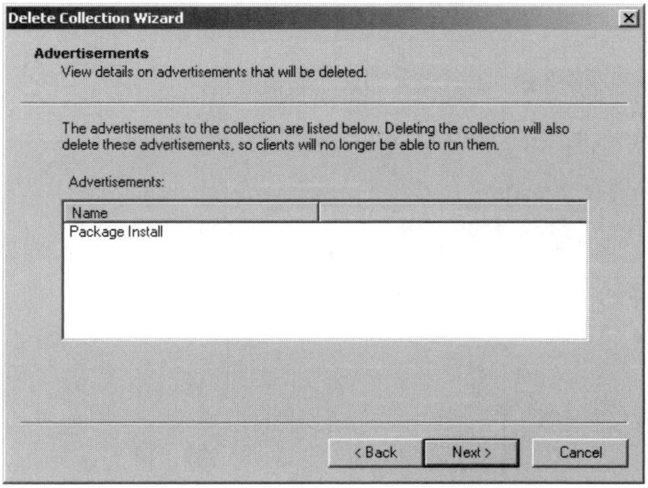

Figure 11-21.   *The Advertisements page.*

7. Click Next to display the Queries page, shown in Figure 11-22, which lists any queries that have been limited to this collection. A similar warning message is provided.

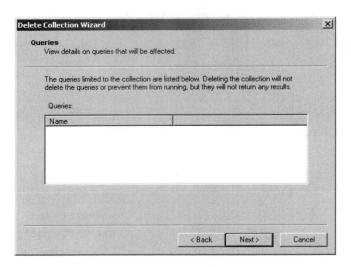

Figure 11-22. *The Queries page.*

8. Click Next to display the Collection Membership Rules page, shown in Figure 11-23. This page displays a list of collections whose membership rules are limited to this collection and warns of possible effects.

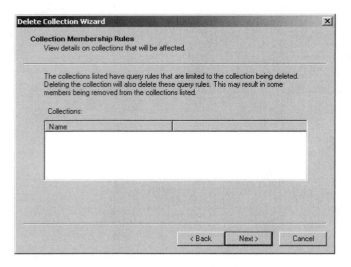

Figure 11-23. *The Collection Membership Rules page.*

9. Click Next to display the Administrators page, shown in Figure 11-24, which lists the administrators who have permissions to view resources in this collection and the effect that the deletion might have on them.

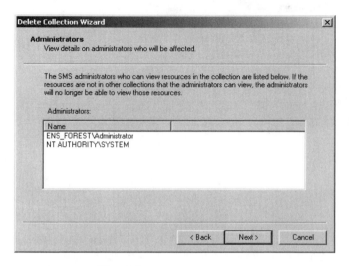

Figure 11-24. *The Administrators page.*

10. Click Next to display the Choose Whether To Delete This Collection page, shown in Figure 11-25. This final confirmation page asks whether you want to proceed with the deletion. Select the Yes option to continue.

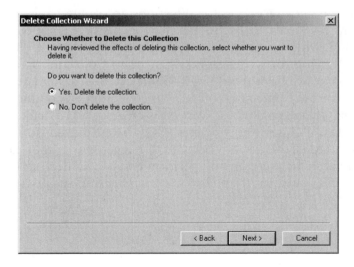

Figure 11-25. *The Choose Whether To Delete This Collection page.*

11. Click Next to display the Completing The Delete Collection Wizard page, shown in Figure 11-26. Click Finish to delete the collection.

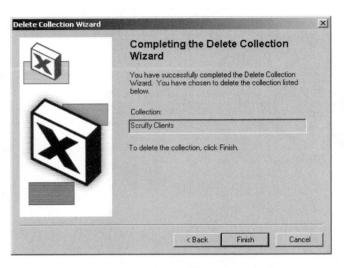

Figure 11-26. *The Completing The Delete Collection Wizard page.*

In this section we've seen SMS administrators update and maintain collections and subcollections. Next, let's discuss how SMS itself can update your collections automatically.

Collection Evaluator Update Process Flow

Collection Evaluator assigns resources to collections according to the most recent data about the resources. Collection Evaluator waits for a file change notification from SQL Monitor before the update process starts. As shown in Figure 11-27, SQL Monitor writes a wake-up file to Collection Evaluator's inbox (SMS\Inboxes\Colleval.box). SQL Monitor writes an update collection (.UDC) file when the update is forced or a collection is modified, an add collection (.ADC) file when a new collection is created, and a delete collection (.DC) file when a collection is deleted. SQL Monitor, like so many other components in SMS 2003, is driven by SQL trigger events that cause the component ultimately to wake up and perform its task. Collection Evaluator then executes the query and updates the membership results in the SMS database.

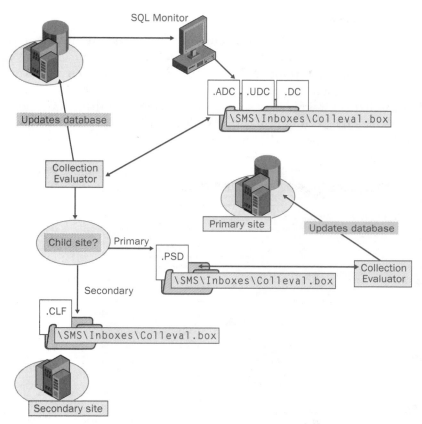

Figure 11-27.   *The Collection Evaluator update process flow.*

If the SMS site has child sites, Collection Evaluator also creates a .PSD file that contains the collection definition and membership. It writes this file to Replication Manager's inbox (SMS\Inboxes\Replmgr.box) so that the file can be scheduled and copied to Collection Evaluator's inbox on the child site. If the child site is a secondary site, the file is rewritten to disk as a .CLF file and contains only the collection memberships. If the child site is a primary site, the collection will be processed in much the same fashion as described in the beginning of this section.

When a child site changes its parent site affiliation, Collection Evaluator is responsible for removing any collections that the parent created (and are therefore locked at the child site). When the child site joins the new parent site, the collections created at the parent site are passed down to the child site, and Collection Evaluator locks them and keeps them updated.

Status Messages

As with all SMS components, Collection Evaluator generates status messages as it processes collections and subcollections, as well as a log file if you've enabled logging for this component. The Status Message Viewer window shown in Figure 11-28 displays typical status messages generated by Collection Evaluator. Notice that this component's message IDs lie within the $25xx$ range. For example, message ID 2516 indicates that Collection Evaluator was notified that a new collection was added (by the SMS administrator, of course). The .ADC file is a wake-up file written by SQL Monitor.

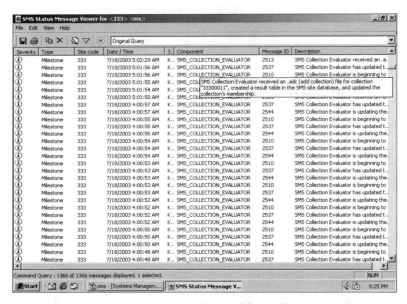

Figure 11-28. *Status messages generated by Collection Evaluator as it processes SMS collections.*

The pairing of messages 2539 and 2510 indicates when the membership rules for a collection were processed and when the collection was updated. A 2508 message indicates that Collection Evaluator is set to replicate the site's collections and subcollections to child sites.

In addition to these status messages, Collection Evaluator writes its thread activity to a log file named Colleval.log if you enabled logging for this component. Figure 11-29 displays log entries as viewed using Microsoft Notepad. As you can see, there's really nothing remarkable here, except that you can view on a per-thread basis when Collection Evaluator processes each collection, updates or deletes wake-up files, and so on.

Figure 11-29.   *Log entries generated by Collection Evaluator during normal processing.*

Collections and the SMS Site Hierarchy

Because the manner in which collections are handled within an SMS site hierarchy can be confusing, let's take a brief look at this topic. Collection definitions created at a parent site will be propagated to that parent's child primary sites. However, the configurations of these collections will be locked to the child site's SMS administrator. As shown in Figure 11-30, a small lock icon appears next to these collections in the SMS Administrator Console showing that the collections are locked and can't be modified. The lock feature is by design. Collections created at the parent site can be modified only at the parent site. Child sites that receive these collections will evaluate them and populate them based on their SMS database if they're also primary sites. You can delete all the members of a locked collection by right-clicking the locked collection and choosing Delete Special from the context menu. However, if the deleted members are still valid at the parent site, they will reappear the next time the collection is evaluated and updated.

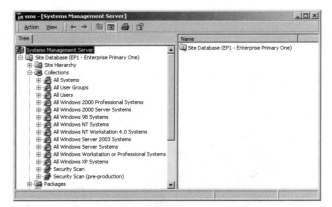

Figure 11-30. *Locked collections in the SMS Administrator Console.*

Child sites can create their own collections. These collections are fully manageable by the child site's SMS administrator and are not forwarded back up to the parent site. They will be propagated to their child sites and, of course, will be locked at the child sites.

Because secondary child sites don't maintain an SMS database of their own, their collections will be created and maintained at their parent sites. The secondary child sites will receive only the list of collection members that belong to their secondary site.

Note If a collection hasn't been updated for a week, SMS will automatically send the entire collection from a primary site to its child sites to synchronize the collections.

Checkpoints

There's not much danger lurking as far as collections are concerned. Any potential problems lie mostly in the setup of the collection. For example, remember that the most useful collections are those based on queries. Query-based membership rules allow the collection to be updated on a regular schedule that you define, ensuring that the collection will be kept up-to-date. However, this regular updating won't take place unless you enable that option in the Membership Rules tab of the Collection Properties window. Since this option isn't enabled by default, it can be easily missed.

Another "gotcha" comes through the SMS Administrator Console. To view the members in a collection, you expand the Collections folder and select the collection entry. Remember that the collection members are not updated in the console automatically. After Collection Evaluator reevaluates the collections' memberships, you still need to refresh the console by right-clicking the Collections folder and choosing Refresh from the context menu. And if you force an update to one or all of the collections, you still need to refresh the console—an update does not also refresh.

Summary

In this chapter we've seen how much easier the life of the SMS administrator can become when the appropriate collections have been created, updated, and evaluated. Good collections, like properly configured Windows groups, can facilitate other SMS management activities, such as accessing clients for remote control, targeting clients for package distribution, troubleshooting remote clients, and so on. Chapter 12 will build on this management theme as we begin our examination of the package distribution capabilities of SMS 2003.

Chapter 12
Package Distribution and Management

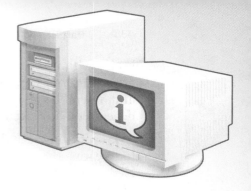

One of the primary features of Microsoft Systems Management Server (SMS) 2003 is its ability to distribute packages to, and run programs on, SMS client computers. This process consists of three main elements:

- Creating and distributing the package
- Advertising a package program to a collection
- Receiving the advertisement and executing the program on a client

The package distribution process is the focus of this chapter. Let's begin with a discussion of what package distribution is all about. First we'll define some terms and outline just what SMS does throughout the distribution process. Then we'll explore the administrative tasks involved in the creation of packages and advertisements. Finally, we'll learn how to monitor status messages and log files for the appropriate SMS components involved and how to test the package and its programs to ensure that they execute properly on the target clients.

Defining Package Distribution

Somehow, SMS administrators and users often misunderstand or mislabel the package distribution process. It's important to remember that SMS 2003 is fundamentally a package delivery tool. Basically, SMS is designed to make a package that you create available to a specified target or targets. The key here is that you are responsible for creating the package. You're also responsible for ensuring that the package will execute as intended when it reaches its target. SMS will get it there for you, but SMS won't "error-correct" it for you—nor should you expect it to.

Look at it this way. Suppose you're sending a bicycle to your nephew. You box up the parts carefully, including instructions on how to assemble it, go to your nearest package delivery service office, fill out the appropriate forms, pay the appropriate fees, and hand over the box. The responsibility of the package delivery service now is to get the box containing the bicycle to your nephew's house within the time frame you specified and paid for. When the package arrives at your nephew's house, he opens the package, reads the instructions, and assembles the bicycle. The extent to which your nephew is successful depends on how accurate and easy to understand the instructions were.

SMS works in much the same way. You, the SMS administrator, are responsible for creating the package and ensuring that all the appropriate pieces are assembled: source files, scripts, executables, command switches, and so on. You identify where the package must go and who should receive it. SMS carries out your instructions and even "opens" the package when it arrives at the target. However, the package's ability to execute—or the user's ability to use the application, for that matter—isn't SMS's responsibility.

Terminology

This description of the basic package distribution process uses some terms that you're probably familiar with. Let's take a moment here to review these terms in more detail.

An *SMS package* generally represents a software application that needs to be installed on an SMS client computer. However, a package might also contain update programs or software patches, single files such as a virus update file, or no files at all—just a command to execute a program already resident on the client. You need to identify to SMS exactly what the package consists of.

Every package must contain at least one program. An *SMS program* identifies what should occur on the client when the package is received. Perhaps a setup routine is executed, or a virus scan is performed, or a file is copied to a particular directory. Perhaps the user needs to supply information such as the program directory, or perhaps no user intervention is required at all. A package may have several programs associated with it, allowing the application to be run in a variety of ways on different clients. Consider a Microsoft Office XP installation. You can choose to perform one of several types of software installation, including Typical, Custom, or Laptop installation. If this software were an SMS package—and it could be—you would have to include a program for each of these installation methods if you intended to use them. Once again, you must define the program to SMS and include any and all appropriate references to script files or command switches. The program also defines the platform and environment within which the package can run. For instance, can the package run on any platform or only on Microsoft Windows XP computers with Service Pack 1 installed? Can the program be executed by any user or can it run only in an administrator context?

Some applications include predefined scripts called package definition files that can be used with SMS. Package definition files contain all the package and program information required for SMS to successfully distribute the package and, usually, to deploy it. Package definition files often come with the application's source file, or they can be obtained from the developer. You can also create package definition files using various tools and utilities from Microsoft. We'll return to package definition files later in this chapter in the section "Creating a Package from a Definition File."

An *advertisement* makes the program and package available to a specified collection. Recall from Chapter 11, "Collections," that collections can contain not only SMS client computers but also Windows users and groups. This means that a program can be advertised to clients as well as to users and groups. So before you create the advertisement, you'll need to have created the appropriate collections.

Advertisements are often used to schedule when a program runs and to specify whether the user can reschedule the program. Advertisements can also be configured to recur—that is, to make a program available on a recurring basis. For example, if you distribute virus update files on a monthly basis, you might create a virus update package and program and then an advertisement that makes the virus update file available on a monthly basis.

The Advertised Programs Client Agent (also sometimes referred to as the Advertised Programs Agent) is installed and started on the SMS client. As with other client agents, this agent is optional and the SMS administrator must configure and enable it. The Advertised Programs Client Agent's job is to monitor the client access point (CAP) for available advertised programs that target the client or the user at the client. When an advertisement is found and the program is ready to be run, the agent connects to an available distribution point—as defined in the package details—to execute the program. If the program runs an existing file on the client, the agent executes the program appropriately.

Three SMS site systems, in addition to the site server, are involved in the package distribution process: CAPs, management points, and distribution points. The CAP is always the point of interchange between the site server and the SMS Legacy Clients, and the management point performs the same function for the SMS Advanced Clients. In this exchange, package detail information and advertisements are copied to the CAP for access by the Advertised Programs Client Agent on the Legacy Client and to the management point for access by the Software Distribution Client Agent on the Advanced Client. To simplify this discussion, I'll refer to both agents as the client agent and make any distinctions in functionality as they're necessary. The actual source files that constitute the package are copied to distribution points. Before you can distribute any packages, you need to have assigned CAPs, management points, and distribution points. Remember that the site server becomes a CAP and a distribution point by default when you install SMS 2003. Remember, too, that you can have only one management point defined per site. (The role of site systems and how they're assigned is discussed in Chapter 3, "Configuring Site Server Properties and Site Systems.")

Preparing for Package Distribution

As you can see from the previous section, many components are involved in package distribution. Before we continue our discussion of package distribution, let's outline the actions required for the distribution process:

- Define your CAPs, management points, and distribution points for the package
- Create appropriate collections
- Gather all source files, setup routines, scripts, and so on needed for the package
- Create the SMS package
- Define at least one program for the package
- Distribute the package to the distribution points
- Advertise the programs to one or more collections
- Execute the advertised program on the client

After reviewing these elements of the distribution process, you'll have a solid foundation to build on. The following sections of this chapter will cover how to configure various components for package distribution.

Creating Packages for Distribution

Now we can delve into the package distribution process in more detail, beginning with package creation itself. In this section we'll explore the package creation process, including identifying distribution points and creating programs.

Gathering Source Files

If your package involves the accessing of source files, such as performing a software installation, you must define a location for the source files. The location can be a shared folder on the site server or on a remote server, including a

CD-ROM drive. The most important characteristic of the source file location is that it must be accessible to the SMS site server either using the SMS service account if running SMS in standard security mode or using the site server's computer account if running SMS in advanced security mode. If your program involves using a script file or files, be sure to include them as part of your source files as well or the program will fail.

Creating a Package from Scratch

As in all things SMS, you'll begin in the SMS Administrator Console. You can create a package either from scratch—one for which you provide all the configuration details—or from a package definition file that already contains all the package details. In this section we'll look at the former technique.

To create a package from the ground up, follow these steps:

1. Navigate to the Packages folder, right-click it, choose New from the context menu, and then choose Package to display the Package Properties dialog box, shown in Figure 12-1.

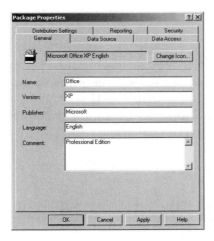

Figure 12-1. *The Package Properties dialog box.*

2. In the General tab, enter the name of the package, its version, its publisher, its language, and a descriptive comment if desired. The only required value here is Name. Notice that the full package name is displayed in the text box to the left of the Change Icon button.

3. Click Change Icon to enter or browse for an icon file or Setup.exe file to display the correct icon for the package. The default icon is the SMS package icon.

4. Select the Data Source tab, shown in Figure 12-2. This tab lets you define details concerning the source files for the package. If the package contains source files—even a single file—select the This Package Contains Source Files check box to enable the options in the Source Directory frame.

Figure 12-2. *The Data Source tab.*

5. Click Set to display the Set Source Directory dialog box, shown in Figure 12-3. In this dialog box you define the location of the source files. The location can be either a local drive path or a UNC path to a remote share. Enter the location or click Browse to look for the directory. Then click OK to return to the Data Source tab.

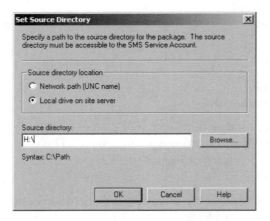

Figure 12-3. *The Set Source Directory dialog box.*

6. If your source files aren't likely to change or are on a removable medium such as a CD-ROM, or if the source path is likely to change, select the Use A Compressed Copy Of The Source Directory option. This option causes SMS to create and store a compressed version of the source files on the site server. When the package needs to be sent to a new distribution point or updated on existing distribution points, SMS will access the compressed files, uncompress them, and send them to the distribution points.

7. If your source files are likely to change periodically—for example, if they include a monthly virus update file—select Always Obtain Files From Source Directory. Selecting this option also allows you to select the Update Distribution Points On A Schedule check box. Setting an update schedule ensures that as the source files change, the distribution points will be updated regularly.

8. Select the Data Access tab, shown in Figure 12-4. The Data Access tab defines how SMS will store the package source files on the distribution points. The default setting is Access Distribution Folder Through Common SMS Package Share. With this setting, SMS will define a share point on the distribution points and place the source files in a folder in that share. The share will always be SMSPKGx\$$, where x represents the drive with the most free disk space. This share is a hidden share to keep prying eyes from browsing for it. When SMS runs out of disk space, it will find the next drive with the most free space and create an additional SMSPKGx\$$ directory and share there.

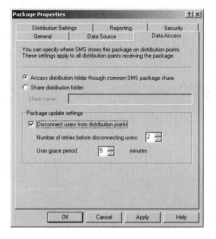

Figure 12-4.   *The Data Access tab.*

9. If you prefer to create your own folder organization and access shares, you may do so first and then reference the share by selecting the option Share Distribution Folder and entering the UNC path to the share. This value can be a share or a share and a path, but whatever value you enter must be unique among all packages. Also, the share and path must already exist on the distribution points that you target. If you enter only a share name (in the form *server**appshare*), any file or subfolders created within the share will be deleted and re-created whenever the package is updated or refreshed. If you enter a share that includes a path (*server**appshare**word*), only the down-level folder will be deleted and re-created.

10. Select Disconnect Users From Distribution Points to do just that. If you want to ensure that no users are connected to the package folder on the distribution points when files are being refreshed or updated, this option will cause SMS to inform users that they will be disconnected. Users will be disconnected after the time period you specify in the User Grace Period text box. The default value is 5 minutes, but you can specify from 0 to 59 minutes. The Number Of Retries Before Disconnecting Users option indicates how many times SMS will attempt to refresh the distribution points before disconnecting users. This value can range from 0 to 99.

11. Select the Distribution Settings tab, shown in Figure 12-5. In this tab you identify the sending priority and preferred sender to use when sending this package to distribution points in a child site. If you have no child sites, these settings will have no effect. (Refer to Chapter 4, "Multiple-Site Structures," for a discussion of parent-child relationships and the role of the sender in transferring information between sites in the hierarchy.)

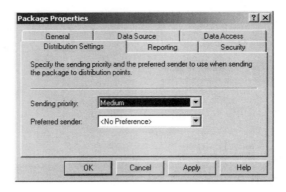

Figure 12-5. *The Distribution Settings tab.*

12. Select the Reporting tab, shown in Figure 12-6. This tab lets you identify how SMS reports installation status Management Information Format (MIF) files from the client when the package is run. Select Use Package Properties For Status MIF Matching to simply use the values you supplied in the General tab to identify status MIF files generated during installation. Or select Use These Fields For Status MIF Matching and fill in the fields if you want to specify different values.

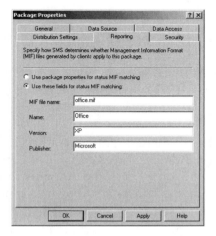

Figure 12-6. *The Reporting tab.*

13. Select the Security tab to set class and instance security rights for the package. This type of security is discussed in Chapter 17, "Security."

14. Click OK to create the package.

We haven't quite finished creating this package. If you expand the new package entry you just created in the SMS Administrator Console, as in the example shown in Figure 12-7, you'll see that three areas of configuration remain. The first area, defining access accounts, allows you to further secure who has access to the distribution source files. The other two areas are absolutely essential to the successful distribution of the package: defining distribution points, without which the client has no access to the source files, and defining programs, which specifies how to install or run the source files. Let's configure the access account first.

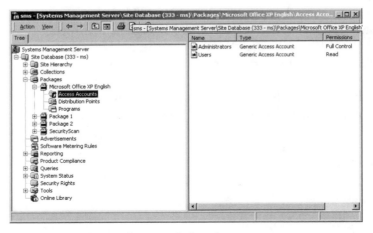

Figure 12-7.   *A sample expanded package entry.*

Defining Access Accounts

By default, when SMS creates the SMSPKG$x$$ share, it grants Read access to the local Users group and Full Control to the Administrators group. The default Users and Administrators entries map to the local Users and Administrators groups for Windows distribution points. These accounts are known as generic package access accounts.

Since the default share is a hidden share, the only way a client should know that a package is available to it is through the package distribution process. In other words, the client agent will see an advertisement for that package that targets a collection the client is a member of. Bear in mind that users will be users, and it's possible that they will find the hidden share, navigate to a package folder, and execute any programs they find there. This could also happen if you create your own shares.

There are a couple of ways to deal with this little breach of security. One would be for you to evaluate the share (or NTFS) security for the SMS shares or for the package folders within the share. This is a time-consuming and potentially destructive process if you happen to lock out SMS from accessing the share. The other solution is to define access accounts for the package through the SMS Administrator Console. When you define an access account, you also define the level of access or permission for the specified user or group. This is much like creating ACLs in Windows.

To define an access account, follow these steps:

1. Navigate to the Packages folder, find your package entry, and expand it.

2. Right-click Access Accounts, choose New from the context menu, and then choose the type of access account you want to create.

3. The two types of access accounts are listed here:

   • *Windows User Access Account*—Defines a Windows user or group account and the level of permission to allow

   • *Generic Access Account*—Defines additional or replacement user, guest, or administrator accounts and the level of permission to allow that maps to an operating system–specific account

   Select the appropriate option to display the Access Account Properties dialog box, shown in Figure 12-8.

Figure 12-8. *The Access Account Properties dialog box.*

4. Click Set to specify the account information as follows:

   • For a Windows user account, the Windows User Account dialog box will appear, as shown in Figure 12-9. Enter the user or group account in *Domain\user* format, and select User or Group.

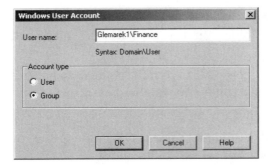

Figure 12-9. *The Windows User Account dialog box.*

- For a Generic account, the Generic Account dialog box will appear, as shown in Figure 12-10. Select the account type.

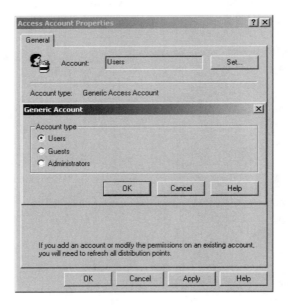

Figure 12-10. *The Generic Account dialog box.*

5. Click OK to return to the Access Account Properties dialog box. Select the appropriate level of permissions from the Permissions drop-down list, as shown in Figure 12-11. For most applications, Read permission will be sufficient. However, if the program requires any kind of writing back to the source directory, you'll need to assign at least Change permission.

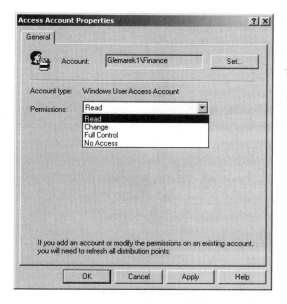

Figure 12-11.   *The Permissions list of the Access Account Properties dialog box.*

6. Click OK to create the account.

Defining Distribution Points

An essential configuration detail for any package is identifying the distribution points on which the package can be found. You should have already assigned the distribution point role to one or more site systems in your SMS site, as well as at any child sites. You now need to tell SMS which of those distribution points will host the package.

> **Note**   If you're distributing the package to a child site, even if the SMS administrator for that site will ultimately distribute the package to its clients, you still must identify at least one distribution point at that child site when you create the package.

To define distribution points, follow these steps:

1. Navigate to the Packages folder, find your package entry, and expand it.

2. Right-click Distribution Points, choose New from the context menu, and then choose Distribution Points to activate the New Distribution Points Wizard, shown in Figure 12-12.

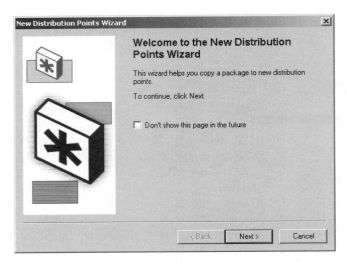

Figure 12-12. *The New Distribution Points Wizard welcome page.*

3. Click Next to display the Copy Package page, shown in Figure 12-13. This page shows a list of available distribution points. Scroll through the list and select the distribution points you want.

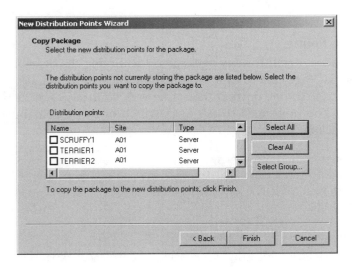

Figure 12-13. *The Copy Package page.*

4. Click Select Group to open the Browse Distribution Point Group page, shown in Figure 12-14. Here you can view a list of distribution point groups and their member site systems. If you select one of the

distribution point groups and click OK, all the site systems that are members of that group will be selected in the Copy Package page.

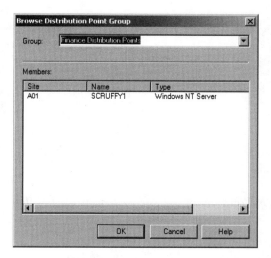

Figure 12-14.   *The Browse Distribution Point Group dialog box.*

5. Click Finish to add the distribution points you selected to the package details.

Once you have added a distribution point to the package, that distribution point will no longer appear in the list of available distribution points if you run the New Distribution Points Wizard again—the wizard displays only distribution points that are available. If you need to remove a distribution point from the package, select it, right-click it, and choose Delete from the context menu. When you delete a distribution point, you'll also delete the package source directory on that distribution point.

It's often desirable to group distribution points so that packages can be distributed to them as a block rather than having to name the distribution points individually. Distribution point groups are defined through the site settings of your site—in the same place that you assign the distribution point role.

To define a distribution point group, follow these steps:

1. In the SMS Administrator Console, navigate to the Site Systems folder under your site name, then Site Settings.

2. Right-click one of the distribution points you defined and choose Properties from the context menu to display the Site System Properties dialog box. Select the Distribution Point tab, shown in Figure 12-15.

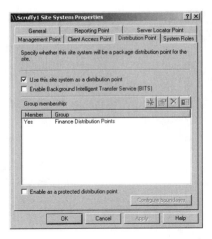

Figure 12-15. *The Distribution Point tab of the Site System Properties dialog box.*

3. To add a new distribution point group, in the Group Membership section click the New button (the yellow star) to display the Distribution Point Group Properties dialog box, shown in Figure 12-16. Enter the name of the group and indicate whether this site system is to be a member of the distribution point group. Then click OK to return to the Site System Properties dialog box.

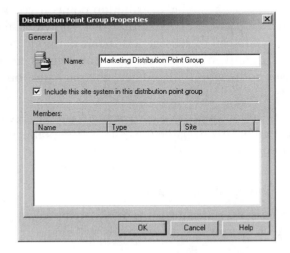

Figure 12-16. *The Distribution Point Group Properties dialog box.*

4. Select the next site system you want to include in the distribution point group, right-click it, choose Properties from the context menu, and

select the Distribution Point tab. Notice that any distribution point groups you have created will be listed in this tab for each site system, as shown in Figure 12-17.

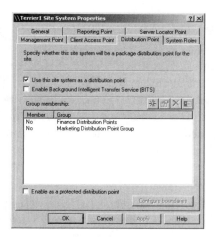

Figure 12-17. *The updated Group Membership list in the Distribution Point tab.*

5. Select the distribution point group that this site system should be a member of and click the Properties button (the hand holding a piece of paper) to display the Distribution Point Group Properties dialog box, shown in Figure 12-18.

Figure 12-18. *The updated Distribution Point Group Properties dialog box.*

Select the Include This Site System In This Distribution Point Group check box and then click OK to return to the Distribution Point tab. The site system now shows that it's a member of the distribution point group. Click OK again.

6. Repeat step 5 for every site system that needs to be a member of a distribution point group.

If you need to remove a site system from a distribution point group, simply repeat step 5 of this procedure, but clear the Include This Site System In This Distribution Point Group check box. If you need to remove a distribution point group altogether, select any site system, open its Site Systems Properties dialog box, and select the Distribution Point tab. Select the distribution point group in the Group Membership list and click the Delete button (the black "X").

Creating Programs

Finally, it's necessary to create at least one program for each package. This program specifies how the package is to be executed at the client. Many packages can have more than one program associated with them. For example, a package might have different installation methods such as Custom, Typical, Unattended, and Manual. This is where you really have to know your package. The command-line information you provide here will either make or break the package when it's run on the client.

To create a program, follow these steps:

1. Navigate to the Packages folder, find your package entry, and expand it.

2. Right-click Programs, choose New from the context menu, and then choose Program to display the Program Properties dialog box, shown in Figure 12-19.

3. In the General tab, enter a descriptive name for the program—for example, Custom Installation or Unattended Installation. Enter additional descriptive information in the Comment text box.

4. In the Command Line text box, enter the command that should be executed at the client. For example, this could be a Setup.exe file, a batch file, or an .MSI file; however, you must include any and all command-line arguments required for successful execution. For example, if you run the Setup program, which uses a script file called Custom.inf, and the Setup program invokes this script file through a "/c" command-line switch, you must enter the full command as it references the script: setup.exe /c:custom.inf.

5. In the Start In text box, enter the name and path of the directory in which you want the program to start. This field is optional, and by default the distribution folder on the distribution point is used.

6. From the Run drop-down list, select an option—Normal, Minimized, Maximized, or Hidden—to specify how the program will be displayed to the user. Hidden does mean that nothing will be displayed; this option is best used with fully unattended, or silent, installations.

7. From the After Running drop-down list, select an option—No Action Required, SMS Restarts Computer, Program Restarts Computer, or SMS Logs User Off—to specify what action, if any, will be performed after the program completes.

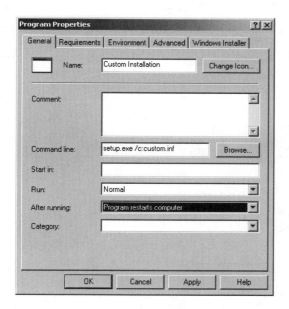

Figure 12-19. *The Program Properties dialog box.*

8. Select the Requirements tab, shown in Figure 12-20. This tab lets you specify descriptive elements regarding the program's estimated size and installation run time. More importantly, it allows you to identify which operating system platforms the program can run on. This enables you to filter out those clients on whose platform the program can't run.

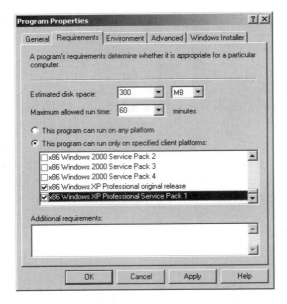

Figure 12-20. *The Requirements tab.*

9. Select the Environment tab, shown in Figure 12-21.

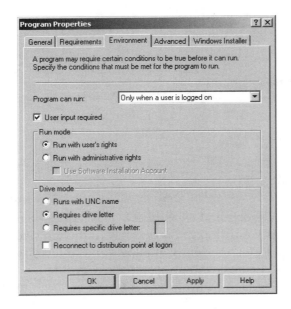

Figure 12-21. *The Environment tab.*

In this tab, user level and drive mode requirements are defined. First specify when the program can run. The drop-down list options are Only When A User Is Logged On (which can apply to all clients, but Windows 98 clients in particular); Whether Or Not A User Is Logged On; and Only When No User Is Logged On. These last two options are specific to computers running Windows NT 4.0 and later. If either of these options is selected, the User Input Required check box and the Run With User's Rights under Run Mode option are automatically disabled.

10. If the program requires the user to click even a single OK button, you must select Only When A User Is Logged On from the Program Can Run drop-down list and then select the User Input Required option. Clear this option only if the program is fully scripted (that is, automated). If the program must be run in the local administrative security context, select the Run With Administrative Rights option in the Run Mode frame. If you have specified a particular account to use on Windows computers when running programs that require administrative privileges, select the Use Software Installation Account check box. If you require that the logged-on user also be able to interact with the program while it's running with administrative rights, select the Allow Users To Interact With This Program check box.

Caution Selecting the Allow Users To Interact With This Program check box allows any connected user to interact with the program in an administrative security context. This could provide an opportunity for a security breach on that client. Choose this option only if absolutely necessary for the successful execution of the program.

11. In the Drive Mode frame, select the option that best fits the program. As you have no doubt experienced, although most programs understand UNC paths, some do not and require a drive letter mapping. If you need to have the client reconnect to the distribution point each time the user logs on, select the Reconnect To Distribution Point At Logon check box. This option could be useful if the application needs to write information back to the distribution folder on the distribution point, retrieve startup files, and so on.

12. Select the Advanced tab, shown in Figure 12-22, which provides several additional options. If you need to run another program before this one—for example, to install a service pack or a patch, select the Run Another Program First check box and then select the appropriate package and program. This assumes, of course, that you have already created the other package and program. In this example you won't need to advertise the other program separately.

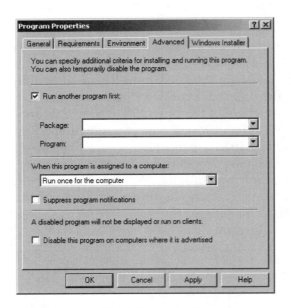

Figure 12-22. *The Advanced tab.*

13. If you've assigned a program to run on a computer, you can either execute it once for the computer or once for every user who logs on to the computer by choosing one of two run time options in the When This Program Is Assigned To A Computer section. Select Run Once For The Computer, the default, to execute the program once for use by all users on the computer. Select Run Once For Every User Who Logs On to execute the program once for each user when the user logs on. Use the Suppress Program Notifications check box to turn off notification and countdown icons and messages for this program.

14. To temporarily disable the program from being run—even if it has been assigned a specific time—select the Disable This Program On Clients Where It Is Advertised check box. This option can be handy if you need to update files, test an installation, and so on.

15. Select the Windows Installer tab shown in Figure 12-23 to specify Windows Installer product information to enable SMS to manage the location of source files for Windows Installer-based programs. This feature is available only for Advanced Clients and is valuable for determining the location of source files when Windows Installer needs to initiate a repair. Click Import to locate and select the Windows Installer package associated with the program and populate the Windows Installer Product Code and Windows Installer File fields.

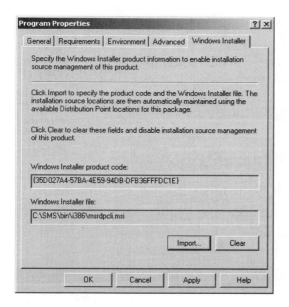

Figure 12-23.   *The Windows Installer tab.*

16. Click OK to save the program.

If you decide to delete a program later, right-click the program in the SMS Administrator Console and choose Delete from the context menu to activate the Delete Program Wizard. This wizard walks you through the process and helps you decide whether to delete the program. Deleting a program does produce a ripple effect for other SMS components. Any advertisements of the program will also be deleted and will no longer be made available to the client. The wizard displays all the affected advertisements and prompts you once more to confirm the deletion.

In Chapter 11 we examined the advantages of using collections whose membership rules are query-based when advertising programs. When a new member joins the collection, it automatically receives any advertisements made to that collection. In general, you should leave programs advertised until they're no longer needed or until they should be retired.

Creating a Package from a Definition File

We've seen what's involved in creating a package from the ground up. Now let's see how much simpler the process becomes when you're creating a package from a package definition file.

To create a package from a predefined definition file, follow these steps:

1. Navigate to the Packages folder, right-click it, choose New from the context menu, and then choose Package From Definition. This will initiate the Create Package From Definition Wizard, shown in Figure 12-24.

Figure 12-24. *The Create Package From Definition Wizard welcome page.*

2. Click Next to display the Package Definition page, shown in Figure 12-25. Select one of the definitions provided by SMS 2003 from the Package Definition list and then click Browse to search for an SMS 2003 compatible .SMS or .PDF file or for a Windows Installer (.MSI) package file.

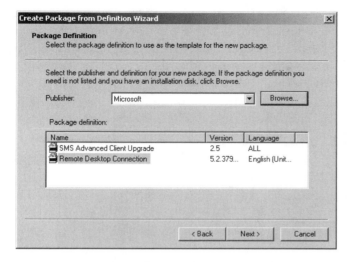

Figure 12-25.   *The Package Definition page.*

3. Click Next to display the Source Files page, shown in Figure 12-26. Here you specify how SMS should manage source files.

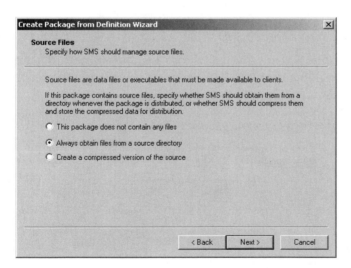

Figure 12-26.   *The Source Files page.*

4. If you select This Package Does Not Contain Any Files and click Next, you'll proceed directly to step 5. If you select one of the other options and click Next, the Source Directory page appears, as shown in Figure 12-27. In this page, identify either the network or local drive location of the source files and click Next.

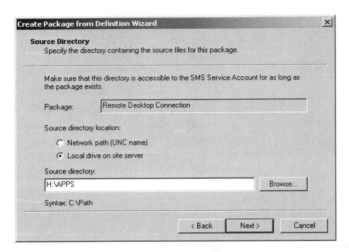

Figure 12-27. *The Source Directory page.*

5. The Completing The Create Package From Definition Wizard page appears, as shown in Figure 12-28. Review your choices and then click Finish.

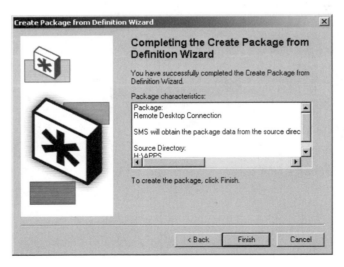

Figure 12-28. *The Completing The Create Package From Definition Wizard page.*

Right-clicking the package you just created in the SMS Administrator Console will display the Package Properties dialog box. The result will be the creation of a package with the essential package details filled in and the appropriate programs created with their essential details filled in in the General, Data Source, and Reporting tabs of the Package Properties dialog box. The Data Access and Distribution Settings tabs are left with the default values. Figures 12-29 through 12-35 will give you an idea of the type of information generated by the package definition file used in the example. Of course, although SMS 2003 or any other application developer provides the package definition file itself, you'll still need to obtain a copy of the source files for the application.

The General tab of the Package Properties dialog box, shown in Figure 12-29, contains the package detail information.

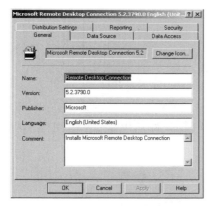

Figure 12-29.   *The General tab of the Package Properties dialog box.*

The settings in the Data Source tab, shown in Figure 12-30, are based on the parameters you defined using the Create Package From Definition Wizard.

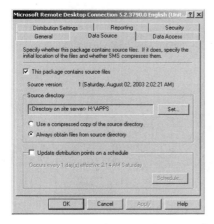

Figure 12-30.   *The Data Source tab of the Package Properties dialog box.*

Package definition files don't always provide status MIF information for the Reporting tab. However, the package definition file we used here does fill in this information, including the MIF filename, as shown in Figure 12-31.

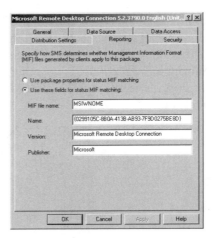

Figure 12-31. *The Reporting tab of the Package Properties dialog box.*

The package definition file is designed to generate all appropriate programs for the application package. The package definition file used in this example created six programs, as shown in Figure 12-32.

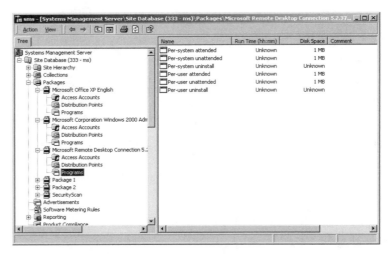

Figure 12-32. *The SMS Administrator Console showing programs generated by the package definition file.*

Right-clicking the Per-System Unattended entry displays the General tab of the Per-System Unattended Program Properties dialog box, shown in Figure 12-33, which provides the appropriate command-line executable and switches.

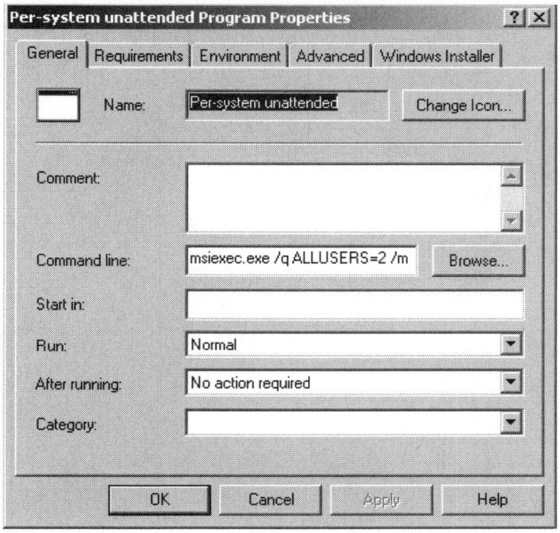

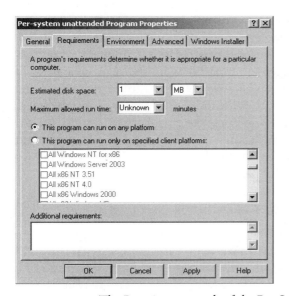

Figure 12-33. *The General tab of the Per-System Unattended Program Properties dialog box.*

The Requirements tab, shown in Figure 12-34, displays the estimated disk space value and platform specification as provided by the package definition file.

Figure 12-34. *The Requirements tab of the Per-System Unattended Program Properties dialog box.*

Because this program requires administrative level access at the client, the program definition file specifies that option in the Environment tab, as shown in Figure 12-35.

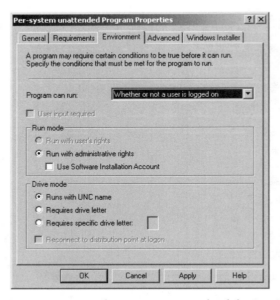

Figure 12-35. *The Environment tab of the Per-System Unattended Program Properties dialog box.*

In general, the package definition file will provide package details for the General and Data Source tabs of the Package Properties dialog box, which should make sense. Distribution settings, for example, define how a package is sent from one site to another, and only the SMS administrator for each site can modify those settings. On the other hand, the package definition file will usually provide most of the property settings in the Per-System Unattended Program Properties dialog box. The exceptions are the options in the Advanced and Windows Installer tabs. The package definition file typically doesn't provide any property settings for the Advanced and Windows Installer tabs. Again, it's up to you to decide whether to run another program first, temporarily disable the advertisement, or whether it's necessary to provide Windows Installer path and file information.

Package Distribution Process Flow

The process behind the creation and distribution of a package, illustrated in Figure 12-36, is fairly straightforward. We begin, as always, with the SMS administrator defining the package, distribution points, and programs. The SMS Provider writes this information to the SMS database. This action triggers

SQL Monitor to write a package notification wake-up file to Distribution Manager's inbox (\SMS\Inboxes\Distmgr.box). The wake-up file takes the form of a site code and package ID as the filename with a .PKN extension. For example, a package notification file for site A01 might be named A0100003.pkn.

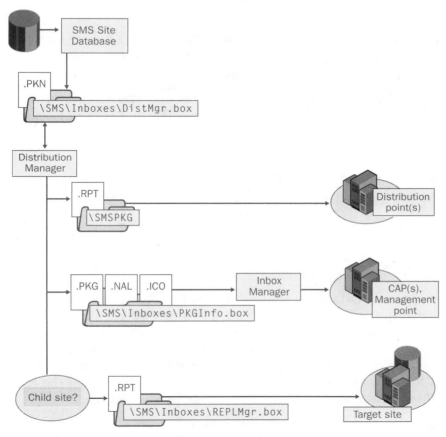

Figure 12-36.   *The package distribution process flow.*

The Distribution Manager component wakes up and processes the package based on the package details you provided. Distribution Manager performs the following general tasks:

- Compresses the source files, if necessary
- Copies the package source directory to the specified distribution points
- Creates various instruction files for clients that are copied to the CAPs and management points by Inbox Manager
- Creates replication files for sending the package to child sites

If you specified that a compressed version of the files should be used, Distribution Manager will compress the files and store them either in the location specified when the Software Distribution component was configured (this process is discussed in the next section) or by default in the SMSPKG folder created on the drive on which SMS was installed on the site server, with the same filename and the extension .PKG.

Distribution Manager then copies the source file directory to the SMSPKGx$ folder created on each specified distribution point within the site. If the package files were compressed, Distribution Manager uncompresses them first.

Distribution Manager generates three files and writes them to the \SMS\Inboxes\Pkginfo.box folder on the site server. These files (with filenames as described earlier) are the following:

- **.PKG** Package program detail information
- **.NAL** Location of distribution points
- **.ICO** Icon file information

The Inbox Manager component, as it's wont to do, copies these files to the Pkginfo.box folder on each CAP. These files serve as instruction files for the client after it receives an advertisement. At this point, the process stops unless the package needs to be sent to a child site.

If the package does need to be sent to a child site, Distribution Manager writes a package replication file (.RPT) to Replication Manager's inbox (\SMS\Inboxes\ Replmgr.box\Outbound). If a compressed copy of the package source directory doesn't already exist, Distribution Manager also compresses the source directory into a temporary directory on the site server and then moves the file to the SMSPKG folder (on the SMS installation drive on the site server or the drive you specified when configuring the Software Distribution component).

Now Replication Manager takes over and begins the sending process. This process is discussed in detail in Chapter 4, so we'll look at only the highlights here. Replication Manager creates a minijob for the Scheduler and places it in the Scheduler's inbox (\SMS\Inboxes\Schedule.box). The Scheduler creates the package and instruction files needed for sending the data in question, as well as a send request file for the sender. The package and instruction files are placed in the \SMS\Inboxes\Schedule.box\Tosend directory. The send request file is written to the preferred sender's outbox (\SMS\Inboxes\Schedule.box\Outboxes*sender*, where *sender* is the sender folder, such as LAN, RASAsynch, or RASISDN). Recall that both the sending priority and the preferred sender are identified in the Package Properties dialog box.

When the send request file is written, the sender reads the file. It also examines whether the address properties have placed any restrictions on when requests of this priority can be sent and whether there are any bandwidth limits. It then changes the extension of the send request file to .SRS and writes status information to it.

The sender connects to the target site's SMS_SITE share—the \SMS\Inboxes\ Despoolr.box\Receive directory—where the Despooler component on the target site will complete processing of the information at the target site. When the data has been completely transferred, the send request file is updated to a status of "completed" and the file is then deleted. Distribution Manager on the target site will carry out any necessary tasks. For example, if you identified distribution points at the target site, the Despooler will decompress the package and pass it to Distribution Manager, which will process the package for those distribution points.

Configuring the Software Distribution Component

You can configure additional settings for the package distribution process if the SMS defaults aren't appropriate within your environment.

To access these settings, in the SMS Administrator Console, navigate to the Component Configuration folder under the site name, the Site Settings, expand it, right-click Software Distribution, and select Properties to display the Software Distribution Properties dialog box, shown in Figure 12-37.

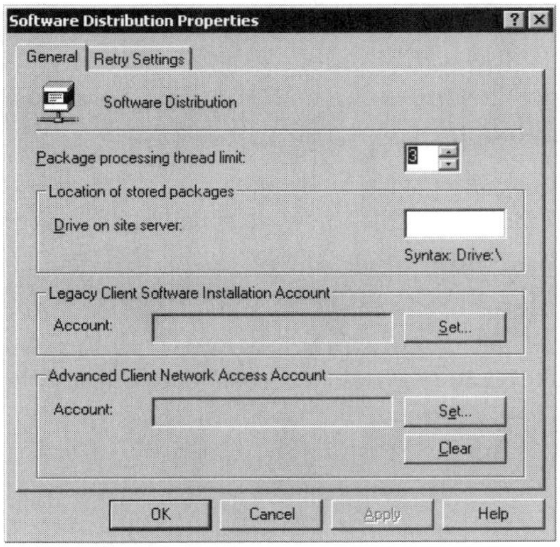

Figure 12-37.   *The General tab of the Software Distribution Properties dialog box.*

The Package Processing Thread Limit option in the General tab lets you identify how many threads to allocate to Distribution Manager to process packages for the site. The default value is 3, but it can range from 1 through 7. In this case, more is not always better. If your site server were only processing packages—and not performing any other functions—you might bump up this number, monitor the site server's performance, and determine what value achieves an optimum level of performance between package processing and other server functions. A higher number of allocated threads might be appropriate and assignable.

However, if the site server has all SMS functions enabled—package distribution, Remote Tools, inventory collection, all site system roles, and so on—increasing the number of threads might prove to be detrimental to the site server's overall performance. The best rule of thumb would be to try adjusting the number if you think you need to improve package processing performance and then use the various tools available to monitor the site server's performance and its other functions to find the best balance.

Three other options you can configure in the General tab are Location Of Stored Packages, which identifies for SMS the drive on which it should create the compressed package folder (SMSPKG), the Legacy Client Software Installation account, and the Advanced Client Network Access account. When programs are executed at the client computer, they will run under the local user account's security context unless otherwise noted in the program properties. Since most users are logged on as users and not as administrators, this means that these programs will run under the local user context. As you have probably discovered, most application software installs .DLL files, modifies registry entries, stops and starts services, and performs other tasks that require an administrative security context on the client. For Windows 98 clients, this security context is not usually a big issue. However, it's a big issue for SMS clients running Windows NT 4.0 or later since they maintain a local account database and provide more security over system modifications.

Security poses a problem when you're dealing with SMS packages. One of our main objectives here is to be able to remotely install software on clients without the user's—or the administrator's—intervention.

SMS 2003, however, does provide solutions to the security issue for both the Legacy Client and the Advanced Client. The first involves the use of an internal account that SMS creates on the Legacy Client when a higher level of security access is required to run a program. This account, named SMSCliToknAcct&, is created automatically and is granted Act As Part Of The Operating System,

Log On As A Service, and Replace Process Level Token user rights on the client. The SMSCliToknAcct& account will be sufficient in most cases. However, if the program execution requires that the program connect to network resources other than the distribution point, SMSCliToknAcct& will fail because it's created as a local account rather than a domain account. In this case you should identify and use the Legacy Client Software Installation account.

You create the Legacy Client Software Installation account in the Windows domain (or domains) your clients are members of. The easiest thing to do, of course, would be to make the account a member of the Domain Admins global group in the domain that the Windows client is a member of. As you know, when a computer running Windows joins a Windows domain, the Domain Admins global group is made a member of the local Administrators group on that computer. Making the account a member of the Domain Admins group would give it the appropriate level of local rights on the Windows client (provided you haven't altered the local Administrator group memberships to exclude the Domain Admins group), but this arrangement isn't secure. Ideally, this account should be made a direct member of the local Administrator's group on each client computer or be given the appropriate level of security access required to run the programs you create.

After you create and configure the account appropriately, identify it to SMS in the General tab of the Software Distribution Properties dialog box by clicking Set next to the Legacy Client Software Installation Account text box and entering the name of the account in the Windows Account dialog box.

Ideally, for Windows 2000 clients and later, you should install the SMS Advanced Client, as this is a more secure SMS client. One of the ways in which this security is manifested is in its use of computer accounts to carry out tasks like installing software on the client. When the client connects to a distribution point, it uses the security context of the local user to do so. You can specify an optional Advanced Client Network Access account to make this connection more secure. Create this account in the domain as you would the Legacy Client Connection account.

After you create and configure the account appropriately in the domain, identify it to SMS in the General tab of the Software Distribution Properties dialog box by clicking Set next to the Advanced Client Network Access Account text box and entering the name of the account in the Windows Account dialog box.

The Retry Settings tab of the Software Distribution Properties dialog box is fairly self-explanatory, as shown in Figure 12-38. It lets you alter the retry settings for Distribution Manager's attempts to deliver packages and for Advertisement Manager's attempts to advertise programs and specify the delay between attempts.

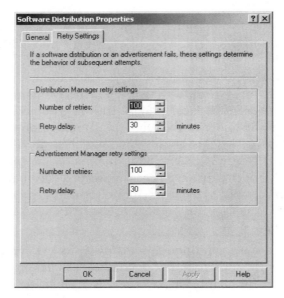

Figure 12-38. *The Retry Settings tab.*

Using the Distribute Software To Collection Wizard

In addition to the methods described earlier in this chapter for creating and distributing a package and an advertisement, SMS 2003 includes an alternative tool called the Distribute Software To Collection Wizard. This wizard walks you through each step in the process of creating or identifying a package and program, defining a distribution point, creating or identifying a collection to a target, and creating an advertisement.

Note The procedure described below varies slightly depending on where you start the wizard.

To run the Distribute Software To Collection Wizard, follow these steps:

1. Right-click any collection, resource, package, program, or advertisement in the SMS Administrator Console, choose All Tasks from the

context menu, and then choose Distribute Software to launch the Distribute Software To Collection Wizard, shown in Figure 12-39.

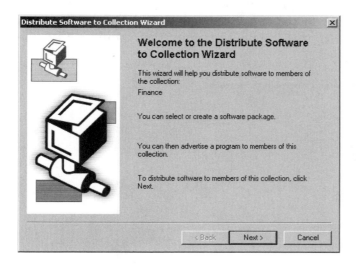

Figure 12-39. *The Distribute Software To Collection Wizard welcome page.*

2. Click Next to display the Package page, shown in Figure 12-40. Here you can create a new package and program from scratch or from a definition file or you can select an existing package.

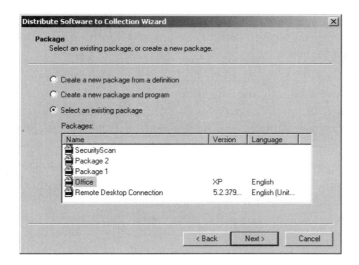

Figure 12-40. *The Package page.*

3. Click Next. The next few pages will vary depending on whether you're creating a new program from scratch or from a package definition or by selecting an existing program. If you selected an existing package, the Select A Program To Advertise page is displayed, as shown in Figure 12-41. Select the distribution point that should receive the package source files.

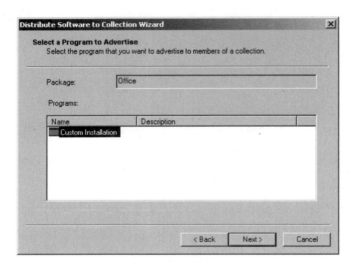

Figure 12-41. *The Select A Program To Advertise page.*

If you selected Create A New Package From A Definition, you're presented with pages asking you to select the package definition file and define the source file directory.

If you selected Create A New Package And Program, the wizard will prompt you for a package name and identification, the location of source files (if there are any), the program name and command line, as well as ask whether user input is required or administrative rights are needed.

4. Click Next. The next few pages prompt for advertisement properties. On the Advertisement Name page, shown in Figure 12-42, enter a descriptive name and comment for the advertisement.

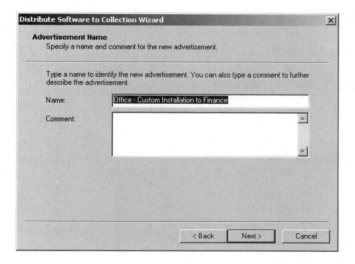

Figure 12-42.   *The Advertisement Name page.*

5. Click Next to display the Advertise To Subcollections page, shown in Figure 12-43. Here you can specify whether to advertise to the collection's subcollections if any exist.

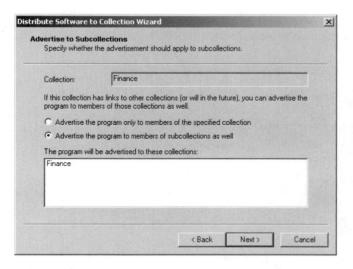

Figure 12-43.   *The Advertise To Subcollections page.*

6. Click Next to display the Advertisement Schedule page, shown in Figure 12-44. This page lets you specify when the advertisement should be offered and whether it expires.

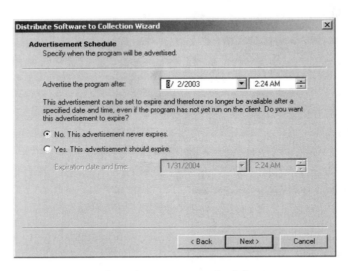

Figure 12-44. *The Advertisement Schedule page.*

7. Click Next to display the Assign Program page, shown in Figure 12-45. Here you can specify an assigned time if necessary.

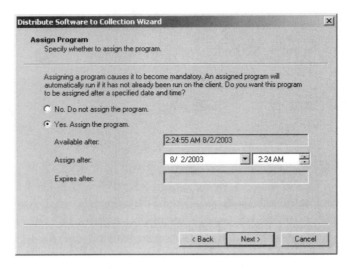

Figure 12-45. *The Assign Program page.*

8. Click Next to display the Completing The Distribute Software To Collection Wizard page, shown in Figure 12-46. Review your selections and then click Finish to begin the package distribution and advertisement processes.

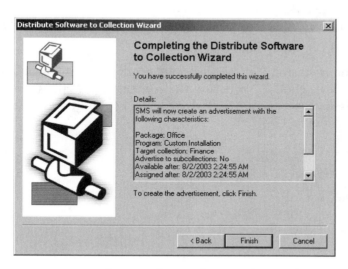

Figure 12-46. *The Completing The Distribute Software To Collection Wizard page.*

As you've probably noticed, the Distribute Software To Collection Wizard doesn't present you with all possible options available for packages, programs, and advertisements. For example, you can't create a recurring advertisement using this wizard. However, the wizard does provide a fine method for generating general packages, programs, collections, and advertisements. There's also a neat technique for targeting one computer without having to create a collection of one: use the wizard to create the collection for you. Simply start the wizard by right-clicking the computer resource you want to target.

> **Note** In case you were wondering, you can't use Ctrl+click to select more than one client at a time in a collection. There is currently no way to target a group of two or three computers that are part of a larger membership without creating a separate collection for them. Perhaps we'll see this functionality in a future release of SMS.

Creating an Advertisement

After you have created your packages and programs, the next step is to create an advertisement. Remember, before you configure an advertisement, you must have identified and created the collections that you'll advertise the programs to. Programs are always advertised to collections—even if it's a collection of one.

To create an advertisement, follow these steps:

1. In the SMS Administrator Console, navigate to the Advertisements folder, right-click it, choose New from the context menu, and then choose Advertisement to display the Advertisement Properties dialog box, as shown in Figure 12-47.

Figure 12-47. *The Advertisement Properties dialog box*

2. In the General tab, begin by entering a descriptive name for the advertisement. Enter a descriptive comment to add more detail. Select the package and program to advertise from their respective list boxes. Enter the collection name, or browse for it by clicking Browse. If the collection has subcollections and you want to include them in the advertisement, select the Include Members Of Subcollections check box.

3. Select the Schedule tab, shown in Figure 12-48. Begin by selecting the start time and date for the advertisement. This setting represents the

time at which the program is advertised and made available for the client to run. By default, the advertisement will be made available in all time zones at the same time, meaning that if the advertisement start time is 3:00 in New York, it's made available in New York at 3:00, in Chicago at 2:00, in London at 8:00, and so on. If you want the advertisement to be made available at a specific hour in each time zone—for example, at 3:00 in New York, Chicago, and London, select the Greenwich Mean Time check box.

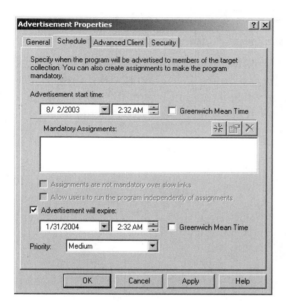

Figure 12-48. *The Schedule tab.*

4. If the advertisement will be available for only a specific period of time, select the Advertisement Will Expire check box, select an expiration date, and select Greenwich Mean Time if desired. The priority you specify is a sending priority only and is used when the advertisement is sent to a child site.

5. You can also assign a run time to the advertisement. To configure this option, click New (the yellow star button) in the Mandatory Assignments section of the Schedule tab to display the Assignment Schedule dialog box, shown in Figure 12-49. Here you can assign a mandatory time and date for the advertised program to run. If the program is not run by this time and date, the Advertised Programs Client Agent on the client will execute it.

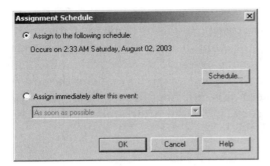

Figure 12-49. *The Assignment Schedule dialog box.*

6. If you select Assign To The Following Schedule and click Schedule, the Schedule dialog box appears, as shown in Figure 12-50. In this dialog box, you can specify exactly when you want to run the advertised program. You can also set a recurrence interval for advertisements such as monthly virus file updates.

Figure 12-50. *The Schedule dialog box.*

7. If you select the Assign Immediately After This Event option in the Assignment Schedule dialog box, you can choose to have the advertised program execute as soon as possible—meaning as soon as the program reaches the client and all program requirements (correct platform, user logged on, administrator access, and so on) are met; at logoff—the next time a user logs off the client; or at logon—the next time a user logs on to the client.

8. Click OK to return to the Schedule tab. If you configure a mandatory assignment, two additional options become available. Select the Assignments Are Not Mandatory Over Slow Links check box to prevent a potentially large program from running if the Advertised Programs Client Agent discovers that the network is overutilized. Select the Allow Users To Run The Program Independently Of Assignments check box if you want to give the user the option of canceling a mandatory advertisement when it's scheduled to run or to reschedule when the advertisement runs.

9. Select the Advanced Client tab, shown in Figure 12-51. These options are available for use by Advanced Clients only and determine how a program should run when a distribution point is or is not available in the site the Advanced Client is roaming to.

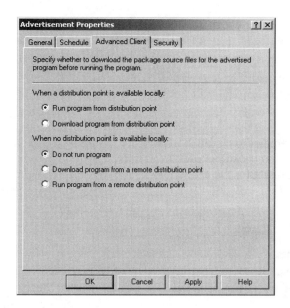

Figure 12-51. *The Advanced Client tab.*

In the When A Distribution Point Is Available Locally section the default option is Run Program from Distribution Point. This means that the program is executed from the distribution point. However, if the computer loses its connection to the distribution point while the program is running, the program will fail. Choose the Download

Program From Distribution Point option to ensure that the entire package is downloaded to the client before the program is executed. If the distribution point supports Background Intelligent Transfer Service (BITS) and the computer becomes disconnected from the distribution point before the files have been downloaded, the download will pick up where it left off when the computer reestablishes a connection.

In the When No Distribution Point Is Available Locally section, the default option is Do Not Run Program. By default, packages aren't run if the distribution point is not local. Since Advanced Clients can roam to the boundaries of other SMS sites in the hierarchy, there might not be a local distribution point available that has the package. If the package is located on a distribution in the Advanced Client's assigned site, the distribution point is considered remote. Choose the Download Program From A Remote Distribution Point option if this package needs to be run on the client and the package is large or the network link to the remote site is slow. Choose the Run Program From A Remote Distribution Point option if the package needs to be run on the client and the package is small or the network connection to the remote site is fast and reliable.

10. Click OK to create the advertisement.

Note If you haven't yet identified a distribution point for the package, you'll be notified of that fact when you click OK. Also, if you haven't yet enabled the Advertised Programs Client Agent for the clients, you'll be given the option to do so.

Real World   Recurring Assignments

As we've seen, you can specify a recurring schedule for your advertisement. This setting can be useful for programs that need to be executed on a regular basis. Let's return to our virus update file example. Suppose you've created a package that distributes a virus update file once a month. On the 14th of every month, you obtain a virus update file and replace the old file in the package source file directory with the new file. You also configure the package to refresh its distribution points once a month, say on the 15th.

When you create the advertisement, give it an assigned schedule. Set it to run on the 16th, maybe at 11:00 P.M. Now all you have to do is remember to update the source file directory once a month. The package and advertisement process will take care of the rest.

You might also consider creating a package that executes the virus-scanning program on the client. Again, you could assign a recurring advertisement to run the virus scan at regular intervals. Here's another twist on this scenario: let's say that you want the virus scan to run immediately after the virus update file is installed. You've seen that when you create a program, you have an advanced option to run another program first. You would then create a program that executes the virus scan but first copies the update file. Then create a recurring advertisement that runs that program once a month at the appropriate time.

You can use recurring advertisements to handle a variety of these kinds of events. Use them to periodically synchronize the system time on your SMS clients with the site server. Use them to perform disk maintenance tasks such as monthly defragmentation or optimization routines. With a little creativity and imagination, you can automate many such tasks and make your job as a system administrator more productive.

Configuring the Client

Of course, life would not be complete if we didn't have a client component to configure, and we do. In order for the client to receive any advertisements we're targeting to it, we must configure the Advertised Programs Client Agent and have it installed on each client. As with other client agents, you can find this agent in the Client Agents folder under Site Settings in the SMS Administrator Console.

Recall that the Advertised Programs Client Agent component files will need to be installed on Legacy Clients. After you enable and configure the agent, the component will be installed on the Legacy Client at the client's next update cycle (every 25 hours by default or at the next computer startup). However, on Advanced Clients, all client agents are installed with the Advanced Client software. So the agent components already exist on the client. After you enable and configure the agent, the Software Distribution Agent will be enabled on the Advanced Client at the client's next policy refresh (once every hour or at the next computer startup).

To configure the Advertised Programs Client Agent, follow these steps:

1. Navigate to the Client Agents folder, select Advertised Programs Client Agent, right-click it, and choose Properties from the context menu

to display the Advertised Programs Client Agent Properties dialog box, shown in Figure 12-52.

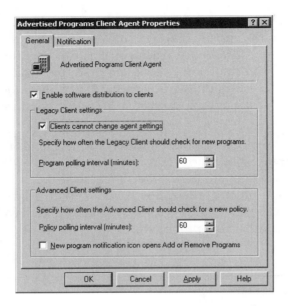

Figure 12-52. *The Advertised Programs Client Agent Properties dialog box.*

2. In the General tab, select the Enable Software Distribution To Clients check box. Note that by default the client agent will check the CAP or management point for new advertisements every 60 minutes. You can substitute a value from 5 to 1440 minutes (24 hours).

Caution Enter a value appropriate to the frequency at which you advertise programs and the urgency of those advertisements. In general, the default 60 minutes or longer should be appropriate.

3. Enable the option Clients Cannot Change Agent Settings to ensure that the settings you configure for the client agent stay that way. Select this option if desired.

Advertised programs are listed on SMS clients in Add Or Remove Programs in Control Panel as well as in the Advertised Programs Wizard on Legacy Clients and Run Advertised Programs on Advanced Clients. When a new advertisement is available, the new program notification icon is displayed on the task bar.

Select the Advanced Client Setting option New Program Notification Icon Opens Add Or Remove Programs to have the notification icon open Add Or Remove Programs to display new advertisements. If you leave this option cleared, the notification icon will open Run Advertised Programs.

4. Select the Notification tab, shown in Figure 12-53. This tab provides several options for defining how the client is notified of an advertisement.

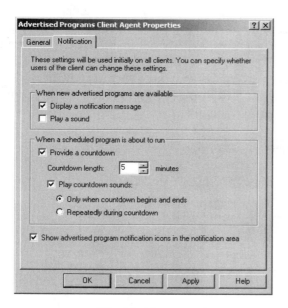

Figure 12-53.   *The Notification tab.*

5. The options in the Notification tab are fairly self-explanatory. Select the options that fit your needs and then click OK to save the configuration and begin the site update process.

   If you don't select any options in this tab, the client agent will check for an advertisement but will never notify the user that an advertisement has been received. The user would have to periodically run the Advertised Programs Wizard (Legacy Clients) or Run Advertised Programs (Advanced Clients) from Control Panel to find and run advertisements. If the advertised program had a mandatory assignment, it would simply run, again without notification to the user. In general, it's not a good idea to not notify the user when an advertisement has been received. Notifying the user can prevent unfortunate occurrences such as the user logging off or shutting down before the program finishes running.

When the client agent is installed or enabled at the client, two new icons will be added to the Control Panel on each client—Advertised Programs Wizard and Advertised Programs Monitor on Legacy Clients; Run Advertised Programs and Program Download Monitor on Advanced Clients.

Running Advertised Programs on Clients

Once an hour, by default, the client agent checks the CAP or management point for new advertisements targeting that client. Advertised programs always appear in both Add Or Remove Programs, as shown in Figure 12-54 (except for clients running Windows 98 or Windows NT 4.0) and in Advertised Programs Wizard (Legacy Clients) or Run Advertised Programs (Advanced Client). After a program has been successfully installed through Add Or Remove Programs, it won't reinstall if the user tries to run it again.

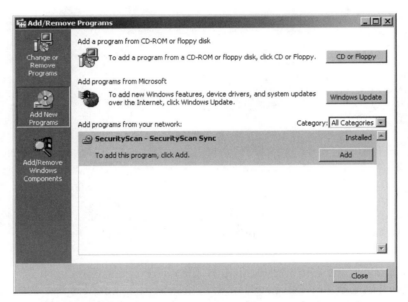

Figure 12-54.   *Add/Remove Programs displaying an advertised program.*

Let's take a look at the other Control Panel programs installed on the Legacy Client and Advanced Client.

Advertised Programs Wizard (Legacy Client)

The Advertised Programs Wizard is installed on Legacy Clients and is used to display available advertisements, select advertisements to run, and execute advertisements. When accessed through the Control Panel, this wizard causes the Advertised Programs Client Agent to check the CAP for new advertisements. When an advertised program is available on the client, the New Advertised Programs icon appears on the taskbar (if you enabled this type of notification). You can also access the wizard through the New Advertised Programs icon.

To run the Advertised Programs Wizard, follow these steps:

1. Click the Advertised Programs Wizard icon in the Control Panel, or double-click the New Advertised Programs Are Available icon on the taskbar (if that option was enabled), or right-click the New Advertised Programs Are Available icon and choose Run Advertised Programs Wizard from the context menu. The Advertised Programs Wizard welcome page is displayed, as shown in Figure 12-55.

Figure 12-55. *The Advertised Programs Wizard welcome page.*

2. Click Next to display the Select Programs To Run page, shown in Figure 12-56. All available advertised programs are listed on this page. Select the program you want to run.

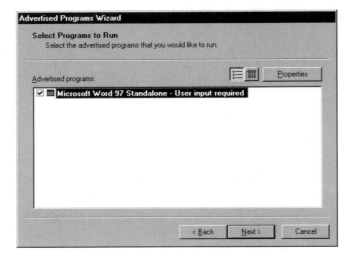

Figure 12-56.   *The Select Programs To Run page.*

3. You can view the properties of each program by clicking Properties to display the Program Properties dialog box, shown in Figure 12-57. This window provides information such as whether the program is scheduled to run, whether it has an expiration date, whether user input is required, and the running time of the program. Click Close to return to the Select Programs To Run page.

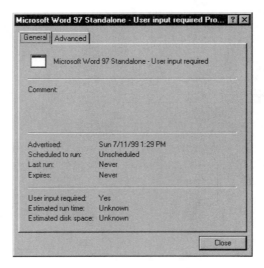

Figure 12-57.   *The Program Properties dialog box.*

4. The two buttons to the left of the Properties button switch between a simple list of programs and a list that displays the following properties in columnar fashion:

   - When the program is scheduled to run
   - When the program was last run
   - When the program was advertised

   The alternative Select Programs To Run page is shown in Figure 12-58.

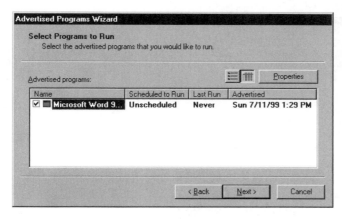

Figure 12-58.   *The alternative Select Programs To Run page.*

5. Click Next to display the Run Programs Now Or Later page, shown in Figure 12-59. You can either let the program run now (the default) or select the Schedule This Program To Run On option and then specify a date and time for the program to run.

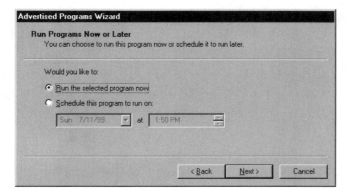

Figure 12-59.   *The Run Programs Now Or Later page.*

6. Click Next to display the Completing The Advertised Programs Wizard page, shown in Figure 12-60. Review your selection and then click Finish.

Figure 12-60. *The Completing The Advertised Programs Wizard page.*

Advertised Programs Monitor (Legacy Client)

The Advertised Programs Monitor is installed on the Legacy Client and provides audit information about programs that have run on the client. When you launch the Advertised Programs Monitor from the Control Panel (or from the taskbar), it displays advertised programs that have run, are running, or are scheduled to run, as shown in Figure 12-61.

Through the Advertised Programs Monitor, you can view the program's properties and reschedule the program if you have permission to do so. You can also modify monitor settings such as the polling cycle for the agent to check the CAP for new advertisements—again, if you have permission to do so.

After a program is run, depending on whether you enabled SMS reporting either through the package details or through a script, the Advertised Programs Client Agent will write its success or failure status back to the CAP.

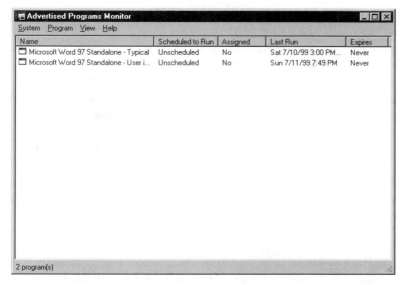

Figure 12-61. *The Advertised Programs Monitor.*

If a program is assigned to run as mandatory and notification to the client hasn't been disabled, the user sees a dialog box similar to the one shown in Figure 12-62. As you can see, depending on the countdown that was configured for the client agent, the user can opt to run the package immediately or click OK and let the package execute when the countdown completes. The user can also view a list of all scheduled programs and the details for this program.

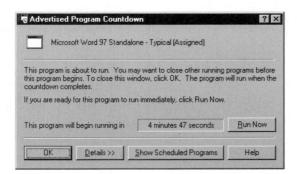

Figure 12-62. *The Advertised Program Countdown dialog box.*

Run Advertised Programs (Advanced Client)

The Run Advertised Programs is installed on Advanced Clients and, like the Advertised Programs Wizard on Legacy Clients, is used to display available advertisements, select advertisements to run, and view the properties of advertisements. Unlike its Legacy Client counterparts, you can't change the configuration of the client agent. When accessed through the Control Panel, Run Advertised Programs causes the Software Distribution Client Agent to check the management point for new advertisements. When an advertised program is available for the client, the New Advertised Programs Are Available icon appears on the taskbar (if you enabled this type of notification). You can also start Run Advertised Programs through the New Advertised Programs Are Available icon (unless you configured this option to always launch Add Or Remove Programs through the agent properties as discussed earlier.)

To start Run Advertised Programs, follow these steps:

1. Click the Run Advertised Programs icon in the Control Panel, or double-click the New Advertised Programs Are Available icon on the taskbar (if that option was enabled), or right-click the New Advertised Programs Are Available icon and choose Run Advertised Programs Wizard from the context menu. The Run Advertised Programs dialog box is displayed, as shown in Figure 12-63.

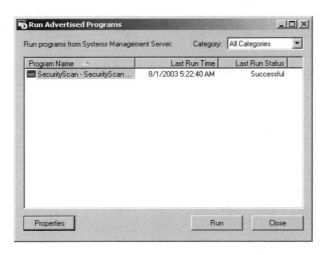

Figure 12-63. *The Run Advertised Programs dialog box.*

2. Select a program from the Program Name list and click Properties to display that program's properties. Properties include any special categories

the administrator assigned the program to, general comments in the General tab, and Advanced tab options, as shown in Figure 12-64.

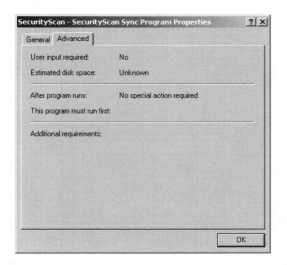

Figure 12-64.   *The Program Properties dialog box.*

3.   Select a program from the Program Name list and click Run to execute the program. If the program requires the package to be downloaded first, the Program Download Required message box is displayed, as shown in Figure 12-65. Here you can view the package's properties and choose to have the program run automatically when the download finishes. Click Download to begin the download or click Cancel to stop.

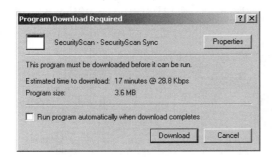

Figure 12-65.   *The Program Download Required message box.*

4. If you click Download in step 3, the Program Download Status dialog box appears, similar to that shown in Figure 12-66. Again, you can view the program's properties, choose to have the program run automatically when the download finishes, cancel the download, or hide the dialog box.

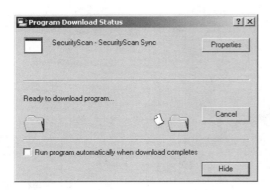

Figure 12-66. *The Program Download Status dialog box.*

Program Download Monitor (Advanced Client)

The Program Download Monitor is installed on Advanced Clients and provides audit information about programs that have run on the client. When you launch the Program Download Monitor from the Control Panel (or from the taskbar), it displays advertised programs that need to be downloaded or are downloading, as shown in Figure 12-67. You can use Program Download Monitor to show status of a download (as seen in Figure 12-66), to cancel downloads, and to specify that a program start automatically after the download completes by highlighting the program in the Program list and selecting the appropriate option from the Download menu.

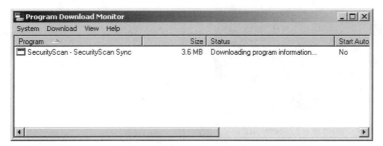

Figure 12-67. *The Program Download Monitor.*

Managing the Advanced Client Download Cache

When you configure the advertisement properties, you can specify whether the package should be downloaded to the Advanced Client before it's run (as shown previously in Figure 12-51). If so, it's stored in the Advanced Client download cache. It can happen that the cache becomes too full to accommodate the download of any additional packages. When a package is downloaded and placed into cache, the client agent locks it. The package is unlocked after 24 hours have passed since the program was run or 30 days have passed and the program hasn't run. After the package is unlocked, it can't be locked again unless it's removed from cache and downloaded again.

When a package needs to be downloaded and the cache is too full, SMS checks the other cached packages to see whether it can delete any or all of the oldest packages to free up enough space to accommodate the new package. If it can, it does so and downloads the package. If it can't, as might be the case if a package is locked, the package isn't downloaded.

Users with administrative credentials on the client can manage this download cache. They can change the size of the cache and its location, as well as delete the contents of the cache. You can manage the Advanced Client download cache by following these steps:

1. Open the Systems Management icon in Control Panel and select the Advanced tab, shown in Figure 12-68. You manage the Advanced Client download cache settings in the Temporary Program Download Folder frame.

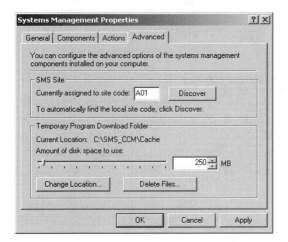

Figure 12-68. *The System Management icon Advanced tab.*

2. Enter the Amount of Disk Space To Use value or use the slide bar to set the amount.

3. Click Change Location to modify the disk location for the download cache folder.

4. Click Delete Files to delete the entire contents of the download cache.

Real World   Synchronizing System Time on Clients

When you schedule an advertised program to run at a predefined time, the Advertised Programs Client Agent on the Legacy Client and the SMS Software Distribution Agent on the Advanced Client will check the assigned time against the system time *as reported on the client*. This can cause significant problems for you if the client's system clock is off. For example, if the client's system clock is set for a different time zone, the package might not run when you expect it to.

Another scenario involves trial software. Suppose a user obtains a trial software application that's timed to run for a specific period—say, 120 days. The user likes the product but doesn't want to actually buy it (a license no-no!) or hasn't finished evaluating it. So the user simply sets the system clock back a month, or a year, or even two years. This can really muck up your package distribution.

To avoid this problem, be sure to build in some kind of time synchronization routine for your clients that periodically synchronizes their time with the site server or some other designated time server. This goes for site systems and the server running SQL Server as well. Windows 2000 and later domains make time-synchronization easy and mandatory.

Advertised Programs Process Flow

The advertisement and its associated files are generated in a process even more straightforward than the package distribution process, as illustrated in Figure 12-69. Just as with the package distribution process, when the advertisement is created and written to the SMS database, a SQL trigger causes the SMS SQL Monitor service to write a wake-up file (.OFN) to Offer Manager's inbox (\SMS\Inboxes\Offermgr.box).

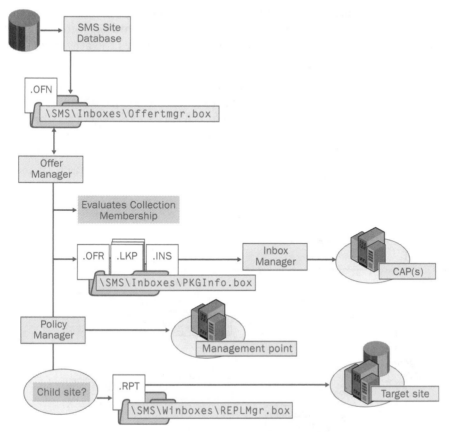

Figure 12-69. *The advertised programs process flow on the server side.*

The Offer Manager component generates instruction files for the Advertised Programs Client Agent on the target client computers and writes these to the \SMS\Inboxes\Offerinf.box directory on the site server. These instruction files consist of an offer file (with a name similar to that of the package but with an .OFR extension), which is the actual advertisement; an installation file (.INS) that references the advertisement ID and the collection ID it's targeting; and up to three lookup files (.LKP), depending on the collection membership. These lookup files act as filters to determine whether the client (*sitecode*systm.lkp), the user (*sitecode*usr.lkp), or the user group (*sitecode*usrgrp.lkp) should receive the advertisement. At this time, Offer Manager also evaluates the collection membership to determine which lookup files to create. Once again, ever-faithful Inbox Manager copies these instruction files to the Offerinf.box folder on the CAPs. For Advanced Clients, the SMS Policy Provider copies the advertisement information to the management point as an Advanced Client policy.

On the Legacy Client, when the Advertised Programs Client Agent runs, it uses the file Launch32.exe to begin the process, as shown in Figure 12-70. Launch32.exe itself starts ODPsys32.exe and ODPusr32.exe, two other threads called Offer Data Providers (ODPs). These threads read the lookup files that were created by Offer Manager and copied to the Offerinf.box on the CAP by Inbox Manager. These files specify whether the client computer, user, or user group should receive the advertisement.

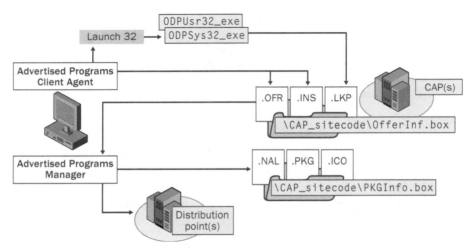

Figure 12-70. *The advertised programs process flow on the client side.*

If the client, user, and user group should receive the advertisement, the Advertised Programs Client Agent reads the instruction and offer file for the advertisement to collect more detailed information. It checks parameters such as the operating system platform on the client and the system time to determine whether to receive the offer. If all is fine, the client agent receives the offer, passes it to the Advertised Programs Manager, generates a status message to that effect, and writes the status message back to the CAP.

The Advertised Programs Manager then reads the .PKG, .ICO, and .NAL files for the package in question from the Pkginfo.box folder on the CAP. Based on the information stored there, the client agent connects to an appropriate distribution point and executes the program. When the program is completed—successfully or unsuccessfully—the client agent again generates a program status message that it writes to the CAP. You can view this status message using the Status Message Viewer in your SMS Administrator Console.

On the Advanced Client, the SMS Agent Host (CCMexec.exe) is responsible for retrieving Advanced Client policy updates from the management point and providing the SMS Software Distribution Agent with advertised program and package information. It's also responsible for forwarding status information back to the management point.

Monitoring Status

Both the package distribution process and the advertised programs process generate status messages. You can monitor status in the same place you have monitored other SMS functions—the System Status folder in the SMS Administrator Console. You can also expand the Component Status folder and view the messages for Distribution Manager and Offer Manager.

You've probably noticed two other folders in the SMS Administrator Console: Package Status and Advertisement Status, located under System Status. These folders pertain specifically to packages and advertisements and are more useful for monitoring their status. As with Component Status, both Package Status and Advertisement Status have status summarizers, which consolidate status messages generated by the SMS components involved in the package and advertisement processes.

In Figure 12-71, the Advertisement Status and Package Status folders have been expanded to demonstrate the information they summarize. Package status detail is summarized at two levels—by site and by distribution point. Advertisement status detail is summarized by site. At each level, you can view the detailed messages that were generated for that particular package or advertisement by right-clicking an entry, choosing Show Messages from the context menu, and then choosing All. After you specify a view data and time range, the Status Message Viewer displays the messages related to the package or advertisement.

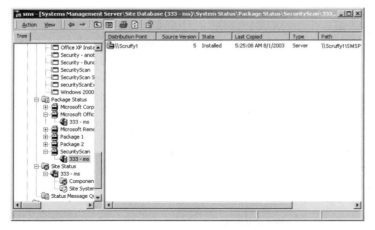

Figure 12-71. *The expanded Advertisement Status and Package Status folders.*

The summary information displayed when a site entry is selected, as in Figure 12-71, shows when the package was copied to the distribution point and last refreshed. The summary information displayed when a specific package is selected, as in Figure 12-72, shows at a glance how many clients installed the package, how many failed, and how many are retrying.

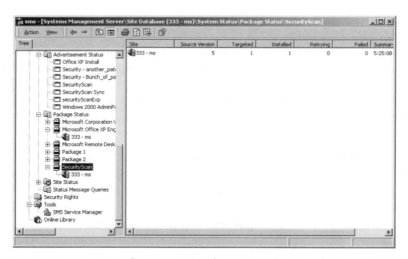

Figure 12-72. *Sample summary information displayed when a package is selected in the SMS Administrator Console.*

Figure 12-73 shows the status messages generated at the site level for a package.

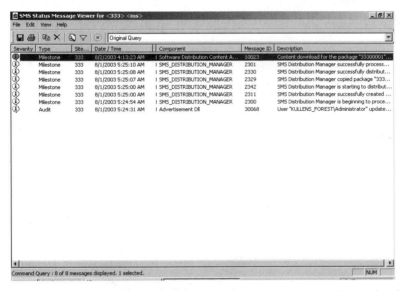

Figure 12-73.   *Status messages for a package generated at the site level.*

Figure 12-74 shows the detailed messages for a specific distribution point in the site.

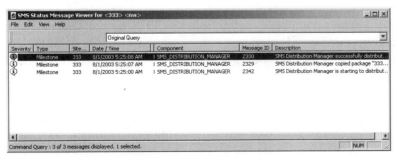

Figure 12-74.   *Status messages for a specific distribution point in a site.*

Notice the difference in messages summarized for each. Messages for the distribution point are specific to that distribution point. Messages in the $23xx$ range refer to Distribution Manager tasks.

Figure 12-75 shows the summary information displayed in the SMS Administrator Console when you select an advertisement. This summary information includes success and failure status generated by the program as it's run on the targeted clients.

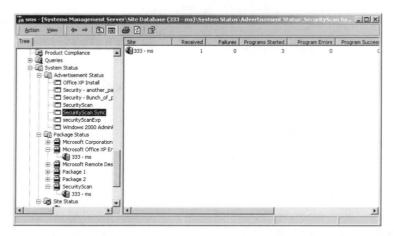

Figure 12-75.   *Advertisement summary showing successful and failed program executions on the targeted clients.*

Figure 12-76 shows some of the detailed messages generated for an advertisement associated with one of the package's programs. The messages that appear vary somewhat depending on the type of SMS client installed. Messages generated by the Offer Manager component fall within the 39*xx* range. The messages generated by the Software Distribution agent in Figure 12-76 came from the client. The complete message text (appearing under Description) tells you when the advertisement was received, when the program started, and when the program completed.

When a program executes at the client and a status MIF is generated, you can determine whether the program completed, how the program ran, and, if it failed, what caused the problem. It should be no surprise, therefore, that we can determine not only whether a program ran, but also how it ran, whether it was successful, and, if it was unsuccessful, why it failed, as shown in Figure 12-76. The degree to which a program can generate this information depends on whether the program generates a status MIF for SMS reporting and the exit codes that are generated. SMS interprets any nonzero exit code as an error or a failure. For example, a Setup.bat file might simply execute an XCOPY of a file to a directory on the client. Even though the XCOPY command is successful, the exit code that it generates is interpreted as an error. Nevertheless, the detailed message is still far more useful and informative.

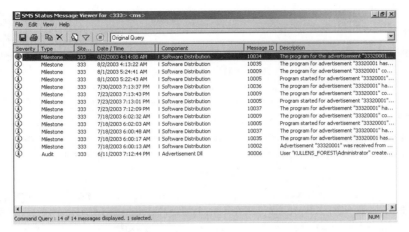

Figure 12-76. *Detailed messages generated for an advertisement associated with one of the package's programs.*

As always, you can also view the log files associated with the Distribution Manager and Offer Manager—Distmgr.log and Offermgr.log. These logs will provide thread activity details, but they're more useful for determining why a source file couldn't be copied to a distribution point or why a program couldn't be advertised—in other words, to troubleshoot the package distribution and advertised program processes. For monitoring the package distribution and program execution process, the Status Viewer will be more than sufficient and probably more efficient.

Checkpoints

As we've seen, the process flows for package distribution and advertised programs are quite straightforward. Outside of normal network traffic issues that might interfere with the copying of source files to a distribution point or the copying of instruction files to a CAP or policy updates to a management point, not much can go wrong. The amount of network traffic generated by updating CAPs and management points with package and advertisement information is relatively small, as the files involved are generally no more than 1 KB to 2 KB in size.

The real traffic comes with the copying or refreshing of source files to the distribution points. Remember that distribution points receive their files in an uncompressed format. That 200 MB application is generating 200 MB worth of network traffic when the source files are copied to the distribution point, and this traffic increases proportionally to the number of distribution points you're targeting. Although you can schedule when the distribution points are refreshed, the initial copy will take place at the time you create the package and identify the distribution points.

Also, keep in mind that when a client accesses a distribution point to run a program, the installation might also generate a significant amount of traffic between the distribution point and the client. The more clients accessing the distribution point at the same time, the more traffic generated and the greater the performance hit taken by the distribution point. In general, if you're targeting large numbers of clients, you should consider distributing the package load across several distribution points, perhaps local to the clients in question.

This same issue of source file size is a reminder to be sure that the proposed distribution points have enough free disk space to host the source files. The client computer needs about 900 KB of space to install the Advertised Programs Client Agent and, of course, enough space to carry out the installation of the application. This concern is not true for the Advanced Client, however. Recall that when you install the Advanced Client software, all the client agents are installed, but not enabled, until you configure the agent at the site server.

If a program fails, start your troubleshooting with the status message system or the log files. Often, simply retracing your steps will be sufficient to spot the problem. Check the package and program parameters. Test the package yourself. Check the clients' system time to be sure that they're receiving the advertisements when you think they should. Check the Advertised Programs Client Agent polling cycle to be sure that the client agent is checking for new advertisements in a timely fashion. Check that the Legacy Client has a CAP available and the Advanced Client a management point. Remember, too, to monitor the Advanced Client download cache and modify it appropriately as well.

Summary

In this chapter we have covered one of the most significant functions of SMS 2003—distributing and advertising packages and programs to clients. This function facilitates remote installation, updating, and maintenance of SMS client computers. However, you should think of SMS as more than a delivery system. As we've seen, it's still your responsibility as the SMS administrator to create (and script, if necessary) the packages you distribute.

A new feature of SMS 2003 is the integration of software update management, a set of tools and processes for keeping your SMS client computers current with security updates and new software updates that are developed after a software product is released. Chapter 13, "Patch Management," discusses this new functionality in more detail, including a description of how it integrates into the package distribution process.

Chapter 13
Patch Management

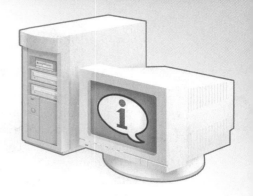

In this chapter we'll cover the following topics:

- The need for effective patch management
- Introduction to the patch management process
- Preparing for patch management
- The four-phase patch management process
- Integrating SMS 2003 into patch management processes
- Responding to emergencies

This chapter's contents are drawn from the patch management best practices documented by Microsoft in the *Patch Management Using Microsoft Systems Management Server 2003 Solution Accelerator*, *Microsoft Solutions for Management (MSM) 2.5*, and the *Microsoft Operations Framework (MOF)*, which provides operational guidance covering reliability, availability, supportability, and manageability of Microsoft products and technologies. For more information about MSM and MOF, see the Microsoft Solutions for Management (*http://www.microsoft.com/technet/itsolutions/msm*) and Microsoft Operations Framework (*http://www.microsoft.com/mof*) Web sites.

The Need for Effective Patch Management

Today's computer systems and networks are under an unprecedented level of threat, ranging from viruses and worms to malicious insiders. Patch management, when properly implemented as part of a defensive strategy, can help organizations adopt a security posture and mitigate vulnerability in their systems. Consequently, patch management is becoming an increasingly important topic for both management who are anxious to demonstrate corporate responsibility to shareholders and for the IT manager, whose job it is to maintain and keep running secure systems.

Trojan Horses, Viruses, and Worms

According to the joint 2003 Computer Security Institute/Federal Bureau of Investigation Computer Crime and Security Survey, 82 percent of respondents detected an attack related to a virus, which was defined as a virus, a Trojan horse, or a worm. The average reported loss due to virus activity was $199,871 per organization. The past 12 months have seen two fast-spreading and debilitating worms: SQL Slammer and MS Blaster. Before that there were Code Red and Nimda. Many organizations had to expend considerable resources defending against and cleaning up after these attacks against their infrastructure.

As alarming as this state of affairs is, what is perhaps more alarming is that in each case updates were available to remove the vulnerability exploited by each worm. Figure 13-1 shows the time from release of an update to discovery of an exploit in the wild for some of the more damaging of the recently discovered Trojan horses, viruses, and worms.

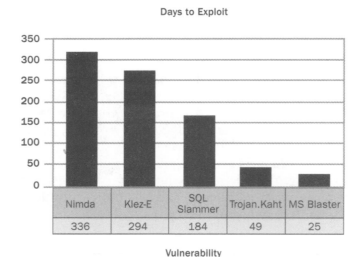

Figure 13-1. *Time from release of update to discovery of exploit in the wild.*

As the chart shows, the trend is moving towards zero-day exploits, where an exploit is discovered on the same day that Microsoft releases an update to remove the vulnerability. The diminishing window between update and exploit is perhaps one of the more compelling arguments for an organization to implement a patch management process, one that's capable of deploying updates quickly, reliably, and efficiently.

Introduction to the Patch Management Process

The remaining sections in this chapter describe a patch management process as recommended by Microsoft. This process, introduced in MSM 2.5, uses a four-phase approach of Identify, Evaluate & Plan, and Deploy and was based on several MOF functions. Also discussed is the implementation of an SMS 2003 infrastructure and its functions in patch management and deployment, along with instructions on responding to patch emergencies and accelerated timelines.

The Microsoft Operations Framework (MOF)

There are many approaches to planning and implementing patch management solutions. The preferred approach is to base a solution upon an existing operations framework, such as MOF. MOF was designed to provide prescriptive guidance to organizations about how to manage their IT operations. MOF consists of three models:

- The process model
- The team model
- The risk model

Of specific interest to patch management, the MOF *process model* is a functional model of the processes performed by operations teams when managing and maintaining IT Services. It's based upon the Office of Government Commerce's IT Infrastructure Library (ITIL), a widely accepted body of practice for operations management. The *team model* and *risk model* might also be of interest, as they provide guidance on the formation of patch management teams, including duties and responsibilities, and a structured approach to managing risk, which is useful when evaluating alerts of vulnerability and software updates and determining the best course of action.

> **More Info**   For more information about the Office of Government Commerce's ITIL, visit its Web site at *http://www.itil.co.uk.*

The MOF process model defines four quadrants of management, as shown in Figure 13-2. The quadrants are Changing, Operating, Supporting, and Optimizing. Each quadrant has a *mission of service*. In the Changing quadrant the mission is to introduce new service solutions, technologies, systems, applications, and processes. The mission of the Operating quadrant is to perform and manage the daily tasks associated with running IT Services. As the name suggests, the Supporting quadrant's mission is to resolve incidents, problems, and inquiries as they arise. Lastly, the Optimizing quadrant's mission is to examine the environment the IT Services run in and drive changes to optimize cost, performance, capacity, and availability.

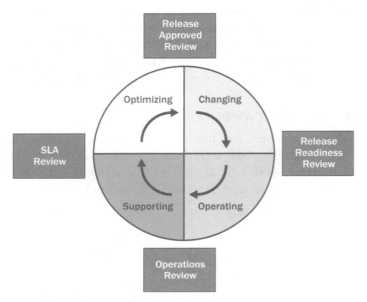

Figure 13-2. *The MOF process model.*

Within each quadrant are major management review processes. These are necessary checkpoints used to guarantee success of the management processes. The reviews are split into two categories: time-based and release-based. The Release Readiness Review and Release Approved Review are release-based reviews and take place before and after a release into the computing environment. The Operations Review and SLA (Service Level Agreement) Review, both time-based reviews, should occur at regular intervals to assess the performance of the internal operations and the agreed-upon customer service levels.

Any comprehensive patch management solution will touch on all four quadrants of the MOF process model—for example, an organization is focused on auditing systems for patch compliance and monitoring alerts for vulnerability and software updates in the Operating quadrant, on assessing and planning response to alerts and downloading and evaluating any updates in the Supporting quadrant, packaging and testing updates in the Optimizing quadrant, and distributing and installing updates as well as auditing and rolling back the update if required in the Changing quadrant.

The Microsoft-Recommended Patch Management Process

Introduced in Microsoft Solutions for Management 2.5 and based on the MOF Change Management, Release Management, and Configuration Management service management functions, the Microsoft-recommended patch management process is a four-phase approach to managing updates to software. The four phases are Assess, Identify, Evaluate & Plan, and Deploy. The process and its four phases are shown in Figure 13-3.

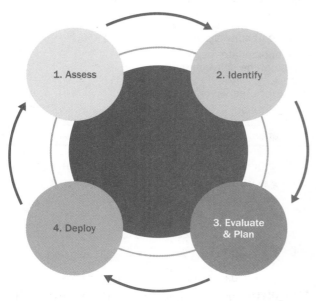

Figure 13-3. *The Microsoft-recommended four-phase patch management process.*

Defined events trigger movement through the phases of the process. Beginning with the Assess phase, the triggering event that causes a move to the Identify phase is notification that a software update exists. The event that causes a move from the Identify phase to the Evaluate & Plan phase is the submission of a formal Request for Change (RFC). The triggering event for a move to the Deploy phase from the Evaluate & Plan phase is the receipt of approval to deploy the software update into the production environment. Finally, the move from the Deploy phase to the Assess phase and the beginning of the process cycle again is triggered by completion of the release of the software update.

Within each phase there are discreet steps that together implement the patch management process. These steps, and the phases they belong to, are described in Table 13-1.

Table 13-1.   Steps in the four-phase patch management process

Phase	Steps
Assess	Inventory/discover existing computing assets.
	Assess security threats and vulnerabilities.
	Determine the best source for information about new software updates.
	Assess the existing software distribution infrastructure.
	Assess operational effectiveness.
Identify	Discover new software updates in a reliable way.
	Determine whether software updates are relevant.
	Obtain and verify software update source files.
	Determine nature of software update and submit RFC.
Evaluate & Plan	Determine the appropriate response.
	Plan the release of the software update.
	Build the release.
	Conduct acceptance testing of the release.
Deploy	Deployment preparation.
	Deployment of the software update to targeted computers.
	Post-implementation review.

Although no technology solution can automate the entire patch management process, they can help somewhat, and SMS 2003 integrates well into patch management processes.

Preparing for Patch Management

Before an organization can implement a patch management process, it needs to prepare for it. Although the four-phase model has an Assess phase, with steps that would appear to cover the initial preparation for patch management, the phase is part of an established and running patch management process. Without careful preparation, a patch management solution is extremely likely to fail. Preparing for patch management is a project in itself, with the defined goal of getting the organization to the point where it can enter the Assess phase of the four-phase model. Among the tasks that need to be accomplished during the preparation project are identifying, inventorying, and bringing the IT assets that will fall under the solution to a known configuration, deployment of the patch management infrastructure, and establishment and training of the patch management team.

Identifying, Inventorying, and Configuring IT Assets

Necessary tasks in the project of preparing for patch management are the identification of assets that will fall under the patch management process, inventorying them, and configuring them so that they conform to a secure baseline.

Not all the IT assets within an organization might qualify for inclusion in a patch management process. Examples of such systems might be legacy systems due for retirement, servers in a perimeter network (also known as DMZ, demilitarized zone, and screened subnet) that need special attention and are patched by hand, development and test systems, and systems leased from a vendor with which there's a support agreement including upgrade maintenance in place. The goal of identifying and inventorying assets is to quantify the number of systems that the patch management process needs to cover, their physical and logical positions within the enterprise, and their hardware and software profiles. You use this information in two ways: to categorize the systems and to determine what the secure configuration or baseline should be in each category and to design the patch management infrastructure to support the patch management process.

Identifying IT Assets

There are many ways to identify IT assets, which can be divided into two categories: manual and automated. In medium and large organizations, manual identification of assets might be infeasible and an automated approach might be favored. SMS 2003 is able to discover assets using a variety of mechanisms, including searching the Active Directory directory service or performing network-based discovery. The quandary here is that you can't deploy SMS 2003 to support the patch management solution effectively without the information that's derived from this task. But with SMS 2003 in place, you can perform this task, and subsequent tasks, more efficiently. One strategy is to deploy a minimal SMS infrastructure that's used solely to gather this information and which is reconfigured when building out the patch management infrastructure.

Inventorying IT Assets

Once you've identified IT assets, you must inventory them. The goal is to determine what the hardware profile of the system is and what software is installed on each. Without this information it won't be possible to determine which systems need to be brought to a secure baseline configuration. A comprehensive patch management solution will need to cope for variations in hardware and software, but it's not possible or desirable for most organizations to manage a large number of combinations. Instead, the organization should categorize IT assets—either by function, such as server or desktop, or by hardware or software configuration. You can use SMS 2003 to help with the inventory process. It will accurately report the operating system, configured services, and any programs or updates that registered themselves with Add/Remove Programs on clients. You can use the SMS 2003 Software Inventory Client Agent to scan SMS client systems for all installed executables, which is useful for inventorying those applications that didn't register themselves. You can examine information about installed applications on any SMS-managed client using the Resource Explorer, which is stored under both Hardware and Software nodes in the Microsoft Management Console (MMC)–based view.

Before you can inventory systems using SMS, the SMS Client must be installed on them. You can do this by pushing the SMS Client software to the systems once they've been discovered, either through Active Directory or network-based discovery. Once the patch management infrastructure is built out, clients can be assigned to SMS sites other than the one in which the SMS Client was deployed.

Configuring IT Assets

Once assets have been identified, an inventory has been performed, and each asset has been categorized, you need to configure the assets and bring them to a secure baseline. Each category will have its own configuration and you should be careful when determining what that configuration should be. The secure baseline should address both the hardware and software configuration for IT assets. As a rule of thumb, each system should be configured for the task to which it is applied, with no extraneous hardware or software and with all appropriate updates applied. Once a secure baseline configuration has been identified for a category, all new systems deployed in that category should conform to the baseline. During the patch management process, as updates to software are deployed, the secure baseline configuration will change. This is discussed in detail later in this chapter.

Until a system is brought to the secure baseline for the category within which it's placed, it can't be included in the patch management process. As with identifying and inventorying IT assets, you can use SMS 2003 to bring systems to a secure baseline configuration in preparation for a patch management process. Of concern to most organizations is ensuring that the software updates necessary to bring a system to a secure baseline configuration are applied. Automating this process with SMS 2003 is discussed in detail later in the chapter in the section entitled "Authorizing and Distributing Software Updates."

Building the SMS 2003 Patch Management Infrastructure

Building out a patch management infrastructure can be a daunting task. A poorly designed infrastructure can have a serious impact on the performance of the patch management process and might result in updates not being applied to systems in a timely fashion. With SMS 2003, organizations have the ability to reconfigure and optimize their patch management infrastructure once it's deployed, but this shouldn't be relied upon in place of a good initial design and implementation. The goal of the implementation should be to build an infrastructure that you can rely on to distribute software updates to systems in a timely fashion. As discussed earlier, you should use the information gathered during the identification and inventorying of IT assets to design the patch management infrastructure. When planning the SMS site hierarchy, take into consideration the categories of assets that will be in each site. For example, SMS sites are comprised of IPv4 subnets and network design best practices recommend placing servers on different subnets from workstations, so it might make sense to create SMS sites designed to achieve the different patch management needs of each category of system on each subnet. An example of an SMS infrastructure that has several sites, each for a specific category of IT asset, is shown in Figure 13-4.

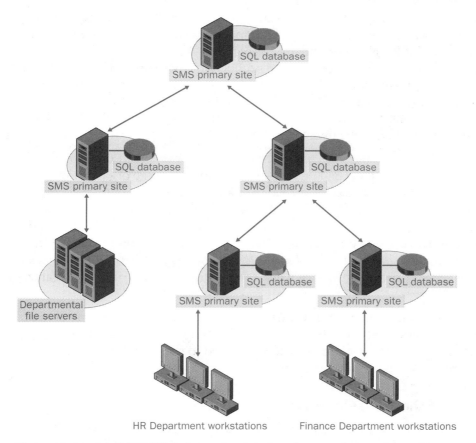

Figure 13-4. *An SMS 2003 infrastructure designed to support patch management.*

Another consideration to keep in mind is how critical each category of system is. Sites with line-of-business systems, such as servers and workstations that are required for the organization to function, should be placed higher up in the SMS site hierarchy. To guarantee that critical updates can be distributed to them as soon as required, intersite links to these sites from the SMS central site shouldn't be configured with bandwidth restrictions. Sites containing noncritical systems can be placed further down in the hierarchy and the intersite links bandwidth restricted as needed. Where a site has multiple categories of assets with a large number of systems in each, it might be desirable to deploy multiple SMS site servers in the site and assign one or more categories to each in order to balance the load against patch management requirements.

Establishing and Training the Patch Management Team

When preparing for patch management, you need to make an effort to establish the patch management team. The patch management team will be responsible for monitoring for alerts of updates to software. When an alert is received, the team needs to assess the impact on the production environment protected by the patch management process. If, as a consequence of an alert, a software update or configuration change needs to be applied to part of or to the entire production environment, the patch management team will be responsible for building, testing, and deploying the update or change.

The makeup of the patch management team will vary from organization to organization and will depend on many factors, including the organization's size, the number of categories of IT assets, the number of systems, and the complexity of the production environment. In larger organizations many people might fulfill a role, while in smaller organizations team members might hold more than one role. The MOF team model white paper, available from *http://www.microsoft.com/technet/itsolutions/tandp/opex/mofrl/mofeo.asp*, is a useful reference and provides guidance when building operations teams for organizations of all sizes.

The patch management team will need to undergo training on the patch management process and on how to use the patch management infrastructure and associated tools. This training should be tailored to the production environment protected by the patch management process.

Entering the Assess Phase

Once the patch management infrastructure is in place and the organization's IT assets have been brought up to the secure baseline configuration, the organization can enter the patch management process. In larger organizations and in those with a complex production environment, it might not be feasible or possible to bring all systems to secure baseline configurations before beginning the patch management process. In these cases the organization might consider rolling systems into the process as they're configured. One of the challenges of rolling in systems over time is that the secure baseline configuration might change in response to an alert of software update before a system is configured, causing the organization to expend considerable resources in updating the baseline before the systems are actually configured—in some cases many times. Several strategies exist for rolling systems into the patch management process, including subnet-by-subnet, category-by-category, site-by-site, and during hardware or software refresh periods. When planning for patch management, the organization needs to consider what strategy it will adopt to roll in systems if it's not possible to bring all systems to a secure baseline before beginning the patch management process.

The Four-Phase Patch Management Process

As detailed earlier, the Microsoft-recommended patch management process is a four-phase process: Assess, Identify, Evaluate & Plan, and Deploy. The process is a continuous cycle, reflecting the reality of operations management. As the result of an alert of software update, the organization shifts from the Assess phase to the Identify phase and begins its journey through the process cycle. It's important to realize that movement through the phases of the process is update-specific. This means that if an organization is in the Evaluate & Plan phase in response to one update when an alert is received for another, the organization will move to the Identify phase for the second update and be in two phases of the process simultaneously. This can pose both logistical and technical challenges to the organization, especially if the alerts are somewhat related or dependencies exist in the updates, and care should be taken.

The Assess Phase

The Assess phase is the first phase in the patch management process. In the Assess phase the organization is concerned primarily with the ongoing assessment of its production environment covered by the patch management process and with monitoring for alerts of software updates. Although many of the steps and tasks in the Assess phase are similar to the tasks undertaken during preparation for the implementation of a patch management process, they're instead focused on optimizing and improving the existing patch management process.

Inventorying and Discovering Existing Computing Assets

As part of the operations of any production environment, IT assets will be added, updated, or retired. This task in the Assess phase is concerned solely with ensuring that the record of IT assets is accurate. As assets are added to the production environment, they should be inventoried and evaluated for inclusion into the patch management process. Assets that are retired should be removed from the record and from the patch management process. Existing assets should continuously be inventoried to ensure that their configuration hasn't changed without a formal change management process or the patch management process. You can automate these tasks somewhat by using SMS 2003's Active Directory and network-based discovery techniques, which are especially useful for discovering unmanaged or rogue systems that were deployed outside a management process.

Assessing Security Threats and Vulnerabilities

Although the IT assets within an organization might have the latest software updates applied to them, there might still be risk from security threats and vulnerabilities introduced by the addition, configuration, or removal of hardware or software components. The organization needs to remain vigilant and check for vulnerability using tools such as the Microsoft Baseline Security Analyzer (MBSA), available from *http://www.microsoft.com/mbsa* and the Software Update Inventory Tools for SMS 2003, which are described later. When vulnerability is discovered, you need to undertake a risk analysis to determine the best course of action. You can find details on how to conduct such an analysis in Chapter 3, "Understanding the Security Risk Management Discipline," available at *http://www.microsoft.com/technet/security/prodtech/windows/secwin2k/03secrsk.asp*. Typically, you'll take steps to mitigate the vulnerability through a configuration change or possibly a software update.

Determining the Best Source for Information About Software Updates

The patch management team needs to remain informed about new software updates for IT assets under control of the patch management process. The team can remain informed by subscribing to e-mail notifications, visiting vendor Web sites, and through regular contact with representatives of software vendors.

Microsoft's authoritative Web site for information about security bulletins is *http://www.microsoft.com/security*, where users can also sign up for e-mail notification of software updates and security bulletins issued by Microsoft.

Assessing the Existing Software Distribution Infrastructure

Although careful planning and implementation might yield a versatile patch management infrastructure that meets the needs of the organization at implementation time, it might not suffice as the organization changes. The patch management team needs to assess the patch management infrastructure continuously to ensure that it continues to meet the organization's needs. SMS 2003 is an extremely flexible management solution and can be reconfigured as needed to support the addition, change in configuration, or removal of categories of IT assets or sites.

If the Assess phase was entered after the completion of the last phase in the patch management process, the Deploy phase, the organization should evaluate how successful the deployment of the software update was. If problems were encountered, the infrastructure should be examined for problems.

Assessing Operational Effectiveness

Lastly, in the Assess phase the patch management team needs to validate the entire patch management process. They need to ask questions such as the following: Does the patch management team have the necessary resources? Do key security stakeholders have the necessary training and understanding of the patch management process? Are formal processes in place for day-to-day operations that have an impact on security? You can find the Microsoft Operations Framework Self-Assessment Tool, designed to gauge an organization's operational excellence, at *http://www.microsoft.com/technet/itsolutions/tandp/opex/moftool.asp*.

As with assessing the software distribution infrastructure for problems after a deployment, the patch management team should assess the operational effectiveness of the process, including their own performance. Lessons learned in this assessment should be applied in order to improve operational excellence for future software updates.

Leaving the Assess Phase and Moving to the Identify Phase

When the patch management team receives notification of a software update that affects the production environment, the patch management process moves into the Identify phase.

The Identify Phase

During the Identify phase of the four-phase patch management process, the organization is focused on gathering information about the software update that triggered entry into the Identify phase, whether or not the update is relevant to the production environment; obtaining the software update itself; and categorizing the update as either an emergency update or one that can be dealt with routinely within the time frame set by the organization for software updates.

Discovering New Software Updates Reliably

When an organization receives an e-mail alert from Microsoft about a software update, the alert contains links to Microsoft's Security & Privacy Web site, found at *http://www.microsoft.com/security*, where more detailed information is made available. Organizations might choose to subscribe to other sources of information about software updates or receive e-mail messages from account representatives or other Microsoft employees. Regardless of where the alert came from, the patch management team needs to verify its authenticity. For alerts detailing software updates to Microsoft products, the authoritative source of information is the Microsoft Security & Privacy Web site, which the team should visit. Of special note, Microsoft never releases software updates as attachments to e-mail messages. If the team receives an e-mail message with an attachment purporting to come from Microsoft and containing a software update, the safest course of action is to delete the message. Similarly, rather than clicking on links contained in e-mail messages that appear to take the reader to a Microsoft Web site, the reader should copy and paste the URL into their browser, as the true Web site that the user will be taken to can be hidden in the formatting of the e-mail message.

SMS 2003 Software Updates, when configured, will automatically poll Microsoft's Web sites, looking for information about software updates in the products that it's aware of. Using the SMS Administrator Console, you can view just about every applicable software update for the production environment, along with the number of systems that are in compliance and those that are not. Figure 13-5 shows a screen shot of software updates listed in the SMS Administrator Console. You can find details on how to configure SMS Software Updates to show this information later in this chapter.

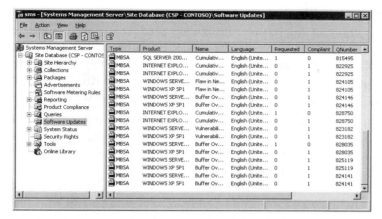

Figure 13-5. *Software updates listed in the SMS Administrator Console.*

Determining Whether Software Updates Are Relevant

Benjamin Franklin wrote, "In this world nothing is certain but death and taxes." Although this was written long before software was invented, today he would no doubt feel compelled to add software updates to the list of certainties faced in life. The fact is that software releases are made on a continual basis and can come from a variety of sources, such as operating systems and application vendors, independent software vendors (ISVs), original equipment manufacturers (OEMs), and hardware manufacturers. Not every released software update will necessarily apply to an organization's production environment, even when it touches a software product in use. The patch management team will need to evaluate and determine whether or not patches are relevant to the production environment covered by the patch management process. For example, a software update to a word-processing package that's deployed within the organization might apply only to a feature that isn't installed or used, or perhaps the risk from not installing the update is considered so low that it can be safely ignored. A good starting point for evaluating the relevance of a software update issued by Microsoft is the detailed bulletin found on Microsoft's Security & Privacy Web site at *http://www.microsoft.com/security*. The bulletin will contain details of the vulnerability addressed by the update, any mitigating factors that might affect the requirement to update a system, and any workarounds if available.

Each software update should be assessed from a risk management perspective, with the organization making a determination about whether or not the update should be applied to its affected IT assets. When considering the risk from not installing an update, the organization must balance it against the risk from installing the update. Risk from installation includes incompatibilities with already-installed applications, system instability, and loss of functionality.

As described earlier, SMS 2003 Software Updates can be configured to poll Microsoft's Web sites for details of available software updates and list them in the SMS Administrator Console. Only updates that are applicable to the production environment are listed. An update is deemed to be applicable when one or more SMS Clients scans itself and determines that the update should be applied and reports this information to an SMS site server. You can find full details on configuring SMS 2003 Software Updates, and details on how the feature works, later in this chapter.

Obtaining and Verifying Software Update Source Files

When assessing the relevance of a software update, it's often desirable to have the source files for the update at hand. The patch management team should take care when obtaining software updates to ensure that they come from legitimate sources only. Every software update that Microsoft releases is digitally signed, and you can verify its authenticity by examining the signature. Although you can do this manually, you can also do it using SMS 2003. When a software update is identified as relevant to the production environment and listed under Software Updates in the SMS Administrator Console, it can be included in a package built by the Distribute Software Updates Wizard. You can instruct the wizard to download software updates automatically, and it will check the signature of each as it does so. If the wizard is unable to download a software update automatically, which might be the case if different updates exist for different platforms and configurations or if the patch management team prefers to download updates by hand, you can verify the software update's digital signature through its properties using Microsoft Windows Explorer. Figure 13-6 shows the dialog box of a software update's digital signature, accessible through Windows Explorer.

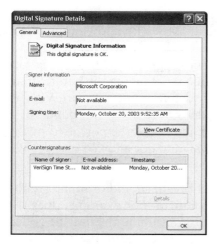

Figure 13-6.   *A digital signatures dialog box, accessible through Windows Explorer.*

Until a software update identified in an alert has been successfully downloaded and verified, the patch management process can't leave the Identify phase.

Determining the Nature of the Software Update and Submitting a Request for Change

Every software update released by Microsoft is assigned a severity rating. The purpose of the ratings is to provide guidance to administrators and patch management teams about the urgency with which the update should handled. These ratings, and their meanings, are listed in Table 13-2. You can find full details of the ratings used by Microsoft in TechNet at *http://www.microsoft.com/technet/security/bulletin/rating.asp*.

Table 13-2.   Software update severity ratings

Rating	Definition
Critical	A vulnerability whose exploitation could allow the propagation of an Internet worm without user action.
Important	A vulnerability whose exploitation could result in compromise of the confidentiality, integrity, or availability of users' data or of the integrity or availability of processing resources.
Moderate	Exploitability is mitigated to a significant degree by factors such as default configuration, auditing, or difficulty of exploitation.
Low	A vulnerability whose exploitation is extremely difficult or whose impact is minimal.

The patch management team should take an update's severity rating into account when determining its nature. Software updates with a low rating might be safely ignored until a predefined refresh cycle is begun, whereas an update rated as critical might need to be deployed as soon as possible. Mitigating factors should also be taken into consideration when determining the nature of an update. For example, with sufficient perimeter defenses and a secure VPN in place, a patch management team might consider not rushing an update for a newly discovered vulnerability that a worm is exploiting if the port used by the worm to propagate itself is blocked at the firewall and not allowed over a VPN connection.

Other considerations that the patch management team should examine are the impact of the update on the production environment. For example, does the update require systems to be restarted after installation and can it be rolled back if it's determined that the update has a negative effect on the production environment?

Once the patch management team has completed determining the nature of the software update, it should submit an RFC to the Change Management Board.

Leaving the Identify Phase and Moving to the Evaluate & Plan Phase

The events that trigger leaving the Identify phase and the handover to the Evaluate & Plan phase are the successful acquisition of the software update and the submission of the RFC.

The Evaluate & Plan Phase

The Evaluate & Plan phase of the patch management process is where the organization needs to examine how it will respond to a software update, how it will release the update, how it will build the update, and how it will conduct acceptance testing for the release.

Determining the Appropriate Response

When an RFC is created, the initiator assigns an initial priority and category to the request. The patch management team should review the RFC and agree to, or change, the priority and category. The finally determined values will have an impact on the remainder of the patch management process, including how and when the software update is released. When the team reviews the initial priority attached to an RFC, it should consider what assets are impacted by the vulnerability the update addresses and whether these are critical systems, whether controls are in place (or can be put in place) to mitigate the vulnerability, and whether the update needs to be applied to as many systems as first thought. It's recommended that the organization define priorities for release of software updates and time frames consistent with their needs, such as those in Table 13-3.

Table 13-3. Release priorities and time frames

Priority	Recommended Time Frame	Minimum Recommended Time Frame
Emergency	Within 24 hours	Within two weeks
High	Within one month	Within two months
Medium	Depending on availability, deploy a new service pack or update rollup that includes a fix for this vulnerability within four months	Deploy the software update within six months
Low	Depending on availability, deploy a new service pack or update rollup that includes a fix for this vulnerability within one year	Deploy the software update within one year, or you might choose not to deploy at all

The organization might wish to consider formalizing the criteria used when determining whether or not to adjust a release's priority. You can find an example of formalized criteria in the form of environmental and organizational factors and the corresponding priority adjustments in Table 13-4.

Table 13-4. Release priorities adjustment criteria

Environmental/Organizational Factor	Priority Adjustment
High-value or high-exposure assets impacted	Raise
Assets historically targeted by attackers	Raise
Mitigating factors in place, such as countermeasures that minimize the threat	Lower
Low-value or low-exposure assets impacted	Lower

Emergency change requests, where vulnerability is being exploited within the production environment or system instability is affecting line-of-business applications, need to be handled expeditiously. These requests might cause other requests with lower priorities to be delayed or halted if already in deployment in order to free the necessary resources required to process them. You can find more information on emergency response later in the chapter.

Not all software updates are the same, and each might have a different effect when applied to a system. Some updates might require a system to be rebooted while others do not. It's possible that some updates will rely on other updates, perhaps a service pack, and can't be installed without them. Also, some software updates, once applied, can't be removed from a system. The patch management team members need to assess the impact that a software update will have on the environment in order to plan for it. This is called categorizing the update.

Once the release priority and category of the software update has been determined, the release needs to be reviewed and authorized for deployment. Before authorization is granted, the patch management team will need to consider various factors, such as what is currently happening in the production environment, the release's projected cost, the best means of distributing the release, the resources required to manage the release, and any dependencies the release requires. Once authorization has been granted, a member of the team should take ownership of the release. The release owner is responsible for assembling the necessary resources to guarantee the building of the release, its testing, and its eventual deployment.

Planning the Release

Once the release has been approved, detailed planning should take place to guarantee the deployment's success. Although considered previously in the Identify phase and when determining the appropriate response in this phase, the IT assets that need to receive the software update need to be identified and recorded. The Software Updates component of SMS 2003 can help identify assets that need updating, but if SMS 2003 can't discover the vulnerability that the update addresses, the patch management team might need to resort to mining through the information recorded by the SMS Client hardware and software inventory agents.

The patch management team will need to determine when to release the software update and whether to allow users to influence the release process. The team might decide, for example, to allow users a seven-day grace period during which they can choose to install the update contained within the release before it becomes mandatory. The team will also have to take into account the release's impact on the production environment. For many organizations it might be easier to release updates over the weekend instead of during the week. The team will need to factor in the size of the update, as larger updates will take longer to download to clients, especially those that connect over slow links such as portable computers on a dial-up connection.

The team might also wish to consider a staged release, where some systems receive the update before others. For example, if the update is determined to be a high priority and is applicable to the patch management infrastructure servers as well as other IT assets, the team might decide to apply the update to the servers first to guarantee their availability while deploying the update even if an exploit has been discovered.

The team will also want to draw up a timetable for the release lifecycle, including packaging the software update, testing both the update and the package, publishing the package in the patch management framework, deploying the package to systems, and validating the deployment. As part of the preparation for patch management, the organization might wish to consider developing templates of release timetables, one for each combination of category of asset and priority level. A sample timetable for a release is shown in Figure 13-7.

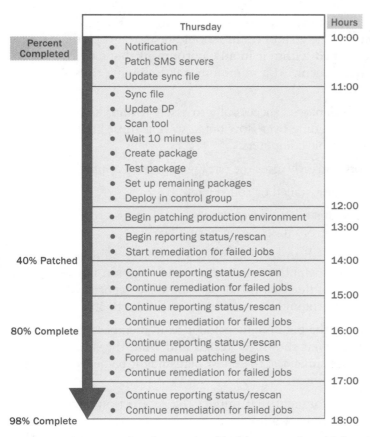

Figure 13-7.   *A sample release timetable for servers for a high-priority release.*

Building the Release

Once the release has been approved, the patch management team needs to build the release package, which will be distributed to affected IT assets using the patch management infrastructure. The package's format will depend on the infrastructure tools. You can use the SMS 2003 Distribute Software Updates Wizard, described later in this chapter, to build a package containing the software update from updates available from Microsoft's Web sites and which are discoverable by the Software Updates feature of SMS.

Conducting Acceptance Testing

When the release package has been built, it must be tested prior to deployment to ensure that no problems will result from application of the package in the production environment. The goal of testing should be to test both the package and the update(s) contained within it in an environment that's representative of the production environment. At a minimum, the following tests should be conducted:

- The package can be deployed successfully to assets within the production environment, including over slow links, such as those connecting remote sites and portable computers.

- The system reboots correctly after the package has been applied.

- The package can be uninstalled or rolled back.

- The package, once installed, doesn't prevent business-critical and infrastructure systems from functioning normally.

Most organizations will wish to conduct more than these minimum tests to ensure that line-of-business applications continue to function normally. The number, range, and detail of the tests will depend on the categories of IT assets in the production environment and the software installed on them.

Before they begin to test, the patch management team members should build test plans, which define what should be tested and what the desired results should be. As with release timelines, these test plans might be developed while preparing for patch management.

Building a patch test environment that mimics the production environment, complete with patch management infrastructure, can be expensive. An alternative to a test environment is to designate certain machines in the production environment as test machines that will receive a package prior to the rest of the production environment. If the package can be deployed and the update applied successfully, the package can be deployed in a general release. This testing strategy needs to be managed carefully, as end users will become the testers and might require additional training. This strategy is also likely to result in acceptance of a patch without the rigorous testing that would be achieved in a test lab.

Leaving the Evaluate & Plan Phase and Moving to the Deploy Phase

The build of a release and the success of the acceptance testing for a package are the triggers for the change to the Deploy Phase.

The Deploy Phase

The last phase of the Microsoft-recommended four-phase patch management process is the Deploy phase, where the patch management team prepares to deploy the packaged software update built in the Evaluate & Plan phase into the production environment. If problems develop during, or as a result of, the deployment, the team might have to roll back or manually apply the update on affected systems. After the package has been deployed, and perhaps rolled back, the team will want to conduct a review of the experience to look for ways to improve future deployments of software updates.

Preparing the Deployment

Once the package(s) containing the software update(s) to be applied to the production environment have successfully passed acceptance testing in the Evaluate & Plan phase and the organization has moved into the Deploy phase, the patch management infrastructure and the organization need to prepare for deployment. Among the steps that need to be taken to prepare the organization are communicating the rollout schedule to affected parties and configuring the patch management infrastructure to prepare to distribute the update.

Communicating information about impending updates to stakeholders such as system administrators and end users is extremely important. A simple and effective communication tool is e-mail. By informing the organization that a software update is pending or in progress, the team can accomplish many things, including reducing the number of calls to the help desk from users wondering what's happening to their systems and giving users the opportunity to install an update when it suits them before forcing a mandatory update on them.

The steps that the patch management team will take to prepare the patch management infrastructure for the update will depend largely on the technology used and how it's configured. With SMS 2003, the team will need to import packages containing software updates from the test environment or build new ones in the production environment, assign distribution points for the package, and stage the updates on the distribution points. In environments where there's a hierarchy of SMS 2003 sites, care should be taken to ensure that each package is assigned an appropriate priority and is distributed to all the sites.

Deploying the Software Update to Targeted Computers

As with the preparation, the steps taken to deploy a package containing updates will depend largely on the technology being used and the way it has been configured. The relative priority of the release and the options chosen when building the package will also figure into the deployment. Essentially, there are three steps to deploying a package containing a software update: making clients aware of the update's availability, monitoring the package's deployment, and recovering from failed deployments.

How the advertisement containing information about a package ready for deployment is configured will depend largely on the update's nature. For example, a relatively low priority update might allow the end user to choose whether or not to accept the package and install the update on the user's system, whereas a high-priority update might be mandatory and leave the user with no choice but to have the update installed. The organization might also wish to create multiple advertisements for the same package, targeting tailored advertisements at different categories of IT assets to reflect different priorities across each.

During the deployment, the patch management team needs to monitor the production environment for problems that might arise on the systems to which the package is being delivered or within the patch management infrastructure itself. Among the variables that should be tracked are the number of systems that have received the advertisement and have successfully applied the update, the number that have received the advertisement but failed to apply the update, the number that have received the advertisement but have not yet attempted to apply the update (for whatever reason), and the number that have not yet received the advertisement. Depending on the technology and how it's configured and used, the patch management infrastructure might be able to reliably report these figures. If the infrastructure is incapable of supporting such reporting, the patch management team might have to use custom scripts (perhaps contained within the package itself) to monitor the deployment. SMS 2003 does provide a reporting mechanism so that the patch management team can gauge the deployment's progress.

If during the deployment's monitoring the patch management team sees a number of systems receive the advertisement but fail while applying the update, they should begin an investigation into why. Of immediate concern should be the possibility that the package is somehow corrupted. A good indicator that this is the case is a high number of failures proportional to successful applications of the package early in the deployment process. If a determination is made that the package is responsible for the failures, the team should stop the deployment and resolve the problem before making the package available again. Not all failures will be attributable to a faulty or bad package, however. Some might simply be due to the system not requiring the update contained within the package, perhaps because the system was manually updated earlier by the user or administrator or because the system was incorrectly identified as requiring the update due to a vulnerability that doesn't exist on the system.

In most deployments there will always be a few systems that can't be updated using an advertised package, either because of their configuration or because they aren't managed by the patch management infrastructure. In these cases the team will likely have to visit each system and apply the update manually. Care should be taken when deploying an update in this fashion to ensure that the correct installation options are used to guarantee the updated system's integrity.

The worst-case scenario for the patch management team is a successful deployment of a package containing an update only to find that the update needs to be rolled back due to unforeseen circumstances, such as application incompatibility that wasn't identified during testing. Complicating factors might be that the update performs as expected on some machines but not on others. If there are no initial reports that the update causes problems to systems and the patch management process leaves the Deploy phase, the subsequent action that needs to be taken to remedy the problem can be considered a software update in its own right and requires movement through the four-phase patch management process.

Reviewing the Implementation

The goal of the review process is to gather information and lessons learned from the deployment that can be used in future applications of the patch management process. Typically held a short time after it has been determined that a package was successfully deployed, the review should focus on ensuring that the IT assets in the production environment have been categorized correctly, that the vulnerability that was mitigated by the software update has been removed, and that the update will form part of the secure baseline configuration for new systems deployed into the production environment. The review should also examine the patch management team's performance.

Leaving the Deploy Phase

Once the Post-Implementation Review has been completed, the organization leaves the Deploy phase of the patch management process and reenters the Assess phase.

Integrating SMS 2003 into Patch Management Processes

Although no technology solution can automate a patch management process completely, a well-rounded patch management infrastructure can certainly help the patch management team by automating many of the routine tasks. SMS 2003 is an extremely flexible tool, and you can easily integrate it into patch management processes, including the Microsoft-recommended four-phase patch management process described earlier in this chapter. SMS 2003 was designed to be extensible to accommodate the changing patch management and software update needs of organizations.

Extending SMS 2003 Functionality for Software Updates

In response to customers' patch management needs, Microsoft released the Software Update Services (SUS) feature pack for SMS 2.0. Much of the functionality of the feature pack has been updated and incorporated into SMS 2003, and new features have been added. You can download the Software Update Scanning Tools for SMS 2003 from Microsoft's SMS Web site (*http://www.microsoft.com/smserver/downloads/2003/default.asp*) to extend the product's functionality. You can also start the SMS Administrator Console, right-click the Software Updates node, select All Tasks, and then select the Download Inventory Scanning Programs option. Currently, two tools exist: the Security Update Inventory Tool, to scan for missing system software updates, and the Microsoft Office Inventory Tool for Updates, to scan for missing Microsoft Office software updates. Microsoft might add more, and ISVs can extend the functionality of SMS 2003 by writing their own. Once they're installed and configured, you can use these tools with SMS 2003 to help automate parts of a patch management process.

Installing the Update Inventory Tools

Installing the Systems Management Server 2003 Software Update Scanning Tools is relatively simple. Once downloaded and unpacked, there should be two installation executables, called OfficePatch_*XXX*.exe and

SecurityPatch_*XXX*.exe, where *XXX* is the language identifier for the executable. Each should be run in turn to install the extensions to SMS 2003. During installation the user will be asked to accept a license agreement; select an installation folder (by default, C:\Program Files\OfficePatch and C:\Program Files\SecurityPatch for the Microsoft Office Inventory Tool for Updates and the Security Update Inventory Tool, respectively); download and install the latest database or catalog of updates from Microsoft's Web site; and create the collections, packages, and advertisements necessary for clients to distribute and run the inventory tools. You're required to enter the name used to identify the package in a dialog box during installation, as shown in Figure 13-8.

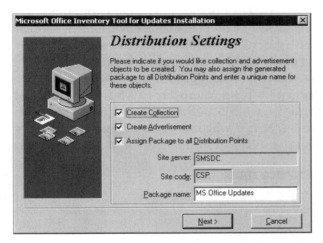

Figure 13-8. *Distribution Settings dialog box during inventory tool installation and setup.*

You're asked whether you wish to retrieve new versions of the database (Office or Security) of software updates automatically. If the answer is yes, you can enter the name of system on which to run the retrieval task. By default, the name is the local server's name. A system that fetches database updates automatically must have Internet connectivity and will fetch updates only when a user with the correct permissions is logged on. As an alternative, you can periodically download and install the Security Patch Bulletin Catalog in MSSecure.XML for Security Updates and Microsoft Office Update Database in Invcif.exe for Office Updates and manually place them into the installation folders for the Security Update Inventory Tool and the Microsoft Office Inventory Tool for Updates, respectively.

Lastly, you're asked for the name of an existing SMS client onto which the inventory tools can be installed and tested. Although a name must be supplied before installation can proceed, any name can be entered, including one for a system that doesn't exist yet (this is useful when you're building out an environment or when you're unsure which system to use).

As part of the installation process, the inventory tools extend SMS 2003 by creating collections, packages, and advertisements. By default, both the Microsoft Office Inventory Tool for Updates and the Security Update Inventory Tool add three collections, a package with three programs, and two advertisements each. The three collections added are used to specify the IT assets in the production environment that will receive advertisements of the packages containing the inventory tools; to specify the IT assets in a preproduction environment that can be used for testing updates (this is the collection into which the SMS client computer named during installation of the update tools is placed); and to specify the host system, called a sync host, that will be responsible for collecting the catalogs of updates and other information from Microsoft's Web site. Figure 13-9 shows collections added with the prefix MS Office Updates and MS Security Updates, as these were the names specified when prompted for a package name during installation of the inventory tools.

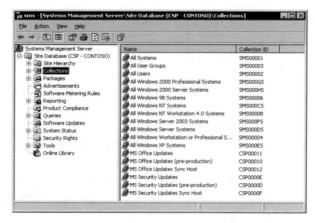

Figure 13-9. *Collections added to SMS 2003 by the Microsoft Office Inventory Tool for Updates and the Security Update Inventory Tool.*

The package created by each of the inventory tools installation programs contains three programs (as shown in Figure 13-10). The first two programs are used to deploy the update scanning tools to SMS clients. As the name suggests, the program marked Expedited is used to run the program in such a fashion that information from the client is made accessible to the SMS site server in an expedited manner. It's not recommended that this be used on production systems for performance reasons, and its use should be limited to test environments. The third program is used to synchronize the database of available Security or Office software updates from Microsoft's Web site with the local copy by downloading the latest revision of the database. Perhaps confusingly, the command executed by both the Office Update Inventory Tool's Sync program and the Security Update Inventory Tool's Sync program is called SyncXML.exe, but these are different programs and each can be found in the respective installation folder for each tool.

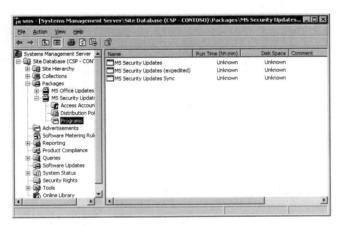

Figure 13-10.   *Packages added to SMS 2003 by the Microsoft Office Inventory Tool for Updates and the Security Update Inventory Tool.*

Lastly, the inventory tools installation programs create two advertisements each (as shown in Figure 13-11). One advertisement is used to inform clients of the program's availability to run the update inventory tools in the corresponding package, and the other is used to kick off the synchronization of the database of updates. The advertisements are installed with a default schedule that should be tuned to the organization's needs.

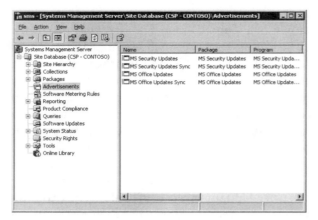

Figure 13-11. *Advertisements added to SMS 2003 by the Microsoft Office Inventory Tool for Updates and the Security Update Inventory Tool.*

Testing the Update Inventory Tools

Once the inventory tools have been successfully installed onto the SMS site server, you should test them. You can do this in several ways. The simplest is to create a new advertisement for the expedited scan program in the Security or Office inventory package you wish to test, as shown in Figure 13-12.

Figure 13-12. *Creating a new advertisement to test the installation of the inventory tools.*

When selecting a collection to advertise the inventory tools package to, select the preproduction environment as it should be prepopulated with the name of the SMS client you specified during installation of the inventory tool you're testing. If you specified a system that doesn't exist during installation, if it has since been removed, or if you want to test the tools across more than one client, you can add systems manually to the collection for testing purposes and then remove them later. Do not specify a production collection in this dialog box, as the expedited program setting can cause problems when run on large numbers of hosts.

To check that a client picked up the advertisement and that the scan tools have run, you can use the Resource Explorer to check the Software Updates node under the Hardware node for an SMS client in the collection that that advertisement was made available to, as shown in Figure 13-13. Software Updates listed under the Hardware node, which are the results of the scan performed by the Update Inventory Tools, are stored as instances of a Windows Management Instrumentation (WMI) class called Win32_Patchstate. Instances of this class are collected and propagated to the SMS site server using the Hardware Inventory Client Agent, where they're collated and processed to give site-level views of the information.

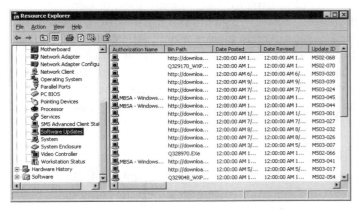

Figure 13-13. *Resource Explorer view of the Software Updates node on an SMS client computer.*

Configuring the Update Inventory Tools

Once it has been determined that the inventory tools have been installed and tested successfully on the preproduction client systems, you need to configure the inventory tools for the production environment. Two areas need careful attention. The first is the removal of limitations on the collections created during the installation of the tools, and the second is configuration of the sync host that's responsible for fetching the latest update and security databases from Microsoft.

Removing Limitations from Collections

The collections created during installation of the inventory tools are limited collections and should be configured for the organization's needs. The collection marked Pre-production should be populated manually with the site systems that will be used to test packages of software updates before general deployment. The other collection should include all production systems in the site that will be scanned for missing software updates. You do this by selecting the collection, editing its properties, and changing the collection query in the Membership Rules tab to remove the limited query. This will make all systems in the SMS site members of the collection and will cause each to receive an advertisement for the inventory tools packages and begin scanning for missing updates.

By default, the advertisements for the inventory tools scanning packages run every seven days. For many organizations this will be too long a period between scans, especially if the reports generated and displayed under the Software Updates node in SMS 2003 Administrator Console are used to determine the update status and compliance across IT assets in the organization. There's also another reason for dropping the advertisement interval, at least initially. A particular software update will be listed in the console only if at least one client runs a scan and finds that the update is applicable, even if it's already installed and therefore not required. You might wish to consider dropping the scan interval to a day or two until all systems in the site have received the package and have performed at least two scans to verify update status.

Configuring the Sync Host

If it's configured, the sync host will attempt to retrieve the latest database of Office updates and security updates from Microsoft's Web sites on a daily basis. The program will run only when a user is logged on to the system. It's possible to configure the program to run when no one is logged on or regardless of whether a user is logged on or not, but these configurations have implications. The program is designed to run under the context of a logged-on user. If no user is logged on, the program runs using the LocalSystem account, if the SMS Advanced Client is installed, or the account SMSCliToknLocalAcct& for those systems with the Legacy Client. As neither of these accounts is afforded network access, the package source folder must be local to the sync host and not on a network share. If a firewall or proxy server is used, it must also be configured to allow unauthenticated outbound access to Microsoft's Web sites where the databases of updates are published. Lastly, the LocalSystem and SMSCliToknLocalAcct& accounts aren't granted access to the package object that's required to update the distribution points after synchronization. To set up unattended synchronization, complete the following steps:

1. When installing the inventory tools, place the synchronization component on the same system as the package source folder specified in the Select Destination Directory page of the installation wizard.

2. Grant the local Administrators group the right to change the contents.

3. Using the Properties dialog box, modify the synchronization command for each inventory tool's package's synchronization program so that it reads as follows:

   ```
   syncxml.exe /s /unattend /site <site server> /code <site code> /target
   <package source> /package <packageID>
   ```

4. Still using the Properties dialog box, select Whether Or Not A User Is Logged In for the option Program Can Run.

5. Using the Package Properties Data Source tab, modify the package so that the distribution points can be updated on a schedule.

6. On the sync host, start Microsoft Internet Explorer and open the Internet Options dialog box from the Tools menu. In the Advanced tab, select Use Http 1.1 Through Proxy Connections and then click OK to save the changes.

7. Ensure that if a firewall or proxy server is used, it allows unauthenticated connections to pass through. If the firewall or proxy server can't be configured to allow unauthenticated connections through, you can use the command PatchDownloader.exe, installed with SMS 2003 in the C:\SMS\bin\i386\00000409 folder, to set credentials used by the synchronization task. For details on the parameters used by this program, use the /? option.

8. Make sure that the source directory for the scan component package is on the synchronization host.

On synchronization hosts that are site servers, there's no need to specify the /unattend option in step 3 and you can omit step 5.

Authorizing and Distributing Software Updates

Once SMS 2003 has been configured to advertise the packages that contain the inventory tools and compliance reports are received, you can begin to authorize and distribute software updates. Several steps are involved in distributing software updates using SMS 2003, ranging from preparing the folders where the packages will be stored, to creating the packages, to testing the packages, to deploying the packages, and, finally, to monitoring the deployment's progress.

Preparing Package Source Folders

Package source folders will contain the files that will be distributed to SMS clients. For this reason their integrity should be strictly maintained. The Access Control List on a package folder should be set so the Administrator account has Full Control and the SMS service account or LocalSystem (depending on configuration) has Read access. No other user or group should have access to the package source folders. Instead of specifying permissions each time a folder is created, you can consider creating a folder hierarchy exclusively for use in storing package sources, securing the top folder, and ensuring that permissions are inherited to all subfolders as they're created.

Building the Package

The next step in distributing a software update is to build the package that contains it. Although a package can contain more than one update, you might wish to restrict the number of updates in a package, especially if you're unsure about the interaction between the updates when they're applied. Before building a package, you should identify the category or categories of IT assets the package is targeted at (the patch management team might provide this information) and be certain that the updates have been tested independently to ensure that they work as expected. For updates that have been identified as required by the inventory tools, you can use the Distribute Software Updates Wizard. You launch it by right-clicking a collection, package, advertisement, or the Software Updates node in the SMS Administrator Console, selecting All Tasks, and then selecting Distribute Software Updates. Be careful not to confuse this wizard with the Distribute Software Wizard (DSW), which is available from the collections nodes.

The first step you're asked to complete after the Welcome page is to select the update type, as shown in Figure 13-14. The list of available update types is driven by the inventory tools updates reported back to the SMS site server by the SMS clients through the Hardware Inventory Client Agent.

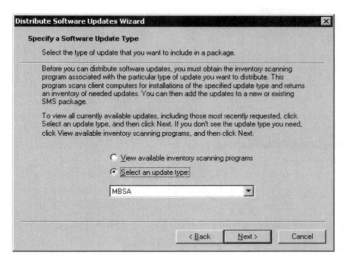

Figure 13-14. *Selecting an update type in the Distribute Software Updates Wizard.*

The next step in the wizard asks you if you wish to create a new package or update an existing one. If you choose to create a new package, you're prompted for the package name. The package name is used to provide a default value for the program name, too. In the next step you're given the option of specifying who the package is coming from. You can also choose to include a Rich Text File (RTF) that provides information to the users about the package and the software updates it contains. For mandatory advertisements there might be little benefit to the organization in specifying that an RTF file be downloaded to the client, but in those situations where the end user is given control over when to install the package there might be more use to this feature.

Before an advertised package containing software updates can be run on an SMS client, an inventory must be performed to ensure that the updates are applicable to the client. The wizard's next step gives you the option of choosing which inventory tools to run, as shown in Figure 13-15. The wizard picks the default scanning program in the inventory tools package created during installation and shouldn't be changed unless you've created an alternate scanning program.

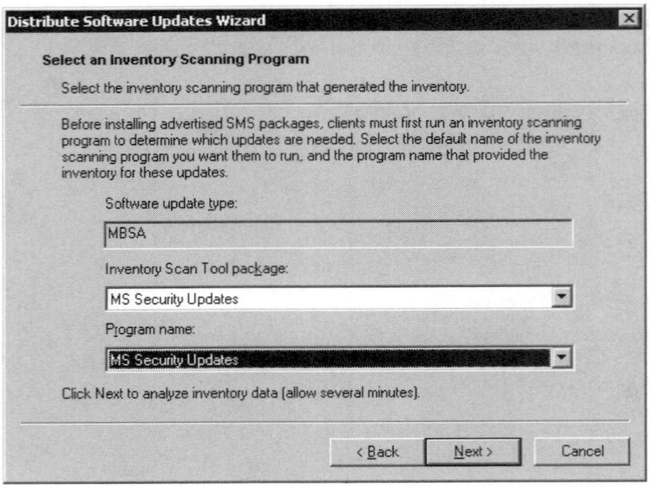

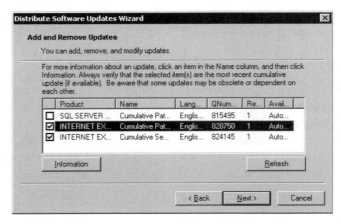

Figure 13-15. *Selecting the inventory program to run.*

The next step in the wizard allows you to select the software updates available in the update type, which need to be applied to one or more machines, as determined by a previous scan. Figure 13-16 shows an example of the updates made available for inclusion in the package. The Information button on the wizard page can be used to go to the authoritative source for information about the selected software update listed in the latest database fetched by the sync host. This provides you with an easy means of researching each update to determine whether or not to include it in the package.

Figure 13-16. *Selecting the software updates to include in the package.*

The next page in the wizard asks you to specify the package source directory, the sending priority for the package, and whether to download the software update automatically from its authoritative source. These options are shown in Figure 13-17. If directed to download update source files, the wizard visits the authoritative location for them, as detailed in the database of updates fetched by the sync host, and checks that they have been signed. If the specified package source folder does not exist, the wizard creates it. You should take care to secure the folder using the guidelines described earlier. You'll need to select the sending priority for the package: Low, Medium, or High. Lastly, on this page of the wizard, you'll need to specify whether to have the wizard automatically download the source files for the updates selected previously to the package source folder. If you choose not to download the source files automatically, or are unable to do so, the files must be copied manually to the package source folder.

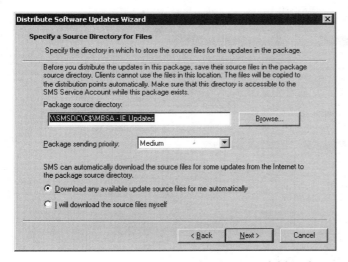

Figure 13-17. *Specifying the package source folder, the priority, and whether or not to fetch the updates.*

If you choose to have the wizard download update source files, several progress windows are displayed, similar to the one shown in Figure 13-18, as each is downloaded. If an update cannot be downloaded, perhaps because the SMS site server does not have Internet connectivity, you must fetch and manually validate the update source files and place them in the package source folder.

Figure 13-18. *The Download Progress status window.*

The next page in the wizard is the Software Updates Status page, shown in Figure 13-19. You are shown information about each of the selected software updates that will be included in the package. The first column, called Ready, is used to show whether each update is ready to be packaged. If an update is not ready, it might be because the update source files are not available or because you are required to verify the command that is run and any arguments before you can apply the update to a system.

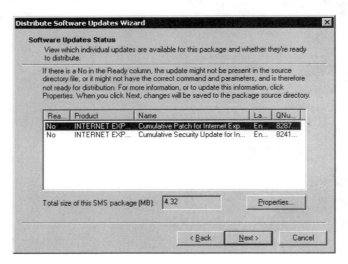

Figure 13-19. *The Software Updates Status page.*

You can check each update listed by the wizard by selecting it and clicking on the Properties button. Figure 13-20 shows the properties for an update. You should ensure that the correct program and parameters are specified to apply the software update on a client system. Many updates are interactive in nature and require command-line parameters to install successfully using SMS 2003. The information about command-line parameters for each update can be found in its bulletin, which can be viewed by clicking the Information button.

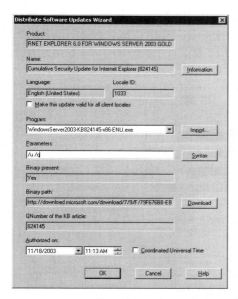

Figure 13-20. *Specifying the properties for a software update.*

You can also download the update source files to the package source folder here by clicking the Download button. The Import button is used to select the program to run, where more than one program was downloaded to the package source folder, and the Syntax button takes you to a Web page that describes in general terms the format of the command line and arguments for an update. Once the properties have been configured, click OK to save the settings.

Once you've verified all the properties for each of the updates to be included in the package, click Next to get to the next page of the wizard. Here you are prompted to select the distribution points for the package, as Figure 13-21 shows.

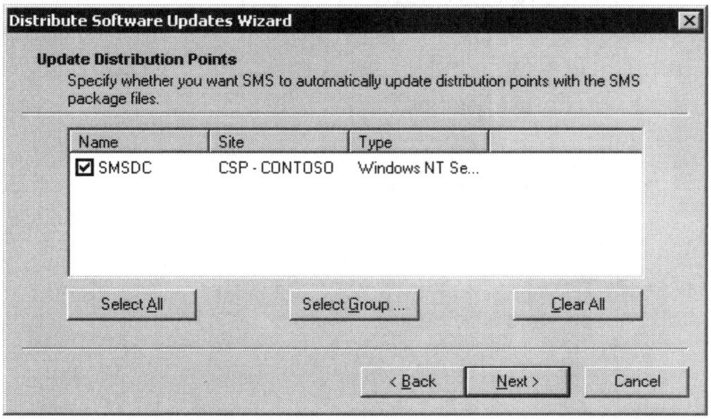

Figure 13-21. *Selecting the distribution points that will be updated with the package.*

The next page in the wizard, shown in Figure 13-22, allows you to configure installation agent settings by choosing whether to perform a client inventory after the update has been applied, whether to create reference templates, whether to postpone a reboot, and to set reboot options. The options available for postponing restarts are Never, Servers, Workstations, and Workstations And Servers.

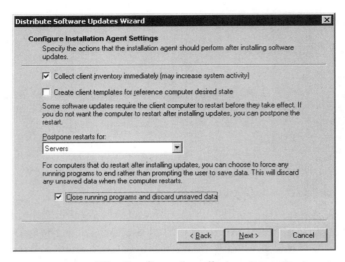

Figure 13-22. *The Configure Installation Agent Settings page.*

The next page in the Distribute Software Updates Wizard, shown in Figure 13-23, allows you to set more installation agent settings. The main choice presented to you is whether to perform an unattended installation of the update, which is recommended. For unattended installations, the logged-on user is either prompted to restart the computer or is warned of an impending restart, depending on the option selected from the After Countdown drop-down list. If the option to perform an unattended installation is not selected, the user is either prompted to install the software or is warned of an impending installation of the software updates contained within the package.

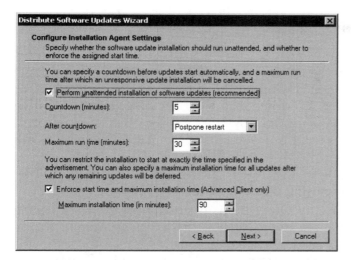

Figure 13-23. *Configuring attended or unattended installation options.*

The last set of installation agent options, displayed on the last page of the Distribute Software Updates Wizard, is used to configure whether users are prompted to run the programs in the package once it is downloaded to the client, or are allowed to postpone the operation (and, if so, for how long). The default options are shown in Figure 13-24.

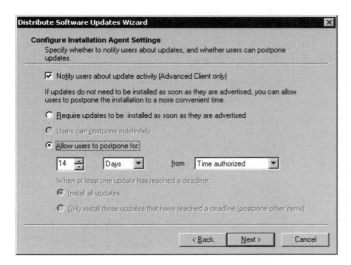

Figure 13-24. *Configuring user notification and the ability to postpone package application to a client.*

In many situations, the default settings will not be appropriate and you may choose to modify them, for example, to force updates to be installed as soon as they are advertised.

When the wizard finishes, a new package is created with programs to apply the software updates contained within it. No advertisements are created for the package, and they must be created manually. The procedure for creating advertisements is the same as it is for any other package, with the same considerations (which systems will the advertisement be made to, how often will it be made, etc.).

Considerations When Deploying Office Updates

Deploying software updates for Office is not as straightforward as deploying security updates. Office applications can be installed as an Administrative installation or as a Client installation. Software updates for each are distributed and applied differently. Administrative installation updates are applied to Administrative installations and Client installation updates are applied to Client installations. An Administrative installation update can be applied to a Client installation, but from then on, only Administrative installation updates can be applied to the installation. Not all Office updates can be applied directly using an update package downloaded from a Microsoft Web site. There are also subtle differences in the way the different versions of Office are updated. When installing updates for various versions of Office in the production environment, or when both Administrative and Client installations of Office are present, it is recommended that different collections be created and used when advertising packages containing Office updates, tailored for each collection.

The Office Resource Kits for various versions of Office contain a tool called Ohotfix.exe, which can be used to execute a series of install instructions and also can determine which updates are necessary for a particular client. The tool, along with instructions for its use with each version of Office, is available from the Microsoft Office Resource Kit Web site, found at *http://www.microsoft.com/office/ork*. To distribute updates that are installed using Ohotfix.exe, use the Distribute Software Updates Wizard to create a package and then perform the following steps:

1. Place the following files, which are used by Ohotfix.exe, into the package source folder:

   ```
   Ohotfix.exe
   Ohotfix.ini
   Ohotfix.dll
   ```

2. Edit the file Ohotfix.ini using the instructions contained within it, on the Office Resource Kit Web site, and in the bulletin for the software update. Make sure the following settings are configured as shown here to ensure a smooth installation:

```
ShowSuccessDialog=0
OHotfixUILevel=q
MSiUILevel=q
```

3. In the package source folder for the Office update, extract each update file using arguments to the update found in the bulletin describing it and then delete the update executable itself. The format of the command to extract each update will look something like the following:

```
<update name>.exe /c /t:<package source folder>
```

4. Run the Distribute Software Updates Wizard and select the package containing the updates.

5. On the Software Updates Status page, select each update in the package that is distributed to clients and click Properties.

6. In the Properties dialog box, click the Import button next to the Program text box, select Ohotfix.exe, and click OK. An error message will appear saying that the executable selected is not the recommended executable for the update and asking if you wish to proceed. Click Yes.

7. Click OK to close the Properties dialog box. An error message will appear saying that no command-line parameters have been specified. This message can be safely ignored.

Monitoring the Progress of the Deployment

Monitoring of deployment of packages created by the Distribute Software Updates Wizard can be accomplished in much the same way that other packages can be monitored, by viewing the Advertisement Status in the SMS Administrator Console. The summary view provides a snapshot of how many clients have received the advertisement and run the package successfully, and how many clients had errors when they ran the package. The detailed messages corresponding to the advertisement also can be viewed. As with other packages, you can create a query that can be used to retrieve details of the systems to which the package has been distributed. Lastly, the Software Updates node in the console also provides a snapshot of the number of systems that have applied each update either from a package distributed using SMS 2003 or by some other method such as the Windows Update Web site.

Responding to Emergencies

Even with the best planning and resources, the chances are high that at some point, an organization will have to cope with an emergency, such as a patch with an emergency release priority, a worm exploiting an unpatched vulnerability in the production environment, or the realization that a previously applied update is causing systems to fail. An organization can react to problems and resolve them more quickly if it is well prepared for the eventuality.

The patch management team should attempt to anticipate the types of emergencies that it will have to deal with, and even conduct fire drills. In the event that the entire patch management team cannot be brought together quickly enough to address an emergency, there should be a core emergency response team that has the authority to handle the problem appropriately. By far the most common emergencies requiring the participation of the patch management team are releases with accelerated timelines and the rollback of previously applied updates.

Releases with Accelerated Timelines

There can be many reasons why a release is deemed to be an emergency and the patch management team needs to accelerate the release timeline. Regardless of the reason, there can be extreme pressure to ignore the patch management process in place and deploy a software update immediately. By circumventing the process, however, organizations risk the integrity of the production environment. The four-phase patch management process recommended by Microsoft is designed to cope with emergencies and should be followed when responding to one.

> **Note** It is important to stress that just because a software update is given a critical rating by Microsoft, it doesn't necessarily translate to an emergency release for the organization. A software update is designated with an initial release priority in the identify phase of the four-phase patch management process. This initial priority is confirmed or adjusted in the Evaluate & Plan phase. If the priority is confirmed as being an emergency release, the patch management team needs to make accommodations from that point on in the process to ensure that it is dealt with in a timely fashion.

The greatest difficulty in dealing with releases with accelerated timelines is that of completing the acceptance testing for packages and the updates contained within them. Often the patch management team is faced with the prospect of having to deploy a package that has not been fully tested in order to meet the accelerated timeline. In such cases the team should concentrate on testing core functionality to ensure that day-to-day operations are not affected by the deployment of the package and application of the update. The patch management team may have to continue testing the release through deployment and afterward in order to confirm that deployment was the best course of action and to satisfy themselves that a rollback will not be required in the future.

SMS 2003 packages containing emergency releases should be advertised as mandatory, forcing clients to install them. By default advertisements that are mandatory have the option Assignments Are Not Mandatory Over Slow Links checked. The patch management team should clear this check box, found on the Schedule tab of the Advertisement Properties dialog box. For large packages which cannot be feasibly downloaded to clients connecting over slow links, such as portable computers over dial-up connections, the patch management team might wish to resort to issuing a call for those systems to be brought in to a local office for updating or some other out-of-band patch management strategy.

When an emergency release affects the servers hosting the patch management infrastructure, the patch management team might choose to patch those systems manually or out-of-band, to ensure that any necessary reboots do not affect the deployment of packages. Another consideration for the patch management infrastructure is how packages are deployed between sites. With SMS 2003, the intersite senders should be configured to remove all restrictions on the intersite senders in order to distribute the updates to other sites as quickly as possible. When links between SMS sites have too little bandwidth to cope with a large package, the patch management team might wish to consider alternatives for distributing updates to the remote sites, such as using the SMS Courier Service.

Rolling Back Software Updates

Occasionally there might be the need to roll back a previously deployed update if it is deemed to be causing or likely to cause problems in the production environment. A rollback might not always be an emergency event, and the patch management team must determine the appropriate priority to place on the event. In all cases, the team should strive to treat a rollback as though it were a software update and follow the established patch management process.

Whether or not the rollback is deemed an emergency, any ongoing deployments of the update in question should be halted. To disable the program for an update which needs to be rolled back, the SMS administrator can select the option Disable This Program On Computers Where It Is Advertised on the Advanced tab of the Program Properties dialog box. For packages that were created by the Distribute Software Updates Wizard, the SMS administrator should re-run the wizard, select the package containing the update that will be rolled back, and clear the update to remove it from the package. This will update the contents of the package, removing the update in question and leaving other updates in the package intact. If there are no other updates in the package, the SMS administrator can delete the advertisement and the package.

The mechanism for rolling back an update is update-specific. Not all software updates, especially updates addressing security vulnerabilities or updates to core components of an operating system, can be rolled back. For those that can be rolled back, the administrator needs to determine what the command to initiate the rollback is, build a package with a program to invoke it, and deploy it. The SMS administrator has two options when deploying a rollback package. The first is to have the rollback program determine whether or not the update has been applied to a system before initiating the rollback and advertise the package with the program to the same systems that the software update was advertised to, and the second is to attempt to identify the systems which applied the update and target an advertisement for a package with the program that performs a rollback to these systems.

Summary

The Microsoft-recommended four-phase patch management process, documented in Microsoft Solutions for Management 2.5, describes a process that can be applied to organizations of all sizes. The four phases, Assess, Identify, Evaluate & Plan, and Deploy, contain prescriptive steps that the organization should follow to ensure successful updates to the configuration of the production environment.

The vulnerability rating for every alert received by an organization's patch management team should be examined for guidance on the level of attention that the software update should receive. The team should look at mitigating factors and factors inherent to their production priority and assign a release priority to the update. The update then needs to be tested and accepted and a release plan developed before deployment can begin. After an update has been successfully applied to systems in the production environment, the organization needs to update the secure baseline configurations for its IT assets and use them when deploying new systems.

SMS 2003 can be extended with the Security Update Inventory Tool and the Microsoft Office Inventory Tool for Updates, both part of the Software Update Scanning Tools download available from Microsoft. The extensions allow SMS to scan clients for recommended security and Office updates from Microsoft and report centrally which updates have been installed and which updates should be installed. The Distribute Software Updates Wizard allows the SMS administrator to quickly build packages containing software updates and advertise them to SMS clients.

Each organization should expect and plan for emergency situations in which a software update has to be deployed in an expedited fashion, or a previously deployed update needs to be rolled back. In both situations, the patch management team should follow through with its patch management process to guarantee the integrity of the production environment.

Scripting an installation is a significant requirement for most organizations that want their package distribution or software updates to be "hands-off" to the user. Chapter 14, "Microsoft Systems Management Server Installer," introduces a utility that can assist you in creating a fully scripted and unattended installation package for SMS to distribute—the SMS Installer.

Chapter 14
Microsoft Systems Management Server Installer

As we saw in Chapter 12, "Package Distribution and Management," SMS 2003's package distribution function is primarily a delivery tool. It's ultimately the SMS administrator's responsibility to create the package, including all scripts and information files, and to test the veracity of the package. Thus the ability to create scripts and somehow bundle the package to ease the installation becomes an integral part of the package distribution process for many organizations and administrators.

For software applications that need to be installed on client computers, the most sought-after characteristic of the script is that it be fully unattended—in other words, you don't want the user to have any interaction with the installation process. This separation ensures a standard installation and minimizes questions and confusion on the part of the user. SMS 2003, of course, doesn't offer this kind of functionality natively. Installation isn't the responsibility of the SMS package distribution process. Remember our package delivery example in Chapter 12. Package delivery services such as Federal Express and United Parcel Service are entrusted with getting your package to its destination, but not with the assembly of its contents—the same holds true for SMS. It's your responsibility to ensure that the package includes everything needed to run successfully on a target computer. SMS just sees that the package gets there and runs.

Fortunately, several third-party applications are available whose main function is to create packages. The Sysdiff utility, one the many utilities included in the Windows 2000 Server Resource Kit for example, essentially takes before and after snapshots of a system in order to bundle application installation with operating system installation. Microsoft provides a package scripting utility for SMS called SMS Installer. The current version of SMS Installer includes the Windows Installer Step-up Utility (ISU). This command-line utility lets you convert setup packages created with SMS Installer to the Windows Installer format.

In this chapter we'll look first at SMS Installer and its initial installation; then we'll explore the software repackaging process. Next, we'll focus on modifying installation scripts using the Installation Expert and Script Editor. Finally, we'll explore rolling back and uninstalling a scripted installation and look at some of the updates to SMS Installer.

More Info The SMS Installer Help is an excellent source of additional information about how to use the application and how to interpret and fill in the various dialog boxes. Another good source of information is Chapter 7 in the *Microsoft Systems Management Server 2003 Operations Guide*, available through Microsoft TechNet and the SMS Web site (*http://www.microsoft.com/ smserver*). Finally, I highly recommend the book *Microsoft SMS Installer* (McGraw-Hill Osborne Media, 2004), written by Rod Trent (who also manages the MYITForum Web site, *http://www.myitforum.com*, an excellent source of peer support for SMS administrators).

Overview

SMS Installer enables you to create customized, self-extracting, software installation files. The SMS Installer–generated executable files let you install software with the SMS package distribution feature. Scripted installation makes installing software easier and less prone to error. The self-extracting executable files contain everything necessary to install the software, including an installation script to control the installation process. The SMS Installer compiler creates the self-extracting files. SMS package distribution is generally used to deliver these files to users. However, you could certainly distribute these files using other methods—for example, by packaging the files on disks, placing them on a Web site, or even attaching them to an e-mail message.

SMS Installer is really more like a developer's tool, and as such it requires intensive study to truly master. The basic process lets you quickly run through an application installation, repackage the application into a script, and distribute it. This basic process is actually quite intuitive and can be learned and accomplished in relatively short order. However, usually you'll want something more elegant than a simple repackaging of the script, and to accomplish this you can use one of two tools: the Installation Expert or Script Editor. Using Script Editor requires a higher level of expertise.

It might take several months of practice creating, testing, and modifying scripts using SMS Installer before you feel truly comfortable. Don't let this scare you off. SMS Installer is a fine, well thought out, and useful tool for amateur and expert script developers alike. At its high end, however, it's certainly not simple and requires effort and motivation on your part. In this chapter we focus on the

Repackage and Installation Expert components of SMS Installer—the two components that are easiest to master. For more specific information, especially regarding use of Script Editor, refer to the SMS Installer Help and Chapter 7 in the *Microsoft Systems Management Server 2003 Operations Guide.*

Installing Systems Management Server Installer

SMS Installer is available for download from the SMS Web site (*http://www.microsoft.com/smserver*). To use SMS Installer, you must first download the self-extracting executable file Smsimain.exe and then run it on an SMS 2003 primary site server. The executable file checks to see whether the server is a primary site server. If the server isn't a primary site server, the installation stops. If the server is a primary site server, the SMS Installer files are copied to a directory you specify or by default to %SystemDrive%:\SMS Installer Setup. SMS Installer itself consists of a single self-extracting file, Smsinstl.exe, that you can copy and run on a reference computer. We'll talk about reference computers in detail later in this chapter. Smsinstl.exe includes all the SMS Installer support files needed to set up the utility on a reference computer.

Identifying and Configuring a Reference Computer

The next phase is to configure a reference computer. SMS Installer supports any computer running Windows 95 and higher and requires about 5 MB of RAM and at least 6 to 11 MB of hard disk space for the installation. The reference computer must be a standard desktop configuration that's representative of your target computers. This computer contains the applications and registry settings that are configured on the end-user systems. It's critical that the reference computer be identical to the computer systems on which you'll be installing the final software package. Be sure to check the following system components:

- **Hardware devices**   The devices installed on the reference computer should match those installed on prospective target clients, including graphics cards, modems, I/O configurations, and disk drive configurations, especially if the application references these components during its installation.

- **Operating system**   The reference computer's operating system should match that of all target systems, including version number and perhaps even service packs installed, especially if the application is platform specific.

- **Installed applications**   The reference computer and all target computers should have the same applications installed. Unless the repackaged application has a specific dependency on an existing application, the reference computer should contain only software that the repackaging process directly needs.

- **Directory structure**   If your script includes telling the application where to place the application's installation files, it's imperative that the reference computer's directory structure and the directory structures of the prospective target clients be standardized. Any changes, however insignificant they might be in the mind of the user—for example, moving or renaming the Program Files directory—can result in failure to run the script.

As you can see, the choice and configuration of the reference computer is one of the keys to creating a successful script using SMS Installer.

> **Caution**   If the original setup program for a software application needs to detect hardware during installation and if subsequent target computers don't have identical hardware and drive configurations that match the reference computer, a repackaged SMS Installer installation will most likely fail. Similarly, if the original installation program updates or modifies data files and the target computers don't contain the same configuration as the reference computer, the SMS Installer–generated files won't be installed correctly. For this reason specifically, it's not recommended that you run SMS Installer on an SMS client.

Installing Systems Management Server Installer on the Reference Computer

Once you've selected and properly configured the reference computer, you can install SMS Installer. Remember, the more closely the reference computer resembles the proposed target computers, the higher the rate of success for using SMS Installer.

To install SMS Installer, follow these steps:

1. Copy the Smsinstl.exe self-extracting executable file to the reference computer.

2. Run Smsinstl.exe to start the Microsoft SMS Installer Installation Wizard. Read the license agreement that displays and click Agree to display the Microsoft SMS Installer Installation Welcome page, shown in Figure 14-1.

Figure 14-1.   *The Microsoft SMS Installer Wizard Welcome page.*

3. Click Next to display the Select Destination Directory page, shown in
   Figure 14-2. Specify the destination directory for the SMS Installer
   files. By default, they will be placed in a folder named Microsoft SMS
   Installer under the Program Files directory.

Figure 14-2.   *The Select Destination Directory page.*

4. Click Next to display the Backup Replaced Files? page, shown in
   Figure 14-3. From this page you specify whether to create a backup of
   all files replaced during the installation. Select Yes to keep a copy of
   the files that are changed during the SMS Installer installation. Select
   No to overwrite these files.

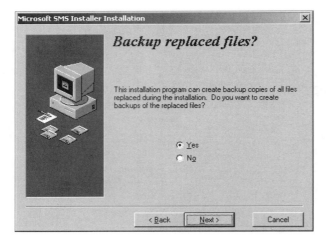

Figure 14-3. *The Backup Replaced Files? page.*

5. Click Next to display the Select Backup Directory page, shown in Figure 14-4, and select a location for the backup files to be written to. (This page won't appear if you selected No in the previous page.) By default, the backup files will be written to a folder named \Backup in the installation folder you defined in step 3.

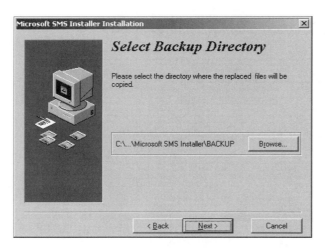

Figure 14-4. *The Select Backup Directory page.*

6. Click Next to display the Ready To Install page, shown in Figure 14-5.

Figure 14-5.   *The Ready To Install page.*

7. Click Next to copy the files and then display the Installation Completed page, shown in Figure 14-6. Click Finish to exit the SMS Installer installation process.

Figure 14-6.   *The Installation Completed page.*

Once the installation of SMS Installer is complete, the utility is ready for use. When SMS Installer is installed, it creates its own program group on the Start menu. You can access the utility by choosing Programs from the Start menu and then selecting the Microsoft SMS Installer program group. Alternatively, you can navigate directly to the Program Files\Microsoft SMS Installer directory through Windows Explorer. With either method, you'll be able to select the appropriate development environment by selecting the appropriate program entry in the SMS Installer program group or by double-clicking Smsins32.exe.

Systems Management Server Installer Tools

Before we go into the details of actually using the SMS Installer utility, let's look at the tools that SMS Installer uses to create and customize the SMS Installer executable files. To create and customize the installation scripts, SMS Installer uses two interfaces: the Installation Expert and Script Editor.

Installation Expert

The Installation Expert automatically creates a basic installation script using the reference computer's configuration. The installation script contains commands that perform the actions necessary to carry out the installation. You can modify the actions performed within the script by configuring the installation attributes; we'll discuss these attributes in the section entitled "Installation Attributes" later in this chapter.

Once the basic script has been created, you can use Script Editor (discussed in the next section) to customize the installation script for specific user functions. However, you'll find it much easier to generate the installation script using the Installation Expert. This technique allows you to create a basic installation script and switch between the Installation Expert and Script Editor to perform modifications. This approach also prevents potential loss of data that can occur if you initially create the installation script using Script Editor and then switch to the Installation Expert. The Installation Expert provides two methods for packaging script files: the Repackage Installation Wizard and the Watch Application Wizard. The application for which you're creating the script file will determine which of these wizards you'll use. The Installation Expert also provides several other tools to test and compile the installation script and to run the installation package. We'll look at each tool in the following sections.

Repackage Installation Wizard

If the application you're attempting to install currently contains a setup file, you might need to repackage the setup file along with the source files and any other support files for distribution to the target clients. You use the Repackage Installation Wizard to accomplish this task. In a single-computer environment, installation of an application typically requires running a setup program. More often than not, during the installation you'll be asked for specific input concerning the setup. For a single workstation setup, this situation is fine. When we talk about distributing these applications to hundreds of users and we want to have control over the input selection, however, we need to provide the input to the setup by some other means. The repackaging process allows us to provide the answers to installation questions and set specific configurations that will apply to all our client machines. When we run the Repackage Installation Wizard, the reference computer is monitored for changes and a script file is generated from the changes made during setup.

Watch Application Wizard

You can use the Watch Application Wizard to create a customized installation file for those applications that don't have their own setup programs by "watching" the files used while the application is run and creating a script from them. In many cases, such as with custom or proprietary applications, a setup file hasn't been created for the application, and we're faced with the problem of how to successfully distribute the application to the clients. The Watch Application Wizard creates an SMS Installer–generated executable file that's used to install the program and all its supporting components, such as DLLs. The wizard runs the existing application on the reference computer and tracks the files being used by the application. Using this list of files, an installation script is created for the application.

The Watch Application Wizard is also useful for applications that make calls for Microsoft Visual Basic support files or run-time files. The repackaging process will catch all the application files, but not necessarily those called from outside the application directory. In this case you can use the Watch Application Wizard to look for these files and add them to the installation script for the application.

Compile

The SMS Installer compiler is used to create the self-extracting installation file. After you have created your installation script and made all the necessary modifications to the installation attributes, the script file is compiled into an executable file. This SMS Installer–generated file contains the script and all the necessary application files. It's the final file that's distributed throughout your organization.

Files created at compile time include the following (*Testapp* represents the file name you provided):

- **Testapp.exe**   The installation executable, including the script and all necessary application files in a compressed format.

- **Testapp.pdf and Testapp.sms**   The standard SMS package definition file used to distribute the SMS Installer–generated file to the target computers through SMS package distribution. Two versions of this file are created: one with the old .PDF extension used with earlier versions of SMS and supported in SMS 2.0 and one with the new, preferred .SMS extension adopted by Microsoft to avoid confusion with other market applications that use the .PDF extension.

Note   These files are created only if the Create Package Definition File option is selected in the SMS tab of the Installation Interface dialog box. For more information about the settings on this tab, refer to the section entitled "Modifying Installation Scripts Using the Installation Expert" later in this chapter.

- **Testapp.ipf**   Text version of the installation script used when making modifications to the script through the SMS Installer utility.

- **Testapp.wsm**   Additional working file used by the installation script to maintain changes made to the script before it gets compiled.

Test

You use the Test tool to test the installation executable file without actually installing it. By running Test from the Installation Expert, you can preview how your setup script will actually run. Are the correct menus presented? Does the installation run unattended? These are the things we can test locally before distributing the installation package.

Keep in mind that Test doesn't really install the application and run it. Test simply copies needed files such as help files and DLL files to the \Temp directory. As always, it's good practice to select a pilot test group for testing the installation before distributing the package to your entire organization.

Run

The Run tool lets you run the installation program on the reference computer. Run will test the SMS Installer–generated file exactly as it will run on the target computers. Run will install the application and make any changes to the system that are required, including registry modifications.

Caution   If you plan to run the installation on the reference computer, you'll need to remove the application (along with any registry settings that were created or modified) that was installed during the repackaging process. Otherwise, the installation might fail when it attempts to create or write to directories needed for the installation.

Script Editor

You use Script Editor to edit the basic installation script generated by the Installation Expert or to create or modify your own installation script. Script Editor allows you to tune the installation script for customization and optimization. You can also modify such items as file locations, registry settings, and user prompts. You can also add many of the functions that can be manually configured through Script Editor to the script by configuring them in the Installation Expert. You can add some functions only through the Script Editor window. For example, you can configure uninstall support using either method, but you can configure support for rollback (which enables you to remove patches rather than uninstalling the application outright) only through Script Editor. We'll discuss uninstall and rollback support in the section entitled "Rolling Back and Uninstalling a Scripted Installation" later in this chapter.

Script Editor provides a much higher level of control over the action of the script. Learning to use this tool effectively takes a long time. It also requires an intimate understanding of how the application's installation routine works—including what files and directories are modified, what registry entries are added or configured, what external DLL support is required, whether a restart is required, and what happens as a result.

Now that you have a working knowledge of the SMS Installer tools, let's look at how to use SMS Installer to create the installation script.

Creating Installation Scripts

To begin the process of creating an installation script, start SMS Installer to launch the Installation Expert interface, as shown in Figure 14-7.

Figure 14-7.   *The Installation Expert interface.*

We'll begin the process of creating an SMS Installer–generated executable by running the Repackage Installation Wizard. In this example we'll create the Microsoft TechNet installation executable.

To create the installation executable, follow these steps:

1. In the Installation Expert interface, click Repackage to launch the Repackage Installation Wizard, shown in Figure 14-8.

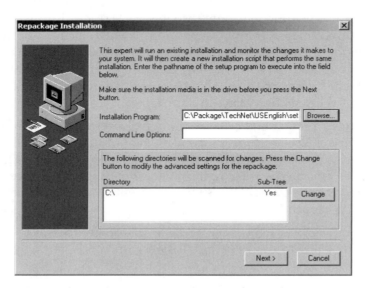

Figure 14-8. *The Repackage Installation Wizard page.*

2. On the Repackage Installation Wizard page, you configure the name and path of the setup program used by the application for installation. You might also need to add any other command-line arguments that the setup program might need.

3. In the Directory list, configure any directories you want to be included in the list of directories to be scanned during the installation process. To add a drive or directory, click Change to open the Repackage Advanced Settings dialog box, shown in Figure 14-9.

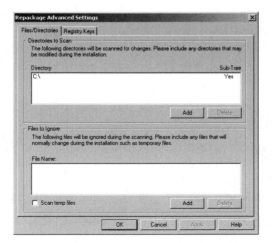

Figure 14-9.   *The Repackage Advanced Settings dialog box.*

4. In the Directories To Scan section of the Files/Directories tab, click Add to display the Select Directory dialog box, shown in Figure 14-10.

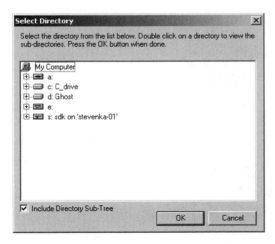

Figure 14-10.   *The Select Directory dialog box.*

5. In the Select Directory dialog box, we can select the root directory or we can select only the specific subdirectories we want to scan. Narrowing the scan can save significant time during the repackaging process. As a general rule, you don't want to scan every directory if you know some directories won't be affected during the installation.

6. When you have added all the directories you want to scan, click OK. The directories are added to the Directory list.

7. Next, we'll configure the directories and files we want to ignore during the scan process. Again, being selective here can improve the performance of the installation process. In the Files To Ignore section of the Files/Directories tab, click Add to display the Open dialog box, as shown in Figure 14-11.

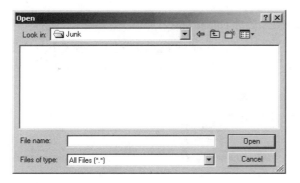

Figure 14-11. *The Open dialog box.*

8. For this example, the C:\junk directory won't contain any files pertaining to our installation of Microsoft TechNet, so we can ignore this entire directory. Select the C:\junk directory by double-clicking on it, and then enter *.* in the File Name text box to include all files in this directory. If you wanted to exclude a specific file in a folder, select that file.

9. Click Open to add the directory, or files, to the File Name list, as shown in Figure 14-12.

Figure 14-12.   *The modified File Name list.*

10. You can also specify whether to ignore scanning of any temporary files during the installation process. To scan temporary files, select the Scan Temp Files check box.

11. To specify the registry keys and values to scan or ignore during the installation process, select the Registry Keys tab, shown in Figure 14-13.

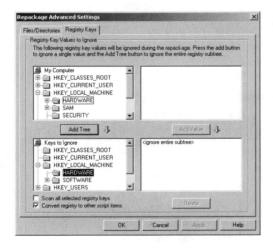

Figure 14-13.   *The Registry Keys tab.*

Caution Selecting registry keys to scan or ignore can be a tricky business. Be especially careful not to overlook or choose to ignore a key that's altered during the setup process—doing so would invariably render your installation script worthless. On the other hand, the installation can change something such as a DHCP address setting by releasing and renewing an IP setting during a system restart, which is unrelated to the installation itself and shouldn't be included in the installation script. Your best bet is to get to know the keys that your installation will affect and once you have created the final script, test, test, test!

12. The Registry Keys tab contains four panes. The top two panes represent the current registry settings read from the reference computer. The lower two panes represent the registry settings that are to be ignored. In the top-left pane, under My Computer, select the registry trees or values you want to ignore. To add the registry subtree to the list of subtrees to ignore, click Add Tree. To add a key you want to ignore, select the key in the upper-right pane, and then click Add Value. The lower-left pane shows where the selected keys are located on the reference computer; the lower-right pane lists their values. Select Scan All Selected Registry Keys to scan for hardware registry entries to ignore. Select Convert Registry To Other Script Items to convert ODBC changes and installation of services to the Install ODBC Driver, Configure ODBC Data Source, and Create Service script items.

13. Click OK to return to the Repackage Installation page, and then click Next to begin the scanning and installation process of our application, as shown in Figure 14-14.

Figure 14-14. *The Repackage Installation page showing the scanning process.*

During the installation phase, the Repackage Installation Wizard will run Setup.exe with any switches you provided in the initial configuration of the wizard The setup will run exactly as it normally does. Remember that you're providing the installation options that will be used during the actual setup of the application on the target computers.

14. After the Repackage Installation Wizard has completed the setup of the application, click Next to rescan the directories and registry settings, as shown in Figure 14-15. The wizard will compare the system image before and after the installation of the software.

Note You might also want to add application setups during this repackaging process—for example, you might want to distribute several applications within one silent installation process. To accomplish this, click Run Setup to run the next setup and add the additional software. Keep in mind the size of these packages as we begin to install larger, more complex applications or multiple applications in a single SMS Installer–generated executable.

Figure 14-15. *The Repackage Installation page showing the rescanning process.*

15. When the rescan of the directories and registry keys is complete, click Finish to complete the repackaging process.

At this point, clicking Compile in the Installation Expert interface will generate a basic script that, while perhaps not very elegant, might certainly be adequate for distribution. You could use the Installation Expert to verify the installation configuration that was created during the repackaging process and then modify and customize the script to meet the particular needs of your users and organization.

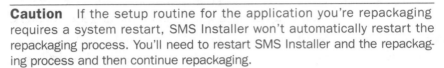

Caution If the setup routine for the application you're repackaging requires a system restart, SMS Installer won't automatically restart the repackaging process. You'll need to restart SMS Installer and the repackaging process and then continue repackaging.

Modifying Installation Scripts Using the Installation Expert

After we've created the installation script, we can begin the process of modifying and customizing it to fit our specific needs. As we've seen, the Installation Expert and Script Editor allow us to modify our installation scripts. In this section we'll look at how to modify installation scripts using the Installation Expert. But first let's look at the installation attributes.

Installation Attributes

You need to consider six sets of installation attributes when modifying installation scripts, as follows:

- **Installation Interface** Enables you to configure the settings used by the SMS Installer–generated executable during installation.

- **Application Files** Enables you to configure specific components to install based on the type of installation you select.

- **Runtime Support** Enables you to configure uninstall support and to add components for Visual Basic or Visual FoxPro. The Visual Basic components you select will affect how the Watch Application Wizard performs.

- **User Configuration** Enables you to set up the program groups and icons and to configure file associations for the installation.

- **System Configuration** Enables you to change or reconfigure the system environment during the installation process.

- **Advanced Configuration** Enables you to configure such items as the screen settings that will be displayed during the installation, language settings, and patch settings, as well as global attributes that will control the actual installation file.

You can configure these attribute sets in the Installation Expert interface, shown in Figure 14-7. Select an installation attribute and click Properties to display its Properties dialog box, where you can customize the installation script through a relatively user-friendly graphical interface.

Modifying the Script

In this section we'll customize the settings for our SMS Installer–generated executable file using the Installation Expert. In this example we'll also modify the script by editing the installation attributes to facilitate an "unattended" installation.

To modify the script using the Installation Expert, follow these steps:

1. From the Installation Expert interface, select Installation Interface from the list in the Installation Attributes section and then click Properties or double-click Installation Interface to display the Installation Interface dialog box, shown in Figure 14-16.

Figure 14-16. *The Installation Interface dialog box.*

2. In the Media tab you can specify whether the SMS Installer–generated executable file will be a single file, used for network or Web distribution; or multiple files, used for floppy disk–based installation. For this example, verify that the Single File Installation option is selected. This

will cause SMS Installer to generate a single executable file when we compile our script. If you choose Floppy Based Installation, you must also select the appropriate disk size in the Settings section at the bottom of the Media tab.

3. Select the Application tab, shown in Figure 14-17. In this tab you can specify the application name that will be used in wizard pages and in the welcome page. This name is also displayed with the program icon. The name you use should be descriptive of the product being installed. You can also enter or modify the default directory that the application will be installed to. This option should be set to the top-level directory used for the application installation. If appropriate, select the Place Default Directory Under Program Files check box to place the default directory in the Program Files folder. SMS installs the application in the Program Files folder on Windows 95 and later by default.

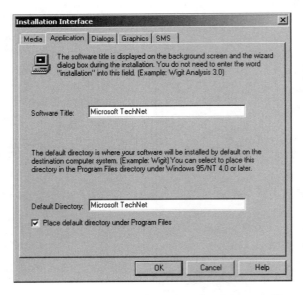

Figure 14-17. *The Application tab of the Installation Interface dialog box.*

4. Select the Dialogs tab, shown in Figure 14-18. This tab represents the dialog boxes the user will see when the script is run at a client computer. (You can also create your own custom dialog boxes and have them displayed through Script Editor.) To suppress all the dialog boxes

that are displayed to the user for an unattended installation, clear all the screen options in this tab. The only item that the user will see will be a progress bar indicating that the installation script for the application is running. To enable uninstall or rollback support, select the Back Up Replaced Files option. If you want to facilitate a "silent" installation, you can also enable this option through Script Editor. For a detailed discussion on enabling this option, refer to the section entitled "Enabling Rollback Support" later in this chapter.

Figure 14-18.   *The Dialogs tab of the Installation Interface dialog box.*

Note   You can effect a fully silent installation—one that doesn't display the progress bar or any dialog boxes—by running the compiled script on the client with a "/s" switch. If you're using SMS to distribute the SMS Installer file, be sure to include the "/s" switch on the command line for the program you create. Fully silent installations are best used on Windows computers, such as servers, which are rarely in a logged-on state. Performing a silent installation on a user's workstation can cause problems because the user will be unaware that anything is happening. Unpredictable results can occur if, for example, the user decides to log off or restart the system while the script is running.

5. Select the Graphics tab, shown in Figure 14-19. You can configure this tab to display custom graphics, such as a custom logo, text boxes that display animation or tips, and so on, in the form of .BMP files during the installation. Figure 14-19 shows a sample bitmap added, although in our example we won't add any graphics. If you select the graphic file and click Details, you can modify several graphic settings, including the file path and where and how the graphic is positioned on the screen.

Figure 14-19.   *The Graphics tab of the Installation Interface dialog box.*

6. Select the SMS tab, shown in Figure 14-20. You use these settings during a rollout of our application using the SMS distribution process. In this tab you can specify whether to have the installation process generate a status MIF file for status reporting to SMS 2003. If you choose to create an MIF file, enter the name for the status MIF files for installation and deinstallation of the application. You must supply a filename and the .MIF extension for both installation and deinstallation if you enable rollback or uninstall support. Select the Create Package Definition File check box if you want to create a package definition file (.SMS) when creating the package for distribution through SMS 2003.

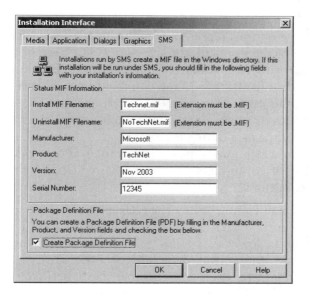

Figure 14-20. *The SMS tab of the Installation Interface dialog box.*

7. Click OK to return to the Installation Expert interface. Select Application Files and then click Properties to display the Application Files dialog box, shown in Figure 14-21.

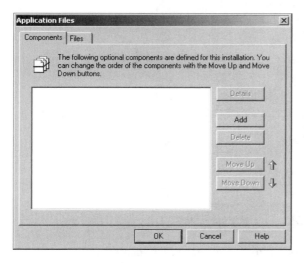

Figure 14-21. *The Application Files dialog box.*

8. In the Components tab you can select a list of optional components for the installation. These options represent components the user can install during execution of the installation of the script. For example, suppose a custom Microsoft Access database installation contains three database files that can be installed. You can identify each database as a component in this tab. (Then, in the Files tab, you can identify which database files are associated with each component.) Components are listed for the user during the execution of the installation script in the order in which they appear in this tab. You can add, sort, or modify the list of components using the Move Up, Move Down, Add, and Delete buttons.

9. Select the Files tab, shown in Figure 14-22. The Files tab contains four panes. In the top two panes, locate the folders or files you want to include in your script. In the lower two panes, select a location on the destination computer at which to install these folders or files. You can add or remove files to your installation. For example, if you needed to include customized Microsoft Word templates as part of the installation, you could add them here.

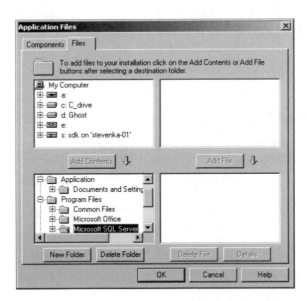

Figure 14-22. *The Files tab of the Application Files dialog box.*

10. Click OK to return to the Installation Expert interface, select Runtime Support, and click Properties to display the Runtime Support dialog box, shown in Figure 14-23.

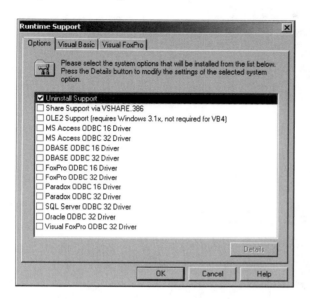

Figure 14-23.   *The Runtime Support dialog box.*

11. In the Options tab you can configure uninstall support, which is enabled by default, and specify the support drivers needed for the SMS Installer–generated executable file. For this example we've left the default setting for Uninstall Support selected for rollback support.

Note   Two additional tabs are available for the Runtime Support attribute: the Visual Basic tab and the Visual FoxPro tab. In the Visual Basic tab you can configure Visual Basic support, including the Visual Basic directory and application type. You can also select Visual Basic options such as runtime support. In the Visual FoxPro tab you can configure Visual FoxPro support, including the Visual FoxPro directory and other options such as runtime support and OLE Control Extension (OCX) support. Refer to the SMS Installer Help for more information about these tabs.

12. Click OK, select User Configuration, and click Properties to display the User Configuration dialog box, shown in Figure 14-24.

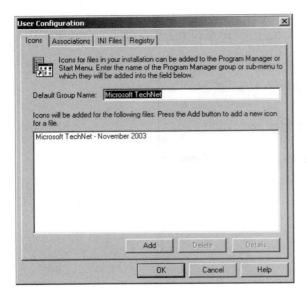

Figure 14-24. *The User Configuration dialog box.*

13. In the Icons tab, specify the name of the program group to which icons will be added. You can also specify additional icons to be added to the program group or even delete icons that shouldn't be added to the program group. For example, you might choose to remove an Uninstall icon that the original setup program included in the program group but that you don't want to expose to the user.

14. To verify modifications to file associations and INI files, select the Associations tab and the INI Files tab. The Associations tab allows you to specify and modify file associations for files being installed; the INI Files tab allows you to specify the INI files and their entries requiring modification during setup. For example, if you know that you need to modify the net heap size entry in the System.ini file on a Windows 98 computer after an application is installed, you could do so in the INI Files tab as part of the installation script.

15. To display the registry changes made during execution of the installation script, select the Registry tab, shown in Figure 14-25.

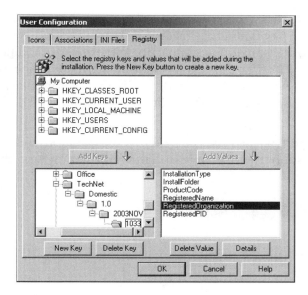

Figure 14-25.   *The Registry tab of the User Configuration dialog box.*

16. You can modify certain registry settings from this tab. For example, in this TechNet installation, we want to change the setting for the registered organization. Under Destination Computer, navigate to the HKEY_LOCAL_MACHINE\SOFTWARE\Microsoft\TechNet\ Domestic\1.0\2003NOV\1033 key, and select RegisteredOrganization.

17. Click Details to display the Registry Key Settings dialog box, shown in Figure 14-26. In this dialog box you can make changes to the registry key settings. Click OK to close the dialog box and click OK once more to return to the Installation Expert window.

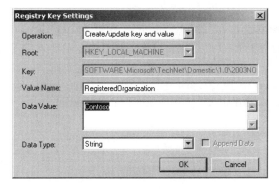

Figure 14-26.   *The Registry Key Settings dialog box.*

You should verify and modify the two remaining installation attributes—System Configuration and Advanced Configuration—according to your specific target computer needs. Although our installation example doesn't make any modifications to these attributes, let's look at the two installation attribute Properties dialog boxes briefly. Keep in mind that you need to verify these settings just as we've verified our other attribute settings. To configure these Properties dialog boxes, follow these steps:

1. In the Installation Expert window, select System Configuration and click Properties to display the System Configuration dialog box, shown in Figure 14-27.

Figure 14-27. *The System Configuration dialog box.*

2. In the Devices tab, you can add or delete devices or modify device properties on 16-bit Windows systems. This tab modifies the [386Enh] section of the System.ini file.

3. Select the Services tab, shown in Figure 14-28. Here you can add system services to, or modify system services in, the Control Panel.

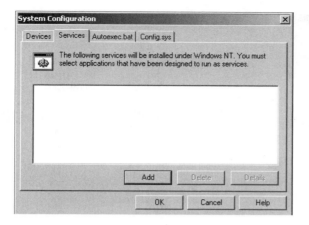

Figure 14-28. *The Services tab of the System Configuration dialog box.*

4. Select the Autoexec.bat tab, shown in Figure 14-29. In this tab, you can produce a script that will modify the system's Autoexec.bat file by adding new lines or appending to existing lines, such as altering the PATH statement or adding SET variable statements.

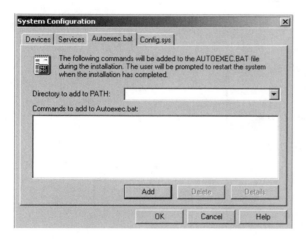

Figure 14-29. *The Autoexec.bat tab of the System Configuration dialog box.*

5. Select the Config.sys tab, shown in Figure 14-30. In this tab, you can produce a script to modify the Config.sys file. After you configure each of these tabs, click OK to return to the Installation Expert interface.

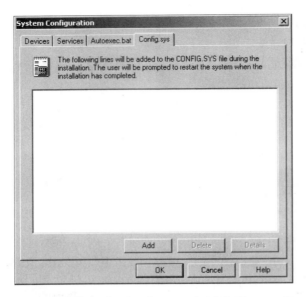

Figure 14-30. *The Config.sys tab of the System Configuration dialog box.*

6. Select Advanced Configuration and click Properties to display the Advanced Configuration dialog box, shown in Figure 14-31.

Figure 14-31. *The Advanced Configuration dialog box.*

7. In the Global tab, you can modify the installation file settings, such as compression, log settings, suppression of reboot message during silent installs, and use of an installation password.

8. Select the Screen tab, where you can select options for the installation progress bar settings and display background gradient of installation dialog boxes. Display color options used during the installation can also be selected here.

9. Select the Font tab to specify the default font used to display all installation screens and dialog boxes.

10. Select the Languages tab to configure the language settings used for the installation.

11. Select the Options tab, where you can specify the Script Editor and compiler settings to be used by SMS Installer. You can also set options for the Watch Application Wizard to ignore specific DLLs.

12. Select the Settings tab, where you can specify the paths (or browse for) the installation executable file, the .INI file that contains language translations for the installation, the setup icon, the directory that contains setup dialog boxes, and the directory that contains temporary files.

13. Select the Patching tab, where you can create patching versions of files. You can select patching threshold levels based on a percentage of change to an existing file, configure memory settings used during the patch process, and configure the compression level for patch files.

14. Select the Compiler Variables tab, where you can configure the compiler used during the compilation of the installation script and enable user-prompted compiler variables when compiling from the command prompt.

15. Select the Signing tab, where you can set up a secure installation environment used in 32-bit installations. From this tab, you can also create a CAB-formatted installation file and supply the contents of Setup.inf, commonly used during setup to provide installation settings.

16. Select the Version tab, where you can enter additional information about the setup program, such as a description, copyright information, company name, product version, and so on.

As you can see, these installation attributes will enable you to modify your installation script and help it to compile and run more smoothly. Although you can configure these options prior to running the Repackage Installation Wizard or the Watch Application Wizard, it's usually a good idea to return to the Installation Expert after running either wizard and verify all your configuration options and settings.

> **More Info** Refer to the SMS Installer Help for more information about each tab in the installation attribute Properties windows.

Modifying Installation Scripts Using Script Editor

As we've seen, we can use SMS Installer's graphical menus and attribute settings to configure our installation scripts to suit our specific needs. Under different circumstances, however, these tools might not give us all the control needed to fully customize our SMS Installer–generated script file. Likewise, specific situations might arise in which it's more efficient or just faster and easier to use a scripting method to make changes.

It really doesn't matter how we go about creating our scripted installation. Remember, we can generate our initial script using either the Repackage Installation Wizard or the Watch Application Wizard. These two methods are probably preferred, as they give us a good basic script that we can customize using the Script Editor utility. Or we can open the Script Editor interface to modify an existing script or even begin scripting from scratch. In this section we'll explore Script Editor variables and actions and then look at how to modify installation scripts using Script Editor.

Script Editor Variables and Actions

The Script Editor provided by SMS Installer is a powerful scripting utility. It provides a vast array of variables and actions (SMS Installer commands) that let you optimize the script files used by the installation process. Script variables contain information about the installation being performed. We can use these variables to hold the information gathered from users about where to place files. Script variables can also be used to hold information about which files users want to install. Additionally, a number of predefined variables contain information about the target computer system on which you're installing software.

Before we look at how to make modifications to a script using Script Editor, let's review some common scripting variables and actions. The following tables aren't intended as a comprehensive list of all the available variables and actions, but rather as a short list of those more commonly used.

> **More Info** Refer to the SMS Installer Help for a comprehensive list of scripting variables and actions.

Table 14-1 lists several predefined variables and the values they are designed to return.

Table 14-1.   Predefined variables

Variable	Returns
WIN	The path of the Windows directory—for example, C:\Windows.
SYS32	The system directory for Win32 files under Windows NT and higher—for example, C:\Winnt\System32.
TEMP	The path of the temporary directory on the reference computer. An application often uses this directory to store DLLs before referencing them.
CMDLINE	The command-line options that are passed to the SMS Installer–generated file.
PASSWORD	The installation password assigned to a password-protected installation.

As we write our script, we can have SMS assign values to existing variables or generate additional variables to perform functions or hold values. During the installation, we can create the variables SMS uses to perform various functions. For example, we can define the values for the four variables listed in Table 14-2 as part of the installation script or have SMS prompt for the values during execution of the installation script. SMS frequently uses these variables—note especially the *DOBACKUP* variable, which is used to support the SMS Installer rollback feature.

Table 14-2.   Functional variables

Variable	Function
BACKUPDIR	Defines where the backup files should be located.
DOBACKUP	Enables the performance of a backup of all files replaced during an installation.
HELPFILE	Identifies the help file to be read and displayed during installation when the user clicks Help.
RESTART	Causes the system to be restarted when the script terminates. This variable is generally set automatically.

Defining Variables

As mentioned, you can also define your own variables in the script. You can use the Set Variable action or the Prompt For Text action from Script Editor. To create variables, follow these steps:

1. In the Installation Expert interface, choose Script Editor from the View menu to display the Script Editor interface, shown in Figure 14-32.

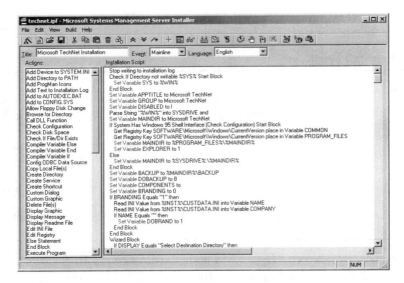

Figure 14-32. *The Script Editor interface.*

Note   If you previously closed SMS Installer from the Script Editor interface, when you next open SMS Installer, Script Editor appears with the Installation Script pane blank. If you open SMS Installer in the Installation Expert interface, it loads a default script, which is displayed in the Installation Script screen when you switch to Script Editor.

2. In the Actions list, double-click the Set Variable action to display the Set Variable dialog box, shown in Figure 14-33.

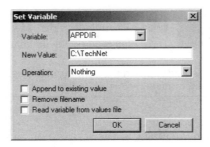

Figure 14-33. *The Set Variable dialog box.*

3. Enter the name of the variable you want to create or select a variable to modify from the Variable drop-down list. Variable names must always begin with a letter, must be no longer than 14 characters, and must contain no special characters except underscores.

4. In the New Value text box, enter the value you want to set the variable to.

5. Select an operation that you want performed on the new value from the Operation drop-down list, if required. Operations include incrementing or decrementing a numeric value by 1, removing trailing backslashes, converting a value to all uppercase or lowercase, converting the path and filename to a short or long filename, or simply performing no action—the default.

More Info   Refer to the SMS Installer Help for examples of how to use the different operations.

6. Three check boxes appear at the bottom of the Set Variable dialog box: Append To Existing Value, Remove Filename, and Read Variable From Values File. If the variable you entered is a counter and you choose to increment or decrement its value, select the Append To Existing Value check box. You can also use this option to append a string value to the current string value. If you want to remove the filename from a value that has a full path, select the Remove Filename check box. If you want SMS Installer to read the variable's value from a file, select the Read Variable From Values File select box. Selecting this option will cause the entered value to be ignored, so select this option only if you're running your script from the command line.

7. Click OK to close the Set Variable dialog box.

To create a variable named APPDIR, for example, in which you set the location of the application's working directory, enter *APPDIR* as the variable name and an appropriate path such as *C:\TechNet* as the value. When you need to invoke this value in your script, reference the variable's value by enclosing the variable name in percent signs. To create a BACKUP directory for rollback that's a subdirectory of the path you entered for APPDIR, your script line would look like this:

Set Variable BACKUP to %APPDIR%\BACKUP

Set Variable is just one of the SMS Installer Script Editor actions. In the next section we'll look at the more common Script Editor actions.

Common Script Editor Actions

The Script Editor window, shown in Figure 14-32, contains a list of SMS Installer Script Editor actions that the installation script can perform. In this section we'll look at some of the more common actions and their functions. Table 14-3 lists these actions.

Table 14-3. SMS Installer Script Editor actions

Action	Description
Add to AUTOEXEC.BAT	Adds or replaces commands and environment variables in the Autoexec.bat file other than the PATH command.
Add to CONFIG.SYS	Adds device driver and other statements to the Config.sys file.
Call DLL Function	Calls specific Win16 and Win32 DLLs.
Check Disk Space	Performs a check of disk space to verify that there's enough free space to complete the installation.
Check If File/Dir Exists	Checks whether a specified file or directory exists on the target computer.
Create Directory	Creates a new directory on the target computer.
Create Service	Creates a service on a target Windows computer.
Delete File(s)	Deletes specified files and directories from the target computer.
Edit Registry	Creates or deletes new keys and values in the registry on Windows 95 or later computers.
Else Statement	Inserts a logical ELSE statement into the script.
Execute Program	Calls an executable to run outside the actual scripted installation.
Exit Installation	Terminates and exits the installation.
If/While Statement	Inserts IF/WHILE logic into the script.
Install File(s)	Finds the source files used during installation and compresses them into the installer executable file. These files are uncompressed on the target computer when the script is run.
Prompt For Text	Generates a dialog box to prompt the user for text input such as a filename or directory path.
Remark	Adds comments to the script.
Rename File/Directory	Finds and renames a file or directory on the target computer.
Set Variable	Creates or modifies a script variable.

As you can see, variables and actions can be set in your script. You can find more details about these options in the SMS Installer Help file accessible through the SMS Installer interface. Don't expect to become proficient at scripting in a couple of hours or even a couple of days. We're talking about a scripting *language* here, and that takes time to learn and appreciate. But with a little perseverance you'll become proficient at using many of these options.

Modifying the Script

Now let's take a look at how to make some simple modifications to our script using Script Editor. To do so, follow these steps:

1. In the Installation Expert interface, choose Script Editor from the View menu to display the Script Editor interface, shown previously in Figure 14-32.

2. Choose Open from the File menu to display the Open dialog box, shown in Figure 14-34, and then select a script (.IPF) file to open for editing. For this example, we'll use the script we created earlier. Click Open to open the script for editing.

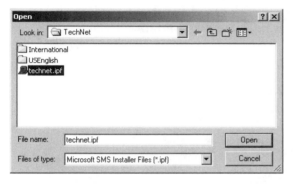

Figure 14-34.   *The Open dialog box.*

3. Next we'll edit the variable that specifies the installation directory the program will use. In this example we're installing to the Microsoft TechNet directory. We'll change this to TechNet.

   Choose Find from the Edit menu to display the Find Text In Installation Script dialog box, shown in Figure 14-35. Enter *Maindir* in the Find What text box, and then click Find Next. The first instance of a script line containing "Maindir" is selected. This is the variable setting for the directory location of the Office installation we want to modify. Click Close to close the dialog box.

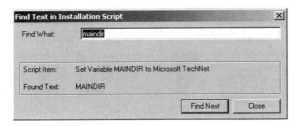

Figure 14-35. *The Find Text In Installation Script dialog box.*

4. Click Edit Script Item button on Installation toolbar or double-click the Set Variable statement containing "Maindir" to display the Set Variable dialog box, shown in Figure 13-36. In the New Value text box, enter *TechNet* and then click OK. The variable setting is modified in the Installation Script pane of the Script Editor interface.

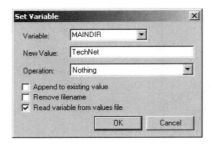

Figure 14-36. *The Set Variable dialog box.*

You'd accomplish any additional script modifications in much the same manner. After we've completed our editing of the script, we're ready to test and compile the installation script file. This will give us the SMS Installer–generated executable file.

Windows Installer Step-Up Utility Buttons

The Script Editor also offers three buttons that you can use to assist you in creating and testing Windows Installer packages. These are the three buttons at the far right of the toolbar in the Script Editor interface as seen previously in Figure 14-32. They are (in order from left to right as seen in the Script Editor window):

- **Compile As Windows Installer Package** Lets you create a new Windows Installer package or convert an existing SMS Installer package to a Windows Installer package.

- **Run As Windows Installer Package** Lets you run the Windows Installer package you create on the reference computer exactly as it would run on the target computers.

- **Uninstall Windows Installer Package** Lets you remove a Windows Installer package that you installed on the reference computer using the Run As Windows Installer Package button.

The use of these buttons is fairly straightforward. You need to have opened or created an SMS Installer or Windows Installer script—an .IPF file. Then click the appropriate button to carry out the task. A command-line version of the Windows Installer Step-Up Utility is also included when you install SMS Installer on the reference computer. Selecting the option ISU Command-Line Utility in the Microsoft SMS Installer program group displays a command prompt window, shown in Figure 14-37, that lists the command-line options that are available and the command syntax, and that places the command prompt in the appropriate directory to run the utility. You can also refer to the SMS Installer Help for detailed instructions for using the Windows Installer Step-Up Utility.

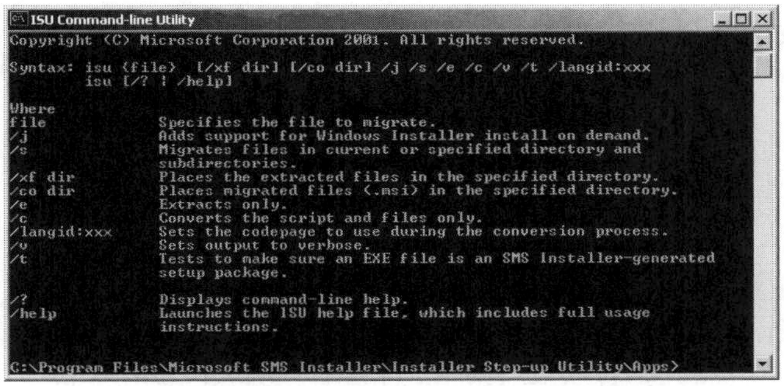

Figure 14-37. *Windows Installer Step-Up Utility command prompt window.*

Real World Sample Script

Occasionally you might encounter a situation in which you don't want to install an application or run the installation script if certain elements aren't in place on the target computer. For example, you might want to verify that there's enough disk space available before proceeding or that a particular program file exists. This example uses a file to indicate whether a computer should execute the installation script. This is a simple text file that you create and copy to all the computers that shouldn't execute the script. If the file is found on the computer, the script will be terminated. If the file isn't found, the script will continue.

The sample SMS Installer script routine shown in Figure 14-38 demonstrates how to test for the existence of a file, and you can incorporate it into larger scripts. It provides a basic structure that you can easily modify to meet other needs.

Figure 14-38. *Sample SMS Installer script designed to find a file and perform an action.*

This script is designed to look for a specific file identified in the script as Findfile.txt using the Search For File action. In the Actions list, double-click Search For File to display the Search For File Settings dialog box, shown in Figure 14-39.

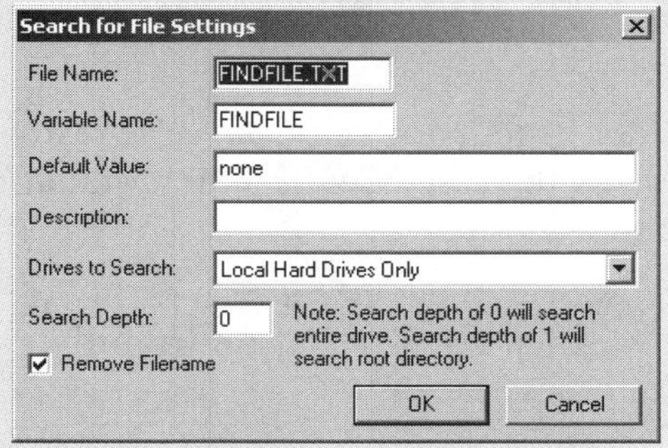

Figure 14-39.   *The Search For File Settings dialog box.*

In the Search For File Settings dialog box, specify the file and path to search for and whether to search all local drives, all network drives, or both. The path that's searched is determined by the Search Depth value. A value of 0 indicates that the entire drive will be searched. A value of 1 indicates that the root drive will be searched. Values of 2, 3, and higher indicate that the first directory level, second directory level, and so on will be searched. In this example we'll search all local drives.

Select the Remove Filename check box. If the file is found, the file and its path will be stored in the variable FINDFILE. This option will remove the file entry and keep just the path, which can be useful if you're trying to capture a specific path or need to rename a file, as we do in this script.

The script begins by using Set Variable to define a variable named FIND-FILE. This variable is set to a default value of None to indicate that no file has been found. The Search For File action looks for the file on all local drives on the target computer. If the file is found, the file and its full path are placed in FINDFILE, and the value of FINDFILE is no longer None. Simple IF/THEN logic tests to determine whether FINDFILE is still None. If it's not, the file has been found, and we'll rename it Findfile.old. If the file hasn't been found, we simply continue on with the rest of the script. The script also includes display messages for debugging purposes to alert us when the file has been found. You can remove these messages after the existence of the file has been tested.

You can easily modify this basic script routine to perform any number of actions or tasks—for example, deleting the file, moving the file to a new location, or creating a new file with the same name as an existing file if that file isn't found.

Testing and Compiling the Installation Script

Now that we've verified and modified our installation settings, we're ready to test and finally compile—or recompile, as the case may be—the installation script. To accomplish this, follow these steps:

1. In the Installation Expert interface, shown previously in Figure 14-7, click the Test button. (You can also click the Test button from the Installation toolbar in the Script Editor interface.)

2. If you haven't already saved the script, a Save As dialog box will appear, prompting you to provide a name for the script (.IPF) file that will be created during the test run of the installation.

3. The SMS Installer–generated script should now run successfully, displaying any dialog boxes you defined. The Test program will notify you of any syntactical problems within the script. If an error is encountered, you can open the Script Editor interface, with the offending line highlighted and waiting to be edited. Correct any problems and continue to retest the script until it runs without error.

4. After you have successfully tested the script file, you can run the installation script in much the same manner as you did when you tested it. The significant difference in running the script is that it will actually perform the installation. Recall that to avoid potential conflicts, you might want to remove the version of the application that was installed during the repackaging process.

5. To run the script file from the Installation Expert interface, click Run. You can also click the Run button from the Installation toolbar in the Script Editor interface.

6. The script will run completely and, as with the Test program, will prompt you with any syntactical errors that are found, giving you the option to correct them. Correct any errors, and repeat the run process until no errors are found.

7. After the installation script has run successfully, click the Compile button to create the SMS Installer–generated executable file. You can also click the Compile button from the Installation toolbar in the Script Editor interface. Once again, any errors will be noted and should be corrected. In addition, when an error in the script is encountered, you're given the option of opening the Script Editor interface so that

you can immediately fix the error. If you choose this option, not only is the Script Editor opened, but also the problem line in the script is highlighted and its properties dialog box is displayed.

Tip   Remember to recompile the script after each change you make, either through the Installation Expert or through Script Editor. You might also want to make a copy of the old script before modifying and recompiling it.

After the final testing has been completed, the SMS Installer–generated executable is ready to distribute to your target systems. Using SMS or any other method of distribution, our scripted package is ready to be rolled out to the client computers.

Rolling Back and Uninstalling a Scripted Installation

Occasionally it might be necessary to remove a software application from the client computers after it has been installed. This might be due to configuration issues or because the application was rolled out to a group of clients that shouldn't have received it. Whatever the reason, at some point you'll likely be faced with the task of uninstalling an application.

In most applications today, the Setup program is used to perform the deinstallation as well as the installation of the application. The biggest problem administrators encounter with these types of uninstall routines is that they usually don't remove everything that was installed with the application. It isn't uncommon to have an uninstall routine leave behind directories, abandoned files, and even unwanted registry entries. This isn't necessarily the application's fault. Install programs are usually not written to keep track of what is or isn't installed.

SMS Installer has both an uninstall and a rollback feature to help alleviate these types of problems. Recall that SMS doesn't actually perform the application's install routine on the target computer. Instead, the Repackage Installation Wizard performs a before-and-after scan of the reference computer and creates a script that defines what should be modified on the target computers. Uninstall and rollback support help to restore the reference computer to the condition it was in before an SMS Installer–generated executable file made any modifications to the system by logging what the script did. Uninstall support is designed for complete removal of an application, including its files, registry modifications, and so on. Rollback support is designed more as a restoration tool—to restore any replaced files and any changed registry entries, such as removing a patch that was applied to an application.

Enabling Uninstall Support

Enabling uninstall support came up in our discussion of modifying the script from Installation Expert earlier in this chapter. Let's recap here. To enable uninstall support, you must configure it from the Installation Expert prior to compiling your Installer executable file. To do so, follow these steps:

1. Select the Runtime Support installation attribute in the Installation Expert interface.

2. In the Summary Information For Runtime Support section, click Runtime Options and then click Properties to display the Runtime Support dialog box, shown previously in Figure 14-23.

3. In the Options tab, verify that Uninstall Support is selected—which it should be by default.

4. Click OK. Uninstall.exe will be included in the installation package and copied to the client computer during the package execution, and an uninstall log file will be maintained on the target computers.

Enabling Rollback Support

Enabling rollback support requires one additional change to the process used to enable uninstall support. To properly restore settings and files, those settings and files must be saved somewhere during the installation of the software package. SMS Installer's trick for rolling back a file such as a patch is to copy the original to a backup location before performing any modifications. To accomplish this, you must specify the backup directory into which to save replaced files.

We also touched on enabling rollback support when we discussed modifying installation scripts using the Installation Expert. To enable rollback support, follow these steps:

1. In the Installation Expert interface, select the Installation Interface installation attribute.

2. In the Summary Information For Installation Interface section, click Wizard Dialogs and then click Properties to display the Dialogs tab of the Installation Interface dialog box, shown previously in Figure 14-18.

3. In the Dialogs tab, select Backup Replaced Files. Selecting this option will cause two dialog boxes to be displayed to the user during the SMS Installer executable file execution. The first prompts the user to specify whether to back up the files. The second prompts for the location of the backup files.

If rollback support is required but your intention is to provide an unattended installation script with dialog boxes suppressed, you need to manually edit the Set Variable DOBACKUP script action as shown in these steps:

1. From the Script Editor interface, choose Find from the Edit menu. In the Find What text box of the Find Text In Installation Script dialog box, enter *Set Variable DOBACKUP To B* and click Find Next.

2. Double-click the selected script action line to display the Set Variable dialog box and change this variable value from B to A. This change causes any replaced files to be backed up during the installation script execution.

3. Click OK to return to the Script Editor interface, shown in Figure 14-40.

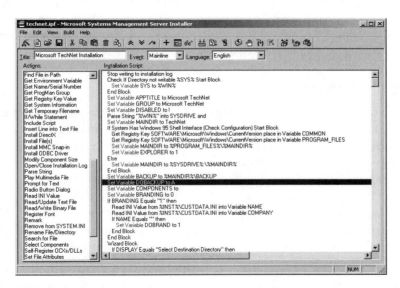

Figure 14-40.   *The Script Editor interface, with a modified script action line selected.*

4. Verify the location of the backup files by searching for the variable Set Variable Backup To. This variable will show the location of the backup files. Modify this value as appropriate for the target computers.

> **Note**   Rollback support is meant for restoring specific files and values and not for uninstalling an application—that's what uninstall support is for. Using rollback to uninstall implies that every file or setting that's modified needs to be backed up, which isn't always practical or desirable.

Performing Uninstall and Rollback

The Uninstal.exe file that's copied to the target computer during the SMS Installer–generated executable file execution is used to perform the actual roll-back. You can use two methods to uninstall or roll back the client computer to its original configuration. If the installation is an application installation, it's automatically added to Add/Remove Programs in Control Panel. All we have to do is select the application in the Add/Remove Programs dialog box and click Remove. The SMS Installer Uninstall Wizard appears, enabling you to perform both the uninstall and the rollback.

The second method is to manually run Uninstal.exe from the application's main directory. The uninstall routine prompts for the name of the installation log generated by the installation package—usually Install.log—and then begins the removal process. Uninstal.exe also supports a silent mode using the /s para-meter from the command line—all of which means, of course, that you could create an unattended SMS package that removes the application for you.

Using the Installation Log

If an uninstall or a rollback has been configured for an SMS Installer–generated executable file, a log file (Install.log) is generated during the installation process and saved in the application directory created on the target computer. This log file contains entries for the files that were copied or installed as well as every registry entry that's created or modified. Additional changes—including icons that were created, shortcuts, and any files that were replaced, such as DLL files—will be archived to the backup location if rollback support is enabled. This log file will be used in the uninstall or rollback process to return files to their orig-inal versions and to return all registry settings to their prior configuration.

Also, when the script needs to modify existing INI files, it comments out the line that needs to be modified by adding ";SMS" at the beginning of the line and then writing the new line above it. This way, when an uninstall or a rollback occurs, the process simply searches for the ;SMS entries, deletes the line above, and removes the comment prefix. Clever, eh?

Creating an Uninstall Status MIF File

As with package installation, you can also configure SMS Installer to generate an uninstall status MIF file to indicate that the application has been removed. As we've seen in the section of this chapter entitled "Modifying Installation Scripts Using the Installation Expert," the configuration of the uninstall status MIF file is done from the SMS tab of the Installation Interface dialog box. To create the uninstall MIF file, you must have configured an uninstall MIF filename, as shown previously in Figure 14-20, before compiling the SMS Installer–generated executable file.

Summary

SMS Installer is a powerful graphical tool as well as a formidable script-editing utility used to generate executable files that can be distributed through SMS or by any other means you might choose. Ideally, the use of SMS Installer will help you in creating and distributing installation script files with a minimal amount of effort and error.

As we've seen, various levels of scripting are supported, each requiring a higher level of learning. Very basic scripts using the Repackage Installation Wizard are sufficient for installations that are uncomplicated or that don't need to be fully unattended or scripted. You can use the Installation Expert to make the basic script perform more specific tasks, such as modifying registry entries or suppressing dialog boxes. You can create elegant scripts using Script Editor actions. The technique you choose should depend on your needs and the amount of time you're willing to invest.

In Chapter 12 we examined the process of creating and delivering packages that install applications to SMS clients. In this chapter we looked at creating application installation scripts using SMS Installer that could then be delivered to and installed on SMS clients using the package delivery feature of SMS. In Chapter 15, "Software Metering," we'll explore the software metering feature of SMS and you'll learn how to monitor application use on your SMS clients.

Chapter 15
Software Metering

With Microsoft Systems Management Server (SMS) 2.0, Microsoft introduced a new application management utility called Software Metering. This feature enabled the SMS administrator to monitor the use of applications among SMS clients, to track license usage, to place restrictions on running applications based on time or permissions, and to spot unauthorized applications when they were run.

This feature in SMS 2.0 required you to identify a server to act as the software metering server for the site. This site server maintained its own data cache and was the point of data exchange between the clients and the site server database. Unfortunately, software metering was not well integrated into the rest of the product and, as a result, proved to be cumbersome to configure and manage, and in its license tracking mode, it tended to generate a significant amount of network traffic. Consequently, SMS administrators didn't much use this feature—at least not the license-tracking part of it.

In SMS 2003 software metering has been completely reengineered. In this chapter we'll look at how software metering has changed and the components that participate in the software metering process. We'll look at how to configure the software metering client agent and at software metering rules. We'll explore how to view reports based on metered data and identify some maintenance tasks.

Overview

Like its counterpart in SMS 2.0, the software metering feature of SMS 2003 gives you the ability to collect and monitor program usage on SMS client computers, including the users running the program, when the program started, and when it was stopped. A program is any executable file that can run in memory on the client computer, especially .EXE and .COM files. You can use this information to help determine how programs are used within an organization, whether and how programs are being used, and whether you're in compliance with license agreements for the programs being run. You tell the clients what programs to meter by creating software metering rules that are copied down to each client.

Unlike its SMS 2.0 counterpart, however, software metering in SMS 2003 no longer requires the implementation of a software metering site system to cache metered data and store and balance program licenses. Instead, it uses Windows Management Instrumentation (WMI) to store software metering rules and collected data. Software metering no longer actively monitors for license usage. To facilitate viewing and analyzing the metered data, SMS 2003 provides specific software metering reports that can be used with the SMS Web reporting tool.

Software metering collects the following information about a program:

- Usage information
  - Start time
  - End time
  - Meter data ID
  - Resource ID (Computer name)
  - User name
  - Users in Terminal Services sessions
  - Still running
- File information
  - File ID
  - Filename
  - File version
  - File description
  - File size (KB)
- Program information
  - Company name
  - Product name
  - Product version
  - Product language

Software Metering Process Flow

Software metering in SMS 2003 is supported on SMS Legacy Clients and Advanced Clients. Two main components make up software metering—the Software Metering Client Agent and software metering rules. The rules represent the programs that you want to monitor on each client, and the agent is responsible for keeping the rules up to date on the client and collecting and reporting metered data back to the site.

Software metering rules are stored in the SMS database and copied to client access points (CAPs) (for Legacy Clients) and management points (for Advanced Clients). The rules are propagated to the SMS clients during the client agent's next update cycle (by default, every two hours for Legacy Clients and every hour for Advanced Clients). Rules created at an SMS site higher up in the hierarchy can apply either to just that site or to that site and all its lower-level child sites.

When the program runs, the agent collects required information about the program, such as the filename, version, and size, when the program started and when it ended, and the client on which it's running. The agent then uploads the data to the CAP or the management point on its next update cycle. If the client isn't connected to the network, the data remains on the client and is uploaded the next time the client connects to the network.

Once the data has been uploaded to the appropriate site server, it's added to the site database, and, if the rule was created at a higher-level parent site, the data is propagated to the higher-level SMS sites.

Configuring Software Metering

Software metering is configured in two areas of reference: software metering rules and the client agent. Let's begin by looking at the server components because without these the client agent is useless. The two server components that need to be configured are the Software Metering component and the software metering site system. Both are definable through the Site Settings node in the SMS Administrator Console.

Configuring the Software Metering Client Agent

Like the other SMS client features we've seen, you enable software metering by configuring a client agent—in this case, the Software Metering Client Agent. And, like the other client agent settings, the options you choose when you configure the agent are considered site-wide options and are propagated to all clients in the site.

To configure the Software Metering Client Agent, follow these steps:

1. In the SMS Administrator Console, navigate to the Client Agents node under Site Settings.

2. Right-click Software Metering Client Agent and choose Properties from the context menu to display the Software Metering Client Agent Properties dialog box, shown in Figure 15-1.

Figure 15-1. *The Software Metering Client Agent Properties dialog box.*

3. In the General tab, select the Enable Software Metering On Clients check box.

4. In the Schedule tab, shown in Figure 15-2, use the Schedule buttons to determine how frequently you want to send collected data from the client back to the site system (Data Collection Schedule) and how often you want to download software metering rules for Legacy Clients (Metering Rules Download Schedule). Note that Advanced Clients download metering rules as part of their Advanced Policy refresh schedule, which is once an hour by default. The minimum actual value that SMS will use for either of these options is 15 minutes.

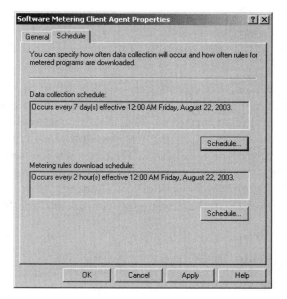

Figure 15-2. *Specifying software metering process flow.*

5. Choose OK to save your settings and configure the agent.

> **Note**   Software metering won't collect a data file that's more than 90 days old. If it finds such a file, it generates status message 5614 and moves the data file to its own folder.

On a Legacy Client, after the next client update cycle (every 25 hours or the next time you start the client), the agent component files will be copied to the client and the agent will be started. On an Advanced Client, all agents are automatically installed when the Advanced Client is installed. So, at the Advanced Client's next refresh cycle (once an hour by default), it receives an Advanced Client policy indicating that the agent has been enabled and the agent is configured and started on the client.

After the rules are downloaded to the client, the agent can begin to monitor programs, even if the program is currently running in computer memory.

Configuring Software Metering Rules

Software metering rules identify for the client agent which programs should be monitored and how they should be monitored. Rules can be identified at any SMS site in your hierarchy and can apply only to that site or, as mentioned earlier, to any lower-level child site below it in the hierarchy. The catch is that any rules created higher up in the hierarchy can be modified only in the site in which they were created. This behavior is consistent with the way package, advertisement, and collection data are handled as well.

The rule configuration information is propagated down the hierarchy to child sites, but maintenance of the rule is effected at the site in which the rule is created. Consequently, it's important that you carefully consider whether the rule you create should be propagated and applied to SMS clients in child sites.

Software metering is supported on SMS clients running Terminal Services or Remote Desktop Connection. Program usage in this case is monitored individually—that is, each program run through a Terminal Services session is counted as a distinct usage of that program, even if the same program is being run in each session. However, the programs run in the Terminal Services session are treated as remote connections and are reported with the same computer name. Programs run using Microsoft Windows 2000 or Windows XP Remote Desktop Connection, however, are treated as local connections and the local computer name is reported.

Creating a Software Metering Rule

To configure a software metering rule, follow these steps:

1. In the SMS Administrator Console, navigate to the Software Metering Rules node.

2. Right-click Software Metering Rules and choose New, Software Metering Rule from the context menu to display the Software Metering Rule Properties dialog box, shown in Figure 15-3.

Figure 15-3. *The Software Metering Rule Properties dialog box.*

3. In the General tab, enter the appropriate information in each field (all fields are required except Version and Comment):

- In the Name field, enter a descriptive name for the rule itself; it's suggested that you include the program name or filename.

- In the File Name field, enter the filename that launches the program or click Browse to search for the appropriate executable file. Keep in mind that some programs are used as placeholders to launch other programs. You should specify the name of the program that ultimately executes the program itself or you might not collect the appropriate tracking information. For example, if you track a command file that launches, say, Solitaire, software metering will track only the command file and not Solitaire. This field isn't required if you specify an Original File Name.

- In the Original File Name field, enter the filename of the program as it appears in the header information contained in the program's executable file. If the executable file is renamed and you were tracking on the File Name value, software metering would no longer recognize the application as the one to monitor. The value in Original File Name, on the other hand, directs the agent to read the application's name from the header information contained in the application's executable file. Thus, even if the file is renamed, the agent would still recognize the application as the one to monitor. This field isn't required if you specify a File Name.

Caution   Not all applications are written to contain the program name in the header information of the executable file. Games, for example, tend not to do this.

- In the Version field, enter the version of the program if you want software metering to monitor a specific version. Here you can use wildcards to broaden or narrow the entry. Use the default asterisk (*) to match on any version. Use the question mark (?) to substitute for any character. For example, if you want to monitor versions 5.0, 5.1, and 5.2, enter 5.? in the Version field.

Caution   If you leave this field blank, software metering will monitor the program only if the version listed in the header information of the program executable file is also blank.

- In the Language field, select the language of the software program from the drop-down list.

- In the Comment field, enter any additional descriptive information that you think can be useful in identifying how or why this rule is used. As always, I prefer to err on the side of having more descriptive information than is needed rather than not enough.

- In the Site Code field, select the site code that the rule should apply to. If you have only one site, or if the site is the lowest in the hierarchy, this field will be dimmed. If the rule should apply to this site and all its child sites, enable the option This Rule Applies To The Specified Site And All Its Child Sites.

4. Click OK to save the rule.

Real World   Monitoring a Suite of Products

In SMS 2.0, it was possible to register several programs as a suite of programs to capture usage information under the suite name rather than for each individual program in the suite. For example, you might want to monitor usage information for Office XP as opposed to Microsoft Word, Microsoft Excel, Microsoft PowerPoint, and so on.

It's possible to do this in SMS 2003 software metering as well. Software metering supports creating metering rules that have the same name. If you want to monitor a suite of programs, create a rule for each program in the suite, but give each rule the same name. Be sure to use the correct version numbers and filenames.

Enabling and Disabling a Software Metering Rule

After you create a new software metering rule, it's automatically enabled and, if you chose to do so, propagated to child sites. However, you might want to stop monitoring a particular program and continue to view data already collected but not completely delete the rule. In this case you can disable the rule and, when you want to run the rule again, enable it again. The client is notified of the change in status of the rule during the next rule update on the client.

To disable a software metering rule, complete the following steps:

1. In the SMS Administrator Console, navigate to the Software Metering Rules node.

2. Right-click the software metering rule you want to disable, choose All Tasks from the context menu, and then choose Disable.

To enable a software metering rule that has been disabled, follow these steps:

1. In the SMS Administrator Console, navigate to the Software Metering Rules node.

2. Right-click the software metering rule you want to enable, choose All Tasks from the context menu, and then choose Enable.

Summarizing Data

The amount of program information that's collected can add up quickly and use a lot of space in the SMS site database. To keep the information manageable, SMS periodically summarizes the collected data as well as deletes old data. You can't view collected metering data until the next summarization cycle—once a day by default—is completed.

Data is summarized based on monthly usage and file usage. File usage tracks the approximate total number of concurrent users who have run a specific program during a specific time interval. The Summarize Software Metering File Usage Data maintenance task (accessible by clicking Site Settings and then Site Maintenance), condenses the individual software metering data records into one record that provides aggregate information about the program—its name, version, language, and number of users—over intervals of 15 minutes and 1 hour. This task runs once a day and summarizes data over 15-minute and 1-hour intervals. Monthly usage tracks the number of times a program is run by a specific user on a specific computer.

Similarly, the Summarize Software Metering Monthly Usage Data maintenance task condenses the individual software metering data records into one record but summarizes the data over monthly periods. This task runs once a day and summarizes data over one-month intervals.

In addition, by default, each day SMS deletes software metering data records older than 5 days and summarized data older than 270 days.

Software metering summarization tasks and deletion tasks are configurable maintenance tasks in SMS 2003. To configure the Delete Aged Software Metering Data task, follow these steps:

1. In the SMS Administrator Console, navigate to the Site Maintenance node under Site Settings, expand it, and, under Site Maintenance, select Tasks.

2. Right-click the Delete Aged Software Metering Data task and select Properties from the context menu.

3. In the Delete Aged Software Metering Data Task Properties dialog box, shown in Figure 15-4, select the number of days after which data will be considered old and the schedule for the task to be executed.

Figure 15-4. *The Delete Aged Software Metering Data Task Properties dialog box.*

4. Click OK when you're finished.

To configure the Delete Aged Software Metering Summary Data task, complete the following steps:

1. In the SMS Administrator Console, navigate to the Site Maintenance node under Site Settings, expand it, and, under Site Maintenance, select Tasks.

2. Right-click the Delete Aged Software Metering Summary Data task and select Properties from the context menu.

3. In the Delete Aged Software Metering Summary Data Task Properties dialog box, shown in Figure 15-5, select the number of days after which data will be considered old and the schedule for the task to be executed.

Figure 15-5.   *The Delete Aged Software Metering Summary Data Task Properties dialog box.*

4. Click OK when you're finished.

To configure the Summarize Software Metering File Usage Data task, follow these steps:

1. In the SMS Administrator Console, navigate to the Site Maintenance node under Site Settings, expand it, and, under Site Maintenance, select Tasks.

2. Right-click the Summarize Software Metering File Usage Data task and select Properties from the context menu.

3. In the Summarize Software Metering File Usage Data Task Properties dialog box, shown in Figure 15-6, select the schedule for the task to be executed.

Figure 15-6. *The Summarize Software Metering File Usage Data Task Properties dialog box.*

4. Click OK when you're finished.

To configure the Summarize Software Metering Monthly Usage Data task, follow these steps:

1. In the SMS Administrator Console, navigate to the Site Maintenance node under Site Settings, expand it, and, under Site Maintenance, select Tasks.

2. Right-click the Summarize Software Metering Monthly Usage Data task and select Properties from the context menu.

3. In the Summarize Software Metering Monthly Usage Data Task Properties dialog box, shown in Figure 15-7, select the schedule for the task to be executed.

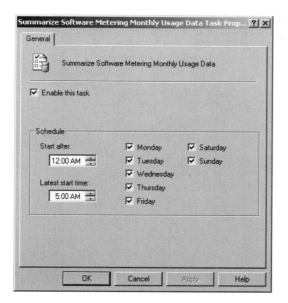

Figure 15-7.   *The Summarize Software Metering Monthly Usage Data Task Properties dialog box.*

4. Click OK when you're finished.

Running Software Metering Reports

The SMS Report Viewer feature of SMS 2003 provides you with several reports for viewing the collected software metering data. Using reports will be discussed in greater detail in Chapter 16, "Queries and Reports." However, I'll give you a brief overview of how to view these reports here.

To launch the reporting tool, complete the following steps:

1. In the SMS Administrator Console, navigate to the Reporting node, right-click it, and select All Tasks, then Run, and then the name of the reporting point that contains the software metering data to start the SMS Report Viewer, shown in Figure 15-8.

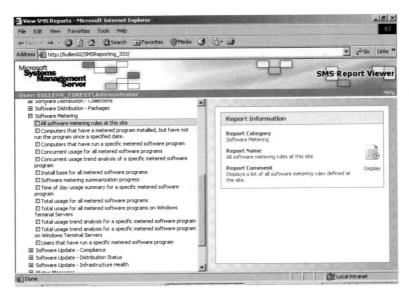

Figure 15-8. *The SMS Report Viewer with Software Metering reports expanded.*

2. Select the report that you want to run from the list of reports on the left side of the viewer.

3. Enter any information required for the report, such as time period or software metering rule name that you're prompted for on the right side of the viewer.

4. Click Display to display the report results.

Figure 15-8 displays a list of the reports available for viewing software metering data. As you select each report, you'll be prompted for information specific for that report. For example, if you select the report All Software Metering Rules At This Site, as highlighted in Figure 15-8, all you need to do is click Display to see a list of all the rules configured for this site. However, if you select the report Users That Have Run A Specific Metered Software Program, you'll need to specify the rule name, the month, and the year for which you want to view reported data, as shown in Figure 15-9. Figure 15-10 shows the result of that last report.

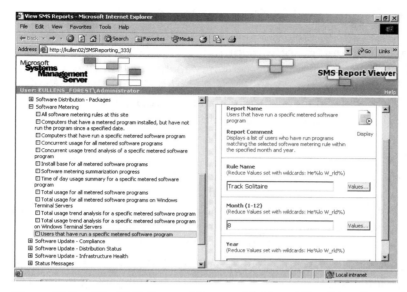

Figure 15-9. *The SMS Report Viewer with Users That Have Run A Specific Metered Software Program selected.*

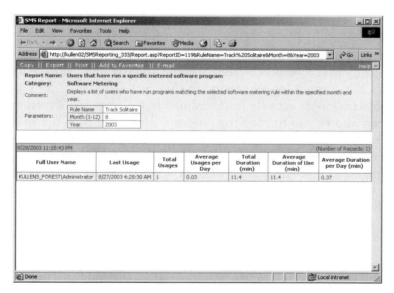

Figure 15-10. *Results of running the report Users That Have Run A Specific Metered Software Program.*

Checkpoints

Because the implementation of software metering in SMS 2003 is so different from SMS 2.0, you can't migrate or view any metered data that you collected using SMS 2.0, nor can you migrate any software metering program properties. Similarly, you can't view metered data collected using an SMS 2003 site in an SMS 2.0 site. SMS 2003 no longer uses the software metering site system role and so won't recognize any SMS 2.0 software metering site systems that might still exist.

Also, remember that after you create a new rule and propagate it to your SMS clients, you'll still need to wait for the next collection and summarization cycles to complete before you can view the data. Since the default for collecting data from the client is seven days and summarization takes place once a day, you might wait for up to eight days for the first data to be viewable.

Finally, be sure to review your rule properties. Check the program name and especially the version number you're trying to match. It might be a good idea to try out your rules in a test environment to be sure that you're actually monitoring the programs you want to monitor.

Summary

In SMS 2003, software metering has been reengineered and streamlined from its counterpart in SMS 2.0. You no longer require the Software Metering site system role, and you can no longer actively track online license usage. This version of software metering allows you to monitor program usage and then use that information to extrapolate data about how programs are used in your organization, who uses them, how long, and so on. Together with software inventory, you can use software metering to determine whether you're meeting the requirements of your software licenses. Through the SMS Report Viewer, you can view statistical information about the programs you're monitoring.

 More Info For more information about using and configuring software metering, see Chapter 8 in the *Microsoft Systems Management Server 2003 Operations Guide*, available through the Microsoft SMS Web site (*http://www.microsoft.com/smserver*) and through Microsoft TechNet.

In this part of the book we've examined various ways to manage client applications. The package distribution process showed us how we can remotely install programs on our SMS clients and how we can maximize the package distribution process using collections. With the SMS Installer, we can fully script our packages to require little or no user input during the package's execution. In this chapter we've seen how to monitor the usage of client applications. In Part 4 we'll explore various ways to retrieve and present information from the SMS database, as well as site database maintenance and recovery.

Part IV
Site Database Maintenance, Recovery, and Upgrade

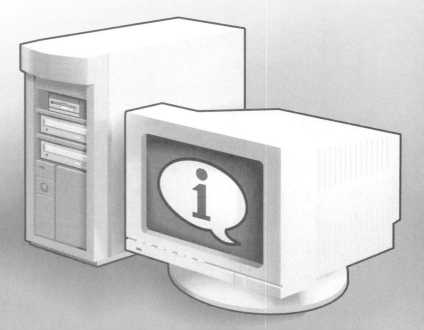

Chapter 16
Queries and Reports

In the first three parts of this book we've covered the primary functions of Microsoft Systems Management Server (SMS) 2003. We've explored the inventory collection process, package distribution and management, software metering, and remote client management. Along the way, a lot of information has made its way into the SMS database, and you've seen periodic references to using a query or a report to extract information from the SMS database—for example, you might use a query as a membership rule to populate a collection or to view status messages generated by various client agents, or you can use a report to view collected software metering data. This part of the book focuses on database maintenance tasks, including extracting and analyzing data, setting security, and recovering data.

Queries are an efficient and relatively easy way to retrieve information from the SMS site database. SMS 2003 also makes a new SMS Report Viewer available as a reporting tool accessible through the SMS Administrator Console. We'll explore both methods of accessing SMS database information in this chapter.

Queries

As you know, the premise behind any database query is the return of information based on a set of criteria. In other words, you define what information you're trying to obtain in the form of a query statement. The query engine then searches the database for entries that match your criteria. The query result then displays the data that matched your criteria.

The same is true for SMS queries. To define a simple SMS query, you would specify an SMS object to search on, one or more attributes of the object, an operator of some kind, and a value. For example, suppose you're querying for computers with processors greater than 700 MHz. In this case, *computer* is an object, *processor* is an attribute of the object, *greater than* is the relational operator, and *700 MHz* is the value.

You can use SMS queries for a variety of purposes. Generally, we think of queries as a means of reporting on data in the database. Indeed, we might use SMS queries to find all the computers that meet a certain memory, disk space, and platform requirement before sending out a package to them. And as we've seen, queries are particularly useful in defining collection memberships. Collections whose members are based on the results of a query can be updated periodically to keep them current. Any programs advertised to a collection are automatically made available to the collection's members. As the query runs and updates the collection, new members automatically receive any advertisements that targeted the collection, and deleted members no longer receive the advertisements.

You can generate SMS queries a couple of ways. The easiest way to create and run a query—and the easiest method to learn—is using SMS Query Builder, which is built into the SMS Administrator Console. This interface provides you with a point-and-click method for building your query. You could also write the query statements yourself; however, this method entails learning a query language—specifically, WMI Query Language (WQL).

Unlike other SQL Server databases, SMS relies on the Windows Management Instrumentation (WMI) layer to expose its database information to the SMS Administrator Console and other tools. Therefore, you can't use regular SQL queries or commands to extract data from the SMS database. Instead, you're specifying WMI object classes and attributes that the query uses to access and search the SMS database. For example, most of the queries that you create and use for collection membership will likely be based on the SMS_R_System discovery class, which contains discovery record properties such as IP Address, OperatingSystemNameandVersion, and Name, and on the SMS_G_System set of inventory classes, such as SMS_G_System_Processor, which includes processor data such as Name and ResourceId, and SMS_G_System_x86_PC_Memory, which includes memory data such as TotalPhysicalMemory.

More Info For more information about SMS object classes and properties, see the *Microsoft Systems Management Server 2003 Software Development Kit (SDK)*, available through the Microsoft SMS Web site (*http://www.microsoft.com/smserver*) and through the Microsoft Developer Network (MSDN) program (*http://msdn.microsoft.com*).

Consequently, it's not recommended that you access the SMS database using regular SQL queries. What you need is a tool that can connect to WMI to access the SMS Provider and collect the information you require. You can use any third-party utility that's WMI Open Database Connectivity (ODBC)–compliant for this purpose. For example, you could use a reporting tool such as Microsoft Excel 2002 or Microsoft Access 2002 with the WMI ODBC drivers to report on SMS data. For more information about how to access a SQL database using a third-party tool, refer to the documentation for that tool.

SMS 2003 loads 21 predefined queries, as shown in Figure 16-1. As you can see, these predefined queries are fairly general in scope and are meant to be more globally oriented, perhaps as the target of an advertisement. However, you can certainly create your own queries—for example, to assist with certain management tasks, including populating and updating collections and viewing client status messages.

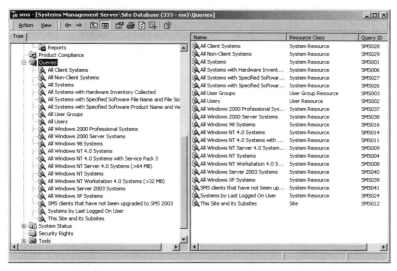

Figure 16-1.   *Predefined queries in SMS 2003.*

Query Elements

Before we review the steps for creating a query, let's take a look at the individual elements that make up a query. The relationship between these elements is illustrated in Figure 16-2. As mentioned, you begin your query definition by selecting a WMI object class to query on. However, when you use the SMS Query Builder, these objects use friendly names that make it easier to select the correct object and attribute. We'll gear our discussion toward these friendly object names.

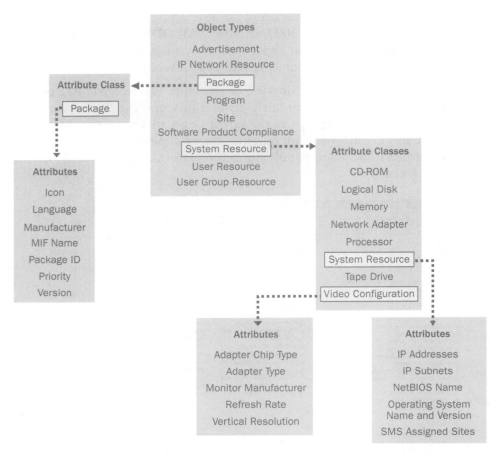

Figure 16-2. *The relationship between objects, their attribute classes, and the attributes of each class.*

SMS provides several object types for generating queries. An object type has specific attribute classes that describe it. For example, the System Resource object type is defined by its memory, environment, logical disk, processor, and network attribute classes, among other elements. An *attribute class* is essentially a category of attributes and contains an attribute list. For example, the System Resource attribute class includes the IP Addresses, IP Subnets, NetBIOS Name, Operating System Name and Version, and SMS Assigned Sites attributes.

Table 16-1 lists the more frequently used object types, some of their attribute classes, and a short list of attributes.

Table 16-1.   SMS objects and some of their attribute classes and attributes

Object Type	Attribute Classes	Attributes
Advertisement	Advertisement	Advertisement ID, Advertisement Name, Collection ID, Package ID, Program Name
Package	Package	Description, Manufacturer, Name, Package ID, Priority
Program	Program	Command Line, Comment, Disk Space Required, Package ID, Working Directory
Site	Site	Build Number, Install Directory, Server Name, Site Code, Site Name
Software Metering Rule	Software Metering Rule	Enabled, File Name, File Version, Language, Rule Name, Site Code
Software Product Compliance	Software Product Compliance	Category, Product Company, Product Name, Product Version, Type
System Resource	Add Or Remove Programs	Display Name, Product ID, Publisher, Version
	Collected File	Collection Date, File Name, File Path
	Logical Disk	File System. Free Space, Volume Name
	Memory	Total Pagefile Space, Total Physical Memory, Total Virtual Memory
	Network Adapter	Adapter Type, MAC Address, Manufacturer
	Operating System	Build Number, Manufacturer, Version
	Processor	Family, Manufacturer, Max Clock Speed
	System Resource	IP Addresses, NetBIOS Name, Operating System Name And Version
User Group Resource	User Group Resource	Name, Resource ID, SMS Assigned Sites, User Group Name, Microsoft Windows NT Domain
User Resource	User Resource	Full User Name, Resource ID, SMS Assigned Sites, User Name, Windows NT Domain

The *criterion type* defines what you're comparing the attribute with. The six criterion types are listed in Table 16-2.

Table 16-2. **Criterion types**

Type	Description
Null Value	Used when the attribute value may or may not be null
Simple Value	Constant value against which the attribute is compared
Prompted Value	Prompts you to enter a value before the query is evaluated
Attribute Reference	Lets you compare the query attribute to another attribute that you identify
Subselected Values	Lets you compare the query attribute to the results of another query that you specify
List Of Values	List of constant values against which the attribute is compared

Along with the criterion type, you will select a relational operator and supply a value to search for. This value can be null, numeric, a string, or a date/time. The list of relational operators is pretty much what you would expect: Is Equal To, Is Not Equal To, Is Greater Than, Is Less Than, and so on. However, the kinds of operators that are available depend on whether the attribute is null, numeric, string, or date/time. Table 16-3 outlines the subtle differences between these operators.

Table 16-3. **Relational operators**

Data Type	Relational Operators
Null	Is Null, Is Not Null
Numeric	Is Equal To, Is Not Equal To, Is Greater Than, Is Less Than, Is Greater Than Or Equal To, Is Less Than Or Equal To
String	Is Equal To, Is Not Equal To, Is Like, Is Not Like, Is Greater Than, Is Less Than, Is Greater Than Or Equal To, Is Less Than Or Equal To
Date/Time	*Unit* Is Equal To, *Unit* Is Not Equal To, *Unit* Is Greater Than, *Unit* Is Less Than, *Unit* Is Greater Than Or Equal To, *Unit* Is Less Than Or Equal To, *Unit* Is
Date/Time	*Unit* Is Not, *Unit* Is After, *Unit* Is Before, *Unit* Is On Or After, *Unit* Is On Or Before

(*Unit* is a date or time unit—millisecond, second, minute, hour, day, week, month, or year.)

When string values are used in a query, the exact string must be provided, without quotation marks, unless the quotation marks are part of the string. If you use either the Is Like or Is Not Like relational operator, you can use wildcard characters as part of the string. Acceptable wildcard characters include those shown in Table 16-4.

Table 16-4.   Wildcard characters

Symbol	Meaning
% (percent)	Any string of characters
_ (underscore)	Any single character
[ ] (brackets)	Any character within a specified range of characters
^ (caret)	Any character *not* within the specified range of characters

For example, if we wanted to query the database for all SMS clients that contained the string FIN in the client name, we might use the value *%FIN%*. String operators are not case-sensitive unless the SQL code page you're using uses case-sensitive comparisons.

In real life, your queries will probably be more complex and will consist of several query statements. These statements are connected using logical operators and are grouped for evaluation using parentheses. The three primary logical operators used with SMS queries are AND, OR, and NOT.

An AND operation finds all data that matches two query statements connected by the AND operator. AND operations generally result in a more restricted search since every expression must be satisfied to generate a result.

An OR operation finds all the data that matches any portion of the two statements connected by the OR. As you might expect, OR operations generally result in a broader search since any expression may be satisfied to generate a result.

A NOT operation finds all the data that doesn't satisfy the statement preceded by the NOT. For instance, in our sample query we might have wanted to exclude all the computers running a version of Windows earlier than Windows 2000 for upgrade purposes.

Creating a Query

Now that you've gotten your feet wet, let's put some of these SMS query elements to use by creating a query. Our test query will search for all computers running Windows 2000 that have at least 2 GB of free disk space (perhaps so that we can install Microsoft Office 2003 or upgrade to a newer version of Windows).

As we've seen in previous chapters, you can create a query from a number of locations—for example, you can create or reference a query when you define the membership of a collection, or you can create a status message query in the Status Message Queries folder in the SMS Administrator Console. The process is essentially the same wherever the query is created. For this example, we'll create a query from the Queries folder in the SMS Administrator Console. To do so, follow these steps:

1. In the SMS Administrator Console, navigate to the Queries folder and expand it to view the existing queries.

2. Right-click the Queries folder, choose New from the context menu, and then choose Query to display the Query Properties dialog box.

3. In the General tab, enter a name for your query. This name can be up to 127 characters, so it can be quite descriptive (as shown in Figure 16-3). You can also select an existing query to copy and modify by clicking Import Query Statement.

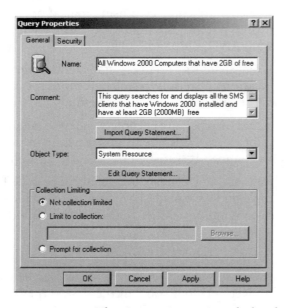

Figure 16-3. *The Query Properties dialog box, showing a descriptive query name.*

4. Enter a more detailed description of the query in the Comment text box if desired.

5. In the Collection Limiting section, you can narrow the query's scope by selecting Limit To Collection and then typing in or browsing for the collection name. You can also make the query more interactive and therefore more useful by selecting Prompt For Collection, in which

case you'll need to supply the collection name whenever the query is run. If you leave the default Not Collection Limited option selected, the query will be run against the entire database, assuming that the administrator executing the query has access to the entire database.

Note As described in Chapter 10, "Remote Control of Client Systems," and Chapter 17, "Security," you can create SMS security rights so that administrators have access to various objects in the database, including specific collections. If an administrator can't access a collection, the query won't run.

6. Select the object type you want to run the query on, and then click Edit Query Statement to display the Query Statement Properties dialog box, shown in Figure 16-4.

Figure 16-4. *The Query Statement Properties dialog box.*

7. In the General tab, you'll define the query results window—that is, the data (the attributes) displayed in the SMS Administrator Console when the query is run. To add a class and an attribute, click the New button (the yellow star) to display the Result Properties dialog box, shown in Figure 16-5.

Figure 16-5. *The Result Properties dialog box.*

8. Click Select to display the Select Attribute dialog box, shown in Figure 16-6, where you define an attribute class and an attribute.

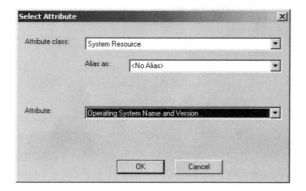

Figure 16-6. *The Select Attribute dialog box.*

9. Enter or select an alias if desired. This must be a valid SQL alias. (Refer to your SQL documentation for more information about aliases.) Click OK to save your selections and return to the Result Properties dialog box.

10. Select a sort order if desired, and then click OK to return to the Query Statement Properties dialog box.

11. Repeat steps 7 through 10 to add as many attributes as you want displayed when the query is run. Remember, the query results displayed are based on your query criteria.

12. Select the Criteria tab. In this tab you will actually define your query statement. Click the New button to display the Criterion Properties dialog box, shown in Figure 16-7. Here you will define the specific query elements.

Figure 16-7.   *The Criterion Properties dialog box.*

13. Select a criterion type from the drop-down list. To select an attribute class and an attribute to fill the Where text box, click Select to display the Select Attribute dialog box and choose the appropriate entries from the drop-down lists. In this example, because we're looking for computers with at least 2 GB of free space (2000 MB), our Attribute Class setting will be Logical Disk and the Attribute setting will be Free Space (MBytes).

14. Click OK to return to the Criterion Properties dialog box and then select an appropriate operator from the drop-down list.

15. Enter a value. If you click Values, SMS will display the Values dialog box, shown in Figure 16-8, which lists all the Free Space values currently recorded in the SMS database. You can select one of these values or enter the appropriate value (2000, in this case) in the Value text

box and then click OK. Notice that the value will then be added automatically to the Value text box in the Criterion Properties dialog box.

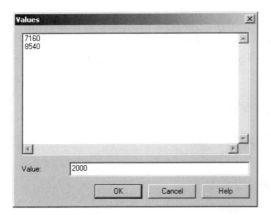

Figure 16-8. *The Values dialog box.*

16. The completed Criterion Properties dialog box is shown in Figure 16-9. Click OK to save your settings and return to the Criteria tab.

Figure 16-9. *The completed Criterion Properties dialog box.*

17. Repeat steps 12 through 16 to add query statements and use the logical operator buttons listed in the Criteria tab to connect these query statements. The New button, used to add a query statement, creates

an AND connection by default. Selecting the AND operator and clicking the &| button will change the AND to an OR, and clicking the ! button will change the AND to a NOT. The two Parentheses buttons are for grouping (or ungrouping) two or more selected statements.

18. Group your statements together using parentheses to define the order of evaluation. For example, Figure 16-10 shows what the query statement would look like if we had not restricted the query to the All Windows 2000 Server Computers collection.

Figure 16-10. *A sample query statement using logical operators and parentheses.*

Notice that this example also specifies more precisely the version number of computers running Windows 2000 Server and that the collection is more generic. Notice too that the operating system name and version are grouped together to ensure that we evaluate clients as those running Windows 2000 Server version 5.0.2195 instead of clients that are running Windows 2000 Server and clients that have any operating system whose version is 5.0.2195 (however likely or unlikely that might be).

Combining Attributes

The Joins tab of the Query Statement Properties dialog box, shown in Figure 16-11, displays the links made between the attribute classes. This linking is done for the most part automatically by SMS as you select attributes from different attribute classes. Sometimes, however, because of the nature of the query, you might need to create joins between different attribute classes manually.

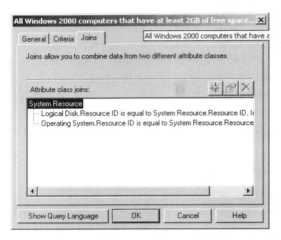

Figure 16-11. *The Joins tab.*

To create your own joins to different attribute classes, follow these steps:

1. Select the Joins tab and click the New button to display the Attribute Class Join Properties dialog box, shown in Figure 16-12.

Figure 16-12. *The Attribute Class Join Properties dialog box.*

2. In the Type drop-down list, select the join type. Four types of attribute class joins exist in SMS:

  - *Inner*—Displays only matching results

  - *Left*—Displays all results for the base attribute and matching results for the join attribute

  - *Right*—Displays all results for the join attribute and matching results for the base attribute

  - *Full*—Displays all results for both the base and the join attributes

3. To select an attribute class and attribute for the Join Attribute text box, click Select to display the Select Attribute dialog box, where you can select appropriate entries from the drop-down lists. The attribute you specified will be connected to the base attribute and becomes a child of the base attribute.

4. Choose an appropriate relational operator from the Operator drop-down list.

5. To fill in the Base Attribute text box, click Select to display the Select Attribute dialog box and choose the appropriate base attribute. The base attribute class is an existing attribute class on which you based the query. Notice that you can't change the base attribute class; you can change only the base attribute.

6. Click OK to close and save your query configuration.

7. Click OK again to save the query.

More Info   Working with joins requires a better-than-good understanding of SMS attribute classes and attributes. For a complete discussion of WQL, refer to the *Microsoft Systems Management Server 2003 Software Development Kit*, as mentioned earlier in this chapter.

Viewing the Query Language

Figure 16-13 shows our sample query using WQL. You can display the WQL version of any query by clicking Show Query Language in the General, Criteria, or Join tab of the Query Statement Properties dialog box. As you can see, writing an SMS 2003 query using WQL is not trivial.

Figure 16-13. *The WQL version of our sample query.*

Prompted Queries

The query we just created will satisfy our immediate quest for information from the SMS database. However, it's static in the sense that it will always check the database for the same information—that is, all computers running Windows 2000 Server that have at least 2 GB of free disk space.

A more useful query would be one that prompts us for value information as the query is being evaluated. For example, instead of hard-coding the value *2000*, it might be more useful to have the query prompt us for the *Size* value. This way, we can use the query repeatedly to find computers with different amounts of free space for different packages and purposes.

To change our query to a prompted query, we need to open it and modify it. You can modify any query by right-clicking it in the SMS Administrator Console and choosing Properties from the context menu to display the Query Properties dialog box. Click Edit Query Statement to return to the Query Statement Properties dialog box, select the Criteria tab, and then double-click the element you want to modify to display the Criterion Properties dialog box. In the example shown in Figure 16-14, we're modifying the Size value. The criterion type has been changed from Simple Value to Prompted Value.

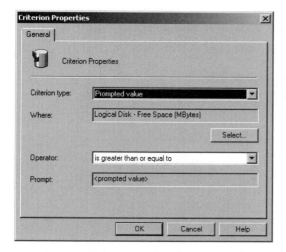

Figure 16-14. *An example of a prompted query.*

Compare this figure with Figure 16-9, and you'll see that the Value field has changed to indicate a prompted value. When this query is executed, it will first ask us to provide the value for Logical Disk-Free Space (MBytes).

Executing Queries

Now that we've seen how to create a query, it's time to explore how to run a query. All SMS queries are run through the SMS Administrator Console. The results of the queries will also be displayed in the SMS Administrator Console. To execute our sample query, follow these steps:

1. In the SMS Administrator Console, navigate to the Queries folder.

2. Right-click the query you want to run and choose Run Query from the context menu.

3. If the query contains any prompts, the Input Query Value dialog box appears, as shown in Figure 16-15. Enter the appropriate value and click OK.

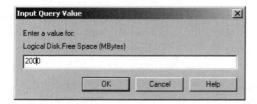

Figure 16-15. *The Input Query Value dialog box.*

4. You can view the results of the query in the result pane of the SMS Administrator Console interface, shown in Figure 16-16. You'll need to scroll to the right to see all the result fields you chose to display.

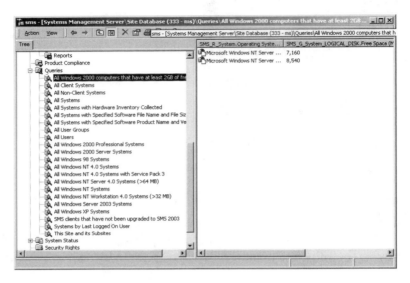

Figure 16-16. *The query results.*

As with other SMS-managed objects, such as collections, packages, and advertisements, only users who have access to the database objects will be able to run the query. The user must have rights to execute the SMS Administrator Console, rights to access the Queries folder, and rights to access data in the SMS database. This permission is assigned by applying object security through the SMS Administrator Console or sometimes through the WMI itself. SMS security is discussed in more detail in Chapter 17.

Reports

SMS 2.0 included a program called Crystal Reports that allowed you to run predefined reports against the SMS site database, as well as to create new reports. Aside from being a snap-in for the SMS Administrator Console, it wasn't really integrated as a feature of the product. However, SMS 2003 contains a fully integrated reporting tool called the Report Viewer that's accessible through the SMS Administrator Console and that uses your Web browser as a report viewer. Another companion feature for reporting is the dashboard. Dashboards are sets of reports that display in grid fashion in a single window.

SMS 2003 provides well over 100 predefined reports in the following categories:

- Hardware
- Software
- Software distribution
- Software metering
- Software updates
- Network
- Operating system
- SMS sites
- Status messages

You can view the list of available reports in two ways. You can view them through the Report Viewer, which in my opinion is the friendlier way because it lists the reports by category, or you can view them through the SMS Administrator's Console, which is basically just a long list of reports.

To view the list of available reports through the Report Viewer, follow these steps:

1. In the SMS Administrator Console, navigate to the Reporting node.

2. Right-click the Reporting node and select Run from the All Tasks context menu.

3. On the Run menu click the name of the reporting point that you want to use. The Report Viewer will be displayed, as shown in Figure 16-17.

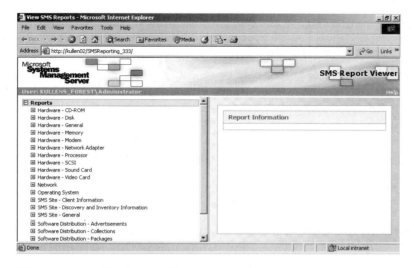

Figure 16-17.   *The Report Viewer.*

4. Select a report category from the list to see the reports contained within that category.

To view the list of available reports through the SMS Administrator Console, follow these steps:

1. In the SMS Administrator Console, navigate to the Reporting node.

2. Click Reports. The list of reports is displayed in the right pane of the console, as shown in Figure 16-18.

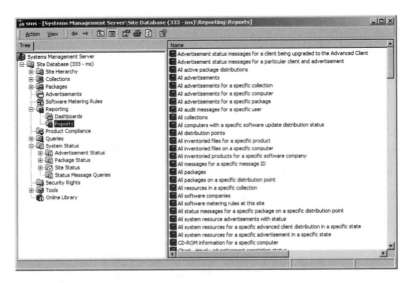

Figure 16-18.   *The Reports list.*

You can create your own custom reports either from scratch or by copying and modifying an existing report. The principal element of an SMS 2003 report is a SQL statement that defines the data to be gathered and how the results should be displayed. If you're going to create or modify reports effectively, you'll need to have a good working knowledge of SQL. Unfortunately, a discussion of SQL statements and syntax is beyond the scope of this book. Chapter 11 of the *Microsoft Systems Management Server 2003 Operations Guide*, available from the Microsoft SMS Web site (*http://www.microsoft.com/smserver*) and Microsoft TechNet, provides several examples of the use of SQL statements in reports.

More Info   For more reading on SQL statements and syntax, consult *Inside Microsoft SQL Server 2000* (Microsoft Press, 2000).

Like queries, you can use report prompts to make a report more flexible. Reports can also include links to additional sources of data to make them more effective, such as other reports, the Computer Details and Status Message

Details pages of the Report Viewer, and a URL that points to any file supported by HTTP.

You can also make reports created outside of SMS 2003 available for viewing. These are called supplemental reports, and although they're primarily Active Server Pages (ASP), they can be any file that can be displayed using Microsoft Internet Explorer 5.0 or later.

Note   SMS 2003 uses the reporting point site system to enable reporting at a site. Chapter 3, "Configuring Site Server Properties and Site Systems," discusses how to define and configure SMS site systems. Reports are run against the database of the site in which they were created. However, because of the way SMS propagates data from child sites to parent sites, you might want to set up reporting points based on where the data resides and on the reporting needs of the administrators at each site. For example, site administrators might want to be able to run reports against the data in their respective site's databases, but company managers might want more generic reports that run against the collected data at the central site.

Using Reports

As stated earlier, creating or modifying a report requires a good working knowledge of SQL, and that's beyond the scope of this book. However, here are some common elements necessary for every report for you to keep in mind:

- Every new report requires a category. You can choose an existing category or create a new category.
- Report names must be unique within each category.
- SMS assigns each report a unique ID.

You can configure each report to refresh results automatically according to an interval. You can also configure some reports to display their data as a chart.

Note   To display data as a chart, you must have a licensed copy of Microsoft Office 2000 Web Components, Microsoft Office XP Web Components, or Microsoft Office 2003 Web Components installed on the reporting point. You can install the Microsoft Office Web Components from the Microsoft Office installation CD.

Creating and Modifying a Report

To create or modify a report, complete the following steps:

1. In the SMS Administrator Console, navigate to the Reporting node.

2. Right-click Reports and select New, then Report, from the context menu to create a new report. Right-click a specific report and select Properties to modify an existing report. For ease of discussion, Figure 16-19 shows the properties of an existing report.

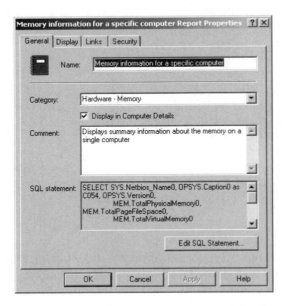

Figure 16-19. *The Report Properties dialog box.*

3. In the General tab, enter the name of the report, select a category, and enter a descriptive comment. Select the Display In Computer Details option if you want the report to be accessible through the Computer Details page of the Report Viewer.

4. Click Edit SQL Statement to display the Report SQL Statement dialog box, as shown in Figure 16-20. The Views and Columns lists display the available SQL views and columns from the SMS database that you can select to insert into your SQL statement. Select a view or column and click Insert to add it to your SQL statement. Select a column entry and click Values to see the values associated with that column entry. Enter or modify the SQL statement for this report in the SQL Statement text box. Click Prompts to view, add, or modify any prompts included as part of the report.

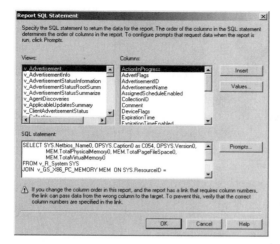

Figure 16-20.   *The Report SQL Statement dialog box.*

5. In the Display tab, shown in Figure 16-21, you can specify whether the report results should refresh automatically, the desired refresh interval, and whether you want to display a chart for the report.

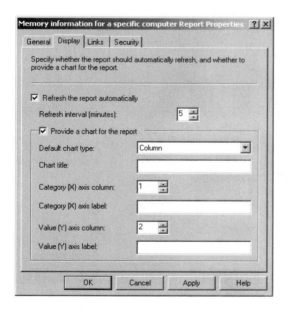

Figure 16-21.   *The Report Properties Display tab dialog box.*

6. In the Links tab, specify whether you want this report to link to another target (another report, the Computer Details page or Status Messages page in the Report Viewer, or a URL) and the appropriate target information. The target information will change based on your choice of link type and is fairly self-explanatory. In the example shown in Figure 16-22, we're linking to another report. You select the target report by clicking Select, selecting the report you want from the list, and clicking OK. The selected report is displayed in the Report text box. The Prompts list box displays any prompts associated with the target report and the column in this report that contains the data for each prompt. Click the Properties button (the icon just above the Prompts list box) to specify the appropriate column.

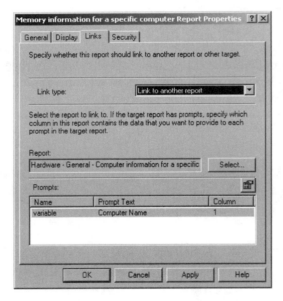

Figure 16-22. *The Report Properties Links tab dialog box.*

7. Click OK to save the report.

Copying an Existing Report

If you modify an existing report, there's really no easy way to return the report to its former state. You probably wouldn't want to directly modify the preexisting reports anyway. The better practice is to make a copy of a report that you want to modify and work with the copy instead of the original.

To make a copy of an existing report, complete the following steps:

1. In the SMS Administrator Console, navigate to Reports under the Reporting node.

2. Right-click the report you want to copy and select Clone from the All Tasks context menu.

3. Enter a name for the new report when prompted and click OK.

Importing and Exporting Reports

SMS 2003 gives you the ability to import into your SMS database report objects that were created in another SMS site and to export report objects from your site. You can export all your reports or a specific report. Report objects are exported to a Managed Object Format (MOF) file, which is a text-based file. Only report object definitions are exported. This means that when you import the report at another site, the report runs against the other site's database and returns results based on the data contained in that site's database. The exported report doesn't contain any information from the source site's database.

If you export a report that includes links, only links to URLs are preserved. Links to other objects, such as other reports, must be manually reconfigured. When you import reports from another SMS site, it's recommended that you use a text editor to review the MOF file entries for any report names that might duplicate reports you already have in your site. If you import a report that has the same name in the same category as an existing report in your site, you'll overwrite the existing report with the imported report, so be careful.

To export a report, follow these steps:

1. In the SMS Administrator Console, navigate to Reports under the Reporting node.

2. Right-click Reports to export all report objects or the specific report you want to export and select Export Objects from the All Tasks context menu.

3. Complete the wizard and click Finish.

To import a report, follow these steps:

1. In the SMS Administrator Console, navigate to Reports under the Reporting node.

2. Right-click Reports and select Import Objects from the All Tasks context menu.

3. Complete the wizard and click Finish.

Scheduling a Report

Each report and dashboard that you create has a unique URL associated with it that contains the report ID and the variable names you used to run the report. You can use this URL to schedule a report or dashboard to run at a specified interval. You can see what the URL is by running a report using the Report Viewer and then copying the URL that displays in the Address box of your Web browser, as shown in Figure 16-23. If you're using a prompted report, you must provide all the prompt information in order to run the report. Thereafter, the scheduled report will always run using the same prompt values that you provided.

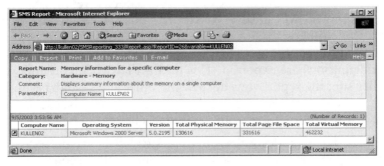

Figure 16-23. *A report showing the unique URL associated with it.*

Schedule the report to run using the Scheduled Tasks feature of your operating system. For example, on a Windows XP computer, follow these steps:

1. Start Scheduled Tasks from Control Panel.

2. Double-click Add Scheduled Task and click Next.

3. Select Internet Explorer from the Application list and click Next. If it's not listed in the Application list, click Browse, navigate to it, and then click Open.

4. Enter a task name, select a time interval, and then click Next.

5. If prompted, select the time and day you want the task to run and click Next.

6. Enter a user name and password that has permissions to run the report and click Next.

7. Select the Open Advanced Properties For This Task When I Click Finish option and click Finish.

8. In the Properties dialog box, insert a space after the entry in the Run text box and enter or paste the URL for the report.

9. Click OK to save the new scheduled report.

Tip You can use the report URL in several ways to facilitate the viewing of specific reports. For example, you could send the URL as a link in an e-mail or add it to a manager's Web browser as a favorite. The important thing to remember is that whoever launches the link must have at least Read permission for the report.

Running a Report

After all that, running a report is easy. To run a report, complete the following steps:

1. In the SMS Administrator Console, navigate to the Reporting node.

2. Right-click the Reporting node and select Run from the All Tasks context menu.

3. On the Run menu, click the name of the reporting point that you want to use. The Report Viewer is displayed, as shown previously in Figure 16-17.

4. Select a report category from the list to see the reports contained within that category.

5. Select a report to run. In the Report Information section of the Report Viewer, enter any required information. In Figure 16-24, the selected report requires that you specify the computer name. You can enter the name or click the Values button to display a list of computer names in the database. Click Display when you're finished to display the report results in your Web browser.

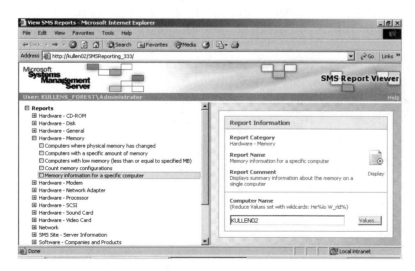

Figure 16-24. *The Report Information section of Report Viewer.*

Note Although it looks like you can use wild cards, the wild cards you enter are used only to reduce the number of values displayed when you click Values. You can't use wild cards to alter the results of the report.

You could also run a specific report by selecting that report directly in the SMS Administrator Console, right-clicking, and choosing Run from the All Tasks context menu, and then proceeding in much the same way as outlined above.

Using Dashboards

A dashboard is a set of reports that you can display in a grid format to facilitate the quick review of one or more specific or related reports. Dashboards can display any report except those that require prompted values. You can view available dashboards through the SMS Administrator Console or Report Viewer in much the same way as you view reports. SMS 2003 creates a unique ID and URL for each dashboard, so you can schedule them, send them out as links, or set them up as a Web browser favorite much the same as you do for reports. However, SMS 2003 doesn't provide any default or predefined dashboards, so you'll have to set them up first.

Creating a Dashboard

To create a new dashboard, complete the following steps:

1. In the SMS Administrator Console, navigate to the Reporting node and expand it.

2. Right-click Dashboards, select New from the context menu, and then select Dashboard to display the Dashboard Properties dialog box shown in Figure 16-25.

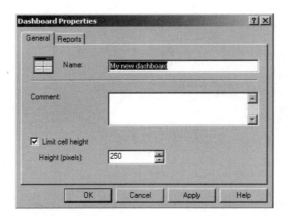

Figure 16-25. *The Dashboard Properties dialog box.*

3. In the General tab, enter a name for the dashboard and a descriptive comment. Select the Limit Cell Height option (possibly for larger reports) and enter the maximum height in pixels you want for the report.

4. In the Reports tab, shown in Figure 16-26, enter the number of rows and columns to display in the dashboard and click Set. For example, if you want to display four reports, you might select 2 rows and 2 columns, or 4 rows and 1 column, or 1 row and 4 columns.

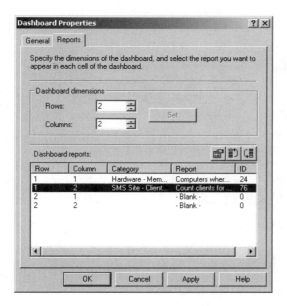

Figure 16-26.   *The Dashboard Properties Reports tab.*

5. In the Dashboard Reports section, identify the report that you want to display in each cell of the dashboard. Click the Properties icon (the first of the three icons immediately above the Dashboard Reports section) to display the list of available reports that you can select.

6. When you have selected all the reports, click OK.

Running a Dashboard

To run a dashboard from the SMS Administrator Console, follow these steps:

1. In the SMS Administrator Console, navigate to the Reporting node and expand it.

2. Select Dashboards and select the dashboard you want to run from the list of dashboards.

3. Right-click the dashboard and select Run from the All Tasks context menu. Then select the appropriate reporting point. The dashboard appears in your Web browser similar to that shown in Figure 16-27.

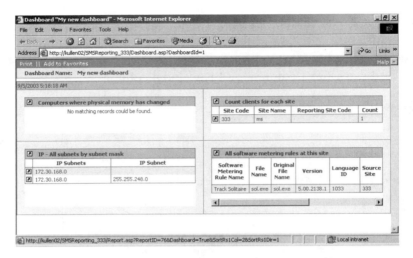

Figure 16-27. *The dashboard displayed in a Web browser.*

To run a dashboard from the Report Viewer, complete the following steps:

1. In the SMS Administrator Console, navigate to the Reporting node.

2. Right-click Reporting, select Run from the All Tasks context menu, and then select the appropriate reporting point to display the Report Viewer.

3. Select and expand Dashboards to see the list of available dashboards, as shown in Figure 16-28.

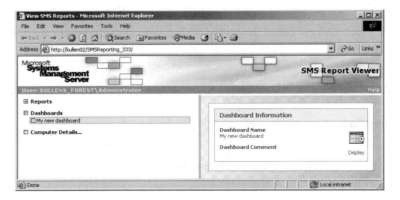

Figure 16-28. *The dashboards displayed in Report Viewer.*

4. Select the dashboard you want to run and click Display.

Checkpoints

The main issues you would encounter when running a query or report, aside from creating the wrong query statement, involve security. It's important to remember that for someone to run a query or report, that person must have access permission to the SMS Administrator Console, the node containing the query or report (such as the Queries, Reporting, or Status Message Queries node), and the database information the query is searching for; otherwise, the request will fail. As mentioned, you'll learn more about security in Chapter 17.

Summary

As you can see, there are several ways to extract and use the data collected and stored in the SMS database. Throughout this book we've looked at examples of queries and reports to view information stored in the SMS database, and now you should have a better understanding of how to create—and improve—them and how to generate queries and reports of your own to view status messages, populate collections, and otherwise search for data based on your specific criteria. Chapter 17 focuses on another database management issue—security.

Chapter 17
Security

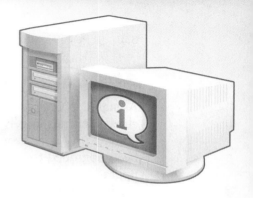

This chapter summarizes some of the security-related issues we've looked at in earlier chapters, such as Microsoft Systems Management Server (SMS) standard and advanced security and the use of Microsoft Windows accounts, and introduces a few new topics. We'll begin with an overview of the NTFS security SMS itself places on various directories. Then we'll review the differences between standard and advanced security modes in SMS and the use of internal and manually created SMS accounts and group accounts. You'll also learn how to set permissions on SMS objects through the SMS Administrator Console and how to create a custom SMS Administrator Console that incorporates SMS object security.

SMS builds several levels of security into its overall security model. You can choose to install standard security mode, which is basically the same security model used in SMS 2.0, or the advanced security mode. This security mode relies primarily on the use of internal and system accounts to carry out site-related and client-related tasks, such as running packages. SMS uses Windows security—NTFS and share permissions—to protect SMS-related folders and files on SMS servers. The SMS Provider and Windows Management Instrumentation (WMI) security are established, including access control over SMS objects, in the SMS Administrator Console. You can apply this level of security at the class or instance level, as we'll see in the section entitled "Permissions and Security Objects" later in this chapter. Finally, security is enforced at the SQL Server level through the use of integrated or standard security, as discussed in Chapter 2, "Primary Site Installation."

More Info This chapter is intended to provide you with information about the most common aspects of SMS security, especially those areas of security that you're most likely to be involved with in a smaller organization. A far more complete and detailed treatment of SMS security can be found in Chapters 5 and 12 of the *Microsoft Systems Management Server 2003 Concepts, Planning, and Deployment Guide*, available on the SMS 2003 CD, through Microsoft TechNet, and as a print book orderable through the microsoft SMS Web site (*http://microsoft.com/smserver/downloads*).

Standard and Advanced Security

As stated in Chapter 1, "Overview," SMS 2003 offers two security modes. Your choice depends largely on the way you've implemented your network Windows servers. If your network still consists of some Windows NT 4.0 servers or hasn't been upgraded to Active Directory directory service native mode, or if you're upgrading an existing SMS 2.0 site, your choice will be standard security, and the installation of SMS will effectively result in an SMS site that functions not much differently from the way SMS 2.0 sites did. In short, it will create many user accounts that it will use to carry out various SMS-related tasks on SMS servers and SMS clients.

If your network is a fully implemented native mode Active Directory network or if all your SMS component servers are running Windows 2000 or later and are registered in Active Directory (a requirement for advanced security), you can choose advanced security.

To be more specific, advanced security requires that the SMS site server and all SMS site systems are running Windows 2000 Service Pack 4 (SP4) or later (or have Windows Quick Fix Engineering (QFE) update 325804 applied) or an operating system in the Windows Server 2003 family in an Active Directory domain. The SMS site database servers must be running SQL Server 2000 SP3 or later, and they must be run in Windows authentication–only mode.

The main advantage of using advanced security mode is that it's certainly the more secure of the two security modes. As we've said, advanced security doesn't require nor rely on the great number of user accounts that standard security needs to carry out SMS-related tasks. In contrast, advanced security uses two security accounts: the local system account and the computer account. Advanced security uses the local system account on SMS servers to run SMS services and make changes on the server and uses computer accounts (rather than user accounts) to connect to other computers and to make changes on other computers. Because only services running in the local system account context can use computer accounts and only administrators can configure services, advanced security is a highly secure mode and therefore the preferred and recommended security mode.

> **Note**   A central site can't run standard security if any other site in that hierarchy is running advanced security.

You can choose advanced security mode during SMS setup, or you can install your SMS site server with standard mode and then upgrade to advanced security later. To upgrade your site to advanced security, complete the following steps:

1. Navigate to the site entry under the Site Hierarchy node in the SMS Administrator Console.

2. Right-click the site entry and select Properties from the context menu.

3. Click Set Security in the General tab shown in Figure 17-1.

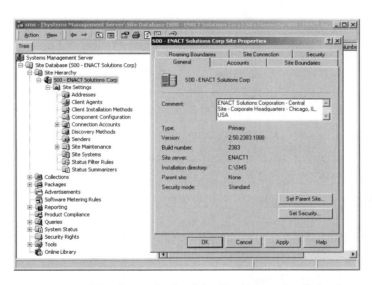

Figure 17-1.   *The General tab of the Site Properties dialog box.*

4. Click Yes when prompted to turn on advanced security mode as shown in Figure 17-2.

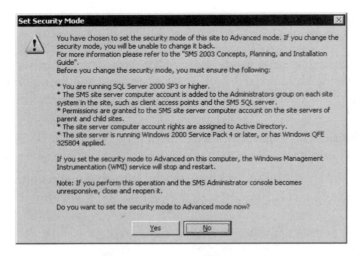

Figure 17-2. *The Set Security Mode prompt.*

I make it a practice to always read the prompts that SMS shows me, and I highly recommend it to you as well. For example, in the prompt that displays in Figure 17-2, SMS is clearly stating several things that you must be aware of:

- Once you make this change, you can't go back.

- There are several server requirements that must be confirmed to support advanced security.

- A service (Windows Management Instrumentation) is stopped and restarted.

- You might have a problem with the SMS Administrator Console that requires you to restart it.

The first point is obvious, although, technically, you *could* revert your site to standard security if you had backed up your site server and its registry and could restore the system state to its previous settings. However, let's just stick with standard procedures and say this: don't upgrade to advanced security unless you're sure you want to do it and you're ready to do it. It's hard to go back.

The second point is perhaps not as obvious, so let's take some time and discuss it. Let's begin with the fact that in advanced security mode, SMS 2003 relies on the local system account mainly to run service-related tasks and on computer accounts mainly to maintain communications. This oversimplifies the case somewhat, but still this is a good rule of thumb to keep in mind.

So with this rule of thumb in mind, note well what the Set Security Mode prompt is telling you to do. The site system requires Administrator access on its site systems and permissions on any parent or child sites that it must communicate with in an SMS hierarchy. You can accomplish the former by adding the SMS site server computer account to the Administrator's group on each site system in the site. Computer accounts are created as hidden accounts, so you can't add the account the way you'd ordinarily do. You need to add the account from a command line. You can add the site server's computer account to the site system's local Administrator's group using the following command line command at the site system:

Net localgroup Administrators *\domain\siteservercomputername*$ /ADD

Similarly, you'll need to add the computer account of each site system to the site server's Site_System_to_Site_Server_Connection group. SMS will automatically do this for the client access point (CAP) and management point site systems to the Site System to Site Server Connection group and will do so for any new site system you add. When you upgrade to advanced security mode, the site server's computer account is automatically added to the Site_to_Site_Connection group on the parent and child sites, allowing communications and the appropriate level of access between sites in the hierarchy. Although this all happens automatically, as a point of troubleshooting, you should, of course, verify that the computer accounts have been given the appropriate level of access they require.

NTFS Security

As you know, an SMS 2003 site server requires the existence of an NTFS partition that's at least 1 GB in size. This requirement extends to the main SMS directory, of course, but it also includes the CAP and management point directories created and maintained generally on the site server. You should invest some time in reviewing the permissions set by SMS both on the directories and on the shares SMS creates to learn why various connection accounts need to be created and how the permissions set by SMS affect the ability of these accounts to carry out a task.

> **Tip** I have found that when organizations make changes to the access levels for Windows administrative shares, either through direct modification of permissions or through application of a group policy, the changes can affect SMS's ability to create and maintain its own folders. If status and log messages indicate a permissions issue when SMS is trying to create or update a folder or file, the first thing to check should be the Windows security you're applying on the SMS server. Often a minor change to a group policy can clear up major permission issues with SMS.

You can use Tables 17-1 through 17-4 to verify the permissions on the site server, CAP, management point, and distribution point. I'll leave it to you to familiarize yourself with the permissions on other site systems (after all, you have to get *some* homework from me). In general, unless otherwise stated, sub-folders inherit their permissions from their parent folder. For the site server, I've identified the main shares and folders rather than iterating the hundreds of folders that SMS creates and maintains. (Well, okay, maybe not hundreds, but there are a lot!)

Table 17-1. CAP folder and share permissions

Share or Directory Name	Administrators	Guests	Users	Everyone
CAP_*sitecode* (share)	Not assigned	Not assigned	Not assigned	Full
CAP_*sitecode*	Full	Read, Execute, List	Read, Execute, List	Not assigned
Ccr.box	Full	Read, Write, Execute	Read, Write, Execute	Not assigned
Clicomp.box	Full	Read, Execute, List	Read, Execute, List	Not assigned
Clidata.box	Full	Read, Execute, List	Read, Execute, List	Not assigned
Clifiles.box	Full	Read, Execute, List	Read, Execute, List	Not assigned
Ddr.box	Full	Read, Write, Execute	Read, Write, Execute	Not assigned
Inventory.box	Full	Read, Write, Execute	Read, Write, Execute	Not assigned
Offerinf.box	Full	Read, Execute, List	Read, Execute, List	Not assigned
Pkginfo.box	Full	Read, Execute, List	Read, Execute, List	Not assigned
Sinv.box	Full	Read, Write, Execute	Read, Write, Execute	Not assigned
Statmsgs.box	Full	Read, Write, Execute	Read, Write, Execute	Not assigned
Swmproc.box	Full	Read, Execute, List	Read, Execute, List	Not assigned

Table 17-2.   Management point folder permissions

Share or Directory Name	Administrators	System	SMS_SiteSystemToSite ServerConnection_*sitecode*
SMS\MP	Full	Full	Read, Execute, List
SMS\MP\Outboxes	Full	Full	Read, Execute, List
Subfolders of SMS\ MP\Outboxes\	Full	Full	Not assigned

Table 17-3.   SMS distribution points folder and share permissions

Share or Directory Name	Administrators	Guests	Users	Everyone
SMSPKGx$ (share)	Not assigned	Not assigned	Not assigned	Full
SMSPKGx$	Full	Read, Execute, List	Read, Execute, List	Not assigned
<package id>	Full	Not assigned	Read, Execute, List	Not assigned

Table 17-4.   SMS site server folder and share permissions

Share or Directory Name	Description	Account	Permissions
SMS_*sitecode* (share)	This share is associated with the \SMS directory—the installation directory for SMS on a site server.	Everyone	Full
SMS	The directory into which SMS is installed on a site server.	Administrators System SMS_SiteSystemToSiteServerConnection_ *sitecode*	Full Full Read, Execute, List
SMS_SITE (share)	This share is associated with the SMS\Inboxes\ Despoolr.box\Receive directory.	Everyone	Full
SMS\Inboxes\ Despoolr.box\ Receive	This directory is used when data is transferred from a child site to its parent site.	Administrators System SMS_SiteSystemToSiteServerConnection_*sitecode*	Full Full Full

Table 17-4. SMS site server folder and share permissions

Share or Directory Name	Description	Account	Permissions
SMS Client	This share is associated with the \SMS\Client directory.	Everyone	Full
SMS\Client	This directory is used to store the SMS client installation executable files.	Administrators System SMS_SiteSystem-ToSiteServerConnection_*sitecode* Guests Users	Full Full Read, Execute, List Read, Execute, List Read, Execute, List
SMS_CPSx$ (share)	This share is associated with the *x*\SMSPKG folder, where *x* represents the drive containing the folder. You identify this drive to SMS through the Software Distribution component properties in the SMS Administrator Console. (See Chapter 12, "Package Distribution and Management," for more information.)	Everyone	Full Control
SMSPKG	This directory is used to store the compressed package source file created during the package distribution process.	Administrators SMS_SiteSystemTo-SiteServerConnection_*sitecode*	Full Read, Execute, List
SMS_SUIAgent	This share is associated with the SMS\SUIAgent folder.	Everyone	Full
SMS\SUIAgent	This directory is used to store the files associated with the Software Update Installation agents.	Administrators System SMS_SiteSystem-ToSiteServer-Connection_*sitecode*	Full Full Read, Execute, List

Accounts and Groups

As we've seen throughout this book, SMS uses a variety of accounts to perform various tasks. Some of these accounts might be created by you, such as a Client Connection account; others are created by SMS automatically, such as the SMS Server Connection account. The number of accounts that SMS creates and requires depends largely on the security mode you've selected. As we've seen, advanced security mode only requires the local system account and computer account.

You can categorize the various accounts that SMS can use in many ways. I have broken these down into four categories as follows:

- Accounts common to both advanced and standard security
- Accounts specific to advanced security
- Accounts specific to standard security
- Accounts specific to clients (advanced and standard security)

In this section we'll review each of these account categories in more detail.

Accounts Common to Advanced and Standard Security

Three user accounts and six group accounts used at the SMS server level are common to both advanced and standard security. These are described in Tables 17-5 and 17-6.

Table 17-5.   User accounts common to advanced and standard security

Account Type	Account Name	Description
Local System	N/A	Required account. Used to run SMS client and server processes and services. Used to run SMS Advanced Client and server processes in Advanced Security.
Client Push Installation	Administrator's choice	Optional account. Used to install SMS components on Legacy Client computers when the SMS Service account doesn't have appropriate rights on the client computer. Can be identified for use by Advanced Clients as well. Default for Legacy Client: SMS Service Account. Default for Advanced Client: client computer account.
Site Address	Administrator's choice	Optional account. Used for site-to-site communications. Default for standard security: SMS Service account. Default for advanced security: site server computer account.

Table 17-6. Group accounts common to advanced and standard security

Account Type	Account Name	Description
SMS Administrators	SMS Admins	Used to provide access to the SMS Provider through WMI to launch the SMS Administrator Console and access the SMS site database.
Internal Client Group	SMSInternalCliGrp	Contains the client token and client service accounts on domain controllers (domain controllers require that all user accounts belong to a group).
Reporting Users	SMS Reporting Users	Controls user access to SMS. Reports through the reporting point.
Site System To Site Server Connection	SMS_SiteSystem-ToSiteServerConnection _sitecode_	Provides site systems access to site server resources.
Site System To SQL Server Connection	SMS_SiteSystem-ToSSQLConnection_ _sitecode_	Provides management points, server locator points, and reporting points access to the SMS site database server.
Site To Site Connection	SMS_SiteToSite-Connection_ _sitecode_	Facilitates communications between sites in an SMS hierarchy. Default members are site address accounts.

Accounts Specific to Advanced Security

When we talk about advanced security, we usually refer to the local system account and the computer account. Strictly speaking, the local system account is sometimes used while running standard security. However, I'm including it here to emphasize its purpose under advanced security. Table 17-7 summarizes these two accounts.

Table 17-7. Accounts specific to advanced security

Account Type	Account Name	Description
Local System	N/A	Used to run SMS client and server processes and services. Used to run SMS Advanced Client and server processes in Advanced Security.
Computer	_Machinename_$	Used by SMS computers to communicate with other SMS computers.

Accounts Specific to Standard Security

Like SMS 2.0, SMS 2003 running in standard security mode uses many accounts to carry out various tasks on the server and on the client. Table 17-8 summarizes these accounts.

Table 17-8.   Accounts specific to standard security

Account Type	Account Name	Description
SMS Service	SMSService by default, but also administrator's choice	Used to run SMS site server processes and services.
Server Connection	SMSServer_*sitecode*	Used to provide CAPs access to the site server.
Site System Connection	Administrator's choice	Optional account. Used to provide sites servers access to site systems. SMS Service account is used by default.
Remote Service	SMSSvc_*sitecode*_xxxx	Used to run the SMS Executive service on remote CAPs and the SQL Monitor service on an SMS database server that isn't the site server.

SMS Service Account

Here's a bit more about the SMS Service account as you're likely to encounter it if you're upgrading from an SMS 2.0 site or need to maintain downward compatibility within your SMS hierarchy for a time. The SMS Service account is the primary account created by SMS in standard security mode. Site server services use this account to create shares and directories on site systems, set permissions, copy files, install services and components, and verify operation of the site system. Specifically, the SMS Executive, SMS Site Component Manager, SMS Site Backup, SMS SQL Monitor, and SMS Client Configuration Manager all use this account. The SMS Service account is created when the SMS site server is installed. By default, it's named SMSService and made a member of the local Administrators group on the site server as well as the Domain Admins and Domain Users groups in the Windows domain the site server belongs to. Because the account is a domain administrator, you should probably rename it and provide password protection with a complex password composed of alphanumeric and special characters. (Just don't forget the password.)

Tip One way to increase security for your Windows domain is to remove the SMS Service account from the Domain Admins group and add it directly to the local Administrators groups on the site server, the server running SQL, CAP, logon point, and software metering server. If you aren't using a Client Push Installation account, add the SMS Service account to the local Administrators group on every SMS Legacy Client as well.

If your SMS site systems are members of trusted Windows domains, you can use the same SMS Service account throughout your site hierarchy for convenience. However, if SMS sites and site systems are in untrusted Windows domains, you must create the account separately in each domain. Although this won't be a concern with Windows 2000 or higher domains, trust relationships might well be a concern if you still need to support Windows NT 4.0 domains. For example, the SMS Service account is used to access the SMS database on the server running SQL. If the server running SQL happens to be in a different, untrusted Windows domain than the SMS site server, SMS will need to use Windows' pass-through authentication method to gain access to the server running SQL. This means that you'll need to create the SMS Service account in the domain of the server running SQL using the same account name and password that are used on the site server.

Caution Do not change this account through the Windows account management tools—for example, the User Manager For Domains utility in Windows NT 4.0. If you need to rename the account or change the password, do so using the Reset function of SMS Setup. This method will ensure that all the SMS services are properly updated with the changed account information.

SQL Server Account

The SQL Server account, created by SQL Server during its installation, is used to provide SMS services with access to the SMS database and the software metering database. The type of account that's used depends on whether or not you're using Windows Authentication mode when accessing SQL Server. Recall from Chapter 2 that you need to tell SMS which security method you've enabled for SQL Server in order for SMS to establish the correct account to use.

By and large, you manage SQL Server accounts through SQL Server Enterprise Manager. If you need to change the account for SMS, first establish the account in SQL Server and then update SMS with the new account information, as shown here:

1. In the SMS Administrator Console, navigate to the *sitecode - site name* entry under Site Hierarchy.

2. Right-click the site entry and choose Properties from the context menu to display the Site Properties dialog box.

3. Select the Accounts tab, shown in Figure 17-3. In the SQL Server Account section, click Set and supply the new account name and password in the SQL Server Account dialog box.

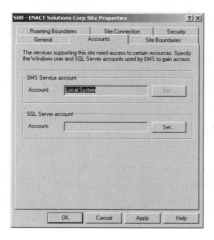

Figure 17-3. *The Accounts tab of the Site Properties dialog box.*

4. Choose OK to save the change and update SMS.

SMS Site Address Account

Here's more information about the site address accounts. The SMS Site Address account is used to establish communications between a parent site and a child site in an SMS hierarchy for the purpose of forwarding data such as discovery data records (DDRs), site control information, inventory, and packages. (Refer to Chapter 4, "Multiple-Site Structures," for more information about the communications process.) Although the SMS Service account can be used to accomplish this task, it's generally recommended that the SMS administrator create a separate account specifically for the purpose of intersite communications. This account can be made fairly secure as well because it need not be a member of the Domain Admins group. In fact, the account needs only Read, Write, Execute, and Delete permissions on the SMS_SITE share (SMS\Inboxes\Despoolr.box\Receive), so it could be simply a guest account with the appropriate permissions to the share.

Server Connection Account

SMS creates the SMS Server Connection account automatically during installation of the site server, and remote site systems use it to connect back to the site server to transfer information. The Inbox Manager Assistant component on CAPs uses this account to transfer client data to appropriate inboxes on the site server. The SMS Provider also uses this account to access SMS directories on the site server as well as the package definition file (PDF) store.

The SMS Server Connection account is named SMSServer_*sitecode* and is assigned a randomly generated password. *Do not modify this account in any way*. In fact, it's a best practice not to modify *any* account created and maintained by SMS itself.

If you change the password for the SMS Server Connection account, you can reset it by running the Reset routine through SMS Setup. However, if you delete the account, calling Reset won't restore it. Instead, you'll need to reinstall SMS.

Accounts Specific to SMS Clients

The accounts used by SMS clients fall into three categories: those common to both the Advanced and Legacy Clients, those specific to the Advanced Client, and those specific to the Legacy Client. As you might have come to expect, the Advanced Client requires far fewer accounts than the Legacy Client does. Table 17-9 summarizes these accounts for you.

Table 17-9. Accounts specific to SMS clients

Account Type	Account Name	Description
Accounts Common to Advanced and Legacy Clients		
Client Configuration Manager (CCM) Boot Loader (Nondomain Controller)	SMSCCMBootAcct&	Used to install the CCM Boot Loader during installation of SMS client components on an SMS client that isn't a domain controller.
CCM Boot Loader (Domain Controller)	SMS#_*domaincontroller*	Used to install the CCM Boot Loader during installation of SMS client components on an SMS client that's a domain controller.
Accounts Specific to Advanced Clients		
Advanced Client Network Access	Administrator's choice	Optional account. Used by the Advanced Client when an advertised program needs to access a share on a server other than the distribution point. The account is a domain account and must have appropriate permissions on the appropriate shares.

Table 17-9.   Accounts specific to SMS clients

Account Type	Account Name	Description
Accounts Specific to Legacy Clients		
Client Services (Domain Controller)	SMS$_*domaincontroller*	Used by SMS client services specifically on domain controllers that are also SMS clients.
Client Service (Nondomain Controller)	SMSCliSvcAcct&	Used by SMS client services on domain SMS clients that aren't domain controllers.
Client User Token (Domain Controller)	SMSCliToknAcct&	Used by SMS client services to execute various component functions on a domain controller installed as a Legacy Client, as well as to run advertised programs in an administrator security context when specified for a package.
Client User Token (Nondomain Controller)	SMSCliToknLocalAcct&	Used by SMS client services to execute various component functions on the Legacy Client, as well as to run advertised programs in an administrator security context when specified for a package.
Client Connection	SMSClient_*sitecode*	Used by SMS client components running on Legacy Clients to connect to CAPs and distribution points to transfer data such as inventory or client configuration updates.
Legacy Client Software Installation	Administrator's choice	Optional account. Used by SMS in lieu of the SMS User Token to install an advertised program on a Legacy Client in an administrator security context when additional network access is required.

Client User Token Account

Here's a bit more detail about the Client User Token account. When programs are executed at the Standard Client computer, they will run under the local user account's security context. Since most users are logged on as users and not as administrators, these programs will run under the local user context. Although this isn't such a big deal for non-Windows systems and for Windows 98 clients, it can be a big issue on Windows NT 4.0 and later clients because they maintain a local account database and provide more security over system modifications such as program installation. Thus, the security context poses a problem when dealing with SMS packages.

When you identify a program to SMS as requiring an administrator context to execute it, SMS uses the Client User Token account, named SMSCliToknAcct& if the client is a domain controller and SMSCliToknLocalAcct& if the client isn't a domain controller, to create a user token on the client with sufficient access to run the program. This internal account is created automatically, assigned a random password, and granted the Act As Part Of The Operating System, Log On As A Service, and Replace A Process Level Token user rights on the client. This account will be sufficient in most cases. Recall from Chapter 12, however, that if the program execution requires that the program connect to network resources other than the distribution point, the client user token account will fail because it's created as a local account rather than as a domain account. In this case you should use the SMS Legacy Client Software Installation account. (See Chapter 12 for a complete discussion of installation accounts.)

Real World Creating Additional Client Connection Accounts

Since client connection account information, such as the randomly generated password, is propagated to each Windows computer that's an SMS Legacy Client, you might encounter account lockout problems in Windows networks that have account lockout policies enabled. When SMS updates a client connection account password, that information is normally passed on to the client computers at the next client update cycle.

But what if a client computer has been shut down for a time—say, while a user was on vacation—and in the interim SMS updated the client account password? In this scenario the client computer would have no way of knowing about the password change. When the client computer was restarted, the client connection account would try to reconnect using the old password and would be locked out—effectively disabling SMS Legacy Clients from sending or receiving updates to the CAP.

The solution to this problem involves creating additional client connection accounts through the site server. You can create two or more client connection accounts for which you control the passwords. Rotate these accounts within the password aging cycle of your Windows account policy so that the client will always have access to a valid account. As you create a new client connection account, you can delete the oldest account. This technique ensures that the client computers will always have current account information and minimizes the possibility of the client connection account being locked out. Or better yet, upgrade your Legacy Clients to the Advanced Client software as soon as possible to take advantage of its streamlined approach to accounts and its superior security.

Permissions and Security Objects

In addition to the security provided by Windows and through SQL Server, SMS 2003 maintains its own object-level security for the SMS site database using the SMS Provider and WMI security. By assigning specific permissions to Windows users and groups, the SMS Provider controls access to specific SMS objects such as packages, advertisements, and collections.

The SMS database is accessed through the SMS Administrator Console, and it's here that SMS object security is defined. The user must have a valid Windows account in the domain in which the site server resides. When a user launches the SMS Administrator Console, the user's account automatically accesses WMI, which validates the user's permission. The user must be a member of the local SMS Admins group on the SMS Administrator Console computer, be a local Administrator, or be specifically granted WMI user rights using the WMI Control tool. The WMI Control tool is a Microsoft Management Console (MMC) snap-in. This utility provides an interface for assigning users and groups Read or Write permission to WMI objects. The user must also be a member of the SMS Admins group on the site server or on the server running SQL if the SMS Provider was installed there.

After WMI security validates the user, the SMS Provider validates the account and launches the SMS Administrator Console, displaying those objects for which the user has been given permission. By default, permission to all SMS objects is granted to the local system account (the NT Authority\System account) and the administrator who first installed the site server, as shown in Figure 17-4. To view the object security of any SMS object, select the Security tab in the object's Properties dialog box.

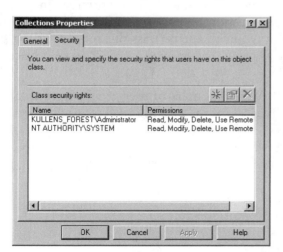

Figure 17-4. *The Security tab of the Collections Properties dialog box.*

Security Objects

Security can be established for the following eight SMS object classes:

- Advertisement
- Collection
- Packages
- Report
- Query
- Site
- Software Metering Rule
- Status Message

For most classes two kinds of security configuration are possible: class and instance. *Class security* is similar to NTFS folder permissions. Just as a folder's NTFS permissions apply by default to all the files within the folder, so is class security applied to all members of the object class. In other words, any permissions you set for the object class Collections will apply to each collection, whether they're the default collections or new collections you create.

Instance security is similar to NTFS file security. Just as you can set permissions on files different from those set at the folder level, you can also set security on individual members of an object class. For example, you might give the Windows group Finance Helpdesk no permission to the object class Collections yet still allow the group to read and manage the specific collection Finance Clients.

Establishing class and instance security for SMS objects is much the same as creating access control lists (ACLs) for Windows files, folders, and printers. In fact, many of the same principles apply. Permissions are always assigned to users or groups. Members of a group implicitly inherit the permissions for that group. No permissions granted is the same as Deny Access—you can't access the object class.

For each class, you'll identify which Windows users or user groups have what level of access. You'll then refine that access at the instance level for each object. The permissions list reads much like NTFS permissions, with the addition of some permissions specific to SMS tasks and functions, such as remote control. Table 17-10 describes the available permissions and their object types.

Table 17-10.   Object permissions

Permission	Object Type	Description
Administer	All security object types	Administers all object classes, including assigning or modifying security rights.
Advertise	Collections	Advertises existing programs to a collection.
Create	All security object types	Creates an instance of an object type, such as a new query or collection.
Delegate	All security object types except Status Messages	Grants rights (that have been explicitly assigned to a user) for any instances created by that user.
Delete	All security object types except Status Messages	Deletes an instance of an object type, such as a package or an advertisement.
Delete Resource	Collections	Deletes a resource from a collection, such as a computer.
Distribute	Packages	Deploys a package to a distribution point.
Manage SQL Commands	Sites	Allows user to create and modify SQL commands through the SMS Administrator Console.
Manage Status Filters	Sites	Allows user to create and manage status filter rules through the SMS Administrator Console.
Meter	Sites	Allows user to apply software metering rules to a site.
Modify	All security object types except Status Messages	Makes changes to an object, such as editing the query statement for a query.
Modify Resource	Collections	Modifies a resource in a collection.
Read	All security object types except Status Messages	Views an instance and its properties.
Read Resource	Collections	Views a resource in a collection.
Use Remote Tools	Collections	Initiates a Remote Tools session with a client in a collection.
View Collected Files	Collections	Views the files collected from a client through the Resource Explorer.

Each object type must have at least one account granted Administer permission to prevent the possibility that SMS administrators could be locked out of the SMS Administrator Console. In fact, SMS doesn't allow you to remove the last account with Administer permission from an object type, nor can you delete your own Administer permission on any given object.

When a user creates a new instance of an object, the user is automatically assigned Read, Modify, and Delete permissions for that instance. Granting Administer permission doesn't automatically grant the other three permissions.

Here's how the Delegate right works. This right allows a user to be able to grant the same level of permissions the user has been granted on an object class to other users or groups on new objects in the same class that the user creates. Simple, right? Here's an example. Suppose that UserX has Create and Delegate permissions on the Collections class. Suppose, too, that UserX has Read, Read Resource, and Use Remote Tools permissions on the Finance collection instance. UserX can create a new collection because UserX has Create permissions on the Collection class. However, UserX can also delegate the Read, Read Resource, and Use Remote Tools permissions to other users or groups for the new collection.

I suggest that you spend a little time experimenting with object permissions if securing SMS objects beyond the defaults is a goal—for example, if you plan to create custom SMS Administrator Consoles, as discussed in the section "Custom SMS Administrator Consoles" later in this chapter. In some cases the combination of class and instance permissions that you set can have an effect on what the user can ultimately do. The best example of this involves collections. For each collection you can set a Read permission and a Read Resource permission. Read allows the user to see the collection and the members contained in the collection. However, if the user tries to view the inventory of a computer contained in a collection, Read permission isn't enough. The user would also require the Read Resource permission.

In a similar fashion, permissions assigned—or not assigned—on one object class can affect a user's ability to use other objects effectively. For example, suppose UserX can execute a query. The query is designed to return a list of computers from the SMS database. If UserX doesn't also have Read permissions on the collections that contain the computers you expect the query to display, UserX won't be able to view those computers in the query results window. As a result, the query results might not be accurate for that user. Like everything else we've talked about with SMS so far, it pays to test out your permission settings before you roll them out into a production environment.

Assigning Permissions

You can assign permissions to an object in four ways: you can use the Security Rights node in the SMS Administrator Console to assign permissions to object classes and instances, you can assign permissions at the specific object class or instance, you can use the SMS User Wizard, or you can clone an existing user. Figure 17-5 shows the list of object classes and specific instances and their permissions that's displayed when you open the Security Rights node. Notice that you can see the default permission as well as specific instances created.

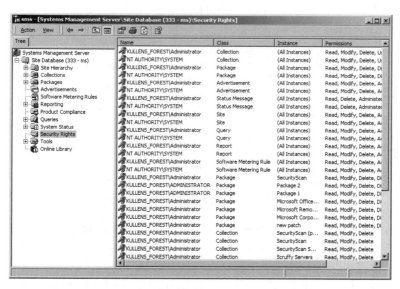

Figure 17-5. *Permissions displayed in the Security Rights node.*

To assign permissions through the Security Rights node, follow these steps:

1. In the SMS Administrator Console, navigate to the Security Rights node, select it, right-click it, and choose New from the context menu.

2. Choose Class Security Right to assign permissions to an existing object class or choose Instance Security Right to assign permissions to an existing object instance.

3. If you choose Class Security Right, the Security Right Properties dialog box for the class is displayed, as shown in Figure 17-6.

Figure 17-6. *The Security Right Properties dialog box for a class.*

Enter the user name (or group name), select the object class, and select the permissions you want to assign. The permissions listed will vary depending on the object class you select.

Notice that the Instance field is disabled here. If you had chosen Instance Security Right in step 2, the Instance field would be available for you to specify an instance of an SMS security object.

4. Choose OK to save your security configuration.

Tip You can modify any entry in the Security Rights node simply by double-clicking it to display its Properties dialog box. Also, once you enter a user or group name, the name is saved for future modifications and can be selected from the User Name drop-down list.

You can also assign or modify permissions at the individual object class or instance level. This technique is preferable because it forces you to specifically choose the object whose permissions you want to modify. Follow these steps to assign or modify permissions at the object class level:

1. In the SMS Administrator Console, navigate to the node whose class permissions you want to modify, right-click it, and choose Properties

from the context menu to display the object's Properties dialog box. For this example, we'll select the Queries object to display the Queries Properties dialog box.

2. Select the Security tab, shown in Figure 17-7. Note the existing class-level security permissions.

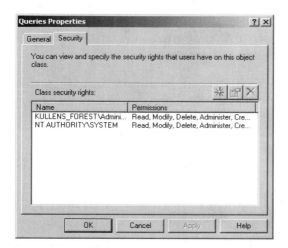

Figure 17-7. *The Security tab of the Queries Properties dialog box.*

3. To add a new user or group to the list, click the New button (the yellow star) to display the Object Class Security Right Properties dialog box, shown in Figure 17-8.

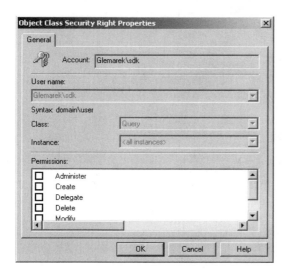

Figure 17-8. *The Object Class Security Right Properties dialog box.*

4. Supply a user or group name and then select the permissions you want to apply. (As mentioned, selecting no permissions is like selecting No Access in NTFS.) Click OK to return to the Security tab of the Queries Properties dialog box.

5. To modify an existing entry, select that entry in the Class Security Rights list and click the Properties button (the hand holding a piece of paper) to display the Object Class Security Right Properties dialog box. Make the appropriate permission changes and then click OK.

6. Click OK again to save your changes.

In the preceding example, we modified the permissions for the user SDK so that SDK has no permissions at the object class level for Queries. Now let's modify permissions at a specific object instance. To do so, follow these steps:

1. In the SMS Administrator Console, navigate to the specific object instance you want to modify, select it, and choose Properties from the context menu to display the Properties dialog box for that instance. For this example, we'll select an instance of the Queries object—Clients With Free Disk Space—to display the Clients With Free Disk Space Query Properties dialog box.

2. Select the Security tab, shown in Figure 17-9. Notice the existing class and instance security permissions—SDK [No Permission] has "trickled down" to this instance.

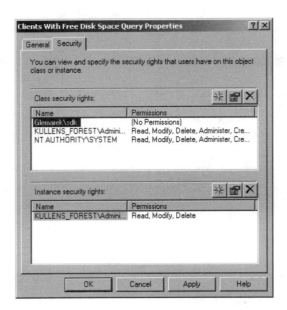

Figure 17-9. *The Security tab of the Query Properties dialog box.*

In this tab you can modify both the class permissions for the Queries object (by clicking the New button, as we did in the preceding example) and the specific permissions for this instance.

3. To modify the instance permissions, click the New button in the Instance Security Rights section of the dialog box to display the Object Instance Security Right Properties dialog box, shown in Figure 17-10.

Figure 17-10. *The Object Instance Security Right Properties dialog box.*

4. Supply a user or group name, select the appropriate permissions, and then click OK.

5. Click OK again to save your configuration.

Figure 17-11 demonstrates how, in the preceding examples, instance security rights take precedence over class security rights. Notice that even though the user SDK has no permissions for the Queries object class, SDK can nevertheless read, modify, and delete the specific query Clients With Free Disk Space. This is wholly consistent with the NTFS security system. Even if you deny a user access to a folder, if the user has permissions to read a file within that folder, the user will be able to access that file through an application or from the command prompt.

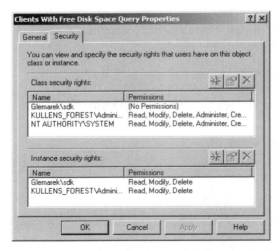

Figure 17-11. *Sample class and instance permissions.*

You can use the SMS User Wizard to add a new user and assign class or instance permissions to that user, modify the permissions of an existing user, or copy the permissions of another user to an existing or new user. This wizard is intuitive to use, so I won't go into a lot of detail about running it.

Follow these steps to use the SMS User Wizard:

1. In the SMS Administrator Console, right-click Security Rights, and from the context menu select All Tasks and then Manage SMS Users to display the Welcome page as shown in Figure 17-12.

Figure 17-12. *SMS User Wizard Welcome page.*

2. Click next to display the User Name page shown in Figure 17-13. On this page you can choose to modify an existing user name or remove an existing user by selecting that user from the drop-down list, or you can add a new user by browsing among existing user names or typing in the new user. If you choose to remove a user, when you click Next, you'll go directly to the Finish page where you can click Finish and you're done. Otherwise, when you click Next, you'll be presented with the Rights page.

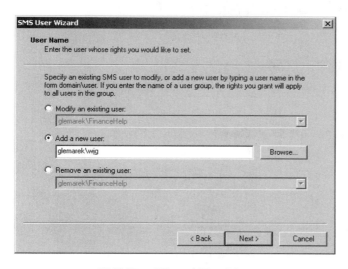

Figure 17-13.   *SMS User Wizard User Name page.*

3. On the Rights page, shown in Figure 17-14, if you select the option The Listed Rights Are Sufficient, you can simply click Next and you'll be taken to the Finish page. This option is a verification that nothing more needs to be done.

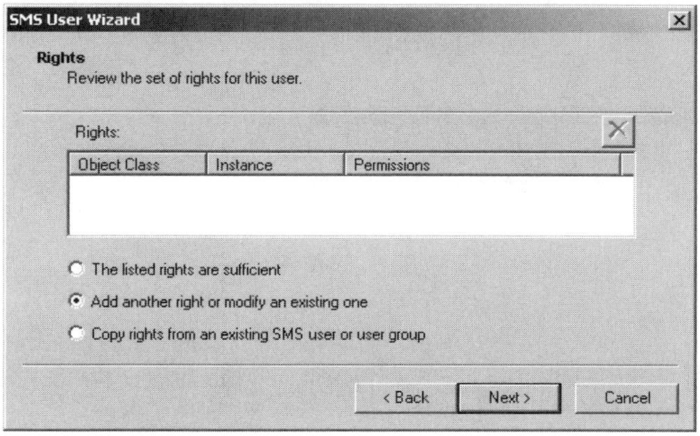

Figure 17-14.   *SMS User Wizard Rights page.*

If you select the option Add Another Right Or Modify an Existing One and click Next, the Add A Right page is displayed, as shown in Figure 17-15. Here you can select the class, instance, and permission you wish to assign and click Next to go back to the Rights page, verify that the listed rights are sufficient, and then click Next to go to the Finish page.

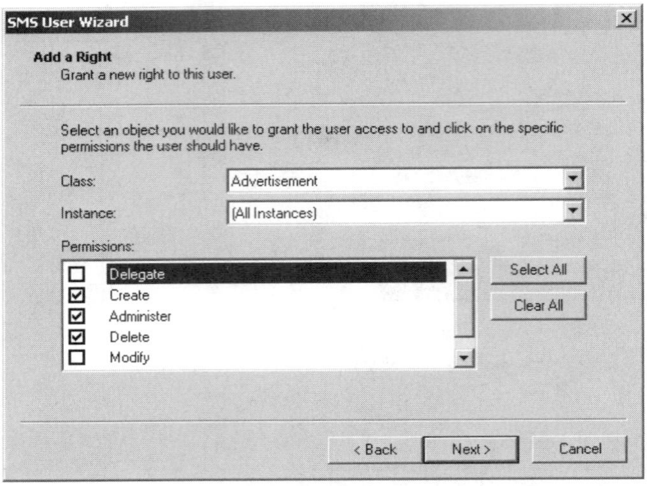

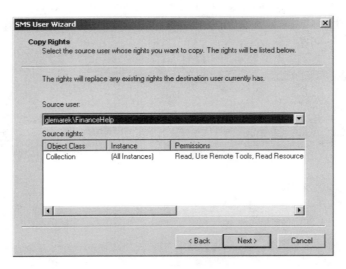

Figure 17-15. *SMS User Wizard Add A Right page.*

If you select the option Copy Rights From An Existing SMS User Or User Group, the Copy Rights page is displayed, as shown in Figure 17-16.

Figure 17-16. *SMS User Wizard Copy Rights page.*

Select the user you want to copy from the Source User drop-down list, select the permissions you want to copy, and then click Next to go back to the Rights page, verify that the listed rights are sufficient, and then click Next to go to the Finish page.

4. When you get to the Finish page, review the information one more time and then click Finish.

Finally, you can copy the class and instance permissions of an existing user to another user. To do so, follow these steps:

1. Navigate to the Security Rights node in the SMS Administrator Console and select it to display the list of all users and their permissions.

2. Right-click the user whose class and instance permissions you want to copy and from the context menu select All Tasks and then Clone SMS User to display the Clone SMS User dialog box shown in Figure 17-17. Enter the name of the user you want to copy the permissions to. Select whether to copy the Class Security Rights or Instance Security Rights and then click OK.

Figure 17-17.   *Clone SMS User dialog box.*

Real World   Using Security

Consider the SMS site hierarchy illustrated in Figure 17-18. In this model SMS administrators are present at each site in the hierarchy. For organizational reasons, the third-level sites are secondary sites. Recall that secondary sites do not have their own SQL Server databases. Therefore, for the administrators at the secondary sites to be able to manage their sites, their SMS Administrator Console computers need to connect to the SQL Server database for their parent site. Using default security, every administrator at every secondary site can manage not only his or her own site, but also any other secondary site that's a child of the same parent.

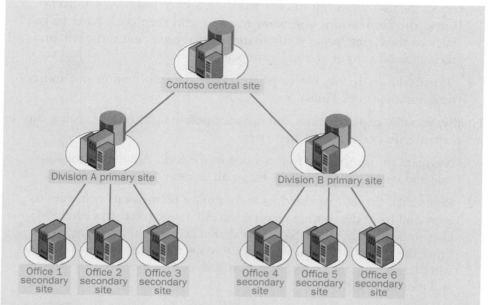

Figure 17-18.   *Sample site hierarchy model.*

To remedy this situation, you can set security on each of the secondary site entries under the Site Hierarchy node in the SMS Administrator Console so that only that site's administrator has access to that site's settings. In this way, you have preserved security for each site and can still maintain the desired site structure.

Custom SMS Administrator Consoles

The SMS Administrator Console is an MMC snap-in, and, consequently, you can create customized versions of the console to distribute to your administrators. You can create a custom SMS Administrator Console that displays only the SMS objects to which a particular administrator needs access to perform delegated tasks such as package distribution, advertising, or initiating remote diagnostic sessions.

Perhaps the most common form of delegation is the help desk function. In a large organization, it wouldn't be unusual to have an administrator or a group whose help desk responsibility is focused on specific departments or regions. It might not be desirable or practical for these individuals to have full access to every object in the SMS database. They really need access only to their assigned department's collection and the ability to initiate remote sessions with their assigned clients.

We can start by providing a custom SMS Administrator Console that displays only the Collections objects. This limitation narrows down what the administrator sees when the SMS Administrator Console is launched. However, this is only a surface modification—any savvy user could restore the other SMS objects to the SMS Administrator Console. The complete solution is to create a custom console and apply appropriate security to all the SMS objects and instances so that administrators see and have access only to what they should.

Setting Security

You begin the process of creating a custom console by applying the appropriate security to the SMS objects. Consider, for example, a help desk group assigned to your organization's finance department. Help desk administrators belong to a Windows group named Finance Help. You have also created an SMS collection named Finance Clients that contains all the SMS client computers in the finance department.

> **Note** The membership rules for this collection are based on a query so that as new computers are implemented in the finance department, they're automatically added to the Finance Clients collection when SMS discovers and installs them.

You set security on all SMS objects in such a way that the Finance Help group has no permissions on any SMS object class. This effectively restricts the Finance Help group members from viewing any SMS objects other than what they need access to—the Finance Clients collection. For that one collection, you'll give Finance Help the permissions the members need to initiate Remote Tools sessions—Read, Read Resource, and Use Remote Tools—shown in Figure 17-19.

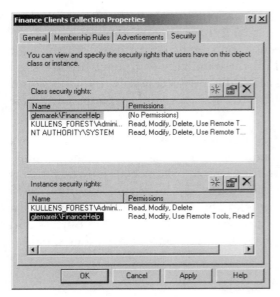

Figure 17-19. *Setting security for the Finance Clients collection.*

Notice that for the Collections object class, Finance Help has no permissions. However, for the Collections object instance Finance Clients, Finance Help has the permissions necessary to initiate a Remote Tools session. The result is that the group has no access to any other collection except this one.

Creating the Custom Console

The next step is to create a custom console to the Finance Help administrators that displays only the Finance Clients collection. To create a customized SMS Administrator Console, follow these steps:

1. From the Start menu on the desktop taskbar of your SMS Administrator Console computer, choose Run and enter MMC to launch a generic MMC, shown in Figure 17-20.

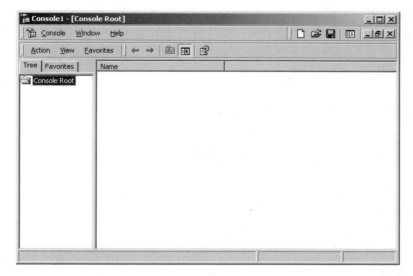

Figure 17-20. *A generic MMC.*

2. Choose Add/Remove Snap-In from the Console menu to display the Add/Remove Snap-In Properties dialog box, shown in Figure 17-21.

Figure 17-21. *The Add/Remove Snap-In Properties dialog box.*

3. In the Standalone tab, click the Add button to display the Add Stand-alone Snap-In dialog box, shown in Figure 17-22. This dialog box lists the MMC snap-ins currently available.

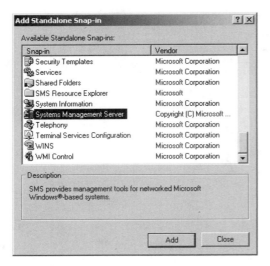

Figure 17-22. *The Add Standalone Snap-In dialog box.*

4. Select Systems Management Server from the list and then click Add to launch the Site Database Connection Wizard, shown in Figure 17-23.

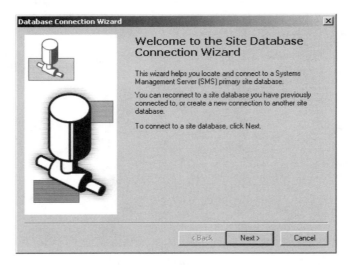

Figure 17-23. *The Site Database Connection Wizard welcome page.*

5. Click Next to display the Locate Site Database page, shown in Figure 17-24. Specify the site server to which you want the console to connect. Remember, this should be the SMS site that the Finance Help administrators need access to.

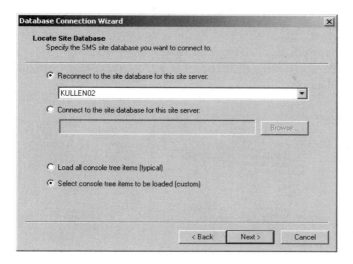

Figure 17-24.   *The Locate Site Database page.*

6. Select the Select Console Tree Items To Be Loaded (Custom) option.

7. Click Next to display the Console Tree Items page, shown in Figure 17-25. Select the SMS console tree entries you want to display in the custom console. In this example you'll choose SMS Collections only.

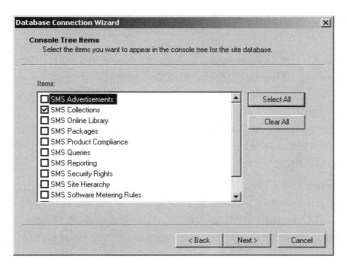

Figure 17-25.   *The Console Tree Items page.*

8. Click Next to display the Completing The Site Database Connection Wizard page. Review your selections and then click Finish.

9. Click Close in the Add Standalone Snap-In dialog box, and then click OK in the Standalone tab in the Add/Remove Snap-In Properties dialog box to save your configuration. The management console shown in Figure 17-26 demonstrates that the only SMS object this console will display is Collections.

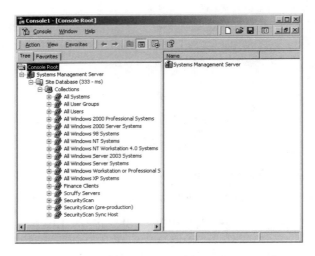

Figure 17-26. *The custom management console.*

10. Choose Options from the Console menu to display the Options properties dialog box, shown in Figure 17-27.

11. From the Console Mode drop-down list, select User Mode - Limited Access, Single Window. This option ensures that the top-level console menus (Console, Window, and Help) are hidden when the console is open and effectively prevents the user from modifying the console in any way. Select the option Do Not Save Changes To This Console to prevent any unintentional modifications later. Click OK to save your settings and return to the console window.

12. Choose Save As from the Console menu to display the Save As dialog box. By default, the file will be saved in the Administrative Tools program folder. Retain that folder or select or create your own. Enter a filename for the console—for example, Finance.msc. Then choose Save.

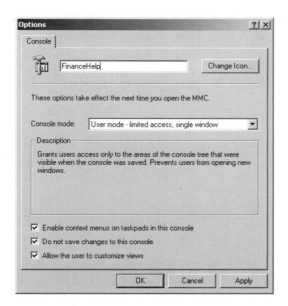

Figure 17-27.   *The Options properties dialog box.*

13. Close the new console.

Distributing the Custom Console

The next step is to distribute the custom console to the administrators in the Finance Help group. Begin by installing the SMS Administrator Console on their Windows NT 4.0 workstations. Next, replace the default SMS.msc file with the console you just created. You can rename the console SMS.msc so that when administrators click the shortcut in the Systems Management Server program group, the correct console is launched.

Caution   Remember that the users in the Finance Help group must be able to access the SMS database, as discussed earlier. One way to do this is to add the Finance Help group to the local SMS Admins group on the site server or the server running SQL (wherever the SMS Provider is installed).

When an administrator in the Finance Help group launches the customized SMS Administrator Console, he or she will see only the Collections object, and because of the security you applied, only one object instance—the Finance Clients collection, shown in Figure 17-28.

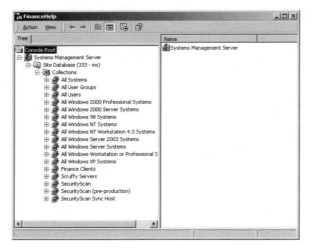

Figure 17-28.   *Sample custom console with security applied.*

Summary

As we've seen, the combination of a custom console with SMS object class and instance security can provide a high level of secure access to the SMS database. Achieving the correct balance of customization and security isn't trivial and, like most aspects of SMS, requires a fair amount of planning. However, the result can be rewarding. Equally rewarding is the recovery of your site server in the event of a problem, as we'll see in Chapter 18, "Disaster Recovery."

Chapter 18
Disaster Recovery

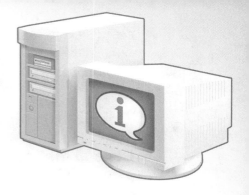

Disaster recovery! No one wants to have to experience it, right? But all systems administrators need to be prepared for the possibility. By the end of this chapter, you'll learn what you need to know about disaster recovery.

The key to a successful disaster recovery effort is, of course, a sound backup strategy. The focus of this chapter is just that—the establishment of a useful backup strategy and strategies for recovering your Microsoft Systems Management Server (SMS) database server, site server, and site systems. This chapter and Chapter 19, "Maintaining the Database Through Microsoft SQL Server," which focuses on database maintenance strategies, provide you with the resources you need to be amply prepared for disaster recovery, but more importantly, teach you how to avoid disaster in the first place.

We'll begin by establishing sound database maintenance practices, including a regular backup process, and then you'll learn how to recover or move the SMS database server, recover or move the SMS site server, and restore an SMS site system.

Database Maintenance

Perhaps the most obvious way to keep your SMS site systems from experiencing failure is to keep them running in top form, much like you might develop an exercise and diet program for yourself or regularly change the oil in your car. In addition to developing a backup and restore strategy, you can do several things for your SMS servers on a regular basis, both to keep them running well and to spot problems before they cause damage. For the most part, these maintenance tasks can be broken down into four groups: general, daily, weekly, and monthly maintenance tasks.

More Info   For more recommendations about database maintenance tasks, see Chapter 13 in the *Microsoft Systems Management Server 2003 Operations Guide*, available as a print book from the Microsoft SMS Web site (*http://www.microsoft.com/smserver*) and through Microsoft TechNet.

General Maintenance Tasks

Probably the most important general task you can perform for any Microsoft Windows system is to develop a backup plan for your servers. At a minimum, you want to develop a backup strategy for your SMS site server and SMS database server, as these are your key systems. Much has been written about backup strategies—full versus differential, daily versus weekly, and so on.

For example, one backup strategy might be that you perform a full, or complete, backup of your database once a week, say on Friday nights, while you perform a differential backup of the database Mondays through Thursdays. Different backup types can take longer to run the backup process and take longer to restore as well. For example, a full backup backs up all the data each time and so will necessarily take longer to back up and restore. A differential backup, in contrast, backs up only data that has changed since the last full backup and will result in reduced backup time and less backup space used.

It all comes down to this ultimate question: how important is it that you recover your data, and how current must that data be? We'll look at the recommended procedure for backing up SMS in the section entitled "Backup Process Flow" later in this chapter.

Other general maintenance tasks might more properly be called troubleshooting assistance tasks, such as configuring the Status Message Viewer, configuring the Performance Monitor and SQL Server alerts, performing a database and site backup, and monitoring the performance of the site systems. We've looked at some of these tasks in previous chapters, such as the following:

- **Configure the Status Message Viewer to view status messages**   Recall from Chapter 5, "Analysis and Troubleshooting Tools," that the status message system is your first and often best source of information regarding the state of your SMS site systems. You can configure the display interval for status messages, set filters, have programs such as pager alerts executed based on message events, and so on. Take some time to determine how the Status Message Viewer might figure into your overall maintenance—and ultimately disaster recovery—strategy.

- **Configure Performance Monitor alerts for key events**   You can set up alerts for the events, such as low disk space, overutilization of the processor and memory, excessive pagefile access, and so on.

- **Configure SQL Server alerts**   You can set up the alerts in the SQL Server Enterprise Manager to monitor database space usage, user locks, and connections. (For more information about setting up SQL Server alerts, refer to the SQL Server product documentation.)

- **Determine a fault tolerance strategy**   If your server supports a fault tolerance method such as RAID 1 (disk mirroring) or RAID 5 (disk striping with parity) either through a hardware method or through Windows, consider configuring one of these fault tolerance methods. Maintaining data redundancy is a hallmark of disaster recovery.

You will undoubtedly think of many other troubleshooting assistance tasks to add to this list. Be as creative—and redundant—as you like. In the following sections we'll explore some specific daily, weekly, and monthly tasks you can perform as an SMS site administrator.

Daily Maintenance Tasks

As the SMS administrator, you decide when various maintenance tasks should be performed within your organization and with what frequency. No single blueprint will provide a perfect fit for every SMS site or site structure. Microsoft recommends that you perform the following tasks daily to protect your SMS servers. You can modify this list to suit your needs.

- **Perform a site backup**   This task ensures that you can recover to at least the previous day's state.

- **Review status messages**   This is especially important if SMS generates a status message alert indicating a potential problem with a component. By default, the Status Message Viewer displays only messages generated since the previous midnight. If you skip a couple of days, you might miss significant status messages. Consider changing the display interval or setting up custom filters so that you will be alerted about serious events. You should review site server and site system status messages every day. However, SMS clients also generate status messages. Although it might be unrealistic to review client status messages on a daily basis, perhaps because of the number of clients you might have installed, you should consider reviewing them on a weekly or monthly basis.

- **Monitor the Windows Event logs and SQL Server logs** Check for errors or warnings that might be indicative of an impending failure of your SMS site. You can view the SQL Server logs in SQL Server Enterprise Manager.

- **Monitor system health and performance through the Performance Monitor and SMS Service Manager tools** Check for performance-related events, such as low disk space, overutilization of the processor and memory, excessive pagefile access, and so on, to help determine when your server isn't running at optimum performance levels and what processes might be affecting performance.

- **Monitor network utilization using a network traffic analysis tool such as Network Monitor** This task is especially important if package distribution or intersite communication appears to be poor in order to determine when and where traffic congestion is occurring.

- **Monitor SMS system folders for file backlogs** The appearance of a large or growing number of files in the SMS system folders might indicate that the site server is unable to process requests for information. You should check status messages and SMS services for errors.

Weekly Maintenance Tasks

Microsoft recommends that you perform the following tasks weekly. Again, you can modify this list to fit your needs.

- **Monitor the size and percentage of database growth of the SMS site database as well as the software metering database, if you've implemented that feature.** SQL Server 2000 automatically monitors the size of the SMS database and makes adjustments appropriately. Of course, this doesn't absolve you from monitoring the database on a regular basis to determine how fast the database is growing and especially whether you might run out of disk space. However, you might not need to look at the database so frequently, and you can set a SQL Server alert to let you know when and how much the database grows.

- **Monitor the amount of free disk space on the SMS database server, the site server, and the site systems (client access points [CAPs], logon points, distribution points, and software metering servers).** Remember, with few exceptions, SMS components will just stop working if they run out of disk space.

- **Purge data that's no longer needed or relevant.** Remove bad Management Information Format (MIF) files, duplicate computer records, aged inventory records, and so on.

- **Perform regular disk cleanup tasks.** This cleanup would include your weekly full virus check or disk optimization routine or monitoring for unused or old Temp files. Check the SMS directories as well for folders that have an unusually high number of files, such as a BadMIFs folder or an inbox with files that aren't being processed, and cross-check these folders with status messages and logs for the specific components involved.

Monthly Maintenance Tasks

Here are some of the recommended maintenance tasks that you might perform on a monthly or an as-needed basis:

- Verify and test your ability to restore the database or the site server.

- Modify SMS accounts and passwords for those accounts you have control over. Refer to Chapter 17, "Security," for a discussion of SMS accounts.

- Review SMS object permissions.

- Review SMS site boundaries and component configuration.

- Review your maintenance plans.

You can protect your SMS site by scheduling and performing these maintenance tasks regularly. In the following section we'll look at how to schedule these tasks.

Scheduling Maintenance Tasks

You can schedule several of the maintenance tasks mentioned above to run on your timetable through the SMS Administrator Console. You can find these tasks in the Site Maintenance node under Site Settings. Two types of database maintenance objects can be configured: SQL commands and tasks.

Scheduling SQL Commands

No predefined SQL commands are available for you to schedule; you must configure these commands yourself. For example, among the recommended weekly tasks is a database size check. You can view database size using the SQL Enterprise Manager, of course, but you can also determine it by executing the SQL stored procedure SP_SPACEUSED.

Caution Before running any SQL stored procedure, be sure to consult the SQL Server documentation for correct syntax and usage.

You can configure this SQL stored procedure to run according to your defined schedule and generate a report based on its results. To do so, follow these steps:

1. Navigate to the SQL Commands node under Site Settings, then Site Maintenance in the SMS Administrator Console and select it.

2. Right-click the folder, choose New from the context menu, and then choose SQL Command to display the SQL Command Properties dialog box shown in Figure 18-1.

3. Enter a descriptive name for the command.

Figure 18-1. *The SQL Command Properties dialog box.*

4. Verify that Enable SQL Command is selected. Enter the command name in the SQL Command text box. Be sure to use the appropriate syntax or the command will fail.

5. In the Log Status To text box, enter the path and filename of the text file you want the command results written to. This must be an existing share.

6. Define your schedule and then click OK.

The SQL command you created will now be listed in the SMS Administrator Console when you select the SQL Commands node. You might consider scheduling other SQL maintenance commands, such as DBCC CHECKDB, DBCC CHECKALLOC, DBCC CHECKCATALOG, and DBCC UPDATEUSAGE. For example, if you recently reindexed the database, you might want to run the DBCC UPDATEUSAGE command to reset space usage reporting so that SP_SPACEUSED returns accurate data. You could schedule this command to run with SP_SPACEUSED or separately, under its own schedule.

When the SQL command is run, it will write the results of its execution to the log file you specified. Figure 18-2 shows the results of the SQL command created in the previous example.

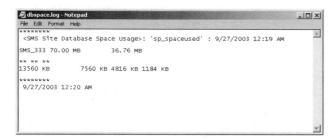

Figure 18-2. *Results of running the SP_SPACEUSED SQL stored procedure as a SQL command.*

The first line of data (beginning with *SMS_333*) indicates the total database size and the available free space. The second line of data indicates the amount of reserved space, breaking this value down into the amount of space used by data, the index size, and unused space.

Scheduling Tasks

The other type of database maintenance objects you can schedule, tasks, is found in the Tasks node in the SMS Administrator Console. The Tasks folder contains 13 predefined tasks; you can't add tasks to this list. Table 18-1 describes these predefined tasks.

Table 18-1. Database maintenance tasks

Task	Description
Backup SMS Site Server	Performs a comprehensive backup of the SMS site database, the software metering database, the \SMS directory on the site server, and the SMS and NAL registry keys on the site server. This task isn't enabled by default.
Rebuild Indexes	Rebuilds indexes created on database tables that are used to more efficiently retrieve data. Enabled by default.
Monitor Keys	Monitors the integrity of primary keys used to uniquely identify all SMS database tables. Enabled by default.
Delete Aged Inventory History	Deletes all hardware inventory that hasn't been updated within a specified period of days (by default, 90 days). By default, this task is enabled and runs every Saturday.
Delete Aged Status Messages	Deletes status messages older than seven days by default and runs every day. Enabled by default.
Delete Aged Discovery Data	Deletes all discovery data records (DDRs) that haven't been updated within a specified period of days (by default, 90 days). By default, this task is enabled and runs every Saturday.
Delete Aged Collected Files	Deletes all collected files that haven't been updated within a specified period of days (90 days, by default). By default, this task is enabled and runs every Saturday.
Delete Aged Software Metering Data	Deletes metered software data that's older than five days to conserve space in the SMS database. This task is enabled by default.
Delete Aged Software Metering Summary Data	Deletes metered software summary data that's older than 270 days to conserve space in the SMS database. This task is enabled by default.
Delete Inactive Client Discovery Data	Deletes all client records that haven't received an updated DDR within the specified number of days—for example, through Heartbeat Discovery. This task is useful when you're using Active Directory Discovery to create DDRs for computers. When you delete a computer in Active Directory directory service, its Active Directory record might remain for some time before being purged. As a result, SMS Active Directory Discovery would continue to report the computer as a valid client, even though the computer is no longer physically present on the network.
Summarize Software Metering File Usage	Enables summarization of collected software metering data to conserve space in the SMS database. This task is enabled by default.

Table 18-1.   Database maintenance tasks

Task	Description
Summarize Software Metering Monthly Usage Data	Enables summarization of collected monthly software metering data to conserve space in the SMS database. This task is enabled by default
Clear Install Flag	Directs SMS to clear the install flag for clients that have been uninstalled. The install flag identifies to SMS those clients that have been installed as SMS clients. When the client is uninstalled, the install flag isn't automatically removed, and the client can't be successfully reinstalled. This task clears the flag so that a client can be reinstalled. This task isn't enabled by default.

Notice that 10 of these tasks are already enabled by default to ensure that vital tasks such as rebuilding indexes are carried out on a regular schedule. All the deletion tasks are designed to keep the database from becoming too large and unwieldy. You can, of course, modify the schedule and disable or enable any of these tasks as you choose. (To enable or disable a task in the Tasks folder, right-click the task and choose Properties from the context menu. In the Task Properties dialog box, select or clear the Enable This Task option.) For example, you could enable the Backup SMS Site Server task to schedule a regular backup of the SMS database (and site server) without having to do so in SQL Server.

The most powerful of these tasks is Backup SMS Site Server. This is by far the most comprehensive backup routine available for SMS. It backs up not only the SMS site database and software metering database, but also the full SMS directory structure on the site server and the SMS and NAL keys in the Windows registry on the site server—all necessary to fully recover a failed site server. This task is discussed in more detail in the section entitled "Backing Up the Site Server" later in this chapter.

Backup Process Flow

The process for completely backing up your SMS site server involves the same basic steps whether you're automating this task through the SMS Administrator Console or carrying out the procedure yourself. In either case, you should have successfully backed up the following data:

- SMS site database
- SMS directory on the site server

- Master site control file (SMS\Inboxes\Sitectrl.box\Sitectrl.ct0)
- SMS and NAL registry keys on the site server

The following sections explore how to back up the data types listed above. We'll begin by discussing SMS Service Manager, first discussed in Chapter 3, "Configuring Site Server Properties and Site Systems," and then again in Chapter 5, to stop all SMS services and components.

Stopping All Services and Components

Before you initiate any manual backup steps, you must of course stop any SMS services and components that might be running so that they don't leave any files open or lock any portion of the database. This includes ending any remote SMS Administrator Console sessions that might be active.

SMS services and components are best managed through the SMS Service Manager tool in the SMS Administrator Console. We discussed how to use this tool in Chapter 5, and we'll review briefly here. To stop a service or component, follow these steps:

1. In the SMS Administrator Console, navigate to the Tools node, select SMS Service Manager, right-click it, choose Select All Tasks, and then choose Start SMS Service Manager.

2. Expand the site server entry and then select Components to display a list of available components, as shown in Figure 18-3.

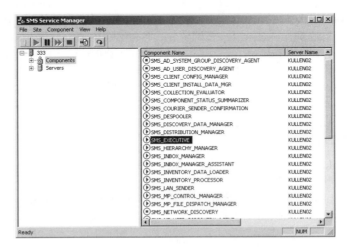

Figure 18-3. *The SMS Service Manager window, showing available services and components.*

3. To view the current status of a component, select it and click the Query Component button (an exclamation point). To disable the component, select it and click the Stop button (the red square).

4. Click the Query Component button again to verify that the component has stopped.

5. To start a component, select it and click the Start button (the green triangle).

Tip   You can stop or start all the components at one time by choosing Select All from the Component menu and then clicking the Stop or Start button.

By stopping the SMS Executive first through the SMS Service Manager, you will stop most of the other SMS components, as many of these components are themselves started by the SMS Executive. After you've stopped all SMS services and components using this technique, verify that at least the following services have indeed stopped by running the Services program in the Administrative Tools folder, accessible by clicking Start and then Programs:

- SMS Executive
- SMS Site Component Manager
- SMS SQL Monitor
- SQL Executive

Only after you've stopped all the services and components should you back up the SMS site database.

Backing Up the Site Database

You can back up this database using a number of techniques. You could use SQL Server's BACKUP command through the SQL Server Enterprise Manager. (This process is described in Chapter 19.) You could use your favorite third-party backup system, such as Veritas Backup Exec, which includes add-ons that back up SQL Server databases. (Review your backup product's documentation to learn how.) You could also use the Backup SMS Site Server maintenance tasks available through the SMS Administrator Console. These tasks are described in the section entitled "Backing Up the Site Through Systems Management Server" later in this chapter.

Backing Up Registry Keys and the Directory Structure

Next, you back up the SMS and NAL registry keys by choosing Save Key from the Windows Registry Editor's Registry menu and then the SMS directory structure. When you back up these elements, you should give the backups similar names. Use the site code in the name and perhaps add a number indicating the date or iteration of the backup. For example, you could name the registry keys SMS*xxx*.reg and NAL*xxx*.reg, where *xxx* represents the three-digit site code for your site.

Save your backups in a single directory for easy reference. This directory can then itself be backed up by your favorite server backup program for added redundancy. Again, consider your naming convention carefully. For example, you could name the directory something like SMSBackup*xxx*.*ddd*, where *xxx* represents your site's site code and *ddd* represents a date or iteration reference.

If you were backing up the site A01 on August 31, for instance, you could create a directory named SMSBackupA01.aug31. You would save the SMS database backup file here, perhaps as SMSDBA01, as well as the registry keys (SMSA01.reg and NALA01.reg) and the SMS directory (SMSA01.dir). You should maintain this master backup location on another server; you should also back up the master backup folder itself as part of your normal network server backup routine.

The Backup SMS Site Server database maintenance task included in the SMS Administrator Console includes most of these steps in one automated package. Because you don't have to perform these backups manually, it's a more effective backup routine. For a detailed discussion of this database maintenance task, refer to the section entitled "Backing Up the Site Server" later in this chapter.

Backing Up the Site Through Systems Management Server

As mentioned, the SMS Administrator Console provides a backup task among its database maintenance tasks. The SMS site database, like other SQL databases, consists of the database file and a transaction log. The database file contains the actual data. The transaction log maintains an audit of database transactions that have taken place to aid in recovery of the database in the event of failure. Because the transaction log contains this audit trail of activity, SQL Server administrators sometimes use it as an alternative to performing frequent full database backups. However, SQL 2000 truncates the transaction log periodically to conserve database space, and there are limitations on when you can back up the transaction log. You can back up the SMS site database through SQL Server, of course, but the SMS backup task is far more comprehensive. Let's take a look at how to configure it.

> **More Info**   Please refer to your SQL Server documentation for detailed
> information regarding how to modify database options, create backup
> devices, and configure backup and restore options through the SQL Server
> Enterprise Manager.

Backing Up the Site Server

This maintenance task essentially performs all the required backups outlined earlier in this chapter in the section "Backup Process Flow." It also backs up some additional information, including the SMS directory structure and files and the site control file.

This task was available in SMS 2.0. However, SMS 2003 has streamlined the backup to include only those components that are necessary to successfully restore a site.

The SMS Site Backup service executes the SMS backup task. This service runs according to the backup schedule you configure. Like other SMS service components, this service comes with a log file (Smsbkup.log) that you can enable through SMS Service Manager (see Chapter 3 for more information). Unlike the other log files, which are best used for troubleshooting tasks, the SMS Site Backup log should be enabled because it maintains a record of what you ran for site backup. When you restore a site, you can use the log to verify that you're restoring from a valid backup. Like other logs, as this log reaches its maximum size (1 MB by default), it's written to Smsbkup.lo_ and a new Smsbkup.log file is created. For a complete backup history, and for redundancy, back up these two files as well. Figure 18-4 shows an example Smsbkup.log file created after the Backup SMS Site Server task is run. Notice that the task first stops SMS components and services before beginning its copy process.

It's not necessary to have predefined a backup device when you enable the Backup SMS Site Server task. You must, however, provide the name of a backup folder location where the SMS Site Backup service will write the backed-up data. This location can actually serve as the main backup location for several site servers because when the task is run, the SMS Site Backup service creates a subdirectory named by the site code and all backup data is written there.

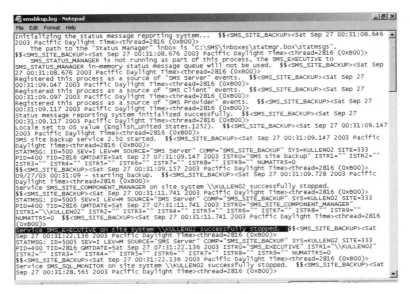

Figure 18-4. *Sample Smsbkup.log file.*

It should be of no little significance, then, that the location of the backup folder must be on a partition with adequate disk space to accommodate the data being written there. It's recommended that you have enough space to accommodate not only the SMS database, but the entire SMS system folder structure as well. You can determine a more accurate accounting of the space required by considering the following factors:

- Amount of disk space used by the entire SMS directory structure

- Amount of space used by the following SQL Server databases: master, msdb, and site server

- At least 10 MB additional space for miscellaneous files such as saved registry keys

At each subsequent scheduled backup, the SMS Site Backup service will first remove the old backed-up data before writing the new data. It will also record each backup event in the Smsbkup.log file, viewable using any text editor.

The Backup Control File

The entire Backup SMS Site Server task is actually governed by a backup control file named Smsbkup.ctl, which is in the SMS\Inboxes\SMSbkup.box folder. This file outlines exactly what will be backed up and where. Smsbkup.ctl is a text file, and, as such, it's fully customizable. It's also well annotated, which will assist you in reading and understanding its flow, as well as in customizing it.

This file contains the names of the files, registry keys, and databases that need to be backed up. It also contains commands that run during the backup operation to gather configuration information. You can customize this file to include additional files, directories, registry keys, and so on. However, it isn't recommended that you remove or modify any of the default entries in this file unless you've tested that, by doing so, you haven't compromised your backup's integrity.

Appendix A, "Backup Control File," presents the code for the backup control file for your reference. Refer also to Chapter 15 in the *Microsoft Systems Management Server 2003 Operations Guide* for additional information regarding the use and customization of this file.

Configuring Backup SMS Site Server

To configure the Backup SMS Site Server maintenance task, follow these steps:

1. In the SMS Administrator Console, navigate to the Site Maintenance node under Site Settings and expand it.

2. Select the Tasks node, select Backup SMS Site Server, right-click it, and choose Properties to display the Backup SMS Site Server Task Properties dialog box, shown in Figure 18-5.

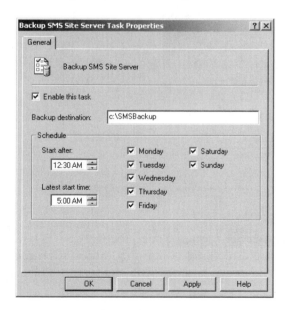

Figure 18-5.   *The Backup SMS Site Server Task Properties dialog box.*

3. Select the Enable This Task check box.

4. In the Backup Destination text box, enter the name of the drive and directory where you've already created a backup folder or where you want SMS to create the folder for you. This name can't contain any extended ASCII characters. You can use a UNC path or a local drive path. Be sure that the destination location has enough disk space available.

5. Specify a schedule for the backup. For active databases, a daily backup is recommended.

6. Click OK to save your configuration and enable the backup.

At the scheduled time, the SMS Site Backup service will find or create the backup destination folders, stop appropriate SMS site server services, and perform the backup. After the backup is complete, you can view the backup folder's contents through the Windows Explorer. Figure 18-6 shows the contents of a sample backup folder.

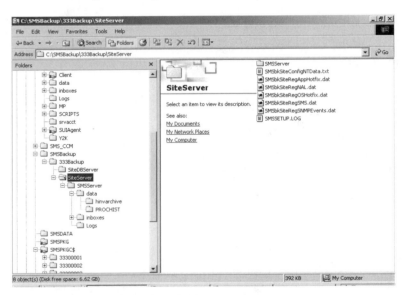

Figure 18-6. *Sample backup folder contents.*

Notice that the SMS Site Backup service created a subdirectory named with the site code. Within this directory are directories containing information relating to the site database server (SiteDBServer), and the SMS site server (SiteServer), which itself contains the entire site directory structure, registry entries, and site control information. The following registry keys are backed up from the Windows Registry on the SMS site server:

- HKEY_LOCAL_MACHINE\Software\Microsoft\NAL
- HKEY_LOCAL_MACHINE\Software\Microsoft\NetworkMonitor
- HKEY_LOCAL_MACHINE\Software\Microsoft\SMS
- HKEY_LOCAL_MACHINE\Software\Microsoft\SNMPEvents

The SiteDBServer directory, shown in Figure 18-7, contains configuration information about the SQL Server installation in particular.

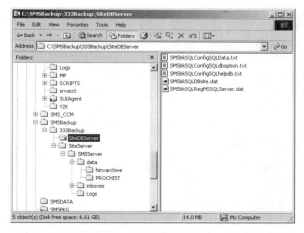

Figure 18-7. *The SiteDBServer directory.*

Notice that this directory contains the backup of the SMS site database (SMS-bkSQLDBsite.dat). It also contains the HKEY_LOCAL_MACHINE\Software\Microsoft\MSSQLServer registry key (SMSbkSQLRegMSSQLServer.dat).

As you can see, this backup routine is quite comprehensive and should be more than adequate to act as your SMS backup routine.

Tip You can change the scheduled time for the Backup SMS Site Server task to whenever you want, but the SMS Site Backup service is engineered to check the schedule only once per day. If you need to execute this maintenance task immediately, configure the task and then stop and start the SMS Site Backup service by running Services in the Control Panel on the site server.

Real World Connection Accounts and Backup

As we saw in Chapter 17, SMS Legacy Client components running on Windows clients use the SMS Client Connection account to connect to CAPs and distribution points to transfer data such as inventory or client configuration updates. SMS creates one such account for the Windows domain named SMSClient_*sitecode*, with a random password that's propagated to each Windows client. This is an internal account that should not be manually modified in any way.

When a site is restored from a backup, the password for the default SMS Client Connection account is reset. If you haven't created any client connection accounts in addition to the default, the SMS Legacy Clients will effectively be unable to connect to a CAP or distribution point because the password recognized by the client will be different from that reassigned as a result of the restore process. The change in password is copied to all site CAPs so that the clients can be updated. Ironically, since the client will be unable to connect to the CAP in the first place, it won't be able to update itself with the new SMS Client Connection account password. There's no way to set the password back to the original because there's no way of knowing what the original password was.

If you have additional client connection accounts specified for the Windows clients and they can't connect using one account, they will try using the others. You control the passwords for the manually created client connection accounts. The site backup and restore scenario is a perfect example of why you should consider creating at least one additional client connection account for your site (preferably before you back up the site). Or better yet, take Microsoft's recommendation to heart and upgrade all your Legacy Clients to Advanced Clients as soon as possible.

Recovering the SMS Site

Recovery of an SMS site generally falls into two categories: recovering the site database and recovering the site server. If the SMS database fails for some reason, you can restore it from its backup using SQL Server Enterprise Manager. You need to have access to a current backup, of course, as well as to the SQL Server Enterprise Manager console. There's no restore function in SMS because, presumably, if you need to restore the site in some fashion, you probably can't open the SMS Administrator Console.

Recovering the Site Database

Recovering the SMS database itself is a fairly straightforward task—which isn't to imply that it's a mundane or trivial matter, but rather that it's cut and dried. You recover the site database by restoring it from a current backup. For example, if you need to move the SMS database to another server running SQL Server for some reason, you would follow these steps:

1. Close all SMS-related tools, such as all SMS Administrator Consoles, that are accessing the current database, as well as all SMS site server services (including the SQL Monitor service on the system running SQL). You don't want anything trying to update the database while you're managing it.

2. Start SQL Server in single-user mode and back up the SMS database, or schedule a database backup through the SMS Administrator Console. The single-user mode option is set through the Properties dialog box for the database accessible through the SQL Server Enterprise Manager, on the Options tab.

3. Locate (or install) the other system running SQL Server, ensuring that the same database sort order has been used as on the original server running SQL, as well as the same hardware platform.

4. Create database and log devices or files (depending on the SQL Server version) that are at least as large as the backed-up database.

5. Restore the backed-up SMS database to the new system running SQL Server.

6. Use the Reset option of the SMS Setup program on the site server to point the site server to the location of the new system running SQL Server containing the database.

You would follow similar steps if the database needed to be restored for any other reason, although if you were restoring to the same system running SQL Server, you might not need to perform step 6.

Recovering the Site Server

If you encounter a situation in which the SMS site server itself needs to be recovered—perhaps it crashed or it had be moved to a different physical system—the steps for recovery are somewhat more involved. First of all, your situation would probably be hopeless if you had not already created a current backup of your SMS database, so let's assume that you've been backing it up regularly.

As we've seen, other significant elements of the site server in addition to the SMS database need to be backed up in order to completely restore the site server to its previous state. These elements include the SMS and NAL registry keys, the site control file (\SMS\Inboxes\Sitectrl.box\Sitectrl.ct0), and the SMS directory structure and files.

The recovery process begins with the restoration of the SMS site database, of course. However, it will also involve the restoration of the backed-up elements. For example, if you need to reinstall SMS on the site server or install it on a new computer, you'll restore the previous site by copying the backed-up SMS directory and site control file over the new installation or over the reinstallation. Similarly, you can restore the SMS-related registry keys by using the Windows Registry Editor to replace the existing SMS keys (created when you reinstalled SMS or installed it to a new server) with the backed-up versions of those keys.

In some cases, you could restore just the database itself and let the SMS site server rebuild itself—which it will do eventually. However, any changes you made that were written to the registry but not yet updated to the database will probably be lost. Restoring the SMS site server completely, as described here, will ensure that all elements of the site server are properly synchronized.

Note If you need to completely reinstall the SMS site server, all vestiges of the old site server must be cleaned off the server first. This includes uninstalling the SMS client software, removing the registry keys, and removing the remainder of the SMS directories and setup files not removed through the Remove SMS option of the Setup program. Then reinstall SMS, and restore the previous site as outlined above.

Real World   Using Preinst.exe

Included on the SMS product CD is the Site Utilities tool (Preinst.exe). This tool must be installed on a site server and is used to help diagnose problems, repair the site control file, delete incorrectly removed sites, or stop SMS site server services, among other things.

Let's look at three of this tool's command-line options here that can be of particular use in the SMS site server recovery and maintenance process: /DUMP, /DELSITE, and /DELJOB. You can run this tool from a command prompt by changing the path to the appropriate directory from the command prompt and executing the tool.

Figure 18-8 displays the command switches available for PREINST. Executing the PREINST /DUMP command causes a new site control image to be written to the root of the partition on which SMS was installed. An *image* is a binary representation of the site control file. This image is based on the current site control data stored in the SMS database and is named SMS_*sitecode*.scf. This file can then be copied to the Site Control Manager's inbox (SMS\Inboxes\Sitectrl.box) and renamed Sitectrl.ct0 to rebuild the site's properties. This function is useful if the site control file becomes corrupted or if you don't have a current backup of it.

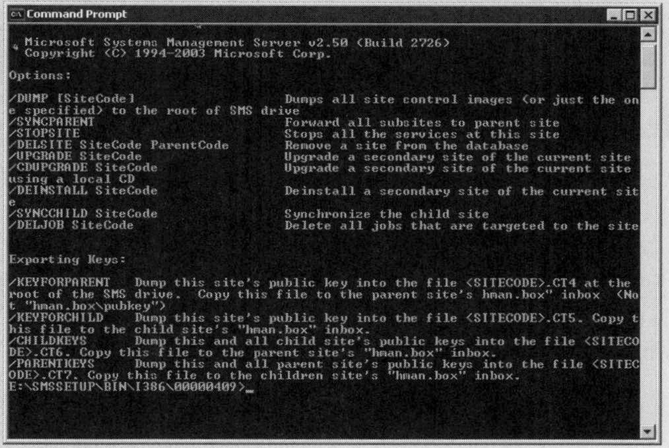

Figure 18-8.   *PREINST switches.*

You can use PREINST /DELSITE to remove a "phantom" child site. When a child site is to be removed from a parent site, the correct process is to break the parent-child relationship through the child site's properties, wait for the parent and child sites to update their respective databases, and then remove the addresses. A *phantom* child site occurs if the child site is removed from the parent site before the relationship has been broken or before the databases can be correctly updated, and references to the deleted child site may remain at the parent.

To delete the removed site from the parent site, execute PREINST /DEL-SITE: {*childsitecode, parentsitecode*}, where *childsitecode* represents the site code of the site that needs to be deleted and *parentsitecode* represents the parent's site code for the site that needs to be deleted. Once executed, the change will be replicated up the SMS site hierarchy.

Last, PREINST /DELJOB is designed to remove jobs or commands targeted to a specific site. You can use this command to remove jobs that might still be in the queue for the removed site but keep trying to be sent or executed, resulting in error status messages. Executing PREINST /DEL-JOB:*sitecode* will delete all commands that are targeting the specified site code.

Restoring Site Systems

Compared to recovering a site server, restoring an SMS site system such as a CAP, management point, distribution point, and so on is rather elemental. Recall from Chapter 3 that the SMS site server builds SMS site systems. You identify the site systems and assign their roles through the SMS Administrator Console. Consequently, if a site system should need to be rebuilt or replaced, it's merely a matter of reassigning that server through the site server.

For example, suppose that a site system such as a CAP or management point goes down and needs to be replaced. When you bring the failed server back on line, SMS will simply restore the appropriate files and components to that site system. If the site system itself needs to be replaced and its computer name has changed, you would remove the old server as a site system from the site server and then add the new server to the SMS site as a site system and assign it the appropriate role.

In a similar fashion, distribution points actually assume their role as packages are distributed and refreshed to these distribution points. Consequently, replacing or recovering a distribution point is simply a matter of refreshing the packages for that distribution point. To do that, follow these steps:

1. In the Packages node of the SMS Administrator Console, select the package you need to redistribute, right-click it, choose All Tasks from the context menu, and then choose Manage Distribution Points to launch the Manage Distribution Points Wizard, shown in Figure 18-9.

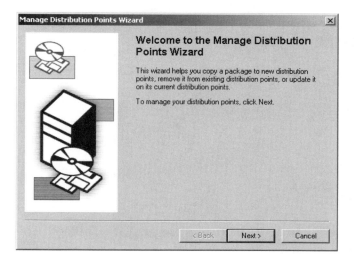

Figure 18-9.   *The Manage Distribution Points Wizard welcome page.*

2. Click Next to display the Manage Distribution Points page, shown in
    Figure 18-10. Select the Refresh The Package On Selected Distribution
    Points option.

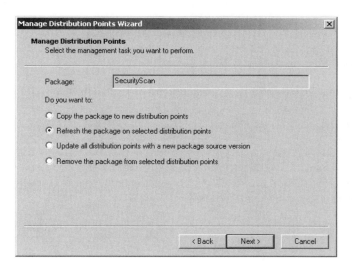

Figure 18-10.   *The Manage Distribution Points page.*

3. Click Next to display the Refresh Package page, shown in Figure 18-11.
    In the Distribution Points list, find the distribution point you just
    recovered and select it.

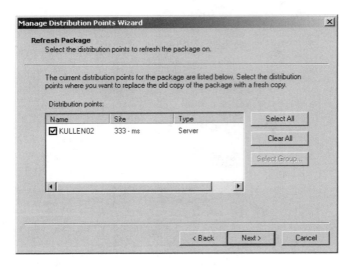

Figure 18-11. *The Refresh Package page.*

4. Click Next to display the Completing The Manage Distribution Points Wizard page, and then click Finish to begin the update process.

Caution   If you're recovering a distribution point that has gone down, the packages must be redistributed to the same drive and directory on which they were originally configured. For example, if you created your own shared folders to which the package was originally distributed, re-create the shares before redistributing the packages.

You can recover other site systems by reassigning them through the SMS Administrator Console.

Tip   If the system running SQL Server or the site server fails, SMS components running on site systems will continue to function correctly, although status messages and data updates won't be forwarded to the site server until it's restored. This means that SMS clients will continue to report inventory data, run advertised programs, and meter software.

Using the Recovery Expert

SMS 2003 includes two tools that can help you automate and facilitate the recovery process: the Recovery Expert and the SMS Site Repair Wizard. Here we will discuss the Recovery Expert.

The Recovery Expert has been, and continues to be, available as a Web-based tool on the Microsoft SMS Web site (*http://www.microsoft.com/smserver*). However, it has been included on the SMS product CD as an option that you can install from the Autorun menu, as shown in Figure 18-12.

Figure 18-12. *The SMS 2003 Autorun menu.*

The Recovery Expert must be installed to a host computer running Microsoft Internet Information Server (IIS) version 5 or later. The installation itself is fairly straightforward and results in the generation of a URL, as shown in Figure 18-13, that you can use to run the Recovery Expert tool.

Figure 18-13. *The final page of the Recovery Expert setup wizard.*

To start the Recovery Expert, open your Internet browser (Internet Explorer version 5.5 or later) and enter the URL that was generated during the installation of the Recovery Expert to display the Recovery Expert Entry Page shown in Figure 18-14. Then click Use The Recovery Expert.

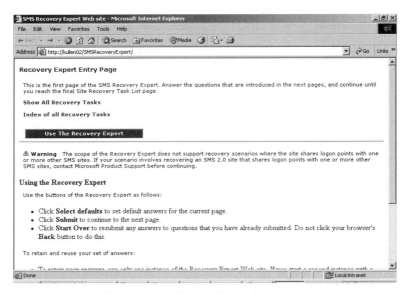

Figure 18-14. *The Recovery Expert Entry Page.*

Through the next few pages of the Recovery Expert, shown in Figures 18-15 through 18-17, you're presented with a series of questions designed to help generate a recovery checklist. As you'll see, these questions are quite specific as to the configuration of your site, the site hierarchy, the currency of your backup, and so on. The result is a comprehensive checklist of steps that you should follow to recover your SMS site. Believe me, this works well, especially if you provide the tool with the correct information. So, my obvious advice to you is to be sure you document your site setup, configuration, and hierarchy well! The time to pull together comprehensive documentation of your site is not after the site crashes.

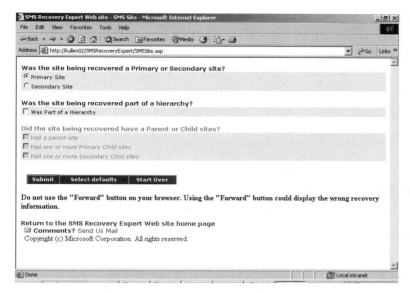

Figure 18-15. *The Recovery Expert Site Information page.*

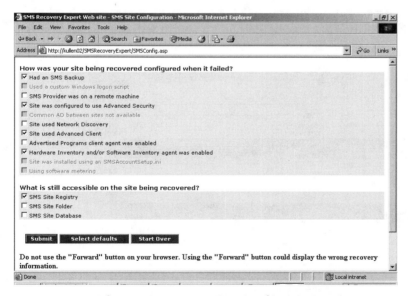

Figure 18-16. *The Recovery Expert Site Configuration page.*

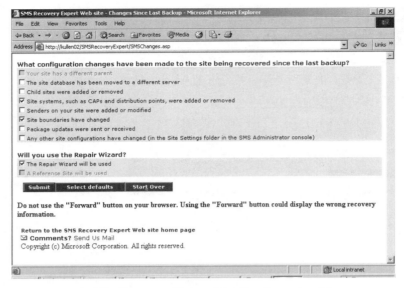

Figure 18-17. *The Recovery Expert Site Configuration Changes page.*

Notice the checklist entries in Figure 18-18. Each of the entries is itself a link to background information that will be helpful to you in successfully completing that task.

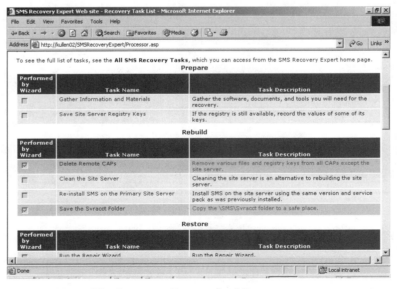

Figure 18-18. *The Recovery Expert checklist.*

For example, if I click the entry Gather Information And Materials, a rather detailed list is displayed, as shown in Figure 18-19, that lists exactly what you should have ready in the way of product CDs, backup files, and so on. You can print out just the checklist steps, or the entire checklist document, including all the background pages. The instructions for doing so are listed at the top of the checklist.

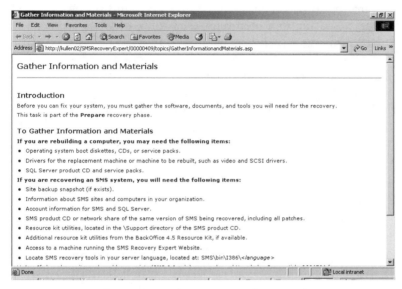

Figure 18-19.   *The Gather Information And Materials page.*

If you selected the option The Repair Wizard Will Be Used on the Recovery Expert Site Configuration Changes page, you'll notice that some of the checklist steps appear dimmed. The Repair Wizard is another recovery tool included with SMS 2003 that's designed to automate many of the recovery tasks for you. As you carry out each Recovery Expert checklist task, skip those tasks that are run by the SMS Site Repair Wizard. When you get to the checklist step that directs you to run the SMS Site Repair Wizard, do so. When the SMS Site Repair Wizard finishes, you can pick up with the next task on the Recovery Expert checklist. Let's see how the SMS Site Repair Wizard works.

Using the SMS Site Repair Wizard

The SMS Site Repair Wizard is automatically installed on your SMS site server during site setup and on any computer running the SMS Administrator Console. The SMS Site Repair Wizard doesn't need to be run on the site that's being recovered, but in many cases it can be more efficient and faster than executing steps across the network. This wizard automates many recovery tasks and is useful in repairing as well as recovering an SMS site server. Here's an example.

When an SMS site server is a member of a site hierarchy, it receives configuration information about packages, collections, and advertisements (among other things) from its parent, sends that kind of information to its own child sites, and sends its database information such as collected inventory and status messages to its parent. Sites participating in a hierarchy keep track of what needs to be sent back and forth by using a series of version stamps. There are version stamps for various objects in the SMS database, and version information is stored in many places—the registry on the site server, the site control file, and in the database itself. If the version stamps get out of sync for some reason, your site might not receive or accept any new information or send information of its own because it can't ascertain whether the information is valid any longer. The SMS Site Repair Wizard helps to put your site server back in sync by resetting the version values.

Another way the SMS Site Repair Wizard can help recover a site is through the use of a reference site. This would be a parent site that the wizard can contact to read the last data set that your site sent to the parent in an effort to restore your site's configuration and reset its version information.

Here is a complete list of the tasks carried out by the SMS Site Repair Wizard:

- Delete remote CAPs
- Save the Svracct folder
- Stop and disable site services on the site server
- Restore the site database
- Restore SMS files
- Restore SMS registry key
- Restore NAL registry key
- Restore the Svracct folder
- Increment the Transaction ID
- Increment the DDM serial number
- Synchronize Advanced Client Policy with the site database
- Increment serial numbers in the site database

- Reset status messages
- Insert the most current site control file
- Start and enable the Windows Management Instrumentation (WMI) service on the site database server
- Reconfigure child sites
- Reconfigure senders
- Reconfigure site systems
- Re-create other configuration changes
- Return the site server to service
- Restart the site server and check SMS services
- Reset the ACL objects on the SMS folders and the registry
- Reset the site again
- Resynchronize the parent and child site servers
- Create addresses for other sites
- Change the site's parent assignment
- Synchronize with other sites
- Delete phantom child sites
- Regenerate orphaned collections, advertisements, and packages

Together with the Recovery Expert, this tool all but guarantees successful recovery and repair of your SMS site. What can go wrong, then? Well, the recovery is only going to be as good as the work you've put into thoroughly documenting your site—its configuration, packages, collections, and so on—and the frequency with which you've backed up your site. Chapter 13 in the *Microsoft Systems Management Server 2003 Concepts, Planning, and Deployment Guide*, available on the SMS product CD, will give you a good detailed approach toward planning for a successful recovery experience.

To run the SMS Site Repair Wizard, follow these steps:

1. From the Systems Management Server program group, click SMS Site Repair Wizard to display the Welcome page shown in Figure 18-20. Enter the name of the site server you need to repair.

Figure 18-20. *The SMS Site Repair Wizard Welcome page.*

2. Click Next to display the Access Rights And Permissions Required page shown in Figure 18-21. This lists the permissions you need when running this wizard.

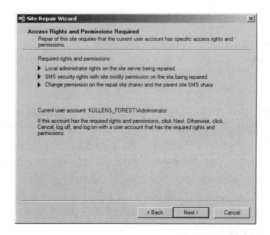

Figure 18-21. *The SMS Site Repair Wizard Access Rights And Permissions Required page.*

3. Click Next to display the Site Restore Steps page shown in Figure 18-22. On this page you can direct the wizard to the location of your most current site backup folder. If you don't have a current backup, you must perform the manual steps listed on this page before continuing. If you select the option The Site Has Been Manually Restored Or Has No Backup and click Next, you'll go right to the progress bar shown

in Figure 18-24 and described in step 4. However, the recommended best practice is that you do have a current backup, so go on to the next step.

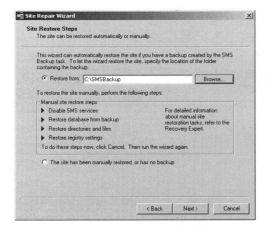

Figure 18-22. *The SMS Site Repair Wizard Site Restore Steps page.*

4. Click Next to display the Restore Database page shown in Figure 18-23.

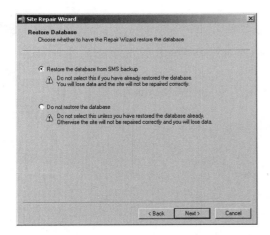

Figure 18-23. *The SMS Site Repair Wizard Restore Database page.*

5. Select whether you want the wizard to restore the SMS site database for you or whether you've already done so and then click Next. At this point the wizard will begin to carry out some initial steps, such as verifying permissions and stopping services, and a progress bar similar to that shown in Figure 18-24 is displayed.

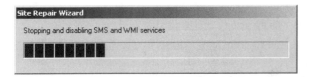

Figure 18-24. *The SMS Site Repair Wizard Site progress bar.*

6. The Site Backup And Failure Dates page, shown in Figure 18-25, is displayed next. Enter the date of the last backup and the date of the failure.

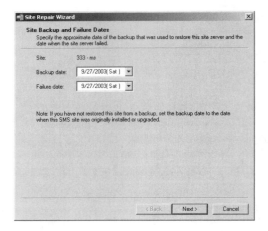

Figure 18-25. *The SMS Site Repair Wizard Site Backup And Failure Dates page.*

7. Click Next to display the Parent Site Setting shown in Figure 18-26.

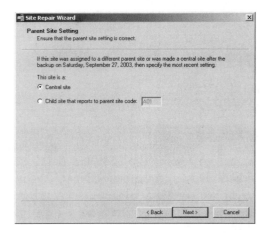

Figure 18-26. *The SMS Site Repair Wizard Parent Site Settings page.*

8. If you choose Central Site and click Next, you'll see the Verify Site Hierarchy page shown in Figure 18-27. Here you must specify any changes to the hierarchy that might have occurred since the last backup—for example, a new child site that was added.

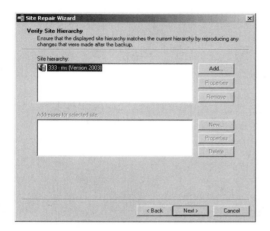

Figure 18-27. *The SMS Site Repair Wizard Verify Site Hierarchy page.*

If you choose Child Site That Reports to Parent Site and click Next, you'll see the Parent Site Connection page shown in Figure 18-28. Here you must specify any changes to site addresses that might have occurred since the last backup. Note that you can specify the name of the parent site for your site to use as a reference server and obtain configuration information for your site. Clicking Next here takes you back to the Verify Site Hierarchy page.

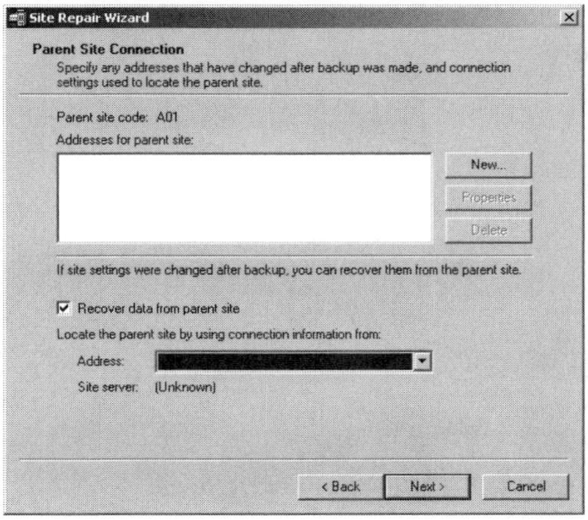

Figure 18-28. *The SMS Site Repair Wizard Parent Site Connection page.*

9. Click Next on the Verify Site Hierarchy page to display the Package Recovery page shown in Figure 18-29. Here you can choose to recover package source files that might have been stored on the site server, as well as refresh distribution points.

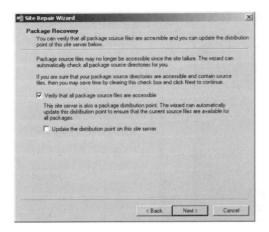

Figure 18-29. *The SMS Site Repair Wizard Package Recovery page.*

10. Click Next to display the SMS Site Repair Wizard Site Completing page shown in Figure 18-30. When you click Finish, the wizard displays a progress bar enumerating the tasks it's carrying out. When the wizard is finished, it displays a completion page that indicates success or failure and any additional steps that you need to carry out.

Figure 18-30. *The SMS Site Repair Wizard Site Completing page.*

Summary

At this point you have developed sound strategies for maintaining, backing up, and restoring SMS within your site. You have configured the database maintenance tasks and scheduled these tasks within appropriate time periods—daily, weekly, or monthly. You have established a regular backup plan that includes backing up not only the SMS database, but also the strategic files, folders, and registry keys contained on the site server. You have outlined and practiced recovery procedures to be followed in the event the SMS database server or site server fails or needs to be moved or a site system needs to be replaced.

Chapter 19 takes us a step further, as we explore maintenance and configuration from the point of view of SQL Server. Together, these two chapters provide the groundwork necessary to keep your SMS site optimized and well prepared should you ever encounter a recovery event.

Chapter 19
Maintaining the Database Through Microsoft SQL Server

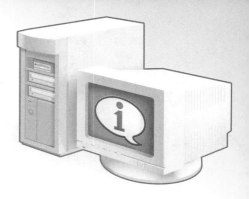

In Chapter 2, "Primary Site Installation," we outlined the prerequisites for a computer running Microsoft SQL Server to host the Microsoft Systems Management Server (SMS) 2003 database successfully. Let's recap those requirements here. Recall that to use SMS 2003, you must have installed either SQL Server 7 with Service Pack 3 or later or SQL Server 2000 with Service Pack 3 or later (required to support advanced security mode). Of the two versions, the recommended version is SQL Server 2000, and that's what we will focus on in this chapter. You can install SQL Server either on its own server or on the same system as the site server. The decision as to which location is more appropriate depends on many factors, not the least of which are the performance capabilities of the server itself.

The same decision also affects the way in which the SMS 2003 installation will proceed. If SQL Server is installed on the same server as SMS 2003, the SMS Setup program can create the necessary database devices and files for you. If SQL Server is installed on a different server, you'll need to define those devices and files prior to installing SMS.

Several SQL parameters affect the way SQL Server handles the SMS database. Some of those parameters, such as the number of open connections and the amount of memory allocated, were discussed in Chapter 2. Other parameters are discussed in this chapter.

In this chapter we'll focus on some specific tasks and terms, beginning with the SQL Server components used by the SMS database. Then we'll look at the management tools available in SQL Server and discuss how to maintain the SMS database using SQL Server 2000. Last, we'll explore how to modify SQL Server parameters and how to solve the problems that might occur with your SQL Server system. This chapter's intent is not to teach you all there is to know about SQL Server. Plenty of good books and courses on SQL Server are available to provide you with that information. Here, however, we'll explore how to maintain the SMS database through SQL Server.

> **Tip** It's possible to install and use SMS 2003 without a working knowledge of SQL Server, but in the long run you'll need to master at least SQL Server administration tasks. SMS 2003 is not itself a database server; instead, it acts as a front end to the SMS database maintained in SQL Server. Therefore, you'll need to initiate many database maintenance tasks through SQL Server. Consider taking a class about SQL Server administration, such as Microsoft Official Curriculum (MOC) 2072, "Administering a Microsoft SQL Server 2000 Database." *Microsoft SQL Server 2000 Administrator's Pocket Consultant* and *Microsoft SQL Server 2000 Performance Tuning* (both published by Microsoft Press) are also good sources of information regarding the execution of administrative tasks and optimizing server performance, respectively.

SQL Server Components

In this section we'll review some basic terminology and see how it relates to the SMS database. Every entity we call a database actually consists of two components: the database and its transaction log. The *database* is a collection of data records, object tables, and indexes organized in a specific structure designed to facilitate the displaying, sorting, updating, and analysis of the information it contains. The *transaction log* is used to record each action performed on the database, such as adding a new record or updating or deleting an existing record.

SQL Server 7.0 and SQL Server 2000 maintain their database and transaction logs in their own files. If SQL Server is installed on the same computer as SMS 2003, SMS can create the database and log files for you during its setup. If not, you'll need to create the files in advance.

If you install SMS on the same computer as SQL Server, SMS will not only create the devices for you, but it will also tune SQL Server for use with SMS. This feature doesn't, of course, relieve you of all responsibility in the maintenance of the server running SQL, but it does ease some of the setup concerns regarding SQL Server, especially if you've had little experience with it.

During the setup process for SMS 2.0, if SQL wasn't already installed on the proposed site server, the SMS 2.0 installation process prompted you for the SQL Server source files and installed a dedicated SQL Server database for itself on that same server. The SMS 2003 installation process doesn't do this. Therefore, you'll need to have installed SQL Server before running SMS setup. If you follow the basic instructions that come with SQL Server and accept all the default values, choosing Windows Only Authentication as the security option, you'll be just fine for SMS.

You can accomplish most of the actions you'll need to perform on the server running SQL through the SQL Server Enterprise Manager. Through this console, you can create databases and transaction logs, set security, back up and restore the database, perform routine database maintenance tasks, and optimize SQL Server parameters for the SMS database. Let's explore the process of creating devices in using SQL Server 2000.

Creating a Device in SQL Server 2000

The SQL Server Enterprise Manager, shown in Figure 19-1, is a Microsoft Management Console (MMC) snap-in. It groups its managed objects into five main categories:

- Databases
- Data transformation services
- Management
- Security
- Support services

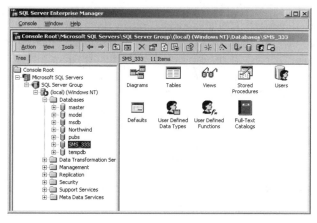

Figure 19-1. *SQL Server Enterprise Manager.*

SQL Server 2000 doesn't require the creation of separate devices before the database can be generated. Instead, it requires the creation of database files that will contain both the actual database objects and the transaction log data. Follow these steps to create a SQL Server 2000 database file:

1. In SQL Server Enterprise Manager, navigate to the Databases folder, right-click it, and choose New Database from the context menu to display the Database Properties dialog box, shown in Figure 19-2.

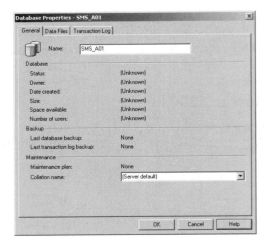

Figure 19-2.   *The Database Properties dialog box.*

2. In the General tab, enter a name for the database, such as SMS_*xxx*, where *xxx* represents the site code for your new site.

3. The database file name will appear as SMS_*xxx*_Data in the Database Files list in the Data Files tab, as shown in Figure 19-3. You can click the ellipsis (Browse) button (found in the Location column) to display the Locate Database File dialog box where you can modify the location of the file. In the Data Files tab you can also change the initial size through this entry.

Figure 19-3.   *The Database Properties Data Files tab.*

4. In the File Properties section, the Automatically Grow File option is enabled by default. This option ensures that SQL Server monitors the size of your database and expands it as necessary according to the File Growth parameter you specify. You can also allow the growth to be unrestricted or set a maximum size.

5. Select the Transaction Log tab, shown in Figure 19-4, and configure the same parameters for the transaction log. The transaction log file will be named SMS_*xxx*_Log.

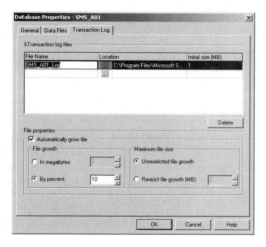

Figure 19-4.   *The Transaction Log tab.*

6. Click OK to create the files.

SQL Server 2000 considers the database and transaction log files combined as representing the database and displays a single database entry.

SMS Database Components

The SMS database contains data objects and their attributes arranged in an organized fashion. Each database consists of four main elements, as follows:

- Tables
- Indexes
- Event triggers
- Stored procedures

A *table* is a database object that contains data in the database organized as a collection of rows and columns. Each row in the table represents a data record, and each column represents an associated field for that record. Generally, each table defines one or more columns (fields) as a key entry that can be used to link tables for the purpose of sorting, searching, and reporting on data in the database. SMS 2003 contains more than 200 predefined tables.

An *index* can be thought of as a companion object to a table. Separate from the table, an index functions much like an index in a book, providing a quick way to search and locate data. If an index is available for a table, your queries will exhibit better performance. If no index is available, the entire table must be searched. The two index types, clustered index and nonclustered index, determine how the data records are searched. The nonclustered index is similar to a book index—each entry contains a bookmark that tells the database where to find the data that corresponds to the key in the index. For example, when you look up an entry such as "site-server" in a book index, you might be directed to several locations in the book. The index doesn't represent the order in which the data is stored in the book. The clustered index is similar to a telephone directory—it contains the data itself, not just the index keys. The clustered indexes are usually based on a primary key defined in each table. Each index entry corresponds to the order in which the data is stored in the book. Like looking up a name in the phone book, when you find the name, you also find the address and phone number.

When you execute a query, you're searching tables for a specific value based on the criteria you enter, using indexes whenever possible. The query result represents the records or data values obtained from records contained in one or more tables. SMS 2003 contains more than 250 predefined indexes.

An *event trigger* is a Transact-SQL statement that's executed whenever a specific event occurs in a given table. The Transact-SQL language is used for communication between applications and SQL Server. It's an enhancement to SQL and provides a comprehensive language for defining tables, maintaining tables, and controlling access to data in the tables. If data is added, deleted, or modified within a specific table, an event trigger will be executed. SMS uses event triggers to notify its components that an event has occurred that a particular component needs to attend to. Event triggers cause components to "wake up" in response to an event rather than waiting for a specific polling cycle to occur. Obviously, this translates to better performance for the site server. For example, when you change a site setting, an event trigger causes SQL Monitor to write a wake-up file in the Hierarchy Manager inbox (see Chapter 3, "Configuring Site Server Properties and Site Systems," for more information). SMS 2003 uses over 200 event triggers.

A *stored procedure* is a group of Transact-SQL statements that have been compiled into a single executable routine. You could think of a stored procedure as a kind of batch file for SQL Server. When a SQL Server event activates a trigger, a corresponding stored procedure is executed that writes the wake-up file into the appropriate SMS component's inbox on the site server. Two common stored procedures that you might execute are SP_SPACEUSED, which displays the amount of reserved and actual disk space used by a table in the database or by the entire database, and SP_WHO, which identifies SQL Server connections (users and processes) currently in use. Both are included with SQL's master database.

SQL Server Management Tools

A quick scan of the SQL Server program group reveals that many tools are installed to assist the SQL Server administrator in maintaining the server running SQL. Unless you're the SQL Server administrator as well as the SMS administrator or you get the necessary education to fully understand and appreciate the product, you'll probably use only two or three of these tools. The SQL Server 2000 program tools are described in Table 19-1.

Table 19-1.   SQL Server 2000 program tools

Tool	Description
Analysis Services	A folder that provides access to the Analysis Manager, another link to Books Online and MDX Sample Application. The Analysis Manager is a console application that provides an interface for accessing and managing analysis servers. For more information about Analysis Services, please refer to Books Online.
Books Online	Provides an online version of the documentation set *SQL Server Books Online* with full searching capabilities.
Client Network Utility	Used to set the custom server connection, DB-Library, and Net-Library configuration for clients.
Configure SQL XML Support In IIS	Used to define and register a new virtual directory in Internet Information Services (IIS) so that HTTP can be used to access a SQL Server 2000 database.
Enterprise Manager	MMC snap-in that facilitates the configuration of the server running SQL and the management of SQL Server databases, including devices and databases, space usage, backups and restores, permissions, data import and export, and so on, through object-level folders.

Table 19-1. **SQL Server 2000 program tools**

Tool	Description
Import And Export Data	Starts the Data Transformation Service Import/Export Wizard, designed to facilitate the import, export, and conversion of data from various data formats.
Profiler	Used to monitor server events, procedure calls, and other real-time server activity; Profiler can also filter events and direct output to the screen, file, or table.
Query Analyzer	Graphical query interface used to execute maintenance tasks such as Transact-SQL statements or stored procedures.
Server Network Utility	Used to configure SQL Server to use Net-Libraries and to specify the network protocol stacks on which the server will listen for SQL Server clients' requests.
Service Manager	Starts, stops, and pauses the SQL Server, SQL Server Agent, and MS DTC services. Also implemented as a taskbar program.

Many SQL Server maintenance tasks specific to the SMS database can be configured and scheduled to run through the SMS Administrator Console, including a complete site server backup (see Chapter 18, "Disaster Recovery," for more information). You can also effect database backups by using a third-party backup program capable of including SQL Server databases as part of its backup routine. Consequently, as an SMS administrator, you're most likely to use Enterprise Manager to perform any additional or advanced maintenance tasks. Through this interface you can create database devices, manage space usage, configure the server, schedule events, back up and restore the database, and so on. You can also use the SQL Server Query Analyzer to execute maintenance tasks such as those described in Chapter 18.

As with most Microsoft BackOffice applications, when you install SQL Server several performance objects and counters are included to assist you in evaluating the ongoing performance and resource use of your server running SQL as well as to facilitate the troubleshooting of specific performance-related problems. To view the available SQL Server performance objects and counters, you can start the Windows System Monitor utility, accessible through the Performance Console. For example, the SQL Server:Database object has a counter called Data File(s) Size (KB) that will help you monitor the cumulative size of your databases, such as Tempdb.

Database Maintenance

As we've seen, some database maintenance tasks should be carried out on a regular basis—either daily, weekly, or monthly. For example, every day you might execute a database backup and review status messages and system performance. Once a week, you might monitor database size usage and purge old data from the database. Once a month, you might verify the integrity of the database backup by testing a restore of the database. Once a month, you might also review security and make appropriate adjustments such as resetting account passwords.

Most of these tasks can be performed or configured and scheduled to run through the SMS Administrator Console. However, you can perform many of these same tasks, and database backup and restores, through SQL Server. In this section we'll review the commands used for performing the essential maintenance tasks and how to perform these tasks.

Commands Used for Performing Essential Maintenance Tasks

Some of the database integrity checking and space monitoring commands you might consider running on a weekly or monthly basis are listed below. These database consistency checker (DBCC) commands are certainly not the only ones available, but they're among the commands that Microsoft most often recommends.

- **DBCC CHECKALLOC**   Checks the specified database to verify that all pages have been correctly allocated and used; reports the space allocation and usage.

- **DBCC CHECKDB**   Checks every database table and index to verify that they are linked correctly, that their pointers are consistent, and that they are in the proper sort order.

- **DBCC CHECKCATALOG**   Checks consistency between tables and reports on defined segments.

- **DBCC UPDATEUSAGE**   Used with a recently reindexed database to reset space usage reporting so that SP_SPACEUSED returns accurate data. You could schedule this command to run with SP_SPACEUSED or to run separately under its own schedule.

Tip   To obtain a complete list and explanation of all Transact-SQL statements and stored procedures, including the DBCC commands, query the online help for SQL Server 2000.

Before you run any DBCC command, remember to set SQL Server to single-user mode. We'll look at how to start SQL Server in single-user mode in the section entitled "Backing Up and Restoring the Database" later in this chapter. We'll discuss how to run these commands in the following sections.

Executing a Maintenance Command Using SQL Server 2000

To execute a database maintenance command in SQL Server 2000, launch the Query Analyzer tool found in the Microsoft SQL Server programs group to display the Connect To SQL Server dialog box, shown in Figure 19-5, and follow these steps:

1. In the Connect To SQL Server dialog box, click the Browse button to choose from a list of servers running SQL located on the network. Select [Local] to specify the use of the local server. If you need to start the service, select the Start SQL Server If It Is Stopped check box.

Figure 19-5.   *The Connect To SQL Server dialog box.*

2. Select either Windows Authentication or SQL Server Authentication, depending on the security mode you enabled for your server running SQL. Supply a login name and password if appropriate.

3. Click OK to display the Query window, shown in Figure 19-6. Select the database you want to query against from the list on the left and enter the command that you want to execute—in this case, DBCC CHECKDB in the Query window.

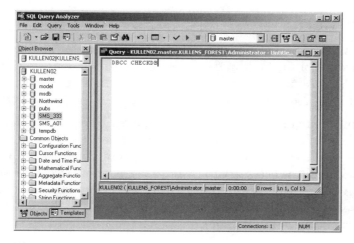

Figure 19-6.   *The Query Analyzer Query window.*

4. Choose Execute from the Query menu or click the Execute Query button (the green arrow) on the toolbar. The results of the query are displayed on the bottom half of the Query window, shown in Figure 19-7.

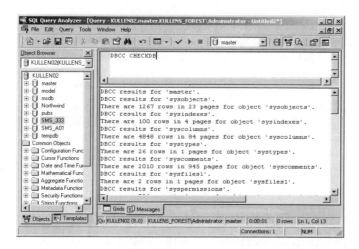

Figure 19-7.   *The Query Analyzer Results window.*

Tip   Each of the DBCC commands and stored procedures might have additional syntax options that will affect how the command is executed. Refer to your SQL Server documentation for a complete description of each command and its syntax.

Backing Up and Restoring the Database

We began our discussion of backing up and restoring the database in Chapter 18, when we explored some of the built-in database maintenance routines configurable through the SMS Administrator Console. In this section we'll review the procedure for backing up and restoring the database directly through SQL Server.

You can back up the contents of the database and transaction log to a device such as a tape drive or to another file location on the server. The frequency of the backup is up to you, the SMS administrator. Generally, you'll back up the SMS database as frequently as necessary to ensure a current and accurate restoration of the data. A common database strategy involves performing a complete backup of the database once a week, with incremental backups of the data that has changed each day between full backups.

Tip As you've seen throughout this book, SMS components have frequent communication with the SMS database. Before implementing a production site, develop and test a backup and restore strategy that will adequately protect your data.

Note Several third-party backup programs, such as Veritas Backup Exec for Microsoft Windows 2000, include modules designed specifically for backing up SQL Server databases. If you have access to such a product, you can have it perform the backup as part of its systemwide backup routine, eliminating the need to configure a backup redundantly through SQL Server or through the SMS Administrator Console. To preserve the data's integrity, it's important that no SMS components try to access the SMS database when the backup or restore is taking place. Be sure that no SMS Administrator Consoles are running and that all SMS components on the site server have been stopped. In addition, when you're restoring the database be sure to set the database to single-user mode. This is set as a property of the database. Note that you won't be able to set the single-user mode option if any open connections exist to the database.

Backing Up and Restoring Using SQL Server 2000

Although the preferred method for backing up the SMS site database is to use the site maintenance task provided in the SMS Administrator console, there's no corresponding restore task. You can back up and restore the SMS site database through the SQL Enterprise Manager.

To back up the SMS database using SQL Server 2000, follow these steps:

1. In Enterprise Manager, navigate to the Databases folder and expand it.

2. Select the SMS database you want to back up, right-click it, and choose Properties to display the Database Properties dialog box.

3. Select the Options tab, shown in Figure 19-8. Select the Restrict Access check box and then select Single User. Click OK to return to Enterprise Manager.

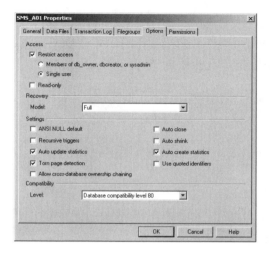

Figure 19-8.   *The Options tab of the Database Properties dialog box.*

4. Right-click the database entry again, choose All Tasks from the context menu, and then choose Backup Database to display the SQL Server Backup dialog box, shown in Figure 19-9.

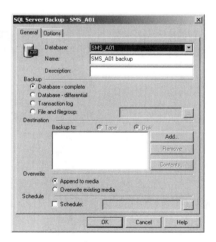

Figure 19-9.   *The SQL Server Backup dialog box.*

5. In the General tab, confirm that your SMS database is selected. Modify the name of the backup if you want and verify that the Database - Complete option has been selected.

6. To specify a backup device, click the Add button to display the Select Backup Destination dialog box, shown in Figure 19-10. Enter a filename and select an existing backup device from the Backup Device list or select New Backup Device to create a new device.

Figure 19-10. *The Select Backup Destination dialog box.*

7. If you select New Backup Device, the Backup Device Properties - New Device dialog box will appear, as shown in Figure 19-11. Enter a name for the device and then click OK to return to the Select Backup Destination dialog box.

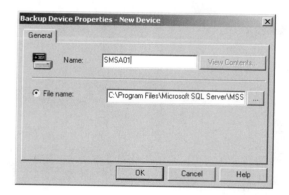

Figure 19-11. *The Backup Device Properties - New Device dialog box.*

8. Click OK again to accept the device destination and return to the SQL Server Backup Properties dialog box.

9. Remove any other backup devices that might be listed in the Backup To list in the General tab, such as a temp file. Set whatever other options you want in the General and Options tabs and then click OK to begin the backup process. (You can click Help for more information about each of the options available in these tabs.)

10. When the backup is complete, a message to that effect will be displayed. Click OK.

To restore the database, follow these steps:

1. In Enterprise Manager, navigate to the Databases folder and expand it.

2. Select your SMS site database, right-click it, choose All Tasks from the context menu, and then choose Restore Database to display the Restore Database dialog box, shown in Figure 19-12.

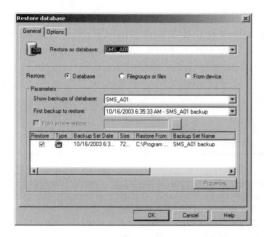

Figure 19-12.   *The Restore Database dialog box.*

3. In the General tab, verify that the correct database is selected and that the Database option in the Restore section has been enabled.

4. In the Parameters section, select the appropriate backup device from the Show Backups Of Database drop-down list. The First Backup To Restore drop-down list displays in chronological order the database backups for this device. This option allows you to restore selective differential backups if you performed them. Select the appropriate entry.

5. Click OK to begin the restore process.

6. When the restore process has completed successfully, SQL Server will display a message to that effect. Click OK.

Note After you perform your backup and restore procedure, be sure to clear the Single User option you set in step 3 of the backup steps outlined previously.

In this section we've looked at the procedures for backing up and restoring SMS databases using SQL Server. Note that what we discussed are only essential procedures. You should consult the SQL Server documentation for other configuration options.

Modifying SQL Server Parameters

Several SQL Server parameters can affect how well the SMS database will be managed. SQL Server self-manages most of these parameters—that is to say, you shouldn't need to fool around with them. In some scenarios, however, you might choose to manually configure one or more parameters—for example, when trying to optimize the use of server resources on the SQL Server system. In those cases, when you install SQL Server you should pay particular attention to the following SQL Server configuration parameters and set them appropriately before installing SMS 2003: User Connections, Open Objects, Memory, Locks, and Tempdb Size. Table 19-2 provides guidelines for setting these parameters for SQL Server 2000.

Table 19-2.   SQL Server configuration parameters

Parameter	Guidelines
User Connections	SMS 2003 requires a minimum of 40 user connections for the site server and 2 connections for each SMS Administrator Console you plan to install. It also requires five additional user connections for each instance of the SMS Administrator Console, if more than five consoles will be running concurrently on your site. You can set SMS 2003 to calculate this number and configure it automatically during setup. Each installation of SMS 2003 requires 20 user connections. In SQL Server this allocation is made dynamically at the time of the connection, providing more efficient memory management.
Open Objects	This parameter indicates the number of tables, views, stored procedures, and the like that can be open at a time. If you exceed the specified number of open objects, SQL Server must close some objects before it can open others, resulting in a performance hit. For most sites, a value of 1000 should be sufficient. For large sites, however, this number could be 5000 or more. Use SQL Server performance counters to track the number of open objects in use to determine the optimum number for the SMS site. Note that SQL Server sizes this number automatically.

Table 19-2. SQL Server configuration parameters

Parameter	Guidelines
Memory	This parameter indicates the amount of RAM that should be used for database caching and management. SMS automatically allocates 16 MB of RAM for SQL Server use. SQL Server allocates memory dynamically in 8 KB units. You can define a range for SQL Server to use.
Locks	This parameter prevents users from accessing and updating the same data at the same time. Because of the volume of information contained in the database, Microsoft recommends setting this value from 5000 to 10,000 depending on the size of the database and the number of SMS Administrator Consoles.
Tempdb Size	This temporary database and log are used to manage queries and sorts. By default, the tempdb database and log information are maintained on the same server running SQL. It's recommended that the tempdb data device size should be at least 20 percent of the SMS database size. SQL Server, as you have by now surmised, sizes the tempdb database dynamically.

Modifying Parameters for SQL Server 2000

To modify these parameter settings for SQL Server 2000, follow these steps:

1. In Enterprise Manager, select your SQL Server entry (the icon of a computer with a white triangle within a green circle), right-click it, and choose Properties from the context menu to display the SQL Server Properties dialog box, shown in Figure 19-13.

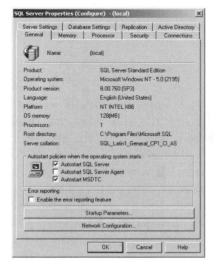

Figure 19-13. *The SQL Server Properties dialog box.*

2. The SQL Server Properties dialog box contains tabs for those parameters for which you can modify settings. (Recall from Table 19-2 that SQL Server dynamically manages most SMS-specific parameters.)

3. Select the Memory tab, shown in Figure 19-14. Notice that the Dynamically Configure SQL Server Memory option is enabled by default, although you can modify the memory range within which SQL Server should manage memory allocation. You can also specify a fixed amount of memory as well as identify the amount of memory to allocate per user for query execution.

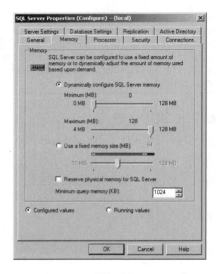

Figure 19-14. *The Memory tab.*

4. Select the Connections tab, shown in Figure 19-15. This tab displays the maximum number of user connections that were configured for SQL Server during the SMS setup. By default, this value is set to 0, which means that SQL Server will dynamically allocate connections and appropriate resources to support them as required. The allocation of user connections is a value you should monitor, especially if you choose to enter your own maximum value. If you add SMS Administrator Consoles or define additional site systems, you might need to increase the maximum number of connections to accommodate the increased resource demand by modifying this setting.

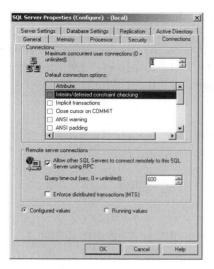

Figure 19-15.   *The Connections tab.*

5. When you have finished making your changes, click OK to save them. You might need to stop and then restart SQL Server to implement your changes. If this step is necessary, a message box will display to that effect.

More Info   Several performance tuning documents are available at Microsoft's SQL Web site (*http://www.microsoft.com/sql/techinfo/administration/2000/perftuning.asp*).

The topic of time synchronization is significant enough to bear revisiting here (you can refer to the "Real World" sidebar in Chapter 2 entitled "Synchronizing System Clocks" for a specific example), especially if SQL Server and the SMS site server are installed on two different servers. Because the time stamp of data objects created will generally be that of the server running SQL, it's important that the SMS site server and the server running SQL synchronize their system times on a regular basis.

It's also important that the SMS clients synchronize their time with the SMS site server and the server running SQL. SMS client computers will check their own system clocks when determining when to execute a program or run an agent. You can see how easily things can go awry if the server running SQL, the site server, and the client computer system clocks are all set to different times. A package might not execute at the time you expected, or an inventory collection might not take place because the scheduled times and the system clock are out of sync.

One way to overcome this situation is to identify one server as your time server for the SMS site. Have all your site systems, the SMS client computers, and the server running SQL synchronize their times with the time server. Or you might even consider making the server running SQL the time server for the SMS site. Fortunately, Windows 2000 and higher domains have this functionality built in.

Using SQL Replication to Enhance SMS Site Performance

Management points, and to a lesser extent server locator points, can access the SMS site database frequently to service requests made by SMS Advanced Clients. This can place a significant strain on server resources on the computer hosting the SMS site database as well as generate a significant amount of network traffic.

You can mitigate these issues by installing a separate instance of SQL Server on another computer in your network and replicating the Advanced Client policy tables from the SMS site database to the second instance of SQL Server. SQL Server database replication will then keep the replicated Advanced Client policy database synchronized with the SMS site database. The replication process is handled entirely by the SQL Server publication and subscription services. Then, configure the management point or server locator point to connect to the SQL Server computer that contains the replicated database rather than the SMS site database server. Refer to Chapter 3 for detailed steps for configuring a management point.

You can run MpPublish.vbs at a command prompt from the SMSSETUP\BIN\ I386\ folder on the SMS 2003 product CD to publish the table and store procedures. The syntax for using MpPublish.vbs is

MpPublish.vbs *SiteDatabaseName PublisherMachineName SQLUserName SQLPassword*

where *SiteDatabaseName* is the name of the SMS site database, *PublisherMachineName* is the name of the SQL Server computer that hosts the replicated database (if not specified, the local computer name is assumed), *SQLUserName* and *SQLPassword* represent the SQL account and password that has access to the replicated database (required if you aren't using Windows Only Authentication for that instance of SQL Server). If the command runs successfully, you'll see the message MpPublish Completed Successfully. After you run this command, you can configure the subscriber and start the snapshot agent on the distributor computer (the SMS site database server). Refer to the SQL Server documentation for information about completing the configuration.

Summary

After reading Chapter 18 and this chapter, you should be well aware of the importance of creating and following an ongoing maintenance schedule for your SMS database. Chapter 18 focused on tasks that can be performed directly through the SMS Administrator Console. This chapter focused on the server running SQL and the tools and procedures that facilitate the management and maintenance of the server and the SMS database.

Up to this point in Part IV, we've explored ways to extract and report on data in the database, how to secure that data, and how to recover in the event of a failure of some kind. We also discussed ways to maintain the integrity of the SMS database and optimize the server running SQL that's hosting that database.

The final chapter, Chapter 20, "Migration Issues," examines the process of migrating from an SMS 2.0 environment to an SMS 2003 environment. You'll learn how to support both versions of SMS within the same hierarchy and how to upgrade from SMS 2.0 to SMS 2003.

Chapter 20
Migration Issues

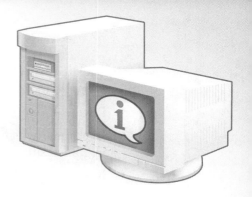

This chapter is designed for those of you who currently maintain Microsoft Systems Management Server (SMS) 2.0 sites and need to either upgrade to SMS 2003 or have the two versions of SMS coexist in the same site structure. Microsoft has published a body of good, detailed information concerning the topic of upgrading your site, including Chapter 6, "Understanding Interoperability with SMS 2.0," Chapter 11, "Planning an Upgrade," and Chapter 14, "Upgrading to SMS 2003," in the *Microsoft Systems Management Server 2003 Concepts, Planning, and Deployment Guide*; and Chapter 1, "Scenarios and Procedures for Deploying SMS," in the *Microsoft Systems Management Server 2003 Operations Guide*. Both guides are available through the SMS Web site (*http://www.microsoft.com/ smserver)* and Microsoft TechNet; the *Concepts, Planning, and Deployment Guide* is also available on the SMS 2003 product CD.

In this chapter I've taken the key elements discussed in the Microsoft documentation and attempted to present them to you in a simplified manner. We'll explore the most significant aspects of the two migration scenarios—interoperability and upgrading—to help you determine which approach is appropriate for your needs and what the main issues are. Our examination of migration is divided into four sections: planning the site structure, maintaining SMS 2.0 and 2003 sites within the same site structure, upgrading from SMS 2.0 to SMS 2003, and reviewing the tasks to be performed after the upgrade.

Planning the Site Structure

Whether you need to upgrade all your SMS 2.0 servers to SMS 2003 or maintain a mixed SMS 2.0 and 2003 environment, you'll need to spend some time thinking through the two scenarios. Both bring up issues that tend to split into server-related and client-related concerns. A checklist of premigration considerations should include the following tasks:

- Review the current SMS site structure
- Determine which client platforms need to be supported within your upgraded site structure
- Review server hardware and software currently in use
- Explore feature differences between SMS 2.0 servers and SMS 2003 servers
- Review and clean up the database to be converted
- Document current site settings that need to be re-created
- Back up the site and the server

Before you upgrade to SMS 2003, you must apply SMS 2.0 Service Pack 4 or later. You'll no doubt add items specific and unique to your own SMS installation, but this checklist should serve as a good starting point as you prepare your SMS 2.0 migration strategy. We'll look at each of these tasks in detail in the sections that follow.

Reviewing the Current Site Structure

The first step in developing a migration strategy is to review your current SMS site structure. The current SMS site structure can play a more significant role in determining your migration strategy than you might realize. In general, the clearer your understanding of the current site structure, the easier it will be for you to manage upgrading the sites and maintaining a mixed site. This means documenting all aspects of your current structure, site by site.

Identify the location of your sites' logon servers, distribution servers, site servers, and other site systems you've specified—an upgrade will affect all of these in one way or another. Identify your Microsoft Windows domain and forest structure and your Windows server platforms. As you've seen throughout this book, SMS 2003 has some specific setup and configuration requirements depending on the Windows server platform you're using.

If your system currently supports SMS 2.0 secondary sites, consider whether you need to retain this support. Perhaps the needs of that site or your organization have changed since the secondary sites were implemented. Although an SMS 2003 primary site can support SMS 2.0 secondary sites, I really recommend that you take the time to review your site requirements. This is an excellent opportunity to rebuild your site structure to better meet your organization's management needs, as well as to consolidate or upgrade hardware.

Determining Which Client Platforms Need to Be Supported

You already know that SMS 2003 supports only client systems running Windows 98 and higher. Prior to upgrading any existing site servers to SMS 2003 or implementing any new site servers using SMS 2003, you need to determine whether you have unsupported clients in your existing SMS sites and whether they still need to be managed by an SMS site. If not, you should remove the old SMS client components from those clients before upgrading the site server to which they belong.

If these clients still need to participate in an SMS site, they can be managed only by an SMS 2.0 site and you'll need to implement a mixed site of SMS 2.0 and SMS 2003 servers. Although this isn't an impossible situation, it's also not without challenges. Mixed-site interoperability will be discussed in detail in the section entitled "Maintaining Mixed Sites Within the Same Site Structure" later in this chapter.

Tip Take this opportunity to review the hardware components for your proposed SMS 2003 clients to be sure that you have adequate resources to support installation of the SMS 2003 client components. For example, installation of all SMS 2003 client components will require at least 40 MB of free disk space for a Legacy Client. Also, consider whether you want your clients to take advantage of the benefits of the Advanced Client. SMS 2003 doesn't support running the Advanced Client on Windows 98 and Windows NT 4.0 systems, and you must decide whether to upgrade these systems, choose not to install the Advanced Client on them, or perhaps even choose not to manage them through SMS.

Reviewing Hardware and Software Currently in Use

Now is an excellent time for you to review the hardware and software currently in use on your Windows servers. Recall from Chapter 2, "Primary Site Installation," that you must meet some minimum and recommended hardware and software requirements to successfully upgrade to or install SMS 2003. For example, you should have at least 256 MB of RAM and 2 GB of available disk space on an NTFS partition, and your server's processor must be at least an Intel Pentium 550 MHz.

By now, you certainly understand that RAM, disk space, I/O, and processor speed are all important factors in maintaining acceptable performance for SMS 2003 site systems, particularly the site server and SMS database server. You must upgrade your servers accordingly before beginning an upgrade or installation process.

In terms of software, you must meet some simple, nonnegotiable terms in order to upgrade to or install SMS 2003. The proposed site server must be running Windows 2000 with Service Pack 3 or later or a server running Windows Server 2003 Standard or Enterprise Edition.

Also, although SMS 2.0 supports SQL Server 6.5 with Service Pack 4 or later applied, SMS 2003 requires SQL Server 7.0 SP3 or higher to support the SMS site database if you're running SMS 2003 standard security and SQL Server 2000 SP3a or higher if you're running SMS 2003 advanced security.

Exploring Site Considerations in a Mixed-Version Environment

If you need to maintain a mixed SMS 2.0 and SMS 2003 site structure, you need to consider several things as you reorganize the structure and roll out the upgrade. Although SMS 2.0 sites can report to SMS 2003 sites, the reverse isn't supported—that is, SMS 2003 sites can report only to other SMS 2003 sites and not to SMS 2.0 sites. Be sure your proposed mixed-site structure reflects this reporting path. This limitation also almost guarantees the necessity of performing a top-down upgrade of SMS 2.0 sites. Begin your upgrade with the SMS 2.0 central site and work your way down to ensure that all SMS 2003 sites always report to another SMS 2003 site.

Note If you'll be supporting a mixed SMS 2.0 and SMS 2003 site structure, the SMS 2.0 site servers must be upgraded with SMS 2.0 Service Pack 4 or higher. This service pack implements several performance and component enhancements that deal specifically with interoperability between SMS 2.0 and SMS 2003 sites.

You can't install or run SMS 2.0 components on an SMS 2003 site system. For example, you couldn't define an SMS 2.0 logon point to be a site server for an SMS 2003 site server. Similarly, SMS 2.0 sites don't recognize SMS 2003 management points, server locator points, or reporting points. However, SMS 2.0 and SMS 2003 sites can share distribution points because no SMS components are installed on those servers, although SMS 2.0 sites can't take advantage of Background Intelligent Transfer Service (BITS) enabled distribution points

Perhaps the most important of these limitations is that SMS 2.0 and SMS 2003 can't share the same SQL Server database, although both sites can maintain separate SMS databases on the same server running SQL. As always, however, it's recommended that each SMS primary site have its own dedicated server running SQL.

Although you can't use an SMS 2.0 Administrator Console to manage an SMS 2003 site, you can use an SMS 2003 Administrator Console to manage an SMS 2.0 site. In fact, this latter scenario is recommended in a mixed-site hierarchy. Of course, administration tasks specific to SMS 2.0 sites wouldn't be available. For example, tasks related to software metering are unavailable, as are the Export Site Database or Export Site Transaction Logs maintenance tasks.

More Info   For a detailed discussion of interoperability considerations, refer to Chapter 6, "Understanding Interoperability with SMS 2.0," in the *Microsoft Systems Management Server 2003 Concepts, Planning, and Deployment Guide* mentioned earlier in this chapter.

Reviewing and Cleaning Up the Database

Although the actual SMS 2003 upgrade process does a fairly good job of converting the SMS 2.0 database, performing whatever maintenance and cleanup tasks are necessary to make the database as error-free as possible before the upgrade is strongly recommended. Otherwise, you could run the risk of migrating "bad" data into the new site, and what's the point of doing that?

Reviewing the Database

Before you upgrade, you should perform the usual recommended SQL Server database maintenance tasks. As we saw in Chapter 18, "Disaster Recovery," Microsoft recommends the following database maintenance commands for consistency checks:

- **DBCC CHECKDB**   Verifies that index and data pages are correctly linked for each database table, indexes are in the proper sort order, pointers are consistent, and page information and offsets are reasonable

- **DBCC CHECKALLOC**   Verifies that all data pages are appropriately allocated and used

- **DBCC CHECKCATALOG**   Verifies consistency in and between system tables

- **DBCC UPDATEUSAGE**   Reports on and corrects inaccuracies in the Sysindexes table that could result in incorrect space usage reports

For details about how to execute these commands, refer to Chapter 18. Also refer to your SQL Server documentation for complete information about these and other database maintenance commands. It's recommended that you take the opportunity to clean up the database before upgrading. For example, check for any duplicate or old client records and remove them. In some cases you might determine that it would be better to start fresh rather than to upgrade and risk importing "dirty" information. As I've recommended in my SMS classes, it does you and your organization no good to preserve data that's questionable; you only end up importing the same database "issues" into the new site. Then, of course, you'll blame your problems on SMS 2003!

If you think that your SMS 2.0 site database might be problematic and you simply must retain that database information for historical purposes, one solution might be to maintain your "old" SMS 2.0 central site as a standalone site or as a child site of the "new" SMS 2003 central site so you still have access to the old site's data when it's needed.

Removing or Disabling Incompatible Features

SMS 2003 no longer supports several features of SMS 2.0. Before you upgrade an existing SMS 2.0 site, therefore, you must disable or remove those features. For example, SMS 2003 doesn't use or recognize SMS 2.0 logon points or software metering server site systems, nor does it use the Event To Trap Translator client agent. You must disable the site systems and remove the client agent before you can proceed with the upgrade.

Backing Up the Site and the Server

Although it's not entirely necessary, especially if you like to live on the wild side, it's a good idea to back up your SMS 2.0 site, including not only the site database but also the SMS directory structure and registry keys. This backup can assist you mightily if you encounter problems with the upgrade and need to restore your site—as will all the other documentation procedures we've discussed.

In addition, consider creating or updating the emergency repair disk or backing up the system state for the Windows server on which your SMS 2.0 site is installed. This disk will assist you in restoring registry keys and SMS services should you need to do so.

> **Tip** You should consider creating a lab environment in which you can test the database upgrade process—and recovery, if need be—outside of a production environment. This testing environment can help you to identify problem records, old settings that need to be documented, and other issues that can, and will be, unique to your installation.

Along these same lines, I strongly recommend that you thoroughly document your SMS 2.0 site settings, configuration settings, packages, advertisements, and especially any custom information you might have created, such as a custom Managed Object Format (MOF) file. Having this information available can greatly simplify recovering the old site in the event that something goes wrong with the upgrade, as well as fine-tuning the new site after the upgrade is complete.

Real World   Preserving Custom MOF Settings

In a mixed-version hierarchy, it's recommended that you use a standard SMS_def.mof file to avoid conflicts in the type of hardware inventory that's collected and propagated up the hierarchy to the central site. In a mixed-version hierarchy, different versions of Windows Management Instrumentation (WMI), the source that the .MOF file uses to collect hardware inventory, are used in SMS 2.0 and in SMS 2003. Having conflicting hardware inventory data in the SMS site database results in having multiple tables for the same class, and reports based on inventory can display incorrect information.

Some organizations customize their .MOF files to collect additional information that the original file doesn't collect. When you upgrade from SMS 2.0, the setup program replaces the old version of the SMS_def.mof file with the SMS 2003 version, and any customizations that you made will be lost. It's important, therefore, that you document any customizations you made to the SMS_def.mof file. You might consider making a copy of it in a directory separate from the SMS installation directory.

In many cases the SMS 2003 version of the .MOF file can now include the extensions that the SMS 2.0 version did not. Compare the .MOF files that you're using with SMS 2.0 against those used for SMS 2003. As you did for SMS 2.0, determine which .MOF extensions you want to use and which you don't need. Also, determine whether existing SMS 2003 extensions can collect the information that you customized the SMS 2.0 version to collect and use the SMS 2003 extensions. After the upgrade you can use your documentation to add any extensions that the SMS 2003 version of the file doesn't already include.

Running the Deployment Readiness Wizard

There's quite a bit to consider before attempting to upgrade your SMS 2.0 site to SMS 2003. I've pointed out only a few of the concerns you must think about. However, Microsoft created a tool to help you determine whether your SMS 2.0 site is ready for an upgrade. You must run the Deployment Readiness Wizard (DRW) on the SMS 2.0 site server before you can run the upgrade.

As you can see in Table 20-1, this wizard runs a rather comprehensive series of tests on your SMS 2.0 site server. When it's finished, it generates a list of the tests and whether they passed. As each test runs, it can either pass with flying colors or generate an error or warning message. A warning message doesn't prevent the upgrade from occurring, but it does identify a potential issue that you might consider resolving before upgrading. An error message, on the other hand, does prevent the upgrade from occurring. You must resolve the issues that caused the error message before you can proceed with the upgrade.

Table 20-1.   Deployment Readiness Wizard tests

Test	Failure Type	Description
Alpha processor clients	Warning	Verifies that no alpha-based client operating systems exist in the SMS site.
IPX site boundaries	Warning	Verifies that no IPX site boundaries are configured.
Non-TCP/IP clients	Warning	Verifies that all clients use TCP/IP.
NetWare server site systems	Error	Verifies that no site system servers are running Novell NetWare.
Secure client configuration	Warning	Identifies those computers in the SMS site that are running Windows 2000 or later that have the SMS 2.0 client installed so that you can easily target those computers with the Advanced Client (which is more secure than the Legacy Client).
Pre–Windows 2000 SP2 site systems	Warning	Verifies that all site systems are running Windows 2000 SP2 or later. SMS 2003 site systems require Windows 2000 SP2 or later.
Unsupported client operating systems	Warning	Verifies that none of the clients assigned to the site are running an unsupported operating system.
Windows 98 FE clients without Internet Explorer 5	Warning	Verifies that all the clients running Windows 98, First Edition that are assigned to the site have Internet Explorer 5 or later installed.
FAT drive on site server	Warning	Verifies that a FAT drive doesn't exist on the site server.
Indirect child sites earlier than SMS 2.0 SP4	Warning	Verifies that all sites below the child sites of the site being tested are running SMS 2.0 SP4 or later.
Pre-SMS 2.0 SP4 sites	Error	Verifies that the site server being tested and all its child sites are running a version of SMS 2.0 SP4 or later.
SMS 1.2 clients	Warning	Verifies that no SMS 1.2 clients are installed in the site.
Collation of temp database and SMS database should be the same	Error	Verifies that the collation of the temporary database and the SMS site database are the same.
Site database SQL Server version less than 7.0 SP3	Error	Verifies that the version of SQL Server used for the SMS site database is SQL Server 7.0 SP3 or later.
Backlogged inboxes	Warning	Verifies that the site server is processing critical inboxes in a timely fashion and doesn't have any files older than one day. Review the test results for more information.

Table 20-1.   Deployment Readiness Wizard tests

Test	Failure Type	Description
Distribution point has latest versions of packages	Warning	Verifies that all distribution points in the site have the latest version of software distribution packages.
Duplicate client IDs	Warning	Verifies that the site doesn't have any duplicate client IDs in its database.
Event to trap translator	Error	Verifies that the SNMP Event To Trap Translator client agent isn't enabled on the site.
Hardware Inventory group map	Warning	Verifies that the inventory definitions for the SMS 2.0 site have not been extended in a way that conflicts with the updated inventory definitions for SMS 2003 and that there are no incorrect NOIDMIF definitions that were created by SMS 2003 Beta 1, duplicate Group-Map table name entries, or GroupMap entries with missing tables.
Inactive clients	Warning	Verifies that all the clients assigned to the site are communicating successfully with the site's client access points (CAPs).
Logon Client Installation disabled	Error	Verifies that SMS 2.0 Logon Client Installation has been disabled.
Logon Discovery disabled	Error	Verifies that SMS 2.0 Logon Discovery has been disabled.
Logon points installed in hierarchy	Error	Verifies that no logon points are currently installed in the hierarchy.
Packages SQL constraint	Error	Verifies that there are no duplicate package IDs.
Multisite assigned clients	Warning	Verifies that no clients are assigned to more than one SMS site.
SMSExec is running	Error	Verifies that SMS Executive is running on site systems such as the SMS site server and the CAPs.
SMSExec Service crashes	Warning	Verifies that no SMS Executive service crashes have happened on the site server within the last 30 days.
Site control file processing backlog	Error	Verifies that site control file changes are being processed in a timely fashion.
Software Distribution: Uninstall registry key usage	Warning	Verifies that no SMS 2.0 programs use the Remove Software When It Is No Longer Advertised option, which uses the Uninstall registry key.
Software metering site systems	Error	Verifies that no software metering site systems are configured in the SMS hierarchy.

To run the DRW, complete the following steps:

1. On the SMS 2.0 site server, navigate to the SMSSetup\Bin\I386 folder on the SMS 2003 product CD and run DRW.exe. The Welcome page is displayed, as shown in Figure 20-1.

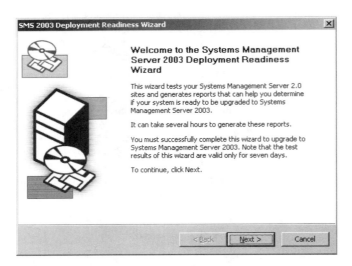

Figure 20-1. *DRW Welcome page.*

2. Click Next to display the Site Selection page, shown in Figure 20-2.

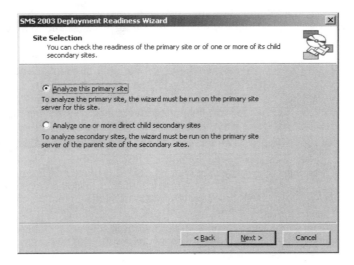

Figure 20-2. *DRW Site Selection page.*

3. Select Analyze This Primary Site if you're running the DRW on the SMS 2.0 primary site you're upgrading or select Analyze One Or More Direct Child Secondary Sites if you want to run DRW against an SMS 2.0 secondary site associated with this primary site. If you select the latter option and click Next, the Secondary Sites page is displayed, as shown in Figure 20-3. Select the site or sites that you want to analyze and then click Next.

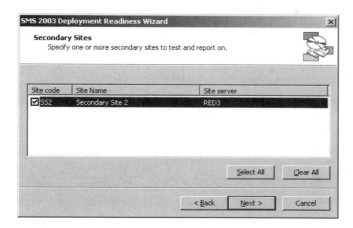

Figure 20-3.   *DRW Secondary Sites page.*

4. Click Next to display the Tests page, shown in Figure 20-4. Select the tests that you want to run and then click Next. Unless you're truly confident about the state of your SMS 2.0 site, I recommend running all the tests.

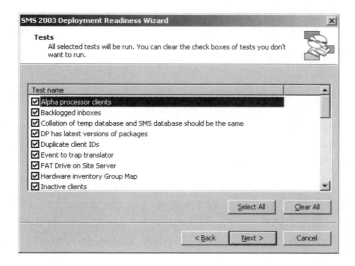

Figure 20-4.   *DRW Tests page.*

5. On the Completing the Systems Management Server 2003 Deployment Readiness Wizard page, shown in Figure 20-5, click Finish.

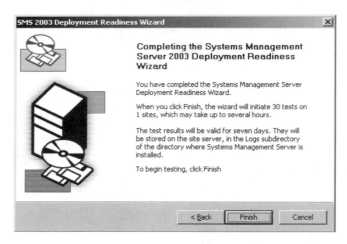

Figure 20-5. *Completing the Systems Management Server 2003 Deployment Readiness Wizard page.*

6. When the wizard has completed running the tests, click Details on the Progress And Results Summary page shown in Figure 20-6 to see the results of each test.

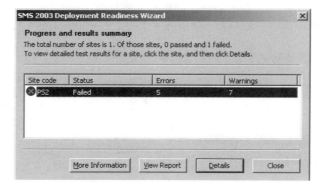

Figure 20-6. *DRW Progress And Results Summary page.*

When you click Details, the Test Results page is displayed, as shown in Figure 20-7. In this page, click View Report to display a report that lists and describes each test that ran or select a test from the list and click Details to display information specific to that test. Click Close when you're finished.

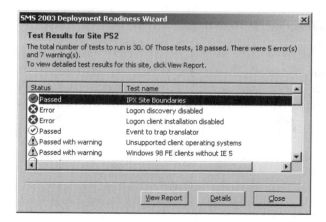

Figure 20-7.   *DRW Test Results page.*

Notice the More Information button on the Progress And Results Summary page. Clicking this button takes you to the SMS 2003 Deployment Readiness Wizard Procedures for Resolving Test Failures Web page, shown in Figure 20-8, hosted on TechNet. This document outlines each test in more detail and includes steps you can take to resolve the warnings and errors that might be generated. You can download a printable version of this document either from TechNet or from the SMS Web site.

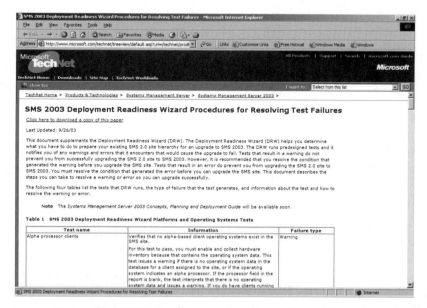

Figure 20-8.   *SMS 2003 Deployment Readiness Wizard Procedures for Resolving Test Failures Web page.*

Maintaining Mixed Sites Within the Same Site Structure

The most pressing reason for maintaining an SMS 2.0 site as part of an SMS 2003 site hierarchy is to enable you to manage those clients that aren't supported by SMS 2003—namely, Windows 3.1 and Windows 95 clients—or to facilitate a phased-in replacement of hardware that can support the operating system platforms that can run the SMS 2003 Advanced Client. Indeed, these should be the only reasons to maintain one SMS 2.0 site server as part of the new SMS 2003 hierarchy.

Holding Sites

Let me introduce the concept of a holding site. This concept is discussed in great detail in the SMS 2003 documents I have referenced at the beginning of this chapter, but I'll summarize its purpose for you here.

Three groups of computer systems can be SMS clients. Group 1 represents those systems that are fully supported by SMS 2003 and run the Advanced Client, although they also can run the Legacy Client. Group 2 represents those systems that are fully supported by SMS 2003, but whose operating systems don't support the Advanced Client. These systems generally run the Legacy Client, but they can also run the SMS 2.0 client. Group 3 represents those systems that can only be supported by SMS 2.0 sites and run the SMS 2.0 client.

After evaluating your options, you might choose to drop your SMS support for Group 3 systems. In this case you can simply start with a fresh installation of SMS 2003, set your site boundaries and client installation methods, and let your supported systems be assimilated into the new SMS 2003 site.

A holding site is the SMS 2.0 site that you identify and maintain in the SMS 2003 site hierarchy that helps you to deal with the Group 3 systems and to maintain manageability of existing Group 1 and Group 2 clients until they finish migrating to an SMS 2003 site. It's a child site of an SMS 2003 site, usually the SMS 2003 central site, and its boundaries overlap with those of the SMS 2003 site to which the SMS 2.0 site's clients are migrating.

You see, Group 1 and Group 2 clients will natively migrate to the SMS 2003 site when you enable a client installation method, because SMS 2003 fully supports them. Group 3 clients, however, will basically "ignore" the client installation method and remain SMS 2.0 clients. Later, you can choose to continue to manage these clients through the SMS 2.0 site, upgrade them so that SMS 2003 sites can support them, or not support them at all.

I've greatly oversimplified the process of migrating clients because the SMS 2003 documentation covers this and other scenarios quite well. (I should know, because I wrote much of it.) But I've given you the gist of the process.

Site Data Propagation

If your migration strategy involves upgrading an existing SMS 2.0 site hierarchy to SMS 2003 and you have taken all the necessary steps to ensure a clean transition as outlined earlier in this chapter, your databases should be up-to-date and all information should have been passed up through the hierarchy. Data will continue to propagate between SMS 2.0 sites and their SMS 2003 parents. Data that normally flows down the hierarchy, such as collection, package properties, and advertisements, continues to flow down from SMS 2003 parent sites to SMS 2.0 child sites. Data that normally flows up the hierarchy, such as inventory and discovery information, continues to flow up from SMS 2.0 child sites to SMS 2003 parent sites. However, data unique to the SMS 2.0 child site, particularly software metering data and inventory Managed Information Format (MIF) files from 16-bit SMS 2.0 clients, will be discarded by the SMS 2003 site.

> **Note** SMS 2.0 SP5 and higher site servers have the capability of signing data that's propagated to a parent site to make it more secure. SMS 2.0 SP4 site servers don't have this capability, so their data transfer is less secure. As a result, you might choose to not allow unsigned data from SMS 2.0 SP4 site servers to be propagated to an SMS 2003 parent site. You can do this by navigating to the site properties dialog box of the SMS 2003 parent site and, in the Advanced tab, selecting the Do Not Accept Unsigned Data From Sites Running SMS 2.0 SP4 And Earlier option.

Upgrading to Systems Management Server 2003

You're now ready to begin the upgrade process. Remember, a top-down upgrade is strongly recommended, as SMS 2003 sites can report only to other SMS 2003 sites and not to SMS 2.0 sites. In this section we'll begin with upgrading the primary site server and then explore upgrading secondary sites. Remember that you must run the DRW before upgrading to identify any problems that you might encounter—for example, an enabled logon point or software metering server. Once you have cleaned up your SMS 2.0 site, existing objects (collections, packages, advertisements, queries) will be migrated to the new SMS 2003 site.

Upgrading a Primary Site

The site upgrade process for a primary site is fairly straightforward, providing you have prepared the SMS 2.0 site server appropriately. Most notably, check that the server meets the hardware requirements, that it's running a supported operating system platform (with all appropriate service packs applied, of course), and that the appropriate version of SQL Server has been installed (with the appropriate service pack applied, of course).

You'll need to log onto the site server using an account that has administrative permissions for the SMS database as well as for the server itself. The account needs to be a member of the local Administrators group. You'll also need access to the SMS 2003 source files.

Log on to the site server and locate the SMS 2003 source files that you'll be using to upgrade the server, either from the application CD or a network share. Then follow these steps to upgrade the primary site:

1. Navigate to the SMSsetup\Bin\I386 folder and then double-click Setup.exe to launch the Microsoft Systems Management Server Setup Wizard Welcome page, shown in Figure 20-9.

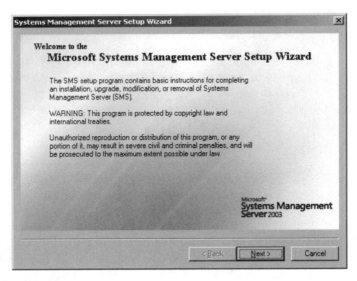

Figure 20-9. *The Microsoft Systems Management Server Setup Wizard Welcome page.*

2. Click Next to display the System Configuration page, shown in Figure 20-10, and verify that Setup has found the SMS 2.0 site. Read the page text before you proceed with the upgrade. Note that in this example you're reminded that the SMS 2.0 site must be running SMS 2.0 SP4 before you can upgrade. This is the kind of issue that the DRW can alert you to before you start your upgrade.

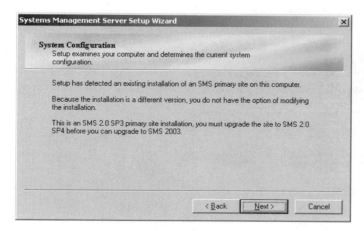

Figure 20-10. *The System Configuration page.*

3. Click Next to display the Setup Options page, shown in Figure 20-11. The option Upgrade An Existing SMS Installation is selected by default.

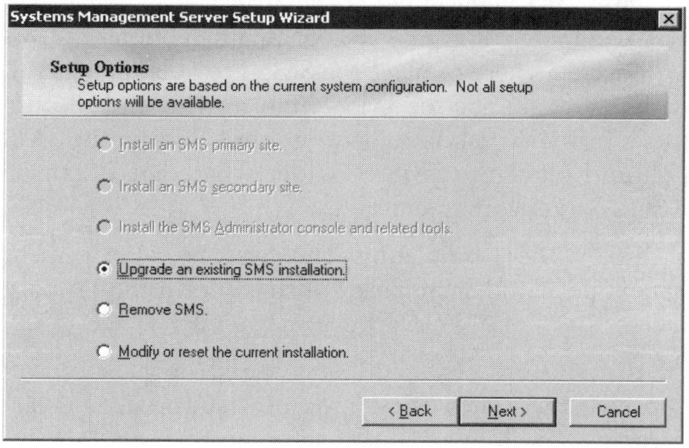

Figure 20-11. *The Setup Options page.*

4. From this point, the remaining installation runs pretty much the same as described in Chapter 2. Click Next to display the Systems Management Server License Agreement page, shown in Figure 20-12. After reading the license agreement, select I Agree (assuming that you do).

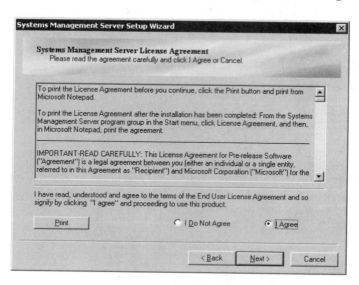

Figure 20-12.   *The Systems Management Server License Agreement page.*

5. If your installation of SQL Server is on a server other than the SMS site server, clicking Next will display the SMS Provider Information page, shown in Figure 20-13. Select either the SMS Site Server option or the SQL Server Computer option. The accompanying notes on this page will help you decide where to place the SMS Provider. In general, for large sites with a large number of SMS administrators and because the SMS Provider's primary task is to access object data in the SMS database, you should place the SMS Provider where the database resides—on the SQL Server computer.

6. Click Next to display the Completing The Systems Management Server Setup Wizard page and then click Finish to begin the primary site upgrade process.

7. At this point, if this site has any child sites the setup process will remind you to upgrade these sites using a top-down approach, as discussed earlier. Keeping this in mind, if this site reports to an SMS 2.0 site, click Cancel to stop the migration process. Remember that SMS 2003 sites can't report to SMS 2.0 sites. Click Finish to continue.

Caution Clicking Cancel stops the migration, but it doesn't leave the existing SMS 2.0 site intact. In this case, use your backup of the SMS 2.0 site to recover it.

8. When the upgrade is complete, a message to that effect is displayed on your screen. Click OK.

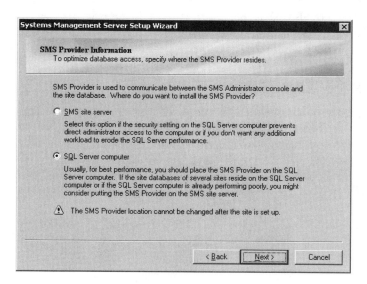

Figure 20-13. *The SMS Provider Information page.*

Upgrading a Secondary Site

When you upgrade the parent site of an SMS 2.0 secondary site to SMS 2003, the secondary site isn't automatically upgraded. This allows you to maintain SMS 2.0 secondary sites if you need to—for example, to support older Windows clients.

If you need to upgrade the secondary site, you can do so using one of the following techniques:

- Initiate the upgrade process wholly from the parent site. This procedure will take up some network bandwidth and is similar to creating a secondary site as outlined in Chapter 4, "Multiple-Site Structures"— that is, you right-click your primary site entry in the SMS Administrator Console, choose All Tasks from the context menu, and then choose Upgrade Secondary Sites to launch the Upgrade Secondary Site Wizard. This wizard is fairly self-explanatory; refer to Chapter 14 in the *Microsoft Systems Management Server 2003 Concepts, Planning, and Deployment Guide*, mentioned earlier in this chapter, for details.

- Initiate the upgrade process from the parent site but place the source files locally at the secondary site to minimize network concerns.

- Upgrade locally at the secondary site server, using the SMS 2003 source files and setup process. Again, this procedure is similar to that outlined in Chapter 4 for creating a new SMS 2003 secondary site. It's almost identical to the primary site upgrade procedure discussed in the preceding section. In this case, however, there will be no database to convert, so the process should take less time.

Post-Upgrade Tasks

Just as this chapter began by outlining some of the more important premigration tasks that you need to consider before upgrading an SMS 2.0 site to SMS 2003, it now ends with a checklist of post-upgrade tasks that you should consider performing as part of your overall migration strategy:

- **Revisit the converted database**   Perform consistency checks, back up the database, and test the restore process.

- **Configure site settings**   Configure site boundaries, enable and configure discovery methods, enable and configure client installation methods, enable and configure the client agents, and identify site systems and assign appropriate roles.

- **Upgrade the SMS 2.0 clients to either the SMS 2003 Legacy Client or the Advanced Client**   If you install a new SMS 2003 site, you can migrate your existing SMS 2.0 clients by enabling one of the client installation methods described in Chapter 7, "Resource Discovery." However, when you upgrade an existing SMS 2.0 site to SMS 2003, by default, SMS 2.0 clients that are supported by SMS 2003 will automatically be upgraded to the Legacy Client. However, for systems running Windows 2000 and higher, the SMS 2003 Advanced Client is the preferred client. It's strongly recommended that you upgrade these clients to the Advanced Client as soon as possible after the site upgrade to take advantage of the enhanced security, Active Directory directory service usage, and other benefits that the Advanced Client provides.

- **Review your security needs**   Configure appropriate object class and instance security for the upgraded site.

Checkpoints

Any potential pitfalls that you might encounter during upgrade should by now be pretty obvious. Your first and best line of defense is to run the DRW before attempting an upgrade. The tests it performs are designed to point out those SMS 2.0 site issues that are likely to, and that will, cause you problems. In addition, I can't stress enough the importance of having performed a complete backup of the SMS 2.0 site before you upgrade, as well as completely documenting your site's configuration settings, client agent settings, collections, package properties, and so on.

Aside from that, I strongly recommend that you read the SMS 2003 Installation Release Notes for updated information regarding upgrading both the site server and the clients. You can find these release notes on the SMS 2003 product CD, but I recommend checking the SMS Web site frequently for the most current version of the release notes. Once the product CD is manufactured, it can't easily be refreshed with newer information. However, the release notes are maintained on the SMS Web site for download so that they can be updated and so that you can have access to the most current information.

Summary

Just as the implementation and installation of a new SMS 2003 site requires more than a little thought and planning to be successful, in this chapter we've seen that at least as much thought and planning are necessary when migrating an existing SMS 2.0 site structure to SMS 2003. Perhaps all your SMS 2.0 sites will be migrated. Perhaps circumstances will necessitate planning for and maintaining a mixed SMS 2.0 and SMS 2003 environment. Whatever your needs might be, the more effort and thought you put into creating a migration strategy, the more successful and, perhaps even more important, the more uneventful your upgrade will be.

Well, it seems we have come to the end of our exploration of SMS 2003. This book has tried to provide you with a clearer understanding of SMS's many features and how to use them. Along with this understanding, you have hopefully developed a greater appreciation of the exceptional management potential this product can bring to your network environment. The inventory, package delivery, Remote Tools, and software metering features, along with the new Advanced Client, advanced security mode, and integration with Active Directory provide you with a complete and scalable management solution.

You can look forward to additional enhancements and integration into the Windows operating system as this product continues to evolve. Good luck as you embark on your own implementation and administration of SMS 2003.

Part V
Appendixes

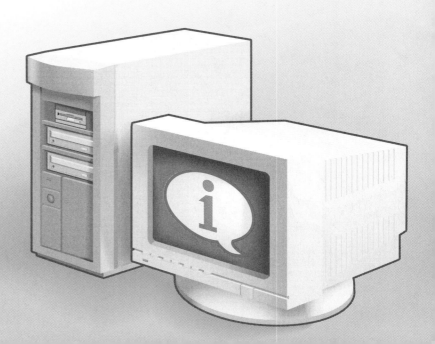

Appendix A
Backup Control File

This appendix presents the code for the backup control file (SMS\Inboxes\
SMSbkup.box\SMSbkup.ctl) used by the SMS Site Backup service when performing
a site server backup scheduled through the Backup SMS Site Server database
maintenance task. This task can be enabled through the SMS Administrator
Console and is discussed at Length in Chapter 18, "Disaster Recovery."

```
# Backup Control File for Backup SMS Site Server task
# Systems Management Server (SMS) 2.5 Release
# Updated August 22, 2001


#!!!!!!!!!!!!!!!!!!!!!!!!!!!!!!!!!!!!!!!!!!!!!!!!!!!!!!!!!!!!!!!!!!!!!!!!!!!!!!!!!!!
#!!!!         Modify only within the blocks designated with          !!!!#
#!!!!
!!!!#
#!!!!                      E d i t i n g   A l l o w e d
!!!!#
#!!!!
!!!!#
#!!!! otherwise you are risking recovery when using the backup snapshot
!!!!#
#!!!! created by this control file.
!!!!#
#!!!!
!!!!#
#!!!! When adding custom commands, make sure there is no "#"
!!!!#
#!!!! (the comment character) at the front of the line.
!!!!#
#!!!!
!!!!#
#!!!! For detailed editing guidelines, refer to the "Backup and Recovery"
!!!!#
#!!!! chapter in the "Administrator Reference."
!!!!#
#!!!!
!!!!#
#!!!!!!!!!!!!!!!!!!!!!!!!!!!!!!!!!!!!!!!!!!!!!!!!!!!!!!!!!!!!!!!!!!!!!!!!!!!!!!!!!!!!!!
!
```

```
#!!!!!!!!!!!!!!!!!!!!!!!!!!!!!!!!!!!!!!!!!!!!!!!!!!!!!!!!!!!!!!!!!!!!!!!!!!!!!!!!!!
!
#!!!!  The backup task FAILS if there are any syntax ERRORS in this file.  !!!!!
#!!!!!!!!!!!!!!!!!!!!!!!!!!!!!!!!!!!!!!!!!!!!!!!!!!!!!!!!!!!!!!!!!!!!!!!!!!!!!!!!!!


#---------#
[Tokens]
#---------#



#------------------------- Default Tokens -------------------------------#
#                                                                         #
# Default tokens and their values:                                        #
# -------------------------------------------                             #
#  SITE_CODE                 (3 character site code)                      #
#  SITE_SERVER               (site server)                                #
#  SITE_DB_SERVER            (site's site system running SQL server)      #
#  PROVIDER_SERVER           (server hosting SMS provider)                #
#  SITE_SERVER_ROOT_DIR      (SMS root directory on site server)          #
#  SITE_DB_SERVER_ROOT_DIR   (site database root directory on the site system#
#                             running SQL server)                         #
#  SITE_DB_NAME              (site database name)                         #
#  SITE_BACKUP_DESTINATION   (BackUP Destination\<SITE_CODE>Backup)       #
#                            (Backup Destination = "Backup Destination" value#
#                             from the "Backup SMS Site Server Properties" #
#                             dialog box in the Administrator console)     #
#                                                                         #
#                                                                         #
# Default destination tokens:                                             #
#                                                                         #
SITE_SERVER_DEST    = %SITE_BACKUP_DESTINATION%\SiteServer
SITE_DB_SERVER_DEST = %SITE_BACKUP_DESTINATION%\SiteDBServer
PROVIDER_SERVER_DEST= %SITE_BACKUP_DESTINATION%\ProviderServer
#------------------------------------------------------------------------#



#******************************************************************************
#                                                                            *
#*-*-*-*-*-*-*-*-*-*-*-* E d i t i n g    A l l o w e d *-*-*-*-*-*-*-*-*-*-*-*
#                                                                            *
# Custom tokens syntax:                                                      *
#  <Token>=<Token Value>                                                     *
#                                                                            *
# Example:                                                                   *
#  MyToken=FOO                                                               *
```

```
#  Where MyToken is the token variable and FOO is its value          *
#                                                                    *
#                                                                    *
# Add custom Tokens here:                                            *


#*-*-*-*-*-*-*-*-*-*-*-*-*-*-*-*-*-*-*-*-*-*-*-*-*-*-*-*-*-*-*-*-*-*-*
#                                                                    *
#********************************************************************
#--------#
[Stop]
#--------#


#------------------------ Default Services    ------------------------#
#                                                                    #
# The following basic services are stopped by default                #
#                                                                    #
# service      \\%SITE_SERVER%\SMS_SITE_COMPONENT_MANAGER            #
# service      \\%SITE_SERVER%\SMS_EXECUTIVE                         #
# service      \\%SITE_DB_SERVER%\SMS_SQL_MONITOR                    #
#--------------------------------------------------------------------#



#********************************************************************
#                                                                    *
#*-*-*-*-*-*-*-*-*-* E d i t i n g   A l l o w e d *-*-*-*-*-*-*-*-*-*
#                                                                    *
# Commands syntax :                                                  *
#  service <service name>                                            *
#  exec <executable name>                                            *
#  sleep <seconds>                                                   *
#                                                                    *
# Examples:                                                          *
#  service \\%SITE_DB_SERVER%\SMS_SQL_MONITOR                        *
#                                                                    *
#  exec runme.exe                                                    *
#  exec runme                                                        *
#                                                                    *
#  sleep 30 (Maximum 900 sec = 15 minutes)                          *
#                                                                    *
# Add custom commands here:                                          *

sleep 30


#                                                                    *
#                                                                    *
#                                                                    *
#*-*-*-*-*-*-*-*-*-*-*-*-*-*-*-*-*-*-*-*-*-*-*-*-*-*-*-*-*-*-*-*-*-*-*
#                                                                    *
#********************************************************************
```

```
#--------#
[Tasks]
#--------#



# DO NOT MODIFY - Default File backup tasks - DO NOT MODIFY:#
#----------------------------------------------------------------
file   %SystemDrive%\SMSSetup.lo*          %SITE_SERVER_DEST%\
file   %SITE_SERVER_ROOT_DIR%\bin          %SITE_SERVER_DEST%\SMSServer\bin
file   %SITE_SERVER_ROOT_DIR%\inboxes      %SITE_SERVER_DEST%\SMSServer\inboxes
file   %SITE_SERVER_ROOT_DIR%\Logs         %SITE_SERVER_DEST%\SMSServer\Logs
file   %SITE_SERVER_ROOT_DIR%\data         %SITE_SERVER_DEST%\SMSServer\data




#****************************************************************************
#                                                                          *
#*-*-*-*-*-*-*-*-*-*-* E d i t i n g   A l l o w e d *-*-*-*-*-*-*-*-*-*-*-*
#                                                                          *
# Command syntax :                                                         *
#                                                                          *
#   file <source> <destination>                                           *
#                                                                          *
# For examples, see default backup tasks.                                  *
#                                                                          *
# Add files to back up here:                                               *




#                                                                          *
#*-*-*-*-*-*-*-*-*-*-*-*-*-*-*-*-*-*-*-*-*-*-*-*-*-*-*-*-*-*-*-*-*-*-*-*-*-*-*
#                                                                          *
#****************************************************************************




# DO NOT MODIFY - Default Configuration backup tasks - DO NOT MODIFY:#
#----------------------------------------------------------------------
machinfo  %SITE_SERVER%         %SITE_SERVER_DEST%\SMSbkSiteConfigNTData.txt
machinfo  %SITE_DB_SERVER%      %SITE_DB_SERVER_DEST%\SMSbkSQLConfigNTData.txt
```

```
#***************************************************************************
#                                                                          *
#*-*-*-*-*-*-*-*-*-*-* E d i t i n g    A l l o w e d *-*-*-*-*-*-*-*-*-*-*-*
#                                                                          *
# Command syntax :                                                         *
#                                                                          *
#   machinfo <source> <destination>                                       *
#                                                                          *
#                                                                          *
# For examples, see default backup tasks.                                 *
#                                                                          *
#                                                                          *
# Add configuration to back up here:                                      *



#                                                                          *
#*-*-*-*-*-*-*-*-*-*-*-*-*-*-*-*-*-*-*-*-*-*-*-*-*-*-*-*-*-*-*-*-*-*-*-*-*-*-*
#                                                                          *
#***************************************************************************


# DO NOT MODIFY - Default Registry backup tasks - DO NOT MODIFY:#
#-------------------------------------------------------------------
# Site Server
reg \\%SITE_SERVER%\HKEY_LOCAL_MACHINE\Software\Microsoft\NAL
%SITE_SERVER_DEST%\SMSbkSiteRegNAL.dat
reg \\%SITE_SERVER%\HKEY_LOCAL_MACHINE\Software\Microsoft\SMS
%SITE_SERVER_DEST%\SMSbkSiteRegSMS.dat
reg \\%SITE_SERVER%\HKEY_LOCAL_MACHINE\Software\Microsoft\SNMP_EVENTS
%SITE_SERVER_DEST%\SMSbkSiteRegSNMPEvents.dat
reg \\%SITE_SERVER%\HKEY_LOCAL_MACHINE\Software\Microsoft\Updates
%SITE_SERVER_DEST%\SMSbkSiteRegAppHotfix.dat
reg `\\%SITE_SERVER%\HKEY_LOCAL_MACHINE\Software\Microsoft\Windows
NT\CurrentVersion\Hotfix`   %SITE_SERVER_DEST%\SMSbkSiteRegOSHotfix.dat

# Site SQL Server
reg \\%SITE_DB_SERVER%\HKEY_LOCAL_MACHINE\Software\Microsoft\MSSQLServer
%SITE_DB_SERVER_DEST%\SMSbkSQLRegMSSQLServer.dat
reg \\%SITE_DB_SERVER%\HKEY_LOCAL_MACHINE\Software\Microsoft\SMS
%SITE_DB_SERVER_DEST%\SMSbkSQLRegSMS.dat

# Presently, the Provider Server is either the Site or Site SQL Server. This
#  registry key has therefore already been backed up.
reg   \\%PROVIDER_SERVER%\HKEY_LOCAL_MACHINE\Software\Microsoft\SMS
%PROVIDER_SERVER_DEST%\SMSbkProvRegSMS.dat
```

```
#*****************************************************************************
#                                                                           *
#*-*-*-*-*-*-*-*-*-*-*-* E d i t i n g   A l l o w e d *-*-*-*-*-*-*-*-*-*-*-*
#                                                                           *
# Command syntax :                                                          *
#                                                                           *
#   reg <source> <destination>                                             *
#                                                                           *
#                                                                           *
# For examples, see default backup tasks.                                  *
#                                                                           *
# Add registry keys to back up here:                                       *



#*-*-*-*-*-*-*-*-*-*-*-*-*-*-*-*-*-*-*-*-*-*-*-*-*-*-*-*-*-*-*-*-*-*-*-*-*-*-*
#                                                                           *
#*****************************************************************************



# DO NOT MODIFY - Default SQL Data backup tasks - DO NOT MODIFY:#
#-------------------------------------------------------------------
smssqlinfo   %SITE_DB_SERVER_DEST%\SMSbkSQLConfigSQL
sitedbdump   %SITE_DB_NAME%  %SITE_DB_SERVER_DEST%\SMSbkSQLDBsite.dat



#*****************************************************************************
#                                                                           *
#*-*-*-*-*-*-*-*-*-*-*-* E d i t i n g   A l l o w e d *-*-*-*-*-*-*-*-*-*-*-*
#                                                                           *
# Command syntax :                                                          *
#                                                                           *
#   Smssqlinfo <destination>                                               *
#   sitedbdump <source> <destination>                                      *
#                                                                           *
# For examples, see default backup tasks.                                  *
#                                                                           *
# Add SQL data to back up here:                                            *



#                                                                           *
#*-*-*-*-*-*-*-*-*-*-*-*-*-*-*-*-*-*-*-*-*-*-*-*-*-*-*-*-*-*-*-*-*-*-*-*-*-*-*
#                                                                           *
#*****************************************************************************
```

```
#---------#
[Start]
#---------#



#*****************************************************************************
#                                                                           *
#*-*-*-*-*-*-*-*-*-*-*-* E d i t i n g    A l l o w e d *-*-*-*-*-*-*-*-*-*-*-*
#                                                                           *
# Commands syntax :                                                         *
#                                                                           *
#   service <service name>                                                  *
#   exec <executable path and name>                                         *
#   sleep <seconds>                                                         *
#                                                                           *
# Examples:                                                                 *
#   service \\%SITE_DB_SERVER%\SMS_SQL_MONITOR                              *
#   exec c:\exec_full_path\runme.exe                                        *
#   sleep 30                                                                *
#                                                                           *
# Add custom commands here :                                    *


#                                                                           *
#*-*-*-*-*-*-*-*-*-*-*-*-*-*-*-*-*-*-*-*-*-*-*-*-*-*-*-*-*-*-*-*-*-*-*-*-*-*-*
#                                                                           *
#*****************************************************************************
```

Recommended Web Sites

By now you should have the insight and information you need as you implement and begin managing your network using Microsoft Systems Management Server (SMS) 2003. As you venture forth into the exciting world of systems management using SMS 2003 as your management tool of choice, it will be important for you to stay on top of the product and to continue to develop your knowledge. The following Internet sites can help you in this regard.

http://www.microsoft.com/smserver

This site is, of course, Microsoft's own Web site dedicated to SMS in all its versions. At this site you'll find the latest information about SMS, including updates and service packs, downloadable products, patches, and so on, as well as links to deployment and technology white papers (several of which have been referenced throughout this book). This site also offers information about SMS 2003 training options.

Links for all of the SMS documentation that we referenced in this book can be found on this site, including

- *Microsoft Systems Management Server 2003 Concepts, Planning, and Deployment Guide*
- *Microsoft Systems Management Server 2003 Operations Guide*
- *Microsoft Systems Management Server 2003 Release Notes*
- *Microsoft Systems Management Server 2003 Frequently Asked Questions*
- *Microsoft Systems Management Server 2003 ToolKit*
- *Microsoft Systems Management Server 2003 Troubleshooting Flowcharts*
- *Microsoft Systems Management Server 2003 Status Message Database*

- *Microsoft Systems Management Server 2003 Deployment Readiness Wizard (DRW) Procedures for Resolving Test Failures (sometimes referred to as the DRW FAQ)*

This site is frequently updated, so be sure to include it as a favorite and check back often.

http://www.microsoft.com/windows2000/ and http://www.microsoft.com/ windowsserver2003

These Microsoft Web sites host links to technical white papers supporting Microsoft Windows 2000 and Microsoft Windows Server 2003 technology, as well as links to other Windows support sites. For example, you can find the following white papers by navigating to *http://www.microsoft.com/windows2000/ techinfo/howitworks*. These white papers can help you draw distinctions between Windows 2000 and SMS 2003 and can help you clarify how the two products work together:

- *Microsoft Windows 2000 Centralized Management*
- *Introduction to IntelliMirror*
- *Introduction to Microsoft Windows Management Services*
- *Introduction to Microsoft Windows 2000 Group Policy*

You can find similar white papers supporting Windows Server 2003 at *http:// www.microsoft.com/windowsserver2003/techinfo/overview*.

http://www.microsoft.com/sql

This Microsoft Web site hosts links to technical white papers supporting Microsoft SQL Server 2000 and Microsoft SQL Server 7.0 technology, as well as links to other support sites, training materials, and so on. For example, you can find the following SQL Server 2000-related white papers by navigating to *http://www.microsoft.com/sql/techinfo/administration/2000*. These white papers can help you understand how to better maintain the SMS 2003 site database and keep your SQL Server installation running at optimum levels:

- *Microsoft SQL Server 2000 Operations Guide*
- *Microsoft SQL Server Performance Tuning Guides*
- *Backup and Restore Strategies with Microsoft SQL Server 2000*

http://www.myitforum.com

MyITforum.com is, in my opinion, the Internet's premier knowledge and information forum for IT professionals focusing on SMS and Windows management. This Web site gives IT administrators the opportunity to gain better insight about what they do by learning from and sharing information with other IT experts throughout the world. Through the Web site, myITforum.com users and contributors can provide tips, share insights, and download utilities and tools to assist in managing IT enterprises.

MyITforum.com is managed by Rod Trent, author of the best-selling books *SMS Installer* (McGraw-Hill Osborne Media, 2000) and *Admin911: SMS* (McGraw-Hill Osborne Media, 2000). Rod Trent is a leading authority on Microsoft SMS and an annual presenter and keynote presenter at the annual Microsoft Management Summits. MyITforum also provides hands-on training, events, and conferences.

Index

A

F

J

K

L

V

Steven D. Kaczmarek MCSE, MCT, Senior Technical Writer, Enterprise Management Content Group, Microsoft Corporation. Steven D. Kaczmarek has been a trainer, author, and consultant since 1991, providing enterprise networking, administration, consulting, and training support through his company ENACT Solutions Corporation. In March 2003, he joined the Systems Management Server documentation team as senior technical writer and assumed responsibility for all SMS 2003–related documentation as project leader. He holds training and professional certifications (MCT and MCP) from Microsoft Corporation for Windows NT and Windows 2000 and Systems Management Server 1.2 and 2.0, as well as the Microsoft Certified Systems Engineer (MCSE) certification.

He is the author of *The Systems Management Server 2.0 Administrator's Guide* published by Microsoft Press. In 2001, he completed work on Mike Meyer's *MCSE Windows 2000 Directory Services Exam Passport* published by Osborne\McGraw-Hill. He was also the author or contributing author of three books published by QUE: *Windows NT Workstation 4.0 Exam Guide, Windows NT Server 4.0 Exam Guide,* and *Windows NT Server 4.0 in the Enterprise Exam Guide.*

In prior positions, Steve provided a variety of client PC support services through the IS departments of several large corporations, including purchasing and installation of PC hardware and software, network management, maintenance and help desk support, and customized training.

Steve has a master of science degree from Loyola University with a specialization in computational mathematics.

Steve can be reached through e-mail at stevenka@microsoft.com.

Inside *security information* you can trust

Microsoft® Windows® Security Resource Kit
ISBN 0-7356-1868-2   Suggested Retail Price: $49.99 U.S., $72.99 Canada

Comprehensive security information and tools, straight from the Microsoft product groups. This official RESOURCE KIT delivers comprehensive operations and deployment information that information security professionals can put to work right away. The authors—members of Microsoft's security teams—describe how to plan and implement a comprehensive security strategy, assess security threats and vulnerabilities, configure system security, and more. The kit also provides must-have security tools, checklists, templates, and other on-the-job resources on CD-ROM and on the Web.

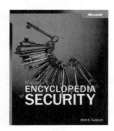

Microsoft Encyclopedia of Security
ISBN 0-7356-1877-1   Suggested Retail Price: $39.99 U.S., $57.99 Canada

The essential security reference for computer professionals at all levels. Get the single resource that defines—and illustrates—the rapidly evolving world of computer and network security. The MICROSOFT ENCYCLOPEDIA OF SECURITY delivers more than 1000 cross-referenced entries detailing the latest security-related technologies, standards, products, services, and issues—including sources and types of attacks, countermeasures, policies, and more. You get clear, concise explanations and case scenarios that deftly take you from concept to real-world application—ready answers to help maximize security for your mission-critical systems and data.

Microsoft Windows Server™ 2003 Security Administrator's Companion
ISBN 0-7356-1574-8   Suggested Retail Price: $49.99 U.S., $72.99 Canada

The in-depth, practical guide to deploying and maintaining Windows Server 2003 in a secure environment. Learn how to use all the powerful security features in the latest network operating system with this in-depth, authoritative technical reference—written by a security expert on the Microsoft Windows Server 2003 security team. Explore physical security issues, internal security policies, and public and shared key cryptography, and then drill down into the specifics of the key security features of Windows Server 2003.

Microsoft Internet Information Services Security Technical Reference
ISBN 0-7356-1572-1   Suggested Retail Price: $49.99 U.S., $72.99 Canada

The definitive guide for developers and administrators who need to understand how to securely manage networked systems based on IIS. This book presents obvious, avoidable mistakes and known security vulnerabilities in Internet Information Services (IIS)—priceless, intimate facts about the underlying causes of past security issues—while showing the best ways to fix them. The expert author, who has used IIS since the first version, also discusses real-world best practices for developing software and managing systems and networks with IIS.

To learn more about Microsoft Press® products for IT professionals, please visit:

microsoft.com/mspress/IT

Microsoft Press products are available worldwide wherever quality computer books are sold. For more information, contact your book or computer retailer, software reseller, or local Microsoft Sales Office, or visit our Web site at **microsoft.com/mspress.** To locate your nearest source for Microsoft Press products, or to order directly, call 1-800-MSPRESS in the United States. (In Canada, call 1-800-268-2222.)

In-depth, daily administration guides
for Microsoft Windows Server 2003

Microsoft® Windows® Server 2003 Administrator's Companion
ISBN 0-7356-1367-2

The in-depth, daily operations guide to planning, deployment, and maintenance. Here's the ideal one-volume guide for the IT professional who administers Windows Server 2003. This ADMINISTRATOR'S COMPANION offers up-to-date information on core system-administration topics for Windows, including Active Directory® services, security, disaster planning and recovery, interoperability with NetWare and UNIX, plus all-new sections about Microsoft Internet Security and Acceleration (ISA) Server and scripting. Featuring easy-to-use procedures and handy workarounds, this book provides ready answers for on-the-job results.

Microsoft Windows Server 2003 Security Administrator's Companion
ISBN 0-7356-1574-8

The in-depth, daily operations guide to enhancing security with the network operating system. With this authoritative ADMINISTRATOR'S COMPANION—written by an expert on the Windows Server 2003 security team—you'll learn how to use the powerful security features in the latest network server operating system. The guide describes best practices and technical details for enhancing security with Windows Server 2003, using the holistic approach that IT professionals need to grasp to help secure their systems. The authors cover concepts such as physical security issues, internal security policies, and public and shared key cryptography, and then drill down into the specifics of key security features of Windows Server 2003.

To learn more about the full line of Microsoft Press® products for IT professionals, please visit:

microsoft.com/mspress/IT

Microsoft Press products are available worldwide wherever quality computer books are sold. For more information, contact your book or computer retailer, software reseller, or local Microsoft Sales Office, or visit our Web site at **microsoft.com/mspress.** To locate your nearest source for Microsoft Press products, or to order directly, call 1-800-MSPRESS in the United States. (In Canada, call 1-800-268-2222.)

The practical, portable guides to
Microsoft Windows Server 2003

Microsoft® Windows® Server 2003 Admin Pocket Consultant
ISBN 0-7356-1354-0

The practical, portable guide to Windows Server 2003. Here's the practical, pocket-sized reference for IT professionals who support Windows Server 2003. Designed for quick referencing, it covers all the essentials for performing everyday system-administration tasks. Topics covered include managing workstations and servers, using Active Directory® services, creating and administering user and group accounts, managing files and directories, data security and auditing, data back-up and recovery, administration with TCP/IP, WINS, and DNS, and more.

Microsoft IIS 6.0 Administrator's Pocket Consultant
ISBN 0-7356-1560-8

The practical, portable guide to IIS 6.0. Here's the eminently practical, pocket-sized reference for IT and Web professionals who work with Internet Information Services (IIS) 6.0. Designed for quick referencing and compulsively readable, this portable guide covers all the basics needed for everyday tasks. Topics include Web administration fundamentals, Web server administration, essential services administration, and performance, optimization, and maintenance. It's the fast-answers guide that helps users consistently save time and energy as they administer IIS 6.0.

To learn more about the full line of Microsoft Press® products for IT professionals, please visit:

microsoft.com/mspress/IT

Microsoft Press products are available worldwide wherever quality computer books are sold. For more information, contact your book or computer retailer, software reseller, or local Microsoft Sales Office, or visit our Web site at **microsoft.com/mspress.** To locate your nearest source for Microsoft Press products, or to order directly, call 1-800-MSPRESS in the United States. (In Canada, call 1-800-268-2222.)

Complete planning and migration information
for Microsoft Windows Server 2003

Introducing Microsoft® Windows Server™ 2003
ISBN 0-7356-1570-5

Get a detailed, official first look at the new features and improvements in Windows Server 2003. Windows Server 2003 provides significant improvements in performance, productivity, and security over previous versions. This official first-look guide shows you exactly what's new and improved in this powerful network operating system—including advanced technologies for XML Web services and components, security, networking, Active Directory® directory service, Microsoft Internet Information Services, support for IPv6, and more. It gives you all the information and tools you need to understand, evaluate, and begin deployment planning for Windows Server 2003, whether you're upgrading from Microsoft Windows NT® Server or Microsoft Windows® 2000 Server.

Migrating from Microsoft Windows NT Server 4.0 to Microsoft Windows Server 2003
ISBN 0-7356-1940-9

Get expert guidance, procedures, and solutions for a successful migration—direct from the Windows Server team. Get real-world guidance for planning and deploying an upgrade from Windows NT 4.0 to Windows Server 2003 for your small or medium-sized business. This book delivers straightforward, step-by-step instructions on how to upgrade to an Active Directory directory service environment; migrate your DHCP, WINS, file, print, remote access, and Web server roles; and implement Group Policy-based administration. Whether you support 10 or 1,000 users, you get the detailed information—plus evaluation software—you need to put Windows Server 2003 to work right away.

To learn more about the full line of Microsoft Press® products for IT professionals, please visit:

microsoft.com/mspress/IT

Microsoft Press products are available worldwide wherever quality computer books are sold. For more information, contact your book or computer retailer, software reseller, or local Microsoft Sales Office, or visit our Web site at **microsoft.com/mspress.** To locate your nearest source for Microsoft Press products, or to order directly, call 1-800-MSPRESS in the United States. (In Canada, call 1-800-268-2222.)

© 2004 Microsoft Corporation. All rights reserved. Microsoft, Microsoft Press, Active Directory, Windows, Windows NT, and Windows Server are either registered trademarks or trademarks of Microsoft Corporation in the United States and/or other countries.

In-depth technical information and tools for
Microsoft Windows Server 2003

Microsoft® Windows Server™ 2003 Deployment Kit: A Microsoft Resource Kit
ISBN 0-7356-1486-5

Plan and deploy a Windows Server 2003 operating system environment with expertise from the team that develops and supports the technology—the Microsoft Windows® team. This multivolume kit delivers in-depth technical information and best practices to automate and customize your installation, configure servers and desktops, design and deploy network services, design and deploy directory and security services, implement Group Policy, create pilot and test plans, and more. You also get more than 125 timesaving tools, deployment job aids, Windows Server 2003 evaluation software, and the entire Windows Server 2003 Help on the CD-ROMs. It's everything you need to help ensure a smooth deployment—while minimizing maintenance and support costs.

Internet Information Services (IIS) 6.0 Resource Kit
ISBN 0-7356-1420-2

Deploy and support IIS 6.0, which is included with Windows Server 2003, with expertise direct from the Microsoft IIS product team. This official RESOURCE KIT packs 1200+ pages of in-depth deployment, operations, and technical information, including step-by-step instructions for common administrative tasks. Get critical details and guidance on security enhancements, the new IIS 6.0 architecture, migration strategies, performance tuning, logging, and troubleshooting—along with timesaving tools, IIS 6.0 product documentation, and a searchable eBook on CD. You get all the resources you need to help maximize the security, reliability, manageability, and performance of your Web server—while reducing system administration costs.

To learn more about the full line of Microsoft Press® products for IT professionals, please visit:

microsoft.com/mspress/IT

Microsoft Press products are available worldwide wherever quality computer books are sold. For more information, contact your book or computer retailer, software reseller, or local Microsoft Sales Office, or visit our Web site at **microsoft.com/mspress**. To locate your nearest source for Microsoft Press products, or to order directly, call 1-800-MSPRESS in the United States. (In Canada, call 1-800-268-2222.)

© 2004 Microsoft Corporation. All rights reserved. Microsoft, Microsoft Press, Windows, and Windows Server are either registered trademarks or trademarks of Microsoft Corporation in the United States and/or other countries.